Books by Robert C. Tucker

PHILOSOPHY AND MYTH IN KARL MARX

THE SOVIET POLITICAL MIND

THE GREAT PURGE TRIAL (CO-EDITOR)

THE MARXIAN REVOLUTIONARY IDEA

THE MARX-ENGELS READER (EDITOR)

ROBERT C. TUCKER is professor of politics at Princeton University. He received his undergraduate and graduate degrees from Harvard University. From 1945 to 1953 he lived in Moscow, where he was a member of the U.S. Embassy and where he met his wife Evgenia. Professor Tucker's other works include *Philosophy and Myth in Karl Marx, The Soviet Political Mind,* and *The Marxian Revolutionary Idea,* and he is also editor of *The Marx-Engels Reader.*

STALIN

AS REVOLUTIONARY

1879-1929

A STUDY IN HISTORY AND PERSONALITY

Robert C. Tucker

The Norton Library

W·W·NORTON & COMPANY·INC·

NEW YORK

Library of Congress Cataloging in Publication Data
Tucker, Robert C.
    Stalin as revolutionary, 1879–1929.
    Bibliography: p.
    I. Stalin, Iosif, 1879–1953. I. Title.
DK268.S8T85   1973   947.084′2′0924   [B]   73-6541
ISBN 0-393-00738-3

Printed in the United States of America
1 2 3 4 5 6 7 8 9 0

To Evgenia

CONTENTS

CONTENTS

Photographs appear following page 266

Maps

PREFACE

THE BIOGRAPHICAL LITERATURE on Stalin has its conventions. The writer typically begins by identifying Transcaucasia, the region lying between the Black and Caspian seas south of the Caucasian mountain range, as an historical mingling-ground of Asian and European peoples. He gives a sketch of the small Transcaucasian country of Georgia, and of the Georgian town of Gori where a boy was born in 1879, Iosif Djugashvili by name, who would later become known to the world as Stalin. Then the story flows on in chronological fashion.

This book, though biographical, follows a somewhat different plan deriving from its particular theme: the rendezvous of a personality with the public political world. My aim is less to tell the story of a life than to illuminate its linkage with history. This being the life of one who in later years made himself the most absolute ruler yet seen in any large contemporary state, the book could also be described as a study in the forming of a dictator and the conditions that made for his dictatorship.

A flood of Russian revelations since Stalin's death in 1953 has removed any possible doubt that his name is going down in history as a byword for tyranny. They make it incontrovertibly clear that he was a man of dictatorial personality. As usual, however, and tragically, much that is evident to hindsight eluded foresight. In the party oligarchy that ruled Russia in the early Soviet years, Stalin does not seem to have been perceived by many as a potential dictator. The ruling group included a forceful though non-tyrannical leader in Lenin, who was surrounded by a galaxy of renowned revolutionary figures of lesser stature: Lev Trotsky, Grigori Zinoviev, Lev Kamenev, Nikolai Bukharin, Karl Radek, and others. Stalin, by contrast, was not yet well known outside higher party circles, and many within them viewed him as a second-rater, hence not someone to be feared. He had risen in the pre-revolutionary Bolshevik movement as a party organizer, one of its "committeemen" working underground in Russia. In November 1917, when the party took power, he became a figure of consequence, though not yet a leader of highest rank, in Lenin's revolutionary Republic of Soviets. Five years later, however, he *was* a leader of highest rank. In addition to belonging to the key policy-making bodies, he had achieved a position of pivotal organizational power as general secretary of the party's Central Committee. Still, in upper Bolshevik circles the condescending view of him persisted.

This helps to explain why the leadership failed to act on a warning that came from Lenin. By late 1922, Lenin was seriously ill and concerned about the party's future. He had also become convinced by this time that certain character traits of Stalin's—notably his "rudeness" and his tendency to be guided by "malice" in politics —made it dangerous for him to be entrusted any longer with the powerful post of general secretary; and in a letter to the coming party congress (a document that later became known as his "testament") he recommended that Stalin be replaced in that post by someone "more tolerant, more loyal, more polite and more considerate of comrades, less capricious, etc." The matter of personality might seem a trifle, he added, but it was one of those trifles that could take on decisive significance. After Lenin died in January 1924, his widow communicated the document to the higher party leaders. They, however, chose to disregard Lenin's recommendation about Stalin. Most of them eventually paid for this decision with their lives.

For an account of the course that history subsequently took, we may turn to Nikita S. Khrushchev, the man who succeeded Stalin as leader of the Soviet Communist party. Addressing a closed session of the party's Twentieth Congress in February 1956, Khrushchev read aloud the part of Lenin's testament that dealt with Stalin, and said: "As later events have proven, Lenin's anxiety was justified." Then he reconstructed these "later events." The burden of his story was that Stalin, having won the role of supreme leader of the party during the nineteen-twenties, proceeded in the thirties to transform the oligarchical single-party system into a true autocracy in which the ruling party itself was subjugated to his personally controlled secret police. He masterminded during those years of party purges a veritable Soviet holocaust. Not only those who had earlier opposed him but many thousands of others were shot or sent to camps as "enemies of the people." Through wholesale purge and terror Stalin created a regime of personal dictatorship in which one man made all the important decisions and his colleagues were forced to be submissive yes-men. He also employed his autocratic power to promote his self-glorification—for example, by secretly editing the draft of his own official biography in such a way as to accentuate the theme of his greatness.

Drawing upon his own experience as one of the dictator's lieutenants from the early thirties to the end, Khrushchev presented in the secret speech to the Twentieth Congress—which did not remain secret for long—a characterization of Stalin the man. He spoke of his intolerance of criticism and of dissenting views, his willingness to inflict suffering or death upon any person whom he came to regard as an "enemy," his intense distrust and suspiciousness, his sense of being surrounded by conspiracies, and his thirst for praise and glory. He underlined the progressive character of Stalin's "negative characteristics," observing that they "developed steadily and during the last years acquired an absolutely insufferable character." In sum, he painted a classic portrait of a tyrant—a portrait, moreover, which has since been redrawn with much added detail by a heterogeneous collection of persons who could likewise, in many instances, speak from firsthand experience: other party leaders important enough to have had direct contact with Stalin; generals who served under him during the Second World War; Soviet journalists and writers; Old Bolsheviks who survived the camps to write their memoirs; a prominent Yugoslav, Milovan Djilas, who dealt with Stalin in the forties; the dictator's daughter, Svetlana, whose corroborative testimony is all the more significant for the fact that she writes from the unique vantage-point of a witness within the family; and a dissident former Soviet party member, Roy Medvedev, who has woven new biographical data into a work on Stalin's career in power.

Scholarship, however, has yet to make full use of the material now available in such abundance. It has scarcely more than begun to formulate the requisite analysis of Stalin's character and the psychological motivations that drove him to seek unlimited autocratic power through purge and terror. Still less has it penetrated the intricate interplay between these psychological motivations and his political goals and ideas. Nor, although much pertinent evidence has long been on the record, has adequate attention been given to the formation of Stalin's political personality in early life. What made him a Marxist, why he dropped out of a theological seminary at the age of twenty to pursue revolution as a career, why he became a Bolshevik follower of Lenin when most Georgian Marxists were choosing Menshevism, and what his personal goals in the revolutionary movement were—all these remain open questions. It is essential to answer them if we are to arrive at a deeper understanding of his actions in later life.

Such leaders of psychological thought in this century as Karen Horney and Erik Erikson (not to mention their predecessor Sigmund Freud) have taught us keener appreciation of the developmental nature of personality. Character and motivation are not static qualities; they undergo growth and change in lives normally marked by crucial junctures and times of future-determining decision. Moreover, the selfhood or (in Erikson's phrase) "psychosocial identity" formed in youth has a prospective or programmatic dimension. It comprises not simply an individual's sense of who and what he is, but also his goals—his clear or inchoate beliefs about what he can, should, and will achieve. Hence later biographical vicissitudes cannot but impinge upon personality profoundly. Fulfillment or nonfulfillment of the inner life-scenario necessarily affects the individual's relationship to himself, and this is something that lies at the core of personality. It is likewise bound to affect his relations with other persons significant to him and thereby, perhaps, his and their lives as a whole. All this is as true of persons who become dictators as of others. In studying such a life, therefore, one should inquire into the structure of aspiration in the formative years, and seek to uncover the view in retrospect, the individual's attitude in middle years towards his intervening life-history.

As the foregoing implies, in speaking of "dictatorial personality" I do not have in mind some hypothetical psychological syndrome that appears in an individual at an early age and functions as a constant quantity thereafter. Such a view would contradict both the developmental concept of personality, as just outlined, and the facts of a classic case like the one before us. We can see the makings of the future tyrant in Stalin as a younger man. Nevertheless, the dictatorial personality was not yet fully formed in him. This may help to explain why many of those around him in the early nineteen-twenties—which were his early forties—failed to perceive the danger looming up. Nor should we assume that he himself, then and earlier, had his eyes firmly fixed upon his future dictatorship as a goal. It is not clear that Stalin *wanted* to become a tyrant. What he seems to have wanted was political power, and with it the role of acknowledged leader of the Bolshevik movement, a second Lenin. He wanted to be the successor, just as he had earlier wished to be the closest comrade-in-arms, of the man whom he had taken in early manhood as his identity-figure and model. His supreme aspiration was to be, like Lenin, a hero in history. Naturally, very many other people, first of all those who were Bolsheviks, had parts to play in the enactment of this life-scenario.

It follows that a study such as this must consider not simply the individual in whom the dictatorial personality is likely to emerge but also the milieu, and the interaction between the one and the other. It must take account of historical factors, including the role to which the individual aspires. Bolsheviks freely accepted and even revered Lenin as their chief. His special position in the party was not a constitutionally defined office, like the American presidency, but an informal leadership role. It had a definite and vitally important place, however, in the party's practice and collective consciousness, or what would today be called its political culture. Lenin's

role in the party had come into existence in the quarter-century of
Bolshevism's history as a revolutionary movement built and led by
him. This study therefore starts with an attempt to delineate anew
the nature of that movement and of Lenin's role as its leader.

Our main subject in this volume is Stalin up to late 1929,
when he completed his long march to political supremacy and won
party recognition as Lenin's successor. Yet, the study is not rigidly
bound to chronology. I have felt free to cite facts and episodes out
of later years when they were pertinent to the argument, and also
to leave aside certain themes of the nineteen-twenties, such as the
development of Stalin's foreign-policy conception, for consideration
in connection with his actions in the thirties. These actions are the
subject of a further volume in preparation, *The Revolution from
Above*.

The new mode of biography to which Erikson has given the
name "psychohistory" offers, as frontiers usually do, both excitement and danger. One danger is that of concentrating so much of
a study's attention upon the personality of a leader that in effect
one conveys a simplified picture of the part this factor played in
influencing the course or pace of history. The challenge facing a
psychohistorical study of an influential political leader is not simply
to examine the subject's personality in as systematic and insightful
way as possible. It is, in addition, to delve into those linkages and
interactions of personality with social milieu and political situation
which alone made it possible for the personal factor to become historically important in the given case.

In the case being considered here, the outcome—Stalin's rise
and later autocracy—has its explanation in the nature of Stalin, in
the nature of Bolshevism as a political movement, in the nature
of the Soviet regime's historical situation in the nineteen-twenties,
and in the nature of Russia as a country with a tradition of autocratic rule and popular acceptance of it. But only by clarifying the
complex conjunction of all these can we discover why it was that
in this instance personality proved to be, as Lenin belatedly but
correctly foresaw, a *decisive* trifle.

ACKNOWLEDGMENTS

MANY PEOPLE have assisted me in this work. My thanks go first to my wife, Evgenia Pestretsova Tucker, whose participation has made the undertaking a shared experience from its earliest beginnings. These go back to Stalin's final years, when she and I were living in Moscow and the idea of writing a psychological study of him first occurred to me. The book owes very much to her help with the research, her linguistic expertise, and her sage counsel on the human realities of Russia—to mention only the more tangible contributions. It owes something as well to her parents, Raisa and Konstantin Pestretsov, who helped make the period covered by the book real to me by sharing their personal memories of Russia in the revolutionary era and the twenties.

George F. Kennan, under whom I worked in the American Embassy in Moscow in 1944–46 and again in 1951–52, was not only deputy chief of mission and later ambassador but a mentor in Russian studies; he was a formative influence on my efforts in this field. I have enjoyed the privilege of bringing the present volume to completion during a period of leave at the Institute for Advanced Study, where Professor Kennan has given generously of his time in discussing various facets of the Stalin problem with me and advising on particular questions concerning the book.

Another friend who stands in a special relationship to this study is my colleague at Princeton University, Professor Stephen F. Cohen. He has been a never-failing source of help of every kind, whether in discussing matters of substance, calling my attention to pertinent new materials, or reading chapters in early draft. Both

Professor Kennan and he have, in addition, done me the favor of giving the whole manuscript a critical reading. Even if we still do not see eye to eye on all points (when have scholars in Russian studies ever done that?) the work is far less imperfect as a result. Among other friends to whom I owe special gratitude for assistance and encouragement are Julius Cohen, Theodore Draper, Robert Adamson, Martin Albaum, Moshe Levin, and my two editor-critics at W. W. Norton: George Brockway and James Mairs.

A number of persons who knew Stalin or had an opportunity to observe him at close quarters were good enough to meet with me individually and share some of their impressions or answer questions that I raised. These include Milovan Djilas, Svetlana Alliluyeva, Ambassador W. Averell Harriman, Ambassador Charles E. Bohlen, Ambassador Gebhardt von Walther, Jean L. Laloy, Dr. Karl Schnurre, and Alexander Bittelman. Their willingness to help is much appreciated.

My large debt to Erik H. Erikson's thought, as well as to that of the late Karen Horney, will be made evident in these pages. In addition to all that I learned from Erikson's writings, I benefited from the opportunity that he kindly offered to discuss the study with him and a group of colleagues at the Austen Riggs Center in Stockbridge, Massachusetts. Later, he read and discussed with me my draft of the chapters on Stalin's childhood and youth. Not only those chapters but others as well bear the imprint of his illuminating comments and questions.

Although this study does not view Stalin as a psychiatric case, I have welcomed opportunities to bring to bear upon it the insight of still other psychiatric minds. Drs. Robert S. Wallerstein, Otto F. Kernberg, and Albert J. Lubin have also read the above-mentioned chapters and reacted with penetrating comments and suggestions, and each has shown a generous interest in the work as a whole. Dr. Wallerstein took the initiative of arranging for me a useful meeting with a Psychoanalytic Association study-group of which he was in charge. Drs. Erich Fromm, Humphrey Osmond, and Gerald Perman individually discussed aspects of the study with me. Finally, a number of psychiatrists have been good enough to respond to my request to evaluate the testimony of Khrushchev's secret report psychologically, and I hope to make reference in the second volume to the responses.

Portions of the manuscript have been read by Bruce Mazlish, Terence Emmons, Felix Gilbert, Arno Mayer, Biserka Limic, Darrell Hammer, and Donald Light. Bertram D. Wolfe, Leonard Schapiro, Helene Carrère D'Encausse, Robert H. McNeal, David M. Lang, Abdurakhman Avtorkhanov, Sidney Ploss, Eugene Lyons, Renata Bournazel, and Warren Lerner kindly corresponded in reply to questions I raised. I am grateful to all these as well as to the numerous other colleagues, friends, and students with whom I have discussed the book's subject over the years.

The Princeton Center of International Studies has been most helpful in providing support and facilities. The Guggenheim Foundation assisted with a fellowship, the American Council of Learned Societies with grants in Slavic studies, and Princeton University with a McCosh faculty fellowship. I was fortunate in being able to spend the 1964–65 academic year as a fellow of the Center for Advanced Study in the Behavioral Sciences at Palo Alto, where the writing of the study began, and the 1968–69 academic year as a member of the School of Historical Studies of the Institute for Advanced Study at Princeton, where it continued. In addition to affording ideal conditions for work, both institutions provided opportunities for searching seminar discussion of problems of my research. I am much indebted to the staff of both and to the Institute's director, Dr. Carl Kaysen.

I am grateful to the staff of the Princeton University Library and particularly its curator of Slavic Collections, Dr. Zed David, for assistance in obtaining materials needed for research; to the Harvard University Library and its late director, Professor Merle Fainsod, for the opportunity to consult the Trotsky Archive; and to the staff of the Hoover Institution Library at Stanford. My special appreciation goes to the late Boris I. Nicolaevsky and to Anna M. Bourguina for their assistance in making available materials of the Hoover Institution's Nicolaevsky Collection. The many hours of conversation with Boris Nicolaevsky about Russian revolutionary history and Soviet politics threw light on many problems and are among my treasured memories of the year in Palo Alto.

Finally, I wish to thank Thomas Robertson, M. L. Bird, Anne Rassweiler, David Fisher, Carl Walter, Anthony Trenga, Jerome Nestor, and Kevin Moore for research assistance, and Lorna Giese, Helena Smith, Janet Smith, and Margaret Van Sant for their able typing of the manuscript at various stages. And I am once again indebted to Emily Garlin for her expertise in the final editing of the manuscript.

Princeton
July 1972

STALIN

AS REVOLUTIONARY

1879-1929

Paraphrasing the well-known words of Luther, Russia might say: "Here I stand, on the borderline between the old capitalist and the new socialist worlds. Here, on this borderline, I unite the efforts of the proletarians of the West and the peasantry of the East in order to smash the old world.

"May the god of history help me."

— STALIN (1920)

Chapter One

RUSSIAN PROLOGUE

I am not the crow but only a fledgling;
the real crow is still flying up above.[1]

AT THE START OF THIS CENTURY, when constitutional government prevailed in most of Europe, absolute autocracy still held sway in Russia. Article I of the Fundamental Laws of the Russian Empire, issued in 1892, read as follows: "The Emperor of All the Russias is an autocratic and unlimited monarch. God himself commands that his supreme power be obeyed out of conscience as well as fear." The tsar could not make all the politically significant decisions personally, and was subject to influence from his chosen advisers in those that he made. But with these qualifications, it could be said that in this instance the formalities corresponded closely to the realities.

The higher organs of government in Russia were emanations of the tsar's autocratic power. Thus the Council of State, a legislative body whose deliberations were conducted in secret, was appointive and merely advisory; it was the tsar himself who made the decisions on passage or repeal of laws. In doing so he often accepted the minority rather than the majority opinion among the advisers, or acted without soliciting an opinion from the council. The Committee of Ministers was not a cabinet in the ordinary sense, but merely a coordinating conference of ministers who were wholly responsible to the tsar himself and dealt with him directly and sep-

---

1. Prophecy attributed to Emelian Pugachev, an insurrectionist who was captured, tried, and executed after leading a peasant rebellion that engulfed the Volga region in 1773–75 and was put down by the Russian army.

arately on matters within their domains.[2] Foreign policy, for example, was decided exclusively by the tsar in company with his foreign minister or any others whom he chose to consult. The government as such not only did not decide foreign policy; it ordinarily was not even permitted to discuss it. According to Gorchakov, one of the nineteenth-century Russian foreign ministers, "In Russia there are only two people who know the policy of the Russian cabinet: the Emperor, who makes it, and myself, who prepares and executes it." And commenting on his own role, Gorchakov compared himself "to a sponge that is caused by pressure from the Emperor's hand to emit the liquid with which it is filled."[3]

Russian government was bureaucratic as well as autocratic. The huge empire stretching from the Baltic to the Pacific was governed from St. Petersburg by a bureaucracy of uniformed officials serving the tsar. The governors of provinces were appointed by, and responsible to, the Ministry of Internal Affairs. They and their subordinate officials in the provincial capitals served as agents of the central government. Nor, with the exception of Finland, were the peoples of non-Russian nationality permitted self-rule within the frame of the Empire. Civil liberties were all but nonexistent for the tsar's subjects. Political parties were prohibited, and could exist only on a clandestine basis. Thus the meeting that founded the Russian Social Democratic Workers' Party in Minsk in 1898 was held underground. Official censorship of publications was still practiced. The internal passport system, a means of control over the movement and residence of people, remained in force. The Okhrana, as the redoubtable Russian secret police was then known, had an extensive network of informers serving as its eyes and ears throughout Russian society. The Russian Orthodox Church, controlled by a state body called the Holy Synod, was a state religion with corresponding official protection and privileges. Government officials

2. Sir Donald Mackenzie Wallace, *Russia* (London, 1912), pp. 374, 392–393.

3. G. H. Bolsover, "Aspects of Russian Foreign Policy, 1815–1914," in *Essays Presented to Sir Lewis Namier*, ed. R. Pares and A. J. P. Taylor (London, 1956), pp. 323, 325.

were obliged to attend communion service at least once a year and to certify their compliance with this rule.

Earlier, Tsar Alexander II had sponsored a series of sociopolitical reforms beginning with the Act of 1861, which abolished serfdom. Although these reforms of the eighteen-sixties brought about the beginnings of local self-government through the *zemstvo*, or local assembly, the autocratic apex of the Russian political structure was left intact. Alexander himself said to Bismarck in 1861 that constitutionalism was not in accord with Russia's political tradition; any move to limit the tsar's autocratic power would, he asserted, shake the belief of the common people that he was their "paternal and absolute God-given ruler." Should he grant the country a constitution today, he remarked on another occasion, "tomorrow Russia would fall to pieces."[4] Ironically, he had reconsidered and was making preparations to grant a parliamentary charter when revolutionaries assassinated him in 1881, ushering in the period of repression and severe reaction that ensued under Alexander III. It took the Revolution of 1905 to extract constitutional innovations from a reluctant tsarist authority. Political parties were legalized, and a mainly elective national parliamentary assembly, the State Duma, came into being. But even then Nicholas II went on trying, in his fumbling and ineffectual way, to act the part of the "unlimited monarch" that the Fundamental Laws had declared the autocratic Emperor of All the Russias to be. No true parliamentary regime developed, and tsarism survived, only to be destroyed in the revolutionary storm that swept over the Russian land in 1917.

But not even a national upheaval of that magnitude changes everything. Such elements of the old political culture as deep-seated popular attitudes toward government tend to persist under the resulting new political order. The centuries of tsarist autocracy, and of the officially sponsored ruler cult accompanying it, had instilled a monarchist mentality in large sections of the populace, particularly the peasants; and the destruction or dispersal abroad of many

4. W. E. Mosse, *Alexander II and the Modernization of Russia* (New York, 1962), pp. 112, 113.

from the numerically small upper and middle strata during the revolutionary years gave the peasant class still greater weight in the society. It should be added that the industrial workers, whose numbers had rapidly grown in the second half of the nineteenth century as Russian industrialization gathered speed, in many cases preserved close ties with the ancestral village.

"Without the tsar the land is a widow; without the tsar the people is an orphan." So the legend of the *Batiushka Tsar'* (Tsar-Father) found expression in proverb. Numerous other old Russian sayings convey the same thought in different ways: "Only God and the tsar know." "Everything is under the power of God and the sovereign." "Through God and tsar is Russia strong." [5] Clearly, the political fidelity of the Russian peasant was not to an abstract institution, the state, but to the ruler in person. Autocracy, along with Orthodox Christianity, appeared to him a part of the natural order of things, corresponding on the higher, national plane to the familiar patriarchal authoritarianism of family life in the village. Only toward the close of the tsarist period did this sentiment begin to lose its hold upon the popular mind.

The grievances felt by the peasant were many and deep, and he was not always averse to voicing them or even to acting upon them violently. But he typically vented his feelings of protest upon the immediate agents of misfortune—above all the landlord—and exempted the tsar himself from blame. For was not the tsar surrounded by ministers and counselors who deceived him and kept him in ignorance of the people's sufferings? Such was the peasant's line of reasoning, and it must have imparted a special poignancy to another of his proverbs: "God is high above, and the tsar is far away." So, a tenacious faith in the tsar's benevolence kept alive the popular tradition of attempting to apprise him of conditions and of directly petitioning him for redress of grievances. It was in this tradition that the priest Georgi Gapon led an icon-bearing procession of workers to the Winter Palace in Petersburg on January 22, 1905, to petition Nicholas for reforms and assistance. The tsar would not

5. Michael Cherniavsky, *Tsar and People: Studies in Russian Ruler Myths* (New Haven, 1961), p. 191 n.

receive his loyal subjects, troops fired upon the procession, and the day went down in Russian history as "Bloody Sunday." The massacre contributed both to the outbreak of the 1905 Revolution and to the decline of credence in the traditional Russian ruler-myth. Its symbolic significance to a tradition-bound Russian mind was expressed in Gapon's tragic words after the shooting: "There is no tsar anymore."[6]

The great popular insurrections that broke out from time to time in Russian history show that the peasant, even at his most rebellious, tended to preserve a loyalty to the tsar or to the idea of being ruled by a tsar. There were the uprisings under Ivan Bolotnikov and others during the Time of Troubles in 1605–13, the rebellion led by Stenka Razin in 1667–71, and the one led by Emelian Pugachev during the reign of Catherine II a century later. Cherniavsky speaks of the "tsar-centeredness" of these insurrectionary movements, pointing out that they advanced against the landed magnates and officials under the banner of the tsar.[7] In no case did the leaders proclaim the movements to be in opposition to the tsar. They held, rather, that the tsar was on their side, or that some other member of the royal family was with them, or that they themselves *were* the tsar. Thus Razin maintained that the tsar's eldest son and heir, the Tsarevich Alexis, was marching up the Volga with his rebels, and Pugachev impersonated the murdered husband of Catherine, Tsar Peter III. It was in deference to the tradition of tsar-centered revolt that the republican Decembrists,[8] in calling upon their troops to rise, did so in the name of a supposed "true tsar," the Grand Duke Constantine. Finally, the historical record offers

6. *Ibid.,* p. 192. Gapon headed a St. Petersburg society of workers' mutual aid which had been formed with government assistance to divert worker dissatisfaction into safe channels.

7. *Ibid.,* p. 70. On this point see also Paul Miliukov, *Russia and Its Crisis* (New York, 1962), pp. 257–261.

8. A group of high-born guards officers, influenced by Western constitutional ideas (in some cases while serving abroad), who made an unsuccessful attempt to stage a troop rising in Petersburg on December 14, 1825, following the death of Alexander I. Some were executed, others exiled to convict labor in Siberia. In later years their action was seen as the opening episode of the Russian revolutionary movement of the nineteenth century.

some evidence for the case in a negative sense. When members of the radical intelligentsia went out into the villages in the "going to the people" movement of the eighteen-seventies and preached socialism to the peasantry in an anti-tsarist spirit, the peasants themselves turned very many of them over to the police. The absence of a monarchist theme from the educated young radicals' socialist propaganda may help to explain the negative peasant response to the movement. Not until the turn of the century did this situation change. By that time the Russian peasant and especially the peasant-turned-worker was finally becoming receptive to revolutionary propaganda of non-monarchist character.

Significantly, the intelligentsia had earlier shown a certain monarchist tendency in its own thinking, and this despite the fact that its characteristic attitude was one of estrangement from the tsarist order. This small stratum of critically minded Russians consisted originally of educated offspring of the landed nobility. By the middle of the nineteenth century it was attracting increasing numbers of commoners from among the fortunate few who gained entry to higher education. Its burning concern was the "social question," which before the emancipation decree of 1861 meant primarily the abolition of serfdom; and some of its representatives pinned their hopes on the monarchy itself as the agency of this great reform. Why should serfdom not be abolished by a progressive tsar acting from above against the resistance of those serf-owning nobles whom Alexander Herzen—a foremost spokesman of the intelligentsia in the eighteen-forties and fifties—called the "planters"? Hence the abolitionist-minded intelligentsia, along with liberal elements in Russian society and within the bureaucracy, inclined not toward a constitutionalist program, realization of which would only strengthen the political influence of the landowners, but to the idea of a progressive autocracy. Vissarion Belinsky, the prominent literary critic and leading intellectual of the forties, oscillated in his thinking between hope for a great serf uprising from below and "hope in a dictatorship of the tsar, acting for the people and against the nobles." [9]

9. Franco Venturi, *Roots of Revolution: A History of the Populist and Socialist Movements in Nineteenth Century Russia* (New York, 1960), p. 49.

Nikolai Chernyshevsky, a writer and critic who assumed intellectual leadership of the intelligentsia in the fifties, had in 1848 confided to his diary the thought that Russia needed an autocracy that would champion the interests of the lower classes in order to realize future equality. He added: "Peter the Great acted thus, in my opinion, but such a power must realize that it is temporary, that it is a means, not an end." [10]

Herzen, living in exile in Western Europe, likewise turned his thoughts in this direction. Disillusioning contact with European reality during and after the 1848 Revolution in France led him to revise his earlier Westernism. Taking his departure from the old Slavophile image of the Russians as a "social people," he propounded the idea that the Russian peasant was an instinctive socialist and that the *mir* (the traditional communal village in Russia) was the nucleus of a future Russian socialist society. If the man of the future in France was the industrial worker, the man of the future in Russia was the peasant, the *muzhik;* and economically backward, not-yet-capitalist Russia, blessed by the survival of its archaic village commune, might in fact be destined to lead the world to socialism. [11] Here in embryo was the socialist ideology of the Russian populist (*narodnik*) revolutionary movement that developed among the radical intelligentsia in the late fifties and sixties.

10. N. G. Chernyshevsky, *Polnoe sobranie sochinenii* (Moscow, 1939), I, 356. On Chernyshevsky's life and views, including his earlier hope for a progressive autocrat and his subsequent abandonment of this hope, see Richard Hare, *Pioneers of Russian Social Thought* (London, 1951), ch. VI. Peter the Great was the tsar during whose reign in the early eighteenth century Russia's capital was shifted from Moscow to the newly built city of St. Petersburg, on the Finnish Gulf, where it remained until after the Bolshevik Revolution. He forcefully sponsored a series of Europeanizing reforms of Russian life and manners, efforts in industrialization, naval expansion, and governmental reorganization.

11. For this reasoning see particularly his essay "The Russian People and Socialism," in A. I. Gertsen (Herzen), *Izbrannye filosofskie proizvedeniia* (Moscow, 1946), II, 128–159. On Herzen and his thought, see Martin Malia, *Alexander Herzen and the Birth of Russian Socialism 1812–1855* (Cambridge, Mass., 1961). In the earlier eighteen-forties Herzen was a leading participant in debates that went on in Moscow intellectual circles between "Westerners," of whom he was one, and "Slavophiles," who saw the Europeanizing of Russia as a tragic disruption of old Muscovite Russian culture based on Eastern Orthodox Christianity and the village commune. On these debates see Hare, *Pioneers*, chs. I–IV.

What is remarkable is that Herzen, in the earlier years of Alexander II's reign (1855–81), combined this "Russian socialism," as it came to be called, with the theory of progressive autocracy. He called upon Alexander to be a "crowned revolutionary," and a "tsar of the land," and to continue Peter the Great's cause of reform by breaking with the Petersburg period as resolutely as Peter had broken with the Moscow period. Mikhail Bakunin, the populist leader and philosopher of anarchism, toyed for a time with revolutionary monarchism. "Alexander II could so easily become a popular hero, the first Russian tsar of the land," he wrote in 1862. "Relying on his people, he could become a savior and the head of the whole Slavic world. He and he alone could carry out in Russia the greatest and most benevolent revolution, without shedding a drop of blood." [12] Four years earlier a young Russian socialist, Nikolai Serno-Solovevich, had addressed himself to Alexander in the same spirit through Herzen's London-based periodical *Voices from Russia,* proposing that the tsar use his absolute power to carry out a socialist program of transferring the landowners' land to the village communes under the auspices of the Russian state. "On the throne of Russia," declared this revolutionary, "the tsar can only be, either consciously or unconsciously, a socialist." [13]

The vision of a "Jacobin Romanov" effecting a socialist transformation of Russia from the throne in St. Petersburg was wildly utopian, and the radicals would obviously have been disillusioned even if the land arrangements under the reform of 1861 had not proved so unsatisfactory as to provoke serious peasant unrest in the aftermath of emancipation. The latter circumstance, however, spurred the growth of the militant populism of the sixties, which declared war on official Russia and saw in Alexander II, whom Herzen himself had earlier christened the "tsar-liberator," the greatest enemy of the Russian people. Chernyshevsky and the other populist revolutionaries relinquished any lingering hope for a people's tsar and a progressive autocracy, took the view that the Russian

---

12. Cited by M. N. Pokrovsky, *Russkaia istoriia s drevneishikh vremen* (Moscow, 1920), IV, 146–147.

13. Venturi, *Roots of Revolution,* p. 256.

monarch was only the pinnacle of the aristocratic hierarchy, and said in effect: "Perish—the sooner the better." So it was that Serno-Solovevich, for example, became a founder of the revolutionary secret society *Zemlia i Volia* (Land and Liberty), predecessor of the *Narodnaia Volia* (People's Will) organization, whose leaders finally carried out the assassination of Alexander. But the change of mind was most clearly reflected in the proclamation written by a student, Karakozov, to explain his unsuccessful attempt on the tsar's life in 1866. Russian history, it said, shows that the person really responsible for all the people's sufferings is the tsar himself: "It is the tsars who through the centuries have gradually built up the organization of the state, and the army; it is they who have handed out the land to the nobles. Think carefully about it, brothers, and you will see that the tsar is the first of the nobles. He never holds out his hand to the peasant because he himself is the people's worst enemy." [14]

Since Karakozov's shot was symbolic of the disappearance of the vision of a progressive tsarist autocracy from the mind of the radical intelligentsia, it might seem an appropriate point at which to end the story of Russian revolutionary monarchism. But we now come to one of those metamorphoses in the history of political thought which show its inner complexity. For in abandoning the notion of a progressive autocracy, the *narodniki* of the sixties and seventies gave it a new incarnation that preserved an essential part of its content while radically changing its form. From the previous idea of a dictatorship of the tsar acting for the people against the nobles, and transforming Russia from above on socialist principles, some deleted the figure of the tsar—*and substituted for it the organization of revolutionaries.* What supplanted the notion of progressive autocracy, then, was the idea that a revolutionary seizure of power from below should be followed by the formation of a dictatorship of the revolutionary party, which would use political power for the purpose of carrying through from above a socialist transformation of Russian society. This theory of revolutionary dictatorship became known as "Russian Jacobinism."

14. *Ibid.,* p. 346.

One of its early formulations appeared in a populist proclamation circulated in 1862 under the title "Young Russia." The author, P. G. Zaichnevsky, was leader of Land and Liberty's secret group at Moscow University. The theory was more fully elaborated by such major figures of the populist movement of the seventies as Pyotr Tkachev and Pyotr Lavrov. According to Tkachev, a ruling elite of revolutionary intellectuals who had conquered political power through "destructive" revolutionary activity from below would utilize this power for "constructive" revolutionary activity from above. Relying chiefly on persuasion of the masses through propaganda rather than on coercion, they would gradually transform the country on socialist lines—building the *mir* into a genuine commune, expropriating private property in the means of production, fostering equality, and encouraging popular self-government to the point where the revolutionary dictatorship would itself no longer be needed. Similarly, the leadership of the People's Will envisaged the establishment of a "provisional revolutionary government" that would carry through a socioeconomic revolution from above, which would be ratified by representatives of the people meeting in a national assembly. Such was Russian Jacobinism in the setting of the populist movement. The old idea of a progressive tsarist autocracy was, no doubt unwittingly, one of its sources. And it had an enduring effect upon history owing to the influence that it exerted upon the political thought of Lenin.

The populists of the seventies had been divided over revolutionary tactics, some advocating the gradual conversion of the peasants to their cause through propaganda (as in the "going to the people" movement of that decade) and others arguing for propaganda "by deed," meaning terrorist action. The latter group saw the Russian peasant as a potential rebel against authority, and reasoned that an act like the assassination of the tsar might spark a general conflagration in the countryside, a greater and successful Pugachev movement. The assassination of Alexander II in 1881, by members of the People's Will, aroused no such peasant response, however, and led to more severe reaction under his successor, Alexander III.

In the sequel many radicals from the populist camp turned away from the tactics of terrorism and lost faith in the peasantry as a revolutionary constituency. Meanwhile, another potential constituency was appearing in the still small but growing Russian industrial worker class, which numbered upwards of three million before the end of the century.[15] Given all these conditions, it is not surprising that a section of the intelligentsia grew receptive to the ideology of proletarian socialist revolution being propagated by Karl Marx and Friedrich Engels. In a number of European countries there existed by this time Social Democratic parties professing Marxism as their program and acting in the name of the industrial working class as their principal constituency. In 1883 a populist turned Marxist, Georgi Plekhanov, launched Russian Marxism on its career as an organized movement by forming a group for "The Liberation of Labor" in Geneva, Switzerland, where he resided.

The initial impulse of the movement, which had in Plekhanov a mentor as well as organizer, was the search for new ways in Russian revolutionary politics. The founding documents were Plekhanov's anti-populist tract *Socialism and the Political Struggle* and its continuation, *Our Differences*. In them he concentrated his attack squarely upon Russian Jacobinism. The conception of a seizure of power by a secret conspiratorial organization was a "fantastic element" in the People's Will program. The very notion of a "provisional revolutionary government" exercising tutelage over the people in the process of building a socialist society was objectionable. A dictatorship of the revolutionary party was unnecessary and undesirable; the workers would not want to exchange one form of tutelage for another, and would no longer need "tutors" by the time of their future graduation from the historical school of revolutionary political self-education. Meanwhile, a premature capture of power by an organization like the People's Will, even supposing it to be feasible, would either collapse for want of popular support or

15. J. L. H. Keep, *The Rise of Social Democracy in Russia* (London, 1963), p. 6. The total population of Russia in 1897 was 129 million. Peasants constituted four-fifths of the total.

else issue in a "patriarchal and authoritarian communism" or "Peruvian [that is, hierarchical and authoritarian] communism" should the government survive and try to introduce socialism from above by decree. Hence the revolutionary movement should cease conspiring to seize power and give up all idea of carrying out "social experiments and vivisections" upon the Russian people under the dictatorship of a revolutionary party.[16] As for Russia's Marxists, they should join with other oppositionist strata of society, including liberals, in a political struggle to overthrow tsarist absolutism and establish free political institutions in their country. This democratic revolution would accelerate the pace of Russian economic development and permit a growing industrial proletariat to build its own independent political party like the Social Democratic parties of Western Europe. In a future socialist revolution the workers would take power as a class.

In these early writings, as it turned out, Plekhanov was laying the theoretical foundations not of the Russian Marxist political movement as a whole but of its Menshevik wing. The opposing, Bolshevik, wing, of which Lenin became leader, showed the influence of some of the very ideas Plekhanov was attacking. But not until much later did all this become clear.

When *Socialism and the Political Struggle* appeared in Geneva in 1883, the future Lenin was a carefree boy of thirteen growing up as Vladimir Ilyich Ulyanov in the town of Simbirsk (now Ulyanovsk), on the Volga. His father, who was school inspector for Simbirsk province and as such a minor member of the nobility, died in 1886. In the following year Vladimir's older brother Alexander, a student at Petersburg University, joined a new People's Will group in a plot to mark the sixth anniversary of Alexander II's assassination by assassinating Alexander III. The plot was foiled. The young man was hanged, having refused on principle, and despite his mother's entreaties, to ask the tsar for clemency. This event greatly helped to propel Vladimir onto his own revolutionary career. His martyred

---

16. G. V. Plekhanov, *Sotsializm i politicheskaia bor'ba. Nashi raznoglasiia* (Moscow, 1939), pp. 59, 60, 65, 88–89.

brother became his hero and the annihilation of tsarism his implacable aim.[17]

Soon after entering Kazan University in the fall of 1877 to study law, Vladimir was expelled for participation in a student demonstration. The police then exiled him to his grandfather's country estate in Kazan province. In late 1888 he received permission to reside in the city of Kazan, where his mother, sisters, and younger brother joined him. A year later the family moved to Samara (now Kuibyshev), farther south on the Volga. He read for the law examinations on his own, passed them in Petersburg in 1891, and later practiced law briefly in Samara. During all this time, however, his obsessive interest, and the main subject of his reading, was not law but revolution. Among the materials into which he plunged were the populist writings of the sixties and seventies. One that had been his brother's favorite, and now became Vladimir's, was the socialist novel that Chernyshevsky wrote upon being incarcerated in the Peter and Paul Fortress prison in Petersburg in 1862: *What Is to Be Done? Stories about New People.*

In the novel's gallery of radical men and women, the legendary character of Rakhmetov particularly stands out. He is the scion of a landowning family of ancient aristocratic lineage. Soon after arriving in Petersburg at the age of sixteen to study in the university, he undergoes a complete conversion through a meeting with a young man of radical views, and dedicates the remainder of his life to the revolutionary cause. He reads prodigiously. On a trip to Western Europe he insists upon giving away the bulk of his inherited fortune to a poverty-stricken great thinker and father of a new philosophy, "a German." He cultivates extraordinary physical strength through

17. This is not to suggest that his motivation in later life may be summed up under a simple formula. On Vladimir's reaction to Alexander's execution, see Bertram D. Wolfe, *Three Who Made a Revolution* (Boston, 1948), pp. 65–66. For the earlier relations between Alexander and Vladimir, their clash of personalities, see Nikolai Valentinov (N. V. Volski), *The Early Years of Lenin* (Ann Arbor, 1969), pp. 118–122. On Vladimir's hero-worship of his executed brother, see Louis Fischer, *The Life of Lenin* (New York, 1964), p. 17. Fischer plausibly speculates that Vladimir's shock and wrath over Alexander's fate were enhanced by "regret not to have been close to the hero brother." For a more recent study which casts valuable further light on Lenin's early life, see Rolf H. W. Theen, *Lenin: Genesis and Development of a Revolutionary* (Philadelphia, 1973).

strenuous exercise, by keeping to a diet of semi-raw beefsteak and black bread, and even by working as a Volga boatman on his wanderings through Russia. He lives ascetically, taking no wine and rejecting the love of a young woman whom he would have wished under normal conditions to marry. On one occasion he tests his capacity to bear pain by spending the night on a bed of sharp nails. Of Rakhmetov and others like him, Chernyshevsky writes in the novel: "They are few in number, but through them flourishes the life of all; without them it would die out and go sour. They are few in number, but they enable all people to breathe; without them people would suffocate. Such ones are few in the great mass of good and honest people, but in that mass they are as the flavor in the tea, the bouquet in the fine wine; the strength and the aroma come from them. They are the flower of the best people, the movers of the movers, the salt of the salt of the earth."

This novel furnished inspiration for several generations of Russian radicals. That it furnished inspiration also for Vladimir Ulyanov is well attested to by, among other things, the fact that he entitled his own revolutionary treatise of 1902—the most important of all his works in historical influence—*What Is to Be Done?* Conversing with friends in a Geneva cafe in January 1904, he confirmed that he had done so with the novel in mind. He angrily rejected a disparaging remark about the literary quality of Chernyshevsky's work, and confessed that it had influenced him profoundly, particularly when he reread it after his brother's execution: "It captivated my brother, and it captivated me. It *made me over completely.* . . . It's something that charges you up for the whole of your life." He went on to explain that "the greatest merit of Chernyshevsky lies not only in showing that any right-minded and truly decent person must be a revolutionary, but also something still more important: he showed what sort of person a revolutionary should be, what rules of conduct he should follow, how he should proceed to his goal, and by what means he should attain it." [18]

Ulyanov's Marxist self-education began in the fall of 1888 in Kazan, where he studied Marx's *Capital* and made contact with a Marxist "circle" (as clandestine study groups were called). It continued intensively after the family's move in the following year to Samara. There too he involved himself in the activities of Marxist circles. But these were not the only contacts that he made. He also sought out and conversed at length with former members of the People's Will who were living in Samara as political exiles. In these conversations with surviving representatives of populism's heroic period, he showed special interest in the old Russian Jacobinists, beginning with Zaichnevsky and his program of revolutionary dictatorship in the manifesto "Young Russia." "In talks with me," wrote one of the exiles much later, "Vladimir Ilyich often dwelt on the question of the seizure of power, one of the points of our Jacobin program. . . . Now more than ever I come to the conclusion that already at that time he was developing the idea of the dictatorship of the proletariat."[19]

There is much to be said for this view. Though initially Lenin accepted Plekhanov's notion of a two-stage revolution in Russia, the thrust of his thinking all along was toward the creation without delay of a revolutionary party dictatorship dedicated to the transformation of Russian society along socialist lines—the dictatorship that he founded in 1917. Thus in 1905 he opposed the Menshevik tactic of supporting the liberals in a strictly bourgeois-democratic revolution against tsarism, and gravitated to the tactic of telescoping the two stages of revolution under a "democratic dictatorship of the proletariat and peasantry."[20] And when he returned from emigration in April 1917 to a Russia in upheaval, he advocated a strategy of pressing forward from the stage of democratic revolution

lution he returned to Russia and worked in the early twenties for a Soviet newspaper, then went abroad and spent the remainder of his long life in emigration. For further biographical particulars see the introduction by Michael Karpovich and foreword by Leonard Schapiro to the English translation, *Encounters with Lenin* (London, 1968), and the introduction by Bertram D. Wolfe to Valentinov's *The Early Years of Lenin*.

19. Valentinov, *Vstrechi*, p. 117.

20. On this see his *Two Tactics of Social Democracy in the Democratic Revolution*.

represented in the Provisional Government to that of socialist revolution via the seizure of power and establishment of a "dictatorship of the proletariat." In an effort to validate this position ideologically, Lenin went back to his Marxist texts during an interval of forced inactivity during 1917 and wrote *The State and Revolution,* his principal work of political theory.

The aim of *The State and Revolution,* as he put it, was to restore to Marxism the "revolutionary soul" that had been let out of it by such leaders of contemporary Social Democratic Marxism as Karl Kautsky in Germany. The soul of the classical Marxism of Marx and Engels was the teaching that the revolutionary proletarian dictatorship was the necessary political instrument of a society's transition to socialism and future communism. To be a genuine Marxist it was not enough to accept the theory of the class struggle; one also had to accept the doctrine of proletarian dictatorship as the goal and terminal point of this struggle. In practice, moreover, a proletarian dictatorship would mean a dictatorship of the revolutionary party *on behalf* of the proletariat. "By educating the workers' party," as Lenin expressed it, "Marxism educates the vanguard of the proletariat which is capable of assuming power and of leading the whole people to socialism, of directing and organizing the new order, of being the teacher, guide, and leader of all the working people and exploited in the task of building up their social life without the bourgeoisie and against the bourgeoisie."[21] Consequently, it would be in no sense un-Marxist for the party to seize power and rule dictatorially in the interest of building a socialist society in Russia. This was the practical political conclusion implicit in every line of Lenin's seemingly scholastic theoretical treatise on Marxist views about the state.

It was a very Russian revolutionary soul that he breathed back into Marxism. Admittedly, the teaching on proletarian dictatorship had a significant place in classical Marxism, and one which later

21. V. I. Lenin, *Polnoe sobranie sochinenii,* 5th ed., 55 vols. (Moscow, 1958–65), XXXIII, 26. This edition will hereafter be cited as *Lenin.* Many of the major writings contained in it are available in English translation in V. I. Lenin, *Selected Works,* 3 vols. (Moscow, 1970–71), and in *The Lenin Anthology,* ed. Robert C. Tucker, forthcoming.

Social Democratic Marxists, including even Engels in his old age, were inclined to downgrade. But it had not the central place accorded it in Lenin's Marxism, nor was the proletarian dictatorship conceived by Marx and Engels as a dictatorship of a revolutionary party on behalf of the proletariat. They did not imagine that the working people, once in power, would have need of a party as their "teacher, guide, and leader" in building a new life on socialist lines. The elevation of the doctrine of the proletarian dictatorship into the "essence" of Marxism, as Lenin later called it,[22] and the conception of this dictatorship as a state in which the ruling party would exercise tutelage over the working people, were a sign of his deep debt to the Russian populist revolutionary tradition. Leninism was in part a revival of Russian Jacobinism within Marxism. Lenin himself must have been well aware of this. It is less clear whether he was aware that indirectly, therefore, his outlook showed the influence of the Russian autocratic tradition that seemed, in 1917, to have reached its end.

22. For his argument on this point, see his treatise *The Proletarian Revolution and the Renegade Kautsky*.

Chapter Two

LENIN AS REVOLUTIONARY

HERO

ULYANOV moved to Petersburg in 1893, ostensibly to practice law but in fact to engage in socialist activity, and quickly acquired a certain reputation as a learned Marxist from the Volga.[1] Among those whom he met in Marxist circles of the capital were two future Menshevik opponents, Julius Martov and Alexander Potresov, and his future wife, Nadezhda Krupskaya, a young noblewoman involved in after-hours socialist activity while holding a clerical job in the railway administration.

In early 1895, he went abroad for four months, going first to Switzerland, where he met and made a strong impression upon Plekhanov and the latter's associate P. B. Axelrod. On his return he undertook with Martov and others to organize a "St. Petersburg Union of Struggle for the Liberation of the Working Class." These efforts led to his (and Martov's) arrest at the end of 1895. After a year of imprisonment in Petersburg, he was sentenced to three years of exile in eastern Siberia. He and Krupskaya were married when she joined him there in 1898.[2] In July 1900, several months after completing the term of exile, he went abroad again and entered the recently founded Russian Social Democratic Workers' party's leadership as one of the editors of *Iskra* (The Spark)—a new foreign-based party organ that he himself had done much to organize. Ex-

1. Nadezhda K. Krupskaya, *Memories of Lenin* (New York, 1930), p. 1.
2. For Krupskaya's life see Robert H. McNeal, *Bride of the Revolution: Krupskaya and Lenin* (Ann Arbor, 1972), and her own *Memories of Lenin*. Their marriage was childless.

cept for his return to Russia during the insurrectionary turmoil of 1905–7, he remained in emigration until 1917, living mainly in Switzerland. Such are the unrevealing externals of his revolutionary biography.

The First Decade

In Petersburg in the early nineties, socialist activity meant discussions in the "circles," writing on issues before the movement, and propagating socialist ideas among workmen. Ulyanov's colossal capacity for work, combined with his powerful and prolific pen, brought him to the fore as a pamphleteer for revolutionary Marxism during that time of controversy between the populist and Marxist branches of the socialist movement, and between militants and moderates within the Marxist branch. In 1894 he struck out at Pyotr Struve, a leading figure among the so-called "legal Marxists," in a critique nearly as long as the book of Struve's it attacked; and he wrote a book-length polemical reply to an anti-Marxist article in a populist journal.[3] The polemic, entitled *Who Are the "Friends of the People" and How Do They Fight Against the Social Democrats?*, went through three illegal hectographed editions and seven "printings" between July and November 1894.[4]

Openly political socialist writings, not legally publishable under then-prevailing censorship practices, would either be published abroad and smuggled back into Russia or, as in this instance, duplicated and circulated clandestinely (a forerunner of the present-day *samizdat,* or "self-publishing," as the circulation of uncensored writings in typescript is called in Soviet Russia). Writings of academic style and bulk, such as Struve's book and Ulyanov's long review of it, were publishable legally although various circumlocutions and code words, known to the radicals as "Aesopian language," fre-

3. The former was "The Economic Content of Populism and Its Criticism in Mr. Struve's Book," the book in question being Struve's *Critical Remarks on the Question of Russia's Economic Development* (1894). On this controversy see J. L. H. Keep, *The Rise of Social Democracy in Russia* (London, 1963), pp. 29–31, 36–37.
4. *Lenin,* I, 656–657.

quently had to be used. As an example, Plekhanov's influential book of 1895 on *The Development of the Monist View of History* came out legally in Russia. "Monism" was a code word for "Marxism," and the author's name appeared as "Beltov." Among the pen names that Ulyanov used during the first decade were "Ilyin," "Tulin," and "Lenin." Some have suggested that in using the latter his inspiration may have been the Lena, a river in eastern Siberia. "Lenin" would thus carry the connotation of "man from the Lena."

The populist-Marxist debates of the nineties were dominated by other issues than those Plekhanov had raised against Russian Jacobinism in his works of the early eighties. The People's Will tradition of conspiratorial terrorism, which still had some support, was only one of several trends among the populist groups that finally united to form the peasant-based party of Socialist-Revolutionaries (SR's) in 1901–2. In the nineties, the two socialist camps were divided chiefly by the *narodnik* rejection of Marxism as a socialist ideology for Russia, and by a series of economic issues. Lenin's contributions to the debate were notable for their uncompromising defense of the Marxist class-struggle interpretation of history as the only correct theory for the Russian (or any other) revolutionary movement, and for their heavy concentration upon economic issues. He especially opposed the populists' view of capitalism in Russia as a regressive tendency that could and should be stopped, and their belief—associated with idealization of the peasant commune—in Russia's exceptionality.[5] His principal attempt to refute these views was *The Development of Capitalism in Russia,* a treatise produced during his Siberian years on the basis of books consulted in libraries that he was able to visit on the way to the place of exile and other materials brought to him by Krupskaya or sent through the mail by his sister. It sought, in Marxist fashion, to refute the populist position by giving statistical proof that Russian capitalism, which it saw as historically "progressive" no matter how painful its impact, had already undermined the old economy, even in the countryside. "The Russia

5. *Lenin*, II, 532–533. On the populist-Marxist debate, see Keep, *Rise of Social Democracy*, pp. 28–38. For later populist thought see James H. Billington, *Mikhailovsky and Russian Populism* (Oxford, 1958).

of the wooden plough and flail, of the water mill and hand loom," it concluded, "has entered upon rapid transformation into a Russia of the metal plough and threshing machine, the steam mill and steam-powered loom." [6]

In the Marxist-populist debates of the nineties Lenin trained his polemical fire upon his populist contemporaries; he did not attack the early Russian populism of Chernyshevsky and his generation. As if to underline how much importance he attached to this distinction, he constructed one of his essays around the theme that the Marxists had more claim than the populists to the intellectual legacy of that early generation. This thesis was based on the highly strained argument that the thinkers of the sixties (whom Lenin called "enlighteners" rather than populists), neither believed in Russia's special character (*samobytnost'*) nor idealized its village life, but desired its "assimilation into general European culture." [7] Evidently it was through this kind of reasoning that Lenin reconciled his adamant opposition to contemporary populism with his continuing conviction that the Marxist party had much to learn from the pre-Marxist Russian revolutionary tradition. He simply refrained from identifying the latter as populist.

His political writings around the turn of the century reflect the emergence of Leninism (a word he himself never used) as an amalgam of the Russian revolutionary heritage and Marxism. One of his themes was the paramount importance of the practical side of the movement—program, organization, and tactics. This he emphasized in *The Tasks of the Russian Social Democrats,* a pamphlet

6. *Lenin,* III, 597–598. This book was sufficiently historical and statistical to pass the censorship, and was legally published in Petersburg in 1899. Lenin, who was still in Siberia then, signed it "Vladimir Ilyin."

7. "What Legacy Do We Renounce?" in *Lenin,* II, 533. Written in Siberia in 1897, this essay was published legally in Petersburg in the following year. To assure its approval by the censors, Lenin had to use considerable Aesopian language. Thus he chose as a representative figure of the men of the sixties an obscure writer of liberal persuasion named Skaldin. In a letter of 1899 to Potresov he revealed that he had used Skaldin as a code-word for Chernyshevsky, and also that he had overstated the case. On these points see *Lenin,* IV, 544, and Keep, *Rise of Social Democracy,* p. 38. Although Chernyshevsky had died in 1882, after twenty years of prison and exile, his name remained unmentionable from the censors' point of view.

written in Siberia in 1897 for uncensored publication abroad and, appropriately, the first of his writings to appear under the name "Lenin." True, he took issue here with a surviving great figure of the populist movement of the sixties and seventies, Pyotr Lavrov. Now living abroad, Lavrov had recently questioned the possibility of creating a workers' party in Russia without organizing "a political *conspiracy* against absolutism" in the tradition of the People's Will. Respectfully referring to him as "a veteran of revolutionary *theory*," Lenin rejected the idea of confining the revolutionary political struggle to a small group's conspiracy to seize power. The battle against absolutism should consist, he said, not in hatching plots but in training, disciplining, and organizing the workers, in propaganda and agitation among them. But save for its focus on workers instead of peasants, this approach also formed a part, as Lenin well knew, of the populist heritage. So did his way of identifying "absolutism" as the supreme enemy. After observing that bureaucracy ("a special stratum of people specializing in government and placed in a privileged position vis-à-vis the people") existed everywhere, he remarked that nowhere was this institution so unchecked as in "absolutist, semi-Asiatic Russia." Consequently, not only the proletariat but many other elements of the people were arrayed against "the all-powerful, irresponsible, corrupt, savage, ignorant, and lazy Russian officialdom." [8] It has been observed that one common characteristic of "classical populism" in all its forms was the feeling that the "Russian state of bureaucratic absolutism has been the primordial enemy of the popular masses and their intrinsic communal-socialist tendencies." [9]

In the editorial of the first issue of *Iskra,* published in December 1900, Lenin again underlined the cardinal importance of practical organizational questions, and added: "In this respect we have lagged greatly behind the old figures of the Russian revolutionary movement." The party should recognize the deficiency, he said, and

8. *Lenin,* II, 445, 455–456, 459–460, 462.
9. Theodore Dan, *The Origins of Bolshevism* (New York, 1964), p. 143. A prominent figure among the Russian Mensheviks, Dan took part in the Russian Revolution, was deported in 1922, and lived abroad for the remainder of his life. This book was originally published in a Russian edition in New York in 1946.

direct its efforts to devising a more conspiratorial arrangement of its affairs, to systematic propaganda of the rules of procedure and methods of evading the police, and to the training of people prepared to devote to revolution not just their free evenings but their whole lives.[10] Lenin returned to organizational questions in his editorial for *Iskra,* No. 4, in May 1901. This time he spoke of the party's need for a fully worked out "plan" of revolutionary organization, and outlined some features of a plan that he promised to present in greater detail in a booklet then being prepared for the press.

"Organizational questions," Lenin's views on them in particular, were a fateful bone of contention when fifty-seven delegates from Russia and abroad met in Brussels in July 1903 for the Russian Social Democratic Workers' party's Second Congress—a meeting with more claim than the earlier one in Minsk to be considered the constituent congress. When it came time to adopt the party's rules, Lenin and Martov submitted different drafts of clause one, which defined the meaning of membership in the party. Though superficially their formulas were very much alike,[11] the small difference reflected a large issue. Lenin's was the "hard" position, Martov's the "soft." Martov at first had a majority, but lost it owing to the withdrawal from the congress of the delegates of the Jewish Workers' Bund and one other small group of his supporters. (The Bund was an organization founded in 1897 to represent the interests of Jewish workers in Lithuania, Poland, and Russia. It entered the Russian Social Democratic Workers' party at its founding congress in 1898, but subsequently withdrew.) Consequently, Lenin and his followers went down in history as the *Bolsheviki* (majorityites); their opponents, as the *Mensheviki* (minorityites).

10. *Lenin,* IV, 376.

11. For details, plus an account of the congress and preceding events, see Leonard Schapiro, *The Communist Party of the Soviet Union* (New York, 1959), ch. 2. The difference was that Lenin's draft required, along with acceptance of the party's program and material support, the member's "personal participation in one of the party organizations," whereas this portion of Martov's draft provided only that the member must give the party "his regular personal cooperation under the direction of one of the party organizations."

The Beginning of Bolshevism

In the aftermath of the congress the split widened as those involved grew more clearly aware of the depth of the divergence over Lenin's centralistic conception of the revolutionary party. Plekhanov, who now joined Martov, Axelrod, Trotsky, and others in the anti-Lenin camp, questioned the authenticity of Lenin's Marxism and drew a comparison between him and Bakunin with respect to their centralism.[12] Trotsky contended that Lenin was more of a Jacobin than a Marxist and made his often-quoted prediction that "these methods lead, as we shall yet see, to this: the party organization is substituted for the party, the Central Committee is substituted for the party organization, and finally the 'dictator' is substituted for the Central Committee."[13] Soon the friction between "hards" and "softs" took on organizational form as a division between factions. During a few years of unpeaceful factional coexistence there were efforts, sponsored by Trotsky among others, toward unification. The split became formal and irrevocable in 1912 when Lenin called an all-Bolshevik meeting in Prague, where his faction constituted itself the "Russian Social Democratic Workers' party (Bolshevik)."

Born in strife, the original party of Russian Marxists died in schism. But this account of events is no adequate explanation of the origin of Bolshevism as a political movement. Underlying the division at the Second Congress was Lenin's organizational "plan." This he set forth prior to the congress in the booklet promised in "Where to Begin?" Printed in Stuttgart in March 1902, under the title *What Is to Be Done? Burning Questions of Our Movement*, the booklet went into Russia by the usual clandestine methods and was soon circulating among Marxists all over the country. During 1902–3,

12. G. V. Plekhanov, *Sochineniia*, XIII (Moscow and Leningrad, 1926), pp. 116–133 and 134 n. The article, entitled "The Working Class and the Social Democratic Intelligentsia," appeared in *Iskra* in July–August 1904.

13. For this see Robert V. Daniels, *The Conscience of the Revolution: Communist Opposition in Soviet Russia* (Cambridge, Mass., 1960), p. 13. Another critic, cited here by Daniels, denounced Lenin in *Iskra* for his "cult of the professional revolutionary."

copies of it were found in searches of Social Democrats arrested in Petersburg, Moscow, Kiev, Nizhni Novgorod, Kazan, Odessa, and elsewhere. Reactions to it were strong.

The Russian Marxist movement was then experiencing serious internal malaise following its rapid growth during the controversy with the populists during the nineties. It had entered a period of "dispersion, dissolution, and vacillation," as Lenin observed in the booklet. The vacillation was reflected in the appearance of "economism," a school of Marxist thought which held that revolutionary struggle for socialist aims was premature in underdeveloped Russia and that her Marxists should therefore confine themselves for the present to assisting the workers in their fight for economic benefits. This of course was deeply dispiriting counsel for militant Marxists impatient to get on with the political task of overthrowing the autocracy. To renounce revolutionary political action for the foreseeable future was completely repugnant to them. Consequently, in the prevailing atmosphere of uncertainty and doubt, they were all the more receptive to the prospectus for political action and the vibrant message of revolutionary hope and faith which came to them in *What Is to Be Done?*

Every page of this pamphlet reflected a Hannibalian hate for "the shame and curse of Russia," as Lenin called the tsarist autocracy. It poured scorn on the "tailism" that invited Marxists to drag along in the rear of the workers' movement instead of marching in the van and giving it direction. It summoned militant Marxists to form a "new guard" under whose aegis Russian Social Democracy would emerge from its crisis into the full strength of manhood. It breathed a spirit of revolutionary voluntarism, of confidence in the capacity of such a small but well-organized elite of Marxist revolutionaries to build up an oppositional mass movement in Russian society and lead it to victory over the seemingly impregnable tsarist government. Most important of all, it prescribed in clear and definite terms what should be *done* towards this end, and thus it pointed the way for Russian Marxists from revolutionary talk to revolutionary action, gave them a practical plan and tasks to perform.

What was to be done, first of all, was to create the right kind of revolutionary party organization for Russia's special conditions. As if to reveal the inspiration that his plan drew from the populist tradition, Lenin devoted some glowing lines in this connection to the memory of "the magnificent organization which the revolutionaries had in the seventies, and which should serve us all as a model." He argued that the Russian Marxist party, unlike its counterparts in Germany and other freer countries in the West, should not seek a mass working-class membership, although it should strive to link itself with masses of workers and other discontented elements of society through party-infiltrated trade unions, study circles, and similar intermediate groups. To meet the needs of conspiratorial operation in the tsarist police state, the party should consist chiefly of persons trained in the art of revolutionary activity and prepared to make it their full-time occupation. It was of course this idea that underlay Lenin's draft of clause one of the rules at the Second Congress. His and Martov's differing formulations on party membership were predicated upon differing conceptions of the party itself. But only one of these—Lenin's—was clearly thought out.

The party's first great task was essentially one of proselytizing. To counteract the workers' spontaneous tendency toward "trade union consciousness"—the assumption that they could accomplish their class goals through reform of the existing order—the members of the Marxist party must go among them and other discontented elements of the population as missionaries of revolutionary "Social Democratic consciousness." Using the various non-party intermediate groups as focal points for their proselytizing activities, they must preach the Marxist revolutionary word by "propaganda," or the theoretical exposition of Marxist ideas, and by "agitation," or the discussion of a particular grievance from a Marxist standpoint. To coordinate all these efforts and provide a nationwide forum for protest and political exposures, the party must have a "collective propagandist and agitator" in the form of an all-Russian revolutionary newspaper, published abroad and clandestinely distributed throughout the country by party members. An increasingly aroused populace would furnish more and more participants for a party-led anti-tsarist mass movement which ultimately, after a series of revo-

lutionary outbreaks alternating with periods of calm, would overthrow the autocracy in a national armed insurrection.

The theme of the pamphlet was the necessity of leadership for
successful revolution. The party was conceived as a leadership group
that would play an essential part in "making" the political revolution
by giving ideological guidance to the masses and directing the revolutionary movement. In Lenin's Archimedean metaphor, "Give us
an organization of revolutionaries, and we shall overturn the whole
of Russia!" If classical Marxism proclaimed the imminence of world
proletarian revolution, Leninism (or "Marxism-Leninism," as it became known in the Soviet Union after Lenin's death) originated in
the proposition that there is no proletarian revolution except through
the party. But it also advanced a further thesis: the leadership to be
furnished by the elite party must be heroic in caliber. To be able to
overturn the whole of Russia, the organization must consist of revolutionaries of special mold. Social Democrats should take as their
ideal not the trade union secretary but the "tribune of the people,
able to react to every manifestation of tyranny and oppression."
They should be prepared to accomplish, as individuals, great revolutionary deeds. Lenin invoked the name of the German Social
Democratic leader Bebel and those of famous Russian populist revolutionaries of the seventies—Alexeyev, Myshkin, Khalturin, and
Zheliabov—to show what "miracles" individuals could perform in
the revolutionary cause. "Or do you think that our movement cannot produce heroes like those that were produced by the movement
in the seventies?" he inquired. And, predicting that "Social Democratic Zheliabovs" and "Russian Bebels" would come forward and
rouse the people to settle accounts with tsarism, he declared: "The
time has come when Russian revolutionaries, led by a genuinely
revolutionary theory, relying upon the genuinely revolutionary and
spontaneously awakening class, can at last—at last!—rise to their
full height and exert their giant strength to the utmost."[14] Clearly,
in taking the title of Chernyshevsky's *What Is to Be Done?* as his

14. *What Is to Be Done?* in *Lenin*, VI, 1–192, *passim*. Andrei Zheliabov
(1850–81) was an organizer and leader of the People's Will. August Bebel (1840–
1913) was one of the founders of the German Social Democratic party.

own, Lenin was saying that the contemporary struggle against tsarism had need of men like Rakhmetov.

This call to revolutionary heroism sounded a new note in Russian Marxist writings. The historical role of individuals was one of the subjects of the earlier controversy with the populists. The latter contended that Marxist economic determinism precluded their opponents from recognizing the influence of great men upon historical events. The Marxists, for their part, accused the populists of disregarding class analysis of social phenomena in favor of a theory of "hero and crowd" according to which historical progress issues from the impingement of outstanding individuals' thought upon the minds of the uncreative mass of humanity. Such, indeed, had been the theme of Lavrov's *Historical Letters,* a series of articles originally published in a Russian journal in 1868–69. For Lavrov the prime movers of change and advance in history were critically thinking, justice-seeking individuals whose awareness of the imperfection of existing social forms was forever disturbing the sleepy peace of the "human ant-heap." Answering the imaginary objection that mere individuals could never avail against the custom-bound mass of people, he wrote: "But how has history proceeded? Who has moved it? Solitary fighting personalities. And how have they managed to do this? By becoming, as they had to become, a force." Then he visualized the method of becoming a force. A small number of critically thinking, committed, and energetic personalities, realizing that "only through organization is victory possible," would form a "social party" of struggle for truth and justice, seeking in the process to enlist the support of allies among the masses "who have not reached the point of critical thought but suffer from the very same social ills that the party is being organized for the purpose of eliminating."[15] This book became the bible of young Russian radicals of the seventies and a major influence on populist thought.

Presenting the contrary, Marxist, view in a pamphlet of 1898

---

15. P. L. Lavrov, *Filosofiia i sotsiologiia. Izbrannye proizvedeniia* (Moscow, 1965), II, 112, 119, 126–128. Lavrov, it may be noted, had presented the main kernel of this philosophy in his *Outlines of Questions of Practical Philosophy* (1859). For this see *ibid.,* I, 459–460. The Lavrovian point of view finds clear expression in Chernyshevsky's *What Is to Be Done?*

on *The Role of Individuals in History,* Plekhanov argued that the personal qualities of historical figures could affect only individual features of events, not the general trend. Had Napoleon Bonaparte been struck down by a bullet early in life, some other individual of comparable capacity would have come forward to accomplish his life work and the course of history would have been the same. But in an effort to show how Marxism could take account of the "particle of truth" in the great-man theory, Plekhanov allowed that individuals could make a mark upon history by *accelerating* the socioeconomically predetermined course of human development. "A great man is great not because his personal qualities give individual features to great historical events," he explained, "but because he possesses qualities that make him most capable of serving the great social needs of his time." [16] This became the generally accepted Russian Marxist position.

Although Lenin did not directly take issue with it, his own outlook differed radically. The novel whose title he took for the exposition of his revolutionary plan could well be described as a dramatization of Lavrov's philosophy of revolution, and the Lenin of *What Is to Be Done?* as a Marxist Lavrov. He too believed that only through organization is victory possible. He too wanted to organize a party of struggle for change whose influence would spread out in concentric circles from a nucleus of committed, energetic, and enlightened leaders—in this case enlightened by Marxist theory. He too saw the social ills of the great, backward, bureaucratically misruled Russian Empire as sources of material suffering that made it possible for the party of heroes to attract a mass following to its banners. Despite his sincere and fervent acceptance of Marxism, Lenin was so much the prototypical radical Russian intellectual, so steeped in the Russian revolutionary lore of the sixties and seventies, that his plan of revolution came out with a striking underlying structural resemblance to that offered in the *Historical Letters.* And like the earlier work, it was received by some as a gospel.

16. G. V. Plekhanov, *The Role of Individuals in History* (New York, 1940), pp. 48–52, 56, 59. On the issue with the populists, see *The Development of the Monist View of History,* in Plekhanov, *Selected Philosophical Works* (Moscow, n.d.), I, 647–649, 742–743, 787, 823.

To Plekhanov, Lenin's mode of reasoning was bound to seem, on reflection, un-Marxist. There was no place in Plekhanovist thinking for an exuberant faith in the power of Social Democratic Rakhmetovs to work wonders in the revolutionary cause and thereby make history. Not surprisingly, Plekhanov charged that Lenin was reviving the old populist theory of heroes and the crowd, with the sole difference that Lenin's revolutionary heroes were to lead a proletarian rather than a peasant crowd. He explained the belatedness of his critical reaction to *What Is to Be Done?* by saying that only *after* the Second Congress had it become clear to him what an "enormous influence" the pamphlet was having upon the party's practical workers, and to what an extent it owed this influence to its very errors. "Lenin," he is also reported to have said, "wrote a catechism for our practical workers, not a theoretical but a practical work, as a result of which many began to revere him and proclaim him a Social Democratic Solomon."[17]

The older man's acid comment paid unwitting tribute to the strength of Lenin's work, its electric appeal to many of the "practical workers" in the movement. Particularly at that time of demoralization, they most needed what Lenin offered: a practical plan and program designed to further the realization of the party's revolutionary goal. It gave the activists in the movement the clear revolutionary perspective that they craved, and an invitation to carry on revolutionary activities not only among the factory workers but in all strata of the population with grievances against an oppressive regime. More important still, it encouraged them to believe that a people's victory over tsarism was a real possibility—as, indeed, 1905 soon showed it to be. No wonder, then, that Lenin's booklet evoked an ardent response from many Russian Marxists. A report from the *Iskra* organization to the Second Congress said that according to their own testimony numerous persons inside Russia were becoming *Iskra* adherents because of this work. "It gave us practical

17. Plekhanov, *Sochineniia*, XIII, 133–134, 139. The comment on Lenin's "catechism," quoted by N. Valentinov in *Vstrechi s Leninym* (New York, 1953), p. 55, may have been made orally. (See note 18, pp. 14–15.)

workers what we particularly needed," recalled a younger brother of Martov's who at the time was a committeeman in Kharkov.[18] Valentinov, then a member of a circle of young Social Democrats in Kiev, remembers that the whole group greeted the appearance of *What Is to Be Done?* with great enthusiasm and even began to view Lenin as the logical man to become leader of the party at the coming Second Congress. He also recalls how receptive the group was to Lenin's theme of individual revolutionary heroism.[19]

However foreign it may have been to the spirit of historical materialism, this appeal to herculean efforts by revolutionary heroes made heady reading for young Marxist revolutionaries carrying on clandestine political activity in the Russian provinces under conditions that were often drearily discouraging. One such person was the future Stalin, then an obscure practical worker in Transcaucasia. He was one of those who began to revere Lenin as a Social Democratic Solomon. In a letter of 1904 to a fellow Georgian revolutionary living in Leipzig, he unreservedly associated himself with Lenin's views and confessed that Lenin was his chosen leader. He scornfully dismissed Plekhanov's criticisms of *What Is to Be Done?* What he found particularly attractive in Lenin's pamphlet was the doctrine of leadership, the theory that it was the mission of the Marxist intelligentsia to raise the proletariat to a consciousness of the socialist ideal rather than "break this ideal up into small change or adjust it to the spontaneous movement."[20]

It is generally accepted that the beginnings of Bolshevism as a separate movement within the Russian Social Democracy date from around 1903. But this development, as suggested earlier, is not to be satisfactorily explained by the conflict to which the movement owed its name. What gave Bolshevism its original impetus, indeed

18. Quoted in Keep, *Rise of Social Democracy*, p. 93, from Levitsky, *Za chetvert' veka* (Moscow and Leningrad, 1926), p. 122. The original family name of Martov and Levitsky was "Tsederbaum." On the report of the *Iskra* organization to the Second Congress, see *Lenin*, VI, 465.

19. Valentinov, *Vstrechi*, pp. 53–55.

20. I. V. Stalin, *Sochineniia*, 13 vols. (Moscow, 1946–52), I, 56–58. Hereafter cited as *Stalin*.

what brought it into being, was not the quarrel at the Second Congress; it was the appearance of *What Is to Be Done?* Even prior to this Lenin was the author of widely read writings and a figure to be reckoned with among Russian Marxists. But it was the inspirational power of his pamphlet of 1902 that elevated him in the eyes of many and made him the central figure of an actual movement. What was reflected in all this, apart from the cogency of Lenin's ideas to the minds of some of his contemporaries, was the appearance on the Russian revolutionary horizon of a charismatic leader-personality. The "real crow" had finally alighted.

The Leader-Centered Movement

Charismatic authority, which Max Weber contrasts with "traditional" and "rational-legal" types of authority, is described by him as repudiating the past and representing a "specifically revolutionary force." It comes into the world proclaiming the need for and possibility of profound change. The classical manifestation is the outlook of the religious prophet who says, "It is written . . . , but I say unto you. . . ." Weber's implication is that charismatic authority occurs in the context of a social movement that may arise outside of and in any event is in some manner opposed to the existing order—a radical movement, be it of religious, political, cultural, or other complexion. Such movements typically attract persons who are experiencing some form of acute distress—social, economic, psychic, or a combination of these—and who respond eagerly to the promise of deliverance from it. An individual in whom this promise appears to be embodied, whether by virtue of his coming forward with a gospel of radical change or his ability to show the way to change, is a candidate for the role of charismatic leader.

Imbued with a sense of mission, he offers himself as one especially qualified to be the leader of a movement for change. His followers, who are also typically his disciples, freely accept his leadership because they perceive him to be the possessor of extraordinary qualities or powers; and this "recognition" of his special qualification is seen by Weber as decisive for the validity of charisma.[21] To say this is not to imply any irrationality on the part of either leader or followers, but only that his charismatic authority has a definite messianic quality. It therefore arouses their intense and enthusiastic devotion. The strong emotional bond that grows up in these circumstances may find expression, either during his lifetime or after his death, in a cult of the leader. Indeed, we may hypothesize that the followers' spontaneous emotional tendency to surround the leader with a personality cult is one of the characteristic signs of charisma.

Charismatic movements have flourished in diverse civilizations from remote antiquity to the present age. But while the phenomenon is thus neither time- nor culture-bound, these movements differ significantly across time and space in the kinds of powers their leaders are expected to display and in the patterns of approved behavior of followers toward the leader. In a religious milieu, for example, the leader may show charisma by performing or appearing to perform miracles. In a setting where complete deference to those in higher authority is an accepted value, the followers of a charismatic leader will render him unquestioning obedience, and dissent from his opinions on any subject will be unheard of. But in the informal atmosphere of a modern radical movement that thrives on internal discussion and debate, the recognition of charisma in the leader need not be incompatible with argument by a follower, especially a high-placed follower, against this or that view of his. Indeed, his unusual powers of discourse and persuasion, demonstrated in such debate, may be, for the followers, a salient source of his charisma, one of the qualities that impel them to set him apart as the leader and accept his authority. Such, as we shall see, was the case in the movement that Lenin founded.

21. Max Weber, *The Theory of Social and Economic Organization* (New York, 1947), pp. 359–362. Also, Max Weber, "The Three Types of Legitimate Rule," *Berkeley Publications in Society and Institutions,* IV, 1 (Summer 1958), 1–11; and *From Max Weber: Essays in Sociology,* ed. H. G. Gerth and C. Wright Mills (New York, 1958), p. 52. For a discussion of the charisma concept and the literature pertaining to it, see Robert C. Tucker, "The Theory of Charismatic Leadership," *Daedalus* (Summer 1968), pp. 731–756.

Charismatic leaders are most likely to arise in times of crisis when widespread distress renders masses of people responsive to movements of change and those who head them. In the history of the modern West, one such time was the era of the Industrial Revolution, which uprooted large numbers of people and created mass misery in the new industrial centers. The socialist doctrines that appeared in the first half of the nineteenth century, Marxism included, were gospels of radical change addressed to the alleviation of this misery. Friedrich Engels himself was one of the first to point out the resemblance between this historical situation and that in which Christianity arose. Observing that both Christianity and modern working-class socialism originated as movements of oppressed people, he noted: "Both Christianity and the workers' socialism preach forthcoming salvation from bondage and misery; Christianity places this salvation in a life beyond, after death, in heaven; socialism places it in this world, in a transformation of society. Both are persecuted and baited, their adherents are despised and made the objects of exclusive laws. . . . And in spite of all persecution, nay, even spurred on by it, they forge victoriously, irresistibly ahead." [22]

The setting was a natural one for the charismatic tendencies that duly appeared. Reviewing the history of European socialism in the latter half of the nineteenth century, Robert Michels found a "cult of veneration among the masses" to be one of its pronounced characteristics. The founders and later leaders of the socialist movements were "temporal divinities" in the eyes of the followers. Thus Rhinelanders received Ferdinand Lassalle "like a god" when he toured their region in 1864. Both Marx and Lassalle underwent posthumous "socialist canonization" in the movements they had helped to found. In central Italy socialist parents were given to naming their boys "Lassallo" and their girls "Marxina." Sicilian farm workers marched in processions carrying the crucifix side by side with the red flag and placards inscribed with sentences from the writings of Marx. In passing from Protestantism to socialism, indus-

22. "On the History of Early Christianity," in Marx and Engels, *Basic Writings on Politics and Philosophy,* ed. Lewis S. Feuer (Garden City, N.Y., 1959), p. 168.

trial workers of Saxony replaced the traditional portrait of Martin Luther in their domestic shrines with one of August Bebel.[23]

The narrowly based revolutionary movement of nineteenth-century Russia produced its heroes, who also in most cases became its martyrs, but no pronounced charismatic leadership emerged. However, there was in the Russian intelligentsia a definite receptivity to such leadership. A profound alienation from official Russian society and commitment to visionary social goals characterized the radical intellectual as a human type. Conditions of life in Russia so filled him with revulsion that fundamental revolution became, in very many instances, an acutely felt personal need, a cause worth dedicating or even sacrificing one's life to. Persons of such outlook were to be found in all sections of the revolutionary milieu, including Marxist circles, and were capable of responding with passionate devotion to a revolutionary leader of extraordinary or charismatic quality when one at last appeared.

Far more than Menshevism and other Russian radical groups of the time, Bolshevism was a leader-centered movement. As a faction and later as an independent party, it was essentially Lenin's political following in Russian Marxism. As Menshevik opponents liked to say, it was "Lenin's sect." Certain currents of political thought and ideology were, to be sure, associated with it. But to be a Bolshevik in the early years was not so much to accept a particular set of beliefs as it was to gravitate into the orbit of Lenin as a political mentor, revolutionary strategist, and personality.

The gravitational pull of Lenin as a personality appears to have been very strong. In a book of sketches of Bolshevik leaders written many years later, A. V. Lunacharsky, one of Lenin's Old Bolshevik companions, spoke of his "magnetism" (*ocharovanie*). "This magnetism is colossal," he asserted. "People who come into his orbit not only accept him as a political leader but in some strange fashion fall in love with him. This is true of people of the most varied caliber and mental disposition—from such a delicately vibrating enormous talent as Gorky to some clumsy *muzhik* from Penza

23. Robert Michels, *Political Parties* (New York, 1959), pp. 64–67. Lassalle (1825–64) was a prominent German socialist leader.

Gubernia, from first-class political minds like Zinoviev to some
sailor or soldier who only yesterday belonged to the Black Hundred
gangs and today is ready at any time to lay down his wild head for
'the leader of world revolution—Ilyich.' " [24] Testimony from a multitude of sources supports this comment.

The historical core of Lenin's following was a little group of
political émigrés in Geneva who became known as the "Bolshevik
colony." A vivid picture of this group and of Lenin as its central
figure comes from Valentinov. Having been won to Lenin's views
from afar by his reading of *What Is to Be Done?* this young revolutionary made his way to Geneva in early 1904, after escaping from
a Kiev jail, and was received into the Bolshevik colony. It proved to
be a group of people who regarded themselves as Lenin's disciples
and were worshipful in their attitude towards him. Although he was
then only thirty-three years old, they habitually referred to him as
the "Old Man" (*starik*), thereby expressing profound respect for his
Marxist erudition and his wisdom in all matters pertaining to revolution. "The *starik* is wise," remarked one member of the group to
Valentinov. "No one before him has taken apart so delicately and
well the levers and screws of the mechanism of Russian capitalism."
A belief in Lenin's great historical mission was also expressed. As
one member of the group put it: "Ilyich will show us all who he is.
Just wait, just wait—the day will come. Then everyone will see
what a big, what a very big man he is." Despite his own enthusiasm
for the leader, Valentinov was abashed at first by the almost religious "reverential atmosphere" that surrounded Lenin in the colony.
Then, little by little, he too became greatly enamored of Lenin: "To
say that I 'fell in love with him' would be a little comical, but this
verb probably expresses best the attitude that I felt toward Lenin
for many months." [25]

Not all the revolutionaries who came into direct contact with

24. A. V. Lunacharsky, *Revoliutsionnye siluety* (Moscow, 1923), pp. 12–13.
(English translation: *Revolutionary Silhouettes* [New York, 1968].) The phrase
"Old Bolshevik," used above of Lunacharsky, refers in Soviet usage to one who
joined the Bolshevik party before 1917 and took part in its revolutionary activity.
25. Valentinov, *Vstrechi*, pp. 72–73, 75, 79.

Lenin had this reaction, and among those who did there were some, like Valentinov himself, who later broke away and rejected Lenin as a mentor and leader. Yet it attests to the remarkable strength of Lenin's magnetism that it at least temporarily drew into his orbit not only those who responded positively to his way of political thinking but even some whose tendency was to oppose it. Martov, to cite a particularly significant example, is said to have "fallen under the spell of Lenin's personality" during the time of their collaboration as editors of *Iskra*, "scarcely realizing whither he was being led." [26] Another fellow editor and subsequent Menshevik leader, Potresov, published much later a memoir that is remarkable both as a personal confession and as a diagnosis of Lenin's charismatic quality:

> No one could so fire others with his plans, no one could so impose his will and conquer by force of his personality as this seemingly so ordinary and somewhat coarse man who lacked any obvious sources of charm. . . . Neither Plekhanov nor Martov nor anyone else possessed the secret radiating from Lenin of positively hypnotic effect upon people—I would even say, domination of them. Plekhanov was treated with deference, Martov was loved, but Lenin alone was followed unhesitatingly as the only indisputable leader. For only Lenin represented that rare phenomenon, especially rare in Russia, of a man of iron will and indomitable energy who combines fanatical faith in the movement, the cause, with no less faith in himself. If the French king, Louis XIV, could say, *L'état c'est moi,* Lenin, without putting it into words, always had the feeling, *Le parti c'est moi,* that in him the will of the movement was concentrated in one man. And he acted accordingly. I recall that Lenin's sense of mission to be the leader at one time made an impression upon me also.[27]

As Potresov pointed out, there was little in Lenin's appearance to explain his "hypnotic effect upon people." Short, stocky, and bald, he struck some as resembling a Russian peasant. Aside from the driving physical energy and strength he exuded, the only physical attribute that particularly impressed others was his eyes, which

---

26. Keep, *Rise of Social Democracy,* p. 126.
27. A. I. Potresov, *Posmertny sbornik proizvedenii* (Paris, 1937), p. 301. The article on Lenin in which this passage appears was originally published in Germany in the journal *Die Gesellschaft,* Book II (1927).

were variously described as "penetrating," "flashing," "all-seeing," "unusual," and "emitting little blue sparks in the corners." [28] He was, it is universally agreed, totally unpretentious in manner, a person of utmost directness and sincerity.

It was on the speaker's platform that Lenin showed the special powers by virtue of which his followers set him apart from ordinary men. These were not gifts of brilliant oratory such as those for which Trotsky became famous. Lenin's speaking style was completely free of histrionics and striving for effect. Speaking in matter-of-fact tones, although articulately and with concentrated intensity, Lenin would launch directly into the subject at hand and present a clear, logically reasoned analysis replete with supporting facts. The effect upon his listeners was often quite extraordinary. Over and over he demonstrated the power to raise his party audiences to a pitch of excitement, a veritable state of exaltation. Listening to his two speeches at the Bolshevik conference of 1905 in Tammerfors, for example, the normally reserved Stalin, like the rest of the company, was carried away. "I was captivated by that irresistible force of logic in them which, although somewhat terse, thoroughly overpowered his audience, gradually electrified it, and then, as the saying goes, carried it away completely," he recalled. "I remember that many of the delegates said: 'The logic of Lenin's speeches is like a mighty tentacle which seizes you on all sides as in a vise and from whose grip you are powerless to tear yourself away: you must either surrender or make up your mind to utter defeat.'" [29] Similar reminiscences abound in the memoir literature. To cite a vivid one, Max Eastman was moved to a state of "Pindaric rapture" while watching Lenin speak in public for the next to last time, in November 1922, and afterwards described him in a note as "the most powerful man I ever saw on the platform." Lenin appeared to him "a granite mountain of sincerity" of whom "you feel that he is all there for you

28. *Zhivoi Lenin. Vospominaniia pisatelei o V. I. Lenine,* ed. N. I. Krutikova (Moscow, 1965), p. 48; *Takim byl Lenin. Vospominaniia sovremennikov,* ed. G. Zhuk (Moscow, 1965), pp. 104, 118, 499, 500. Louis Fischer writes that Lenin's eyes had "an X-ray quality" (*The Life of Lenin* [New York, 1964], p. 625).
29. *Stalin,* VI, 55.

—you are receiving the whole of the man." It was as though a self-less intellectual had at last appeared on the scene of history, and "he was taking us inside his mind and showing us how the truth looks." [30]

Since Lenin wrote as he spoke, his political writings had something of the compelling quality of his political speeches. Not surprisingly, the genre in which he expressed himself to greatest effect was the lengthy pamphlet on the order of *What Is to Be Done?* At intervals in the years after 1902, he produced a whole series of them: *One Step Forward, Two Steps Back; Two Tactics of Social Democracy in the Democratic Revolution; The Right of Nations to Self-Determination; Imperialism, the Highest Stage of Capitalism; The State and Revolution; The Proletarian Revolution and the Renegade Kautsky;* and *Left-Wing Communism: An Infantile Disorder.* These pamphlet-treatises shaped the strategy and outlook of Bolshevism and were landmarks in its history. Although they contained many excursions into Marxist theory, basically they subordinated theoretical concerns to the practical needs and problems of the revolutionary movement. In this they continued the tendency of *What Is to Be Done?,* which made the Marxist theory of revolution into a theory of how to make a revolution. It might therefore be said that they elevated the practical needs and problems of the movement to the level of theory. Even in his one abstract philosophical treatise, *Materialism and Empiriocriticism* (1909), Lenin was preoccupied with practical needs of the movement as he perceived them, in this case with the need for a doctrinaire Marxist theory of the universe as an ideological foundation; and, appropriately enough, one of the book's themes was the "party character" of philosophy itself. Some Russian Marxist minds of speculative theoretical bent were repelled. But this and other writings of Lenin exerted a hypnotic power over many others precisely *because* of the spirit of partisan practicality that permeated them.

30. Max Eastman, *Love and Revolution: My Journey Through an Epoch* (New York, 1964), pp. 334–335. Eastman came to Moscow in the early twenties as an enthusiast of the Revolution. He married the sister of a prominent Bolshevik and was befriended by Trotsky, among others.

There shone through in Lenin's speeches and writings not only an inflexible will to revolution but a belief in it, a confidence that a socialist revolution would come about in Russia and that he and his followers would lead it. Potresov rightly pointed to this quality of revolutionary faith as a prime source of Lenin's charisma. To appreciate its full significance, we must recall how hard it was in the early years of the century for Russian revolutionaries to preserve faith in the success of their cause. In Chekhov's Russia, as the poet Valery Briusov recalled in 1920, people like himself had pictured the revolution as a far-off event that they were not likely to see in their own lifetimes: "Now, for example, there is talk of travel to other planets, but few of us hope to see them. That is exactly how far away the Russian Revolution seemed to us then. To foresee that the Revolution was not so far away and that now was the time to be moving towards it—this was possible only for a man of colossal wisdom. And this is what astonishes me most of all in Lenin." [31] Lenin had managed to communicate to people who yearned for socialist revolution without seriously expecting it a feeling that such a revolution was a real possibility, and in doing this he was ministering to their deep-seated need for confidence in their own commitment.

It is true that the upheaval of 1905 exposed the inner weakness of the monarchy behind its imposing façade of power, and showed that mass revolution was a potentiality in Russia. But as this revolutionary wave receded and the tsarist regime consolidated itself, the rank-and-file of the revolutionary parties deserted en masse. Many members of the radical intelligentsia began to question the revolutionary beliefs by which they had lived. Russian Marxists showed a tendency to renounce clandestine political activity, thereby succumbing to what Lenin saw as the heresy of "liquidationism." The revolutionary movement as a whole experienced a period of disintegration, stagnation, and decline. And another time of severe trial ensued with the coming of the World War in 1914.

Later testimony from prominent Bolsheviks suggests that Lenin's faith and fortitude during those times of adversity may have

31. *Zhivoi Lenin,* p. 238. Briusov gave the speech in the Press Club in Moscow on the occasion of Lenin's fiftieth birthday.

been of decisive importance for the Bolshevik movement. Stalin, for
one, places great stress on Lenin's instilling of confidence in his dispirited Bolshevik followers after their defeat at the Stockholm "Unity
Congress" in 1906 at the hands of a Menshevik majority. Defeat,
he says, "transformed Lenin into a spring of compressed energy
which inspired his followers for new battles and for future victory."
He further recalls how the Bolshevik delegates huddled dejectedly
together, gazing at Lenin and expressing discouragement, and how
"Lenin bitingly replied through clenched teeth: 'Don't whine, comrades, we are bound to win, for we are right.'"[32] Zinoviev, to take
another example, gives—from intimate personal memory—the following account of Lenin's role during the ensuing "dark era" of
counter-revolution: "He alone contrived to collect a close and intimate circle of fighters, whom he would cheer up by saying: 'Don't
be disheartened; these dark days will pass, the muddy wave will ebb
away; a few years will pass and we shall be borne on the crest of the
wave, and the proletarian revolution will be born again.'"[33]

A significant strand in Lenin's revolutionary faith was belief in
the imminence of socialist upheavals in Europe, and his visions of
Russian revolution drew added inspirational strength from a tendency to picture it as part of a larger, international revolutionary
scene. Already in *What Is to Be Done?* he envisaged the Russian
proletariat making itself the "vanguard of the international proletariat" by overthrowing tsarism. Subsequently he gravitated, as did
Trotsky, to the notion of a dialectical link between Russian and
European revolution. In 1905 he presented an alluring image of the
"great perspectives" that a seizure of power in Russia would open
up: "The flame of our revolution will set light to Europe; . . . then
the revolutionary upsurge in Europe will have a reciprocal effect
upon Russia, and will change an epoch of several revolutionary
years into one of several revolutionary decades. . . ."[34]

The belief in the ripeness of the major European nations for

32. *Stalin*, VI, 56.
33. G. Zinoviev, *Lenin. Speech to the Petrograd Soviet Celebrating Lenin's
Recovery from Wounds Received in the Attempt Made on His Life on August 30,
1918* (London, 1966), p. 29.
34. *Lenin*, X, 14.

socialist revolution was one of the factors behind Lenin's espousal of a radical policy in the wake of the February Revolution of 1917, which deposed the tsar and created a Provisional Government in Russia. When news of this revolution reached Lenin in Zurich, he immediately adumbrated a radical position in a set of "theses" dispatched to Stockholm for the guidance of Bolsheviks then on their way back to Russia. Shortly afterwards, in the first of a series of "Letters from Afar," he declared that the revolution in Russia was only the first of the revolutions to be engendered by the World War, and then went on to say that the Russian Revolution itself was still only in its "first stage." [35] These two propositions were intimately interlinked in his mind. And the imminence of European socialist revolutions was a prominent theme of his messages to the Bolshevik Central Committee in October, demanding that the party proceed without delay to carry out the armed rising and seizure of power.

According to Max Weber, a charismatic leader must from time to time furnish "proof" of his charisma. He must demonstrate in action the extraordinary powers with which he is endowed in his followers' minds. In the case of a revolutionary political leader, charisma will be most clearly proved by the demonstration of extraordinary revolution-making powers. Lenin furnished this proof to the Bolsheviks in 1917.

On a party questionnaire of 1921, Lenin gave his pre-1917 occupation as "writer" (*literator*). But the years of literary activity were spent in preparation for the role of revolutionary command that he assumed on his arrival at the Finland Station in Petrograd (as St. Petersburg had been renamed in 1914) in April 1917. To participate in revolution was the highest of his aspirations. As he put it in a subsequent postscript to *The State and Revolution*, which he wrote while in hiding in August and September of that year and left unfinished when he returned to Petrograd in October to take charge of the revolution, "It is more pleasant and useful to go

35. *Lenin*, XXXI, 11. For the "theses" dispatched to Stockholm, see the same volume, pp. 1–6.

through the 'experience of the revolution' than to write about it." [36] As it turned out, however, "writing about it" was for Lenin a primary means of "going through" it.

His direct personal involvement in the developing revolutionary events was terminated in July after an abortive mass outbreak for which he and his party were held responsible by the authorities. In the ensuing anti-Bolshevik terror, he decided to go into hiding, along with Zinoviev, so as to escape probable assassination. In his absence, overall leadership of the Bolsheviks in the capital devolved upon Trotsky, who only now, at long last, became a member of the Bolshevik Central Committee and formally merged his small personal political following, the so-called Inter-Borough organization, with the Bolshevik party. Elected president of the Petrograd Soviet (revolutionary council) in September, Trotsky used this key position to carry out a series of masterly political maneuvers in preparation for the events of late October. Meanwhile, his spellbinding oratory worked its effect upon the masses. As the climax drew near, he directed the organization of the armed rising and capture of power. When Lenin reached the headquarters of the insurrection at the Smolny Institute on the evening of October 24, he found operations proceeding swiftly and effectively under command of the Military Revolutionary Committee, headed by Trotsky. The following evening, the Bolshevik leaders appeared before the Congress of Soviets, meeting in the Smolny, to inaugurate the new regime. As John Reed describes the scene of Lenin's first appearance on the rostrum, "he stood there waiting, apparently oblivious to the long-rolling ovation, which lasted several minutes. When it finished, he said simply, 'We shall now proceed to construct the socialist order!' Again that overwhelming human roar. . . . His great mouth, seeming to smile, opened wide as he spoke. . . . For emphasis he bent forward slightly. No gestures. And before him, a thousand simple faces looking up in intent adoration." [37]

36. *Lenin*, XXXIII, 120.
37. John Reed, *Ten Days That Shook the World* (New York, 1960), p. 172.

Despite his physical absence from Petrograd during the climactic period, Lenin played a decisive part in the October Revolution. From the beginning, when news of the first revolution reached him in Switzerland, he grasped that a more radical Russian revolution was possible. His political instinct informed him that the warweary soldiers, discontented workers, and land-hungry peasants would give increasing support to a revolutionary party that appealed to them with slogans like "Peace, Bread, and Land" and "All Power to the Soviets!" No sooner had he set foot on Russian soil than he unfolded in his "April Theses" a political strategy aiming at a more radical revolution. Having persuaded the Bolshevik leadership to adopt this strategy as the party line, he then took charge of the efforts to put it into practice. Nor did his leadership of the Bolsheviks lapse when he went into hiding in July. While Trotsky took command in Petrograd, Lenin went on making the revolution in the familiar role of a writer.

His essential contribution was to *nerve* the Bolsheviks into making their decisive revolutionary move when the time came. This fundamental concern inspired all of Lenin's writings and messages from his hiding-place. His seemingly theoretical treatise on *The State and Revolution* pursued a supremely practical end: to persuade the Bolsheviks (including, perhaps, himself) of the full Marxist legitimacy of taking power by force and violence and then setting up a "dictatorship of the proletariat" which would suppress the bourgeoisie and other counter-revolutionary elements. His subsequent pamphlet, *Will the Bolsheviks Retain State Power?*, sought to quell doubts and refute the fearful thought that the party might not be able to hold onto political power if it succeeded in attaining it. If 130,000 landlords could rule Russia repressively after 1905, he argued, surely 240,000 Bolsheviks could rule it in the interests of the lowly, particularly if they took swift steps to expand the social base of Bolshevik rule by enlisting millions of the poor in the everyday work of administration through such organizations as the Soviets.[38] In *Marxism and Insurrection,* a letter to the party written at the end of September, he maintained forcefully that a Bolshevik

38. *Lenin,* XXXIV, 113.

victory was now assured, since all objective conditions existed for a successful insurrection: majority support for the Bolsheviks in both the Petrograd and Moscow Soviets, a nationwide rising revolutionary spirit, great vacillation in the ranks of the other parties, and the advantage of a party that firmly knew the path it must follow. Then, in a series of further messages in October, he virtually bludgeoned the party leaders into taking the historic decision despite the doubts that afflicted some and the objections of such prominent figures as Zinoviev and Kamenev. "We must not wait! We may lose everything!" he exclaimed in a final appeal to the Central Committee written on October 24. "History will not forgive revolutionaries for procrastinating when they could be victorious today (will certainly be victorious today), while they risk losing much, in fact, everything, tomorrow." [39]

Whether or not the Bolshevik Revolution would have taken place without Lenin's leadership is one of those historical questions that people feel driven to pose in spite of their ultimate insolubility. The opinion that Trotsky expressed in his diary in exile in 1935 is all the more significant since he himself was the one other individual whose contribution may have been decisive. In the absence of both himself and Lenin, he reasoned, there would have been no October Revolution. In his own absence the Revolution would have taken place on condition that Lenin was present and in command. Without Lenin, however, he alone would probably not have been able to bring the irresolute Bolshevik leadership to the crucial decision. [40] Something similar had been said by Zinoviev many years

39. *Lenin,* XXXIV, 435–436.
40. *Trotsky's Diary in Exile, 1935* (New York, 1963), p. 46. This statement is consistent with the picture that Trotsky gives in his *History of the Russian Revolution* (Ann Arbor, 1957). Isaac Deutscher summarizes as follows the point of view of the *History:* "His [i.e., Lenin's] shrewdness, realism, and concentrated will emerge from the narrative as the decisive elements of the historic process, at least equal in importance to the spontaneous struggle of millions of workers and soldiers. If their energy was the 'steam' and the Bolshevik party the 'piston box' of the revolution, Lenin was the driver" (*The Prophet Outcast: Trotsky, 1929–1940* [London, 1963], pp. 240–241). Taking issue with Trotsky's view that Lenin's presence was a *sine qua non* of the October Revolution, Deutscher points out that this view ill accords with Trotsky's Marxist *Weltanschauung,* and adds that if it were true, ". . . then the leader cult at large would

earlier. Speaking before the Petrograd Soviet in 1918, shortly after the near-fatal attempt on Lenin's life by a former Socialist-Revolutionary, Fanya Kaplan, he said: "The October Revolution—insofar as even in a revolution one may, and indeed, *must* speak of the role played by the individual—the October Revolution and the part played in connection with it by our party are to the extent of nine-tenths the work of Lenin. If anybody could bring into line all those who doubted or hesitated, it was Lenin." [41] Whatever their historical validity, these judgments tell a great deal about the Bolshevik perception of Lenin's role in the October Revolution.

But it was not only in the taking of power that he gave his followers "proof" of his extraordinary quality; he went on doing so in the exercise of power—as a revolutionary from above. One might argue, at the risk of some exaggeration, that it was in the role of revolutionary statesman that Lenin finally found his true element and demonstrated the full measure of his political genius. With that composed self-assurance which had characterized him from youthful years, he began his career in power by drafting and putting before the Congress of Soviets in the first hours the decrees on peace and land by which the new government established its revolutionary credentials and ringingly appealed for mass support in Russia and beyond its borders. Then he took charge of the beleaguered Bolshevik regime in its epic struggle to survive. No sooner had the Revolution been made than it needed to be defended, and its prospects for salvation were unclear during the critical first two years of turmoil, civil war, and foreign intervention. At the outset, a German ultimatum in the peace talks that Trotsky conducted at Brest-Litovsk plunged Lenin's regime into a grave crisis that was both external

---

by no means be preposterous; and its denunciation by historical materialists, from Marx to Trotsky, and the revulsion of all progressive thought against it would be pointless" (*ibid.*, p. 244). That the view ill accords with Trotsky's *Weltanschauung* may speak against the *Weltanschauung* rather than against the view. Nor is this view invalidated by the consideration that its acceptance would make the Lenin cult seem other than "preposterous." For an argument that Lenin's presence was decisive for the outcome of the Revolution, see Sidney Hook, *The Hero in History* (Boston, 1955), ch. X.

41. Zinoviev, *Speech to the Petrograd Soviet*, p. 43.

and internal. Overcoming the opposition of Bukharin and others in a "Left Communist" faction that was calling for revolutionary war, he finally forced through an acceptance of the German terms in the hope of trading space for time, a policy subsequently vindicated by events. On this ground alone, some Bolsheviks came to regard him not only as the *sine qua non* of the Revolution but its savior as well. Needless to add, Lenin had no monopoly upon heroic leadership of the Bolshevik cause during the revolutionary period. Many others rendered exceptional service in saving the Revolution and constructing the new Soviet order. It is particularly noteworthy that Trotsky rose to great heights as the organizer of the Red Army and chief manager of its operations on the far-flung fronts of the Civil War.

The Leader in Power

In deviation from the historic pattern of Russian autocracy, the Soviet Russian state arose as a novel form of party rule. Political power in the one-party system was vested in collective bodies such as the party congress, which met annually in the early years, and its elected interim surrogate, the Central Committee. Yet, the revolutionary party dictatorship had in Lenin an acknowledged individual supreme leader of such pre-eminence that it could properly be described as a "Lenin regime." What was the nature of his role as leader, and on what basis did he exercise his great authority?

It was not on the basis of his tenure of a particular office. Indeed, no office of supreme leader was established in the Soviet system. True, Lenin held the premiership. He was chairman of the Council of People's Commissars, the central Soviet government. But it was the higher party organs, notably the Central Committee and its subcommittee, the Politburo, that decided Soviet policy in both internal and external affairs, and the government evolved as the party's main executive agency. Lenin was an advocate of this arrangement and took care to uphold it in practice. In 1923, he praised the established procedure under which foreign-policy moves were decided in the Politburo for implementation by the Foreign Affairs Commissariat, and held up this "flexible amalgamation" of party and government institutions as a model of the way in which the Soviet party-state ought to function.[42] There were instances in which he would resolve differences between himself and a subordinate government leader not by invoking his superior power as premier but rather by referring the disputed issue to the Politburo for decision by a majority vote. It must be stressed, though, that he gave strong leadership in his role as presiding officer in the government. A participant in sessions of the Council of People's Commissars later recalled: "Lenin was not merely a chairman but a recognized chief to whom everyone brought his thorny problems. The commissars quarreled among themselves in their daily work, but here Lenin had the last word; and all alike left these meetings reassured, as though their quarrels had been those of children now pacified by a wise parent."[43]

Since the party was the ruling political authority in the Soviet state, it was not as chief of government but as head of the party that Lenin acted as supreme leader. On the party side, however, his primacy was not institutionalized in a post corresponding to the premiership in the government. Officially he was merely one of the members of the higher party organs: the Central Committee, which in the early twenties had about twenty-five full members and fifteen or so non-voting candidate members, and the Politburo. The latter in 1922 had a membership of ten (Lenin, Trotsky, Kamenev, Zinoviev, Stalin, Alexei Rykov, and Mikhail Tomsky, with Bukharin, M. I. Kalinin, and Viacheslav Molotov as candidate members). In filling out a questionnaire as a delegate to the Tenth Party Con-

---

42. *Lenin*, XLV, 398–399.

43. Simon Liberman, *Building Lenin's Russia* (Chicago, 1945), p. 13. An ex-Menshevik, Liberman worked for the Soviet government as a non-Communist specialist in the first post-revolutionary years and in this capacity attended meetings of the Council of People's Commissars. He testifies (pp. 180–181) from his own experience on Lenin's practice of referring decisions on disputed issues to the Politburo. When he directly asked Lenin's help in arranging permission for his son to accompany him on a business trip abroad, over opposition from the heads of the Cheka (secret police), Lenin, instead of over-ruling the latter in his capacity as premier, referred the question to the Politburo, where the issuance of the passport was approved by a vote of three to two.

gress only a year earlier, Lenin gave his party office as "member of the Central Committee."[44]

The Central Committee, like the Politburo, operated as a collegial body, taking decisions by majority vote. In neither was Lenin chairman. Formally, he was on a par with the other full members; his vote counted for no more than theirs. There was a great discrepancy, however, between the formality and the reality of his position in these policy-making bodies. In fact he was the dominant individual and his influence was very great. He was *primus inter pares*, recognized by all the other members of the ruling group as their own and the party's supreme leader.

But what did his acknowledged leadership of the party, and hence of the party-state, mean in practice? It may be useful to approach the question from the negative side. The acceptance of Lenin's authority did not mean that the other leaders were indisposed to disagree with him or oppose him on specific policy questions. As supreme leader, he did not simply issue commands to the ruling group; he did not rule by arbitrary *Diktat*. Automatic acquiescence in his position was not expected; the whole previous history of Bolshevik leadership politics militated against any such dictatorial relationship of the leader to his followers. It was not that Lenin hesitated to impose his views or was easily given to compromise when his position and that of his followers diverged, as happened rather frequently. On the contrary, he was a strong-willed and very self-confident leader who repeatedly set himself against the main current of party opinion in questions of revolutionary strategy and politics. He did not compromise with those who opposed him on matters that he deemed of critical importance for the movement. The point is that the powers on which he chiefly relied in exercising this forceful individual leadership were his powers of persuasion. It was so in the long preparatory period before Bolshevism came to power, and it remained so after the Bolshevik Revolution.

Perhaps the best proof of this proposition is the fact that there were repeated occasions when he failed to gain his way or did so

44. *Desiatyi s"ezd RKP/b/. Mart 1921 goda. Stenograficheskii otchet* (Moscow, 1963), p. 643.

only by overcoming heavy opposition within the party. In April 1905, a majority of the Bolshevik faction successfully opposed his effort to force through a final break with the Mensheviks. In December, he had to go along with the general view in the faction in favor of boycotting the elections to the first Duma, despite his own preference for participation. In August 1907, he found himself in a minority in the faction on the similar issue of whether to take part in the elections to the third Duma. In that same year he was overruled in his opposition to a scheme for a joint Bolshevik-Menshevik publishing venture, and in 1910 he found himself at odds with a majority of Bolshevik "conciliators" who favored reunion with the Mensheviks. In the closing period of the World War, according to Trotsky, it took Lenin a full year to secure agreement to his proposal to change the official name of the party from "Social Democratic" to "Communist" as a means of making an organizational break with Social Democratic Marxism on an international scale.[45]

In the ensuing revolutionary crisis, Lenin took a series of positions that initially disturbed many of his followers and encountered formidable resistance in the party. On his return to Russia in April 1917, the demand set forth in his "April Theses" for a radical strategy looking to an early taking of power was at first termed "unacceptable" by the party's own organ, *Pravda,* and all his persuasive powers were required to overcome the intra-party opposition quickly. In September his appeal from hiding to proceed immediately with the armed insurrection and seizure of power was ignored by the party leadership in Petrograd as untimely, and when he raised the same imperative plea again in late October it was opposed in the Central Committee by a group that included Zinoviev and Kamenev. In the first days of the Soviet regime, these two prominent Bolshevik figures joined with other so-called waverers in advocating, against Lenin, a reformation of the Bolshevik government into a broad socialist coalition. Finally, in early 1918 Lenin's insistence on acceptance of the harsh German terms at Brest-Litovsk had to be backed up by his threat to resign in order to secure the support of

45. "Lessons of October," in L. Trotsky, *The Essential Trotsky* (New York, 1963), p. 140.

the Central Committee, which, at that, passed his motion only by a majority of seven to four, with four abstentions. After the treaty was signed, moreover, Bukharin and his Left Communist supporters proceeded to agitate in the party against its ratification.[46]

Events in the revolutionary period so often vindicated Lenin's political judgment that a saying became common in leading party circles: "Vote with Ilyich and you won't be wrong." [47] However, the argumentative tradition persisted in Bolshevik leadership politics after the consolidation of power, and Lenin's views were not automatically endorsed in the high party councils. We have his own testimony on this point in the correspondence of March 1921 with A. A. Ioffe, who wrote privately to protest his rapid reassignment from post to post by orders of the Central Committee. Appealing to Lenin to put a stop to this practice, Ioffe remarked in his letter: "The Central Committee—c'est vous." In his reply, Lenin most emphatically objected to this phrase, saying that Ioffe could have used it only in a state of extreme nervous irritation and fatigue. He went on: "The old Central Committee (1919–20) defeated me on one gigantically important question, as you know from the discussion. On organizational and personal questions I have been in the minority countless times. You yourself saw many instances when you were a Central Committee member." [48] The defeat here referred to was, it appears, the Central Committee vote of December 7, 1920, on a motion made by Zinoviev with Lenin's support to abolish the Joint Central Transport Committee (Tsektran). This organization, presided over by Trotsky, had become a subject of sharp dispute in the course of the then-developing controversy in the party over labor policy and the functions of the trade unions in the Soviet system. The Zinoviev-Lenin motion was defeated by a vote of eight to seven.[49]

46. For details on these and the earlier instances of intra-party opposition to Lenin, see Schapiro, Communist Party, chs. 3–12, passim.

47. E. Preobrazhensky, in Pravda, April 23, 1920.

48. Lenin, LII, 100.

49. Leonard Schapiro, The Origin of the Communist Autocracy (Cambridge, Mass., 1955), p. 280. For a full discussion of the background of the incident, see ch. XIV in Schapiro. For Lenin's discussion of it, see his article "The Party Crisis," in Lenin, XLII, 236.

Although Lenin was no doubt correct about the facts cited in his letter, Ioffe's remark revealed the underlying realities of the Bolshevik authority structure. For Lenin in some sense *could* (though he never would) have said, "The Central Committee—*c'est moi.*" He was so much the dominant Bolshevik figure, his authority in the ruling group and the party as a whole was so great, that he could usually shape and determine the party line on any political issue of major importance. So far as the vote on Tsektran is concerned, it is significant that this was the only case of defeat on a serious political issue that Lenin was able to cite for the entire 1919–20 period. And it might have been pointed out in reply that the vote had come about rather unexpectedly, and that Lenin's position on the trade unions had prevailed soon afterwards at the Tenth Party Congress.

A true measure of his ascendancy was provided by another incident of that period—the military debate at the Eighth Party Congress in March 1919. In closed session, powerful forces in the Bolshevik leadership mounted a determined attack upon the military policy of Trotsky, who had left Moscow before the debate in order to direct operations against Admiral Kolchak's forces on the eastern front. The defeat of this military opposition became a foregone conclusion, however, when Lenin put in a strong plea on Trotsky's behalf; so much so that Lenin did not even remain at the congress to await the outcome.[50] Again, the ill-fated decision of July 1920 to launch the Red Army on an invasion of Poland—a decision for which Lenin himself was largely responsible—did not even shake his commanding authority in the party, although the results proved disastrous. As Zinoviev remarked at the Thirteenth Party Congress, some months after Lenin's death, no one but Lenin would have been able to go before a party congress (as he did in March 1921) and confess responsibility for such an error with complete political impunity.[51] Finally, it may be noted that Lenin, without holding office in the Communist International, dominated its

50. Isaac Deutscher, *The Prophet Armed: Trotsky, 1879–1921* (London, 1954), p. 431.
51. *Trinadtsatyi s"ezd RKP/b/. Mai 1924 goda. Stenograficheskii otchet* (Moscow, 1963), p. 256.

decisions through his personal influence over the Russian representatives who gave leadership to the organization. They quarreled
amongst themselves, recalls a former German Communist who took
part in the Comintern executive's sessions in 1921, but "when
Lenin had had his say, the question was settled. His authority was
simply taken for granted by his comrades. I don't mean they just
obeyed mechanically or were under any kind of threat. I'll admit
even today that his position was the result of his undoubted superiority."[52]

How was Lenin able to dominate the party without being an
all-powerful chief executive who could give orders to its leading
organs? Some might explain it by the prestige accruing to him as
the one who had founded the Bolshevik party and accomplished
the astounding feat of leading it to power in the Revolution of 1917.
Although not without merit, such an explanation can scarcely be
accepted as adequate. For it leaves open the question of how he
acquired his authority in the beginning and how he held onto it
at the end; and here we must recall that the prestige of many an
historical leader has declined very quickly after reaching its peak.
In the final analysis, Lenin's phenomenal authority in the party derived from his extraordinary qualities as a revolutionary leader and
political personality. We may express this in terms suggested earlier
by saying that he conformed to Weber's conception of the charismatic leader who enjoys his authority not through enacted position
or traditional dignity but owing to gifts of grace (charisma) "by
virtue of which he is set apart from ordinary men and treated as
endowed with supernatural, superhuman, or at least specifically exceptional powers or qualities" (the "supernatural" and "superhuman" being excluded in this instance).[53] Alternatively, we may
refer back to words that Lenin used in 1902 in a "Letter to a
Comrade on Our Organizational Tasks." After describing the kind
of revolutionary organization that his plan envisaged, he declared
that its task was to "preserve *leadership* of the whole movement,

52. Bernard Reichenbach, "Moscow 1921. Meetings in the Kremlin," *Survey*, No. 53 (October 1964), p. 17. Reichenbach was a co-founder of the German
Communist party.

53. Weber, *Theory of Social and Economic Organization*, p. 358.

preserving it, of course, not by force of power but by force of authority, by force of energy, by greater experience, greater versatility, and greater talentedness." [54] This formula for the party's preservation of its leadership of the mass movement may be taken as a fair description of how Lenin himself preserved leadership of the party during the following two decades.

He was the veritable hub of the Bolshevik regime in the five years of active life remaining to him after the taking of power. His authority, energy, and tact as a leader enabled him to manage the various strong-willed personalities among the Bolsheviks and to keep the work from being too greatly disrupted by the animosities that developed, as for example between Stalin and Trotsky in the course of the Civil War. He exercised supreme direction of Bolshevik policy and action in the Civil War, in external affairs, in economic life and the organizing of the new system. In March 1921 —a time of profound crisis for the Revolution—he sponsored one of those abrupt and far-reaching shifts of line by which his political style was characterized. The White armies had been defeated by then, but inside the weary and war-torn country the peasants were vocally and in places violently in revolt against the forcible grain requisitions to which the beleaguered regime had regularly resorted under "War Communism." While the Tenth Party Congress was in session in Moscow, sailors and workers at the Kronstadt naval base, on an island outside Petrograd harbor, rose in armed rebellion and issued inflammatory appeals, like "Soviets without Bolsheviks!" The rising was crushed by the Red Army, but its political implications were taken into account by the Lenin regime. Under his leadership the Tenth Congress inaugurated the "New Economic Policy" (NEP) by abolishing forcible grain requisitions in favor of a graduated tax in kind on the peasant proprietors of the approximately twenty-five million small private farms then existing in Russia. It became a congress of transition not only from war to peace but likewise from the

54. *Lenin*, VII, 14. The letter at first circulated among party members in Russia through the then-existing network of *samizdat*. The Siberian Social Democratic organization put it out in hectographed form in June 1903, and it was published as a pamphlet in Geneva in the following year.

"military-proletarian dictatorship"[55] of the first years to a period of civil peace under the NEP, which lasted through most of the twenties.

Basic Soviet strategy in foreign affairs, under which the Comintern and the Foreign Commissariat operated as two arms of a dual policy, one working to overthrow capitalist governments while the other tried to conduct business with them, was essentially Lenin's creation, as was the notion of a Soviet diplomacy designed to reduce the insecurity of the revolutionary state by aggravating the discords between its enemies. Moreover, he closely supervised the conduct of foreign relations, even dictating to Foreign Commissar Georgi Chicherin, on occasion, the texts of diplomatic notes to be sent to foreign governments.[56] In the midst of all these labors of direct political leadership, he prepared and delivered a multitude of speeches, wrote articles for the Soviet press, and produced such major political treatises as *The Immediate Tasks of the Soviet Power, The Proletarian Revolution and the Renegade Kautsky,* and *Left-Wing Communism: An Infantile Disorder.* Toward the end, after illness partially incapacitated him, he set forth guidelines for post-Lenin Soviet policy in a series of shorter writings that Bukharin would later call his "political testament." They had to do chiefly with the great problem of how to transform backward "NEP Russia" into a country that could properly be described as socialist.

It is hardly surprising in the light of all this that Lenin's stature in Bolshevik eyes grew to gigantic proportions. He came to appear the very personification of the miracle of their survival in power, and of the further promise of the Communist revolution at home and abroad. Not only by close associates but by great numbers of party members he was not simply admired but quite literally idolized. The strongest evidence of this is the testimony of those who observed party audiences on occasions when he spoke in public. One such report comes from Walter Duranty: "I have seen Lenin speak to his followers. A small, busy, thick-set man under blinding lights, greeted by applause like thunder. I turned round and their faces were shining, like men who looked on God. Lenin was like

55. *Desiatyi s"ezd,* p. 560.
56. G. Chicherin, in *Izvestia,* January 30, 1924.

that, whether you think he was a damnable Antichrist or a once-in-a-thousand years' prophet. That is a matter of opinion, but when five thousand faces can light up and shine at the sight of him, as they did, and I saw it, then I say he was no ordinary individual." [57] Similar reports abound in the memoir literature. "Their faces shone," said a Russian Communist who was in the audience at one of Lenin's post-revolutionary public speeches. "It was truly an intellectual revel." [58] Ignazio Silone, who first saw Lenin at the Comintern congress in Moscow in 1921, recalls that "whenever he came into the hall, the atmosphere changed, became electric. It was a physical, almost a palpable phenomenon. He generated contagious enthusiasm the way the faithful in St. Peter's, when they crowd around the Sedia, emanate a fervor that spreads like a wave throughout the basilica." [59]

The hero-worship of Lenin was manifested in a tendency of his followers to make him the center of a personality cult. It appeared, for example, in the reactions when he was shot on August 30, 1918, and his recovery remained temporarily uncertain. The Soviet newspapers were filled at that time with messages expressing devotion to him and fervent wishes for his recovery. Trotsky, who in later years was to condemn the cult of Lenin, declared in a speech of September 2, 1918, to the Executive Committee of the Soviets: "Never has the individual life of one or another among us seemed to be of such secondary importance as it does now at a moment when the life of the greatest man of our age is in peril. Any fool can shoot Lenin's head to pieces, but to create this head anew would be a problem for nature herself." And Lunacharsky quotes Trotsky as saying, presumably at this same time although not in public, "When you think that Lenin might die, all our lives seem useless and you stop wanting to live." [60] A few days later, in

57. Walter Duranty, *Duranty Reports Russia* (New York, 1934), p. 170. Duranty was the *New York Times* correspondent in Moscow in the twenties.

58. *Zhivoi Lenin*, p. 283.

59. *Dissent*, September–October 1970, p. 429. The article appeared originally in *Corriere della sera*, April 22, 1970.

60. *Revoliutsionnye siluety*, p. 13. For the text of the speech of September 2, 1918, see Leon Trotsky, *Lenin* (Garden City, 1959), pp. 196–205.

the speech to the Petrograd Soviet cited above, Zinoviev said that the Soviet state had found in Lenin "not only its chief political leader, practical organizer, ardent propagandist, poet and singer, but also its principal theoretician, its Karl Marx," and characterized him as follows: "Take the fanatical devotion to the people which distinguished Marat; take his integrity, his simplicity, his intimate knowledge of the soul of the people, take his elemental faith in the inexhaustible strength of the 'lowest of the lowly,' take all this and add to it the first-class education of a Marxist, an iron will, an acute analytical mind, and you will get Lenin such as we know him now."

Nothing could have been more displeasing to Lenin himself —to whom any craving for personal glory was foreign—than this great public outpouring of emotion and encomium. Consequently, when his health improved sufficiently to enable him to return to work, he was horrified to read what had been printed in the Soviet press after the shooting. V. D. Bonch-Bruevich, his aide in the Council of People's Commissars, recalls being urgently summoned into Lenin's office and listening to him exclaim:

What is this? How could you permit it? Look what they are saying in the papers. Makes one ashamed to read it. They write that I'm such-and-such, exaggerate everything, call me a genius, a special kind of man. And look at this piece of mysticism: They collectively wish, demand, and desire that I get well. Next they'll be holding public prayers for my health. Why, this is horrible! And where does it come from? All our lives we have carried on an ideological struggle against the glorification of personality, of the individual. We long ago solved the question of heroes, and now we are again witnessing the glorification of personality. This is no good at all.[61]

61. V. D. Bonch-Bruevich, *Izbrannye sochineniia*, III, *Vospominaniia o V. I. Lenine 1917–1924 gg.* (Moscow, 1963), pp. 296–298. The statement shows a curious forgetfulness on Lenin's part concerning his own earlier views on the decisive role of revolutionary heroes. In Lunacharsky's remembrance of this episode, Lenin, in ordering Bonch-Bruevich and two other aides to make the rounds of the newspapers, added: "It would not be convenient for me to forbid this kind of thing myself, for that would also be absurd and pretentious in its way. But you must surreptitiously put a brake on this whole business" (*Izvestia*, February 14, 1960).

Not content with privately voicing dismay, Lenin ordered Bonch-Bruevich and two other aides to visit the editorial offices of Soviet newspapers, starting with *Pravda* and *Izvestia,* and explain that the glorification of personality must stop immediately. "The very next day the newspapers were altogether different in tone," continues the memoir, "and Vladimir Ilyich never raised this question again."

A little over a year later, however, Lenin's followers again showed in public their tendency to place him on a pedestal. In speeches at a party meeting in April 1920 in honor of his fiftieth birthday, and in articles published in the Soviet press for this occasion, they acclaimed him as the *vozhd'* [62] of the Russian and world revolution. Maxim Gorky compared him as a history-making figure to Christopher Columbus and Peter the Great. Evgeni Preobrazhensky called him "the soul and brain of the October Revolution." A. Sol'ts portrayed him as a new kind of hero in history, a leader of consciously acting masses whose need was no longer for a hero to whom they could bow but for one who was, like Lenin, "flesh of their flesh, thought, and word." Trotsky described Lenin as a blend of Marxist internationalist and Russian revolutionary statesman with "something about him that is strongly suggestive of a peasant." Since Russia had never experienced a great revolution or reformation at the hands of its bourgeoisie, Trotsky said, its national revolution had devolved upon the working class, led by Lenin: "Our historical past knows neither a Luther, nor a Thomas Münzer, neither a Mirabeau, nor a Robespierre. For that very reason the Russian proletariat has its Lenin." Bukharin paid tribute to Lenin as a teacher who had developed a new theoretical school of Marxism, and on this account spoke of the other party leaders as his "disciples." Stalin, who was one of the last to speak at the meeting, commented that the others had left him with little to say and then devoted his remarks to the modesty of Lenin, recounting two episodes in which "that giant" had erred (one was in not having wanted to await the convening of the Congress of Soviets in Oc-

62. This strong Russian word for "leader" lacks a precise English equivalent. It could be rendered "supreme leader" or "Leader" (capitalized). In these pages I shall frequently use the Russian word itself.

tober 1917 before launching the coup) and later courageously admitted erring. But in his *Pravda* article for the occasion, Stalin offered a general assessment of Lenin as the "organizer and *vozhd'* " of the Russian Communist party. It concluded by contrasting Lenin with two lesser types of proletarian leaders known to history— those who were outstanding practical leaders in times of stress but weak in theory, like Lassalle and Blanqui, and those who were strong in theory but weak in organizational and practical work, like Plekhanov and Kautsky. The greatness of Lenin as a leader lay in combining both kinds of talent.[63]

Lenin responded to the birthday celebration by registering once again, this time publicly, his aversion to being an object of adulation. He absented himself from the jubilee meeting until the speeches in his honor were over. When he appeared after an intermission and was met by an ovation, he drily thanked those present, first for their greetings and secondly for excusing him from listening to them. Then he pointedly expressed the hope that in time a "more fitting" way of marking anniversary dates would be found, and he concluded his talk with a discussion of routine party problems. Even in this part of the short talk, he warned the party against permitting success to go to its head and becoming a "conceited party."[64]

Thus the Bolshevik party, in spite of the great expansion of its numbers resulting from the Revolution, continued, in power, to be essentially what it had been in its small beginnings around the turn of the century—a leader-centered movement. But what was the relation of the masses of non-party people in Russia to Lenin as a political leader? We know that Russian workers and peasants who met him individually or in small groups felt the magnetic spell of his personality. For example, M. A. Landau-Aldanov, a Russian socialist who was politically opposed to Lenin, tells the following

63. *Stalin*, IV, 314–315. This and other articles commemorating Lenin's birthday appeared in *Pravda* on April 23, 1920. Louis-Auguste Blanqui (1805–81) was a French revolutionary leader who favored a seizure of power by a small, disciplined minority operating conspiratorially. Such tactics became known as "Blanquism."

64. *Lenin*, XL, 325–327.

story of a worker who spoke briefly with him on the occasion of
delivering a message: "I saw this workman at the moment when he
returned from his audience with Lenin. He was powerfully moved,
not the same man. Usually a quiet and reasonable being, he spoke
all at once like a man in ecstasy. 'That is a man,' he repeated over
and over, 'that is a man for whom I would give my life! With him
a new life begins for me! Ah, if we had had a tsar like him!' "[65]
Other such examples could be cited. We must take care, however,
in generalizing from such evidence. What can be said with confidence is that, despite the low development of the modern communications media in Russia at that time, Lenin as a personality
made a very strong impression upon the masses of people and
aroused passionate feelings—both positive and negative. The ambivalence of attitudes arose from the fact that ordinary Russians,
aided by the old habit of personifying political power in the tsar,
tended to see in Lenin the personification of Bolshevism, towards
which feelings in the populace were deeply divided in the revolutionary period. Those for whom the Bolshevik Revolution represented a threat to religious and other values perceived in Lenin a
demonic figure, whereas those to whom the Revolution meant hope
of deliverance from misery saw in him a deliverer. Consequently,
Lenin in his own lifetime became, quite literally, a legendary figure
and subject of folklore.

There were legends in Russian Central Asia, for example,
which pictured him as a liberator sent by Allah to make the people
happy.[66] In remote peasant villages in the Urals region, the poetess
Seifullina heard similar tales. One of them, constructed along the
lines of an ancient Russian heroic legend, told of how a man "of
unknown rank and title, without passport, and by name Lenin" had
divided up the nation with "Tsar Mikolashka" (i.e., Nicholas II),

65. Related by René Fülöp-Miller in *The Mind and Face of Bolshevism:
An Examination of Cultural Life in Soviet Russia* (New York, 1928), p. 40.
"The whole success of Lenin," adds Fülöp-Miller, "is plainly due entirely to the
spell of his personality, which communicated itself to all who came into touch
with him, and then penetrated into the cabins of the peasants in the remotest
villages."

66. E. H. Carr, *Socialism in One Country 1924–1926*, II (New York,
1960), p. 3 n.

taking all the common folk onto his side and giving the fine folk to the tsar, and of how Lenin was winning the struggle because the fine folk could do nothing without the common folk and the generals had no soldiers to do their fighting for them. Seifullina found that Lenin had both detractors and defenders in the country districts; all of them, however, were vehement in expressing their feelings. She heard devout Russian Orthodox peasants depicting Lenin as a monstrous evildoer. Reciting whole pages of the Bible in a screaming voice, they would attribute to Lenin the number of the beast, the number 666, the number of Antichrist. Others, likewise with abundant reference to Holy Scripture, would speak out in his favor, saying that Lenin was the bearer of the righteous wrath of God, that he had come to fulfill the prophecies of Isaiah, that he acted according to the Bible when he took away the "broad acres of the rich." In a village of Old Believers there was a thin red-headed man who professed his faith in Lenin by joining the party, slinging on a rifle which he brandished threateningly at every meeting, and bellowing out scriptural texts to prove the justice of Lenin's political acts.[67] So Lenin's following was swelled by numbers of simple Russians for whom Marxism remained as much a mystery as any system of theology. Not in all instances did these people join the party.

As already indicated, peasant feeling toward the regime was deeply affected by its agrarian policy. In the period of War Communism (1918–21), the Soviet leadership appeared to the peasant to be of two minds on this question: while encouraging the peasants to divide up the remaining landed estates and guaranteeing them tenure, it nationalized the land, began to organize communes, and forcibly requisitioned grain in the countryside to feed the town population. That the peasant as a result was of two minds concerning the leadership is vividly shown in a popular saying of the time: "Long live the Bolsheviks, down with the Communists!" To the peasant, it seemed that the regime was inwardly divided between those forces that wanted the peasants to have the land ("Bolshe-

---

67. L. Seifullina, *Sobranie sochinenii*, II (Moscow and Leningrad, 1928), pp. 271–275.

viks") and those that wanted to take it away from them ("Communists"). Significantly, he tended to identify Lenin with the former. Valentinov, who had returned to Russia at the time of the Revolution and was working in the editorial offices of the *Torgovopromyshlennaia gazeta* (Commercial-Industrial Gazette), records a typical expression of this thinking. A peasant in the village of Vasilievskoe, not far from Moscow, explained to him in a conversation that took place in 1922: "Lenin is a Russian man, he respects the peasants, does not allow them to be robbed and driven into communes, while that other ruler, Trotsky, is a Jew, cares nothing for the peasants, knows nothing of their work and life, and does not want to know anything." [68] One of the sources of this positive image of Lenin as a pro-peasant "Russian man" was his personal identification in the popular mind with the NEP, under which town-country relations had been placed on a firm basis of trade and the country was beginning again to enjoy a modest measure of prosperity.

Lenin died on January 21, 1924, after having been incapacitated for many months by his third stroke. Since his illness had been announced, there had been time for people to make a mental adjustment in advance of the event. Nevertheless, there appears to have been a spontaneous and very widespread feeling of sorrow among the population as well as in the party. Memorial meetings in cities and villages throughout the country were attended by masses of people. In Moscow tens and hundreds of thousands of people braved some of the bitterest cold in living Russian memory to await their turns to file through the Hall of Columns, where the body was lying in state, and to come to Red Square on the day of the funeral. Eliena Eastman, the sister of a prominent Bolshevik, obtained a pass enabling her to spend two hours in the Hall of Columns. In a letter to her husband, who was absent from Moscow at the time, she described the scene: "Mothers lift up their children for one look at him, hysterical women fall on the floor crying

68. N. Valentinov, *Novaia economicheskaia politika i krizis partii posle smerti Lenina. Gody raboty v VSNKH vo vremia NEP. Vospominaniia* (Stanford, 1971), p. 88.

'tovarishch Lenin,' three strong men in white suits are there to lift them and carry them out, and they cry so terribly that your blood becomes cold." Outside, the city presented the following picture: "The red flags with black hems, the black-red sash on the right arm of many people, many people selling little picture-brooches of Lenin, and his small white bust and small white statue, the white bright snow, the thick cold air, the frosted hair and furs, white smoke from the mouths and red fires in the street at night. That is Moscow of these days." [69]

69. Eastman, *Love and Revolution*, p. 399.

Chapter Three

KOBA: THE FORMATIVE
YEARS

Georgian Prologue

THE NATIVE LAND OF Iosif Djugashvili has great natural beauty, an ancient culture, and memories of an heroic past under the independent Georgian monarchy that flourished in the eleventh and twelfth centuries. Its conversion to the Orthodox Christianity of the Eastern Roman Empire at Byzantium took place in the year 330, over six centuries prior to Russia's conversion. There is a rich Georgian literary tradition and a record of notable achievement in architecture and the fine arts. The people, according to an eighteenth-century Georgian's characterization,

are doughty warriors, lovers of arms, haughty, audacious; and so avid of personal glory that they will sacrifice their fatherland or their sovereign for the sake of their own advancement; they are hospitable to guests and strangers, and cheerful of disposition; and if two or three are assembled together, they are never at a loss for amusement; they are generous and prodigal of their own goods and of other people's, and never think of amassing possessions; they are intelligent, quick-witted, self-centered, and lovers of learning. . . . They lend loyal support to one another, will remember and repay a good turn but will exact retribution for an insult. They change rapidly from a good mood to a bad one; they are headstrong, ambitious, and apt both to flatter and to take offence. . . .[1]

1. Prince Vakhushti Bagration, *Déscription géographique de la Georgie*, pp. 62–65, as quoted in David M. Lang, *A Modern History of Soviet Georgia* (New York, 1962), p. 18.

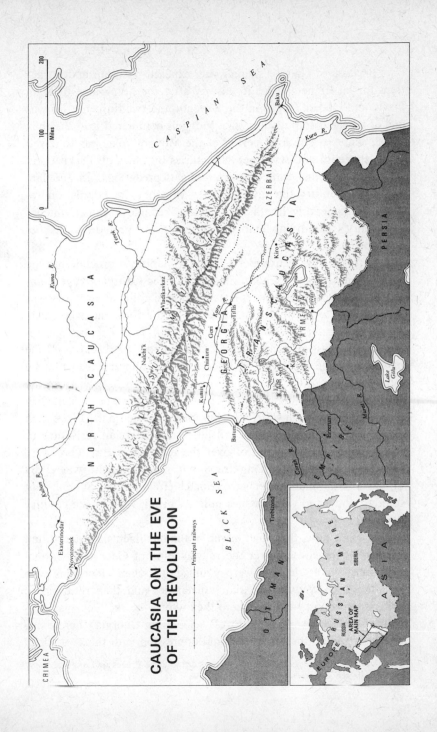

CAUCASIA ON THE EVE
OF THE REVOLUTION

Principal railways

200

100

0

Miles

CRIMEA

Novorossisk
Ekaterinodar

Kuban R.

NORTH CAUCASIA

Kuma R.

Terk R.

CAUCASUS MOUNTAINS

Nalch'k

Vladikavkaz

Gori

Kutais

Chiatura

Batum

BLACK SEA

Trebizond

OTTOMAN EMPIRE

Corah R.

Erzerum

Murat R.

Lake
Gölü

PERSIA

Araks R.

AZERBAIJAN

Baku

Kura R.

CASPIAN SEA

TRANSCAUCASIA

GEORGIA

Tiflis

Kura R.

Kiro

Lake Sevan

Erivan

ARMENIA

Kars

KAR S

RUSSIAN EMPIRE

EUROPE

RUSSIA

SIBERIA

A S I A

AREA OF
MAIN MAP

Because of Georgia's small size, exposed position, and attractions for larger neighbors, its history after the heroic age of King David and Queen Tamar in the eleventh and twelfth centuries was one of repeated subjugation. The Mongols conquered it in the thirteenth century. The long period of the Mongol yoke was followed in the sixteenth and seventeenth centuries by times of Turkish and Persian dominion, with accompanying depredations. In the late eighteenth century the ravaged little kingdom, its population reduced to something like a half million, became a vassal state of Petersburg's expanding empire. This was the prelude to its occupation.

In 1801 Tsar Alexander I issued a manifesto proclaiming the annexation of eastern Georgia to Russia. The Georgian royal family was removed from power. Later, supreme political authority was invested in a series of Russian viceroys of the Caucasus who made their headquarters in Georgia's capital city, Tbilisi, better known then by the Russian name "Tiflis." In 1811 the Russians ousted the patriarch of the Georgian Orthodox Church and replaced him by a metropolitan of the Russian Orthodox Church who was given the title "Exarch of Georgia." Russian administrators were installed in large numbers. Meanwhile, Russian forces wrested parts of western Georgia from the Turks and crushed local Georgian resistance to the extension of their control over the remainder. But there were rebellions, including a long-drawn-out guerrilla fight waged by mountain tribesmen under a warrior chieftain, Imam Shamil. Not until around 1860 was Russia's military pacification of the country complete.[2]

By that time, there had arisen in the intelligentsia a social and literary movement to foster the reawakening of Georgian national consciousness. Its leaders were young upper-class Georgians who went north to study in Russian universities and then returned to Tiflis or to country estates where they wrote—in the Georgian language—stories, poems, and novels celebrating Georgia's heroic age and intertwining themes of national oppression with those of social

2. This summary of Georgian history draws upon Professor Lang's account. For details see *A Modern History*, chs. I–IV.

protest. Daniel Chonkadze, Akaki Tsereteli, and Raphael Eristavi were prominent members of this group. Its principal leader was Prince Ilia Chavchavadze, who promoted the movement, among other ways, by founding in 1877 a literary journal called *Iveria* (an ancient name for Georgia). By then there was in existence a further group, called *Meore Dasi*, or the "Second Group," which continued the effort in a more radical spirit.[3]

A notable characteristic of the Georgian intelligentsia was its blending of the ideas of national liberation and social change. Influenced by the Russian populist revolutionary literature, and realizing, no doubt, that the yoke of tsarist autocracy could not be lifted from Georgia without deep changes in Russia itself, some Georgian intellectuals in the seventies and eighties made common cause with the Russian *narodniki*. Later in this period, others proceeded along the Marxist path. The leading figure in the latter group, which in 1892–93 became known as *Mesame Dasi*, or the "Third Group," was Noi Zhordania. He went abroad after attending, in the eighties, the Tiflis theological seminary, an institution whose overseers' harsh Russifying ways had made it into more of a school of Georgian nationalism than the training center for loyal priests of the Russo-Georgian Orthodox Church that it was supposed to be. Studying in the veterinary institute in Warsaw, Zhordania became acquainted with Marxist ideas through the writings of the German Social Democratic theorist Karl Kautsky. He returned to Georgia in 1892 a convinced Marxist and helped shape the program of the new *Mesame Dasi* accordingly. This group was the nucleus of Georgian Social Democracy.

Shortly after its formation Zhordania, who was in danger of arrest, went abroad again and stayed for four years. During that time he met both Kautsky and Plekhanov. Upon his return to Georgia in 1897, he and his associates took over the editorship of *Kvali* (The Furrow), a Georgian-language weekly newspaper initiated some years earlier by members of the "Second Group." They made it the voice of their Marxist view that Georgia's hope lay not in the strictly national and liberal reforms advocated by the Chavchavadze

3. *Ibid.*, pp. 99–102, 109–111.

generation but in alignment with the international working-class movement. Paradoxically, these Georgian Marxists initially enjoyed a certain preference in the eyes of the Russian authorities, for whom less menace was apparent in their class themes than in the separatist message of the liberals.[4] *Kvali,* if not an organ of "legal Marxism," was at any rate published legally. Zhordania and the moderate majority of *Mesame Dasi,* including such figures as Nikolai Chkheidze and Sylvester Djibladze, eventually aligned themselves with Russian Menshevism, while a more radical minority, among them the future Soviet historian of the Transcaucasian revolutionary movement, Filipp Makharadze, gravitated toward Bolshevism. Zhordania himself became president of the independent Georgian Republic that arose in 1918 and was overthrown by a new Russian army—the Red Army—in 1921.

By the beginning of the twentieth century, the Russian authorities in Transcaucasia could no longer view the Social Democratic movement without alarm. Although the Transcaucasian economy was still predominantly agrarian, industrial development was making rapid strides owing to the region's rich mineral resources. On the Caspian seashore, at the southeastern tip of Transcaucasia, stood the oil-producing city of Baku, future capital of the Azerbaijan Soviet Socialist Republic. Tiflis, with a population of about 200,000, had a multitude of factories employing an aggregate labor force of well over 25,000, not counting the large numbers employed in its extensive railway workshops and depots. The port of Batum, on the Black Sea coast of western Georgia, was the terminus of an oil pipeline from Baku and a center of oil-refining and other industries. Many workers labored in the manganese mines of Chiatura, in central Georgia. Much of this industrial development was financed by foreign capital. Working conditions were generally bad. Strikes and trade union activities were forbidden. The restive labor force was understandably receptive to approaches from Marxist revolutionaries, and it is not surprising that the main centers of the Transcaucasus contributed their full share to the turbulence that swept over

4. *Ibid.,* p. 136.

large parts of the Russian Empire in the early years of the twentieth century.

Growing Up in Gori

Of four children born to Vissarion and Ekaterina Djugashvili, only Iosif, the last-born, survived. His birthday was December 21, 1879. As a boy he was called "Soso," the common Georgian nickname for "Iosif." The parents, who were at best semi-literate, were of peasant stock, the descendants of serfs. They were poor and lived in a small rented house on the outskirts of Gori. That neighborhood was then still known as *Rusis-ubani* (Georgian for "Russian quarter") because of the old Russian troop barracks that stood nearby.

Gori, which takes its name from the Georgian word for "hill," lies in the hill country of eastern Georgia, about forty-five miles northwest of Tiflis, and was then a district center in Tiflis province. Repeatedly in history it was devastated by earthquakes. At one time a stopping-place for caravans, it became a station on the main railway line, completed in 1871, between Poti, on the Black Sea coast, and Tiflis. At the time of Soso's birth, it had a population of eight or nine thousand.

Nineteenth-century accounts describe it as a picturesque little town spread out on one bank of the Kura River and dominated by a high hill with a fortress at its top. The writer Maxim Gorky, who visited Gori on one of his far-flung travels of the nineties, found a heavy flavor of "apartness and wild originality" in the place. In a report to a hometown newspaper, he went on to picture "the sultry sky overhead, the raging muddy waters of the Kura, the nearby mountains pocked with well-spaced holes—it's a town of caves—and farther off on the horizon those eternally still white clouds: the peaks of the main Caucasus range covered with never-melting snow." [5] Such were the scenes amidst which Soso Djugashvili spent his boyhood.

5. V. Kaminsky and I. Vereshchagin, "Detstvo i iunost' vozhdia: dokumenty, zapisi, rasskazy," *Molodaia gvardiia*, No. 12 (1939), p. 24. Gorky's report appeared in *Nizhegorodskii listok* on November 26, 1896.

Not much is known of his forebears. A paternal great grand-father, Zaza Djugashvili by name, took part in an anti-Russian peasant rising in the early years of the nineteenth century and later found refuge in the village of Didi-Lilo, near Tiflis. Zaza's son Vano tended vineyards in Didi-Lilo, and Vano's son Vissarion, nicknamed "Beso," was born there. After Vano's death, Beso settled in Tiflis and found a job in the Adelkhanov leather-goods factory, where he learned the shoemaker's trade. When a man named Baramov opened a shoe-repair shop in Gori some time later, Djugashvili was one of those whom he hired to come and work for him. There, in Gori, Beso met and married Ekaterina Geladze. She had been born into a family of serfs living in the nearby village of Gambareuli. When the serfs were emancipated in Georgia in 1864 (three years later than in Russia itself), the Geladze family moved to Gori.[6] She was then nine years old. When Soso was born, she was in her early twenties and had buried three infants.

The Djugashvilis' rented house consisted of a single all-purpose room of modest dimensions furnished with a table and four stools, a bed, a small buffet with a samovar, a mirror on the wall, and a trunk containing the family's belongings. A copper kerosene lamp stood on the table. Clothes and dishes were kept on open wall shelves. A winding stairway led down to a cellar which had a fire-place where Ekaterina must have done her cooking. Beso kept leather and shoemaking tools there. The sole furnishings were an unpainted stool and Soso's cradle.[7]

Beso Djugashvili is described as thin, with coal-black hair, beard, and mustache; according to a contemporary, his son, as a young man, bore a strong physical resemblance to him. Beso, it is well attested, was also a rough and violent-tempered man and a heavy drinker; he eventually died in a barroom brawl. Both Soso and Ekaterina suffered beatings at his hands. In 1885, when Soso was five, Beso returned to his old work at the Adelkhanov factory, in Tiflis. He did not break his ties with his family, however, and

6. Kaminsky and Vereshchagin, "Detstvo," pp. 24–25.
7. Ibid., pp. 27–28. The house has been preserved as a memorial.

came home to them from time to time. Meanwhile, Ekaterina earned a meager living as a washerwoman, seamstress, and cook in the homes of better-off families in Gori.

Soso Djugashvili appears to have been a precocious boy, quick at learning, bright-eyed, energetic, physically agile, and fond of games. He had a good, high-pitched singing voice and sang in the Gori church school choir. He grew up to be small of stature, probably not more than five feet four or five inches tall.[8] A childhood case of smallpox left his face pock-marked. As a boy he had his share of mishaps. At the age of ten or eleven, while standing in a crowd by the river on a religious holiday, he was knocked unconscious by a runaway carriage and suffered injuries from which it took him about two weeks to recover. A great wail of grief came from Ekaterina when the procession carrying Soso's limp form reached her house.[9] Whether then or at some other time, blood poisoning developed from an infected bruise on his left arm, resulting in a chronic stiffness of the left elbow joint. Many years later he told his sister-in-law that this minor infirmity was the cause of his being rejected as unfit for military service when he was called up in 1916.[10]

An important source of information on Djugashvili's early life is the memoir published in Berlin by his one-time close friend and schoolmate in Gori, Iosif Iremashvili. The two boys made each other's acquaintance one day on the school playground as protagonists in a wrestling match that Soso Djugashvili won by seizing Soso

8. According to Hugh Lunghi, who served as a British interpreter in high-level meetings during World War II, "Stalin can hardly have been more than 5 ft. 5 in. in height; strongly and squarely built, but not broad" ("Stalin Face to Face," The Observer Weekend Review, February 24, 1963). Other eyewitness testimony agrees with this estimate.

9. Kaminsky and Vereshchagin, "Detstvo," p. 37. He is reported in this same source to have opened his eyes and said: "Don't worry, Mama. I'm all right."

10. A. S. Alliluyeva, Vospominaniia (Moscow, 1946), p. 167. Stalin explained to the Alliluyevs that along with other political exiles he was brought to Krasnoyarsk in October 1916 for induction into the Russian army. He attributed his rejection also to the fact that he was regarded as a potential "undesirable element" in the army.

Iremashvili from behind as he was dusting himself off. Iremashvili, for whom the Djugashvili household became a second home, remembered his friend as a thin but muscular boy, with lively dark eyes gazing unafraid out of a freckled face, head cocked back and prominent nose sticking pertly in the air. Less childishly carefree than most of his schoolmates, he would occasionally go off and apply himself with single-minded persistence to such enterprises as mastering the ascent of a high cliff or distance throwing with stone markers by the riverside. He lacked feeling for living things, was unmoved by the joys and sorrows of schoolmates, and never was seen crying. "To gain a victory and be feared was triumph for him," the character sketch concluded. "He was devoted to only one person—his mother. As a child and youth he was a good friend so long as one submitted to his imperious will." [11]

Iremashvili describes Ekaterina Djugashvili as a devout and industrious woman who was deeply attached to her son. She customarily dressed in the Georgian woman's traditional costume. She was much respected in the community and dedicated her life in the old-fashioned way to serving God, husband, and child. We should not deduce from this account, however, that Ekaterina was a soft and submissive soul. Such an inference would be belied by the picture that Stalin himself gave of her in conversations with his daughter, Svetlana, during the nineteen-forties. According to Svetlana, Stalin held his mother in high regard throughout his life. He described her as an intelligent woman, albeit uneducated. He recalled that she used to "thrash" (*kolotila*) him when he was small, and that she would hit Vissarion too when he was drunk. She wanted her son to become a priest and always regretted his failure to do so. When he came to see her in 1936, shortly before her death, she told him—to his de-

---

11. Joseph Iremaschwili, *Stalin und die Tragödie Georgiens* (Berlin, 1932), pp. 5–6. Iremashvili (to use the normal English transliteration) was later a schoolmate of Djugashvili's in the Tiflis theological seminary. Subsequently he became a Menshevik and the two friends drifted apart. Iremashvili taught school in Tiflis after the Revolution and emigrated in the early twenties. See Kaminsky and Vereshchagin, "Detstvo," pp. 39, 72, for Soviet confirmation that Iremashvili was a boyhood companion of Djugashvili and, later, a member of the same secret study-group in the Tiflis seminary.

light—"What a pity you never became a priest." From all that she learned Svetlana concludes that Ekaterina was a woman of strict and decisive character, firm and stubborn, puritanical in her standards, unbending in her nature, and highly demanding toward herself; and that she transmitted all these qualities to her son, who was "much more like her than like his father." [12]

The devotion that Soso Djugashvili felt toward his mother contrasted sharply with his feelings toward his father. Iremashvili tells of brutal blows inflicted upon the boy by the frequently drunk Vissarion, and of the gradual growth of an aversion in Soso for his father. Living under the threat of Vissarion's wrathful temper, watching resentfully how his mother had to work nights over the sewing-machine because Vissarion drank up most of his small wages, Soso began to detest the man and avoided him as much as possible. He also developed the vindictiveness that would characterize him in later life, and became a rebel against paternal authority in all guises: "Undeserved dreadful beating [Schläge] made the boy as hard and heartless as the father himself was. Since all people in authority over others owing to power or seniority seemed to him to be like his father, there soon arose in him a vengeful feeling against all people standing above him. From childhood on the realization of his thoughts of revenge became the aim to which everything was subordinated." [13] In 1890, when Soso was eleven years old, Beso died in a drunken brawl after being stabbed with a knife. "The early death of the father made no impression upon the boy," comments Iremashvili. "In the man he was supposed to call father he lost nothing." [14]

Ekaterina was also a victim of Vissarion's blows. Very likely

12. Svetlana Alliluyeva, *Twenty Letters to a Friend* (New York, 1967), pp. 153–154, 204. Iremashvili's description of Ekaterina (*Stalin*, pp. 10, 11) is fully consistent with Alliluyeva's.

13. Iremaschwili, *Stalin*, pp. 6, 11–12. Iremashvili attributes Vissarion's coarse and brutal nature (perhaps unfairly) to Ossetian ancestry. The Ossetes were a Caucasian mountain clan known for their vendettas.

14. Iremaschwili, *Stalin*, p. 12. On the manner of Vissarion's death see Svetlana Alliluyeva, *Twenty Letters*, p. 153 n. A Soviet source (Kaminsky and Vereshchagin, "Detstvo," p. 44 n.) gives 1906 as the year of Vissarion's death, but this statement appears erroneous. The date of 1890 is generally accepted among the non-Soviet biographers.

the strong-willed woman stood up to her husband at times, with violent results. "The mother would beat the boy," writes Svetlana on the basis of her conversations with her father; *"her husband would beat her."* [15] On one occasion, she relates, the boy incurred his father's wrath by making a futile effort to protect his mother from attack. He threw a knife at Beso, and then fled from the furiously screaming man and found refuge with neighbors, who hid him. Whether there were more such harrowing episodes we do not know, but it is significant that Djugashvili still remembered this one in his old age. And the horror that the beating of his mother inspired in him may help to explain why in later life he thought of beating— symbolic or real—as a form of punishment merited by the worst of offenders. Thus, in a letter that he wrote to Lenin in 1915 from Siberian exile, he mentioned the "liquidators," saying: "There is no one to beat them, devil take it. Can it be that they will go unpunished?! Make us happy by informing us that there will soon appear an organ in which they will be lashed across their mugs [*gde ikh budut khlestat' po rozhe*], good and hard, and without letup." [16] And toward the end of his life, when a group of Kremlin doctors was imprisoned on charges of conspiring to shorten the lives of Soviet leaders, he is said to have called the investigative judge and instructed him as follows on the methods to be used in order to make the accused confess: "Beat, beat, and, once again, beat." [17]

Soso Djugashvili grew up, then, in the midst of severe parental conflict as well as material poverty. One of the parents' most serious quarrels, moreover, had to do with the boy's future. Ekaterina wanted to send him to the church school in Gori as the first step toward a career in the priesthood, and the school admitted him in September 1888. He received a stipend of three rubles monthly in recognition of the family's poverty, and arrangements were made permitting Ekaterina to earn ten rubles a month by working for the

15. Svetlana Alliluyeva, *Only One Year* (New York, 1969), p. 360. Italics added.

16. *Proletarskaia revoliutsiia,* No. 7 (1936), p. 167. Stalin for some reason did not later include this letter in his collected works.

17. Nikita Khrushchev, "Special Report to the Soviet Twentieth Party Congress," *The New York Times,* June 5, 1956, pp. 13–16.

school and the teachers.[18] All this did not occur, however, without strong opposition from Beso, who did not share his wife's ambition to see their son rise to a higher place in life than he himself occupied. He was repeatedly heard to say to her: "You want my son to become a metropolitan? You will never live to see it! I am a shoemaker, and my son must become one too, and will!" According to this account, Vissarion finally decided to carry out his resolve to make a shoemaker out of Soso. He came to Gori, removed the boy from school, took him to Tiflis, and put him to work for several days as a helper in the Adelkhanov factory (this proved the sole proletarian episode in the life of Stalin). Ekaterina, taking counsel with persons in authority, was advised by both teachers and church officials to accept the situation, and the latter tried to ease things for her by promising to place Soso in the church choir of the Georgian Exarchy in Tiflis. But the determined woman disregarded their advice, brought the boy back to Gori, and returned him to the school.[19] This story was subsequently confirmed in all essentials by Ekaterina herself. In an interview with Soviet correspondents in 1935, she said of her son: "He studied extremely well, but his father —my deceased husband Vissarion—decided to take the boy out of school and train him in his shoemaking trade. I objected as strongly as I could and even quarreled with my husband, but in vain; he insisted on having his way. A little later, however, I managed to put the boy back in school." [20] When Vissarion died a year or so after this incident occurred, Soso must have felt that an ominous shadow had passed out of his life. By now, however, the boy was showing a vindictiveness and mean streak reminiscent of the father whom he despised. The alien force that his father represented had somehow been internalized within him.

The parent with whom he identified positively was his mother. Whether or not we think of him as directly assimilating her traits of mind and character, it is evident that he formed a strong mother-

18. Kaminsky and Vereshchagin, "Detstvo," pp. 34, 35. Ekaterina must have been known to the local clergy and school authorities as a person of strong loyalty to the church.
19. Kaminsky and Vereshchagin, "Detstvo," pp. 44–45.
20. Pravda, October 27, 1935.

attachment which greatly influenced the development of his personality. The nature of the influence is suggested by Freud's remark that "a man who has been the indisputable favorite of his mother keeps for life the feeling of a conqueror, that confidence of success that often induces real success." [21] In this case it was not a matter of being a favored son, since the others had not survived, but of being an enormously admired one in whom all the mother's aspirations were invested. Manifestly, her existence centered in Soso and his future. She lavished her devotion upon him, and made him the vehicle of ambitions for success that she could not realistically feel for herself. He responded by developing that "feeling of a conqueror" and "confidence of success" to which Freud refers. He began to view himself as a person for whom it would be natural to excel in whatever activity he chose to pursue, whether wrestling or cliff-climbing or studies in school. He imbibed his mother's belief in his capacity to achieve big things; and we may note that there was a strong basis for this belief in real talents that he began to demonstrate as soon as he entered school. Unconditionally admired by his mother, he grew up taking such admiration as his due, expecting to be idolized and to be worthy of it. Encouraged by her idealization of him, he started idealizing himself, and showed it by a number of identifications with hero-figures which will be discussed in the following pages. Anxieties and threats to self-esteem that beset him in early life from his father's side must have spurred him on in the process of self-idealization, making a compensatory fantasy life psychologically indispensable.

This interpretation of Soso Djugashvili's character development finds support in his behavior and record in the Gori school. He showed from the start a strong self-confidence, sense of rightness, and driving need to excel. "Firm, persistent, and energetic" was one former schoolmate's recollection of him. Another recalled: "He was always prepared for lessons—waiting to be called on. He was always exceptionally well prepared and carried out assignments to the letter.

21. Sigmund Freud, *Collected Papers*, IV (London, 1952), p. 367. Concerning the influence of a strong mother-attachment on personality development, see also Erich Fromm, *Sigmund Freud's Mission* (New York, 1959), pp. 20 ff.

He was considered the best pupil not only in his class but in the whole school. During class periods he would strain not to miss a single word or idea. He was all attention—this ordinarily very brisk, mobile, and vivacious Soso." [22] Soso's very strong scholastic showing is said to have accentuated the tension that existed in the school between the sons of the well-off and those of the poor. Moving from grade to grade at the head of his class, he graduated in July 1894, at the age of fourteen, with a special certificate of honor that would not often come to a pupil from one of the lowly families. And having done quite well on the entrance examination for the theological seminary in Tiflis, he was admitted to that institution as a boarding student with all expenses paid.

The gifted, intense, and hard-working shoemaker's son was obviously bent on succeeding. All the more significant, therefore, is the fact that he was not noted for being deferential toward the school authorities. Instead of rendering the humble obedience to superiors which the educational system sought to cultivate, he showed himself an independent spirit who would, for example, forthrightly speak up to a teacher on the reasons why this or that pupil was falling behind and how his work might be improved. Soso himself, on the other hand, did not easily submit to being corrected. Always confident of his rightness, he would not take back words once spoken. According to a former schoolmate, teacher Iluridze, who often tried to put down Soso as a leader of the pupils whom he called "children of the poor and unfortunate," asked him on one occasion to state the distance between St. Petersburg and Peterhof. After giving the answer, Soso stubbornly repeated it when told that he was mistaken, and simply stood still, his eyes widening with anger, when the indignant teacher began to shout threats and demand apologies. On another occasion, when a group of older boys went on an outing in the country with a school supervisor, Soso was the first to take a running leap across a stream; and when one of the others helped the hesitant teacher across by standing in the middle of the stream and making a stepping-stone of his back, Soso muttered: "What are

22. Kaminsky and Vereshchagin, "Detstvo," pp. 36, 41. Iremashvili (*Stalin*, p. 8) also recalls that Soso was the best pupil in the school.

you, an ass? I wouldn't offer my back to God himself, much less to
a supervisor." [23] (Soso reportedly had ceased believing in God by
the age of thirteen, after reading something by or about Darwin.[24])

Iremashvili writes that Soso was the ringleader of a corridor incident in which a group of pupils whistled and hooted at a particularly offensive teacher, and calls the incident "the first of Soso's
revolts." But it seems inadvisable to attach large importance to this
episode. Soso could hardly have made the outstanding scholastic
record that he did, or have graduated with an unusual certificate of
honor, if his rebellious tendencies had been very conspicuously manifested. Furthermore, the atmosphere in the Gori school in the early
nineties was rebellious, so that an incipient young rebel could avoid
attracting much attention to himself in this capacity. For the school
officials were following practices that might seem (if we did not
know better) deliberately designed to make rebels out of all the
pupils, and the latter were responding as could have been expected.

When Soso entered the school in 1888, the language of instruction was Georgian, and Russian was still taught as a foreign language.
Two years later, in the heyday of the tsarist government's policy
of Russification in the borderlands, Georgians were replaced by
Russians in leading positions in the Gori school, Russian was made
mandatory for classroom use, and *Georgian* became the foreign
language (two lessons per week). Being unable at first to speak
Russian, the naturally voluble Georgian boys were unable to contain the urge to talk in their own language. For this they were
penalized by blows with fist or ruler, by being forced to kneel bare-
legged on pebbles for one to two hours, or by being made to stand
facing a corner. Or, when the word "guilty" rang out, the guilty one
would be made to hold a wooden stick in his hand, sometimes for as
much as a whole morning, until another culprit took it. Some of the
newly installed persons in authority, like school inspector Butyrsky
(the object of the corridor incident mentioned above), made matters

23. Kaminsky and Vereshchagin, "Detstvo," pp. 38, 41, 43, 64.

24. *Rasskazy starykh rabochikh zakavkaz'ia o velikom Staline* (Moscow,
1937), pp. 18, 20. See also Iremashvili, who reports (*Stalin,* p. 8) that by this
time religion had lost all meaning for Soso Djugashvili, although he enjoyed singing in the church choir.

still worse by showing open contempt for the Georgian language and all things Georgian. The boys' patriotic Georgian pride was of course only intensified by the crude effort to make little Russians out of them. Many began to hate the Russians in the process of learning their language.[25]

They also became avid readers of Georgian fiction outside of school. Georgian books, poorly represented in the school's library, were obtainable through a local Georgian bookseller who ran a small lending library on the side. The first book Soso took out was Daniel Chonkadze's *Surami Castle,* a passionate novelistic tract against serfdom with themes similar to those of *Uncle Tom's Cabin;* and he was so fascinated that he stayed up nearly all night reading it.[26] He and his friends also read the poems and stories of Ilia Chavchavadze, Akaki Tsereteli, and Raphael Eristavi. Still another writer of this group was the romantic novelist Alexander Kazbegi. A native of the hill country and a fervent Georgian nationalist, Kazbegi wrote stirring stories of resistance by the Caucasian mountain clans to the Russian military conquest of their land. They were tales, as it were, of the white man's Indian wars, told from the standpoint of the Indians. One of them, *The Patricide,* made a particularly deep and lasting impression upon Soso Djugashvili.

It wove a story of love, intrigue, and adventure into actual historical events of 1845, when mountaineer forces led by Imam Shamil clashed with a Russian military expedition led by the Russian viceroy of the Caucasus, Count Vorontsov. The story tells of Iago and Nunu, a young village pair whom fate constantly separates, and of their faithful friend Koba, who tries to help them with all he possesses—mainly his bravery, clear and quick-thinking mind, and ability to get out of any situation. Iago is imprisoned and Nunu abducted through the machinations of Girgola, a village renegade who collaborates with the Russians. Koba becomes an outlaw after killing one of the abductors in an attempt to prevent them from carrying off Nunu, and then, in a daring escapade, frees Iago. The

25. Iremaschwili, *Stalin,* p. 7. See also Kaminsky and Vereshchagin, "Detstvo," pp. 38–39.
26. Kaminsky and Vereshchagin, "Detstvo," pp. 51–52.

two young men lead a Robin Hood existence in the mountains, befriending peasants, fighting Cossacks, and capturing some Russian officers whom they bring to Shamil. Just as they are on the point of rescuing Nunu, after which they plan to join Shamil's warrior band, misfortune overtakes them. Trapped by Girgola and his men, they fight against impossible odds. Iago is killed, Nunu dies after being falsely accused of murdering her own father, and Koba alone escapes. At the end Koba's avenging shot rings out, and the mortally wounded Girgola confesses his guilt for all his misdeeds.

In the fearless and laconic Koba Soso Djugashvili found the first of his hero-identifications, a fit name and symbol for the heroic Soso that he envisaged himself as being: "Soso's ideal and dream-figure [*Traumgestalt*] was Koba. . . . Koba had become Soso's god, the sense of his life. He wanted to become another Koba, a fighter and hero as famous as he. The figure of Koba was to resurrect in him. From now on he called himself Koba, and would not have us call him by any other name. His face would shine with pride when we called him 'Koba.'" [27]

Because of the importance of the Koba-symbol in our subject's life, it may be well to consider further what it originally meant to him. The Koba of *The Patricide* is not a complex and subtle character, but rather the one-dimensional idealized hero-type that one would expect in such a novel: a strong silent man, chivalrous, intrepid, redoubtable in battle, an unerring marksman, and cunningly resourceful when in difficulty. Such qualities would obviously appeal to a combative youth with an urge to cast himself mentally in a hero-role. But in the setting of Kazbegi's story, Koba has one further characteristic that must have powerfully recommended him to Soso Djugashvili: he is an avenger.

The theme of vengeance runs through the novel like a red thread. Thus, the Caucasian mountaineer custom of the vendetta is mentioned approvingly more than once. The Georgian common people are described as burning with the desire to take revenge on

---

27. Iremaschwili, *Stalin,* p. 18. For Soviet confirmation that Soso derived the nickname "Koba" from Kazbegi's novel, see Kaminsky and Vereshchagin, "Detstvo," p. 53.

the arrogant Russian conquerors who have despoiled and down-trodden them in the process of annexing their country. Shamil himself, presented as a "man of iron" and brave warrior-leader adored by his followers, appears as the head of the popular movement for revenge, as one "who embodies the people's wrath." [28] The friends, Iago and Koba, crave to avenge themselves not only upon their immediate oppressors, Girgola and the village bailiff, but likewise upon the Russian authorities who support such scoundrels; and they see in service to Shamil a heaven-sent opportunity to take part in collective acts of vengeance. So *The Patricide,* besides furnishing Soso with an idealized image of the hero as avenger, conveyed to him the message that vindictive triumph is a cause to which a person can worthily devote his life.

There was, finally, a very significant social theme in the novel. In portraying the conflict between Georgians and Russians, it showed a Georgian society divided along class lines. Shamil's forces, wrote Kazbegi, were recruited from among mountaineers and simple peasants whose villages had been burned, crops destroyed, and women ravished by the Russian invaders. Meanwhile, Georgian princes and nobles, eager for honors and for appointments that would enable them to live like European aristocrats, were fighting on Vorontsov's side. Because of their deep roots in the traditional institution of serfdom, the Georgian feudal lords were ready to sacrifice the good of the country to their own selfish interests. And seeing this, the illiterate mountaineer Shamil realized that it would be desirable to extend to all Georgians the free and equal existence enjoyed by his own Chechen tribesmen, who had never been serfs. Thus, in some rudimentary sense Kazbegi's Shamil stands for a new social order; and so does Koba. When, for example, a village woman appeals to Koba for protection against Girgola, Kazbegi comments: "How strange! Under an organized administration, with headmen, judges, bailiffs, police officers, and all kinds of other officials spreading over the land like ants and pretending to mete out justice, a simple,

28. Alexander Kazbegi, *Otseubiitsa,* in *Izbrannye proizvedeniia* (Tbilisi, 1957), pp. 229, 237. For information on Kazbegi, see Lang, *A Modern History,* pp. 114–115.

utterly innocent woman begged a man who had committed a murder to defend her from injustice!"[29] Although such passages were not direct calls to social revolution, they inclined the reader's mind in that direction. To a boy of Soso's background who longed to be a new Koba, they could suggest—or at any rate prepare the mind for—a vision of the hero as revolutionary.

The Seminarian

When the fourteen-year-old Djugashvili entered the three-story stone building of the Tiflis theological seminary in August 1894, he found himself in a world very different from the one he had known in Gori. The students, numbering about six hundred, were confined to the barrack-like building (which some called the "stone sack") for all but an hour or so in the afternoon and led a highly regimented existence inside: up at seven, prayers, tea, classes until two, dinner at three, roll-call at five, evening prayers, tea at eight, study-period, and to bed at ten. Theology, Holy Scripture, literature, mathematics, history, and the Greek and Latin languages were among the subjects taught. On Sundays and religious holidays the boys had to stand through church services three to four hours long. The subjects were taught in a dull and dogmatic manner guaranteed to stifle intellectual interest. As in Gori, Russification was the order of the day. Not only was Russian enforced as the regular seminary language, but it was forbidden to read Georgian literature and newspapers, and going to the theater was considered a mortal sin.[30]

To make matters worse, the seminary functioned under an authoritarian regime of informing, constant surveillance by the monks, and the threat of incarceration in the "dark room" for infractions of the repressive rules. As Stalin recalled in 1931—by way of explaining to the German author Emil Ludwig why he became a Marxist revolutionary—it was a "humiliating regime" based on "Jesuitical methods." When Ludwig asked if he saw no good points

---

29. Kazbegi, *Otseubiitsa*, p. 197.
30. Kaminsky and Vereshchagin, "Detstvo," pp. 64–67; Iremaschwili, *Stalin*, p. 16.

in the Jesuits, he replied: "Yes, they are systematic and persistent in the pursuit of bad ends. But their chief method is surveillance, spying, invasion of the inner life, the violation of people's feelings, and what can be positive in that? The surveillance in the dormitory, for example. At nine o'clock the bell rings for morning tea, we go to the dining-room, and find on returning that all our clothes drawers have been searched and ransacked. What can be positive in that?" [31] Clearly, the memory still rankled. The "humiliating regime" undoubtedly contributed something to the transformation of seminarian Djugashvili into a revolutionary. But other factors were also involved, among them the fact that rebellion had already become a tradition in the seminary.

The institution had long been turning out young Georgian revolutionaries as well as Georgian-born Russian Orthodox priests. Expulsions on political grounds were numerous as early as the eighteen-seventies, when many of the students began applying their knowledge of Russian to the study of the populist literature coming from up north. Secret study and discussion groups flourished from that time on, and rebellious actions flared up on occasion. In 1885 an expelled student, the future *Mesame Dasi* leader Sylvester Djibladze, beat up the rector, a Russian named Chudetsky who called Georgian "a language for dogs," [32] and in the following year another expelled student murdered the man. A week-long student protest strike took place in 1890 and another at the end of 1893. In the latter case, the students' demands included an end to the spying, the dismissal of some especially odious school officials, and the creation of a department of the Georgian language.[33] The authorities responded by closing down the seminary for a month and expelling eighty-seven students, of whom twenty-three were also prohibited from residing in Tiflis. One of the deported ringleaders of the strike was a former schoolmate of Djugashvili's from Gori, Lado Ketskhoveli, who would subsequently influence his younger friend's choice of career.

31. *Stalin*, XIII, 113, 114.
32. Lang, *A Modern History*, p. 109.
33. Filipp Makharadze, *Ocherki revoliutsionnogo dvizheniia v Zakavkaz'i* (Tbilisi, 1927), pp. 57–58.

Revolt, then, was not only a living tradition but something still reverberating in the seminary when Djugashvili entered a few months after the strike. From the start he turned against the institution. On his first homecoming holiday, in October 1894, he was overheard in a Gori pastry shop complaining to an acquaintance about the school's regime and the behavior of the monks.[34] Soon he joined with a number of other students, including his friend Iremashvili, in organizing a clandestine young socialists' circle. Meanwhile, his attitude toward studies changed. He ceased striving to excel, did well only in two subjects that particularly interested him (secular history and logic), and gave to the others no more time than was needed to obtain passing marks.[35] His general bearing and relations with others also underwent a change. Fellow seminarians who remembered him from Gori as a vivacious boy, rather cheerful and sociable, now saw him become serious, reserved, and introverted. "Comrade Soso changed noticeably after entering the seminary," recalled David Papitashvili. "He became pensive, and boys' games no longer interested him." From another who knew him well, Lado Ketskhoveli's younger brother Vano, comes similar testimony: "At this time Comrade Soso's character changed completely. He lost his love for games and childhood pastimes. He became reflective and, somehow, withdrawn [zamknutym]. He gave up games but not books, and would go off in a corner and read assiduously."[36] Thus, young Djugashvili began to show the reticence and brooding aloofness from others that would characterize him in later years. He also became known as one who was quick to take offense, even if spoken to in jest. Sergo Ordzhonikidze, a fellow Georgian revolutionary from the early days, remembered him as having a "touchy character" (obidchivy kharakter) even as a very young man. He also recalled in later years how common friends from the Tiflis seminary would marvel at this quality in Djugashvili, which struck them as quite un-

34. Kaminsky and Vereshchagin, "Detstvo," p. 65.

35. Ibid., p. 68. According to the slightly different picture given by Iremashvili (Stalin, p. 20), he set out at first to excel in studies but gave up after being convinced by his first collision with the school authorities that scholastic success was out of the question for him.

36. Kaminsky and Vereshchagin, "Detstvo," pp. 65, 67.

Georgian. "Koba just cannot take a joke," they would say sadly. "Strange Georgian—doesn't understand jokes. Replies with fists to the most innocent remark." [37]

Although the erstwhile exemplary pupil stopped striving for scholastic success soon after entering the seminary, he continued to feel the need to be outstanding. His drive for achievement was simply transferred to other fields, such as his socialist self-education and—as time went on—revolutionary activity. Nor did his new-found introversion and reserve prevent him from asserting himself as a leader of group activity. The self-confident "feeling of a conqueror" did not abandon him. As he entered upon his rebel career through the young socialists' study circle that he and Iremashvili joined, he took it for granted that he belonged at the head of the movement. The circle elected as its leader an older student named Devdariani, who drew up for the new boys a six-year reading program designed to make them educated Social Democrats by the time they graduated from the seminary. Before long, however, Djugashvili was organizing one or more new study circles of which he himself was the mentor.[38] Again, a quality by which he was distinguished in later years—the urge for personal power—was finding expression in the seminary period. So was his intolerance of dissenting opinions. In discussions among the young socialists of the seminary, according to Iremashvili, Soso would adamantly insist upon the rightness of his own views, and express withering scorn toward those who voiced contrary ones. The group consequently divided into those who were cowed into becoming his dependable followers and the more independent-minded boys who would not submit to his domineering ways.[39]

He became, according to all accounts, a prodigious reader of "outside" books. The students would obtain these from a cheap lending-library and other sources in Tiflis, and smuggle them into the seminary. They would read in all manner of places: in bed at night by candle, in a hiding-place behind the woodpile in the schoolyard,

37. I. Dubinsky-Mukhadze, *Ordzhonikidze* (Moscow, 1963), p. 92.
38. Kaminsky and Vereshchagin, "Detstvo," p. 67.
39. Iremaschwili, *Stalin*, pp. 21–22.

on the back stairway of the seminary church, and inside the church as well: "Secretly, during classes, services, and sermons, we read 'our' books. The Bible was open on the desk, but on our laps we held Darwin, Marx, Plekhanov, or Lenin." [40] At first, Iremashvili recalls, he and Soso read widely in Georgian literature. One of their favorite works was the twelfth-century Georgian epic poem by Shota Rusta-veli, *The Man in the Panther's Skin,* in which three knightly friends rescue a beautiful maiden from captivity in a castle and from the threat of a forced marriage. It may be noted here that during his first period in the seminary, Soso wrote a number of poems in Georgian which appeared in print in 1895 in the Tiflis literary magazine *Iveria.* He also applied himself to Russian and Western literary classics, including *Dead Souls* and *Vanity Fair,* and acquired a con-siderable knowledge of literature.[41] Thanks in part to the fact that the monks repeatedly caught him reading smuggled books, we know the titles of some of them. Thus, an entry in the seminary's conduct-book for November 1896, signed by inspector Germogen, reads:

Djugashvili, it transpired, has a card for the "Cheap Library" and is checking books out. Today I confiscated from him V. Hugo's *Toilers of the Sea,* in which I found the aforementioned card.

Punish by lengthy confinement in the cell—I had already issued him a warning in connection with the outside book *Ninety-Three* by V. Hugo.

A subsequent entry (for March 1897) records that Djugashvili was apprehended for the thirteenth time reading books from the Cheap Library. On that occasion he was found on the church stairway read-ing Letourneau's *Literary Evolution of the Nations.*[42]

As usually happens in such a process of self-education by read-ing, one kind of book led to another. It may have been Hugo's *Ninety-Three* that stimulated Djugashvili's interest in books he is said to have read on the French Revolution, 1848, and the Paris Com-

40. *Ibid.,* p. 20.
41. Kaminsky and Vereshchagin, "Detstvo," p. 69. In memoirs published after Stalin's death, Kliment Voroshilov recalled that when he first met Djugash-vili and shared a room with him during the party congress in Stockholm in 1906, the young Georgian was able to recite passages from literature by heart (*Rass-kazy o zhizni. Vospominaniia* [Moscow, 1968], p. 247).
42. Kaminsky and Vereshchagin, "Detstvo," p. 71. He read Russian trans-lations of the books by Western authors.

mune. He became more and more absorbed in historical and political literature, socialist writings in particular. Reportedly he read Volume One of *Capital* in a hand-copied (and perhaps abridged) version that students had prepared from the one copy available in the Tiflis library. At what point he began reading the Russian Marxist literature, and when he made his first acquaintance with Lenin's writings, we do not know. There is some indication, however, that Lenin (under his pseudonym "Tulin") made an impression upon him even before he left the seminary in 1899. A former fellow student, P. Kapanadze, recalls an agitated discussion that he witnessed one day in 1898 in the square outside the seminary building. Djugashvili was sharply criticizing the views of *Kvali*'s editor, Noi Zhordania. After the bell rang and the group dispersed, he told Kapanadze that he had been reading articles by Tulin which he liked very much, and added: "I must see him at all cost." [43]

The study groups afforded a first experience of underground life, soon followed by more. On Djugashvili's proposal, according to his seminary friend D. Gogokhiia, a room was rented in town for five rubles monthly (contributed by the students whose families provided them with pocket money), and there they would meet for weekly or twice-weekly discussions during the afternoon periods of freedom.[44] This form of outside activity led to others. One evening Djugashvili and Iremashvili sneaked out of the seminary and made their way to the house of a worker of the Tiflis railway station to attend a meeting of the Social Democratic organization of railway workers. An escaped revolutionary dressed in a black shirt with a red tie, his fiery blue eyes set in a thin pale face, held them spellbound for hours with his stories of the sufferings endured by political prisoners in the Siberian wilderness. A further point of contact with Social Democracy was the editorial office of *Kvali,* which some of the students visited regularly. Iremashvili recalls that "Koba went with us a time or so, but afterwards ridiculed the men in the office." [45]

43. *Rasskazy starykh rabochikh,* p. 26. Kapanadze, who later became a teacher in Georgia, adds: "I recalled these words, spoken in 1898, when I met Comrade Stalin in 1926, and he remembered the episode."
44. *Rasskazy starykh rabochikh,* p. 13.
45. Iremaschwili, *Stalin,* p. 22.

His memory is consistent with Zhordania's own later recollection that a young man showed up one day in late 1898 at the *Kvali* office, introduced himself as a seminary student named Djugashvili and a regular reader of the Marxist periodical, said that he had decided to quit the seminary and devote himself to activity among the workers, and asked for advice. After questioning him for a while, Zhordania concluded that his theoretical knowledge was insufficient for a party propagandist and advised him on this account to stay in the seminary another year and continue his Marxist self-education. "I'll think it over," said Djugashvili, and went away. About a half-year later, Zhordania's colleague Djibladze told him in great agitation that the young man in question had been entrusted with a workers' circle and had proceeded to propagandize its members not only against the government and capitalists but "against us." [46]

The example of Lado Ketskhoveli was undoubtedly a factor in Djugashvili's decision to devote himself full time to Social Democratic work. After being banished, Ketskhoveli went to Kiev to continue his studies. In 1897, he returned illegally to Tiflis, joined *Mesame Dasi,* and began living the conspiratorial life of a professional revolutionary. He went to work in a Tiflis printing establishment in order to learn the printer's trade and managed while there to print some illegal pamphlets and proclamations as well as the first illegal Georgian book: a translation of Dickstein's *Story of a Piece of Bread.* Convinced that a legal Marxist journal like *Kvali* could only corrupt the masses, this energetic radical went on to found the underground Marxist press in the Transcaucasus and trained numerous comrades in the conspiratorial technique of illegal printing. After moving to Baku in early 1900, he set up an underground print-shop (known by the party code-name of "Nina") where *Iskra* and the illegal Georgian Marxist paper *Brdzola* (The Struggle) were turned out beginning in 1901. Earlier, his admiring former neighbor Djugashvili had made contact with him in Tiflis. Djugashvili, who was friendly with Lado's younger brother Vano in the seminary,

---

46. N. Vakar, "Stalin po vospominaniiam N. N. Zhordania," *Poslednye novosti* (Paris), December 16, 1936. Zhordania's discouraging reception of Djugashvili may help explain both the episode on the square that Kapanadze witnessed and the ridiculing of *Kvali* that Iremashvili remembered.

would come frequently to the Ketskhoveli apartment to read, and there he met and talked with Lado. Once, according to Vano's much later recollection, Lado came home to find Plekhanov's book *The Development of the Monist View of History* lying open on the table; when told by Vano that Soso was reading it, he remarked on the latter's penetrating mind and forecast for him a big role in the revolutionary movement.[47]

Whatever the attitude of Lado toward Soso was, it seems that Soso felt for the elder Ketskhoveli brother something akin to hero-worship. Arrested in 1902, Ketskhoveli was shot dead by a prison guard in August 1903 after shouting through the window of his cell: "Down with the autocracy! Long live freedom! Long live socialism!" Twenty years later Abel Yenukidze, at one time a Transcaucasian revolutionary and by now a high Soviet official, reminisced about him as follows in a talk before the Old Bolsheviks' Club in Moscow: "Comrade Stalin has many times emphasized with astonishment the outstanding capabilities of our deceased comrade, Ketskhoveli, who already at that time was able to raise questions in the spirit of revolutionary Marxism. Stalin frequently recalls that Comrade Ketskhoveli already then took a perfectly sound Bolshevik position. I and Comrade Stalin do not doubt that if Ketskhoveli had lived until the split of the RSDWP, he would have been wholeheartedly with the Bolsheviks and one of the strongest and most influential figures in our party." [48] Not—it seems—because of anything he did, but by virtue of what he was, Ketskhoveli exerted a formative influence upon Djugashvili. In this dedicated and fervent revolutionary who was four years his senior, the eighteen-year-old seminary youth found an immensely appealing model. Ketskhoveli had preceded him through the church school in Gori and the seminary in Tiflis and thence into

47. Kaminsky and Vereshchagin, "Detstvo," p. 92.
48. A. Yenukidze, *Nashi podpol'nye tipografiii na Kavkaze* (Moscow, 1925), p. 24. Yenukidze also said in his speech: "In 1895–97 Vlado Ketskhoveli was senior comrade in illegal circles in Tiflis and in particular the senior one in the circle in the seminary, in which, by the way, Djugashvili-Stalin, presently secretary of the Central Committee of the Russian Communist party, also took part" (*ibid.*, p. 5). If this is true, Ketskhoveli must have returned illegally to Tiflis earlier than other Soviet records indicate. Few, however, were as knowledgeable on these matters as Yenukidze.

the conspiratorial world of revolutionary politics. He was a living example of an individual making revolution his profession, and a proof of the practical possibility of Djugashvili's making the same choice for himself. So, in 1898, he too joined *Mesame Dasi*.

The decision to quit the seminary before graduating must have followed pretty much as a matter of course. Iremashvili urged him not to do so, reminding him that completion of the sixth and final year (1899–1900) would qualify him to enter a Russian university. But Djugashvili was by now committed to the idea of revolution as a career, besides which he feared that the school authorities would not allow him to complete the final year.[49] This fear was probably well founded. By his fifth year he had long since acquired the reputation of being a troublemaker, and he no longer bothered to conceal his rebellious attitude. On one occasion, inspector Abashidze caught him reading an outside book and snatched it out of his hands, whereupon Djugashvili snatched it back. When the angry monk exclaimed, "Don't you see who is before you?" the youth rubbed his eyes, peered, and said: "I see a black spot before me, nothing more."[50] The inspector's initials appear at the end of the following entry in the seminary conduct-book for 1898–99:

> *Djugashvili, Iosif* (V, I), during a search of the belongings of certain fifth-class pupils, several times spoke up to the inspectors, giving voice in his remarks to discontent over the searches carried out from time to time among the seminary students. In one of them he asserted that in not a single seminary were such searches made. In general, pupil Djugashvili is rude and disrespectful toward persons in authority and systematically fails to bow to one of the teachers (A. A. Murakhovsky), as the latter has repeatedly informed the inspectors.
> Reprimanded. Confined to the cell for five hours by order of Father Rector.[51]

Things having come to this pass, it is not surprising that pupil Djugashvili left the seminary in May 1899. What his mother's re-

---

49. Iremaschwili, *Stalin*, pp. 23–24.
50. Kaminsky and Vereshchagin, "Detstvo," pp. 66–67. Since Abashidze was appointed inspector in 1898, the episode must have occurred during one of Djugashvili's last two years in the seminary.
51. *Ibid.*, p. 84.

action was we do not know but can easily guess. According to school records published in the journal of the Georgian Exarchy for June–July 1899, he was expelled because "for unknown reasons" he failed to appear for final examinations at the end of the school year.[52] Characteristically, he later dramatized the event. On a questionnaire for a district party conference in Moscow in 1931, the one-time seminary dropout replied as follows to the question on schooling: "Kicked out of an orthodox theological seminary for Marxist propaganda." [53]

The Professional Revolutionary

Djugashvili began serving his apprenticeship as a professional revolutionary before leaving the seminary. The study circle assigned to him in 1898 by *Mesame Dasi* consisted of workers from the Tiflis railway workshops. At that time, he recalled in later years, "I received my first lessons of practical work in the apartment of Comrade Sturua in the presence of Djibladze (he was also one of my teachers), Chodrishvili, Chkheidze, Bochorishvili, Ninua, and other foremost workers of Tiflis." [54] Evidently, some of the older party comrades were present to coach him if necessary and to make sure that he could cope with a party propagandist's task, which was to tutor the workers in the Marxist view of things. Possibly on the basis of this early practical experience, he drew up in 1898 a "Program of Study in Marxist Worker Circles." [55]

After leaving the seminary, Djugashvili continued his activity as a propagandist in study groups of Tiflis railway workers, who

52. *Ibid.*, p. 86. This explanation of the expulsion appeared in *Dukhovny vestnik gruzinskogo ekzarkhata*, Nos. 12–13 (June 15–July 1, 1899), p. 8.
53. *Istoricheskie mesta Tbilisi: putevoditel' po mestam sviazannym s zhizn'iu i deiatel'nost'iu I. V. Stalina* (Tbilisi, 1944), p. 29. Stalin's official biographies explain that he was expelled from the seminary for "unreliability."
54. *Stalin*, VIII, 174. The occasion of his reminiscence was a talk that he gave on June 8, 1926, to workers of the main railway workshops in Tiflis.
55. A foreword by the Marx-Engels-Lenin Institute to Volume I of Stalin's works, published in 1946, states that two of his writings of the 1901–7 period, the "Program" of 1898 and a "Credo" written in 1904, had not been found (*Stalin*, I, x). For further reference to the "Program," see *Ocherki istorii kommunisticheskikh organizatsii Zakavkaz'ia. Chast' pervaia. 1883–1921 gg.* (Tbilisi, 1967), p. 47. Hereafter cited as *Ocherki istorii*.

knew him as "Soso." According to a later official biography, he "eked out a living" at this time by giving lessons.[56] At the end of December 1899 he found part-time clerical employment and lodgings in the Tiflis Observatory. These arrangements lasted, however, for only three months. The police raided his room at the observatory during a roundup of local Social Democratic activists in late March 1900, a time of widespread unemployment and rising worker unrest in Georgia. Not being there when they came and getting wind of the situation before returning, he evaded arrest by going underground, at the cost of the observatory job. Our only indication of how he managed to live afterwards is Iremashvili's recollection that in the post-seminary period some former fellow students "stood together to support him now and then in his need." [57]

Of his activities in the following months little is known. He played some part, along with Djibladze and others, in preparations for the large but unsuccessful Tiflis railway workers' strike of August 1900. He made the acquaintance of a friend of Lenin's, Victor Kurnatovsky, who came to Tiflis at that time as an emissary of *Iskra* and its views, and found in this Russian Marxist revolutionary one of his early mentors. He worked with Lado Ketskhoveli and the latter's associate Alexander Tsulukidze in creating *Brdzola,* the Georgian-language paper that was turned out in 1901 by the underground printing press "Nina," along with reprints of the Russian-language *Iskra.* Djugashvili's first published writings appeared in this short-lived illegal Georgian paper.[58] By and by he carried enough weight in local Marxist circles to be made a member of the Tiflis Social Democratic Committee when this group was re-elected at a party

56. "Iosif Vissarionovich Stalin. Kratkaia biografiia," in *Malaia sovetskaia entsiklopediia,* X (Moscow, 1940), p. 321. Hereafter cited as *Malaia* biography.
57. Iremaschwili, *Stalin,* p. 24.
58. The first two writings included in Volume I of Stalin's works are an editorial foreword that appeared unsigned in the first issue of *Brdzola,* published in September 1901, and an article, "The Russian Social Democratic Party and Its Immediate Tasks," which also appeared unsigned in *Brdzola,* Nos. 2–3, later that year. Stylistically neither piece is clearly recognizable as his in the way later writings are, and one of them has been cited in the post-Stalin literature on party history without reference to his authorship. They may have been collectively written articles in which he had a hand. The third item in Volume I, an article on the nationality question from *Proletariatis brdzola* of late 1904, seems clearly his.

conference held in November 1901 on the premises of the underground Avlabar printing press in Tiflis.[59] The Tiflis committee itself had been in existence since 1898.

During these first years Djugashvili involved himself in the internal politics of the local Marxists as well as in their revolutionary activities. There was a division, corresponding roughly to that between "softs" and "hards" on *Iskra,* between the dominant majority, which followed Zhordania's tendency, and a more militant minority (composed of Makharadze, Ketskhoveli, Tsulukidze, Mikha Tskhakaia, and others), which scorned the legal-Marxist tendencies of *Kvali,* favored underground methods, and wanted the movement to go beyond clandestine propaganda activities into a new "street" phase based on mass agitation. These were the proto-Bolsheviks, so to speak, and Djugashvili joined them. But he promoted the militant position in an offensive factional manner that gained him a reputation among Georgian Marxists of being a difficult character, someone who was always stirring up trouble. This may explain why he moved to Batum shortly after being elected to the Tiflis Committee.

The move took place under circumstances which, although not fully clarified to this day, did not reflect credit upon him. Émigré Georgian Menshevik sources have persistently reported that he went to Batum after being expelled from the Tiflis organization by a party tribunal on charges of intrigue and slander against Sylvester Djibladze.[60] According to another version, which has a certain plausibility, the move was precipitated by an argument as to whether or not workers as well as party professionals (meaning intellectuals, for the most part) should be members of the Tiflis committee. Djugashvili unsuccessfully opposed this on the grounds that it would com-

---

59. *Ocherki istorii,* p. 61. The Avlabar press was underground in the literal sense. It was set up in caverns dug into the wall of a well sunk inside a house in the Avlabar district on the outskirts of Tiflis. The police did not discover it until 1906.

60. *Brdzolis khm* (Paris), No. 3 (1930). Quoted in Bertram D. Wolfe, *Three Who Made a Revolution* (Boston, 1948), p. 420, where the story is pronounced plausible. See also Vakar, "Stalin," and Grigori Uratadze, *Vospominaniia gruzinskogo sotsial-demokrata* (Stanford, 1968), pp. 66–67. Isaac Deutscher, who does not accept this story, suggests that Djugashvili's move was precipitated by personal and political antagonisms between himself and Djibladze (*Stalin: A Political Biography,* 2nd ed. [New York, 1966], p. 46).

plicate conspiratorial operation and that the workers themselves
were not yet sufficiently developed for the role of committeemen.
This version has its source in a history of Transcaucasian Social
Democracy first published in Geneva in 1910 and republished in
Moscow in 1923.[61] The author, himself a Social Democratic participant in events recounted in the book, did not name Djugashvili
directly. He wrote that worker participation on the committee was
resisted by one young intellectual whom he described as motivated
by personal caprice and love of power. After being badly defeated
in the committee vote, the young man departed Tiflis for Batum,
"whence the Tiflis workers received information concerning his improper behavior, his hostile and disorganizing agitation against the
Tiflis organization and its members." [62] In fairness it should be
mentioned that the Social Democratic leaders in Batum at the time
of Djugashvili's arrival there around the beginning of December
1901 were two exponents of the moderate position, Chkheidze and
Ramishvili, who might have been expected to oppose his efforts
to organize a more militant and conspiratorial Social Democratic
operation along the lines favored by men like Ketskhoveli and
Kurnatovsky.

Acute worker unrest in Batum created a favorable environment
for the kind of agitational leaflets that Djugashvili is reported to have
cranked out on a simple hand-press set up in the hut where he lived.
But we do not know whether these leaflets made any significant contribution to the strikes that broke out in the Matashev works and the
Rothschild oil refinery in Batum in February 1902. The dismissal of
389 Rothschild workers precipitated the latter. An ensuing work
stoppage at the refinery led to the arrest of thirty-two workers on
March 8, after which six hundred workers went to the police depart-

61. S. T. Arkomed, *Rabochee dvizheniia i sotsial-demokratiia na Kavkaze
(s 80-x godov po 1903 g.)* (Moscow, 1923), pp. 83–84. The second edition was
unchanged save for the addition of notes and a preface. Arkomed's real name is
given as G. A. Kardjian in *Ocherki istorii,* p. 51, where it is confirmed that he
was elected to the Tiflis Committee at the same time as Djugashvili.

62. Arkomed, *Rabochee dvizheniia,* pp. 83–84. Trotsky, who accepts Arkomed's version, states that Djugashvili was the only member of the Tiflis Committee
who moved to Batum in the fall of 1901. On this see Leon Trotsky, *Stalin: An Appraisal of the Man and His Influence* (New York, 1967), p. 30.

ment and demanded that their comrades be released or that they themselves be arrested. The police arrested them. On the following day a great mass of workers appeared with the same demand and, refusing the command to disperse, were fired upon by soldiers. Fourteen died and many were wounded.[63] What role—if any—Djugashvili played in these events is not clear.

As industrial unrest mounted in several Transcaucasian centers, partly, perhaps, under the impact of the Batum demonstration of March 9, the authorities decided to crack down on Social Democratic activists in various places. On the night of April 5, 1902, the members of the Batum Social Democratic Committee, Djugashvili included, were arrested during a committee meeting.[64] He was confined in the Batum prison for more than a year and in the Kutais prison for about six months before being sent to three years of exile in an eastern Siberian village called Novaia Uda, located in Irkutsk province. He arrived there in late November 1903, escaped early in the following January, and made his way back to Tiflis. This was a sequence of events destined to be repeated. Between 1902 and 1913, according to his official biography, he was arrested eight times, was sent into exile seven times, and escaped from exile six times.[65] The exile from which he did not escape was the one to which he was sentenced in 1913 and from which he was freed by the February Revolution of 1917. That time he was sent to so remote a spot in the far north of Siberia that escape was impossible.

Upon returning to Tiflis in February 1904, following his first escape, Djugashvili took refuge in the apartment of a Social Democratic activist, Micho Bochoridze. This we know because of his chance meeting there with his future father-in-law, Sergei Alliluyev, who published his memoirs many years later. Alliluyev, a Russian, was a skilled mechanic who came south in the early eighteen-nineties, found employment in the Tiflis railway workshops, married, and settled down. He also became a Social Democrat, and his home in a Tiflis suburb was a favorite meeting-place of revolutionaries.

63. Makharadze, *Ocherki*, pp. 83–84.
64. *Ocherki istorii*, p. 67.
65. *Malaia* biography, p. 329.

When he went one evening to see Bochoridze on party business, the latter introduced him to Djugashvili, who told him something about his recent escape from Novaia Uda. He had tried to flee after the first few days, but without sufficient warm clothing, and he was forced to go back because his face and ears were freezing. His second attempt was successful.[66] As reported in the memoirs of Alliluyev's older daughter, Anna, who was eight at the time but heard the story from her father, Djugashvili could not get away at first because the surveillance-man kept too close an eye on him. But after awaiting his chance and getting hold of some warm things, he went off on foot, nearly froze his face, and made it.[67]

We know still less concerning details of the subsequent escapes. It may be noted, however, that such escapes were not uncommon among Russian revolutionaries. The system of administrative exile to places in the far north of European Russia or to Siberia should not be confused with the more severe and rigorous, but also more sparingly applied, sentence of penal servitude. Nor was the vaunted Okhrana so abundantly staffed and efficient as its Soviet successor-organization would one day be. Once at the place to which they were sent, the exiles were free to take lodging with local inhabitants and live their own lives, subject only to a surveillance which varied in intensity and effectiveness. They could correspond, although at the risk of having their mail read by the authorities. As we have seen in Lenin's case, they might even produce major scholarly dissertations, not to mention revolutionary manifestoes that could be spirited abroad. Escape itself was difficult, sometimes hazardous, but quite often possible.

On returning to Tiflis in February 1904, Djugashvili plunged back into underground party activity. In his absence, the Social Democratic movement had taken on changed organizational form.

66. S. Alliluyev, *Proidennyi put'* (Moscow, 1946), p. 109.
67. A. S. Alliluyeva, *Vospominaniia*, p. 37. She adds (p. 38) that this "first meeting" between her father and Djugashvili took place at the beginning of January 1904. Since the date of Djugashvili's successful departure from Novaia Uda is given in official sources as January 5, she may have been mistaken on this point. At the time of Alliluyev's first meeting with Djugashvili, his younger daughter, Nadezhda (whom Stalin would marry in 1919), was three years old.

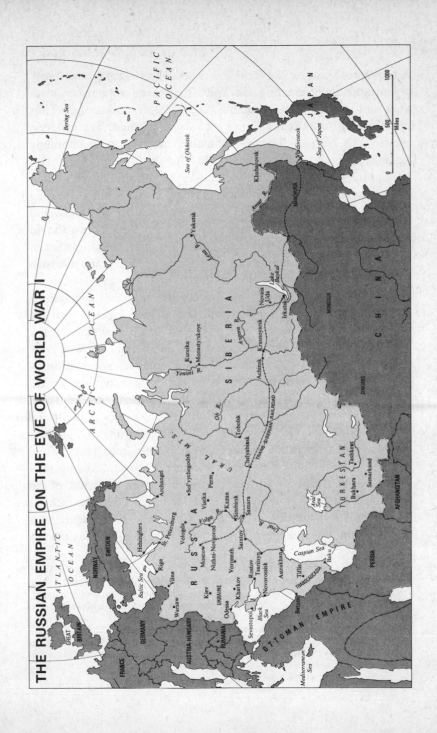

THE RUSSIAN EMPIRE ON THE EVE OF WORLD WAR I

A constituent congress of Transcaucasian Social Democratic party organizations, representing the Tiflis, Baku, and Batum organizations and smaller party groups in lesser centers, had met in Tiflis in early 1903 to unify the Transcaucasian movement. The congress created a "Caucasian Union Committee" of nine as a continuing leadership group, and at some point after his return Djugashvili became a member of it.[68] In the following months he moved around the Transcaucasus on party affairs, visiting Baku in June, spending September and October in the west Georgian town of Kutais, and stopping more briefly in Batum and Chiatura. Perhaps we should say "factional affairs," however, because his chief preoccupation at this time was the strengthening of his side in the Transcaucasian version of the emerging party schism.

It has been suggested, by Trotsky for one, that Djugashvili began his activities as a Menshevik and aligned himself with the Bolsheviks only on the eve of 1905, after much hesitation.[69] The evidence offered is a tsarist police report, dated 1911, in which the following appeared: "According to newly obtained agent information, Iosif Djugashvili was known in the organization under the names of 'Soso' and 'Koba,' worked in the organization from 1902, first as a Menshevik and then as a Bolshevik, as a propagandist and head of District I (Railway District)." This document was published in the Tiflis paper of the Georgian Communist party, *Zaria vostoka* (Dawn of the East) on December 23, 1925, among reminiscences of Stalin by former comrades on the occasion of his forty-sixth birthday. A copy of it is on file in the Okhrana archives at the Hoover Institution in Stanford, California. Its authenticity is not in doubt, but its accuracy is. Apart from the erroneous placing

68. Makharadze, *Ocherki*, p. 76; and *Ocherki istorii*, pp. 70–72. The original nine, according to the latter source (p. 72), were Bochoridze, Djibladze, Zhordania, Zurabov, Knuniants, Makharadze, Topuridze, Tsulukidze, and Tskhakaia; and Djugashvili was one of nine others who "entered at various times." This statement of the 1967 official Georgian party history implicitly contradicts the contention of Soviet sources in the thirties that Djugashvili was elected to the committee *in absentia* at the time of its original creation. The false claims about his election *in absentia* led Isaac Deutscher to infer wrongly that "at the age of twenty-two he was already some sort of 'grey eminence' in the underground of his native province" (*Stalin*, p. 50).

69. Trotsky, *Stalin*, pp. 50–51.

of Djugashvili in Tiflis during a year that he spent in Batum, it is an obvious anachronism for the author of the report (the chief of the Tiflis province Gendarme Administration) to ascribe Menshevism to him from 1902. For Menshevism in any tangible sense had its inception only in the aftermath of the Russian party's Second Congress, i.e., around 1904. The police officer might have been misled by the fact that most of the Social Democrats with whom Djugashvili associated in Tiflis in 1900–1901 subsequently became Mensheviks.

One of the few things about which we can be quite definite in speaking of his early revolutionary career is that he adopted Bolshevism unhesitatingly as soon as the issues in the developing intra-party dispute became clear to him. On this we have the independent testimony of two one-time Georgian Social Democrats who wrote their memoirs after emigrating.[70]

Upon returning from Siberian exile, Djugashvili espoused the Lenin position on his travels around Transcaucasia. A Georgian memoir confirms that he was taking this position when he came to Kutais in the fall of 1904 to head the local Social Democratic Committee.[71] Further evidence of an unusual kind appears in two private letters that he sent from Kutais in October to a fellow Georgian revolutionary then living in Leipzig, M. Davitashvili, who passed them on to Lenin and Krupskaya (in whose correspondence they later turned up).

Djugashvili revealed himself in these letters as a completely committed Lenin follower—the term "Bolshevik" was not yet in wide currency. In the first he asked his friend to send him *Iskra*, which by then was under the control of an anti-Lenin majority and printing articles critical of Lenin's position. He explained the request by saying that "though it's without a spark [*iskra*], it's still needed: at least it has a chronicle, devil take it, and you have to know well your enemy." That he meant "enemy" seriously is best

---

70. Iremaschwili, *Stalin,* pp. 21–23; Uratadze, *Vospominaniia,* p. 67.

71. Baron (Bibineishvili), *Za chetvert' veka* (*Revoliutsionnaia bor'ba v Gruzii*) (Moscow and Leningrad, 1931), pp. 80–81. The retrospective rewriting of Georgian party history to embellish Stalin's role was not yet customary at the time this memoir was written.

shown by the scorn the letter heaped on Plekhanov for attacking *What Is to Be Done?*, which for Djugashvili was evidently a kind of credo. One of Plekhanov's arguments against Lenin was that the working class does not need a proselytizing Social Democratic intelligentsia in order to acquire revolutionary consciousness. On this the ardent Leninist from Kutais commented:

The man has either gone off his nut completely or is showing hate and hostility. I think it's both. I think Plekhanov has lagged behind the *new questions*. He sees in his imagination the old opponents and goes on repeating: "social being determines social consciousness," and "ideas don't just fall from the sky." As if Lenin were saying that Marx's socialism would have been possible in the time of slavery and serfdom. Now even schoolboys know that "ideas don't just fall from the sky." But that's not the question now. . . . What interests us now is . . . how particular ideas and insights become linked in one orderly system (the theory of socialism), and by whom they are worked out and linked together. Does the mass give the leaders the program and its argumentation, or do the leaders give it to the mass? [72]

Not surprisingly, Djugashvili's first published article following his return from exile was a thumping defense of Lenin's position on the controversial clause one of the party rules. It appeared in a new illegal Georgian Marxist paper, *Proletariatis brdzola* (The Proletariat's Struggle), on January 1, 1905,[73] as revolutionary stormclouds gathered on the horizon.

The "dress rehearsal," as Lenin much later called the Russian Revolution of 1905, was a massive and spontaneous insurrectionary movement of nationwide scope. Smoldering grievances in large groups of the populace were transformed into a rebellious mood by the economic depression at the start of the century and the humiliat-

72. *Stalin*, I, 56–57. The two letters were first published here, in 1946. An editorial note (p. 396) states that they were found in the correspondence of Lenin and Krupskaya with Bolshevik organizations in Russia. This is a plausible explanation of the manner in which they were recovered for publication. They bear the stamp of authenticity in their style and the coarse simplicity of the language, which would be natural considering that Djugashvili was writing not for publication but privately to friends.

73. "The Proletarian Class and the Proletarian Party (Concerning Point One of the Party Rules)," in *Stalin*, I, 62–73.

ing Russian defeats in the war being waged with Japan during 1904. In this atmosphere Petersburg's Bloody Sunday in January 1905 touched off an explosion. There were waves of strikes, street demonstrations, disorders in the countryside, and acts of armed violence. The latter ranged from episodes like the mutiny on the battleship *Potemkin* at Odessa (later immortalized in Sergei Eisenstein's film) to armed uprisings in Moscow and a number of other centers. Something approaching a general political strike developed during October. At that time a soviet (i.e., council) of workers' deputies, in which Trotsky played a prominent part, was formed in Petersburg, and political parties for the first time emerged into the open. On October 17, the tsar issued a manifesto proclaiming civil liberties and the creation of an elective national legislature, the Duma. But not until the beginning of 1907 did the revolutionary mood subside completely.

In Transcaucasia, where deep social discontents were intensified by frustrated national feelings, the 1905 upheaval was exceptionally violent. Peasants rose up in arms against landlords, workers struck en masse, street demonstrations erupted. Violent reprisals by Russian troops and whip-wielding Cossacks, including a terrible massacre of people gathered for a meeting in the Tiflis town hall in late August, failed to quell the insurgency, and Georgia entered a state of near-anarchy by the end of the year. The Social Democrats were not responsible for the emergency but took full advantage of it to press for their goals. Here as well as elsewhere in the country, however, their internal division deepened as differences over revolutionary tactics compounded those that had caused the intra-party conflict in the first place. The Revolution of 1905 thus accelerated the transformation of the two warring factions into warring parties.

Djugashvili was actively involved in the 1905 events in Georgia but did not play a conspicuous revolutionary role. He addressed some mass meetings, issued a few agitational leaflets, and wrote some articles dealing with the revolutionary situation and with intra-party differences. He moved around Georgia as an itinerant organizer and propagandist of Bolshevism, investing much energy in the factional politics of the revolutionary movement. Thus, the chronicle of his doings in 1905 that appeared much later, in Volume I of his collected works, records that in April he "speaks at a big discussion session in Batum against the Menshevik leaders N. Ramishvili, R. Arsenidze, and others," and that in July he "speaks at a two-thousand-strong discussion meeting in Chiatura against the anarchists, federalists, and SR's." [74]

But there was a further way in which Djugashvili participated in events of that time. In various sections of the country, including Transcaucasia, fighting groups of the party carried out a series of "expropriations," i.e., armed robberies of banks, mail coaches, and so on. Although these operations (known among the revolutionaries as "exes") aroused much opposition in the party, especially from the Mensheviks, Lenin approved and relied heavily upon them as a source of funds to finance political activity. With his connivance they continued in the aftermath of 1905 despite the fact that a Menshevik-sponsored resolution forbidding them was passed at the party's Fourth Congress—the so-called Unity Congress—held in Stockholm in 1906. One of the most notorious was a raid on the Tiflis State Bank in June 1907, which netted a huge sum of money for the Bolshevik treasury. The Tiflis operation was led by a daring adventurer, S. A. Ter-Petrosian ("Kamo"). Djugashvili, however, is believed to have played a covert directing role in this and other "exes" in the Transcaucasus.

It is true that none of his later official biographers ever alluded to this facet of his revolutionary career, and that he himself avoided giving a direct reply when the German writer Emil Ludwig, interviewing him in 1931, observed: "Your biography contains instances of what may be called acts of 'highway robbery.' " [75] Nonetheless, it is fairly well attested that Djugashvili, while never a direct participant, functioned behind the scenes as the planner and organizer of

74. *Stalin*, I, 422, 423.
75. *Stalin*, XIII, 112. According to the Soviet transcript of the interview, Ludwig coupled the comment here quoted with a query on Stalin's view of Stenka Razin as an "ideological highwayman." Stalin took advantage of this opening and confined himself to the historical aspect of the question, denying an analogy between Bolsheviks and leaders of peasant rebellions like Razin.

various "expropriations." [76] Menshevik sources have alleged that he was expelled from the party by the Transcaucasian organization for his part in the Tiflis raid of June 1907. In March 1918, before Menshevik activities had been wholly suppressed by the victorious Bolsheviks, Martov wrote in his Moscow newspaper that Stalin in his time had been expelled from his party organization for having something to do with expropriations. Stalin thereupon brought charges against Martov before a party tribunal and denied that he had ever been tried or expelled by his party organization. But he did not deny involvement in expropriations. [77]

The Mensheviks emerged from the Revolution of 1905 as the dominant Social Democratic faction in Georgia. One factor in their success was the vigor with which they adopted the general Menshevik-favored tactic of participating in the elections for the first Duma. The Bolsheviks, meeting for a conference in the Finnish town of Tammerfors in December 1905, decided (over Lenin's objections) to boycott these elections. A result of the course taken by Georgia's Mensheviks was that five of the eight Georgian deputies to the first Duma, and all of the Georgian deputies to the second Duma, were Mensheviks. The success of Georgian Menshevism is probably also to be explained by its more nationalist orientation and by the fact that its leaders were more genuinely revolution-minded than the Russian Menshevik leaders. So overwhelming was the Menshevik influence among Georgian Social Democrats that the sixteen delegates elected from Georgia to the Stockholm congress included but one Bolshevik—Djugashvili. At the Fifth Congress, held in London in April–May 1907, *all* the voting delegates from Georgia were Mensheviks. Lacking sufficient local bases of support for similar mandates, Djugashvili and Tskhakaia, the two Bolshevik representatives from Georgia, were admitted only in the

76. This is one of the points on which the non-Soviet biographers of Stalin are generally agreed. See, for example, Trotsky, *Stalin*, pp. 100–101; Deutscher, *Stalin*, pp. 87–88; and Wolfe, *Three Who Made a Revolution*, pp. 390–391.

77. R. Arsenidze, "Iz vospominanii o Staline," *Novy zhurnal*, No. 72 (June 1963), p. 232. On the Martov episode, see Trotsky, *Stalin*, pp. 101–102; Wolfe, *Three Who Made a Revolution*, pp. 470–472; and G. Aronson, "Stalinskii protsess protiv Martova," *Sotsialisticheskii vestnik*, Nos. 7–8 (1939), p. 84.

lower category of delegates with "advisory vote," and at that only over protests from the Menshevik side. When Lenin, who presided at the fourteenth session of the congress, called for a vote on the credentials commission proposal to admit Ivanovich (Djugashvili), Barsov (Tskhakaia), and two others with the right of advisory vote, Martov moved that information be sought on the individuals concerned, saying "one cannot vote without knowing who is involved." Lenin then said: "That in fact is unknown. But the congress can have confidence in the unanimous opinion of the credentials commission." Martov's motion was voted down and the commission's proposal was adopted by a majority of votes, with a considerable number of abstentions—at which point Kostrov (Zhordania) called out from the floor: "We protest." [78]

Although the Bolsheviks were an oppositional minority in Georgian Social Democracy, Georgian Bolshevism did nevertheless exist as a movement. Djugashvili, however, was not initially a leading figure in it. It is a measure of his relative unimportance in the first period that he was not one of the fifteen delegates from local groups who gathered in Tiflis in November 1904 for the first conference of Transcaucasian Bolsheviks. Nor did he travel to London in April 1905 as one of the four Transcaucasian delegates to the all-Bolshevik Third Party Congress, which Trotsky has described as "the constituent congress of Bolshevism." [79] The Tammerfors meeting later that year marked his debut in higher Bolshevik councils. By that time he was emerging as a figure of consequence on the local Bolshevik scene, though not yet in central party affairs. His two brief trips to attend the party congresses in Stockholm and London in 1906 and 1907 were, by the way, his first exposures to foreign life, and it is doubtful that he spent much time outside the meeting-halls. A six-week sojourn in Cracow and Vienna at the

78. *Piatyi (Londonskii) s"ezd RSDRP. Aprel'–mai 1907 goda. Protokoly* (Moscow, 1963), pp. 226–232, 241. Party practice was to use fictitious names even at the congress and in its records.

79. Trotsky, *Stalin*, p. 59. The four were Kamenev, Tskhakaia, Djaparidze, and Nevsky. The Third Congress was convened by the Bureau of Committees of the Majority, contrary to the desire of the Mensheviks, and it was at this congress that the Bolshevik faction of the party informally organized itself as a separate and independent unit.

beginning of 1913 was his only other known venture abroad before he traveled to Teheran in 1943 to confer with Prime Minister Churchill and President Roosevelt on the war against the Axis.

On his return to Transcaucasia from London in June 1907, Djugashvili stopped only briefly in Georgia and then settled down for a time in the Caspian port city of Baku, in Azerbaijan. Social Democratic activities in Baku were focused upon the polyglot population of oil-field workers, who made up nearly a quarter of the city's population of 200,000. There as well as in Georgia the aftermath of the 1905 Revolution found the Mensheviks in the ascendancy, and Bolshevik efforts were aimed at changing this situation. Djugashvili joined the factional fray in his familiar capacity as an underground party organizer. Since the Baku Social Democratic Committee was in Menshevik hands, he was at first a *komitetchik* (committeeman) without a committee. But organizational maneuvers, in which he involved himself along with such leading Baku Bolsheviks of that period as Stepan Shaumian, Abel Yenukidze, Alyosha Djaparidze, Suren Spandarian, and Sergo Ordzhonikidze, led to the formation in October of a rival Bolshevik Baku Committee, of which Djugashvili was a member.[80]

In the ensuing months he concentrated his attention upon what was for him a new field of revolutionary work: trade union activities. Looking back much later, he reminisced that his experiences in the stormy conflicts of those years between the oil workers and employers had taught him "what it means to lead large masses of workers." [81] The leadership comprised practical efforts in the organizing of strikes and influencing of trade union policy, and the writing of articles on labor issues for a legal Bolshevik trade union paper, *Gudok* (The Whistle). At first Djugashvili appears to have taken a militantly leftist position favoring maximum party control over the unions and a no-compromise orientation toward a general strike, whereas Djaparidze and some other Bolsheviks of more

80. For a detailed account of these machinations and of Djugashvili's subsequent trade union activities in Baku, see Ronald Grigor Suny, "A Journeyman for the Revolution: Stalin and the Labour Movement in Baku, June 1907–May 1908," *Soviet Studies*, January 1972, pp. 382–384.

81. Speech of June 1926 to Tiflis railway workers, in *Stalin*, VIII, 174.

moderate outlook preferred to recognize the autonomy of trade union activity and probe the possibilities of less extreme forms of labor action. Eventually he was overruled, and he wound up supporting a more flexible Bolshevik policy which paved the way for marked Social Democratic and specifically Bolshevik successes in elections of worker delegates in early 1908 to a council charged with preparing positions for a planned conference with the employers.[82]

These very successes, however, led to the arrest of a number of Social Democratic activists. Djugashvili (who was then operating under the pseudonym "Nizheradze") was arrested on March 25, 1908, and confined in the Bailov prison in Baku until early November, when he was exiled for two years to Vologda province, in the far north of European Russia. He proceeded there, according to the usual practice, "by stages"—i.e., in a group that moved under convoy from prison to prison, picking up prisoners along the way. From the Vologda city prison he was assigned in January 1909 to the small town of Sol'vychegodsk as his place of exile. On the way there, again "by stages" and possibly on foot, he fell ill with typhus and was temporarily hospitalized in the town of Viatka, finally reaching Sol'vychegodsk at the end of February. Four months later he escaped, made his way south, and reappeared in July 1909 in the Baku party underground. Arrested again in March 1910 and held a second time in the Bailov prison, he was dispatched in early September back to Sol'vychegodsk, after being handed an edict in which the viceroy of the Caucasus banned him from residing in Transcaucasia for five years. After completing the two-year term of exile in Sol'vychegodsk, he chose Vologda as his place of residence

82. Suny, "Journeyman for the Revolution," pp. 382, 386–389. On Djugashvili's initial militance, Suny cites 1923 reminiscences of A. Stopani, one of the Baku Bolsheviks of that earlier time, who wrote: ". . . we had our own 'Left' (Koba-Stalin) and 'Right' (Alyosha Djaparidze and others, including myself); the disagreements were not on fundamentals but with reference to the tactics or the methods of establishing that contact." Suny plausibly infers that Djugashvili was concerned above all with protecting the underground's primacy, and comments: "As a *komitetchik* he was the last to adjust to the new possibilities for legal activities by the workers." Stopani's reminiscence appeared in *Iz proshlogo: stat'i i vospominaniia iz istorii bakinskoi organizatsii i rabochego dvizheniia v Baku* (Baku, 1923), p. 18.

under surveillance (in accord with the ban). He illegally quit Vologda in September and went to Petersburg under a false passport
bearing the name "Chizhikov." There he made contact with Sergei
Alliluyev, among others. Arrested again in December, he was exiled
to Vologda for three years but escaped in early 1912.[83] This was
not the last such sequence.

In concluding this account of Djugashvili's early life, a word
must be said about his first marriage. It will have to be brief because
our information is so scanty. The official biographies make no mention of the marriage, and what little we know comes mainly from
the Iremashvili memoir. The bride was Ekaterina Svanidze, whom
Djugashvili may have met through her brother Alexander, a fellow
student of his in the Tiflis seminary. Although Iremashvili gives the
year of the marriage as 1903, it probably took place in 1902, before
Djugashvili's first arrest and exile, or in 1904, following it. It may
be indicative of the mother-attachment discussed above that the
bride, in addition to bearing the same first name as his mother, resembled her in other ways. She was not an intellectual and revolutionary, like her brother Alexander, but a traditional Georgian
woman for whom wifely duties were a mission in life. Like Ekaterina
Djugashvili, she was a devout daughter of the church, and according
to Iremashvili she would even pray at night for her husband to be
moved to renounce his nomadic life as a professional revolutionary
and turn to respectable pursuits. She likewise resembled the other
Ekaterina in being completely devoted to Iosif, whom she "looked
upon as a demigod." [84] Where the couple lived during their occasional interludes together we do not know. Very possibly Ekaterina
kept house for him in some part of her family home. This is believed
to have been located in the village of Didi-Lilo, near Tiflis, where
earlier generations of Djugashvilis had lived.

In 1908 Ekaterina bore her husband a son whom they named
Yakov, and a year or so later she died of an illness.[85] Having been

83. On these arrests and escapes, see *Stalin*, II, 411–416.
84. Iremaschwili, *Stalin*, pp. 30, 39.
85. Iremaschwili, *Stalin*, p. 40, gives the year of her death as 1907. This
must be mistaken, for we know from other sources that Yakov was born in
1908. Stalin's daughter, Svetlana, a child of his later marriage to Nadezhda

deeply fond of her, Djugashvili was grief-stricken. Iremashvili, although now a Menshevik and thus a political enemy, came to offer condolences and attended the Orthodox funeral service that was held in accordance with the deceased wife's last wishes and those of the Svanidzes. When the small procession reached the cemetery entrance, "Koba firmly pressed my hand, pointed to the coffin, and said: 'Soso, this creature softened my heart of stone. She died and with her died my last warm feelings for people.' He placed his right hand on his chest: 'It is all so desolate here inside, so inexpressibly empty.' " [86] Their son was brought up in Georgia by his mother's sisters.

The Question of Police Connections

Djugashvili had a way of leaving places under a cloud after some ugly incident, brought on in part by his own tendency to become embroiled with others. His move from Tiflis to Batum was a first case in point. His departure from the Georgian scene for Baku may, as indicated earlier, have been a second. And his departure from Baku itself may in some sense have been a third. In any event, his Baku period appears to have been clouded by a rivalry that developed between himself and Stepan Shaumian, and he was reportedly suspected by local Bolsheviks of causing Shaumian's arrest in 1909 by informing on him to the police.[87]

This report is one of several—chiefly emanating from Georgian Menshevik circles—which show that he was suspected in certain quarters of informing to the police on people whom he wished to

---

Alliluyeva, writes that Yakov was only seven years younger than her mother, whose year of birth was 1901 (*Twenty Letters,* p. 100). Also, on being captured by the Germans in 1941, Yakov, who had served as a Red Army officer, gave his place and date of birth as Baku, March 16, 1908. For the German source of this information, see Edward E. Smith, *The Young Stalin: The Early Years of an Elusive Revolutionary* (New York, 1967), p. 392. On Didi-Lilo as Ekaterina's Georgian home, see Smith, p. 127. On the couple's small house in Baku, see S. Alliluyev, *Proidennyi put',* p. 182.

86. Iremaschwili, *Stalin,* p. 40.
87. Uratadze, *Vospominaniia,* p. 67; Arsenidze, "Iz vospominanii," p. 224.

see removed from the scene. According to Semeon Vereshchak, a one-time SR who was a fellow prisoner of Djugashvili's in the Bailov prison in 1908, he began the practice of informing (although not, in this instance, to the police) shortly after leaving the Tiflis seminary. In reminiscences published in a Paris Russian paper in 1928, Vereshchak cited other prisoners who had been schoolmates of Djugashvili as sources for the story that soon after being expelled he caused the expulsion of the other members of his secret socialist group in the seminary by reporting their names to the rector. According to these sources, he admitted his action and justified it to the expelled boys on the ground that they would become good revolutionaries now that they had lost the opportunity for careers as priests.[88] Although further evidence of Djugashvili's involvement is lacking, we do have confirmation that a group of forty or so students was forced to leave the seminary in the fall of 1899 in a manner very strongly suggesting that the school authorities found them to be engaged in forbidden clandestine activities.[89]

Additional hearsay evidence of possible dealings by the young Djugashvili with the police has recently come from Old Bolshevik sources. Roy Medvedev cites the unpublished personal papers of one E. P. Frolov, a party member since 1918, as the source of a story that in the early nineteen-thirties a Soviet party historian named Professor Sepp, then working in the Georgian party's Central Committee, came upon an old tsarist police file containing a request by Iosif Djugashvili to be released from arrest, and a note written on it saying: "Free him, if he agrees to give the Gendarme Department information about the activity of the Social Democratic party." In a further instance, there was reportedly found in the Kutais archives a denunciation of a group of Social Democrats, signed by Iosif Djugashvili. According to a third story, again from the Frolov papers, a party member once called on young Djugashvili in a conspiratorial apartment in Tiflis and found him with a high-ranking

88. S. Vereshchak, "Stalin v tiur'me (Vospominaniia politicheskogo zakliuchennogo)," *Dni,* January 22, 1928.

89. Kaminsky and Vereshchagin, "Detstvo," p. 88.

gendarme officer. Afterwards, when questioned about the latter's presence, Djugashvili allegedly said: "Ah . . . he's helping us, in the gendarmerie." [90]

Djugashvili came to maturity in an extremely rough political milieu, and his lack of squeamishness in the choice of means is well attested. It is, furthermore, an established fact that the Okhrana made a practice of trying to pressure arrested revolutionaries, particularly younger ones, into becoming informers.[91] There is no reason to doubt that Djugashvili was subjected to such pressure after his first arrest, as one of the hearsay reports quoted above would indicate. Furthermore, although none of the evidence yet advanced is conclusive, it is not implausible that Djugashvili agreed at some point to give information to the police, or that at one or another time he did so—more for his own personal or factional purposes than for those of the police. The Baku suspicions, for example, were quite possibly well founded.

But we can make allowance for this without accepting the thesis, which has been advanced in some books of recent years, that he became an agent of the tsarist police, an *agent provocateur* like Roman Malinovsky, who rose high in pre-revolutionary Bolshevik councils only to be exposed in 1917 and later executed by the Soviet government. No evidence of such a relationship was turned up by the Extraordinary Investigatory Commission of the Provisional Government, which from March to November 1917 investigated the relations between the Okhrana and the revolutionary movement. Djugashvili's name did not appear on the detailed list of police

90. Roy A. Medvedev, *Let History Judge: The Origins and Consequences of Stalinism* (New York, 1971), pp. 319–320. This important work by a Soviet scholar and former Communist party member has circulated clandestinely inside Russia and has been published, so far, only abroad. It incorporates valuable materials obtained by the author from surviving Old Bolsheviks in a single-handed project of oral history. Medvedev, it should be noted, dismisses the hearsay evidence just cited on the ground that it is based on questionable second- or third-hand stories whose purveyors, some of whom spent years in Stalin's labor camps, may be swayed by understandable anti-Stalin feelings.

91. For a detailed account of one experience of this kind, in the Tiflis prison in 1900, see S. Alliluyev, *Proidennyi put'*, pp. 69–72. The means of pressure employed were solitary confinement and threats of unpleasant consequences for the prisoner's family.

agents which the commission compiled on the basis of its study of the archives and interrogation of prominent former police officials.[92] Nor, incidentally, does the above-quoted 1911 gendarme report on him suggest that he was well known to the Tiflis police.

One other circumstance merits mention in this context. In 1918 a Moscow publishing house brought out a book of documents from the Okhrana archives bearing on the history of Bolshevism. Twelve persons, including Malinovsky, were named in it as having been police agents in the Social Democratic movement. Djugashvili was not one of them. But it has been taken as a suspicious fact that one of the twelve was identified not by a full name but only as "Vasili," which was one of the party cover-names that Djugashvili used at various times in the revolutionary movement. Reporting all this, Roy Medvedev observes that the "Vasili" in question might just as well have been some other party member who also used that pseudonym. He also observes that police records show Stalin's more common party cover-names to have been "Koba" and "Kavkazets." [93] To this it should be added that if Djugashvili had entered the service of the Okhrana as one of its agents in the revolutionary movement, he would not have been likely to use as his cover-name in that capacity one of the same pseudonyms that he was using in the movement itself.

The only documentary evidence so far put forward in support of the thesis that Stalin became a police agent is the "Eremin letter." Purportedly written in 1913 by Colonel A. M. Eremin of the St. Petersburg Police Department to Captain A. F. Zhelezniakov in Yeniseisk, this document describes "Djugashvili-Stalin" as someone who served the Okhrana as an agent between 1908 and 1912, after which he broke off the relationship. In 1956 Isaac Don Levine made it the basis of his book *Stalin's Great Secret*, which argued that the Great Purge of the nineteen-thirties in Russia was motivated by the

92. Gregory Aronson, "Was Stalin a Tsarist Agent?," *The New Leader*, August 20, 1956, p. 24.

93. Medvedev, *Let History Judge*, pp. 315, 320. The book in question, published by the Zadruga publishing house in Moscow, was *Bol'sheviki (Dokumenty po istorii bol'shevizma s 1903 po 1916 gg. byvshego Moskovskogo Okhrannogo Otdeleniia).*

need to eliminate all those who might have heard about the guilty secret of the one-time liaison with the tsarist secret police. The "Eremin letter," however, has been exposed as a forgery.[94]

A later book mainly devoted to the thesis that Stalin became a police agent, Edward E. Smith's *The Young Stalin*, does not rely upon the "Eremin letter." Here the case rests upon a series of speculative interpretations of Djugashvili's early actions and of events in his life. The difficulty is that these actions and events are subject to alternative interpretations. To cite an example, and one which plays an important part in the book, Smith suggests that the Tiflis Gendarme Administration may have approached Djugashvili shortly after his departure from the seminary in May 1899 with a proposal that he become a secret agent, and that he, being unemployed, penniless, alone, and friendless, had no alternative but to accept the proposal. The six-month period of unemployment following his departure from the seminary, Smith adds, would have been about the right amount of time for the training of the new recruit by one of the Tiflis gendarme officers. After stating that "we are entitled to consider the possibility" that all this occurred, Smith proceeds to treat the possibility as though it were a fact.[95]

But there is no proof that Djugashvili was so down and out at that time, and so bereft of the companionship of friends, that it would have been possible for the police (assuming they did approach him) to force him to enter their service. On the contrary, we have the testimony of Iremashvili, cited above, that some former fellow students of his in the seminary got together to assist him from time

94. On the forged character of the document see Aronson, "Was Stalin a Tsarist Agent?" and Martin K. Tytell, "Exposing a Documentary Hoax," a paper presented at the New York meeting of the American Association for the Advancement of Science, December 29, 1956. In a communication to *The New Leader* (October 1, 1956, p. 28), Mr. Don Levine admitted the possibility that the document might prove to be of "dubious origin." For the text, see his *Stalin's Great Secret* (New York, 1956).

95. Smith, *The Young Stalin*, pp. 67–68. On his treatment of the hypothetical possibility as though it were a fact, see, for example, pp. 70 and 76 of Smith's book. A review of the work by George F. Kennan appears in *The American Historical Review*, October 1968, pp. 230–232. Smith's valuable bibliography contains the fullest listing in English of sources in various languages pertaining to the early life of Stalin.

to time, and the further testimony of his official biography that he made a little money at first by giving lessons. Furthermore, there is no indication that Djugashvili was ever in police custody prior to his arrest in Batum in early 1902. And later on, as he began to emerge as a *komitetchik* in the Social Democratic party, he must have acquired access to such funds, lodgings, and so on as party sources of support could provide for a professional revolutionary of his station. By the time he moved to Baku, or, as is more likely, before the move, his Bolshevik role was significant enough to assure that. The sources of support in question were diverse. In an article of 1906 on "Partisan Warfare," Lenin declared that funds obtained through "expropriations" were used in part for the maintenance of the "expropriators"—the "persons waging" the revolutionary struggle[96]— and Djugashvili, as we have seen, certainly belonged to that category. Donations to the party by wealthy persons were a further major source of financial support.

Medvedev notes that although many papers in the Petersburg police archives were destroyed by a fire during 1917, the documents that survived have yielded no confirmation of the suspicion that Djugashvili served the police as an agent. He reproduces two letters from the Central State Historical Archives of the USSR which suggest the reverse. In one of them, a letter dated August 17, 1911, the Okhrana chief of Moscow warned the Okhrana chief of Vologda province that an "active and very serious member of the Russian Social Democratic Labor party" bearing the pseudonym "Koba," then completing a term of administrative exile in Vologda, had been in touch with the party center abroad and had been directed to go abroad in order to receive instructions on further duties as a traveling agent for the party Central Committee. As will be seen later in the present study, this warning was founded on fact. In his letter of re-

96. *Lenin*, XIV, 4. According to J. L. H. Keep, "Some of [the activists] received a modest salary (approx. 25–30 rubles per month) from party funds, but this was the exception rather than the rule" (*The Rise of Social Democracy in Russia* [London, 1963], p. 181). According to Leonard Schapiro, the expropriations "gave Lenin a great advantage over the impoverished Mensheviks in providing him with wages for his professional agents" (*The Communist Party of the Soviet Union* [New York, 1959], p. 108).

ply, dated August 21, 1911, the Okhrana chief of Vologda, one Colonel Konisskii, identified "Koba" as Djugashvili, described his party political activities while in exile, and stated that he would be accompanied by "an observer" on his forthcoming departure from Vologda. Colonel Konisskii went on as follows:

Taking into consideration the fact that Djugashvili is very careful and could therefore be lost by an observer, it would be better to make a search and arrest him now in Vologda. To this end, please inform me whether you have at your disposal information necessary to make a case against Djugashvili, and whether there are any objections on your part to a search of him in Vologda, in view of the extremely conspiratorial nature of his actions. Simultaneously with the search of Djugashvili all the people with whom he is in contact here will also be searched.

Medvedev comments, quite rightly in my view, that it is hard to imagine such letters being exchanged concerning an *agent provocateur* of the police.[97]

In sum, the question of Stalin's possible police connections during his early years as a revolutionary should be broken down into two questions: (1) Did he enter into certain transitory dealings in the course of which he informed on others—dealings which he tried to use for his own personal and factional purposes while the police sought to exploit them for their own? (2) Did he become in the full sense a police agent, working systematically from within to undermine the movement to which he was ostensibly devoting his life? On the basis of the inconclusive evidential material presently on the historical record, we are justified in regarding the answer to the first question as very probably an affirmative one. As for the second, a negative answer is indicated not only by the complete lack of evidence of such a deep and enduring police connection, but also by our appraisal of the young Stalin as a revolutionary personality.[98]

97. *Let History Judge,* pp. 320–323.
98. I have added the last paragraph in order to render fully explicit the conclusions that follow from the final section of this chapter.

Chapter Four

DJUGASHVILI AS STALIN

Koba's Marxism

WHY DJUGASHVILI became a revolutionary is a question posed above but not adequately answered. We noted, first, that he himself explained it in later life as a reaction against the Jesuitical regime in the seminary; and secondly, that revolt was a living tradition in the institution when he entered it. A further contributing factor was personality. The boy's childhood experiences with his father gave him a general predisposition to rebel against paternalistic authority. In the school at Gori, and again in the seminary, he was confronted with forms of authority that were not only paternalistic but punitive. His rebelliousness began to appear in the first of the two schools, flared up strongly soon after he entered the second, and continued to develop. By the time he left the seminary in 1899 he was a committed revolutionary, in revolt against that great punitive system of paternalistic authority known as tsarism. As he went out into the world, writes Iremashvili, he took with him "a grim and bitter hatred against the school administration, the bourgeoisie, and all that existed in the country and represented tsarism." [1]

That this rebel became a Marxist is not surprising: Marxism was in the air in Tiflis during those years. Inside the seminary, student Social Democrats like Devdariani tutored still younger students like Djugashvili and Iremashvili in Marxist ideas. Outside, Marxism was becoming the dominant strain of thought among the Georgian

---

1. Joseph Iremaschwili, *Stalin und die Tragödie Georgiens* (Berlin, 1932), p. 24.

radical intelligentsia. Social Democratic propagandists were eliciting a remarkably positive response from workers, especially the railway workers of Tiflis. Members of *Mesame Dasi* were contributing articles to the columns of *Kvali*, which became a weekly after Zhordania returned from Europe in late 1897 and was made editor. In Zhordania himself, moreover, Georgian Social Democracy had an imposing leader.

Having gravitated in this direction, Djugashvili became deeply interested in Marxist theory and well versed in it. After leaving the seminary he continued the Social Democratic self-education that had not been sufficient to satisfy Zhordania in the interview of late 1898, and before many years had passed he was a rather well read Marxist. This statement may seem surprising in view of his own later memory of himself as having been one of the party's "practical workers" in those years, and in view of the often-encountered image of the mature Stalin as a sort of Bolshevik pragmatist with a greater interest in "nuts and bolts" than in general ideas.[2] It must be borne in mind, however, that his original function as a Social Democratic "practical worker" was propaganda. Spreading Marxist ideas among the workers was essentially a form of teaching, all the more so as the propagandist was normally dealing with poorly educated people to whom the material had to be explained very simply. As a teacher, he was bound to gain a fuller mastery of his subject matter. A knowledge of the fundamentals of Marxism and the ability to explain them to ordinary workers were Djugashvili's chief stock-in-trade as a professional revolutionary. Having a retentive mind and the habit of constant reading, he acquired, before long, an impressive Marxist erudition; and the seminary experience gave him a catechistic approach to teaching and a facility for finding homely examples which must have been effective in his worker classes. On

2. For Stalin's characterization of himself as having been one of the party's practical workers around the turn of the century, see his 1946 Preface to Volume I of his collected works (*Stalin*, I, xiii). The "pragmatist" image of Stalin is conveyed in Isaac Deutscher's statement: "Stalin was in a sense less dependent on Lenin than were his colleagues; his intellectual needs were more limited than theirs. He was interested in the practical use of the Leninist gadgets; not in the Leninist laboratory of thought" (*Stalin: A Political Biography*, 2nd ed. [New York, 1966], p. 235).

the basis of experiences in the Bailov prison in Baku in 1908, Simeon Vereshchak remembered him as someone who always had a book in his hand and was the most knowledgeable Marxist among those who led the study groups and the organized discussions to which the political prisoners devoted much of their time:

Looking at that low brow and small head, you had the feeling that if you pricked it, the whole of Karl Marx's *Capital* would come hissing out of it like gas from a container. Marxism was his element, there he was invincible. No power on earth could dislodge him from a position once taken, and he could find an appropriate Marx formula for every phenomenon. Such a man made a strong impression on young party men not well versed in politics. In general Koba enjoyed the reputation in the Transcaucasus of being a second Lenin. He was considered "the best authority on Marxism." [3]

Somewhat earlier, Djugashvili had furnished evidence in writing of the theoretical learning that he was to display in the Baku prison. In a series of articles published in Bolshevik newspapers in Tiflis under the general title *Anarchism or Socialism?*, he defended Marxism against critical attacks that were being leveled against it by Georgian followers of the Russian anarchist philosopher Pyotr Kropotkin. The first version of the articles, published in mid-1906, was followed by an expanded second version that appeared in late 1906 and early 1907 but remained incomplete owing to Djugashvili's departure for the London congress in April and his subsequent move from Tiflis to Baku. The expanded version takes up nearly eighty pages in Volume I of his collected works. Had it been brought to completion, the result would have been a short book on Marxist theory in the form of a polemic against its anarchist detractors. But even in its incomplete state, the tract leaves no doubt that the writer's mind was steeped in the classical Marxist texts then available. Among the works of Marx and/or Engels that it directly quotes are *Anti-Dühring, Ludwig Feuerbach and the End of German Classical Philosophy, The Communist Manifesto, The Critique of the Gotha Program, The Eighteenth Brumaire of Louis Bonaparte,*

3. S. Vereshchak, "Stalin v tiur'me (Vospominaniia politicheskogo zakliuchennogo)," *Dni,* January 22, 1928.

The Class Struggles in France, The Civil War in France, The Poverty of Philosophy, Revolution and Counter-Revolution in Germany, The Communist Trial in Cologne, and *The Origin of the Family, Private Property and the State.* It also shows familiarity with several major writings of Kropotkin, Paul Louis' *History of Socialism in France,* and of course the writings of the Georgian anarchists whose views were being contested.

Besides displaying the author's Marxist erudition, this work throws light on what it was in Marxism that originally appealed to him. The three sections that he completed deal respectively with dialectics, materialism, and the theory of socialism, along with the anarchist criticisms of Marxism on all three counts. To expound Marxism, he explained at the start of the first section, one must first of all expound dialectical materialism, for "Marxism is not only a theory of socialism; it is an entire world-view, a philosophical system from which Marx's proletarian socialism flows logically." [4] Then he set forth the principles of the dialectic and of Marxist materialism in terms strikingly similar to those he would employ thirty years later in preparing the section on "Dialectical and Historical Materialism" for the *Short Course* of party history published in 1938. This exposition contained nothing notably original; it was what could have been expected from someone with a philosophically awakened mind, a good knowledge of basic texts like *Anti-Dühring* and the philosophical writings of Plekhanov, and a propagandist's experience of expounding Marxism to workers' study-groups. The point is that the mind *was* philosophically awakened, that it felt the need for a coherent overall philosophical image of the world. To young Djugashvili, it was quite evidently a mark of Marxism's special strength as a socialist ideology that it had dialectical materialism—"an entire world-view"—as its matrix. No doubt his receptivity to Marxism as a general *Weltanschauung* owed something to the theological training he had received in the seminary. The seminary influence was also visible in his dogmatic style of exposition, the way in which he would invoke the classical Marxist texts to establish points of philosophical doctrine. *Anarchism or Socialism?* was

4. *Stalin,* I, 297–298.

the product of a religiously formed mind that had found in dialectical materialism an irrevocable and enormously satisfying intellectual
commitment.

But it was not only as a philosophical system that Marxism
exerted its appeal. What may have been its most magnetic feature
for this rebel against established authority was the grand theme of
class war that permeates the teaching of Marx and Engels. Judging
by the pervasiveness of this theme in Djugashvili's early writings,
and the way he emphasized it, he was strongly attracted to Marxism's vision of past and present society as a great battleground where-
on two hostile forces—bourgeoisie and proletariat—are locked in
mortal combat. There is no "Russia one and indivisible," he declared
at the beginning of an article published on January 1, 1905: "A
grandiose picture of struggle between two Russias, bourgeois Russia
and proletarian Russia, has opened up before us. Two great armies
have appeared on the arena of struggle: the army of proletarians
and the army of the bourgeois, and the struggle between these two
armies has embraced our whole social life." [5] The reality behind the
apparent class complexity of contemporary society, we find him
writing in an article of late 1906 entitled "The Class Struggle," is
that Russia is splitting into two great opposing "camps" of bourgeois
and proletarians, around which all other groups are gathering and
between which the class struggle is intensifying day by day.[6] Again,
the opening sentence of *Anarchism or Socialism?* reads: "The axis
of contemporary social life is the class struggle." Later in the work,
the author stresses that the proletariat cannot achieve socialism by
reconciliation with the bourgeoisie, but only by the path of a class
struggle that must end in the victory of the one class and the defeat
of the other: "Either the bourgeoisie with its capitalism, or the proletariat with its socialism." Then he enumerates with seeming relish
the various weapons that the proletarian warriors have at their disposal for this struggle: the strike (particular and general), the boycott, sabotage, street actions, demonstrations, and participation in
representative institutions. But none of these can alone be decisive,

5. *Ibid.,* pp. 62–63.
6. *Ibid.,* p. 277.

he continues. They are all at best preparatory means of destroying capitalism, beyond which lies the decisive means: socialist revolution. This itself should be seen not as a brief and sudden coup but as a "protracted struggle of the proletarian masses" commencing with the seizure of power and establishment of a proletarian dictatorship. Afterwards, the proletariat will continue the socialist revolution from above by expropriating the bourgeoisie as prescribed in the *Communist Manifesto* and by using military force, its own "proletarian guard," to quell the dying class enemy's counter-revolutionary attacks.[7]

Clearly, the young Djugashvili saw in Marxist socialism first of all a gospel of class war. We can hardly doubt that needs of his militant rebel-personality were involved. Here was a socialist doctrine that structured the existing social universe into "we" the downtrodden and oppressed and "they" the powerful oppressors who now dominate all the institutions of society. It invited the former to wage incessantly and by all possible means a mortal struggle against the latter, and envisaged the socialist revolution itself as a culminating series of battles in the protracted social war. Not only did such an ideology legitimize the young man's resentment against the various forms of established authority, it identified his enemies as history's, bestowed higher meaning on his urge to live a life of combat against forces of evil, and sanctified his quest for vindictive triumphs along the way. The latter point is illustrated by a fiery proclamation that he wrote in January 1905, entitled "Workers of the Caucasus, It Is Time to Take Revenge!" It drew a vivid picture of a "discontented Russia" rising in revolt against a tsarist autocracy whose "senile flabbiness" had finally been exposed by the troop casualties, the loss of the fleet, and the shameful surrender of the Manchurian naval base of Port Arthur to the Japanese. Now, in the face of growing popular unrest, the autocracy was donning sheep's clothing (after shedding its old skin like a snake—a typical Djugashvili mixing of metaphors), and proclaiming a domestic policy of reconciliation: "Do you hear, comrades? It is asking us to forget the swish of the

7. *Ibid.*, pp. 294, 344–346.

whips and the whistling of the bullets, the hundreds of murdered hero-comrades, their glorious ghosts that are hovering around us and whispering: 'Avenge us!' " But the voices of the ghosts would be heeded. It was high time to avenge the comrades brutally killed by the tsar's bashi-bazouks. Time to call the government to account for those fallen on Far Eastern battlefields, and dry the tears of their wives and children. Time to settle scores for all the sufferings and humiliations visited upon the people for so long. Time to *destroy* the tsarist government! [8]

Before Russian Marxists became divided into opposing factions called "Bolshevik" and "Menshevik," they became aware of a division of tendency among them between the more and the less militant, those who were "hard" and those who were "soft." We have seen earlier that there was a comparable division within the *Mesame Dasi* between the undergrounders and those who (like Zhordania) preferred legal political activity. Lado Ketskhoveli was one of the undergrounders, and so was his seminary protégé. Long before he adopted the revolutionary pseudonym "Stalin" as a symbol of steel-like hardness,[9] Djugashvili was a "hard." In his disputes with Devdariani and other young Marxists in the seminary, he showed an affinity for revolutionary extremism as against more moderate leftist views.[10] It was inevitable, therefore, that he would espouse Bolshevism as soon as he became aware of the factional division among the Russian Social Democrats and its political meaning. Having gravitated to Marxism in part because of the powerful appeal of the class-war doctrine to his fighting nature, he needed no persuading to accept the militant revolutionary line that Lenin was taking in the interpretation of Marxism. What inspired him to become one of the leading advocates of the Bolshevik cause among Georgians was first of all the fact that in Bolshevism, as a doctrine of the "hards," he found himself in his spiritual element.

8. *Ibid.*, pp. 74–77. The proclamation was printed on the Avlabar underground printing press in Tiflis.

9. The Russian word for steel is *stal'*, giving "Stalin" the connotation "man of steel." For Zhordania's later recollection of the division in *Mesame Dasi*, see his memoir *Moia zhizn'* (Stanford, 1968), pp. 25, 29.

10. Iremaschwili, *Stalin*, p. 22.

The Appeals of Lenin

According to his own later testimony, Djugashvili became aware of Lenin "from the end of the nineties and especially after 1901, after *Iskra* began publishing." Speaking at a memorial meeting of the Kremlin military school on January 28, 1924, a few days after Lenin's death, he said also that he first made contact with Lenin "by correspondence" from Siberian exile in 1903, after becoming convinced that only Lenin "understood the inner essence and needs of our party." He had written of this to a friend then living abroad, and Lenin—to whom the friend showed the letter— had sent him a reply containing a fearless criticism of the party's practices and a remarkably clear and concise exposition of a complete plan of party work in the coming period, all of this set forth in those characteristically bold and succinct phrases that "do not simply speak but shoot." He concluded: "I cannot forgive myself for the fact that, in accordance with the habits of an old undergrounder, I consigned this letter of Lenin's, as well as many other letters, to the flames." [11]

This story was a blend of fact and fantasy. Djugashvili could not have written a letter abroad and received a reply in the very short time he spent in Novaia Uda, nor would tsarist administrative practice have allowed him to know long before arriving there that this village was his destination. On the other hand, his claim to have written an enthusiastically pro-Lenin letter to a friend living abroad finds support in his two-part letter of October 1904 from Kutais to his friend Davitishvili in Leipzig, and Lenin reportedly did reply (after Davitishvili sent him the letter) to the extent of commenting that the Kutais correspondent was a "fiery Colchian." [12] Moreover, there exists a Lenin letter corresponding very closely to the one allegedly received in exile, only it was not personally ad-

---

11. *Stalin*, VI, 52–54.

12. The reported source of the story about this reply is the reminiscences of D. Suliashvili, one of the Georgian Bolsheviks then living in Leipzig. On this see *Stalin*, I, 396. "Colchian" derives from "Colchis," the name by which the ancients designated the western part of Georgia.

dressed to Djugashvili. It is Lenin's "Letter to a Comrade on Our Organizational Tasks," which was issued in hectographed form by the Siberian Social Democratic organization in June 1903 and was circulating among political exiles in that region at the time of Djugashvili's travel to Irkutsk and Novaia Uda.[13] That Djugashvili knew this document well and valued it highly is proved by the concluding request in his correspondence from Kutais: "Did you receive the six rubles or not? More will be coming any day. Don't forget to send by the same individual *Letter to a Comrade*—many here haven't read it."[14]

The obviously legendary character of the story told to the military school in no way detracts from its significance. Putting the facts together, we can infer that Djugashvili, who already had heard about Lenin, obtained a copy of the "Letter to a Comrade" during his movement through Siberia to the place of exile, and was enormously impressed. And no wonder. This compressed exposition of Lenin's organizational plan fairly throbbed with the intensity of his enthusiasm for the project of an underground party organization, and in bold sharp strokes (just as Stalin recalled in 1924) it laid out the plan with a richness of organizational detail not seen before in the Marxist literature. Something else that could not fail to please and impress a committed young *komitetchik* from the party underground was Lenin's argument in the "Letter" that the local party committees, consisting of professional revolutionaries, "must direct *all* aspects of the local movement and have charge of *all* local institutions, forces, and funds of the party."[15] So completely attuned to Djugashvili's thinking was this that when he read the "Letter" in Siberia in 1903 it may well have seemed *personally addressed to him*. Hence, in telling the story in the talk of 1924, he may have felt that he had license to transpose the facts a little and tell it in that way. In addition, the choice of 1903—the year of Bolshevism's be-

13. On the "Letter to a Comrade," see pp. 53–54 and note 54, above. The hypothesis that this was the Lenin document in question originates with Bertram D. Wolfe. On this see his *Three Who Made a Revolution* (Boston, 1948), p. 426.

14. *Stalin*, I, 61. The "Letter" had appeared in Geneva in 1904 as a printed pamphlet.

15. *Lenin*, VII, 9.

ginning—as the year in which his direct relationship with Lenin began was, in the immediate post-Lenin context, a way of symbolically bolstering his qualifications for the succession.

So he must have returned to Tiflis in early 1904 primed to join the intra-party fray on the side of Bolshevism, as in fact he did; and in his correspondence later that year from Kutais, he showed the enthusiasm that he felt for Lenin as his chosen leader and mentor in the revolutionary movement. By this time, moreover, he had read the full-scale exposition of Lenin's party plan in *What Is to Be Done?*, and it was probably his most exciting reading experience since *The Patricide.* In any event, he revealed himself in the correspondence as a doctrinaire, fiercely partisan defender of this charter document of Bolshevism. He not only unconditionally accepted Lenin's reasoning, but offered suggestions on the best way to refute its critics (among them P. B. Axelrod, Rosa Luxemburg, and Vera Zasulich, as well as Plekhanov). He called Plekhanov's theoretical arguments against Lenin a war against windmills, thereby dismissing Plekhanov's great reputation as a Marxist sage (no small thing for an obscure young provincial undergrounder to do at that time). The real issue was whether the leaders give the program and the reasoning behind it to the masses, or the masses to the leaders: "Who elevates whom to an understanding of the program, the leaders the led or vice versa?" If the theory and program of socialism originate in the minds of intellectuals rather than arising directly out of the spontaneous mass movement, then they must be instilled into the movement from without. The proletariat must be elevated to a consciousness of its true class interests. Such was the Leninist idea, emphasized Djugashvili, and it could rightly be called Leninist because no one in the Russian party literature had propounded it so clearly as Lenin.[16]

The correspondence from Kutais reveals Djugashvili as an admiring disciple for whom Lenin was the supreme exponent of Marxism in the Russian movement as well as the "mountain eagle" that one of the letters called him. The reasons for the rapturous response

16. *Stalin,* I, 57–61.

were numerous. First, Lenin's concept of the organization of professional revolutionaries as an essential factor in "making" the political revolution was implicitly an exaltation of the role of people like Djugashvili; it cast them as the real makers of future revolutionary history. Furthermore, their activity as propagandists and agitators—introducing Marxist revolutionary consciousness into the working-class mind—was made out to be the party's main mission at present and the *sine qua non* of the coming socialist revolution. This idea gratified Djugashvili immensely. In writings like *Briefly about the Disagreements in the Party* and "Reply to *Social Democrat*," he lashed out against Georgian critics of Lenin's "remarkable book" *What Is to Be Done?* [17]

Secondly, Djugashvili could not fail to be deeply impressed by the militance of Lenin's teaching. Having found Marx's doctrine of class struggle strongly appealing, he could not help liking a version of Marxism which placed such heavy emphasis on class struggle as Lenin's did. Here was no calm professorial Marxist like Plekhanov, but a passionately angry man summoning popular Russia to war against official Russia in the name of socialism. One could not read a page of Lenin without seeing in him an implacable foe and hater of tsarism and the whole upper-class Russian society linked with it. No other Russian Marxist's writings were so imbued with the martial spirit of class war. It was expressed, for example, in the militaristic terminology abounding in Lenin's discussions of the revolutionary party. The organization of revolutionaries was repeatedly likened to an elite military organization whose members were to place themselves, as professional soldiers of revolution, at the head of a "mobilized army" of the people. They should make every factory "our fortress" in the process of building a "proletarian army" whose

17. For these two articles, see *Stalin*, I, 89–130 and 160–172. Whether Lenin knew at the time that Stalin was the author of the articles is uncertain. The first article appeared above the name of the Union Committee, and the second originally appeared unsigned. Nevertheless, Stalin began it with an unusual assertion of individual authorship: "I must note this: Many consider that the author of *Briefly about the Disagreements in the Party* was the Union Committee and not an individual. I must declare that the author of this pamphlet is myself. Only the editing of it comes from the Union Committee" (*Stalin*, I, 160). Evidently, at the time of writing he was planning to sign the article.

ranks would become "more and more serried" until, finally, it would storm tsarism in a "national armed insurrection." [18]

To the young Georgian disciple, who not only harbored a vengeful hatred of official Russia but fancied himself a fighter and conqueror like Koba, all this made heady reading, as did the passages in which Lenin argued the need for keeping the party organization small, select in composition, centralized, and clandestine in much of its activity. The military imagery became even more conspicuous in Djugashvili's writings on the party than it was in Lenin's. In an article of January 1, 1905, "The Proletarian Class and the Proletarian Party," he visualized the two warring Russias as "two great armies," each with an "advance detachment" in the form of a political party. The "army of proletarians" had the Social Democratic party as its vanguard, and the "army of the bourgeois" had the liberal party. The party of the proletariat was not a philosophical school or religious sect but a "party of *struggle*" whose mission was to "direct the *fighting* proletariat." As a "fighting group of leaders," the party should be numerically much smaller than the proletarian class, higher than the proletarian class in consciousness and experience, and a compact organization. Only as such could it provide the requisite leadership for the "proletarian army." The latter phrase recurred constantly in the article.[19]

Besides appealing to Djugashvili's martial mentality, Lenin's conception of the revolutionary party gave him a psychologically vital new sense of group identity, of membership in a community of the chosen. In assessing the significance of this, we must bear in mind that being a rebel against society was a decidedly lonely role for him in turn-of-the-century Georgia, particularly after he dropped out of the seminary. One might even speculate that a frustrated need for companionship drove him to pressure numbers of former fellow students into the revolutionary life by provoking their expulsion from the seminary in the fall of 1899 (if, in fact, he was responsible for their expulsion, as Vereshchak reported). He was at

18. *Lenin*, VI, 177, and VIII, 404.
19. *Stalin*, I, 62–73.

odds with the dominant Social Democratic group in Tiflis. Lado
Ketskhoveli departed for Baku in January 1900 to evade arrest by
the Tiflis police. Although Djugashvili entered into a new association when Victor Kurnatovsky arrived in the city in the summer of
that year as an emissary of Lenin, it is not clear that he belonged
more than marginally to a social group.

We have already noted a certain tendency in him to become a
loner. There were intimations of it in his boyhood and it was clearly
evident soon after he entered the seminary, although he was capable
of forming personal friendships. Voroshilov found him a sociable
sort when they met and roomed together during the Stockholm congress in 1906, and remembered that "he had astonishingly shining
eyes, and he was a bundle of energy, gay and full of life." [20] He
developed rather close personal ties with a number of Caucasian
Bolsheviks, notably Yenukidze and Ordzhonikidze. Furthermore, as
we have seen, he acquired a family.

It is clear that Djugashvili, despite his semi-isolation, felt a
need for community. But for the reasons mentioned above, plus the
fact that he was a difficult person to get along with, life was not
fulfilling this need. Here is one of the keys to his enthusiasm for
the Leninist conception of the party as an elite corps of revolutionary leaders united by bonds of mutual trust. In *What Is to Be Done?*
Lenin argued against the flexible rule of party membership accepted
in the German Social Democracy. Under Russia's special conditions,
he held, membership should be open not to all who supported the
party's program, but only to those who in addition were willing and
competent to work in one of its organizations, normally as full-
time revolutionaries. Given the necessity of clandestine operation,
democratic procedures such as election to party office would not be
practicable as a general rule. Instead, the organization must be
based upon "complete, comradely, mutual trust among revolutionaries." Should the trust prove misplaced, the organization would
"stop at nothing to rid itself of an unfit member." Furthermore, did

20. K. Voroshilov, *Rasskazy o zhizni. Vospominaniia*. Kniga pervaia (Moscow, 1968).

not the notion of revolutionary "comradeship" (*tovarishchestvo*) really contain within itself the substance, as distinct from the toy forms, of democratism? [21]

Lenin freely admitted that this idealized picture of a revolutionary fraternity was something to which the existing Russian Social Democratic party bore very little resemblance. At the end of his discussion of the militant centralized organization, he exclaimed: "That is what we should dream of!" But did a Marxist have the right to get ahead of reality by dreaming such dreams? Lenin's only reply was to quote the words of Dimitry Pisarev, a Russian radical of the eighteen-sixties: "Divergence between dreams and reality causes no harm if only the dreamer believes seriously in his dream, deeply observes life, compares his observations with his cloud castles, and in general works conscientiously to realize his fantasy. So long as there is some contact between dream and life, all is well." [22] The efficient, harmonious, close-knit community of like-minded revolutionaries existed on paper only. But as a paper conception it proved intensely meaningful and satisfying to Djugashvili, assuaging his frustrated need for community. Here was a fighting association of which he could proudly conceive himself a member. No matter that it was still in its formative stage, and hence a community in which, for the present, one must live more in imagination than in actual fact. Why not believe seriously in this dream and help to translate it into reality? Why not think of himself as belonging to a nascent community of revolutionaries destined to lead the proletarian army into victorious battle against tsarism?

That this was the direction of his thinking is best shown by "The Proletarian Class and the Proletarian Party." Here he took up the cudgels for the Bolshevik position in the great controversy that was splitting the party in two: who had the right to call himself a party member? Lenin's "splendid formulation" was the only right one. The party should be seen as "an *organization* of leaders," and membership as entailing action on its behalf. A mere "platonic

21. *Lenin*, VI, 141–142.
22. *Ibid.*, p. 172.

acceptance" of the party's program and tactics was not enough. To admit any windbag willing to declare verbal support of the program would be "a desecration of the party holy of holies." And further: "Until this day our party has been like a hospitable patriarchal family ready to take in all who sympathize. But now that our party has turned into a centralized *organization,* it has thrown off its patriarchal appearance and come to resemble in all respects a *fortress,* the doors of which are open only to the worthy." The fortress metaphor recurred repeatedly in the article. Thus, "we must be extremely vigilant and not forget that our party is a fortress whose doors are open only to those who have been tested." Again, the trouble with Martov's Menshevik formulation of the rule on party membership was that for him "the party is not a fortress but a banquet, to which any sympathizer is free to come." [23]

The imagery in this exposition of Leninist doctrine revealed the disciple's mind much more than the teacher's. Djugashvili had found in Lenin a community-concept that met his inner needs, and was elaborating it in his own way. The party was not to be thought of in Menshevik fashion as a loose assemblage of unorganized supporters of a program. No, it was an organized association of the elect, with all that this implied by way of commitment and qualification. It could even be compared to a religious community, as in the comment that membership was the party's "holy of holies." This was one of the ex-seminarian's occasional lapses into religious idiom. It suggested that being a party member was something like belonging to the priesthood of a revolutionary church—an interpretation which finds reinforcement in his contemporaneous statement that *"only the party committees can worthily lead us, they alone light up for us the path to the 'promised land' called the world of socialism!"* [24] But the party community was above all else an association of fighters. Not a banquet or a hospitable family but a "for-

---

23. *Stalin,* I, 64, 65–67, 70, 73. In a footnote (p. 68) Stalin introduced Lenin to the Georgian reader as "an outstanding theoretician and practician of revolutionary Social Democracy."

24. *Ibid.,* p. 79. The statement appears in Stalin's proclamation of January 1905 to the Caucasian workers.

tress" with doors open only to the worthy and the tested. This metaphor was of a piece with Djugashvili's much later characterization of the party as "a kind of order of *swordbearers* within the Soviet state. . . ."[25] It also pointed toward the vision of the party that would appear in a speech he gave at the time of Lenin's death:

Comrades, we Communists are people of a special cut. We are made of special stuff. We are those who form the army of the great proletarian strategist, the army of Comrade Lenin. There is nothing higher than the honor of belonging to this army. There is nothing higher than the title of member of the party whose founder and leader was Comrade Lenin. It is not given to everyone to be a member of such a party. It is not given to everyone to withstand the trials and storms that go with membership in such a party. It is sons of the working class, sons of want and struggle, sons of incredible privation and heroic effort, who above all should be members of such a party.[26]

Thus was Lenin's party "dream" refracted through the mind and emotions of his Georgian follower.

The Hero-Identification

As a boy Djugashvili found in Kazbegi's Koba an identification that expressed his need to imagine himself in a hero's role. When he entered the seminary and started upon his career of rebellion, he did not cease feeling this need. Iremashvili ascribes to him a boundless urge to be a hero to the masses, and even suggests that he rejected Christianity's God because he was a godlike figure to himself.[27] However that may be, he was certainly a person of sensitive pride who took himself very seriously. We have seen evidence of this in the reputation he acquired among his fellow students as a "touchy character" with an un-Georgian inability to take a joke. Further testimony may be present in the poetry that he wrote soon after entering the seminary. Particularly notable is the recurring

25. *Ibid.*, V, 71. The phrase appears in a prospectus, written in 1921, for an article on party strategy and tactics.
26. *Ibid.*, VI, 46.
27. Iremaschwili, *Stalin*, p. 23.

theme of a mighty "hope." The following stanzas, taken from two different poems in the series that appeared in *Iveria* in 1895 under the pseudonyms "J. Dj-shvili" and "Soselo," will illustrate:

> And worn out from this hope
> I am joyful and my heart beats high.
> Can the beautiful hope that came to me in that instant
> Really be fulfillable?

> Know this: He who fell like ashes to the ground,
> He who was ever oppressed,
> Will rise higher than the great mountains
> On the wings of a bright hope.[28]

Insofar as these verses say something about the poet's inner life at the time of writing, they tell of soaring ambition and longing for future glory.

It was not hard for Djugashvili to visualize revolution as a field of the quest for glory. Some of the books he read in the early seminary period undoubtedly stimulated his imagination along those lines. In Hugo's *Ninety-Three,* which he presumably read either before or after inspector Germogen confiscated it from him, the great revolutionary year unfolds as an epic struggle of opposing armies, a saga of heroism and adventure. The chief figure in the novel's gallery of revolutionary heroes is the ex-priest Cimourdain, of whom Hugo writes that he "had a pure but gloomy soul" and "there was something of the absolute within him." The rebellious seminarian, who could already easily see himself as an *ex*-priest, must have read with interest the further characterization contained in the following passage:

He was a faultless man, who believed himself to be infallible. He had never been seen to weep. His was an inaccessible and frigid virtue; a just, but awful, man. There are no half measures possible for a revolutionary priest. A priest who embarks on an adventure so portentous in its aims, is influenced either by the highest or the lowest motives; he must

---

28. V. Kaminsky and I. Vereshchagin, "Detstvo i iunost' vozhdia: dokumenty, zapisi, rasskazy," *Molodaia gvardiia,* No. 12 (1939), pp. 69–70, where these passages from the Georgian original are rendered in Russian.

be either infamous or sublime. Cimourdain was sublime, but isolated in rugged inaccessibility, inhospitably repellent—sublime in his surrounding of precipices. Lofty mountains possess this forbidding purity.[29]

Believing that the revolutionary regime must show pitiless severity toward those who fail in the defense of the new order as well as those who represent the old, Cimourdain condemns his one-time pupil, the valorous young revolutionary commander Gauvain, to be executed for letting some captured enemies of the Revolution go free. He does this despite the fact that Gauvain is the only person in the world dear to him. He supervises the guillotining, and then ends his own life with a pistol shot.

However deeply he may have been impressed by the revolutionary priest, Djugashvili preserved his earlier hero-identification when he entered the revolutionary movement. He took "Koba" as his conspiratorial pseudonym in the party.[30] The signatures of his earliest signed articles were "Koba" and "Ko." Later, the name or initial would appear in diverse combinations, such as "Koba Ivanovich," "K. Ko.," or "K. Cato." Nor was it abandoned when Djugashvili, around 1910, adopted "Stalin" as his party pseudonym; "K." or "Ko." continued to appear as the initial.[31] "Koba Stalin" was the name by which he became known in the revolutionary movement. When he wrote to Lenin from Siberian exile in 1915, he signed the letter "Your Koba." He was still using the signature "K. Stalin" in 1917, and his real initial made its first appearance after the October

29. Victor Hugo, *Ninety-Three* (Boston, 1888), pp. 133, 141.
30. Anna Alliluyeva, basing herself on a Caucasian source, writes that he began to be called "Koba," meaning "the fearless" in Turkish, after summoning the workers of Batum to a street demonstration in 1902 (*Vospominaniia* [Moscow, 1946], p. 110). See also Deutscher, *Stalin*, p. 46, where this version is repeated It is, however, legendary and inaccurate. Iremashvili's contention that Djugashvili was already "Koba" in the seminary is supported by other memoir evidence (Kaminsky and Vereshchagin, "Detstvo," p. 87) that "Koba" became his conspiratorial pseudonym when he first joined the Social Democratic organization in Tiflis, before moving to Batum in 1901.
31. The signature "Stalin" first appeared under an article published in 1913 in *Sotsial demokrat*. But in his own mind he appears to have adopted the pseudonym earlier, for some of his articles of 1910 were signed "K. S." and "K. St." See *Stalin*, II, 187, 196.

Revolution, when he began signing documents "People's Commissar I. Stalin."

That he entered the revolutionary movement thinking of himself as "Koba" is not surprising. Kazbegi's Koba was an heroic fighter against oppressors on behalf of the lowly and oppressed (the fact that the former were mainly Russians could easily be seen as secondary). And as we have observed, the revolutionary movement was for Djugashvili first of all a war against an oppressor class. Being at once a Koba and a Marxist revolutionary was therefore quite possible. It must have seemed all the more natural to him when he encountered Lenin's theory of the party as an all-Russian league of skilled and dedicated fighters against tsarism. What was this design for a revolutionary party if not the picture of a warrior band—like Shamil's? Was not a younger intrepid fighter needed, then, to play a role like Koba's? Djugashvili could not have doubted it after he read in *What Is to Be Done?* that Lenin was dreaming of the emergence of "Social Democratic Zheliabovs from among our revolutionaries and Russian Bebels from among our workers who would take their place at the head of the mobilized army and rouse the whole people to settle accounts with the shame and curse of Russia." Here was a clarion call for Marxist Kobas, and Djugashvili eagerly enlisted in Lenin's revolutionary band.

In the far-off figure of Lenin he found a new hero-identification, the decisive one of his life. He saw Lenin as a great and fearless fighter summoning proletarian Russia to battle against bourgeois Russia and taking his place at the head of the former. In his talk to the Kremlin military school in 1924, he recalled that in 1903 Lenin appeared to him not as one party leader among others but as an extraordinary (*neobyknovennyi*) man. "When I compared him with the other leaders of our party, it all the time seemed that his comrades-in-arms—Plekhanov, Martov, Axelrod, and others—were a whole head lower than Lenin and that by comparison with them he was not just one of the leaders but a leader of the highest type, a mountain eagle knowing no fear in the struggle and boldly leading the party forward along uncharted paths of the Russian revolutionary movement." [32] This recollection takes on all the more credibility from the fact that the 1904 letters from Kutais, in addition to comparing Lenin favorably with Plekhanov, Axelrod, and others, did describe his hero as an eagle. One of the things about Lenin that impressed Djugashvili was his manner, the self-confident forthrightness with which he propounded his views. "A man who takes up our position must speak with a firm and determined voice," he declared to Davitishvili. "In this respect Lenin is a real mountain eagle." [33]

This subtly Caucasian imagery strongly suggests that Koba saw in Lenin at that time a kind of Social Democratic Shamil. His further reminiscences before the Kremlin military school support the impression. When he came to the Tammerfors conference in 1905, where he was to see Lenin for the first time, "I was hoping to see the mountain eagle of our party, a great man, great not only politically but, if you like, physically too, for Lenin had taken shape in my imagination as a giant, stately and imposing. What then was my disappointment when I saw the most ordinary man, below average height, in no way, literally in no way, different from ordinary mortals." He was disappointed, too, to find that Lenin, instead of appearing a little late as befitted a "great man," had come early and was chatting in a corner with "the most ordinary delegates to the conference." Only afterwards did he realize that this simplicity and modesty, this desire to remain unnoticed or at least not to be conspicuous and accentuate his high position, was "one of Lenin's strongest aspects as a new *vozhd'* of new masses, the simple and ordinary masses of the deepest 'depths' of humanity." [34]

The careful scrutinizing of Lenin's behavior on that occasion doubtless reflected the desire of the younger man to model himself upon his hero.[35] Lenin was for Djugashvili everything that a revo-

32. *Ibid.*, VI, 53.
33. *Ibid.*, I, 56.
34. *Ibid.*, VI, 53, 54, 55.
35. As regularly happens in the psychological process of identification, Djugashvili wanted to become like the person with whom he admiringly identified. According to Freud, who originated the concept, "identification endeavors to mold a person's own ego after the fashion of the one that has been taken as

lutionary leader ought to be, and that he too would like to be insofar as his capacities permitted. On his return to the Caucasus, he acquired the reputation of being a "second Lenin" not only by forcefully defending Leninist positions but also by emulating Lenin's mode of argument and mannerisms. From Arsenidze, who knew Djugashvili in those years and whose bias as a memoirist is not in his favor, comes valuable corroborating testimony: "He worshiped Lenin. He lived by his arguments and by his thoughts. He copied him peerlessly, to such a degree that we jestingly called him 'Lenin's left foot.' " [36] It is likely, moreover, that the identification with Lenin played a part in Djugashvili's decision to adopt "Stalin" as his party name. Unlike such revolutionary pseudonyms as "Trotsky," "Kamenev," Zinoviev," and "Molotov," "Stalin" resembled "Lenin."

Djugashvili's hero-worship of Lenin in no way conflicted with his own ambition and self-admiration. On the contrary, it fortified these feelings. For one thing, Lenin was living proof of the attainability of eminence in the arena of revolutionary politics. For another, Lenin insisted that there was room for more than one giant in this field. He called upon others to join him at the head of the movement and share in the glory of victory. In *What Is to Be Done?* he dwelt on Social Democracy's present need for "heroes" like those produced by the *narodnik* movement of the seventies. He treated membership in the revolutionary party as synonymous with leadership of the masses. He offered an image of the "ideal" Social Democrat who would be not a trade union secretary but a "tribune of the people," able to react to every manifestation of tyranny and oppres-

---

a model" (*Group Psychology and the Analysis of the Ego* [New York, 1960], p. 47). Nevitt Sanford writes that identification, unlike conscious imitation, is more or less unconscious. "Most important, perhaps, identification tends to be *identical,* that is to say, the subject strives to behave in a way that is *exactly* like that of the object" ("The Dynamics of Identification," *Psychological Review,* No. 2 (1955), p. 109).

36. R. Arsenidze, "Iz vospominanii o Staline," *Novy zhurnal,* No. 72 (June 1963), p. 223. Arsenidze knew Stalin at the time as a fellow participant in the Social Democratic movement. See also his statement (p. 220) that Stalin repeated Lenin's arguments "with gramophonic exactitude." And further (p. 235): "Stalin, I would say, was better than Shaumian in copying Lenin and repeating his thoughts."

sion, skilled in the arts of concealment and conspiracy, steeled to sacrifice and hardship. Why not, then, carve out a place of eminence alongside that of the mountain eagle? Why not become Lenin's partner, his right-hand man, his alter ego, Lenin II?

We have no way of knowing whether Djugashvili framed his thoughts in just such words. But he showed that this was the direction of his thinking by strongly emphasizing the theme of revolutionary heroism in his early writings. Thus, in 1910 he hailed the seventy-year-old German Social Democratic leader August Bebel in an anniversary article that began: "Who does not know Bebel, the venerable *vozhd'* of the German workers, once a 'mere' turner, but now a famous political figure before whose criticism 'crowned heads' and diploma'd savants have more than once retreated as from hammer blows, whose word is taken as the word of a prophet by the many millions of the German proletariat?" Then he told the story of how Bebel had emerged from the "worker depths" to become "a great fighter of the world proletariat," adding that only Marxism could offer sufficient scope for the seething nature of such an eager destroyer of the rotten old capitalist world. He concluded, with obvious allusion to Lenin's vision of "Russian Bebels from among our workers," by saying: "Let him serve as an example for us Russian workers, who have special need for Bebels of the working-class movement." [37] Earlier, in a eulogy for a deceased comrade, G. Telia, he had sounded a similar note. After praising Telia as "an apostle of revolutionary Marxism (Bolshevism)" who had possessed inexhaustible energy, deep love of the cause, heroic inflexibility, and the apostolic gift, he went on: "Only in the ranks of the proletariat do we meet such people as Telia, only the proletariat gives birth to such heroes as Telia, and this same proletariat will strive to take revenge on the accursed order of which our comrade, *the worker G. Telia,* was a victim." [38] In both eulogies, Djugashvili spoke of individuals who had risen from humble origins like

37. *Stalin,* II, 201, 208. See also his article "The Party Crisis and Our Tasks," where he speaks of the movement's great need for "Russian Bebels, for experienced and tested leaders from among the workers (*ibid.,* p. 152).

38. *Ibid.,* pp. 30, 31. The article appeared in March 1907 in the Georgian party paper *Dro.*

his own to become, in their different ways, revolutionary heroes. Notable, too, is his view that the supreme function of the revolutionary hero is to take revenge. Appropriately, the signature under the article on Telia was "Ko."

Clearly, Djugashvili did not become an ardent Leninist solely because of the persuasive force of Lenin's political arguments. Becoming a Leninist also involved, in this case, a rebellious young man's emotional need for psychosocial identity.[39] Not only did he derive from Lenin a community-concept that helped him to live his lonely life of an underground party worker and outlaw; he acquired at the same time a self-concept that accorded both with his need to idealize himself and with his anti-social social role as a revolutionary. Leninism confirmed him as Koba the heroic people's avenger while offering membership in the select fraternity of professional fighters against the existing order that Lenin called "the party." It thus assisted him to fashion for himself an exalted revolutionary persona. In Lenin himself, moreover, it gave him a leader to revere and a living example of the glory to which he too might aspire as one of the leader's comrades-in-arms. It is no wonder that he turned into one of the most zealous Lenin men in the Caucasus and tried in every way possible to pattern himself upon his hero. He now had an inner compass by which he would try to steer for the rest of his days.

The Change of National Identity

All this profoundly affected Djugashvili's sense of nationality, wrenching him away from his psychic moorings in the Georgian people. It was not so much the fact that the party he joined was called the Russian (*rossiiskaia*) Social Democratic Workers' party. After all, many other Georgians joined this party without ceasing to feel themselves Georgians. What made party membership carry a different connotation in Djugashvili's case was, above all, the

39. On the concept of psychosocial identity, see the writings of Erik H. Erikson, including *Childhood and Society* (New York, 1963), pp. 261–263, 412 n.; *Insight and Responsibility* (New York, 1964), chs. III, V; and *Identity: Youth and Crisis* (New York, 1968), ch. IV.

hero-identification with Lenin. Besides being a Great Russian by nationality, the mountain eagle was an archetypal example of the Russian revolutionary intellectual. To become like him was to become, among other things, a Russian. Djugashvili had the linguistic equipment for this. Although he spoke Russian with a Georgian accent, it was no longer really an alien tongue for him. By the time he moved to Baku in 1907, he wielded Russian with such facility that he could write his articles in it as well as use it as his regular speaking language. So, becoming a Russian was essentially a matter of coming to regard himself primarily as one, and of making the requisite psychic break with his native Georgianness.

If the Lenin-identification spurred him to do the former, other feelings impelled him toward the latter. As we have seen, he had antagonized various prominent Georgian Social Democrats and acquired a reputation in the Georgian party milieu as a difficult character and a troublemaker. He was not successful in the Georgian revolutionary arena, nor was the current of Social Democracy with which he associated himself. But if Georgia was not warmly receptive either to him or to Bolshevism, he for his part was disposed to take this as a poor reflection not upon himself or Bolshevism but upon Georgia. He seems to have rationalized it in terms of Georgia's relative backwardness. Thus, in one of his "Letters from the Caucasus" in 1910, he contrasted Tiflis and Baku in a manner that told something about his feelings as well as those cities. Baku he admiringly portrayed as the humming center of the oil industry, where the sharp class position of the Bolsheviks was finding a lively response among the workers. Tiflis, however, with its mere twenty thousand or so industrial workers, fewer than the number of soldiers and policemen, could be of interest only "as the administrative-commercial and 'cultural' center of the Caucasus." The weakness of its connection with Russia's markets, big and always animated, placed a stamp of stagnation upon Tiflis, and the absence there of the sharp class collisions characteristic only of big industrial centers made it "something like a marsh, awaiting impetus from without." [40] A certain contempt was expressed in and between these

40. *Stalin,* II, 188.

lines, as though their author had dismissed Georgia, from the revolutionary point of view, as a provincial backwater. They also reflected a respect for bigness that probably played a part in the mental process. of Djugashvili's Russification. To identify himself with Russia was to take as his revolutionary arena not simply little Georgia but the whole of a great empire covering a sixth of the world. His sense of historic mission called—at that time—for no more. To the future prophet of socialism in one country, viewing things from Baku in 1910, the colossal one country looked adequate to his highest aspirations.

We should not overlook the class component in his self-concept as a Bolshevik. There are passages in his writings at this time that express pride in Bolshevism as the truly proletarian faction in the Social Democratic party. On his return from the London party congress of 1907, he reported in the Russian-language *Bakinskii proletarii* (Baku Proletarian) that there had been a substantially higher representation of factory workers among the Bolshevik delegates to the congress than among the Mensheviks:

Evidently, the tactics of the Bolsheviks are the tactics of the proletarians of big industry, the tactics of the regions where class contradictions are especially clear and class struggle especially acute. *Bolshevism is the tactics of real proletarians.* On the other hand, it is no less evident that the tactics of the Mensheviks are chiefly the tactics of handicraft workers and peasant semi-proletarians, the tactics of those regions where class contradictions are not fully clear and class struggle is masked. Menshevism is the tactics of the quasi-bourgeois elements of the proletariat.[41]

But in the next breath Djugashvili declared that the faction of real proletarians was also the faction of real Russians. Analyzing the composition of the delegations by nationality, he pointed out that whereas the majority of the eighty-five Menshevik delegates were Jews, with Georgians in second place numerically and Russians in third, the great majority of the ninety-two Bolshevik delegates were Russians, with Jews coming next, then Georgians, and so on. He proceeded to quote the jest of a Bolshevik delegate named Alexinsky, who had described the Mensheviks and Bolsheviks at the con-

41. *Ibid.,* pp. 49–50. Italics added.

gress as, respectively, the "Jewish faction" and the "true-Russian faction" and had suggested that it might not be a bad idea for the Bolsheviks to "conduct a pogrom in the party." [42] His heavy-handed treatment of this theme and his lack of embarrassment about quoting Alexinsky's anti-Semitic remark add credibility to Arsenidze's memory of his speaking as follows to Georgian workers in Batum in 1905: " 'Lenin,' Koba would say, 'is outraged that God sent him such comrades as the Mensheviks! Who are these people anyway! Martov, Dan, Axelrod are circumcised Yids. And that old woman V. Zasulich. Try and work with them. You can't go into a fight with them, or have a feast with them. Cowards and peddlers!' " [43]

So, via Bolshevism, Djugashvili joined the Russian nation. With his revolutionary identity as a Lenin man and a member of the "true-Russian" faction came a sense of national identity as a Russian. This may have been reflected in his choice of "Ivanovich" —a name typifying Russian man in the way that "Schmidt" typifies the German—as the party name under which he attended the congresses in Stockholm and London in 1906 and 1907. [44] In subsequently choosing "Stalin" as the name by which he would be known, Djugashvili undoubtedly realized that, besides suggesting a man of steel and resembling "Lenin," it had a Russian sound.

Since his acquired Russianness was merged with his consciousness of class identity as a member of the Russian Empire's party of the proletariat he did not feel compelled to surrender all sense of Georgian nationality. In an essay on "How Social Democracy Understands the National Question," published in *Proletariatis brdzola* in September 1904, he pointed out that the Social Democratic party

42. *Ibid.*, pp. 50–51. The expression "true-Russian" (*istinnorusskii*) was used by the tsarist minister of education, Count Uvarov, in 1832 when he spoke of the "true-Russian conservative principles of orthodoxy, autocracy, and nationality." It eventually became a byword of and for the nationalistic far Right in Russia. The Alexinsky whose jest was repeated by Stalin is identified in a note to the text (p. 382) as one who later left the party and "after the October socialist revolution was a white émigré."

43. Arsenidze, "Iz vospominanii," p. 221. Arsenidze also recalls Stalin's perplexity at the negative response among workers to this line of attack.

44. His report on the London congress in *Bakinskii proletarii* was signed "Koba Ivanovich." "Ivanovich" is quite common in Russian as a patronymic but is also a surname. It may be noted that Vissarion Djugashvili's patronymic was "Ivanovich," his father's given name having been "Vano."

called itself *rossiiskaia* (which we could translate as "all-Russian") rather than *russkaia* (which would more directly connote Russian nationality), and explained that the party thereby wanted to declare its intention of gathering under its banner not only the Russian proletarians but also those of *all nationalities* in Russia, and that, accordingly, it would take every measure to destroy the national barriers between them. Hence the party's position, continued the future commissar for nationality affairs, was that "national interests" and "national demands" have no particular value and are worthy of attention only insofar as they promote the proletariat's class-consciousness and development.[45]

This essay was also notable for its harsh condemnation of Georgian nationalism in all its forms. It originated as a polemic against a group of nationalistic Georgian radicals who had set themselves up recently as a party of "Social-Federalists" and whose Paris-based paper, *Sakartvelo* (Georgia) was voicing the party's demands not only for Georgia's national autonomy in the Empire but for Georgian party autonomy within the socialist movement. Djugashvili commented sarcastically that Georgian nationalism, which had historically gone through one form with the nobility and another with the bourgeoisie, was now reappearing in proletarian guise. He lashed out against the idea, propounded not only by the Georgian Social-Federalists but also by an Armenian Social Democratic organization, that there should be separate national parties within the revolutionary movement of the Russian Empire, and accused these groups of drawing their inspiration from the example of the Jewish Workers' Bund.[46] Every line of this first writing of Djugashvili's on the national question betrayed the revulsion that he now felt toward Georgian nationalism.

To the reasons adduced for his adoption of a Russian self-identity something needs to be added. We have seen how this disadvantaged but gifted boy, the sole survivor of four Djugashvili children, grew up believing himself to be a person of destiny. We have observed in him a yearning for future glory, and also a deep horror of being beaten. Now these were two sides of one coin. In

45. *Stalin*, I, 42.
46. *Ibid.*, pp. 37–40.

Russian, as in English, "beat" has a double meaning: to strike or chastise, and to win or conquer. Djugashvili's early determination *never to be beaten* expressed not only his refusal ever to be chastised if he could avoid it, or to be weak—since weakness invites a chastising—but also his driving need to excel and to always be on the winning side, his fear and scorn of ever being a loser in the battles of which life, as he saw it, consisted.[47] As he himself put it in the essay just referred to, "the object of any struggle is victory."[48]

From this standpoint, the conversion from his original identification with Georgia to the later one with Russia signified a move on Djugashvili's part from a losing to a winning side in history. Weak because of its smallness, a perennial victim in the centuries-old contest among the powers of the area, Georgia had an unhappy past experience of repeatedly being beaten (in both senses) and subjected to alien rule—Persian, Turkish, and finally Russian. From what he learned of the past, plus his own early experiences in school and seminary, Djugashvili could not have failed to draw the conclusion that Georgia was one of history's losers. Russia, on the other hand, whatever beatings it might have suffered in the past (and it is not clear how deeply Djugashvili had looked into Russian history by the turn of the century), was now the greatest of all countries in territory, and a mighty power—a likely winner in history. These thoughts alone could not have produced a psychological change of nationality, but they could have greatly facilitated the conversion to Russian identity that Lenin and Bolshevism inspired. Such an hypothesis takes on added force from the fact that Djugashvili did not simply drop his self-identification with Georgia; he actively rejected it. He conceived a certain animus against Georgia, ostensibly on account of its supposed insignificance in the revolutionary movement of the Russian Empire. This animus persisted, and may help to explain the harshness with which he dealt with Georgia as commissar for nationality affairs in the early nineteen-twenties. It also found verbal expression in his sarcastic reference in a speech of 1923 to "a little piece of Soviet territory called Georgia."[49]

47. I am indebted to Erik Erikson for pointing out to me the significance of this twofold association.
48. *Stalin,* I, 36.
49. *Ibid.,* V, 232.

Djugashvili's anti-Semitism, which would grow over the years and finally become an obssession toward the end of his life, may also, in part, have been an expression of contempt for whatever was small and weak. The Jews were a dispersed people without a territory of their own, and very often (especially in Russia) a helpless object of pogroms and other forms of persecution. Because they were frequently being *beaten* he could not respect them, and pity was not a feeling that came easily to him if it came at all. Hence his willingness to repeat Alexinsky's crude jest about the "Jewish faction" and the desirability of a pogrom in the party.

It remains to be said that Lenin made the transition to Russian identity all the easier for Djugashvili by virtue of his anger against official Russia and everything associated with it. In the Leninist *Weltanschauung* there was still a Russia one could hate, indeed must hate, as well as a Russia one was invited to join in the class struggle. So, the Georgian disciple could change his national identification without renouncing the anti-Russian feeling acquired in childhood; it was merely a question of redefining it in Marxist terms. The Russia with which he identified himself at this early time was not yet the Russian state, but revolutionary Russia. His identification with the state would come later.

It should be added that in taking Lenin as his object of heroworship and imitation, Djugashvili did not assume an attitude devoid of potential ambivalence. We may harbor unconscious competitive feelings or jealousy toward the very persons with whom we admiringly identify. The likelihood of such feelings would be all the greater if, as in the present instance, the individual in question identified with the older person as *leader* of the movement and wished to emulate him in that capacity. Hence Djugashvili's identification with Lenin did not, as we shall see, keep their future relations free of friction and ultimately of conflict.[50]

---

50. I have added the final paragraph to this chapter in the second printing in order to clarify a point not made sufficiently clear in the initial printing. In this connection I wish to acknowledge with gratitude a personal communication from Dr. Robert S. Wallerstein, head of the Department of Psychiatry of Mount Zion Hospital and Medical Center in San Francisco, who explains on the basis of clinical experience and his knowledge of the psychoanalytic literature that "one can struggle with and against one's identification figures."

Chapter Five

BECOMING A BOLSHEVIK
LEADER

In the Party Underground

FROM THE TIME HE LEFT the seminary, Stalin's life was entirely devoted to the Marxist movement. He knew no other calling than that of revolutionary politics, and he endured his full share of the experiences of prison and exile that normally befell those who pursued this hazardous profession in Russia. His arduous revolutionary career was not, however, a distinguished one. For upwards of a decade he remained a provincial revolutionary operating in his native Transcaucasus. He had no dramatic anti-tsarist exploits to his credit, and prior to 1913 he contributed no writings that helped shape Bolshevism as an ideological current. He was one of the party's practical workers—an organizer, conspirator, propagandist, and journalist.

Because Stalin's early revolutionary career was not an outstanding one, the question arises: how did he come to be elevated to membership of the Bolshevik Central Committee? To be sure, he was not elected to this post *in absentia* by the Prague Bolshevik conference of January 1912, as later asserted by Stalinist party historians, but co-opted by the Central Committee elected there.[1] This was Lenin's doing. How did he come to regard Stalin as suitable for

1. From the fact that Stalin entered the Central Committee "through the back door" Trotsky infers that his candidacy was opposed when put forward at

membership in the inner circle of Bolshevik leaders?

We have mentioned the story (possibly but not necessarily apocryphal) that Stalin first came to Lenin's attention when the enthusiastically pro-Lenin letters that he wrote from Kutais in late 1904 were forwarded by his Leipzig friends to Lenin, who in reply called their Georgian correspondent "the fiery Colchian." Direct correspondence dates from May 1905, when Stalin, writing as a member of the Caucasian Union Committee, reported to Lenin on the comparative influence of Bolsheviks and Mensheviks in the party organizations of the region.[2] Meanwhile, he came out as a zealous disciple of Lenin in polemics against the Georgian Mensheviks. In *Briefly about the Disagreements in the Party,* a pamphlet issued in Georgian, Armenian, and Russian in the spring of 1905 by the Avlabar underground printing press in Tiflis, he assailed Zhordania for criticizing the views that Lenin had presented in his "remarkable book" *What Is to Be Done?* The chief issue was Lenin's contention that revolutionary (as opposed to trade unionist) consciousness had to be instilled in the working class by organized Social Democracy. Marshaling quotations from Karl Kautsky and from Marx and Engels, Stalin stoutly maintained that Lenin's position was not in fundamental contradiction with Marxism, as Zhordania had argued, but fully in accord with it. In July, Krupskaya wrote from abroad to Tiflis requesting copies of the pamphlet, from which we may surmise that Lenin was informed about it. In August, Stalin returned to the subject in a polemical refutation of Zhordania's reply to his pamphlet. This so pleased Lenin that in his contribution to a review of the Russian-language edition of the Georgian party paper in which Stalin's second piece had appeared, he especially praised, and then

---

the Prague conference (*Stalin: An Appraisal of the Man and His Influence* [New York, 1967], pp. 136–137). Another possibility is that, being relatively unknown, he simply did not receive a sufficient number of affirmative votes. The fact that he originally entered the Central Committee by co-optation was shown in official party documents of the twenties, and has again been recognized in party documents of the post-Stalin period, but was suppressed in the intervening years.

2. *Ocherki istorii,* p. 141.

paraphrased, its "splendid formulation of the question of the celebrated 'introduction of consciousness from without.' "[3]

What impression Stalin made upon Lenin when they first met
face to face, at Tammerfors later in 1905, is not known. But he
must have made a definite (if not wholly happy) impression when,
at the Stockholm congress in 1906, in a session over which Lenin
presided, he took the floor in the debate on agrarian policy to support neither the platform of land nationalization, which Lenin favored, nor the Menshevik platform of municipalization, but rather
the confiscation of the landed estates and their division among the
peasants—a position that received majority support in the Bolshevik delegation though not in the congress as a whole.[4] In spite of,
and perhaps also because of, their difference over the question at
hand, Lenin may have come to realize by this time that in "Ivanovich" (Stalin's pseudonym at the congress) he had a forceful and
incisive young Georgian follower who was worth watching.

Such a reaction would have been all the more understandable
in view of a further general circumstance: Bolshevism's failure in
Georgia. There, as we have noted in an earlier chapter, the Mensheviks emerged from the Revolution of 1905 as the dominant Social
Democratic faction. Stalin was thus in the advantageous position of
being one of the relatively few prominent Georgian Social Democrats adhering to Bolshevism. In addition, he showed his usefulness
to the Bolshevik cause by his behind-the-scenes role in the "expropriations" that took place during and after the 1905 upheaval in
the Transcaucasus. He must have thereby recommended himself to
Lenin as an underground worker who could safely be entrusted with
secret assignments of great delicacy and importance.

Such an individual was all the more certain to come to the
fore in Lenin's circle under the conditions of party crisis that prevailed from 1907 to 1912. That period of reaction saw a cata-
strophic decline in party fortunes. Discouragement, apathy, and

3. *Lenin*, XI, 386. Whether Lenin knew at the time that Stalin was the
author of the pamphlet and follow-up article is uncertain, since both originally
appeared unsigned. On this see note 17, p. 125, above.

4. The position that Stalin supported was presented to the congress by the
preceding Bolshevik speaker, S. A. Suvorov.

political quietism took over in the aftermath of the 1905 Revolution. The party practically fell apart as former activists deserted it en masse and arrests took a heavy toll of those still willing to carry on. By the summer of 1909, not more than five or six of the Bolshevik underground committees were still functioning regularly in Russia.[5] Meanwhile, those in the party whom Lenin contemptuously dubbed "liquidators" took the view that instead of rebuilding the illegal party, Social Democrats should now concentrate on such limited legal activities—in the Duma, for example—as conditions allowed. It was a time, then, when Lenin felt an acute need for men who were absolutely unswerving in their dedication to revolutionary politics and to the illegal party as its organizational medium—in short, for men like Stalin, who during those years, between arrests and periods of exile, went on doggedly working in what was left of the underground organization to prepare for a new revolutionary period. Writing now in the Russian language in party organs read by Lenin, Stalin strongly espoused the cause of orthodox revolutionary politics. To make the party's activity as legal as possible and abandon revolutionary demands, he wrote in the *Bakinskii proletarii* in August 1909, would bury the party rather than renovate it. In order to overcome the present state of party crisis, it was necessary, first, to end the isolation from the masses and, second, to unify party activities on a nationwide basis. And speaking like the Lenin of *What Is to Be Done?*, Stalin suggested that the latter objective could best be achieved by creating an all-Russian party newspaper. There was, however, one difference: Stalin insisted upon the paper's being based inside the country rather than abroad, where party organs, being "far removed from Russian reality," could not effectively fulfill the unifying function.[6]

A seasoned professional revolutionary, a completely committed

5. Leonard Schapiro, *The Communist Party of the Soviet Union* (New York, 1959), p. 101. Bertram Wolfe writes: "By 1909 the party had crumbled away until Krupskaya could write 'we have no people at all.' In retrospect, Zinoviev, very close to Lenin then, would say, 'at this unhappy period the party as a whole ceased to exist'" (*Three Who Made a Revolution* [Boston, 1948], p. 486).

6. *Stalin*, II, 147.

Bolshevik whose wnole world lay in party affairs and who found his element in clandestine activity, Stalin was too rare a resource for Lenin to ignore. Nor did he permit himself to be ignored. The proposal for a Russia-based party organ carried an overtone of self-nomination to the editorial role that Stalin in fact came to play when *Pravda* was founded in Petersburg three years later. In a resolution of January 22, 1910, written by Stalin, the Baku party committee not only repeated the proposal for an all-Russian party organ but called for "the transfer of the (directing) practical center to Russia."[7] The implicit bid for inclusion in such a practical center became virtually explicit in a letter that Stalin sent abroad at the end of 1910 from his exile in Sol'vychegodsk. Although addressed to a Comrade Simeon, the letter was clearly meant for Lenin, to whom Stalin at the outset sent hearty greetings. He argued that there was urgent need to organize a central coordinating group in Russia, to be called something like "Russian section of the Central Committee" or "auxiliary group of the Central Committee," and he offered his services upon the expiration of his term of exile in six months' time, or sooner if necessary.[8] The proposal may have taken on added weight from the fact that Stalin by this time had been appointed an "agent" of the Central Committee—that is, a roving official maintaining liaison with and giving guidance to local party organizations on behalf of the Bolshevik center.[9] In any event, when the Bolshevik faction was recast as a separate party at the Prague conference in 1912, the Central Committee, now all-Bolshevik in composition, not only co-opted Stalin but also elected him as one of the four members of a "Russian Bureau" for direction of party activities inside Russia. Indeed, it is possible that Lenin brought Stalin into the Central Committee primarily so that he could be-

7. *Ibid.*, pp. 198–199.
8. *Ibid.*, p. 211.
9. *Iosif Vissarionovich Stalin. Kratkaia biografiia* (Moscow, 1947), p. 50, where Stalin is said to have held the status of an *agent* or *upolnomochenny* of the Central Committee from 1910 to 1912. One might question the statement, especially in view of its absence from earlier versions of Stalin's official biography. It has been confirmed, however, in a footnote to protocols of the Central Committee Bureau's meeting in March 1917 (*Voprosy istorii KPSS*, No. 3 [1962], p. 156).

come a member of this auxiliary organ whose creation he had persistently solicited.[10]

Lenin appears to have had certain reservations concerning the young man he was sponsoring for these high posts. For he had learned of some letters of Stalin's commenting on developments among the émigrés in a way that he found objectionable. Writing in June 1908 to Mikha Tskhakaia, who was then living in Switzerland, Stalin had characterized Lenin's philosophical polemics with the Bogdanov group over Machism ("empiriocriticism") as a "tempest in a teacup," and had found some "good sides" in Machism itself. Bogdanov was the leader of a group of party intellectuals who wanted to ground Marxist philosophy in a theory of knowledge derived in part from the teachings of Ernst Mach. Later, after *Materialism and Empiriocriticism* came out, Stalin had written to a certain M. Toroshelidze (also then in Switzerland) a letter in which, while praising Lenin's book as a compendium of the tenets of materialist epistemology, he also commended Bogdanov for pointing up some "*individual* faults of Ilyich," and for correctly noting that "Ilyich's materialism differs in many ways from Plekhanov's, which Ilyich, contrary to the demands of logic (for diplomatic reasons?) tries to cover up." Then, on January 24, 1911, Stalin had written a letter from Sol'vychegodsk to Vladimir Bobrovsky saying: "We have of course heard about the 'tempest in a teacup' abroad: the blocs of Lenin-Plekhanov on the one hand and Trotsky-Martov-Bogdanov on the other. So far as I know, the workers' attitude toward the first bloc is favorable. But in general the workers are beginning to look upon the emigration with disdain: 'Let them crawl on the wall to their hearts' content; but as we see it, let anyone who values the interests of the movement work, the rest will take care of itself.' "[11]

10. Since the other members of the Russian Bureau (Ordzhonikidze, Suren Spandarian, and F. Goloshchekin) had all been elected to the new Central Committee by the Prague conference, it would have been awkward to make Stalin a member of the bureau without simultaneously co-opting him onto the Central Committee itself.

11. These letters do not appear in Stalin's collected works. The text of the third, which at the time of its dispatch was intercepted by the tsarist police, was

Ordzhonikidze, while attending a party school in France, in the summer of 1911, learned directly from Lenin that Stalin's letters had come to his attention and had vexed him greatly. While strolling with Ordzhonikidze in Paris one day, Lenin suddenly asked him whether he was familiar with the expression "tempest in a teacup abroad." Ordzhonikidze, who knew about the letters and immediately saw Lenin's point, tried to defend his fellow Georgian and friend, but Lenin continued: "You say, 'Koba is our comrade,' as if to say, he's a Bolshevik and won't let us down. But do you close your eyes to his inconsistency? Nihilistic little jokes about a 'tempest in a teacup' reveal Koba's immaturity as a Marxist." Lenin softened the reproof by saying that he had the most favorable memories of Stalin and had commended some of his earlier writings from Baku, especially the previous year's "Letters from the Caucasus." [12] In view of this, and of the fact that Ordzhonikidze was about to return to Russia, it seems likely that Lenin was taking the opportunity to communicate to Stalin his strong feeling about the letters. Perhaps he wanted thereby to clear the way for collaboration with a man whom he saw as very valuable for the movement even if immature as a Marxist.

Theorist of the National Question

Not long after Stalin's co-optation into the new all-Bolshevik Central Committee, his political relationship with Lenin was cemented by their joint work on the national question. This question was very much on Lenin's mind when Stalin came to Cracow in November 1912 to confer with him on party business. Lenin had written an article that same month expressing adamant opposition to what he called "the adaptation of socialism to nationalism" and

---

disinterred from police files and published among the materials on Stalin in the Tiflis paper *Zaria vostoka* on December 23, 1925. The full texts of the other two have not been published, but excerpts appear in I. Dubinsky-Mukhadze, *Ordzhonikidze* (Moscow, 1963), p. 93, and in *Vladimir Ilyich Lenin. Biografiia*, chief. ed. P. N. Pospelov, 2nd ed. (Moscow, 1963), pp. 179–180.

12. Dubinsky-Mukhadze, *Ordzhonikidze*, pp. 92–94.

an "Austrian federation" within the party.[13] The latter phrase referred to the situation in the Austrian Social Democratic party, which had evolved over the years into a federation of autonomous Social Democratic groups organized along national lines (German, Czech, Polish, Ruthenian, Italian, and South Slav). Lenin was extremely fearful lest a similar tendency gain the upper hand in Russia. There the Social Democratic party had originally been conceived as a non-federal association of workers of all nationalities in the Russian Empire.[14] In practice, however, the Jewish Workers' Bund (after its return to the party fold in 1906) and the Social Democratic organizations of Poland, Latvia, and Lithuania had enjoyed autonomy within the Russian party, introducing into the latter what a resolution of the Bolshevik conference in Prague called "a federation of the worst type." And now, in 1912, attempts were being made in certain Social Democratic quarters, notably the Bund and the Georgian Menshevik organization, to gain acceptance by the Russian party of the Austro-Marxist slogan "national-cultural autonomy." Lenin, for whom national separatism had no place within Social Democracy, was infuriated at what he saw as one more manifestation of "liquidationism." Any move to divide the Russian Social Democracy along national lines could only hurt it as a class-conscious revolutionary movement against tsarism. All Social Democrats, regardless of nationality, should work together in the party organization of their territory. The Transcaucasian organization, uniting revolutionaries of Georgian, Armenian, Russian, and other nationality, could be taken as a model.[15]

Stalin's arrival in Cracow at just this time must have struck Lenin as very opportune. For if the views being fostered by non-

13. " 'Bol'nye voprosy' nashei partii: 'likvidatorskii' i 'natsional'ny' voprosy," in *Lenin*, XXII, 223–230. Although written in November 1912, this article was not published until August 1913.

14. This was reflected in the use of the term *rossiiskaia*, referring to the Russian Empire, in the party's name, rather than *russkaia*. For Lenin's emphasis upon the transnational meaning of *rossiiskaia*, see his "Tezisy po natsional'nomu voprosu," in *Lenin*, XXIII, 320.

15. A brief summary of these views of Lenin appears *ibid.*, p. 59. For an expanded version of them, see *ibid.*, pp. 314–322.

Russian "nationals" of the Social Democratic movement needed combating, other "nationals"—being least suspect of indifference to the concerns of national minorities—were good ones to do it. Moreover, Lenin may have seen in Stalin a potential source of light on the complexities of the nationality problem in the Transcaucasus. If so, he was not disappointed, for Stalin was well informed on this subject. More important (as Lenin may now have learned for the first time), he had a long record of opposition to local nationalism in the Transcaucasian revolutionary movement. In 1904, as we have seen, he took a strong stand in print against the nationalist tendencies of certain Georgian and Armenian socialist groups, and championed the idea of a centralized Russian Social Democratic party that would gather the proletarians of *all* Russia's nationalities under its banner and work to destroy the national barriers dividing them. He had continued to adhere to this position when, in 1906, a group of Social Democrats from Kutais raised the question of national-cultural autonomy at a Transcaucasian regional party conference, and now again, in 1912, when Zhordania and the Georgian Mensheviks veered in the same direction. So Lenin encountered in Stalin a "national" who would eagerly take his side in the fight over the national question and do so out of long-standing personal conviction. The gratification this gave him was reflected in his letter of February 1912 to Maxim Gorky: "About nationalism, I fully agree with you that we have to bear down harder. We have here a wonderful Georgian who has undertaken to write a long article for *Prosveshchenie* after gathering *all* the Austrian and other materials. We will take care of this matter." [16]

Stalin wrote the bulk of the work during a stay in Vienna in January 1913. In an introductory theoretical section he dealt with the problem of defining the concept of a "nation." On this there were a number of differing positions in the Marxist literature. For Otto Bauer a nation was in essence a community of character and culture. For Karl Kautsky, the nation was a modern phenomenon resulting from the formation of large territorial economies under

16. *Lenin*, XLVIII, 162. *Prosveshchenie* (Enlightenment) was the party's theoretical journal.

capitalism. His definition of the nation found it to be distinguished
by a community of language and a community of territory founded
on the capitalist process of economic consolidation. Stalin criticized
Bauer's psychological approach from a Kautskyan perspective, but
he included national character—under the heading of "community
of psychological makeup"—as the last of four constitutive characteristics of a nation. The first three were community of language,
community of territory, and community of economic life. Here he
followed both the content and the sequential order of Kautsky's
definition, though without reference to the latter's relevant writings
(most of which had been translated into Russian) as his source.[17]
As we shall have occasion to observe at further points, the failure
to acknowledge intellectual debts, save the one to Lenin, was a
recurrent practice with Stalin.

After concluding the general theoretical part of the work, he
opened fire on the Austro-Marxist concept of "national-cultural autonomy" as developed by its two chief exponents, Karl Renner and
Otto Bauer. It was not the business of Social Democrats to organize
nations or to "preserve and develop the national attributes of peoples" (as the Austrian Social Democratic program expressed it),
but to organize the proletariat for class struggle. "National-cultural
autonomy" was a masked form of nationalism, and all the more
dangerous because (as he put it) it was encased in socialist armor.
It was an anachronism in an age when, as Marx had prophesied,
national barriers were everywhere falling. Moreover, it created the
psychological prerequisites for the division of a single workers' party
into a group of parties organized on national lines, and for similar
national separatism within a country's trade union movement. Such
had been the experience of the Austrian Social Democracy, and
menacing tendencies in that direction were visible in Russia. Although Marx, Kautsky, and even Bauer had envisaged for the Jews

17. *Stalin*, II, 292–302. On Stalin's unacknowledged debt to Kautsky, see
Roy A. Medvedev, *Let History Judge: The Origins and Consequences of Stalinism*
(New York, 1971), p. 509, and Iu. I. Semenov, "Teoreticheskaia razrabotka V.
I. Leninym natsional'nogo voprosa," *Narody Azii i Afriki*, No. 4 (1966), esp.
pp. 119–121. Semenov describes the first two sections of Stalin's work as "even
stylistically utilizing the works of K. Kautsky. . . ."

not nationhood but assimilation, the Bund had broken with internationalist Social Democracy in an effort to take the Jewish workers
of Russia down the road of national separatism. Now some Transcaucasian Social Democrats were raising a demand for national-
cultural as well as regional autonomy for their area. Trying to
reduce such a demand to an absurdity, Stalin argued that it would
entail the granting of national-cultural autonomy also to many small
Transcaucasian nationalities of primitive culture, like the Ossetes
and Mingrelians, which in turn would reinforce them in their cultural primitivism and assist the local forces of political reaction.
Regional autonomy was acceptable for the Transcaucasus because
it would help the backward nations there to cast off the shell of
small-nation insularity. But *national-cultural* autonomy would work
in the opposite direction, shutting up these nations in their old shells.
The national question in the Transcaucasus could only be resolved
by drawing the backward nations and nationalities into the common
stream of a higher culture.

As for the argument that the demand for national-cultural autonomy was not in contradiction with the right of national self-
determination proclaimed in the Social Democracy's program, it
was of course true that nations have a right to arrange their affairs
as they please. But Social Democracy, while proclaiming and upholding this right, ought nevertheless to fight and agitate against
harmful institutions and inexpedient demands of nations, just as it
ought to agitate against Catholicism, Protestantism, and Orthodoxy
while upholding the right of all people to freedom of religious wor-
ship. The duty of Social Democracy was to influence the will of
nations to arrange their affairs in the manner best corresponding
to the interests of the proletariat. For example, Social Democrats
would agitate against Tartar secession or against national-cultural
autonomy for the Transcaucasian nations. The correct general solution for the national question in Russia was regional autonomy,
with full provision for national minorities in every region to use
their native language, possess their own schools, and so on. And on
the party side, the workers should not be organized according to
nationality. Workers of all nationalities should be locally organized

within the single integral party, thus becoming conscious of themselves not primarily as members of a given nation but as members of one class family, the united army of socialism.[18]

In a conversation with Milovan Djilas in 1948, Stalin said that he had expressed Lenin's views in *Marxism and the National Question*, and that Lenin had edited the work.[19] It is very likely, indeed, that Stalin, in addition to writing it on Lenin's suggestion, benefited greatly from the discussions in Cracow on the nationality problem and incorporated various specific points that Lenin had made in those discussions. On the other hand, there is no good reason to credit Lenin—as Trotsky did—with virtual authorship of the work. Stalin's polemic against national-cultural autonomy flowed easily from views on the national question that he had expressed in writing as early as 1904. The language of the work and its style of argumentation are consistently recognizable as his. Footnotes to the work show that most of the required Austrian materials on the national question were available to him in Russian translation.[20] He needed little if any assistance in those important sections of the

18. *Stalin*, II, 290–367. Later known as *Marxism and the National Question*, the work was entitled (like Bauer's) *The National Question and Social Democracy* when originally published in *Prosveshchenie* in 1913.

19. Milovan Djilas, *Conversations with Stalin* (New York, 1962), p. 157. Stalin made the remark in reply to a question from Djilas on the distinction between "people" and "nation." An ambiguity in Djilas' English text at this point makes it unclear whether Stalin was referring to that distinction or the whole of *Marxism and the National Question* when he went on to say: "That was Ilyich's—Lenin's—view." Djilas has informed me that he believes Stalin was referring to the work as a whole.

20. For example, Otto Bauer's *The National Question and Social Democracy* was used by Stalin in a Russian translation by M. Panin. Stalin referred to the translation by way of correcting a minor mistranslation of the German phrase *nationalen Eigenart*, thereby giving the impression that he knew German well, although he had only a smattering of it. For Trotsky's argument that Stalin's work was a product of Lenin's inspiration and further assistance from Bukharin and Troyanovsky, see his *Stalin*, pp. 156–158. Others who have viewed the work as Lenin's in substance include Isaac Deutscher (*Stalin: A Political Biography*, 2nd ed. [New York, 1966], p. 117), Boris Souvarine (*Stalin: A Critical Survey of Bolshevism* [New York, 1972], p. 133), and Wolfe (*Three Who Made a Revolution*, pp. 578–581). The contrary position, which I share, has been argued by Richard Pipes in *The Formation of the Soviet Union* (New York, 1968), pp. 40–41, and by Robert H. McNeal in "Trotsky's Interpretation of Stalin," *Canadian Slavonic Papers*, No. 5 (1961), p. 90, and in *Stalin's Works: An Annotated Bibliography* (Stanford, 1967), pp. 43–44.

work that dealt with the Bund and the national question in the Transcaucasus. Finally, Lenin, although he had begun intensive thinking on the national question by 1912, had not yet produced any major writings on it and was still in the process of working his thoughts into a systematic whole. Furthermore, when he came out in 1914 with his most significant contribution, *The Right of Nations to Self-Determination,* his treatment of the national question was strikingly different from Stalin's in its underlying emphasis. His main theme of national self-determination—in the meaning of secession and the formation of an independent nation-state—had not been heavily stressed by Stalin. Indeed, Stalin seemed to give it no more than grudging recognition in those few passages of the work that spoke of this right.

Marxism and the National Question was basically Stalin's, and the collaboration with Lenin that underlay it seems to have been mutually beneficial. Lenin, at any rate, was greatly pleased by the work. When his party colleague Alexander Troyanovsky suggested that it be published in *Prosveshchenie* under the editorially noncommittal heading "discussion" (explaining that his wife, E. Rozmirovich, was for national-cultural autonomy), Lenin wrote to Kamenev: "Of course, we are absolutely against that. The article is *very good.* The issue is a fighting one and we will not surrender one iota of our principled opposition to the Bundist trash." [21]

By his work on the national question Stalin established himself in Lenin's mind as a developed Marxist. It may be more than a fanciful comparison to say that he presented his mentor with a successful dissertation. Yet this coming together of the two men, milestone though it was in Stalin's party career, was not yet the beginning of a close personal association. Shortly after returning to Petersburg in the middle of February 1913, and before seeing his work on the

21. Letter of February 25, 1913, in *Lenin,* XLVIII, 169. On March 29, he wrote again to Kamenev: "Koba has managed to write a big (for three issues of *Prosveshchenie*) article on the national question. Good! We have to fight for the truth against the separatists and opportunists from the Bund and from among the liquidators" (*ibid.,* p. 173). And in an editorial of December 1913 on the national program of the party, Lenin wrote that Stalin's article "stands out in first place" in the recent theoretical Marxist literature on the national question (*ibid.,* XXIV, 223).

national question in print, Stalin was apprehended by the police while attending a benefit concert organized by the local Bolsheviks. The betrayal of his whereabouts to the police has been attributed to the *agent provocateur* Roman Malinovsky.[22] Stalin spent the ensuing years in Siberian exile. His name appears a few times in Lenin's wartime correspondence, but in a manner that illustrates the absence of a close relationship. "Koba" and "Koba Ivanovich" were the names by which Lenin had come to know Stalin, who indeed signed himself "Koba" when he wrote to Lenin from Siberia. "Do you remember the last name of Koba?" Lenin inquired in a letter of 1915 to Zinoviev, and later that year he wrote to V. A. Karpinsky: "Big request: find out (from Stepko or Mikha, etc.) the last name of 'Koba' (Iosif Dj . . . . . ?? have forgotten). It's very important!!"[23]

Siberian Interlude

After some months of imprisonment in Petersburg, Stalin was sentenced to four years of exile in the Turukhansk territory, in north-central Siberia. In early July 1913 he was sent under guard by rail to the city of Krasnoyarsk and thence by boat northward down the Yenisei River to the village of Monastyrskoe, the administrative center of the Turukhansk territory. There the exiles' colony, having been informed in advance of his impending arrival, welcomed him with a room and provisions. The newcomer, however, proved a disappointment. Instead of following the usual custom and reporting to the group on the political situation in Russia, Stalin disappeared into the room and was uncommunicative. To make things worse, on being transferred to an outlying place he

22. A. S. Alliluyeva, *Vospominaniia* (Moscow, 1946), p. 117.
23. *Lenin,* XLVIII, 101, 161. The first of the two letters appears here for the first time; the second was first published in 1929 in *Leninskii sbornik,* XI. The only clue as to what the important matter referred to by Lenin may have been is the statement by Anna Alliluyeva (*Vospominaniia,* p. 118) that Stalin sent to her father from Siberian exile the finished manuscript of his work on the national question for transmission to Lenin, and that the Alliluyevs transmitted it. Lenin's inquiry to Karpinsky may have been made in this connection.

took with him the books of a recently deceased member of the colony. The exiles had agreed that these books would become a circulating library for the use of them all. One of their number, Filipp Zakharov, went to see Stalin about this matter, only to be received in a haughty manner, as though by a general receiving an ordinary soldier.[24]

The organizer of the warm welcome for Stalin at Monastyrskoe was Yakov Sverdlov, an old acquaintance of Stalin's from a previous period of shared exile. Sverdlov was also a fellow member of the Central Committee's Russian Bureau and was destined to become secretary of the party Central Committee and Soviet head of state until his early death in 1919. At the beginning of 1914, after getting wind of some possible escape plans, the authorities transferred Sverdlov and Stalin to the remote fishing settlement of Kureika, beyond the Arctic Circle, where at first they shared a room. In a letter of March 1914 to a friend, Sverdlov reported: "I am much worse off in the new place. Just the fact of not being alone in a room. There are two of us. With me is the Georgian, Djugashvili, an old acquaintance whom I already know from another exile. A good fellow, but too much of an individualist in everyday life. Myself, I believe in minimal order. This makes me nervous sometimes. But it's not so important. Much worse is the lack of separation from the hosts. The room adjoins theirs and has no separate entrance. They have children. Naturally they spend hours with us and sometimes interfere."[25] By the end of May the two men had moved into separate quarters, and Sverdlov wrote to his friend: "A comrade is with me. But we know each other too well. And saddest of all, in exile or prison conditions a man bares himself before you, shows himself in all his petty aspects. The worst thing of all is that only from the standpoint of the 'petty aspects of life' is a person seen. There's no room to display the big features. Now the comrade

24. Medvedev, *Let History Judge*, pp. 5–6. Medvedev cites as his source for these facts the unpublished memoirs of Filipp Zakharov's wife, R. G. Zakharova. A short selection from her reminiscences has been published in Iu. Trifonov, *Otblesk kostra* (Moscow, 1966), pp. 47–48.

25. E. Gorodetsky and Iu. Sharapov, *Sverdlov. Zhizn' i deiatel'nost'* (Moscow, 1961), pp. 84–86.

and I are living in different quarters and rarely see each other." [26] The full meaning of this estrangement will be evident when it is mentioned that these two were then the only political exiles living in Kureika.

For the rest, what little we know about Stalin's life in the Turukhansk exile comes chiefly from the Alliluyev family. Having made each other's acquaintance in Tiflis days, Stalin and Sergei Alliluyev met again in Baku. Subsequently the Alliluyevs moved to Petersburg, where Sergei found work with the electric light company and clandestinely continued to maintain his party connections. In 1911, during a brief appearance in Petersburg between periods of Vologda exile, Stalin found shelter with this always hospitable family. They were especially friendly toward comrades from the Caucasus and continued to look after him when he reached Turukhansk in 1913. They sent him some money from the party assistance fund and parcels with warm clothing. In a letter of late 1915 to Sergei's wife, Olga, Stalin thanked them warmly for a recently received parcel and asked that they not spend any more of their much-needed money on him. What he now wished for was postcards with natural scenes. He explained. "Nature in this accursed region is shamefully poor—in summer the river and in winter the snow, that's all nature offers here—and I'm crazy with longing for natural scenes, if only on paper." [27] Truly, Kureika was a long way from Gori.

Later, upon his return to Petrograd (as Petersburg was renamed in 1914), Stalin told the Alliluyevs a little more about his life in Kureika. The villagers, who were from one of the native nationalities of the north, had taken to calling him "Osip," and had taught him how to fish in the Yenisei. Because of his success (gained by moving around, whereas the peasants would stay by a

26. Ya. M. Sverdlov, *Izbrannye proizvedeniia* (Moscow, 1957), I, 276–277. A note to the first sentence states: "The reference is to I. V. Stalin, with whom Ya. M. Sverdlov was in exile in the village of Kureika." Sverdlov's letter was first published in *Pechat' i revoliutsiia*, Bk. 2 (1924), p. 66.

27. A. S. Alliluyeva, *Vospominaniia*, pp. 117–118. For Stalin's meeting with Sergei Alliluyev in Baku, see S. Alliluyev, *Proidennyi put'* (Moscow, 1946), p. 182.

single spot whether or not the fish were biting there), they thought he had magic powers, and would say: "Osip, thou knowest the word!" Once, after fishing through a hole in the ice in the winter, he had become lost in a snowstorm on the way back home. He later learned that two villagers whom he had unsuccessfully accosted while searching for the village had fled because, on account of his ice-covered face, they had taken him for a goblin.[28] He found a society of sorts among the local people, and the Alliluyevs heard later, whether directly from him or from some other source, that he had lived with a local peasant woman and had a son by her.[29] If this story is well founded, it may help to explain why Stalin and Sverdlov lived separate lives in Kureika.

In October 1916, the government responded to the increasingly serious situation at the front by declaring political exiles eligible for military service. Stalin was among those called up in the Turukhansk territory and went back to Monastyrskoe with orders to report at Krasnoyarsk for induction into the army. Here again he displayed the stiffness and aloofness that had antagonized the other revolutionaries on his arrival. Apparently he felt in need of emphasizing—and gaining recognition of—the special position of eminence which he was conscious of occupying by virtue of being a member of the Central Committee. Not only did he remain aloof from the other exiles, but he also failed to resume ties with Sverdlov and one other member of the Russian Bureau who were present in Monastyrskoe at that moment. As a fellow Bolshevik exile, Boris I. Ivanov, has recalled in unpublished memoirs: "The necessary reconciliation did not take place. Djugashvili remained as proud as ever, as locked up in himself, in his own thoughts and plans. . . . As before, he was hostile to Sverdlov, and would not move toward reconciliation, although Sverdlov was prepared to extend the hand

28. A. S. Alliluyeva, *Vospominaniia*, pp. 167, 189–190.
29. Svetlana Alliluyeva, *Only One Year* (New York, 1969), pp. 381–382. According to the author, "My aunts told me that during one of his Siberian exiles he had lived with a local peasant woman and that their son was still living somewhere—he had received a slight education and had no pretensions to the big name." The exile in question must have been the one in Turukhansk, as Stalin did not remain long enough in Siberia during either of his two previous exiles there to start a family.

of friendship, and was willing to discuss problems of the workers' movement in the company of the three members of the Russian Bureau of the party Central Committee." [30]

From Monastyrskoe the exiles with induction orders were sent up the Yenisei—by dog- and reindeer-drawn sleigh and on foot— to Krasnoyarsk. The medical examination took place at the beginning of February 1917, and Stalin was rejected for military service. As mentioned earlier, he told the Alliluyevs that the doctors rejected him because of a stiff left arm resulting from a poorly healed childhood injury, and also because they considered him "an undesirable element" for the army. Afterwards, taking into account that his four-year term of exile was close to completion, the authorities permitted him to settle in Achinsk, a small town on the Trans-Siberian railway line, for the remainder of the time. Among the exiles then living in Achinsk were Lev Kamenev and his wife, Olga (Trotsky's sister), and Stalin was a regular guest at their home in the evenings. According to the recollection of one who saw him there on occasion, and subsequently emigrated from Russia, "Osip"—as Stalin was still called in Achinsk—would take little part in the conversation, and when he did Kamenev would cut him off with a slighting comment, after which he would relapse into silence and re-light his pipe. Once, when the talk touched on the war and the question of how it would end, Kamenev forecast a German victory followed by a bourgeois-democratic revolution in Russia. As for a socialist revolution, he thought twenty or thirty more years would be needed for that. "Osip" was observed nodding his agreement with Kamenev's position. [31]

Before the end of that very month of February 1917, Russia was engulfed in revolution. The town population was growing increasingly restive as the hardships associated with a terrible and seemingly endless war culminated in a partial breakdown of essential services. Disturbances broke out in Petrograd on February 23

30. Quoted in Medvedev, *Let History Judge*, p. 7.

31. A. Baikalov, "Moi vstrechi s Osipom Djugashvili," *Vozrozhdenie* (Paris), March–April 1950, p. 118. Baikalov states that he himself was at the time a member of the board of the Yenisei Union of Cooperatives and in that capacity frequently had occasion to travel from Krasnoyarsk to Achinsk.

among people waiting in line before food shops. A wave of spontaneous strikes and street demonstrations thereupon spread through
the capital and its suburbs, and the unwillingness of soldiers of the
garrison to obey orders to quell the disturbances by force made the
situation unmanageable. In these circumstances, high-placed persons prevailed upon the tsar to abdicate. Attempts to preserve the
dynasty by creating a regency, with the tsar's young son as future
emperor, were ineffectual. On March 2 formal authority devolved
upon a Provisional Government formed under the auspices of the
State Duma and headed by Prince Lvov.

Autocratic, authoritarian, police-state Russia suddenly became
—as Lenin expressed it in his "April Theses" not long after—"the
freest of all the belligerent countries in the world." Political exiles
in distant places were among the first to experience the new freedom. A group of them, including Stalin, boarded an express train
on March 8 at Krasnoyarsk and reached Petrograd four days later.
Cheering throngs greeted them from station platforms along the
way. On his arrival Stalin sought out the Alliluyevs, who were
living in an apartment on the outskirts of the city, and was given
a warm welcome. Sergei and Olga were there, as well as their son,
Fyodor, their older daughter, Anna, and their younger daughter,
Nadya, then a schoolgirl of sixteen. They plied the newcomer with
questions about exile, Siberia, and the trip back. He employed his
unusual powers of mimicry as he recounted for them what it was
like when the train for Petrograd would stop at provincial stations
enroute and local orators would beat their breasts and proclaim in
high-flown language how "holy revolution, long-awaited, dear revolution has, finally, arrived." The next morning Stalin joined Fyodor, Anna, and Nadya in boarding a steam-driven tram for the
center. They were looking for an apartment in the city, and he was
heading for the *Pravda* office. As they parted, he waved good-bye
and called out: "Be sure to set aside a room in the new apartment
for me. Don't forget."[32]

At party headquarters (which had been set up in a mansion
formerly occupied by the ballerina Kseshinskaia) an embarrassing

32. A. S. Alliluyeva, *Vospominaniia*, pp. 165–169.

experience awaited him. By then the Bolshevik party was emerging from underground, and its directorate, the Russian Bureau of the Central Committee, was taking in various leading figures as they returned from prison or exile. Protocols of its meetings, first published in 1962, show that the question of Stalin's admission came up during the meeting of March 12—the day of his arrival on the scene. The bureau heard a report that Stalin had earlier been an agent of the Central Committee and would on that account be desirable as a bureau member. However, "in view of certain qualities inherent in him, the bureau expressed itself to the effect that he should be invited with advisory vote." [33] The protocols did not elaborate on the nature of Stalin's "certain qualities." Undoubtedly, however, the allusion was to his arrogance, aloofness, and uncomradely behavior during the Turukhansk exile.

Nineteen-Seventeen

In addition to the deeper historical causes, the 1917 Revolution was brought on by a long losing war in which an under-equipped and poorly led Russian peasant army suffered an estimated seven million casualties in dead, wounded, and missing. As the slaughter went on and on, defeatism spread among the populace and demoralization became rife in the army. "Everybody is impatiently waiting for the end of this 'damned war,'" said a secret police report of October 1916 later made public by the Soviet government. "I am firmly convinced," wrote Seventh Army Commanding General V. J. Selichev in his diary on March 10, 1917, "that the common soldier today wants only one thing—food and peace, because he is tired of the war." [34] What more than anything else doomed the Provisional Government was its failure to recognize war-weary Russia's imperative need for peace. Moreover, in the

---

33. "Protokoly i resoliutsii Biuro TsK RSDRP (b) (Mart 1917 g.)," *Voprosy istorii KPSS*, No. 3 (1962), p. 143. The protocol on the bureau's meeting of March 15 (p. 149) records that Stalin was on that day elected a member of the bureau's presidium. By this time he must have acquired full voting rights.

34. Both documents as quoted in Michael T. Florinsky, *Russia: A History and an Interpretation* (New York, 1955), II, 1377, 1378.

face of the spontaneously developing movement among the peasants to partition the landowners' estates, the new government espoused a futile policy of deferring the agrarian revolution pending
convocation of the Constituent Assembly to which it was committed
under its program. A new political upheaval was a strong possibility
under these conditions, particularly given the situation of "dual
power" arising out of the presence, side by side with the Duma, of
the Petrograd Soviet of Workers' and Soldiers' Deputies—a potential political base for a radically revolutionary regime. But this fact
was not immediately apparent to many, Bolsheviks included.

Stalin did not long rest content with a merely advisory vote
in the Central Committee's reconstituted Russian Bureau. After his
chilly initial reception, he successfully asserted his authority. Along
with Kamenev and M. K. Muranov, he joined the editorial board
of *Pravda,* the bureau's organ, which had resumed publication on
March 5 under the editorship of Viacheslav Molotov (an acquaintance of Stalin's since pre-war days). In the absence of Lenin and
other party leaders who were still enroute to Russia or arranging
their return, Kamenev and Stalin dominated party decisions in Petrograd during a three-week interval in March and the beginning of
April. In doing so, moreover, they took a position consistent with
Kamenev's forecast in Achinsk that a long interval of years would
separate Russia's coming bourgeois-democratic revolution from the
eventual socialist one. That is, they espoused a policy of moderation
toward the Provisional Government, predicated upon the view that
the democratic revolution was still incomplete and that the overthrow of the new regime was therefore not yet an operational objective. Nor did this policy envisage the removal of the Provisional
Government as a pre-condition of taking Russia out of the war.
Thus in his *Pravda* editorial for March 17, "On the War," Stalin
called only for "pressure on the Provisional Government with the
demand that it consent to the immediate opening of peace talks." [35]

At first, under Molotov's editorship and while the Russian Bureau was headed by A. Shliapnikov, *Pravda* had taken the more
radical line of no support for the government. Now the tune changed.

35. *Stalin,* III, 8.

According to the memoirs of Shliapnikov, "Comrades Kamenev, Stalin, and Muranov decided to take over *Pravda* and give it 'their' line. . . . On the basis of their formal rights they completely took into their hands the editing of the regular issue No. 9, of March 15, employing their majority and formal prerogatives to prevail over the representative of the Central Committee Bureau, Comrade V. Molotov." Shliapnikov recalled further that this "editorial revolution" caused great indignation in Petrograd worker districts, where there was little sympathy for a moderate policy toward the war and the Provisional Government, and that demands were even heard for the expulsion of the three new editors from the party.[36]

At about this time the editors of *Pravda* were receiving from Switzerland the first two of Lenin's "Letters from Afar." These letters anticipated the argument of his "April Theses" that the democratic revolution had already taken place in Russia, that socialist revolution was in the offing, and that the way out of the war was to overthrow the Provisional Government and create a Republic of Soviets. Recoiling from Lenin's revolutionary militance, Kamenev and Stalin permitted only one of the letters (the first) to appear in *Pravda* and even then deleted about one-fifth of it, including passages that attacked the Provisional Government and characterized a policy of support for it as treason to the proletarian cause.[37]

They were also silent about Lenin's letters when party members gathered in Petrograd for the all-Russian Bolshevik party conference that took place behind closed doors at the end of March and beginning of April. Reporting to the conference on party policy toward the Provisional Government, Stalin cautioned against "forcing events" for fear of prematurely alienating the middle strata of the bourgeoisie. To those comrades arriving from the provinces who wanted (as he put it) to pose immediately the question of seizing

---

36. A. Shliapnikov, *Semnadtsaty god. Kniga vtoraia* (Moscow and Petrograd, 1923), p. 180. For further details, see E. N. Burdzhalov, "Eshche o taktike bol'shevikov v marte–aprele 1917 goda," *Voprosy istorii*, No. 8 (1956), pp. 110–112.

37. E. N. Burdzhalov, "O taktike bol'shevikov v marte–aprele 1917 goda," *Voprosy istorii*, No. 4 (1956), pp. 48–50. See also the historical note on "Letters from Afar," in *Lenin*, XXXI, 503–504.

power, he replied that it was still untimely to pose that question; the Provisional Government was "not so weak." And, again taking his cue from Kamenev, Stalin urged a policy of conditional support for the Provisional Government insofar as it "fortifies the steps of the revolution." Meanwhile, the party was to bide its time and permit events to show up the government's "hollowness." Later in the conference, Stalin submitted and defended a motion for entering into negotiations with the Mensheviks on unification of the party on a platform of moderate opposition to the war. When this controversial motion passed by a narrow majority of fourteen votes to thirteen, he was appointed to head the Bolshevik negotiating committee.[38] The negotiations for unification with the Mensheviks were not, however, destined to take place. Lenin's return on April 3, the day after the March conference ended, reversed the party line. Even before he set foot on the platform of the Finland Station, in Petrograd, Lenin made clear his opposition to the position that Stalin and Kamenev had taken. F. F. Raskolnikov, who with Kamenev and others boarded Lenin's incoming train at the Beloostrov Station, outside Petrograd, recalled in 1923, in the party journal *Proletarskaia revoliutsiia* (Proletarian Revolution), how Lenin, immediately upon entering their compartment, lashed out at Kamenev: "What is that stuff you people are writing in *Pravda*? We saw several numbers and roundly berated you." [39]

In the sequel, the Kamenev-Stalin policy of conditional support for the Provisional Government was discarded in favor of the revolutionary intransigence of the "April Theses." Furthermore, unification with the Mensheviks was rudely rejected by Lenin when he presented the "Theses" before a meeting of Bolsheviks on April 4. "I hear there is a unification tendency in Russia," Lenin declared at the close of his speech. "That is a betrayal of socialism. I think it is better to stand alone like Liebknecht—one against a hundred

---

38. "Protokoly vserossiiskogo (martovskogo) soveshchaniia partiinykh rabotnikov 27 marta–2 aprelia 1917 goda," *Voprosy istorii KPSS*, No. 5 (1962), p. 112, and No. 6 (1962), pp. 139–140. These protocols of the March conference, first published in Russia in 1962, appeared in slightly incomplete form in 1937 in L. Trotsky, *The Stalin School of Falsification* (New York, 1962).

39. *Proletarskaia revoliutsiia*, No. 1 (13) (1923), p. 221.

and ten." [40] Thus did the curtain ring down upon the inauspicious first weeks of Stalin's participation in the Russian Revolution.

In anti-Bolshevik political quarters of Petrograd, Lenin's radical position seemed indicative of a mind out of touch with reality. Such reactions, typified by Plekhanov's commentary "On the Theses of Lenin, Or Why Delirium Is Sometimes Interesting," led the American ambassador in Petrograd, David F. Francis, to cable to Washington: "Extreme socialist or anarchist named Lenin making violent speeches and thereby strengthening government; designedly giving him leeway and will deport opportunely." [41] For their part, many Bolsheviks were thunderstruck by the audacity of Lenin's proposed position and filled with consternation over what struck them at first as a misreading of the Russian situation. As Stalin recalled much later, he and other Bolshevik "practical workers" assumed in the pre-1917 years that there would be a substantial interval between the bourgeois and socialist revolutions and did not, "because of inadequate theoretical preparation," grasp Lenin's view that the bourgeois revolution would "grow into" a socialist one.[42] This may help to explain why he and others initially resisted the strategy Lenin now advocated. He was still fighting against the "April Theses" at Kamenev's side when the Central Committee's Russian Bureau discussed them on April 6. The Central Committee minutes preserved a summary recording of his remarks, saying: "A scheme but no facts, and so does not satisfy. No answers on small nations." [43] The former criticism paralleled Kamenev's comment in the same meeting that

40. *Lenin,* XXXI, 112. Lenin's reference was to the refusal of the German Social Democratic leader Karl Liebknecht to go along with the decision of the other 110 Social Democratic members of the Reichstag to join in voting war credits to the Kaiser's government on the outbreak of war in 1914.

41. Quoted by Florinsky in *Russia,* II, 1403–1404. The date of Ambassador Francis' cable was April 21 new style, or April 8 old style. Following Soviet usage, I have been giving dates according to the old-style calendar through this period. The old-style Russian calendar was changed after the October Revolution, which occurred on October 25 old style (November 7 new style).

42. *Stalin,* I, xii–xiii. This statement appears in the author's preface, written in 1946.

43. Burdzhalov, "Eshche o taktike," p. 114. These minutes have not been published. Burdzhalov refers to documents in the archives of the Moscow Institute of Marxism-Leninism as his source. I share his interpretation (p. 114) of Stalin's quoted remarks.

the "Theses" failed to give concrete directions, as well as his statement at the all-Russian Bolshevik party conference of April 24–29
that "the general sociological scheme has not been filled in with concrete political content." [44] By the time this conference met, however,
Stalin (unlike Kamenev) had abandoned his dissident position and
was steering a general course of support for Lenin.

Despite the importance—and retrospective unfortunateness—
of the role that events had enabled Stalin to play in party affairs during the early weeks, his March conduct was not subsequently held
against him. When the April conference re-elected the party Central
Committee, Stalin finally became a member by election as distinct
from co-optation. Indeed, he received the third highest number of
votes, exceeded only by the numbers of votes cast for Lenin and
Zinoviev.[45] A major reason for this success may have been the fact
that Stalin was now assuming the role, for which Lenin had groomed
him in earlier years, of party spokesman in the field of national-
minority affairs, where he was in his element and could be of much
value. Inaugurating a practice which he would follow frequently in
the ensuing years, he addressed the April conference as *rapporteur*
on the national question. Before the office was formally created,
Stalin was acting as the Bolsheviks' commissar for nationality affairs.

As the April conference showed, moreover, the national question was emerging as one of the urgent and thorny issues before the
party. With a view to encouraging the revolutionary disintegration
of multi-national empires—particularly Russia's—Lenin had espoused in *The Right of Nations to Self-Determination* the idea that
each national community had every right to secede and form its own
independent nation-state. Now the disintegration was beginning.
Finland, which had been a part of the Tsarist Empire with special
privileges of internal autonomy, was seeking the Provisional Gov-

44. Burdzhalov, *ibid.*, and *Sed'maia ('aprel'skaia') vserossiiskaia i petrogradskaia obshchegorodskaia konferentsii RSDRP (b). Aprel' 1917 g.*, ed. M. D. Orakhelashvili (Moscow, 1934), p. 72.
45. *Sed'maia konferentsii*, p. 190. The Central Committee was re-elected on
this occasion with nine full members (Lenin, Zinoviev, Stalin, Kamenev, Vladimir
Miliutin, Nogin, Sverdlov, Ivan Smilga, and G. F. Fyodorov) and five candidates.
Lenin received 104 votes (out of a possible 109), Zinoviev 101, Stalin 97, Kamenev 95, and the others considerably fewer.

ernment's permission to secede. Poland was likewise a candidate for
secession, and separatist movements were ripening in the Ukraine,
the Transcaucasus, and elsewhere. Under these conditions, should
the Bolsheviks adhere to Lenin's position? Stalin's report and proposed resolution gave a qualified affirmative answer. The right of
secession was enunciated as a correct general principle, and the justice of Finland's case was recognized. But Stalin's draft resolution
contained some significant "fine print" in the statement that one
should distinguish between the right of secession and "the expediency of this or that nation separating at this or that moment." The
latter question should be decided by the "party of the proletariat" in
accordance with the interests of "social development and the class
struggle." [46]

In short, the *right* of self-determination was proclaimed and its
implementation endorsed in a special case like Finland's (as well
as Ireland's, another case singled out by Stalin as an example), but
without committing the Bolsheviks to a *policy* of supporting secession in the many other cases close to home that were likely to arise.
Indeed, Stalin cautiously adumbrated a contrary policy when he said
in his conference report: "I can acknowledge a nation's right to secede, but this does not mean that I have obligated her to do this. . . .
Personally, I should be opposed, for example, to the secession of
Transcaucasia, taking into account overall development in Transcaucasia and Russia, certain conditions of the proletariat's struggle,
etc." Furthermore, he said, now that tsarism and its policies no
longer existed, the national minorities of the Empire should lose
their past mistrust of the Russians and show an increased attraction
toward Russia. Nine-tenths of the nationalities would not wish to
secede. The party, moreover, would propose regional autonomy for
non-seceding nationalities with distinct languages and cultures. But
this was not, Stalin emphasized, the same thing as acceptance of the
Austro-Marxist principle of national-cultural autonomy as urged by
the Bund, which would make Russia into a "union of nations" not
based on territoriality.[47] An insightful listener might have perceived

46. *Ibid.*, pp. 230–231.
47. *Ibid.*, pp. 192–193.

that the author of this tortuous argumentation delivered in a Georgian accent was a Russia-oriented centralist from one of the national minorities. But no one present seems to have been that interested in Stalin's real views.

Georgi Piatakov, a rising young Bolshevik leader of leftist persuasion then closely associated with Bukharin (who had not yet arrived back in Russia), took the floor as "counter-*rapporteur*" to argue that the party should *not* espouse the right of national self-determination. Piatakov had a special interest in Ukrainian affairs deriving from a youth spent in Kiev. He and Felix Dzerzhinsky, a Pole, urged the view that separatist movements of the minorities, whether of Poland or the Ukraine or elsewhere, would be used by the bourgeoisie of these areas to stave off revolution. The struggle for socialism should be waged by Social Democrats under the slogan "Down with borders." Answering Piatakov, Lenin said that ever since 1903 the Polish comrades had been opposing the idea of national self-determination. In effect, they were asking their Russian comrades to take the position of Russian chauvinists who denied the right of Poland, the Ukraine, or Finland to separate from Russia. No Russian socialist could fail to recognize Finnish or Ukrainian freedom without descending to chauvinism. The hope was that "if the Ukrainians see that we have a Republic of Soviets, they will not secede. . . ." [48] In the end Stalin's resolution was adopted by a vote of fifty-six to sixteen, with eighteen abstentions, and Piatakov's was rejected. But the issue was Lenin's position, of which Stalin had undertaken to be the spokesman. Indeed, Stalin's speech was scarcely mentioned in the impassioned debate that it touched off.

In the course of the developing revolutionary events, Stalin reverted to his old role of a special assistant to Lenin for delicate assignments. His astuteness, conspiratorial skills, and total reliability were now put to good use. His conspiratorial skills became especially valuable during the time of Bolshevik adversity that followed the popular outbreaks in Petrograd in late June and early July. Although Bolsheviks were involved in the disturbances, Lenin and the Bolshevik Central Committee, fearful of a premature rebellion,

48. *Ibid.*, pp. 194–203.

neither planned nor willed them in advance.[49] Following the July demonstration, however, the Provisional Government ordered the arrest of Lenin and Zinoviev on conspiracy charges, and caused reports to appear in the press that the Bolshevik leader and his associates were agents of the German General Staff. Lenin at this time went into hiding with Stalin's friends the Alliluyevs, who had moved into an apartment on Rozhdestvenka Street soon after Stalin's earlier visit. What recommended this hiding-place, apart from the trustworthiness of the Alliluyev family, was the fact that because they had occupied it for only about two months it was not known as a party address. Lenin occupied the very room that the Alliluyevs had set aside for Stalin at his request and that Stalin himself had not yet used.[50]

Some prominent Bolsheviks thought that Lenin and Zinoviev should go on trial as a means of publicly repudiating the government's charges; others opposed their appearance for trial for fear that they would be assassinated if they surrendered themselves to government custody. On July 7, Krupskaya, Stalin, Ordzhonikidze, Victor Nogin, and others discussed the matter with Lenin in the Alliluyev apartment. When Nogin suggested tentatively that Lenin should appear in open court to do battle with his accusers, Lenin expressed the view that there would be no open trial—to which Stalin added: "The Junkers will not take you as far as prison, they will kill you on the way." [51] But when Elena Stasova entered with news of a government-inspired rumor that Lenin was a police agent, he determined to turn himself in, and decided to stay in hiding only after Ordzhonikidze and Nogin failed in their attempt to elicit from the Petrograd Soviet a guarantee of safe treatment and a public

---

49. On this episode see Alexander Rabinowitch, *Prelude to Revolution: The Petrograd Bolsheviks and the July 1917 Uprising* (Bloomington, Ind., 1968), esp. pp. 234–235.

50. A. S. Alliluyeva, *Vospominaniia*, pp. 170, 176–177.

51. Dubinsky-Mukhadze, *Ordzhonikidze*, p. 178; A. S. Alliluyeva, *Vospominaniia*, p. 181. Somewhat later Stalin told the Alliluyev sisters that when the same question was discussed at a Central Committee meeting at that time, the temperamental Ordzhonikidze reached for an imaginary Caucasian dagger and shouted: "I'll cut up anybody who wants Ilyich to be arrested (*Vospominaniia*, p. 190).

trial. A week later, the newspaper *Proletarskoe delo* (Proletarian Cause) published a letter from Lenin and Zinoviev in which they announced their decision not to submit to arrest and declared that there could be no guarantees of justice in Russia at the present moment and that no Russian revolutionary could any longer harbor constitutional illusions.

Because of the comings and goings of party comrades, it became apparent after a time that Lenin should change hiding-places. It was decided that he should move out of the city to the small resort town of Sestroretsk, located on the Gulf of Finland about twenty miles northwest of Petrograd. A disguise was necessary so that he could go there without being recognized on the way. Lenin suggested that his beard and moustache be shaved off, and Stalin acted as barber. Then Lenin donned a cap and a long coat belonging to Sergei Alliluyev. Looking like a Finnish peasant, he left the apartment in the company of Stalin and Alliluyev, walked through side streets to the Primorsky Station, and took a crowded suburban train to his destination.[52]

In addition to assisting a revolution, Stalin was by now acquiring a home. After Lenin's departure for Sestroretsk he began to spend a few hours when possible—usually at night—with the Alliluyevs, and became a part of the family. One day in September he brought with him a Caucasian friend who turned out to be the legendary Kamo and who regaled the family with stories of his incredible escapes from captivity. Stalin deposited in the room that the family had set aside for him a small wicker bag containing all his earthly goods—some books, manuscripts, and a few clothes. Olga Evgenievna, a typical Russian mother in her ruthless insistence that everyone under her roof eat well, sought to improve his diet; and after vainly trying to repair the one worn-out suit that he owned, she went out and found him a new one. At his request, she had a high-necked dicky made for him to wear with it; he was not fond of neckties.

The older daughter, Anna, was now working at revolutionary

52. A. S. Alliluyeva, *Vospominaniia*, pp. 183–184.

headquarters in the Smolny Institute, and Nadya was still attending high school. Often they would wait up until late at night in hopes that Stalin would come. When he did, he would try to bring some bread, fish, or other food for the family. On occasion he and the two girls would gather in his room for tea so as to avoid awakening Sergei and Olga, who slept in the dining room. He would entertain them with tales of his Siberian exile or by mimicking persons he had met that day. Or he would take his Chekhov volume down from the shelf and exercise the talent for mimicry again as he read aloud to them from "Chameleon" or "Dushechka"—his two favorites among the stories; the latter he knew practically by heart. Sometimes, instead, he would choose something from Pushkin or Gorky to read to them.[53] Very likely it was during this period that he began to look appreciatively upon Nadya, an attractive high-spirited girl whose musical gifts went along with a bent for housekeeping and who, like all the Alliluyevs, was ardent in her Bolshevik sympathies. Two years later they were married.

The reaction following the July days temporarily decimated the revolutionary leadership. With Lenin and Zinoviev in hiding and Trotsky and Kamenev, among others, in jail, Stalin was one of the lesser figures whom events propelled to the fore in Bolshevik affairs. The July days, like the February Revolution, placed him temporarily in a position to wield serious influence in the determining of overall party strategy. Now, however, he had earned the role by becoming in the interim an amanuensis of Lenin and one who could be counted upon to represent the absent leader's views in higher party councils. Accordingly, when 267 Bolshevik delegates met in Petrograd in early August for the Sixth Party Congress, which was held clandestinely, Stalin gave not only the Central Committee's report (always the first major address at a party congress, and Lenin's prerogative), but also the lead-off speech on the current political situation.

The Stalin of this speech was a far cry from the party moderate of March who had considered a socialist revolution in Russia premature, though such views were still very alive in the party and

53. *Ibid.*, pp. 184–190.

found expression in the debate on the current situation. He was an unconditional Lenin man for whom the issue between the Provisional Government and the revolution was now *"Kto kogo?"* (Who will eliminate whom?): "What is the Provisional Government? It's a puppet, a miserable screen behind which stand the Kadets, the military clique, and allied capital—three pillars of counter-revolution. . . . But since the forces of revolution are developing, there will be explosions, and the moment will come when the workers will rise and rally around them the poor strata of the peasantry, raise the banner of worker revolution, and open the era of socialist revolution in the West." Prior to the July days, Stalin concluded, a peaceful transfer of power to the Soviets was possible. But no longer: "The peaceful period of the revolution has ended; the non-peaceful period, the period of clashes and explosions, has come." [54]

Stalin made a particularly notable statement during the discussion of the draft resolution accompanying this speech. The final part of the draft declared that when the moment of national crisis arrived, the task of the revolutionary classes would be to seize power and direct it, in alliance with the revolutionary proletariat of the advanced countries, toward peace and the socialist reconstruction of society. Evgeni Preobrazhensky, a future leading figure of the Trotskyist faction, moved that the concluding words be reformulated: ". . . and direct it toward peace and, *on condition of a proletarian revolution in the West,* toward socialism." Stalin objected, saying:

The possibility is not excluded that Russia will be the country that blazes the trail to socialism. So far no country has enjoyed such freedom as exists in Russia; none has tried to realize the workers' control over production. Besides, the base of our revolution is broader than in Western Europe, where the proletariat is completely alone in its confrontation with the bourgeoisie. Here the workers have the support of the poorest strata of the peasantry. Finally, in Germany the machinery of state power is functioning incomparably better than the imperfect machinery of our bourgeoisie, which is itself a payer of tribute to European capital. *It is*

---

54. *Shestoi s"ezd RSDRP /bol'shevikov/. Avgust 1917 goda. Protokoly* (Moscow, 1958), p. 114. The Kadets were the liberal Constitutional Democratic party.

necessary to give up the outworn idea that Europe alone can show us the way. There is a dogmatic Marxism and a creative Marxism. I stand on the ground of the latter.[55]

All the more significant because of its spontaneity, this remarkable statement revealed for a brief moment Stalin's underlying Russo-centrism. Indeed, the future party debate over the possibility of building a socialist society in Soviet Russia without revolutions in Europe was prefigured in the exchange, and the notion of socialism in one country was embryonic in Stalin's "creative Marxism" of 1917. A further portent of things to come was the defeat of Pre-obrazhensky's amended wording when put to a vote.

Stalin came out less well in another dispute that arose at the congress. In the reply to the debate on his Central Committee report, he spoke of the party's need to issue a manifesto explaining recent events and then went on to the matter of whether Lenin and Zinoviev should appear for trial. At present, he said, it was unclear who really held power, and there was no guarantee that the leaders would be safe if arrested. Were the court to be democratically organized and a guarantee given that they would not be harmed, things would be different. There was no point in their surrendering themselves now, but they would do so under a regime of at least some degree of honor which would guarantee them against violence.[56] "This contradictory statement envisaging the possibility of Lenin's placing himself, under certain conditions, at the disposal of a bourgeois government was deeply mistaken," declared the official Soviet journal of party history in the post-Stalin period.[57] And such appears to have been the opinion of the great majority of the delegates to the Sixth Congress. In the debate, Ordzhonikidze argued that the party must in no event surrender Lenin for trial. Dzerzhinsky supported him. Nikolai Skrypnik objected to Stalin's idea of a conditional offer of appearance for trial, and proposed simply to register a protest against the slander campaign. Even V. Volodarsky, who with the

55. *Ibid.*, p. 250. Italics added.
56. *Ibid.*, pp. 27–28.
57. *Voprosy istorii KPSS*, No. 4 (1962), p. 47. See also *Istoriia kommunisticheskoi partii Sovetskogo Soiuza*, chief. ed. P. N. Pospelov, Vol. III (Moscow, 1967), p. 178.

support of two others from Trotsky's Inter-Borough organization submitted a draft resolution authorizing Lenin and Zinoviev to appear under certain conditions, found unacceptable Stalin's allowance for "an honorable bourgeois court." Then Bukharin took the floor and stated that there must be no scholasticism in this question. He ridiculed the idea of an honorable bourgeois court ("Won't an honorable bourgeois court seek first of all to cut off our heads?"), and submitted a draft resolution denouncing "the shocking prosecutor-spy-police hounding of the leaders of the revolutionary proletariat" and ruling out all possibility of their appearance for trial. The congress adopted this resolution by an overwhelming majority.[58]

In fairness to Stalin, there is no indication that he seriously contemplated the course of action mentioned in the statement that so many found objectionable. Certainly his characterization of the Provisional Government in the speech on the current situation quite excluded its ever being regarded by the Bolsheviks as "a regime of at least some degree of honor." The fact is that Stalin was manifesting a tendency which had shown up in his speech at the April conference on the national question: a tendency to equivocate on tactical issues where principle and policy found themselves at odds. He was prepared to proclaim the right of national self-determination in principle while espousing a policy that in practice was contradictory to this principle. Now he was suggesting that the party take a position—in principle—that would envisage Lenin's and Zinoviev's appearance in court, but under conditions that could not possibly be realized. In circumstances that seemed to many Bolsheviks to call imperatively for an unequivocal stand, he was inclined to follow a devious course.

Later Stalinist literature on the Revolution would contend that he worked in complete harmony with Lenin in 1917. The historical record does not, however, support this contention. Apart from his dissidence of early April, there were two episodes of the revolutionary period in which Stalin diverged from Lenin on matters that the latter considered of decisive importance. The first occurred on the

58. *Shestoi s"ezd*, pp. 30–36.

eve of the October action, when Kamenev and Zinoviev broke ranks and divulged the insurrection plan in the newspaper *Novaia zhizn'* (New Life). In letters of October 18 and 19 to the Central Committee, Lenin denounced them for "strike-breaking" and demanded their expulsion from the party. There was some reluctance among Central Committee members to take such extreme action. When the question was discussed at the committee meeting of October 20, with eight members in attendance, Sverdlov argued that the Central Committee had no authority to expel people from the party and proposed simply to accept Kamenev's proffered resignation from the Central Committee. Stalin, who had taken it upon himself to publish in the party paper that day a letter from Zinoviev replying to Lenin's charges, and also to append to it an editorial note saying that "the question may be considered exhausted," suggested first that action on the matter be deferred pending a plenary session of the committee. When this move failed, he stated that Zinoviev and Kamenev would submit to Central Committee decisions, argued against their expulsion from the party, and even proposed that they be allowed to remain members of the Central Committee. After the committee voted (five to three) to accept Kamenev's resignation, Stalin offered to resign as editor of the party organ. His resignation, however, was not accepted.[59]

The other episode occurred in February 1918, when the Lenin regime faced possible destruction at the hands of an advancing German army. On February 10, the Bolsheviks rejected the extremely harsh peace terms which the Germans had presented to Trotsky at Brest-Litovsk. A week later, amid indications of renewed German offensive action, a bitterly divided Central Committee voted to inform the German government of Bolshevik willingness to conclude peace on the terms recently rejected. On February 23, the committee met to consider the German reply, which was an ultimatum containing still harsher terms. Lenin, de-

59. *Protokoly tsentral'nogo komiteta RSDRP/b/. Avgust 1917–fevral' 1918* (Moscow, 1958), pp. 106–107. On this episode see *Istoriia kommunisticheskoi partii*, III, 309–310. On Stalin's editorial note to Zinoviev's letter, see McNeal, *Stalin's Works*, p. 56.

claring that the "politics of the revolutionary phrase" were over, moved immediate acceptance of the new German terms and thereupon presented his own ultimatum: if the terms were not accepted he would leave the government and the Central Committee. In the ensuing debate, Stalin suggested: "We could refrain from signing, but open peace negotiations." To this Lenin shortly afterwards replied: "Stalin is wrong when he says that we could refrain from signing. Those terms have to be signed. If you do not sign them, you will sign the Soviet regime's death warrant in three weeks." [60] In the sequel Stalin cast his vote with the majority that supported Lenin. But the leader's sharp rebuke to him must have been indelibly recorded in the minds of those present as well as in the minutes of the meeting.

Stalin was not really in his element in the turbulent mass politics of 1917, and did not rise to greatness as a revolutionary leader. In no way did he show himself as a colorful personality. Lacking oratorical gifts, he did not make it a regular practice to address mass meetings. His articles in the Bolshevik press were not those of an inspired pamphleteer. Above all, he failed to show the distinctive qualities of outstanding revolutionary leadership in a time of crisis and fluidity: quick adaptability, innovative thinking, sensitive insight into mass feeling and response, and decisiveness. Not surprisingly, then, he did not figure in Bolshevism's later collective memory as one of the heroes of the revolutionary period. Nor was he represented as such in the early memoirs and historical literature. One widely read non-Bolshevik source, the journal kept by Nikolai Sukhanov, a participant observer of the revolutionary events, even contained a slighting comment on Stalin's appearance in March 1917 in the Executive Committee of the Petrograd Soviet. Observing that the Bolshevik party had a whole series of impressive figures and able leaders among its "generals," Sukhanov went on: "Stalin, however, during his modest activity in the Ex. Com. produced— and not only on me—the impression of a gray blur, looming up now and then dimly and not leaving any trace. There is really noth-

60. *Protokoly tsentral'nogo komiteta RSDRP/b/*, pp. 211–213.

ing more to be said about him." [61] Stalin went unmentioned in John Reed's *Ten Days That Shook the World*, which appeared in Russian translation in 1923 with an enthusiastic foreword by Lenin recommending it to the workers of the whole world and lauding its "truthful and most vivid exposition of the events. . . ." [62] Further, as we have seen, he did not fare very well in such early Bolshevik writings on 1917 as the memoirs of Shliapnikov.

Yet, it would be misleading to end with that. Nineteen-seventeen was a large milestone on the path of Stalin's rise. Being at the center of revolutionary events, taking part in the deliberations of the Bolshevik Central Committee, acting as one of the party's leading organizers, he greatly matured as a man of politics. It was then, as Trotsky much later observed, that he achieved the status of a recognized member of the Bolshevik general staff and "definitely became Stalin." [63] He established himself as the party's foremost specialist on the national minorities. Moreover, although he won little glory during the year of revolution, he gained much influence in party affairs. His earlier experience as a *komitetchik* and his penchant for that kind of work found a field of application now in the committee that headed the whole party. As the Central Committee itself grew in size (from nine full members and five candidates in April 1917 to twenty-one full members and ten candidates in August, after the Sixth Congress), he was one of the dozen or so persons who constituted the inner circle of party leaders. When, for example, the Central Committee at one of its October meetings created a "Political Bureau" to exercise political leadership during

61. N. N. Sukhanov, *The Russian Revolution 1917. A Personal Record* (London, 1955), p. 230. In his editorial foreword to this abridged English translation of Sukhanov's memoir, Joel Carmichael points out that it created a great stir when circulated in Russia in 1922 and was made required reading for party study circles. It is indicative of the interest it aroused that Lenin devoted one of his last articles ("Our Revolution: Apropos of Sukhanov's *Notes*) to a critique of Sukhanov's view of the Russian Revolution.

62. Lenin wrote the foreword in 1919 after receiving a presentation copy from Reed. In his introductory notes and explanations, Reed named Lenin, Trotsky, and Lunacharsky as leaders of the Bolsheviks in the revolutionary period.

63. Trotsky, *Stalin*, p. 238.

the period just ahead, Stalin was one of the seven men chosen as its members (along with Lenin, Zinoviev, Kamenev, Trotsky, Grigori Sokolnikov, and Andrei Bubnov). And when, a week later, the Central Committee organized a "Military Revolutionary Center," which was designed to function inside the Petrograd Soviet's Military Revolutionary Committee, headed by Trotsky, Stalin was one of its five members (along with Sverdlov, Dzerzhinsky, Bubnov, and Mikhail Uritsky).[64] The tide of events was then swiftly rising, and neither of these organizational steps proved consequential in the decisive days and weeks that followed. But both were a measure of Stalin's emergence as one of the party's leaders.

64. *Protokoly tsentral'nogo komiteta RSDRP/b/*, pp. 86, 104.

Chapter Six

A REVOLUTIONARY IN
POWER

The People's Commissar

STALIN'S INCLUSION in the Council of People's Commissars as the man responsible for national minority affairs must have been a foregone conclusion in Lenin's mind when he drew up the government roster on the morrow of taking power. The final entry on the list of a dozen or so names read: "president for nationality affairs— I. V. Djugashvili (Stalin)." Four names higher on the list appeared the commissar for foreign affairs, "L. D. Bronstein (Trotsky)." And at the head of it: "chairman of the council—Vladimir Ulyanov (Lenin)."

The unusual new institution over which Stalin was to preside was first conceived as a special commission rather than a commissariat.[1] It came into being, however, as the People's Commissariat for Nationality Affairs, and became known in Soviet jargon as Narkomnats. As its chief Stalin acquired the proud title of "people's commissar" by which these revolutionaries in power sought to distinguish themselves from the ministers who make up ordinary governments. But at first there was no institution to preside over, only a mandate to create one. In doing so Stalin enjoyed the assistance of one S. S. Pestkovsky, a Bolshevik of Polish extraction who approached him in search of work in the revolutionary government and became his vice commissar. Their first "address" was a room in

1. E. N. Gorodetsky, *Rozhdenie sovetskogo gosudarstva (1917–1918 gg.)* (Moscow, 1964), p. 158.

the Smolny Institute where Pestkovsky found a vacant table, placed it against the wall, and pinned above it a notice saying: "People's Commissariat for Nationality Affairs." When he suggested that they would need some money, Stalin made an inquiry and then instructed him to see Trotsky, saying: "He has money. He found it in the former Ministry of Foreign Affairs." Pestkovsky obtained three thousand rubles from Trotsky, and the commissariat was in business.[2]

In March 1918 the hard-pressed Lenin regime moved the capital from Petrograd to more centrally located and less vulnerable Moscow. Stalin, like others in high posts, acquired an office as well as living quarters in the Kremlin. One of his first concerns was to secure a suitable building for his commissariat. The Moscow Soviet at first assigned it two former mansions located in different streets. Desiring the entire institution to be under one roof, Stalin tried to obtain the building of the Great Siberian Hotel, in Zlatoustinsky Street. Nadya Alliluyeva, who was now working in Stalin's commissariat as a secretary, typed some notices saying: "These premises occupied by Narkomnats." Stalin and Pestkovsky ordered a car and drove to the hotel. On the front door was a notice saying: "These premises occupied by Supreme Council of National Economy." They tore it off and replaced it with one of their own, then entered the darkened building by a rear entrance and lit their way through it with matches, tacking up more Narkomnats notices here and there. But the battle for the building was won by the Supreme Council. "It was one of the few instances," Pestkovsky later observed, "when Stalin suffered a defeat."[3]

During the frenetic first months of Bolshevik rule, Stalin could devote no more than a portion of his time to the commissariat. He was heavily involved in the decisions being taken by the inner circle of party leaders, and the discussions concerning them. At its meeting of November 29, 1917, the Central Committee delegated to a *chetverka* (foursome) of Lenin, Stalin, Trotsky, and Sverdlov the

2. L. Trotsky, *Stalin: An Appraisal of the Man and His Influence* (New York, 1967), p. 245.

3. S. Pestkovsky, "Vospominaniia o rabote v narkomnatse (1917–1919 gg.)," *Proletarskaia revoliutsiia*, No. 6 (June 1930), pp. 129–130.

right to decide "all emergency questions," but with the proviso that any other Central Committee members present in the Smolny at the time of such a decision must be invited to participate.[4] The Political Bureau elected by the Central Committee on the eve of the insurrection had been stillborn, and a functioning Politburo was not created until early 1919. Because Sverdlov's energies were mostly absorbed by his work in the Central Committee's Secretariat and by various other duties that kept him away from the Smolny much of the time, the *chetverka* became in fact, according to Trotsky's later recollection, a *troika* (threesome). Stalin at this time functioned more than ever in his now-familiar role as Lenin's right-hand man for special assignments. The room that he and Pestkovsky occupied in the Smolny was not far from Lenin's. He would frequently be summoned by phone, or Lenin would simply appear at the door and ask Stalin to join him. On one such occasion Pestkovsky entered Lenin's office and found the two of them standing on chairs before a large wall map of Russia tracing out something with their fingers in the northern part of what appeared to be Finland.[5] At night Stalin would spend hours at the direct wire in a room in the Smolny, making contact with key individuals in different parts of the country. Trotsky, while disputing Pestkovsky's memory of Stalin functioning as Lenin's "deputy," does confirm, however, that he "played the role of chief-of-staff or of a clerk on responsible missions under Lenin."[6]

One of Stalin's first missions as people's commissar was to go to Helsinki as an emissary of the new Russia and spokesman of Lenin's policy of recognizing Finland's right of national self-determination. Addressing a convention of the Finnish Social Democratic party on November 14, 1917, he proclaimed in ringing words that his government would carry out that policy in practice. In the following month he went before the All-Russian Central Executive

4. *Protokoly tsentral'nogo komiteta RSDRP/b/. Avgust 1917–fevral' 1918* (Moscow, 1958), p. 157. At the same meeting Stalin was appointed (along with Trotsky, Sokolnikov, and Bukharin) to the editorial board of *Pravda*.

5. Pestkovsky, "Vospominaniia," p. 128.

6. Trotsky, *Stalin*, pp. 246, 247. On how the *chetverka* functioned more as a *troika* because of Sverdlov's frequent absence, see the same source, pp. 240–241.

Committee (as the Soviet legislative assembly was called) to present for ratification a decree in which the Council of People's Commissars recognized Finland's independence. He expressed regret, however, that Russian socialists were granting independence to a Finland ruled by the bourgeoisie, and assailed the Finnish Social Democrats for the "indecisiveness and incomprehensible cowardice" that underlay their failure to seize power.[7]

Finland aside, it was not Stalin's job to preside over the dissolution of the former Russian Empire. Under Lenin's guidance he sought, rather, to engineer the retention of as much of it as possible in the new state formation whose official name, under the constitution adopted in July 1918, was the "Russian Socialist Federative Soviet Republic" (RSFSR). Prior to the adoption in January 1924 of the second Soviet Constitution, under which the country's official title became "Union of Soviet Socialist Republics," the Russian Federation (as the RSFSR was commonly called) stood in treaty relations with nominally independent Ukrainian, Byelorussian, and Transcaucasian Soviet republics; subsequently it joined these republics as one of the four "union republics" composing the USSR of 1924. Stalin had a hand in the constitution-making process at both stages. Representing Narkomnats on the commission formed under Sverdlov's chairmanship to draft the 1918 Constitution, he advocated a form of federalism based on national territorial units.[8] His draft was adopted by the commission and reflected in Article 11 of the 1918 Constitution, which provided that regions distinguished by a special way of life and ethnic composition could enjoy regional autonomy within the RSFSR.

What recommended the policy of national-territorial autonomy to Stalin, and certainly to Lenin as well, was first of all the need to compete with other forces in seeking the support of national minor-

---

7. *Stalin,* IV, 24.

8. This was one of several contending positions. One of the others envisaged the RSFSR as a federation of socioeconomic groups on non-territorial lines. Its leading proponent was Mikhail Reisner, who argued that the national-territorial approach involved "hidden centralism under cover of a federal structure." On this point and the contending views in the commission, see Richard Pipes, *The Formation of the Soviet Union,* rev. ed. (New York, 1968) pp. 111–112. For Stalin's position, see *Stalin,* IV, 79–80 and 74–78.

ities. During the revolutionary disintegration of the Russian Empire, movements for national-territorial autonomy had arisen under non-Bolshevik auspices in various parts of the country—among the Tartars of the Volga region; the Bashkirs of the Urals region, farther east; and the Moslem peoples of the Trans-Caspian territory of Turkestan (known today as Soviet Central Asia). Autonomy under such "bourgeois" auspices was entirely unacceptable, Stalin declared in a document issued by Narkomnats in April 1918 as an appeal to the Soviets of the above-named territories. In order to detach the masses from bourgeois leadership, the task was "to 'take over' autonomy from them, first cleansing it of bourgeois filth, and to convert it from a bourgeois into a Soviet autonomy." In short, national-territorial autonomy was conceived as an instrument of sovietization. Stalin was unequivocal on this point: "It is necessary to elevate the masses to the level of the Soviet regime, and to fuse their best representatives with the latter. But this is impossible without autonomy of these outlying regions, i.e., without organizing local schools, local courts, a local administration, local organs of authority, local sociopolitical and educational institutions with guaranteed full right of use of the local native language of the masses in all spheres of sociopolitical work." [9] So arose the nationality policy which would later find a formula in the idea of Soviet culture as "national in form and socialist in content."

Implementing the policy of national-territorial autonomy was one of the chief tasks of Narkomnats. To that end the commissariat was structured along national lines. Polish, Byelorussian, Latvian, Jewish, Armenian, and Moslem national commissariats were created within it, and national sections were set up to concern themselves with such smaller national groups on Russian territory as the Estonians, the Germans, the Kirghiz, the Kalmyks, and the mountain tribes of the Caucasus. The Moslem commissariat was renamed "Tartar-Bashkir" after the autonomous republic of that name was organized in 1918 as a pilot project of autonomization. Narkomnats published a weekly official gazette called *Zhizn' natsional'nostei*

9. *Stalin*, IV, 75–76. The appeal was also published as a *Pravda* article on April 9, 1918.

(Nationality Life) and various publications in non-Russian languages. Under a reorganization carried out in 1920 the national commissariats became regular departments of the central organization, and affiliated sections were created in the executive committees of regional soviets. In that same year a Council of Nationalities was formed as a Narkomnats collegium in which each nationality in the RSFSR had representation. Under the 1924 Constitution, the Council of Nationalities became the second chamber of the USSR's legislative assembly, and Narkomnats was dissolved on the ground that it had fulfilled its essential mission.[10]

In May 1918 Stalin opened a preparatory conference on the creation of the Tartar-Bashkir Autonomous Soviet Republic with a short address that restated with studied clarity his centralist philosophy of Soviet nationality policy. He rejected as divisive and anti-Soviet a "purely nationalist" type of autonomy under which bodies representing a given national or ethnic group would have charge of the affairs of this group without regard to areas of residence on Soviet territory. The only acceptable type of autonomy was one exercised through the Soviet organization of a region in which one or more distinct national groups predominated. Further, it was undesirable to provide nationality representation through a bicameral legislature like those in North America and Switzerland, with their attendant red tape and anti-revolutionary bias. What the country needed in the present historical situation was "a strong Russia-wide state authority capable of conclusively quelling the enemies of socialism and of organizing a new, communist economy." Regional and local organs of authority set up on a sovereign basis would only stand in the way of solving these tasks. Hence it was necessary to leave in the hands of the central authority "all functions of importance to the country" and to endow the autonomous region mainly with administrative-political and cultural functions of a

10. A. Denisov, "Narodnyi kommissariat po delam natsional'nostei," *Bol'-shaia sovetskaia entsiklopediia*, Vol. XLI (Moscow, 1931), pp. 213–214. For details on the structure and activities of Narkomnats, see E. H. Carr, *The Bolshevik Revolution 1917–1923*, I (London, 1951), pp. 281–291. On the disintegration of the Russian Empire in 1917–18 and its reconstitution under Soviet rule, see Pipes, *Formation of the Soviet Union*, chs. II–V.

purely regional character, such as schools, courts, and the use of the native language.[11]

Stalin's deputy Pestkovsky took the lead in setting up Narkomnats, and because of Stalin's inability to give this work his undivided attention the vice commissar very likely continued to provide much of the organizational direction during the twenty months of his service in the commissariat. He later recalled having sympathized with the Left Communist elements in Narkomnats who favored an economic approach over Stalin's national-territorial one, and also that Stalin had personally retained overall responsibility for policy toward eastern nationalities while allowing him to oversee the work among the western ones, such as the Poles and Latvians.[12] Another figure upon whom Stalin learned to rely at this time was Ivan P. Tovstukha, a thirty-year-old revolutionary veteran who had entered the party in 1913. Tovstukha, a Ukrainian, joined Narkomnats in early 1918 and showed pronounced organizing talent. He left it in 1921 to become head of Stalin's personal secretariat.[13] This able and self-effacing man, the first of Stalin's private secretaries, would in time become also the first of his biographers.

Going to War

For about two years, starting in June 1918, Stalin's regular governmental duties took second place to activity connected with the critical situation confronting the regime. Like many of the other party leaders, he devoted his energies to the supreme end of ensuring the Revolution's survival in the military struggle against the Whites. In brief, he went to war.

Although heavily dependent upon the upheaval in the country-

11. *Stalin*, IV, 87–89.

12. Pestkovsky, "Vospominaniia," pp. 127, 130. For documentary evidence on Pestkovsky's role in organizing Narkomnats, see M. P. Iroshnikov, *Sozdanie sovetskogo tsentral'nogo gosudarstvennogo apparata: sovet narodnykh komissarov i narodnye komissariaty. Oktiabr' 1917 g.–ianvar' 1918 g.*, 2nd ed. (Leningrad, 1967), p. 237 and pp. 238–239 n. Iroshnikov also emphasizes the organizing role of F. M. Seniuta, the first office manager of the institution.

13. For Tovstukha's career, see his obituary in *Pravda*, August 16, 1935, and "I. P. Tovstukha," *Voprosy istorii KPSS*, No. 4 (1969), pp. 128–130.

side, the Bolshevik Revolution was urban-based. The taking of
power in Petrograd, Moscow, and other main cities was accomplished in a few weeks and without great bloodshed. But given the
presence of social forces unreconciled to the Revolution, the chaotic
conditions prevailing in much of the vast country, the difficulties
of transport and communication, and the availability of staging-
grounds for armed counter-revolution, the relatively easy initial
phase was bound to give way, as it did, to the fury of Russia's
Civil War of 1918–20.

White (i.e., anti-Soviet) Russian armies took the field under
such former tsarist officers as Generals Denikin, Yudenich, and
Wrangel. Anti-Bolshevik regional governments arose, among them
the regime headed by Admiral Kolchak and based at Omsk, in
Siberia. Military intervention by outside powers—chiefly France,
Great Britain, Japan, and the United States—brought the Whites
not only munitions and supplies but also some support, however
indecisive, in fighting men. Meanwhile, the Reds found their talented
war leader in Trotsky, who relinquished the Foreign Commissariat
to become war commissar and chairman of the Revolutionary War
Council of the Republic. Through mobilization—initially of workers
in Petrograd and Moscow—the Red Army grew into a force of
800,000 by the end of 1918 and nearly four times that number a
year later.

The fortunes of the Bolshevik regime reached their lowest
point in the summer of 1918. The German Army occupied the
Ukraine and other territories detached from Russia under the
Brest-Litovsk Treaty. Anti-Bolshevik movements controlled parts
of the Volga region to the east and the Don Cossack region to the
southeast. The territory actually under Soviet rule was reduced to
the historic Russian heartland—the provinces around Petrograd and
Moscow and in the black-earth region farther south and southeast
of the capital. The crisis was made all the more desperate by hunger.
With industry in a state of partial collapse and inflation rife, normal
exchange between town and country was disrupted. The peasants
had little incentive to supply the towns with grain and other produce.
In these circumstances, the regime's struggle for survival became in

RUSSIA AFTER
THE REVOLUTION

1918 } Limits of counterrevolutionary
1919 } movements

large part a battle for bread. Armed requisitioning detachments were sent into the countryside to take grain by force. To mobilize peasant assistance in the confiscation policy, the government organized "committees of the poor" in many villages. These consisted of poorer peasants who were often hungry themselves and who were given the task—in return for a share of the confiscated food—of helping Soviet organizations to extract grain from the "kulaks" (as the more well-to-do peasants were called) and any others suspected of harboring a surplus. So the countryside itself became the scene of class war, very often of a bloody kind.

Such were the circumstances under which the system of War Communism came into being and which prompted the government to proclaim the Soviet Republic a "military camp" in a decree of September 2, 1918. War Communism has been described as a compound of war emergency and socialist dogma. Its main features, in addition to the forcible food requisitions, were extreme centralization of economic life, the state's effort to take both production and distribution into its own hands as far as possible, the compulsory mobilization of labor, and the attempt to abolish money in favor of direct exchange in kind.[14] It remained in force until 1921, when the regime proclaimed the New Economic Policy in order to revive the shattered economy. Under the NEP, forcible grain requisitions were replaced with a graduated tax in kind upon the peasant farmsteads, a money economy was restored, and private enterprise was legalized in agriculture, the service trades, and parts of light industry.

On May 29, 1918, during the most difficult period, Stalin was appointed director of food supplies in southern Russia. A few days later he set out from Moscow in a special train, accompanied by a detachment of Red Army men, and traveled southeast to the city of Tsaritsyn, on the lower Volga (renamed Stalingrad in 1925, and Volgograd in 1961). This key center, a gateway to the grain-producing North Caucasus, was defended by the Tenth Army, a largely

14. William H. Chamberlin, *The Russian Revolution 1917–1921*, 2 vols. (New York, 1965), Vol. II, *1918–1921: From the Civil War to the Consolidation of Power*, pp. 96–103.

partisan Red fighting force under the command of Stalin's old friend Kliment Voroshilov, who had served during the war years as a noncommissioned officer in the tsarist army. The city was gaining renown as a "Red Verdun"; its retention by the Bolsheviks was of great importance in preventing a possible link-up of White forces in the Cossack lands of the North Caucasus with those farther east. Stalin arrived on June 6. The next day he wired Lenin that he was taking urgent steps to bring order to the city's economic life and was organizing the shipment of large quantities of grain by rail.[15]

He took command of the situation with his customary imperiousness and dispatch. According to Voroshilov's later reminiscences, Stalin's arrival in Tsaritsyn was followed in a short time by both a reorganization of the forces at the front outside the city and "a ruthless purge of the rear, administered by an iron hand." When, for example, an engineer named Alexeyev and his two sons arrived on the scene from Moscow and came under suspicion of being in the service of counter-revolution, Stalin's order was: "Shoot them." Not only Alexeyev and his sons, but numbers of others merely suspected of conspiring against the Bolsheviks, were likewise summarily shot.[16] It should be borne in mind in this connection that the crisis facing the regime was aggravated by events that transpired in Moscow shortly after Stalin's departure. Leading figures among the Left Socialist-Revolutionaries, a radical element hitherto represented in the Lenin government, acted on their opposition to the Brest-Litovsk Treaty and to aspects of Bolshevik peasant policy by assassinating the German ambassador, Count Mirbach, and staging an abortive anti-government revolt in the capital. Terrorism against the revolutionary regime intensified the terrorism on its part, and this was not confined to the operations carried out by the official

15. *Stalin*, IV, 116–117.
16. K. E. Voroshilov, *Stalin and the Armed Forces of the USSR* (Moscow, 1951), pp. 18–19. Voroshilov cited as his source for this episode an article by one Colonel Nosovich, who was chief of operations of the Tenth Army when Stalin arrived at Tsaritsyn but later went over to the White side and gave an account of his Tsaritsyn experiences in an anti-Bolshevik paper, *Donskaia volna,* on February 3, 1919. According to Nosovich's article, as cited by Voroshilov, Alexeyev was in fact involved in anti-Bolshevik activity.

security police, Dzerzhinsky's Cheka. On July 7, the day after the murder of Mirbach and the attempted SR coup, Lenin telegraphed Stalin: "It is necessary mercilessly to suppress these pitiful and hysterical adventurists who have become an instrument in the counter-revolutionaries' hands. . . . So, be ruthless against the Left SR's and keep us informed more often." To this Stalin replied: "Your communication received. Everything will be done to forestall possible surprises. Be assured that our hand will not tremble." [17] There is no indication that it did.

In August 1918 Trotsky went east in his armored train and set up headquarters at the small town of Sviazhsk, near Kazan, on the Volga. There he rallied the demoralized Red units into a fighting force that in early September captured Kazan in a battle that has been called "the Valmy of the Russian Revolution." [18] In the aftermath of this victory, anti-Soviet forces were cleared from the Volga region. During the summer months of 1918, however, the Reds at Tsaritsyn were under heavy pressure. The seizure of nearby points by hostile Cossack bands not only interfered with Stalin's food mission but endangered the city itself. In these circumstances he directly involved himself in military matters. On July 7 he wrote to Lenin:

I am rushing to the front. I write on business only. The line south of Tsaritsyn has not yet been restored. I am driving and bawling out everyone who needs it, and hope we will restore it quickly. You may be sure that we will spare no one, neither ourselves nor others, and we will, no matter what, produce the grain. If only our military "specialists" (bunglers!) had not been idle and asleep, the line would not have been broken; and if it is restored, this will not be due to them but in spite of them. . . . In view of poor communications with the center, it is necessary to have a man on the spot with full powers so that urgent measures can be taken promptly.

In a further message sent three days later, Stalin said: "For the good of the cause, I must have military powers. I've already written

17. *Stalin*, IV, 118, 420.
18. Chamberlin, *The Russian Revolution*, II, 118. At the original Valmy the French revolutionary forces for the first time decisively checked the invading pro-monarchist armies.

about this, but have received no reply. Very well. In that event I myself, without formalities, will remove those army commanders and commissars who are ruining things. That's what the interests of the cause bid me to do, and naturally the absence of a paper from Trotsky won't stop me." [19] This bold assertion of superior authority won the day for Stalin. On July 19 the Revolutionary War Council of the Republic created a War Council of the North Caucasus military district and appointed Stalin as head of it. He was charged with "establishing order, consolidating the detachments into regular units, and establishing a proper command, at the same time dismissing all insubordinates." The telegram of appointment carried the notation: "The present telegram is sent with Lenin's approval." [20] Apparently Trotsky had not wished to sign it himself.

The hostilities in which Stalin became involved at Tsaritsyn were thus directed not only against the Whites but also against Trotsky. The ostensible issue was the role of the military specialists. With Lenin's support, Trotsky at this time was building up the Red Army as a professional military organization. Because of the shortage of officers (then called "commanders") from the working classes, large numbers of former tsarist officers were being recruited as "military specialists." They served in command capacities but under the supervision of Bolshevik political commissars who, according to the system then devised, had to countersign their orders. The policy of heavy reliance upon the old officers encountered opposition from some Red commanders who scorned "bourgeois" military men and favored partisan methods of warfare. The main center of this "miltary opposition" (as it subsequently came to be called) was the North Caucasus. The ringleaders were Voroshilov and some other Red commanders, including a colorful former sergeant-major of the cavalry named Semeon Budenny, who became famous during the Civil War as the leader of a Red cavalry army. At Tsaritsyn Stalin espoused their cause. This, undoubtedly, was the reason for Trotsky's great reluctance to endow him with the

19. *Stalin*, IV, 118–121. The second of the two letters to Lenin was first published in this volume, in 1951.
20. *Stalin*, IV, 450; Voroshilov, *Stalin and the Armed Forces*, p. 14.

plenipotentiary military powers that he insistently solicited from Lenin.

Asserting these powers, Stalin encouraged the local Red commanders' insubordination to orders from the high command. After the restoration of the line south of the city in mid-July, he ordered the arrest of A. E. Snesarev, the senior local military specialist, and a large number of the headquarters staff. The latter were imprisoned on a barge in the middle of the Volga. On a telegram of protest from Trotsky, who insisted that the military staff and commissariat be permitted to function at Tsaritsyn, he inscribed the notation "Disregard." [21] After an inspection commission arrived to investigate these matters, Snesarev was released and shifted to a command position in another sector. But the headquarters staff was not so fortunate; the barge sank unexpectedly with all aboard.[22] When N. N. Sytin, another military specialist, was appointed commander on the southern front, Stalin—in defiance of instructions from Moscow not to interfere with the military commander in operational matters—countermanded Sytin's initial orders and afterwards removed him from his command.[23] Responding to the challenge, Trotsky cabled Lenin on October 4:

I insist categorically on Stalin's recall. Things are going badly at the Tsaritsyn Front in spite of superabundant forces. Voroshilov is capable of commanding a regiment, not an army of fifty thousand. However, I shall leave him in command of the Tenth Army at Tsaritsyn, provided he reports to the commander of the Army of the South, Sytin. Thus far Tsaritsyn has not even sent reports of operations to Kozlov. . . . If that is not done by tomorrow, I shall remand Voroshilov and Minin to court martial and shall publish the fact in an Army Order. . . . Tsaritsyn must either submit or take the consequences. We have a colossal superiority of forces, but there is utter anarchy at the top. I can put a stop to it in twenty-four hours, provided I have your firm and clear-cut support. At all events, this is the only course I can see.[24]

21. Voroshilov, *Stalin and the Armed Forces,* p. 19.

22. Roy A. Medvedev, *Let History Judge: The Origins and Consequences of Stalinism* (New York, 1971), p. 13.

23. *Ibid.*

24. Trotsky, *Stalin,* pp. 288–289. On the following day, Trotsky sent Lenin a further wire saying that he had received from the commander-in-chief, Vatsetis, a telegram saying: "Stalin's military order No. 118 must be canceled. I have issued

Lenin gave way, and Stalin was recalled from Tsaritsyn in the second half of October. According to Trotsky's account, Sverdlov personally went to Tsaritsyn in a special train and brought Stalin back. On the way Sverdlov arranged a meeting on board the train between Stalin and Trotsky. The ensuing conversation, as later recounted by Trotsky, concerned the Tsaritsyn Red commanders: "Do you really want to dismiss all of them?" Stalin asked in a tone of exaggerated subservience. "They're fine boys." "Those fine boys will ruin the Revolution, which can't wait for them to grow up," I answered him. "All I want is to draw Tsaritsyn back into Soviet Russia." [25]

Although Stalin had done what he could to expedite the shipment of grain from the south, this first major episode of his participation in the Civil War was militarily unsuccessful. Soviet military historians have concluded on the basis of their archival researches since his death that he failed to grasp the role of the military specialists, clung to guerrilla methods, and did not take the requisite initiative to assist the North Caucasian army and the troops fighting in Baku. Along with Voroshilov, he showed lack of discipline toward the high command and the commander of the southern front. His intervention in the affairs of this front "complicated" the organization and supply of the front's forces and their battle employment. He showed "sectionalism and separatism" in allocating supplies to the troops of the Tsaritsyn sector. He overrated the importance of this sector and drew the best forces and equipment to it, thereby weakening other, no less significant sectors.[26] On the latter point, the published correspondence shows that Stalin, while in Tsaritsyn, bombarded Lenin with urgent requests for military equipment and drew alluring pictures of what it would mean for the progress of the war if he could obtain it. One such message promised the capture of Baku, the North Caucasus, and Turkestan if Lenin would "smash all obstacles" and send him immediately several light minesweepers

---

full instructions to the commander of the southern front, Sytin. Stalin's activities undermine all my plans." Order No. 118 must have been the one dismissing Sytin.

25. *Ibid.*, pp. 288, 289.

26. *Ocherki po istoriografii sovetskogo obshchestva,* chief ed. P. A. Zhilin (Moscow, 1965), p. 18.

and two submarines. This letter, dated August 31, 1918, ended with the words: "I press the hand of my dear and beloved Ilyich." [27]

The inglorious ending of Stalin's mission to Tsaritsyn caused him no serious political setback. On October 11, before his departure for Moscow, he was appointed a member of the Revolutionary War Council of the Republic—very likely in order to salve his sensitivity in connection with the impending recall. Nor did the unflattering circumstances surrounding the recall receive any publicity. The people's commissar was interviewed on his return by a *Pravda* correspondent, who reported in detail his assessment of the situation on the southern front. Stalin spoke of Tsaritsyn as the enemy's central objective in the south on account of its special strategic significance in separating the White forces of the Don region from those near Astrakhan and in the Ural mountains to the east. He praised the capable administrators in the rear whose mobilization and supply work had been instrumental in saving Tsaritsyn, and explained the successes of the army "primarily by its awareness and discipline." [28]

Moreover, Stalin now acquired new governmental duties in addition to his responsibility for Narkomnats. In November he was elected to the All-Russian Central Executive Committee, and also to membership of its directorate, or Presidium. More important, when the Central Executive Committee on November 30 passed a resolution setting up a Council of Workers' and Peasants' Defense under Lenin's presidency, as an overlord committee to direct the mobilization of all the country's resources for war, Stalin became a member of this body along with Trotsky; the commissar for railways, Vladimir Nevsky; the assistant food commissar, N. Brukhanov; and the chairman of the extraordinary commission for supply, Leonid Krasin. Stalin took office as representative of the Central Executive Committee and became Lenin's deputy on the council. [29] Commenting on the appointment, Trotsky later wrote: "Lenin wanted to give

27. *Stalin*, IV, 127. The obvious occasion of the tender concluding expression was the previous day's attempt on Lenin's life by Fanya Kaplan.

28. *Ibid.*, pp. 148–151. The interview appeared in *Pravda* on October 30, 1918.

29. *Stalin*, IV, 455; Chamberlin, *The Russian Revolution*, II, 35.

Stalin some satisfaction for removing him from the army in Tsaritsyn; I wanted to give Stalin the chance to formulate openly his
criticisms and proposals, without wetting the powder in the War
Department." [30] Even accepting this explanation, it is inconceivable
that Lenin would have wanted Stalin to sit on the defense council,
particularly as his deputy, had he not continued to set great value
upon the man's executive capacities and dependability, not to mention his unswerving loyalty to the cause. Very likely he saw the
conflict between Stalin and Trotsky as the result of an unfortunate
personal incompatibility between two proud and strong-willed lieutenants, each of whom was devoted to him, and both of whom, in
different ways, were indispensable.

Their conflict of course quickly became reciprocal. Trotsky,
for example, complained privately to Lenin that Stalin was re-
establishing in the army a "regime of grand dukes"—an allusion to
the tsarist tradition under which grand dukes given army assignments would disregard their superior officers and cause chaos in the
command.[31] However, the quarrel was one-sided in its origins; the
aggressor was Stalin. Further, the issue of the military specialists,
for all its importance, was not the conflict's cause but only the first
of the many arenas in which it was fought. The underlying motivation on Stalin's part was psychological. What impelled him to take
the offensive against Trotsky was, it seems, a powerful animosity
against a man who, by virtue of the role he was playing in the Revolution, was spoiling his own life-scenario.

As a very young man Stalin had formed a hero-identification
with Lenin. He had dreamed of becoming the leader's alter ego and
closest companion-in-arms. Now, in spite of all that he had done
to realize the dream, in spite of the special relationship that he had
achieved with Lenin in 1917 and their continuing closeness, the
shadow of Trotsky—this latecomer and interloper among the Bolsheviks (as Stalin saw it), this erstwhile fellow-traveler of the Mensheviks and opponent of Lenin in the revolutionary movement, this

30. Trotsky, *Stalin,* pp. 291–292. One would have thought Trotsky's motive
more pertinent to the appointment of Stalin to the Revolutionary War Council of
the Republic because of the latter's direct concern with military operations.
31. *Ibid.,* p. 270.

Jew—had fallen across the whole enterprise. He had appeared in Petrograd in the midst of the Revolution and taken a prominent part in ensuing events; and now, as war commissar, he was continuing to do so. He was invading Stalin's special relationship with Lenin. In sum, he was trying to cheat Stalin of his just deserts, to rob him of his hard-won role as Lenin II of the revolutionary movement. Not because of any one thing that Trotsky had done but because of what he had become, a hero of the Revolution alongside Lenin and a much-acclaimed figure, Stalin felt threatened in his very depths. And because he was incapable of scaling down his ambition to the size of his real accomplishments and potentialities, he reacted with jealousy, resentment, and vindictive hostility toward the source of the threat. As his correspondence from Tsaritsyn shows very clearly, he attempted to tear Trotsky down, first of all in the eyes of Lenin. Trotsky, who was both ignorant of and uninterested in Stalin's inner world, made it all the easier for him to act upon his animosity simply by being his imperious unbending self and making no concessions to Stalin's *amour-propre*. But it is hard to imagine that a more understanding response by Trotsky would have seriously altered the outcome. This conflict was not accidental.

Stalin's impulse to tear down Trotsky had, in part, a retrospective bearing. He wanted not only to disparage and discredit Trotsky's present performance as war commissar but also to belittle his role in the epic events of the previous year. An opportunity to begin doing this arose shortly after the return from Tsaritsyn to Moscow. Stalin wrote a short article on "The October Coup (24 and 25 October 1917 in Petrograd)," which appeared in *Pravda* on the coup's first anniversary, now celebrated as Soviet Russia's national holiday. A passage which would be deleted when the article was reprinted in later years paid tribute to Trotsky: "All the work of practical organization of the insurrection took place under the immediate direction of the chairman of the Petrograd Soviet, Comrade Trotsky. One may confidently say that the party is obliged primarily and chiefly to Comrade Trotsky for the swift passing over of the garrison to the side of the Soviet and for the able handling of the work of the Military Revolutionary Committee. Comrade

Trotsky's chief assistants were Comrades Antonov and Podvoi-sky." [32] Overall, however, the article was a subtle put-down of Trotsky, whose role—in this very passage of praise—was treated as essentially technical rather than as the political as well as technical one that it actually was. In Stalin's narrative the political hero of the events of the two crucial days (aside from the Baltic sailors and the Red Guards from the Vyborg district, who played a supporting role), was made out to have been the party Central Committee: "The inspirer of the overturn from beginning to end was the party Central Committee headed by Comrade Lenin." Trotsky was not in error when he said many years later: "The purpose of the article was to strike a blow at my prestige, turning against me the authority of the Central Committee headed by Lenin." [33]

The Quest for Martial Glory

The Tsaritsyn experience appears to have whetted Stalin's appetite for a role in the war, and opportunities were plentiful. Before long he went off on a new mission. Together with Dzerzhinsky, he traveled east to Viatka in January 1919 to investigate for the Central Committee the causes of the surrender of the Urals city of Perm by the Reds' Third Army. Then, in May, he was assigned to Petrograd to bolster the panicky Zinoviev in the face of menacing movements by General Yudenich's Estonia-based White army and threats of desertion and mutiny in the city and its environs. He remained in Petrograd through the month of June, acting with his customary unceremoniousness. On June 16, after the recapture of the fort of Krasnaia Gorka on the Gulf of Finland, the garrison of which had mutinied a few days earlier, he sent Lenin a telegram saying:

Naval experts assert that the capture of Krasnaia Gorka from the sea runs counter to naval science. I can only deplore such so-called

---

32. *Pravda*, November 6, 1918, and reprinted without this passage in *Stalin*, IV, 152–154. Because of the change of Russia's calendar in February 1918 from the old style to the new, between which there was a difference of thirteen days, the revolutionary events of October 24–25 old style came to be celebrated on November 6–7 of each year.

33. Trotsky, *Stalin*, p. 291.

science. The swift capture of Gorka was due to the grossest interference in operations by me and civilians generally, even to the point of countermanding orders on land and sea and imposing our own.

I consider it my duty to declare that I shall continue to act in this way in future, despite all my reverence for science.[34]

This boastful message, rationalizing Stalin's high-handedness in terms of military results, may be read as an attempted retrospective self-justification for his behavior toward the military specialists—and Trotsky—at Tsaritsyn. But it is also significant as a revelation of a wish to make his mark in military history. The clear implication is that this "civilian" could teach some lessons in strategic art to the military professionals.

That Stalin harbored military ambitions is not surprising. One obvious spur was a desire to challenge the laurels that Trotsky (another "civilian") was winning by his dynamic direction of the Red Army. But we may also recall that Stalin's earliest dreams of future glory were martial in character, centering on an urge to emulate the exploits of the intrepid fighter Koba—the name by which close friends addressed him, even now. This may help to explain an interest that he had long taken in the military side of revolution. Under the inspiration of the 1905 events, Stalin wrote an article on "Armed Insurrection and Our Tactics" for *Proletariatis brdzola*. In it he took issue with the idea that the party's role should or could be confined to political leadership preparatory to armed insurrection. The party must likewise take charge of the "technical" aspect, for example by organizing workshops for the manufacture of explosives, by creating specially trained fighting squads capable of leading the rebellious populace into battle, and by enlisting the aid not only of military persons belonging to the party but also of other comrades "who by their innate capacities and inclinations will be quite useful in this area." [35] There can hardly be any doubt that the article's author classified himself as one of the comrades in the latter category.

---

34. *Stalin*, IV, 261. Trotsky says that "Lenin was annoyed by this tone of provocative braggadocio" (*Stalin*, p. 307).
35. *Stalin*, I, 132–137. The article was originally published in July 1905.

Stalin returned to Moscow on July 3, 1919, after completing his mission to Petrograd. The Petrograd front had become quieter after mid-June, and it remained so until Yudenich launched his big offensive against the city in the autumn of 1919. It was then that Trotsky went to take charge of the situation. He rallied the Red defenders, helped turn imminent defeat into victory, and returned to Moscow to find himself hailed on all sides as Petrograd's savior. At a meeting of the recently created Politburo, whose members were Lenin, Trotsky, Stalin, Kamenev, and Nikolai Krestinsky, with Bukharin, Zinoviev, and Kalinin as candidate members, it was decided to confer the Order of the Red Banner upon Trotsky in honor of the great Petrograd victory. According to Trotsky's account, Kamenev, in some embarrassment, moved at the close of this meeting that the same decoration be conferred upon Stalin. "For what?" inquired Kalinin. Afterwards, Kalinin was cornered by Bukharin, who explained: "Can't you understand? This is Lenin's idea. Stalin can't live unless he has what someone else has. He will never forgive it." At a celebration meeting held a few days later in the Bolshoi Theater in Moscow, Trotsky reported on the military situation and received the decoration. When the chairman announced toward the end that Stalin, too, had been awarded the Order of the Red Banner, Trotsky tried to applaud and two or three hesitant claps followed his. "A sort of bewilderment crept through the hall; it was especially noticeable after the ovations that had gone before. Stalin himself was wisely absent." [36]

Stalin's next major war assignment after Petrograd was in the south, where General Denikin's forces captured Kursk, Voronezh, and Orel in September–October 1919 in what was envisaged as a march on Moscow. The question of the strategy of the counter-offensive against Denikin was a controversial one. A strategic plan favored by the Soviet commander-in-chief, S. S. Kamenev,[37] called for an advance against Denikin from the southeast via the Don

36. L. Trotsky, *My Life* (New York, 1930), pp. 432–433.
37. Not to be confused with the Bolshevik leader Lev Kamenev. S. S. Kamenev was a former tsarist staff officer. He served as Red Army chief of staff under Trotsky as war commissar.

steppes. From July onward Trotsky opposed that plan, arguing instead for a southward push on the central sector. As late as September 6, in reply to a message from Trotsky, Leonid Serebriakov, and M. Lashevich along these lines, the Politburo upheld the commander-in-chief's strategic plan. Under the pressure of Denikin's further advance, however, the Politburo on September 14 commissioned Trotsky to transmit to the commander-in-chief a new directive on the necessity of capturing Kursk and moving upon Kharkov and the Donets coal basin (Donbas).[38] Consequently, when Stalin joined the revolutionary war council of the southern front on October 3, a new strategic plan was being implemented. Reserves were massed for a counteroffensive in the Kursk-Kharkov direction; the central sector of the southern front was now the decisive one. Although Stalin had concurred in the Politburo decision of September 6 to support the commander-in-chief against Trotsky, he now saw the validity of the new plan. Also, he became alarmed over indications that the commander-in-chief still wanted to maintain pressure from the southeast. On November 15 he wrote a letter to Lenin declaring that "the old plan, already repealed by life, must not under any conditions be galvanized. . . ." In explanation he pointed out that the old plan envisaged an advance through hostile Cossack territory without passable roads, whereas in the Donbas the Red forces would be in an area with a friendly population and a good railway network.[39] Since on the basis of this letter

38. Trotsky, *Stalin*, pp. 318–320, 324; M. Markin, "Stalin and the Red Army," in Trotsky, *The Stalin School of Falsification* (New York, 1962), pp. 223–225. See also Chamberlin, *The Russian Revolution*, II, 210, 246–247; and N. Kuzmin, S. Naida, Iu. Petrov, and S. Shishkin, "O nekotorykh voprosakh istorii grazhdanskoi voiny," *Kommunist*, No. 12 (1956), pp. 64–66.

39. *Stalin*, IV, 275–277. The letter is here dated October 15, 1919. A Soviet military historian, N. F. Kuzmin, has shown (*Voprosy istorii*, No. 7 [1956], pp. 30–32) that the date must have been November 15. He reveals that the original typescript of Stalin's letter, preserved in Soviet archives, bears the obviously wrong date "15.IX" (September 15). The date of October 15 was chosen when the letter was reprinted in Stalin's works in 1951. Kuzmin's demonstration that November 15 must have been the date is reinforced by the consideration that the typist could easily have typed "IX" instead of "XI." His argument further confirms Markin's surmise that "Stalin must have written his letter of criticism sometime early in November, and hardly prior to that time . . ." ("Stalin and the Red Army," p. 226).

he would later be credited with authorship of the winning strategy against Denikin, it should be mentioned that the arguments used in it repeated those Trotsky had vainly been urging upon the Politburo for some time.

Stalin was appointed political commissar on the southwestern front in May 1920, after the Polish Army under Marshal Pilsudski invaded the Ukraine and captured Kiev. When the Red Army repulsed the Poles, the Soviet leaders had to decide whether or not to push the counteroffensive onto Polish territory. Trotsky, supported by Dzerzhinsky and Karl Radek (both of whom knew Poland well), opposed a march on Warsaw, believing that it could succeed only in the event of a workers' uprising in Poland itself, which in turn seemed improbable. Stalin, too, expressed misgivings, but he wound up voting with the majority of leaders who supported Lenin in his desire to open a door to European Communist revolution via Poland.[40] In early July, the Red Army forces on the western front, commanded by an outstanding young former tsarist officer turned Bolshevik, Mikhail Tukhachevsky, began an advance that brought them to the outskirts of Warsaw by mid-August. The forces on the southwestern front, commanded by A. I. Egorov, had meanwhile abandoned their plan of northwesterly advance toward Brest and Lublin and were pushing southwest toward Lvov in the expectation that capture of this major center would provoke a revolution in Galicia. Permission for this change of direction was obtained from the commander-in-chief in Moscow. Lenin reportedly opposed it, commenting: "Who would ever go to Warsaw by way of Lvov?"[41]

After it became clear at the end of July that the drive for Lvov was not succeeding, the Politburo decided, on August 2, to redirect major elements of the southwestern front, including Budenny's mounted army, toward Brest and Lublin according to the

40. Trotsky, *Stalin*, pp. 327–328; Isaac Deutscher, *Stalin: A Political Biography*, 2nd ed. (New York, 1966), pp. 215–216. For the life of Radek, see Warner Lerner, *Karl Radek: The Last Internationalist* (Stanford, 1970).

41. S. F. Naida, in *Materialy vsesoiuznogo soveshchaniia zaveduiushchikh kafedrami obshchestvennykh nauk* (Moscow, 1958), p. 166. Professor Naida cites Lenin's aide V. D. Bonch-Bruevich as the source for the remark. Bonch-Bruevich first quoted it in 1931 in his book *Na boevykh postakh fevral'skoi i oktiabr'skoi revoliutsii*.

original plan, so as to cover Tukhachevsky's dangerously exposed left flank. The remainder of the southwestern front's forces were to be transferred to a new southern front directed against General Wrangel's forces in the Crimea. Stalin did not object to these instructions when informed of them by Lenin, although his telegram of reply, dated August 3, cautioned against disrupting the southwestern front's administrative setup. In a further telegram sent the following day, he spoke—overconfidently, as it turned out—of Poland's war exhaustion and the possibility of defeating Wrangel in a matter of days.[42] Despite Stalin's lack of objection to the new directive, however, the forces ordered north were for the time being kept in the fighting for Lvov. On August 11, Commander-in-Chief Kamenev sent a new directive demanding abandonment of the Lvov operation and immediate transfer of these forces to Tukhachevsky's command. The necessary transfer order received the signature of Egorov as commander of the southwestern front but required countersigning by at least one political commissar to become valid. Stalin, now in open insubordination, would not countersign. On August 13, after fresh representations from the commander-in-chief and direct intervention by the Central Committee, the other political commissar of the southwestern front, R. I. Berzin, was prevailed upon to sign.[43] But even after that date, Budenny's cavalry continued—evidently at Stalin's behest—to engage in heavy fighting in the Lvov area. On August 17, Stalin was recalled to Moscow. When, some days later, the mounted army finally went to assist the western front, it was too late to save the situation. The Polish Army had opened its counteroffensive on August 16 with a drive into the vacuum between the two fronts, and Tukhachevsky's forces were in general retreat.[44]

No single cause explains the Soviet debacle. But it is clear

42. Naida, in *Materialy*, pp. 163–164. Unlike some other telegrams sent by Stalin during the Civil War, these two were not included in his collected works.

43. *Ibid.*, pp. 165–166; *Ocherki po istoriografii*, p. 167 n. Berzin at first declined to countersign on the grounds that his province was affairs of the rear and that he was not in touch with military operations at the front.

44. Naida, in *Materialy*, pp. 166–167; *Ocherki po istoriografii*, p. 167 n. See also Kuzmin *et al.*, "O nekotorykh voprosakh," pp. 67–70.

from the account just given, which is based upon writings of Soviet
military historians published after Stalin's death, that his insubordination was an extremely significant contributing factor. The historians' researches have completely confirmed the conclusion of
Trotsky that Stalin, considering it more important to take Lvov
than to help others take Warsaw, "was waging his own war." [45]
This conclusion appears to have been widely shared in Bolshevik
circles during the twenties. When the causes of the defeat were debated at a closed session of the Tenth Party Congress in 1921,
Stalin reportedly laid responsibility upon Ivan Smilga, who had been
the chief political commissar on the western front. Smilga, he said,
had deceived the party by failing to fulfill his promise to take Warsaw by a certain date. Protesting, Trotsky replied that Smilga's
"promise" had really been no more than a hope and in any event
could not eliminate the element of the unexpected. "In silent hostility the congress listened to the sullen orator with that yellow glint
in his eyes," Trotsky recalled. "With that speech of his Stalin hurt
no one but himself. Not a single vote supported him." [46] In *The
Campaign for the Vistula,* based on his lectures of February 7–10,
1923, at the Red Army Military Academy, Tukhachevsky stated:
"For a whole series of unexpected reasons, the high command's
efforts to bring about a regrouping of the great bulk of the southwestern front's forces in the Lublin direction were unsuccessful,
and the regrouping remained hanging in air." [47] Numerous Soviet military writings of the twenties made the same point in one
or another way. In his monograph *Lvov–Warsaw,* put out in 1929
as an apologia for the southwestern command, Egorov complained
that the disastrous role of the southwestern front had come to be
taken for granted in Soviet military teaching. Not even Egorov,
however, praised Stalin's performance in the Polish campaign.

45. Trotsky, *Stalin,* p. 329.
46. *Ibid.* Trotsky adds: "Lenin, terribly upset by the dissensions, joined
in the discussion and expressed himself to the effect that we did not want to blame
anybody personally. Why does not Stalin publish the stenographic record of this
debate?" In 1973 the record in question remains unpublished.
47. M. N. Tukhachevsky, *Izbrannye proizvedeniia,* I, *1919–1927* (Moscow,
1964), p. 154.

Although Stalin acquired valuable military experience in the Civil War, he did not emerge from it with a party reputation for having a first-class military mind. He was not one of the principal organizers of the Red Army, nor did he show the qualities of an outstanding military leader. He gave plentiful evidence, moreover, of those objectionable personal qualities to which reference was made in March 1917 when the matter of his reappointment to the Central Committee's Russian Bureau came up. His grudge against Trotsky became a palpable fact of political life inside the party. On his travels to the front he frequently flaunted his authority and acted in a high-handed way. His behavior during the Russo-Polish war showed that he was capable of disregarding the party's best interests in order to fulfill his need to play a heroic part. And at times he was guilty of outbursts of ill temper. Thus, on February 20, 1920, he replied as follows to a message from Lenin asking him to take emergency measures to speed up the transfer of two divisions to the Caucasian front: "I am not quite clear as to why the chief concern about the Caucasian front falls primarily upon me. The strengthening of the Caucasian front properly and entirely falls upon the War Council of the Republic, the members of which, according to my information, are in good health; it is their concern and not that of Stalin, who is overburdened with work as it is." [48] Such incidents could not fail to strengthen the impression in higher party circles that Stalin was a person of difficult character.

On the other hand, there was no question about his dedication to the party cause, instinct for command, sharp intelligence, and formidable capacity for work. Whatever his military failings, he recommended himself by his wartime services as a forceful leader with an ability to size up complex situations quickly and take decisive action. When, for example, the Defense Council appointed a subcommittee to expedite the supply of cartridges, rifles, and machine guns to the army, Stalin was made head of it and was able

---

48. Markin, "Stalin and the Red Army," p. 228. Stalin's message evoked from Lenin the reproof: "It is generally necessary to give all possible assistance and not to bicker about departmental jurisdiction" (ibid.).

to report back one week later on the results of its work. When he and Dzerzhinsky went to Viatka in January 1919 to investigate the causes of the fall of Perm, they returned before the month was out with a comprehensive report that not only analyzed the local situation and outlined measures to be taken, but drew conclusions for the whole Soviet governmental process. They had found in Viatka that liaison between the governmental organizations of Moscow and this provincial center was nonexistent, that the committees of the poor in the surrounding countryside were dominated by the kulaks they were supposed to be combating, and that practically all the Soviet civil servants in Viatka—4,467 out of a total of 4,766—were holdovers from the tsarist bureaucracy. They proposed that a "control-auditing commission" be set up to investigate such "defects in the mechanism" of the people's commissariats and their local branch offices, and that this commission be directed, as one of its tasks, to create a special agency to provide training in Soviet procedures for those mostly young and experienced local officials who were showing themselves to be honest, dedicated, and hard-working.[49]

The latter proposal appears to have made a favorable impression upon Lenin, who wanted to enlist people of proletarian origin, women in particular, for a Soviet inspectorate that would become a kind of school of training for governmental administration. Perhaps as a result, Stalin was drawn into planning the reorganization and expansion of the People's Commissariat of State Control, a department that had been created in 1918 to oversee the official acts of Soviet economic organizations, the execution of governmental directives in this sphere, and the expenditure of funds. As chairman of the commission on reorganization, he reported out a plan at a meeting of the Council of People's Commissars in March 1919 and shortly afterwards was appointed commissar of the agency he had helped to reorganize. As such, one of his first official acts was to announce in the Soviet government newspaper, *Izvestia,* that the commissariat was opening a Central Bureau of Complaints and Statements. Renamed the "People's Commissariat of Worker-Peas-

49. The text of the Stalin-Dzerzhinsky report is in *Stalin,* IV, 190–224.

ant Inspection" in a further reorganization carried out in 1920, the inspectorate became familiarly known as Rabkrin. Stalin's appointment to head it was a measure both of the importance that Lenin attached to this agency and of his appreciation of Stalin's capacities. He later had occasion to make this appreciation explicit. At the Eleventh Party Congress, held in early 1922, Preobrazhensky protested that many higher party leaders were devoting too much of their time to governmental duties of secondary importance, and, citing Stalin as an example, he questioned whether any man could carry the work of two commissariats in addition to party responsibilities such as Stalin's. In reply Lenin admitted that this problem existed, and then, to show how unavoidable it was, said:

What can we do now to maintain the present situation in Narkomnats and get to the bottom of all those Turkestan, Caucasian, and other questions? These are all political questions! . . . We are resolving them and we have to have a man to whom any national representative can go and explain in detail what the problem is. Where can we find him? I don't believe that Preobrazhensky could name any candidate other than Comrade Stalin. The same applies to the Rabkrin. A gigantic job. But in order to cope with the inspection work, you have to have at the head of it a man with authority, otherwise we'll bog down and drown in petty intrigues.[50]

One further circumstance should be borne in mind in explaining why Stalin's star continued to rise in the Civil War period. In the party milieu his rude and autocratic ways were less likely to be questioned during the years of War Communism than either before or after. That "Heroic Period of the Great Russian Revolution," to use the title of Lev Kritsman's later book about it, left a deep mark upon the spirit and style of Bolshevism. The political culture of the movement underwent a certain militarization and grew more authoritarian. Lenin's writings of the time show this military-authoritarian strain despite the fact that his overall legacy to the movement was the idea of the preferability of persuasion in the party's relations with the masses. Proletarian dictatorship should not mean "a

50. *Odinnadtsatyi s"ezd RKP/b/. Mart–aprel' 1922 goda. Stenograficheskii otchet* (Moscow, 1961), pp. 84–85, 143.

jellyfish proletarian government," he wrote in 1918. No great revolution, let alone a socialist one, was conceivable without a civil war and therefore the merciless use of compulsion. "Dictatorship is iron rule, government that is revolutionarily bold, swift, and ruthless in suppressing the exploiters as well as hooligans," he went on. "But our government is excessively mild, very often it resembles jelly more than iron." Nor should the conferring of dictatorial powers upon individuals, as in the administering of the railways, be seen as something contrary to democratic Soviet principles of government; for "in the history of revolutionary movements the dictatorship of individuals was very often the expression, the vehicle, the channel of the dictatorship of the revolutionary classes. . . ." Lenin concluded: "What we need is the measured tread of the iron battalions of the proletariat." [51] Clearly, in this "iron" age of the Revolution there was maximum need and tolerance of a capable commissar of dictatorial tendency whose name signified steel.

Finally, Stalin's failure to win military laurels in the Civil War must be balanced against his success in accumulating political influence in the Soviet regime. Unlike Trotsky, who single-mindedly devoted himself to building the military organization and waging the war—and trod on no few Bolshevik toes in the process—Stalin combined his war work with politics. That is, he took full advantage of his special assignments at the front and in the rear to develop old political associations and form new ones. Some of the people he cultivated politically were the very ones whom Trotsky had antagonized by his brusque, no-nonsense approach.[52] Those years, accordingly, were the formative period of the Stalin faction in the party. Whereas Trotsky emerged from the war with much glory and little power, Stalin emerged with little glory and much power.

Glory, however, remained his aim.

51. *Lenin,* XXXVI, 190, 195, 196, 198–199, 208. The work cited is *The Immediate Tasks of the Soviet Regime.*
52. Trotsky, *Stalin,* p. 289. The reference in this passage is to Stalin's cultivation of the Tsaritsyn group of Red commanders. Elsewhere in the same book (p. 271) Trotsky writes that the Tsaritsyn group became the nucleus of the Stalin faction in the party.

The Party Politician

In a view of him widely held in the West, Stalin was the supreme "organization man" of the early Soviet period, a nonintellectual who differed from the brilliant revolutionary literati of Bolshevism in his bent for plodding, practical work in constructing the party-state. Like so many historical stereotypes, this one is seriously flawed. Insofar as it applies at all, it fits not Stalin but his former fellow exile Sverdlov, who presided over the initial organizing of the party apparatus and Soviet state structure.

Some intellectuals in the Bolshevik leadership, like Bukharin and Radek, did in fact have little taste for organizing work or administration. But others—among them Lenin, Trotsky, and Kamenev—showed formidable capacity in this field. Stalin fell somewhere in the middle of the spectrum. Whether or not one counts him among the party intellectuals (and not many did in those days), he was, as we have seen, a would-be theoretician of distinction. On the other hand, he was not particularly gifted as an organizer and administrator, although he could be quite effective in setting critical situations to order in an authoritative manner. To neither of his two commissariats did he give the sustained and imaginative direction that agencies so innovative in design especially called for. The notion of the worker-peasant inspectorate as essentially a public force against "bureaucratism" came from Lenin, and Stalin never seems to have felt at home with it. His one public pronouncement, a speech of 1920 to a conference of Rabkrin officials, was notable for its contention that the public controllers should abjure the old tsarist inspectors' search for criminal malfeasance in the bureaucracy in favor of an approach aimed at "perfecting" the institution under inspection.[53] Even before he remarked that the Rabkrin needed "a man with authority" at its head, Lenin

53. *Stalin*, IV, 367. For the difference between Lenin and Stalin in their approach to public control, see A. P. Konstantinov *et al.*, *Leninskie traditsii partiino-gosudarstvennogo kontrolia* (Leningrad, 1963), esp. pp. 11, 18; and V. Donskoi and S. Ikonnikov, "Razvitie leninskikh idei o partiino-gosudarstvennom kontrole," *Kommunist*, No. 18 (December 1962), p. 32.

had indicated dissatisfaction with Stalin's stewardship of it, and would later (as we shall see) hold the inspectorate up to scorn as a prime example of how a commissariat should *not* be operated.

Stalin was not temperamentally well constituted for success as an organizer and administrator. He was deficient in such qualities as patience, even temper, cooperativeness, and the capacity to subordinate oneself, in small ways and large, to the needs of an institution. The little commissar in Russian leather boots and party tunic—his habitual costume in the twenties and thirties—was not in fact the person of steel self-control that his adopted name and normal public demeanor suggested. Behind the scenes, according to testimony from numerous sources, he was frequently moody and prone to outbursts of temper.[54] He could work with prodigious energy, but he could also be indolent. His vindictive disposition became proverbial in upper party circles owing to a remark he made in conversation with Kamenev and Dzerzhinsky over wine one summer day in 1923. The three men began to speak of what they loved most in life. As Kamenev later related the story to Trotsky, Stalin said: "The greatest delight is to mark one's enemy, prepare everything, avenge oneself thoroughly, and then go to sleep." [55] This became known among Stalin's party comrades as his theory of sweet revenge. They considered it a self-revealing confession.

The great change from a revolutionary's underground existence to the life of a man of state influenced Stalin's personal ethos less than that of many other Old Bolsheviks (as those with a pre-1917 party past were now coming to be called). He continued, for example, to show from time to time the aloofness that we observed in him earlier, the tendency to be a loner. A revealing passage in Pestkovsky's memoir highlights this fact. He recalls how Stalin

54. One such incident occurred around 1929 or 1930, during a time of food rationing. As later told to Stalin's daughter by her nurse, who was an eyewitness, he threw a cooked chicken out of the window of his Kremlin apartment because of pique at the lack of variety in his diet. On a later occasion, he angrily tore a telephone apparatus from the wall when he wanted to make a call and was getting a busy signal. For both episodes, see Svetlana Alliluyeva, *Only One Year* (New York, 1969). See also Svetlana Alliluyeva, *Twenty Letters to a Friend* (New York, 1967), *passim*.

55. L. Trotsky, *Trotsky's Diary in Exile, 1935* (New York, 1963), p. 64.

would lose patience during the interminable discussion meetings that went on in Narkomnats. Instead of showing his impatience openly, he would rise, say "Back in a minute," and leave the conference room. A phone call from Lenin would occasionally come through at such times. When told that Stalin had disappeared, Lenin would request Pestkovsky to find him at once. Then the vice commissar would set off down the long corridors of the Smolny or the Kremlin in search of his missing chief. On more than one occasion, he found him in the apartment of a sailor named Vorontsov, lying on a couch in the kitchen, smoking his pipe, and mulling over his "theses." [56] One cannot picture Stalin's more austere colleagues among the Bolshevik leaders acting in this manner.

The truth is that the administrative-organizational side of things was not in itself of great interest to him. Not organizational work, save in one important aspect still to be discussed, but general political leadership of the movement was what beckoned him. That, after all, was Lenin's cardinal function as *vozhd'*, and Lenin was his model. Stalin wanted to lead the party in great new revolutionary deeds at home and abroad. But how was he to position himself for leadership? Lacking the extraordinary qualities that had assisted Lenin to acquire a following and dominate a political movement primarily by being the person he was, contributing the ideas that he contributed, and writing as he wrote, Stalin's only course was to build a commanding position for himself by the politics of power and influence. The distinction being made here is not absolute: Lenin was no stranger to the politics of power, nor was Stalin, as later events would show, incapable of attracting followers by showing prowess as a political leader. But at the start, in the early Soviet years, he proceeded by cultivating a political clientele.

Politics in this sense, as distinguished from administration, genuinely appealed to him. It is reported that he spent many hours during his final Siberian exile poring over a copy of that classic manual of advice for the power-seeker, Machiavelli's *The Prince*.[57]

56. Pestkovsky, "Vospominaniia," p. 128.
57. Personal conversation with Boris I. Nicolaevsky, whose source was L. B. Kamenev.

His own writings of the twenties show that politics as an art, with its inherent rules of strategy and tactics, was a subject of absorbing interest to him. Nor did his difficult traits of character incapacitate him for the dealings with others that go with being a successful politician. If he was obnoxious at times, he could also be charming and ingratiating in the presence of someone whom he wished to impress. He was wily and knew how to keep his own counsel. He had a keen intuitive eye for people's strengths and failings, an ability to size up their potential as political friends or enemies; and his inclination throughout life was to divide political associates into the one category or the other.

The wealth of personal contacts resulting from his two decades of immersion in the Bolshevik movement were an invaluable resource to him now. Bolshevik revolutionaries of yesterday's Russia were the ruling class of today's, directing the new state apparatus; leading the Red Army; managing the economy; overseeing the trade unions, youth leagues, and other public organizations. Their ranks were being swelled by many thousands of younger party members from the generation now coming of age—a group in which Stalin showed special interest. This expansion and renewal of the movement's membership brought inevitable changes in patterns of motivation. Whereas persons oriented chiefly toward career success were not likely to become revolutionaries in the pre-1917 days, career motives were naturally common among those now joining a ruling Bolshevik party. So this period was a propitious one for the politics of influence-building that Stalin pursued. His war work, the contacts that he made on his travels to different parts of the country, and his leadership of two commissariats were of great assistance to him. But in order to build up and maintain a large personal following, Stalin needed a base of political operations in his old element, the party. Here fortune intervened: Sverdlov, who had managed the party's organizational affairs during its first period in power, died suddenly.

Like some other imposing bureaucratic structures, the Soviet Communist party's central apparatus was very modest in origin. Its initial whereabouts were Lenin's lodgings in emigration, and the party secretary was his faithful helpmate Krupskaya, who carried on the correspondence, dispatched party literature, communicated in code and invisible ink, kept accounts, paid out money, and took care of such details as housing and false passports for party comrades.[58] After the February Revolution, the secretarial functions were taken over by another veteran woman revolutionary of noble origin, Elena Stasova. When the party moved into the Kshesinskaia mansion in March 1917, the Central Committee acquired office space on the second floor, along with a spacious bathroom which was used as a storehouse for party literature. Stasova, with three or four women assistants, handled the correspondence, received callers, sent out directives, kept records of Central Committee sessions, and managed the finances.[59]

In August, following the Sixth Party Congress, the Central Committee formally instituted a Secretariat, which was to consist of five persons holding Central Committee membership and to be entrusted with "the organizational part of the work." The five delegated to serve on it were Sverdlov, Stasova, Dzerzhinsky, Ioffe, and M. K. Muranov, the last-named as treasurer.[60] Sverdlov, who had recommended himself as a general secretary by his impressive organizing of the just-completed party congress, took charge. He installed Stasova and her clerical assistants in new quarters in the former house of the Brotherhood of St. Sergei, in Furshtadtskaia Street, and set up another part of the Secretariat—in Stasova's words, "the operational part"—in the Smolny, under his own direction. In Moscow later on the Secretariat and its staff were housed in a Central Committee office building situated not far from the Kremlin.

Sverdlov ran the party organization single-handedly in addition to discharging the many duties connected with his presidency of the All-Russian Executive Committee of the Soviets. He personally made the decisions on assignments and transfers of party workers, recording these in his private notebooks. When he fell ill with the

58. Robert H. McNeal, *Bride of the Revolution: Krupskaya and Lenin* (Ann Arbor, 1972), pp. 101–102, 144.

59. E. D. Stasova, *Vospominaniia* (Moscow, 1969), pp. 133–134, 136.

60. *Protokoly tsentral'nogo komiteta RSDRP/b/. Avgust 1917–fevral' 1918* (Moscow, 1958), p. 13.

Spanish flu and died on the eve of the Eighth Party Congress, in March 1919, the need for new arrangements was obvious. Increasing the size of the Central Committee itself to nineteen members and eight candidates, the congress made provision for two smaller bodies, each to consist of five Central Committee members: the Politburo and an Organizational Bureau (Orgburo). The latter was entrusted with the "organizational work," meaning the party appointments required for effectuating policy decisions taken in the Politburo or the Central Committee. The Secretariat was reconstituted. A further decision, passed by the Ninth Party Congress a year later, provided that the Secretariat be composed of three Central Committee members regularly devoting themselves to this function, and that it handle current questions of an organizational and executive character, general direction of organizational work being reserved for the Orgburo.

The Secretariat thus evolved as a collegium of Central Committee members overseeing the central party bureaucracy and, through the latter, the hierarchy of regional and lower party organizations down to the many thousands of party cells formed in Soviet institutions of all kinds. Its staff increased from a mere thirty employees in 1919 to 150 in 1920 and 600 in 1921, not including the military guard and communications unit. It became the custom for each of the three secretaries to oversee one major sphere of activity embracing the work of more than one department. The principal departments were Records and Assignments (known familiarly as Uchraspred), which handled personnel matters and the mobilization of party forces for special needs as the occasion arose; the Organizational-Instruction Department, which directed the activities of the local party organizations by correspondence and by the use of a corps of roving Central Committee instructors; and the Department of Propaganda and Agitation (Agitprop), which administered special schools and journals concerned with indoctrination of the party membership, and press and propaganda activities among the population at large, including the work of a number of special agitation trains with names like "Red East" and "Soviet Caucasus" which spread the Bolshevik revolutionary message on whistle-stopping tours through outlying areas. There was also a special women's section, a secret section, an administrative section, and a printing press.[61]

Stalin became a member of the Orgburo upon its formation in 1919, but it took him another three years to achieve headship of the central party bureaucracy through a seat on the Secretariat. The secretarial trio elected by the Central Committee after the Ninth Congress in 1920 consisted of Krestinsky, Preobrazhensky, and Serebriakov—all three of them men of the party Left with links to Trotsky—and these same three plus Stalin and Alexei Rykov made up the Orgburo. Following the Tenth Party Congress a year later, the three secretaries lost their seats on the Central Committee, and therefore their secretarial roles as well, as a result of an intra-party conflict in which Lenin and Trotsky found themselves pitted against each other. Stalin, who was not a principal protagonist in this controversy, showed himself an artful politician by his conduct in it and thereby became the chief beneficiary.

The party conflict of 1920–21 reflected the grave problems of the time of transition through which the country was passing. By the close of 1919 the Reds were clearly on their way to victory in the Civil War, but the prize—Soviet Russia—was a war-ravaged land with a hungry and dispirited people, an industry in shambles, an inflation-debased currency, a railway system in a state of virtual collapse, and a peasantry with no incentive to supply food for the towns. It took the revolt of the Kronstadt sailors in March 1921 and other ominous signs of popular unrest to galvanize the regime into its decision—made at the Tenth Party Congress that very month— to abandon War Communism for the NEP. Meanwhile, however, Trotsky had offered a plan prescribing the militarization of the labor force as a way out of the crisis, and this precipitated the party conflict.[62]

61. The sources of this information are the organizational report of the then party secretary, Nikolai Krestinsky, at the Tenth Party Congress (*Desiatyi s"ezd RKP/b/. Mart 1921 goda. Stenograficheskii otchet* (Moscow, 1963), pp. 805–813), and the article on the Communist party in *Bol'shaia sovetskaia entsiklopediia,* Vol. LX (Moscow, 1934), p. 552.

62. My treatment of the trade union conflict relies on the detailed accounts

Trotsky's plan, which was presented in *Pravda* in December 1919, involved such measures as the reassignment of workers serving in the Red Army to new duties in armies of labor and the use of the War Commissariat for industrial administrative purposes. Although Lenin gave the plan his full support, many in the party leadership were vociferously opposed. The next act unfolded in 1920 after Trotsky undertook, at Politburo urging, to put the nearly paralyzed railway system into commission and did so in part by mobilizing the railwaymen for duty under martial law and creating his own new transport authority, Tsektran, over opposition from the railwaymen's union. This action, and his subsequent warnings of the possible need to "shake up" still more unions, brought him into sharp conflict with trade unionist elements in the party. Lenin, alarmed over the latter development, withdrew his support, and Trotsky found himself under attack for policies that allegedly violated proletarian democracy in favor of a militarized bureaucratic centralism. The trade union question was posed for resolution by the impending Tenth Congress, with various platforms competing for support. Trotsky's, with which Bukharin and others associated themselves, called for incorporation of the unions into the state economic administration. The "platform of the ten," representing Lenin's position, allowed the unions a separate existence as workers' organizations. As such, however, they were to function under the party's tutelage as "schools of communism" for a working class not yet qualified to run the economy on its own. Direct worker administration of the economy via the unions was the platform of a group calling itself the "Workers' Opposition," led by the unionist Shliapnikov. To this both the Trotsky and Lenin positions were quite opposed.

Zinoviev, an ambitious man with his own motives for promoting Trotsky's defeat, took a prominent part in the pre-congress party debate as a defender of the Lenin position and "proletarian democracy" against Trotsky. Stalin, for whom the whole situation

in Isaac Deutscher, *The Prophet Armed: Trotsky, 1879–1921* (London, 1954), ch. XIV; and Leonard Schapiro, *The Origin of the Communist Autocracy* (Cambridge, Mass., 1955), chs. XIV–XV.

was a windfall of the first order, astutely permitted Zinoviev to spearhead the attack. He was one of the ten signatories of the Lenin platform, however, and took advantage of the opportunity afforded by the debate to publish his first polemical article against Trotsky. In it he championed "democratism" in the trade unions against Trotsky's "military-bureaucratic method," and argued that reliance upon persuasion of the working class was all the more necessary now that the war danger had given way to the less tangible but equally serious danger of economic breakdown.[63] Behind the scenes, moreover, Stalin was one of the movers of the anti-Trotsky campaign. Indeed, one speaker at the Tenth Congress, representing the oppositionist group of "Democratic Centralists," ironically pictured the campaign as having been waged in Petrograd under Zinoviev's generalship and in Moscow under that of "the military strategist and arch-democrat, Comrade Stalin."[64]

The congress endorsed Lenin's position by an overwhelming majority, defeated Trotsky's resoundingly, and stigmatized the platform of the Workers' Opposition—in a resolution drafted by Lenin —as a "syndicalist and anarchist deviation" in the party. It passed a "Resolution on Party Unity," which Lenin also drafted and which expressed his belief that under existing conditions, when (as Kronstadt showed) Bolshevik rule was threatened by a petty-bourgeois counter-revolution more dangerous than all the former White Guard armies, the party could not tolerate the discords recently displayed. Accordingly, the resolution declared such "factionalism" inadmissible, instructed the Central Committee to root it out, and ordered the disbanding of all party groups formed around particular platforms. Still another congress resolution spoke of the need to recruit more worker members and cleanse the party of non-Communist and unstable elements.[65]

The Tenth Congress was a political setback for Trotsky. He came out a loser in the trade union controversy, and the NEP was

63. *Stalin*, V, 8–10. The article appeared in *Pravda* on January 5, 1921, under the title "Our Differences."

64. *Desiatyi s"ezd*, p. 98. The speaker was R. B. Rafail. The Democratic Centralists took a position not unlike that of the Workers' Opposition.

65. *Ibid.*, pp. 564, 571–573.

implicitly a repudiation of the line that he had publicly been taking in economic policy. All this, combined with adept maneuvering in the intra-party politics of the time, explains the otherwise paradoxical fact that Stalin's political fortunes rose at the very congress which listened in hostile silence when he tried to justify his conduct in the Soviet-Polish war. Numbers of persons who had aligned themselves with Trotsky in the trade union debate—among them Krestinsky, Preobrazhensky, and Serebriakov—lost their seats on the Central Committee as re-elected by the congress, while a number of persons associated with Stalin gained seats. These included his old friends Voroshilov and Ordzhonikidze, and two able and promising younger men who had been active respectively in Turkestan and Caucasian affairs and who would become key figures in his faction: Valerian Kuibyshev and Sergei Kirov. Molotov, by now Stalin's factional confederate, not only moved up from candidate to full membership of the Central Committee but was elected to the candidate membership of the Politburo vacated by Zinoviev, who replaced Krestinsky as one of the five full members of that body. The Secretariat and Orgburo seats lost by Krestinsky, Preobrazhensky, and Serebriakov went to Molotov, who became the senior secretary, Emelian Yaroslavsky, and V. M. Mikhailov—men better qualified than their more liberal predecessors to carry out the policy of tightened intra-party discipline that the congress had proclaimed. The first large-scale party purge of the Soviet period took place during the ensuing months, under the direction of the secretarial trio, and Molotov reported to the Eleventh Party Congress in March 1922 that the party's membership had been reduced from 660,000 to about 500,000 through the expulsions and forced resignations that resulted. "Now," he said, "those numerous currents and semiformed factions do not exist." [66]

Stalin's move into the Secretariat was predetermined by the outcome of the Tenth Congress. The post-congress reshuffle of the Orgburo made him the clearly dominant figure in it. Molotov di-

---

66. *Odinnadtsatyi s"ezd*, pp. 46, 47. A party purge (*chistka*) at that time consisted of a process of re-registration of members by control commissions and weeding out of those deemed unfit. Those purged were not arrested.

rectly involved him in Secretariat affairs as the Central Committee member responsible for overseeing the activities of Agitprop.[67] It was now mainly a question of formalizing the *de facto* control of the party organization that Stalin had attained. This was done when the Central Committee's organs were re-elected following the Eleventh Congress. Stalin was elected a member of the Secretariat and accorded the title "general secretary" in token of his seniority in a new secretarial trio whose two other members were Molotov and Kuibyshev. The base of operations was now securely in his possession.

Stalin was not the builder of the central party machine. When he took over as general secretary in the spring of 1922, he found himself at the head of a sizable, satisfactorily functioning Central Committee bureaucracy that had been organized over a five-year period, during the successive tenures of Sverdlov, Krestinsky, and Molotov. This was no longer a small-scale establishment operating on an emergency basis, as in Sverdlov's time. It was a well-developed apparatus fulfilling all the ruling party's administrative functions, including the supervision of a nationwide network of province, town, and district party committees. Mass public organizations like the Communist Youth League (Komsomol) and trade unions were operating under its tutelage. The internal structure of its departments had undergone a series of improvements. Uchraspred was far along in the process of taking censuses both of the party's membership as a whole and of its "responsible workers" in the province and district centers. Cards had been prepared on twenty-six thousand of these full-time party functionaries, and the information on the seven thousand working at the province level had been set aside for detailed further study by Central Committee officials, with a view to defining a still smaller category of more important figures.[68]

Stalin found a party machine in being. Where he differed from his predecessors in the secretaryship was in turning the position to his own political advantage. He set about building up a personal machine as an informal political reality within the official one, a

67. *Ibid.*
68. *Ibid.*, pp. 49, 56.

Stalin empire in the party-state. The bodies in which he now had a controlling voice were, among other things, a sort of all-Russian employment agency for the new ruling elite. The Orgburo was shifting leading personnel around in implementing policy decisions taken in the Politburo. Lower-level personnel decisions were within the jurisdiction of the Secretariat, and the latter, through Uchraspred, was able to effect appointments and transfers in the system of party organizations throughout the country. Here was a boundless field of opportunity for empire-building by a man of Stalin's ambitions and aptitudes. He appears to have plunged into it with zest.

The one kind of organizing activity that really engaged his interest and aroused his effort was "organizational work" in the special Bolshevik sense of personnel placement. He saw himself in this regard as the successor of Sverdlov, whom he eulogized in a memorial article of 1924 as "an organizer through and through, an organizer by nature, by habit, by revolutionary training, by intuition, an organizer in all his intense activity." To be a leader-organizer (*vozhd'-organizator*) of Sverdlov's caliber in present-day conditions, Stalin said, meant, firstly, to know party workers, to appreciate their strong and weak points, and to know how to treat them; secondly, it meant the ability to place them in positions where each could feel in his element and be of maximum service to the Revolution, with the overall result of coordinated performance and fulfillment of the political idea underlying the assignment of the workers to their posts.[69] But the Stalin school of organizational work differed from the Sverdlov in one fundamental aspect that Stalin did not mention: it applied a self-serving test in selecting candidates for advancement in the party hierarchy. No longer did it suffice to give good indication that one was a person of ability, energy, and devotion to the Bolshevik cause. One must, in addition, evince a favorable disposition toward the party regime of the general secretary, usefulness to the Stalin organization. One of the early signs of the importance attached to this qualification was Stalin's choice of a zealous follower named Lazar Kaganovich to head the Central

69. *Stalin*, VI, 277–278.

Committee bureau responsible for supervising the provincial party organizations—the Organizational-Instruction Department. An ex-worker from a poor Jewish family in the Ukraine and a Bolshevik since 1911, Kaganovich acquired the pivotal Secretariat post in 1922 at the age of twenty-nine and in the following year was made a candidate member of the Central Committee.[70] He filled Stalin's specifications for a political protégé in being able, tough, hard-driving, deferential to his patron, and unreservedly prepared to link his own career with the patron's. He could satisfactorily apply to those he supervised Stalin's tests of qualification for political advancement because he himself met them so well.

Stalin, as many in the party soon began to perceive, was acting in the manner of a political boss. But we should take care not to assume that he saw himself in this light. There is no indication that he thought of himself as a "machine politician" in our sense of that phrase. The evidence, some of it already cited, suggests rather that he perceived his secretarial activity as that of a *vozhd'-organizator* in the high Sverdlov tradition, a man wholeheartedly serving the cause of Bolshevism and the Revolution. What made it possible for Stalin to take this view was his deeply ingrained way of personalizing political relationships. As we shall see, being a good Bolshevik was something indissolubly associated in his mind with being well disposed toward Stalin, and the converse was just as true: an enemy of Stalin's was an enemy of the party. Because of this, the "organizational work" that appears to us a crass form of machine politics was for him essentially a process of finding and promoting those best qualified to be of "maximum service to the Revolution."

It remains to be said that Stalin's career in party politics was well served in a number of ways by his marriage to Nadya Alliluyeva in 1919. Unlike the simple, traditional Georgian girl of his previous marriage, Nadya was a person for whom Bolshevism was a birthright and public activity a deep need. She joined the Communist

70. *Politicheskii slovar'*, ed. G. Alexandrov *et al.* (Moscow, 1940), p. 235.

party in 1918 and served its cause by working for a time in Tsaritsyn. Nor did she retire to a domestic existence upon her marriage. She took a job in 1919 in Lenin's personal secretariat. At the height of the Civil War she worked there for long hours, often into the night, as a typist and as a coder and decoder of telegrams; she was entrusted, according to the later recollection of her superiors in that office, with work of the most secret character. Subsequently she found employment on a journal called *Revoliutsiia i kul'tura* (Revolution and Culture), published by *Pravda*, and was active in the party organization of *Pravda*'s editorial offices. Still later she enrolled at Moscow's Industrial Academy for training as a specialist in synthetic fibers.[71]

Nadya also became the mother of two children and showed herself to be a good homemaker and hostess. The family's way of life was not proletarian. While maintaining an apartment in the Kremlin, Stalin and Nadya made their home in a roomy country house that they took over in 1919. It was located near the village of Usovo on a lovely stretch of the Moscow River about twenty miles from Moscow. They called it "Zubalovo" after the name of the oil magnate who had owned it before the Revolution. The house was remodeled during the twenties, and under Stalin's management the place was transformed into a thriving, well-kept estate with various outbuildings, gardens, orchards, a turkey run, and a duck pond. In order to remain active outside the home, Nadya relied heavily on nursemaids and private tutors to care for her son, Vasily, and her daughter, Svetlana. But she herself presided over Zubalovo, making it a lively social scene and a center of hospitality for a constant flow of guests from among their numerous friends in high party circles.[72] A rising figure in Soviet politics, especially one characterized by a solitary streak, could not have been more fortunate in his choice of a wife.

71. *Pravda,* November 10, 1932. This career information appears in obituary notices published upon Nadya's death, which is believed to have been by suicide. Whether her work at Tsaritsyn took place during Stalin's three-month stay there in 1918 is not indicated.

72. Svetlana Alliluyeva, *Twenty Letters,* pp. 31–34.

Return to Transcaucasia

The revolutionary years were a time of troubles in Transcaucasia's history. Local political forces asserted themselves after the breakdown of tsarist authority, but without enduring result. An effort to create an independent federal government for the whole region foundered on the rocks of national separatism and religious animosity. In May 1918 the three component lands were proclaimed independent nation-states under governments of the Musavat party in predominantly Moslem Azerbaijan, the Dashnak party in Armenia, and the Mensheviks in Georgia. These arrangements in turn foundered on the rocks of world politics. Turkish and German intervention gave way, after the defeat of the Central Powers, to a smaller intervention by the British and finally to a decisive one by the Soviet government, which reconquered the region for Russia in 1920–21. These military actions could be seen as the Reds' final victories in the Civil War, save that the non-Communist Transcaucasian regimes were not contesting Bolshevik rule in Russia proper but only exercising that right of national self-determination to which Lenin and his party in theory subscribed.

The Transcaucasian Bolsheviks did play a part in the political life of the region during the interregnum. Stepan Shaumian was elected president of the Soviet that arose in Baku, capital city of Azerbaijan, following the February Revolution. In August 1917 Shaumian became a member of the Bolshevik Central Committee, and in December he was named by the Lenin government as its commissar extraordinary for Caucasian affairs. In the midst of great turmoil in Baku in March 1918, the local Bolsheviks maneuvered themselves into power and formed a government, headed by Shaumian, which called itself the "Baku Commune" in honor of its Parisian predecessor of 1871. The imminence of a Turkish invasion brought about the fall of the commune after ninety-seven days. Its twenty-six Bolshevik commissars—including Shaumian and the prominent Baku Bolshevik Alyosha Djaparidze—were shot after falling into hostile Russian hands during their attempt to flee by boat across the Caspian.[73] Bolshevik political activities in Transcaucasia then continued on an illegal basis. Nothing decisive could be done without outside help, and the embattled Lenin regime was not able to provide that.

The situation changed upon the winding up of the British intervention in the summer of 1919 and the collapse of General Denikin's cause in south Russia in early 1920. In preparation for the coming new time of opportunity, a group of Transcaucasian Bolsheviks approached Lenin in late 1919 to seek financial and other aid. A young Armenian named Anastas Mikoyan was one of its members; the others were A. Stopani and an Azerbaijani, Nariman Narimanov. Their views on the party's Caucasian policy were then considered by the Politburo, which forwarded them for comment to Stalin and Ordzhonikidze, who were away on war assignments. On Stalin's advice, the Politburo decided to confine the sphere of activity of the Caucasian Revolutionary Committee for the present to the North Caucasus and to reconstitute this committee as the "Bureau for Restoration of Soviet Power in the North Caucasus." Ordzhonikidze was named as its chairman; Sergei Kirov (who was in Astrakhan directing Soviet activities in the North Caucasus) as vice chairman; and Stopani, Narimanov, and a Georgian Bolshevik named P. G. (Budu) Mdivani as the other members.[74]

Tukhachevsky was appointed military commander of the Caucasian front; Ordzhonikidze and Kirov were his commissars. In early 1920, under this leadership, the Soviet Eleventh Army took the offensive in the North Caucasus against Denikin's remaining forces, twenty-two thousand of whom were taken prisoner at the end of March while seeking to embark on French and British warships at the port of Novorossiisk. In the wake of this victory, the Reds maintained their momentum. Ordzhonikidze, who had been

73. Pipes, *Formation of the Soviet Union*, pp. 200–204, and for further details Ronald Grigor Suny, *The Baku Commune 1917–1918: Class and Nationality in the Russian Revolution* (Princeton, 1972).

74. G. K. Zhvaniia, *V. I. Lenin, Ts. K. partii i bol'sheviki Zakavkaz'ia* (Tbilisi, 1969), pp. 228–231.

pressing Lenin long and hard for a decision to take Transcaucasia by armed force,[75] received Moscow's permission in late April to move the Eleventh Army into Azerbaijan. The Musavat government took flight in the midst of this operation, and Ordzhonikidze, accompanied by Kirov and Mikoyan, arrived in Baku by armored train on April 28, 1920. The takeover of Armenia followed in early December. It was accomplished by a combination of armed action and successful pressure upon the Dashnak government, more fearful of a Turkish than of a Soviet occupation, to consent to the latter.[76]

Georgia, for a variety of reasons, was harder for the Bolsheviks to take over. The impetuous Ordzhonikidze was all for marching into his homeland immediately upon the triumphal entry into Baku. Following the technique of forcible self-determination already employed in the Azerbaijani operation, he set in motion a plan involving the instigation of Georgian popular outbreaks by local Bolsheviks as a pretext for the Red Army to intervene in support of an internal revolutionary uprising. In telegrams of May 3 and 4, 1920, to Lenin and Stalin, he urgently requested permission to order the Eleventh Army to cross the Georgian border, giving assurances that "it will go brilliantly" and promising to be in Tiflis by the twelfth or fifteenth. But Moscow, currently confronted with the Polish invasion of the Ukraine, turned him down. In a telegram of May 5, sent on Politburo authority and signed by Lenin and Stalin, he was categorically forbidden "to self-determine Georgia" and instructed to continue negotiations with the Georgian government.[77] In one of the abrupt turnabouts characteristic of Lenin's political style, Moscow thereupon concluded a treaty in which it

75. I. Dubinsky-Mukhadze, Ordzhonikidze (Moscow, 1963), p. 283.
76. Pipes, Formation of the Soviet Union, p. 234. For further details see Firuz Kazemzadeh, The Struggle for Transcaucasia (1917–1921) (New York, 1951), ch. XIX.
77. Lenin, LI, 424; Zhvaniia, V. I. Lenin, pp. 238–239. According to the latter source (p. 240), Ordzhonikidze and Kirov replied two days later, signifying their compliance but outlining five reasons for intervening without delay. They argued that a non-Soviet Georgia would be a focal point of counter-revolution in the south; that the Georgian operation would be a repetition—with, at most, small changes—of the easy one in Azerbaijan; and that "with Georgia in our possession, we knock the British off the eastern coast of the Black Sea."

formally recognized the Georgian government headed by the Menshevik leader Noi Zhordania. Under its terms, the Georgian Communist party was guaranteed legal status. Kirov then went to Tiflis not as a conquering commissar but as the diplomatic envoy of the RSFSR in a neighboring state. But this situation did not long endure.

The on-the-spot director of Soviet Russia's policy in the Caucasus was Ordzhonikidze. He headed the Central Committee's Caucasian Bureau (Kavburo), created in April 1920 as the directing center for all Caucasian party organizations, and stayed on in the early twenties as Bolshevism's proconsul in Transcaucasia. Stalin's role, though no less important, was different in character. He functioned as Lenin's chief of staff and high-level adviser on policy in the Caucasus, and handled much of the liaison with Ordzhonikidze, Kirov, and others on the spot. While not a member of the Kavburo, he would on occasion take part in its deliberations, and in high Bolshevik councils he spoke with authority on Caucasian matters. Lenin, for example, sent a wire on November 18, 1920—at which time Stalin was in Vladikavkaz (now Ordzhonikidze) on an inspection tour of the North Caucasus and Azerbaijan asking whether, in his opinion, it would be wise to make war on Georgia at the risk of a break with Great Britain and "even a new war." The telegram concluded: "Reply, and I will put it before the Politburo." We do not have the full reply, but on Stalin's return to Moscow five days later, the Politburo heard his report on the situation in the Caucasus and decided "to pursue toward Georgia, Armenia, Turkey, and Persia a maximally conciliatory policy, that is, aimed primarily at avoiding war." [78]

Before visiting Vladikavkaz, Stalin spent more than a week in Baku, where Ordzhonikidze was his host. On his first return to Transcaucasia since 1912, the former inmate of Bailov prison received a warm welcome. The Central Committee of the Azerbaijan Communist party published an announcement which struck a note of adulation that was quite out of keeping with Bolshevik customs of

78. S. V. Kharmandarian, *Lenin i stanovlenie zakavkazskoi federatsii. 1921–1923* (Erevan, 1969), pp. 47–48.

that time and that must have reflected Ordzhonikidze's awareness of his guest's thirst for recognition and acclaim as the chief:

Comrade Stalin, a worker leader of exceptional self-dedication, energy, and stalwartness, the only tested and generally recognized authority on revolutionary tactics and *vozhd'* of proletarian revolution in the Caucasus and the East, has come on a visit. Knowing Comrade Stalin's modesty and dislike of official pomp, the Central Committee of the Azerbaijan Communist party (Bolshevik) had to give up the idea of special meetings connected with his arrival. The Central Committee believes that the best greeting and reception which our party, the Baku proletarians, and working people of Azerbaijan could give our dear *vozhd'* and teacher would be to bend every effort again and again to improve party and Soviet work in every way. All out for harmonious militant work worthy of the seasoned proletarian fighter Comrade Stalin —the first organizer and *vozhd'* of the Baku proletariat.[79]

While in Baku, Stalin met privately with the local party leaders, and on November 6, the eve of the Revolution's anniversary, he addressed a ceremonial meeting of the Baku Soviet. The talk gives a view of the world as this revolutionary saw it after three years of being in power.

He went back in memory to that November 6–7 of 1917 when "we, a small group of Bolsheviks headed by Comrade Lenin, having in our hands the Petrograd Soviet (it was then Bolshevik) and an insignificant Red Guard, having at our disposal nothing more than a small, not yet fully formed Communist party of 200,000 to 250,000, took power from representatives of the bourgeoisie and transferred it to the Second Congress of Soviets." Many, said Stalin, had seen this band of Bolsheviks as being at best oddities and at worst agents of German imperialism. Since then the Revolution had gone through a first period of utter isolation and a second period of open war with the Entente, and now had entered a third period of being not only recognized abroad but even a little feared. "And so, going through fire and storm, Russia has forged itself during this time into the greatest socialist power in the world." The

---

79. This announcement appeared in the Baku paper *Kommunist* on November 4, 1920. It is quoted in *Istorik-marksist*, No. 11 (1940), p. 12, and in Pipes, *Formation of the Soviet Union*, p. 230.

once weak government that possessed only a small armed guard of Petrograd workers now had the millions-strong Red Army. The not yet fully formed Communist party had grown into a steel-like party of 700,000 which at a wave of the Central Committee's hand could reform its ranks and move against the foe. A party that three years ago had only small groups of sympathizers in the West was now the main nucleus of the world socialist movement via the Third International, while Mr. Kautsky, head of the defeated Second International, was forced to seek refuge from the German revolution in "backward Tiflis, among the Georgian social-innkeepers." And the countries of the East, quiescent three years ago, were now coming into motion in a series of liberation movements against the Entente and imperialism. No doubt the path ahead would not be easy. But difficulties were not to be feared, said Stalin, and he concluded:

Paraphrasing the well-known words of Luther, Russia might say: "Here I stand, on the borderline between the old capitalist and the new socialist worlds. Here, on this borderline, I unite the efforts of the proletarians of the West and the peasantry of the East in order to smash the old world.
"May the god of history help me." [80]

But Stalin's mind could switch easily from this religious image of revolutionary Russia to a view of her as a power in world politics with interests to pursue in the normal way of great powers. He made the following statement, for example, in a private meeting with the Baku party leaders, held three days after his appearance before the Soviet: "Georgia is now in the position of a girl with lots of suitors. They're all wooing and she's putting on airs. We are wooing, too, trying to get what we can out of it. The Entente wants to build an alliance against us. We won't bring Georgia onto our side, of course, but we will cause greater deterioration in the Georgian government, and by giving each a drop of oil we'll slow down the forming of a fighting alliance between Georgia and the Entente. Then the facts will show what's best to do next." [81] And on his return to Moscow

80. *Stalin*, IV, 382–393. The talk was originally published in the Baku *Kommunist* on November 7 and 11, 1920.

81. Kharmandarian, *Lenin i stanovlenie*, p. 47, based on documents of the Azerbaijan branch of the Institute of Marxism-Leninism.

later in November, Stalin opened an interview with a *Pravda* correspondent about the situation in the Caucasus with an appraisal of that region's significance which may have brought a gleam to the eye of the German theorist of geopolitics, Dr. Haushofer, if he ever read it:

The Caucasus' important significance for the Revolution turns not only on its being a source of raw materials, fuel, and food, but also on its position between Europe and Asia, between Russia and Turkey in particular, and on the presence of highly important economic and strategic roads (Batum–Baku, Batum–Tabriz, Batum–Tabriz–Erzerum). The Entente takes all this into account. Now in possession of Constantinople, that key to the Black Sea, it would like to keep a direct road to the Orient through Transcaucasia. Who will establish himself finally in the Caucasus, who will use the oil and the extremely important roads leading to the heart of Asia, the Revolution or the Entente—that is the whole question.[82]

For Stalin, we may be sure, there was no inconsistency between the speech to the Baku Soviet and the *Pravda* interview. Between the visionary mystique of the one and the geopolitical realism of the other there was a connecting link in his idea of Russia as at once the embodiment of the world socialist revolution *and* a great national state fighting its battles on the world arena according to calculations that necessarily had to match those of its adversaries.

The *Pravda* interview was also notable for a statement which clearly implied that Menshevik Georgia's respite was running out: "The Georgia that enmeshed itself in the toils of the Entente and was consequently deprived both of Baku oil and of Kuban grain, the Georgia that became the main base of imperialist operations by Britain and France and hence entered into hostile relations with Soviet Russia—this Georgia is now living out its last days." The prediction took on special meaning from events just transpired or transpiring. The Reds' Crimean victory of mid-November 1920 over the White army led by Baron Pyotr Wrangel marked the effective ending of the Civil War. The sovietization of Armenia was

---

82. *Stalin*, IV, 408. The interview originally appeared in *Pravda* on November 30, 1920.

taking place at the very time when Stalin spoke. At this point, and doubtless with his connivance, the Kavburo became a pressure group for armed action against Georgia. In mid-December Ordzhonikidze presided over a session of it in Baku, attended by representatives of the Eleventh Army, and afterwards wired Lenin that the meeting had decided "on the immediate rendering of aid to the working people of Georgia and the establishment of Soviet power." A Soviet historian of Georgian nationality comments in his narrative of this event that the decision suffered from the fact that "primary attention was given not to internal conditions of the immediate taking of power but to the Eleventh Army." [83] Lenin replied that such a decision was radically contrary to Central Committee policy, that the consequences might be disastrous, and that he categorically demanded the repeal and non-execution of the decision. Two days later, on December 17, a plenum (as Central Committee plenary sessions are called) reaffirmed the "peaceful direction" of the RSFSR's policy in the Caucasus. Pressure from the south then subsided, but not for long. In early January Ordzhonikidze and Kirov dispatched a letter to the Central Committee's members urging the immediate sovietization of Georgia. Another plenum thereupon reconsidered the question and decided that neither from the internal nor from the external standpoint was the time yet ripe for action. There the matter rested for another week, after which Stalin directly intervened on the side of the Kavburo.

He timed his move well. On January 20, 1921, the commissar for foreign affairs, Georgi Chicherin, sent Lenin a lengthy letter detailing charges that the Zhordania government had violated the Soviet-Georgian treaty and contending that an internal revolutionary crisis was brewing in Georgia. Stalin, who saw this letter, made use of it when, on January 24, he circulated a letter of his own to the Central Committee members. Referring to Chicherin's materials and to others which he claimed were in his possession, he stated

83. Zhvaniia, *V. I. Lenin*, p. 261. My account of the process of decision leading up to the intervention in Georgia in February 1921 is largely based on Zhvaniia's book, which is documented from archival sources, and his article, "V. I. Lenin i partiinaia organizatsiia Gruzii v period bor'by za sovetskuiu vlast'," *Zaria vostoka*, April 21, 1961. See pp. 261–268 of the book for details.

that a revolutionary situation now existed in Georgia and proposed
that Ordzhonikidze and the Georgian Communist party organization be instructed to prepare an armed rising and that the Revolutionary War Council of the Republic be directed to prepare immediately to render assistance to the Georgian insurgents in event
of necessity. To this document he added a postscript saying: "I
request a reply before six o'clock." Some Central Committee members wanted to delay consideration of the matter for several days.
But Lenin's notation to the Stalin letter, saying "Not to be de-
layed" (*ne otlagat'*), brought quick action. A Central Committee
plenum met on January 26 and passed a resolution in which the
Foreign Commissariat was asked to make an exact record of the
alleged treaty violations and to demand of the Georgian government
that it permit munitions to pass through its national territory en
route to Armenia. The resolution provided that armed assistance
be rendered the Georgian working people in event of necessity.
Preparations went forward in the Caucasus, and on February 6
Ordzhonikidze addressed a wire to Lenin and Stalin strongly urging immediate commencement of the armed uprising. Replies from
Lenin, dated February 8 and 14, gave the solicited authorization
subject to various provisos, including the curious one that international norms be observed.[84] On the night of February 11–12, disturbances broke out in a Georgian border area inhabited in part by
Armenians and Russians. On February 15, 1921, the Red Army invaded Georgia.

At his post in Tiflis, Zhordania had felt the pressure building up
from Russia during December and January. Based on information
from various sources, he formed the impression that a struggle was
going on in Moscow between advocates and opponents of war, with

84. *Lenin*, LII, 71, where the text of the telegram of February 14 is given.
It began: "The Central Committee is inclined to permit the Eleventh Army to give
active support to the uprising in Georgia and to take Tiflis, with observance of
international norms and on condition that all members of the Eleventh Army's
revolutionary war council, after serious consideration of all the facts, guarantee
success." For the reference to armed assistance in the January 26 resolution, see
Ocherki istorii, p. 473. On Stalin's knowledge and use of the Chicherin letter, see
Zhvaniia, "V. I. Lenin i partiinaia organizatsiia Gruzii."

Stalin and Trotsky at the head of the first camp and Lenin at the head of the second; and he tried to stave off invasion with a policy of offering concessions compatible with the preservation of his country's independence.[85] He was not in fact confronted with an internal revolutionary crisis. Although there was unrest among the Armenians in the border area where the disturbances were incited, the Menshevik regime had entrenched itself rather solidly with the Georgian population by its policies of land reform, limited national- ization in the economy, and Georgian cultural nationalism. But financially and militarily the regime was weak, and it lacked serious international support. Despite all this, the underequipped and poorly led Georgian forces resisted. It took the Red Army ten days to smash its way across the little country from the south and take Tiflis, and fighting continued in the western part of the country for another three weeks.[86] Full-scale armed aggression was required for Georgia's "self-determining." Meanwhile, Moscow sought to cam- ouflage its Georgian operation from the international public—and the Soviet public as well—by presenting it as an intervention in an Armenian-Georgian conflict during which internal revolutionary changes happened to occur. Speaking before the Moscow Soviet on February 28, Lenin touched on the Caucasian events, saying: "The clash between Armenia and Georgia could not but upset us, and

---

85. N. Zhordania, *Moia zhizn'* (Stanford, 1968), pp. 109, 112. Zhordania was mistaken about the role of Trotsky, who appears to have taken the soft line on this issue. He himself later recalled having espoused the view that peace with Poland and the defeat of Wrangel made it possible to safely postpone the inevitable sovietization of Georgia, so as to allow for "a certain preparatory period of work inside Georgia, in order to develop the uprising and later come to its aid" (Trotsky, *Stalin,* p. 268). Moreover, Trotsky, though he was war commissar, was so com- pletely bypassed in the military planning for the invasion that on February 21, 1921, he sent a wire from Ekaterinburg, in the Urals, to his deputy Sklyansky, in Moscow, saying: "Please compile for me a short note on the military operations against Georgia, when these operations began, by whose order, and so forth." For this document, see *The Trotsky Papers 1917–1922,* ed. Jan M. Meijer (The Hague, 1971), II, 385.

86. On Georgia under the Menshevik regime and on the armed conquest, see David M. Lang, *A Modern History of Soviet Georgia* (New York, 1962), chs. X and XI. He writes: "Red Army detachments headed by Sergo Orjonikidze en- tered Tbilisi on 25 February. The city was given over to murder, pillage and rape" (p. 235).

these events led to the Armenian-Georgian war's turning into an uprising in which a certain portion of Russian troops took part. And the outcome was that the Armenian bourgeoisie's design against us boomeranged against them, so far at any rate, and boomeranged in such a way that in Tiflis, according to the latest information, still unconfirmed, there is a Soviet regime." [87]

Lenin was worried over Georgian response to sovietization and also over reaction in the international socialist movement to the spectacle of Soviet overthrow of a Social Democratic government. Consequently, he put pressure on his colleagues to deal gently with conquered Georgia. In an interview of February 9 with Makharadze, who was leaving to head the "revolutionary committee" being set up in Georgia as a provisional new governmental authority, Lenin stressed that it was a petty-bourgeois country, that the Mensheviks were strong down there, that it was necessary to act very cautiously and not to apply the RSFSR's experience mechanically in solving Georgia's problems.[88] On March 3 Lenin wrote to Ordzhonikidze urging him to seek an acceptable compromise for a bloc with Zhordania or some other Georgian Mensheviks not absolutely hostile to the idea of a Soviet system in Georgia under certain conditions; and he bid the Georgian Communists "not to apply the Russian stereotype but skillfully and flexibly to create tactics of their own based on great willingness to make concessions to all manner of petty-bourgeois elements." [89] The suggested bloc with Zhordania did not materialize. Having departed for western Georgia just before Tiflis fell, Zhordania and his government boarded an Italian steamer on March 17 and sailed abroad.

In the wake of the military invasion came an influx of Soviet civilian officials into Georgia. On Stalin's proposal, the Orgburo decided on February 27 to mobilize party personnel immediately for service there. The Cheka and various commissariats took similar steps. On March 1, before arriving in his homeland, Makharadze

---

87. *Lenin*, XLII, 356. This speech appeared in *Pravda* on March 2, 1921.

88. Kharmandarian, *Lenin i stanovlenie*, p. 59.

89. *Lenin*, XLII, 367. A postscript said: "*To Stalin*. Request you to dispatch; if you have objections, talk over by phone." The letter was published in the Tiflis Bolshevik paper *Pravda gruzii* (Georgia's Truth) on March 6.

reported to Lenin from Vladikavkaz: "I see that countless 'in-chiefs' and 'especially empowereds,' representatives with earth-shaking mandates, are already descending upon us from various 'centers' and 'head offices.' " [90] In an effort to stem the southward flow of these Soviet carpetbaggers (as one is tempted to call them), Lenin instituted special procedures for high-level clearance of each assignment of a commissariat representative to Georgia. He also continued to urge upon his associates the necessity of a modulated approach in Transcaucasia. In a letter of April 14, 1921, to the Communists of all three Transcaucasian republics, he pointed out that there was no present danger of Entente intervention there, that the Caucasian republics were peasant societies to an even greater extent than Russia was, and that the Caucasus could develop trade and co-existence with the capitalist West still more quickly and easily than Russia could. More mildness, carefulness, conciliatoriness toward the petty bourgeoisie, intelligentsia, and peasantry were called for. A slower, more cautious, more systematic transition to socialism than in the RSFSR was both possible and necessary.[91]

But the forces set in motion by the invasion were not so easily contained. Bolshevism's Caucasian lobby, having pressed successfully for the decision to intervene in Georgia, was now in charge of the situation down there. Its leader, Ordzhonikidze, and its *éminence grise,* Stalin, were not disposed to deal with their fellow countrymen, or Caucasians in general, in the conciliatory manner prescribed by Lenin. The Kavburo, with Ordzhonikidze at its head, set up headquarters in Baku and asserted supreme authority in Transcaucasian affairs, laying down policy for the region in anything but a mild way. Ordzhonikidze was a tough administrator with a style more attuned to the heroic era of War Communism than to the dawning age of the NEP. It is true that certain elements in the party leaderships of all three Transcaucasian republics favored the cautious and discriminating line of policy that Lenin counseled.

90. Kharmandarian, *Lenin i stanovlenie,* p. 63. On the Orgburo decision proposed by Stalin, see this source, p. 57.

91. *Lenin,* XLIII, 198–200. This letter was published in *Pravda gruzii* on May 8, 1921.

But with Stalin's powerful assistance as chief of the Orgburo, Ordzhonikidze was able to secure the appointment of trusted men to
the key local positions. In August 1921, for example, Kirov was
sent down to Baku to take over the secretaryship of the Azerbaijan
Communist party organization. The Georgian party organization
was placed in the charge of one of Ordzhonikidze's more pliable associates, Mamia Orakhelashvili.

Georgia, however, was a special case. Unlike Azerbaijan,
which was less formed as a nation, and Armenia, whose people
perforce saw in Russia a protector against Turkey, Georgia had
taken readily to independent existence as a nation-state. Menshevik-
ruled Georgia had been a going concern. Here forcible sovietization
was a greater shock, experienced by many as a heinous violation of
the country's nationhood. The arrival of representatives of the
Cheka to take over police functions and of a large number of other
party and governmental officials from the north gave the place the
air of an occupied country. Moderates in the local leadership, like
Makharadze and Stalin's former brother-in-law Alexander Svanidze
(who became foreign commissar of the Georgian Soviet regime),
were appalled at the situation confronting them and wanted to follow
a policy of assuaging the Georgians' wounded national feeling. But
the higher leadership was not so inclined.

This became vividly apparent after Stalin arrived in Tiflis at
the end of June 1921 to take part in an important plenary meeting
of the Kavburo, with local leaders in attendance, to consider policy
questions affecting Georgia and Transcaucasia as a whole. His first
visit in many years to his native land proved a very different experience from the return to Baku eight months before. The plenum,
which was held behind closed doors in accordance with normal
party practice, opened on July 2 and continued for six days. During
this time Stalin agreed to speak at a mass meeting of railway workers.
His appearance on the speaker's platform was met with hisses, and
old women in the audience shouted epithets like "Accursed one,"
"Renegade," and "Traitor." Isidore Ramishvili and Alexander Dge-
buadze, two veteran Menshevik revolutionaries present in the audience, received an ovation, and the latter said to Stalin: "Why have

you destroyed Georgia? What have you to offer by way of atonement?" Stalin is reported to have turned pale and left the meeting-hall surrounded by his Russian Cheka bodyguard, and to have furiously upbraided Makharadze the next day as the man responsible for his humiliation.[92] According to a present-day Soviet historian's account, Ramishvili was carried up to the platform by some of those present, and the crowd would not let Stalin speak. Inflamed by this incident, Stalin made a behind-the-scenes demand for a tougher policy and complained that the Mensheviks were being treated too leniently. He also brought about—over considerable local opposition—the shift of Makharadze from the chairmanship of the Georgian Revolutionary Committee to the lesser post of republic commissar for agriculture. Some months later, Makharadze was recalled to Moscow at the request of Ordzhonikidze and assigned by the Orgburo to duties in the Central Committee office.[93] Ironically, Budu Mdivani, whom Stalin had nominated as the new head of the Revolutionary Committee, turned out to be a more forthright Georgian national leader than Makharadze.

Stalin also showed his anger when he appeared on July 6 before a more docile audience—a meeting of the Tiflis party organization—to deliver a major address on the tasks of Communism in Georgia and the Transcaucasus. He announced some benefits: Moscow would issue a loan of over six million gold rubles to the three Transcaucasian republics, and Azerbaijan would provide some oil products gratis to Georgia and Armenia. But the heart of the speech was a stern lecture to the Georgians on the necessity to "stamp out the hydra of nationalism." Returning to Tiflis after a lapse of years, Stalin said, he was unpleasantly struck by the lack of the solidarity that had existed in 1905–17 between workers of the different Transcaucasian nationalities, and by the way that nationalism had developed among the workers and peasants. Evidently, three years of life under nationalist governments had left their mark. So the Georgian Communists were faced with the task of carrying on a

92. Lang, *A Modern History of Soviet Georgia*, pp. 238–239.
93. Kharmandarian, *Lenin i stanovlenie*, pp. 85, 104. Makharadze was relieved of the chairmanship of the Revolutionary Committee on July 7.

"ruthless struggle against nationalism"—indeed, of "burning out" the remnants of nationalism "with a red-hot iron." Still another task was to unify the economic efforts of the three republics. Finally, the Communist party of Georgia must take care to preserve its purity and staunchness, remembering the sad fate of the German Social Democrats, who had gone down to ruin as a party by opening their ranks to all manner of "petty-bourgeois trash." In this connection, Stalin observed that "Lassalle was right in saying that a party strengthens itself by purging itself of filth." [94] To make sure that the message would reach a larger local audience, the speech was published in the Tiflis party paper a week later, as Stalin was about to depart.

For many years now, as we have seen, he had harbored a certain scorn for Georgia. The effect of the experience that he had just been through could only have been to harden this animosity and reinforce him in the feeling that his true homeland was not little Georgia but great Russia. To the long-standing estrangement from the land of his birth was added a new vindictiveness. This helps to account for a remark he made when an uprising broke out in 1924 in Georgia's Chiatura mining district and its environs. Georgia, said Stalin, must be "replowed anew." [95]

94. *Stalin*, V, 95–100. Stalin's speech was published in *Pravda gruzii* on July 13.

95. Trotsky, *Stalin*, p. 268.

Chapter Seven

CONFLICT WITH LENIN

On a Collision Course

GIVEN THE DIFFICULTY that associates had in getting along with Stalin, it may seem remarkable that his relations with Lenin held up as long and well as they did. Tensions had arisen between them from time to time, ever since the episode of 1911, but never of such seriousness as to jeopardize their relationship. Lenin seems to have sensed the need for special tact in dealing with Stalin, and evidently considered the effort involved worth making. He appreciated Stalin's strengths as a leader, valued his judgment in certain areas, and never doubted his supreme dedication to the cause. Also, he may have been influenced, if only subconsciously, by Stalin's personal feeling for him. He could not have been insensitive to the fact that this rough Caucasian, ten years his junior, had all along regarded him with the admiring eyes of a disciple and understudy and even harbored a certain unwonted tenderness toward him. Stalin, for his part, probably was on his best behavior in Lenin's presence, so that the latter was spared—at least until a very late date—some of the trying experiences that various other high Bolsheviks had with him.

Around 1921, however, their relationship began to show signs of strain. One contributing factor was Lenin's victory at the Tenth Congress and the resulting resolution of the intra-party conflict that had alienated him from Trotsky. These developments cleared the way for a renewal of Lenin's close ties with the man whom Stalin saw as his own arch-enemy; and *rapprochement* between Lenin and Trotsky could not fail to stir resentment in Stalin. Moreover, various episodes of the Civil War years that brought out Stalin's negative traits and the consequences to which they could lead—such as intrigues and ugly disputes—finally aroused in Lenin a foreboding about him as a personality. "This cook will concoct nothing but peppery dishes," he reportedly commented when Zinoviev—still maneuvering against Trotsky—pressed Stalin's candidacy for the party secretaryship in a private meeting of Lenin and a group of intimates during the Eleventh Congress.[1] By the same token, his acquiescence in Stalin's designation as general secretary may have been a reflection of the other side of an ambivalent attitude: his awareness of Stalin's valuable qualities as a leader.

But the misgivings remained. At a certain point, it seems, Lenin began to see personality in Stalin's case as a political problem. He began to perceive Stalin not only as a difficult man for colleagues to work with but as one whose personal failings could harm the Bolshevik cause. This concern must have deepened as his health deteriorated. Lenin spent most of the summer of 1921 resting at his country home in the village of Gorki, near Moscow. In December he became ill and returned to Gorki to recuperate, remaining there until March 1, 1922. In April he underwent an operation for removal of a bullet fired at him in 1918 by Fanya Kaplan. At the end of May, while resting again at Gorki, he had a stroke which caused partial paralysis of the right side. He soon recovered sufficiently to resume work, but suffered further strokes on December 13 and 22, after which he had to submit to a regime of greatly reduced activity.

During 1922 events moved swiftly toward a crisis in Lenin's relations with Stalin, who by this time felt sufficiently secure in his power base to assert views and persist in them even if they oc-

---

1. L. Trotsky, *Stalin: An Appraisal of the Man and His Influence* (New York, 1967), p. 357. In *My Life* (New York, 1930), Trotsky dates this incident at the Tenth Congress a year earlier. The earlier date is also given in his speech of October 23, 1927, in the Central Committee, for which see Trotsky, *The Real Situation in Russia* (New York, 1928), p. 7. If it did occur during the Tenth Congress, that might explain why the senior secretaryship went then to Molotov rather than Stalin in the post-congress voting on Central Committee offices.

casionally ran counter to Lenin's. One episode in the developing pattern of conflict was a dispute over proposed measures to relax the Soviet state's monopoly on foreign trade. The proposal emanated from Sokolnikov, Bukharin, and others who were both anxious to develop Soviet foreign trade and doubtful of the Foreign Trade Commissariat's capacity to do so successfully.[2] Sokolnikov, then commissar of finance, wanted to replace the foreign-trade monopoly with a regime of trade concessions, and sought permission for Soviet trusts and cooperatives to purchase foodstuffs directly from abroad. Lenin was incensed, foreseeing dangerous consequences if any move were taken to weaken the foreign-trade monopoly. He fought hard for his view but encountered persistent high-level opposition, some of which came from Stalin. Thus, when Lenin on May 15, 1922, wrote to Stalin and the vice commissar of foreign trade, M. Frumkin, proposing "formally to prohibit" all discussion of a relaxation of the monopoly, Stalin replied: "I have no objection at the *present* stage to the 'formal prohibition' of steps toward a *relaxation* of the foreign-trade monopoly. Still, I think the *relaxation* is becoming inevitable."[3] In the sequel Lenin enlisted Trotsky's assistance and finally won the behind-the-scenes battle over the foreign-trade monopoly.

Stalin was not the chief opponent of Lenin in this issue, but he did take the contrary position, and he held to it tenaciously in the face of Lenin's attack. When Trotsky cited the episode in his speech before the Comintern Executive Committee in late 1926, Stalin admitted having committed an error in regard to the foreign-trade monopoly. Minimizing it, he said that at a time when the procurement agencies were in chaos he had proposed the temporary opening of one Soviet port for grain export, and added: "But I did not per-

2. Moshe Lewin, *Lenin's Last Struggle* (New York, 1968), p. 35. Professor Lewin's is the fullest treatment of this episode in English, and his book is the most comprehensive study of the final period of Lenin's life. Its value is enhanced by a series of appendices giving the pertinent documents in English translation. See *Lenin*, XLV, for the correspondence on the dispute over the foreign-trade monopoly, and the note on pp. 548–549 of that volume for a brief Soviet account of the development of the dispute.

3. *Lenin*, XLV, 548.

sist in my error and, after discussing it with Lenin, at once rectified it." [4] This certainly understated both the seriousness of the matter and the amount of friction it generated. Still, the disagreement over the foreign-trade monopoly could not be compared in gravity with the conflict that broke out over the national question, and here Lenin was pitted directly against Stalin.

On the national question, Lenin's thinking was originally dominated by two distinct considerations, one relating to the revolutionary party and the other to revolution. Wanting to maintain a unified and strictly centralized Russian revolutionary movement, he saw the Austrian Social Democrats' "national-cultural autonomy" as a dangerously divisive idea in the party context; it was this aspect of his thinking that Stalin elaborated very effectively in *Marxism and the National Question*. But the very centrifugal forces of national separatism that appeared menacing to Lenin from the party standpoint were hopeful from the standpoint of revolution itself: they could contribute to the revolutionary break-up of the Tsarist Empire. Hence he espoused with great forcefulness the slogan of the "right of nations to self-determination"—something all the easier for him to do because of his revulsion for Great Russian nationalism and the tsarist idea and practice of "Russia One and Indivisible."

When the Empire did in fact collapse and disintegrate under the impact of war and revolution, Lenin was confronted with a political dilemma. As a foe of Great Russian nationalism, he was inclined to respect the right of national self-determination. But as a revolutionary statesman, he wanted to preserve as much as possible of the Empire under Bolshevik rule. Nor could he ignore such considerations as, for example, the economic value of Baku's oil industry or the strategic and political significance of such areas as Transcaucasia and Central Asia, inhabited predominantly by non-Slavs, or the immense importance from all points of view of the Ukraine,

4. *Stalin,* IX, 74–75. Proof that Stalin *did* persist in his "error" was first published in 1964 in the memoirs of Lenin's secretary, Fotieva, who reported that Stalin appended a note to a further letter from Lenin of October 13, 1922, saying: "Comrade Lenin's letter has not made me change my mind. . . ." See L. A. Fotieva, *Iz vospominanii o V. I. Lenine. Dekabr' 1922 g.–mart 1923 g.* (Moscow, 1964), p. 28.

with its population of Slavs of non–Great Russian ethnic stock. He tried to resolve the dilemma by, on the one hand, bowing to the overwhelming pressures to accept the secession of Poland, Finland, and the Baltic countries, and, on the other hand, seeking to retain the remainder of the vast former empire for the Revolution. Russified minority representatives like Stalin and Ordzhonikidze, who had no qualms about imposing Soviet Russian rule upon minority nationalities, were eager and effective instruments of the latter process. Stalin, as we have seen, never really felt at ease with the national self-determination slogan, although he repeated it on occasion. He tended to hedge the position, as, for example, when he told the Third All-Russian Congress of Soviets in January 1918 that it was necessary "to interpret the principle of self-determination as the right of self-determination not of the bourgeoisie but of the working masses of the given nation. The principle of self-determination should be an instrument in the struggle for socialism and should be subordinated to the principles of socialism." [5] In other words, self-determination should be construed in practice to mean sovietization.

Lenin was not inclined to reason away the problem with a casuistical formula of this sort. While permitting revolutionary and practical political considerations to take precedence over observance of the principle of national self-determination—as in Transcaucasia—he felt uneasy about this course of action. He therefore became doubly determined to prevent a revival of the Russification policies that the tsarist government had pursued toward the national minorities. Detesting the old-fashioned Russian national arrogance that he called "Great Russian chauvinism," he was intensely concerned that the Soviet Republic should not be guided by such an attitude in its dealing with the 65 million of its 140 million citizens who were ethnically either non-Slav or (in the case of the Ukrainians and Byelorussians) Slav but not Great Russian. Furthermore, he saw an enlightened policy on the national question as one of the ways in which Soviet Russia could contribute to the further progress of world revolution. If it could show the world the spectacle of a

5. *Stalin*, IV, 31–32.

genuine socialist commonwealth of nations, the socialist idea would become more attractive—es˜˜cially to those peoples of the East still suffering national oppressiᴜn under alien rule. So, in the same speech of February 1921 to the Moscow Soviet in which he spoke disingenuously of events then transpiring in Georgia, Lenin declared: "What we have succeeded in showing in the West—that wherever the Soviet power exists, there national oppression has no place—we shall show also in the East." [6]

At the beginning of the Soviet period Lenin had to contend with opposition on the national question from the Left Communist group led by Bukharin, Piatakov, and others, and it may be for this reason that he was slow to perceive the still more serious difference that he had with Stalin. Left Communism, as we have seen,[7] took exception to the idea of national self-determination on the ground that Marxists should approach society and politics in terms of internationalism and class, and not take nations as such too seriously. Reporting to the Eighth Party Congress in March 1919 on the party program, Bukharin argued (with a reference to Stalin's above-cited statement to the Third Congress of Soviets) that self-determination should refer to the working classes of a nation and not to the nation per se. The will of the Polish workers should be respected, for example, but not that of the Polish bourgeoisie. For the purposes of the anti-imperialist struggle, however, the principle of *national* self-determination could still be recognized for colonial peoples like the Hottentots, Bushmen, Negroes, and Hindus.[8]

In a rejoinder, Lenin contended that nations were still a basic fact in the life of society and must be accepted as such by the party. He observed drily that while there were no Bushmen in Russia and he had not heard of any Hottentots demanding an autonomous republic, there were Bashkirs, Kirghizes, and numerous other small non-Russian nations that *must* be recognized. Externally, too, and not only in the colonial world, nations were a political reality. By

6. *Lenin*, XLII, 357.
7. See p. 170, above.
8. *Vos'moi s"ezd RKP/b/. Mart 1918 goda. Protokoly* (Moscow, 1959), p. 47.

granting the Finns the right of national self-determination, Soviet Russia had made it impossible for the Finnish bourgeoisie to convince the working people that the Great Russians wanted to swallow them up. Later in the debate, Lenin returned to the subject of Finland. He recalled that when territorial concessions were made in a treaty concluded with the short-lived Red Finnish government, he had heard objections from Russian Communists: "Those were good fisheries and you gave them up." Such objections had provoked him to say: "Scratch certain Communists and you find a Great Russian chauvinist." Again, there were Communists in or around the Commissariat of Education who wanted a unified school system in which only the Russian language would be taught: "In my view such a Communist is a Great Russian chauvinist. He sits in many of us and we have to fight him." [9]

Many prominent Communists shared Lenin's worry. At the Tenth Party Congress two years later, where Stalin as commissar for nationality affairs gave the report on party policy in this sphere, a number of speakers showed deep concern over Great Russian nationalism. A co-report by G. I. Safarov, representing the Turkestan delegation, deplored the persistence of colonial relations between Great Russians and natives in Turkestan, and proposed that the theses which Stalin had submitted to the congress on nationality policy be supplemented with a clause approving "national-cultural self-determination" for the peoples of the Soviet East. V. P. Zatonsky, a delegate from the Ukraine, protested against the tendency of many Communists to think of the Soviet federation as Russian (*rossiiskaia*). Not only in the non-Russian borderlands but in central Russia itself, he said, the Revolution had awakened a national movement. The fact that Russia had led the way in Communist revolution, and had transformed itself from an appendage of Western Europe into the center of a world movement, had inspired a kind of "Russian Red patriotism" among some Russian Communists. They tended not simply to be proud of being Russians but to consider themselves first and foremost as Russians and to think of the

9. *Ibid.,* pp. 52–53, 106.

new state more as a Russia One and Indivisible than as a *Soviet* regime and federation. Significantly, Stalin ignored this contention in his reply to the discussion. Also, he dismissed Safarov's proposed amendment on national-cultural self-determination on the ground that it "smacked of" Bundism: "That is a Bundist formulation: national-cultural self-determination. We long ago dropped nebulous slogans on self-determination, and there is no need to revive them." [10]

Although his party comrades may only now have begun to realize it, the commissar for nationality affairs was himself one of the Communists infected with "Russian Red patriotism." He tended to take the viewpoint of Russia One and Indivisible. It is ironic but not surprising, therefore, that he and Lenin should finally have become antagonists over the very question that had once served to cement their association—not surprising, because Russian nationalism was as alien to Lenin's makeup as it was congenial, deep down, to Stalin's. As we have seen in an earlier chapter, Stalin acquired a sense of Russianness as a youthful revolutionary, seeing in Bolshevism the "true-Russian faction" of the Marxist movement. Paradoxically, the man whom Lenin himself regarded as a valuable party asset primarily in his capacity as a spokesman of minority nationalities, and who accepted for a long while that definition of his principal party role, was inwardly a budding Russian nationalist even before the two men met, and many years prior to Lenin's shocked discovery of his fully formed Russian nationalist outlook.

Stalin's self-identification with Russia underlay the *hauteur* toward minority-nation cultures, particularly Caucasian, which we earlier detected in *Marxism and the National Question,* and the eagerness with which he entered the lists for Lenin against "national-cultural autonomy" inside the party. True, in one passage of this work he based the argument for the "international type" of Social Democratic organization in Russia upon the view that "the workers are *primarily* members of one class family, members of a single army of socialism," adding that this view had "huge educational signifi-

10. *Desiatyi s''ezd RKP/b/. Mart 1921 goda. Stenograficheskii otchet* (Moscow, 1960), pp. 191–192, 201–203, 213, 300.

cance" for the workers.[11] But the primacy of class identity was not heavily emphasized; and in any case there was, as we have observed, no contradiction in Stalin's mind between simultaneously having class identity as a "real proletarian" and national identity as a "true Russian." On the contrary, they coalesced.

Bolshevism or Leninism, as he saw it, was an authentically Marxist, class-conscious revolutionary movement of international complexion *and* Russian through and through. In revealing words that he would use in an internal party document of April 1926, addressed to Kaganovich and other members of the Ukrainian party Politburo, Leninism was "the highest achievement of Russian culture." The document was a memorandum of a conversation between Stalin and a prominent Ukrainian Communist, O. Shumsky, who had pressed the case for bringing more Ukrainians into the Ukrainian Republic's party and trade union leadership and taking other measures of "Ukrainization," apparently including promotion of the Ukrainian language in public life. He had done so on the ground that a growing movement of intellectuals for Ukrainian culture might otherwise bypass the party. Stalin agreed that such a movement existed, but found Shumsky's proposals objectionable. Any forcible Ukrainization of the proletariat from above (it is not at all clear that Shumsky had advocated this) would only stir up anti-Ukrainian chauvinism among the non-Ukrainian elements of the working class in the Ukraine, he wrote. Was it not incongruous, moreover, that some Ukrainian intellectuals were urging a "de-Russification" of the Ukrainian proletariat and a cultural orientation *away* from Moscow at the very time when the proletarians of Western Europe and their Communist parties were looking *toward* Moscow and gazing with admiration at the flag flying over this citadel of the international revolutionary movement and of Leninism? Shumsky failed to see the seamy side of the new movement for Ukrainian culture and public life, the danger that "this movement, which is very often led by the non-Communist intelligentsia, may in places take on the character of a struggle to alienate Ukrainian culture

11. *Stalin*, II, 365.

and public life from general Soviet culture and public life, the character of a struggle against 'Moscow' in general, against Russians in general, against *Russian culture and its highest achievement—Leninism.*" [12]

It would never have occurred to Lenin and Russian revolutionaries like him to describe Bolshevism (Lenin never used the word "Leninism") as the highest achievement of "Russian culture." As a theory and practice of proletarian revolution and dictatorship it was for them simply a valid Russian manifestation of Marxism, which in turn was supra-national in essence and envisaged the eventual fusion of all nations in a higher unity. The fact that it bore a certain Russian impress due to circumstances of origin and growth —and everyone was aware that it did, especially in organizational practices—was not a source of satisfaction. Where Stalin differed was that he took positive pride in the Russianness of Leninism, rather as a radical patriotic Frenchman might see Jacobinism as the grand manifestation of the quintessential France. Stalin saw the rendezvous with Leninism as historic Russia's glorious fate. This did not, in his mind, impugn Leninism's worldwide relevance. In *The Foundations of Leninism,* he was insistent upon the international character of Leninism, which he defined as the Marxism of the contemporary era of wars and revolutions. As the 1926 memorandum makes plain, however, his internationalism was Moscow- and Russia-oriented. The point was again made clear in the following year, when he defined an "internationalist" as "he who is unreservedly, unhesitatingly, and unconditionally ready to defend the USSR, because the USSR is the base of the world revolutionary movement and it is impossible to defend and advance this movement without defending the USSR." [13]

Two decades later, in 1947, Stalin would issue a proclamation hailing Moscow, on the eight-hundredth anniversary of its founding, as the historic center of centralized Russian statehood. But that was only a further expression of an attitude already developed in him in the early twenties, his pride in Moscow as the citadel of the interna-

12. *Ibid.,* VIII, 149–153. Italics added.
13. *Ibid.,* X, 51.

tional revolutionary movement and of Leninism. He was intensely proud to be a Muscovite and a Russian. In a dispatch sent to Tiflis in February 1922, he identified himself as "a Muscovite." [14] The phrases "we Russian Marxists" and "we Russian Bolsheviks" appear frequently in his writings of the twenties. In his interview with Emil Ludwig in 1931, he even Russified his personal revolutionary origins by remarking that he had entered the revolutionary movement at the age of fifteen, "when I made contact with underground groups of Russian Marxists then living in the Transcaucasus." [15] In actuality, as he himself had admitted in his talk to the Tiflis railroaders in 1926, the Marxists with whom he first made contact were Georgian, not Russian. On that very visit to Tiflis, however, he was showing his Russianness. While attending a Georgian opera and chatting with the composer Balanchivadze during the intermission, he made a point of noting the influence of Russian operatic works, Tchaikovsky's in particular, upon the Georgian composers.[16]

On one occasion—at the Twelfth Party Congress in 1923—Stalin strongly condemned Great Russian chauvinism along with the various local chauvinisms, which were, he said, largely reactive in origin. A wish was abroad in certain quarters "to accomplish by peaceful means what Denikin failed to accomplish, i.e., to create the so-called 'One and Indivisible.' " The main danger was that "owing to the NEP, great-power chauvinism is growing in our country by leaps and bounds, striving to obliterate all that is not Russian, to gather all the threads of government into the hands of the Russian element, and to stifle everything that is not Russian." [17] This was a fair description of the Russian nationalist tendency that aroused anxiety in the minds of Lenin and others in the party, but it did not express Stalin's real attitude. He spoke at that congress under circumstances which, as we shall see presently, made it imperative for him to conceal his own bias toward the very thing he was condemning. An earlier statement not made under those polit-

14. Richard Pipes, *The Formation of the Soviet Union*, rev. ed. (New York, 1968), p. 281 n.
15. *Stalin*, XIII, 113.
16. *Ibid.*, VIII, 396.
17. *Ibid.*, V, 238–239, 245.

ical pressures gives a better view of his real position. On January 1, 1921, he opened a conference of Communists from the Turkic peoples of the RSFSR with a short extemporaneous speech in which he said that these and other peoples which had suffered national oppression in the past were now faced with a problem of overcoming remnants of nationalism and even a "nationalist deviation." In contrast, the fight against nationalist deviation had never had any serious significance in the history of Russian Communism. Having been a ruling nation, the Russians—and the Russian Communists in particular—had not experienced national oppression and consequently had not had to contend with nationalist tendencies in their midst, save for certain leanings toward great-power chauvinism, and hence had little or no problem of overcoming such tendencies.[18] Stalin seemed oblivious of the nationalist phenomenon among historically ruling nations, and failed to see Great Russian chauvinism, despite his perfunctory reference to it, as a serious problem. Between his proudly Russocentric outlook and Lenin's there was a mental chasm of which Lenin became grimly conscious in 1922.

The Constitutional Issue

Deep political conflicts often emerge in terms of issues that seem on the surface to be of secondary importance. An issue that played such a part in the present instance had to do with the formalities of the Soviet constitutional structure. It began to arise as early as January 1920, when Stalin, then on the southern front, wrote a letter to Lenin commenting on the latter's draft theses on the national and colonial questions for the Second Congress of the Comintern. In clause seven of the theses, Lenin affirmed "federation" as an interim method of organizing the state relations between the working people of different nations. Federation had shown its expediency, he said, both in the relations of the RSFSR with other Soviet republics, such as the Ukraine, and in the practice of pro-

18. *Ibid.,* p. 2. One may infer that the speech was extemporaneous from the fact that it is described here as a "record in the minutes of the meeting." As such it first appeared in *Pravda* on January 12, 1921.

viding an autonomous state existence within the RSFSR for such smaller nationalities as the Bashkirs. This was a reference to the constitutional distinction between "union republics," with which the RSFSR was in treaty relations (the Ukraine, Byelorussia, Azerbaijan), and "autonomous republics," which were constitutionally granted a certain political competence but not formally regarded as independent. Stalin, in his letter to Lenin, expressed doubt that a future Soviet Germany, Poland, Hungary, or Finland would soon wish to federate with Soviet Russia, and suggested that this problem be solved by providing for a future "confederation" or "union of independent states." The distinction between the two types of federative relations *inside* the Soviet federation—Ukrainian and Bashkirian—would be of no help, he said, since "in actual fact there is no such distinction, or it is so small as to equal zero." [19] Stalin's coming conflict with Lenin over nationality policy was foreshadowed in this exchange.

In 1922 the party leadership decided to redefine the constitutional system of federal relationships, and Stalin was appointed to head a Central Committee commission on the project. Higher party circles were sharply divided over this question. Some wanted to incorporate the Ukraine, Byelorussia, and the Transcaucasian Federation (into which Azerbaijan had meanwhile been merged, along with Armenia and Georgia) directly into the RSFSR as autonomous republics. A few still more extreme centralizers favored the merger of all the existing Soviet republics into a "Russian Soviet Republic" that would no longer even be federally organized—an outright Russia One and Indivisible in Soviet form. On the other side, there were Georgian, Bashkir, and other local party leaders who desired a looser federal state in which even the existing "autonomous republics" would be elevated to union status. Stalin drafted for the commission a set of theses that took the first position: the Ukraine, Byelorussia, Azerbaijan, Georgia, and Armenia were to enter the Russian Federation as autonomous republics, and the supreme governmental organs of the RSFSR were to become

19. Lenin, *Sochineniia,* 2nd ed., XXV (Moscow, 1928), p. 624.

supreme for these republics as well.[20] He was clearly a centralizer.

When circulated to the Central Committees of the borderland republics for their reactions, Stalin's "autonomization" plan was not very well received. The Ukrainian and Byelorussian party leaderships, although not openly opposed to the plan, were also less than enthusiastic. The Azerbaijani party's Central Committee gave it unqualified support—no doubt a tribute to Kirov's commanding position in that party. So did Ordzhonikidze's Kavburo and the Armenian Central Committee. The Central Committee of Georgia's Communist party was, however, in open opposition. On September 15, it passed a decision—over the negative votes of Ordzhonikidze and Kirov, who were both present—pronouncing the autonomization proposed in Stalin's theses premature. Unification of economic efforts and general policy among the several Soviet republics was necessary, "but with preservation of all the attributes of independence."[21] Nevertheless, the Central Committee commission, meeting September 23–24, 1922, with Molotov in the chair, accepted the autonomization plan with one abstaining vote (that of Mdivani, who represented Georgia on the commission). On the following day, Stalin's draft, the commission's resolution, and the protocols of its meetings were sent to Lenin in Gorki. At the same time, and without awaiting Lenin's comments, the Central Committee Secretariat (i.e., Stalin) circulated the commission's resolution to all members of the Central Committee in preparation for its plenum, scheduled for October 5.[22]

Lenin's response was quick and negative. After talking with Stalin on September 26, he summed up his position in a letter of the same date to Kamenev for members of the Politburo. The issue is one of supreme importance, he began, and "Stalin has a little

20. On the three positions and Stalin's stand, see V. V. Pentkovskaia, "Rol' V. I. Lenina v obrazovanii SSSR," *Voprosy istorii,* No. 3 (1956), pp. 16–17. Also, Pipes, *Formation of the Soviet Union,* pp. 271–272.

21. Pentkovskaia, "Rol' V. I. Lenina," pp. 17–18.

22. The full details of this story and ensuing developments have been revealed only since Stalin died. See, in particular, *Lenin,* XLV, 556–560, and Pentkovskaia, "Rol' V. I. Lenina." Lewin, *Lenin's Last Struggle,* ch. 4, and Pipes, *Formation of the Soviet Union,* ch. VI, both present detailed accounts based on recent Soviet materials.

tendency to be in a hurry." Stalin, he went on, had agreed to one concession: instead of referring to the other republics' "entry" into the RSFSR (i.e., to their autonomization), the resolution would convey a spirit of equality of the Russian Federation with the other republics by speaking of "their formal unification, together with the RSFSR, in a union of Soviet republics of Europe and Asia." Other changes, however, were still needed. Instead of making the Central Executive Committee of the Russian Federation into the supreme governmental organ of all the Soviet republics, there should be a new *federal* Central Executive Committee. Similarly, certain services should be placed under the jurisdiction not of existing RSFSR commissariats but of new federal commissariats situated in Moscow. It was important, Lenin explained, not to supply fuel to the "advocates of independence," and not to destroy their independence but rather to create a "new *level,* a federation of equal republics." [23]

Stalin received Lenin's letter with hostility. On September 27, he circulated it to the Politburo members along with a letter of his own explaining some objections to Lenin's proposals. To set up a Central Executive Committee of the federation alongside that of the RSFSR, he said, would only generate conflict and debate by creating two such organs in Moscow, one of which would obviously become a "lower house" and the other an "upper house." Showing how wounded he was by Lenin's remark on his tendency to be in a hurry, Stalin went on to say that Comrade Lenin himself had "hurried a little" in proposing the merger of certain existing commissariats with new federal ones. "There is hardly a doubt," he added, "that this 'hastiness' will 'supply fuel to the advocates of independence,' to the detriment of the national liberalism of Comrade Lenin." [24] Despite this outburst of pique, however, Stalin reworked the Central Committee commission's resolution in accordance with Lenin's proposals, which adumbrated the federal system of the USSR as re-fashioned under the new Soviet Constitution of 1924. In this altered form the

23. *Lenin,* XLV, 211–213.

24. This letter of Stalin's has never been published in full. Reference to it, and specifically to the charge of "national liberalism" against Lenin, is made in *Lenin,* XLV, 558. A partial text was made public by Trotsky in *The Stalin School of Falsification* (New York, 1962), pp. 66–67.

resolution came before the Central Committee when it gathered on October 5 for a two-day plenum. A severe toothache kept Lenin from attending on October 6, but he wrote a brief note that day to Kamenev saying—with obvious reference to the events just recounted—"I declare a life-and-death war on Great Russian chauvinism." [25]

The Georgian Affair

The conflict reached a climax later in the year under the impetus of events in Georgia. In 1921 Ordzhonikidze became embroiled with an influential group of Georgian Communist leaders over controversial questions of state organization in Transcaucasia. Some form of unification seemed desirable for economic reasons, among others, but there was no agreement on the best form. One plan, which Stalin and Ordzhonikidze decided to espouse, called for a "Transcaucasian Federation" within which Georgia, Azerbaijan, and Armenia would continue to exist as separate but closely interrelated Soviet republics. In effect, this would create an all-Transcaucasian governmental body subordinate to the Kavburo and thus facilitate the latter's control over the political life of the whole region. At a later point in the dispute, Ordzhonikidze implicitly admitted this motive by saying before a congress of Transcaucasian party organizations: "This truth—about the necessity to organize an administrative-political center in the Transcaucasus—was something that even obtuse Russian tsarism realized." [26]

On November 3, 1921, the Kavburo, meeting in a plenary ses-

25. *Lenin,* XLV, 214. For an alternative view of the constitutional issue and the Lenin-Stalin difference over the national question, see Lewin, *Lenin's Last Struggle,* pp. 58–63. Proceeding from Isaac Deutscher's suggested division of the Bolshevik leaders into two types—power-oriented "activists" and idealistic "theoreticians"—Professor Lewin sees the nub of these issues not in Stalin's Russian nationalism but in the contrast between his activist approach to the national question, concerned only with administrative efficiency, and Lenin's more ideological approach.

26. S. V. Kharmandarian, *Lenin i stanovlenie zakavkazskoi federatsii. 1921– 1925* (Erevan, 1969), p. 361. The central governing organ in the tsarist period was the viceroyship, the entire Transcaucasian region being divided into five gubernias.

sion in Baku with Molotov (then the senior Central Committee secretary) in attendance, decided to go ahead with the federation plan. This decision was communicated to the Politburo, which was taken by surprise and asked Ordzhonikidze for further information on the matter. Local circles were also taken by suprise, for the Kavburo passed the decision without preliminary discussion by the three Transcaucasian party central committees and in the absence of Mdivani, who was one of its members. It then secured the approval of these party bodies, but in the Georgian case over strenuous opposition from a sizable group of Communist leaders headed by Mdivani, who pronounced the federation plan "premature." [27]

Conscious of Georgian Communism's special predicament vis-à-vis the population and anxious to preserve at least the outer trappings of the country's national independence, these Communists were uneasy about early federation, disinclined to see Ordzhonikidze increase his power of control over them, and incensed at the hasty and high-handed manner in which the Kavburo had taken its action. They undertook to slow down the creation of the federative structure, and in the process Georgian tempers grew hotter. At a meeting of the Georgian Central Committee's presidium on November 23, Mdivani declared that the whole Georgian Central Committee, with the exception of only three members, considered Ordzhonikidze the "evil genius" of the Caucasus and thought it necessary to secure his recall. Two days later Mdivani telegraphed Stalin a personal message protesting the procedures that had been followed, complaining that "Sergo is accusing the Georgian Communists, me in particular, of chauvinism," and proposing that the composition of the Kavburo be changed. Apprised of Mdivani's action, Ordzhonikidze and Orakhelashvili pressured the Georgian Central Committee into adopting a rule forbidding any member to communicate with higher party organs without submitting a copy of the communication to the Central Committee itself. This evoked a stern rebuke from the Moscow Central Committee, which ordered Ordzhonikidze to re-

27. *Ibid.*, pp. 96–98, 202–203. On the lack of advance discussion by the three central committees, see *Lenin*, XLIV, 566.

peal the rule and warned him not to institute a censorship of that kind. All party members were to continue enjoying the right to communicate their impressions on any matter directly to the Central Committee.[28]

The appeal to Stalin over Ordzhonikidze's head necessarily failed, since Stalin was masterminding Ordzhonikidze's course of action on the federation. When the Kavburo toward the end of November responded to the Politburo's request for more information by sending the pertinent documents to Moscow, Stalin went through these materials and drafted a Politburo decision which he sent to Lenin for approval. This communication has never been published (according to present-day Soviet historians it is missing from the Central Party Archive), but judging from Lenin's reply—a note to Stalin of November 28, 1921—it approved the federation scheme, and did so in a manner that failed to stress the need to move slowly and make a concerted effort to persuade the local parties and people of the advantages of a federation. On November 26, Lenin had received a telegram from Mikhail Frunze, a Bolshevik leader and Central Committee member then traveling through the Caucasus, speaking of the opposition among the Georgian Communists to the federation scheme and of their objections to the way in which it had been sprung on them. In his note of two days later to Stalin, Lenin accepted the latter's draft decision in the main but suggested that it be formulated "just a little bit differently." Then he phrased it to read that the federation plan was absolutely correct in principle "but premature in the sense of immediate practical fulfillment, i.e., requiring several weeks of discussion, propaganda, and promotion from below through the soviets." The three Transcaucasian central committees were directed to raise the matter for discussion by their parties and the masses of workers and peasants, to carry it through congresses of soviets in each republic, and to inform the Politburo right away in the event of any considerable opposition. Stalin replied that same day, accepting Lenin's draft but suggesting that the phrase "several weeks" be amended to read "a certain period of time." He explained that several weeks would not be enough

28. Kharmandarian, *Lenin i stanovlenie*, pp. 203–205, 214–215.

time to put the plan through the Georgian soviets, which were "only beginning to be organized." [29] So amended, Lenin's draft resolution received Politburo approval on the following day.

But Georgian Communist resistance to the federation plan did not end at this point, nor did Ordzhonikidze's embroilment with its leaders. On December 6, 1921, shortly before returning to Georgia as the republic's commissar for agriculture, Makharadze sent Lenin and the Central Committee a memorandum in which he said that Transcaucasia's economic unification had been carried through from above without advance preparation and "by way of battle orders." As for the federation, this was a formal kind of political unification, likewise imposed from above, that would accomplish nothing, and signified "simply the creation at the top of one more superfluous bureaucratic apparatus, extremely unpopular in the eyes of the masses and utterly isolated from them." [30] On December 13, Svanidze wrote a personal letter to his high-placed relative saying:

Dear Iosif!

Not a single Central Committee has taken place lately that didn't start and end with stormy scenes between Sergo and Budu. Ordzhoni-kidze is beating us with the heavy club of the Center's authority, some-thing, by the way, for which we have no less respect and confidence than the comrades from the Kavburo do. One request I urgently make of you is that you somehow reconcile Sergo and Budu, if that's objectively pos-sible. Teach them to treat each other with respect.

P.S. I shall be boundlessly grateful to you for tearing me out of this atmosphere and giving me the chance to work in some mission abroad.[31]

Svanidze's request for a foreign assignment was granted (he sub-sequently became Soviet trade representative in Berlin), but there is no indication that Stalin undertook to reconcile Ordzhonikidze and Mdivani. While operating in the background—as was his habit—and letting others do the open fighting, he was himself a principal protagonist in the conflict.

29. *Ibid.*, pp. 206, 217. For the text of Lenin's draft, see *Lenin*, XLIV, 255.
30. Kharmandarian, *Lenin i stanovlenie*, p. 217.
31. *Ibid.*, p. 218.

The federation finally became a reality at the end of 1922.
Meanwhile, however, the conflict entered a new phase when the
constitutional issue emerged in the fall of that year. Mdivani and
his friends were unhappy with Stalin's "autonomization" plan and
greatly heartened by the discovery—in personal interviews with
Lenin—that he was also against it and in favor of a union of formally equal Soviet republics. Mdivani saw Lenin on September 27
to discuss the constitutional problem, and two days later Lenin had
a talk with three of Mdivani's supporters: M. S. Okudzhava, L. E.
Dumbadze, and Kote Tsintsadze. During the latter interview Lenin
asked: if "autonomization" is bad, what about a "union"? The delighted Georgians replied that if little Georgia were to enter the
USSR on a par with the huge Russian Federation, this would be a
"trump card" to play in the effort to win over the Georgian masses.[32]
The Central Committee plenum of October 5–6, 1922, accepted
Lenin's plan for a USSR, but with the proviso that both the Russian
Republic and Transcaucasia enter it as federations. Although the
Georgian opposition thus received only partial satisfaction, its
leaders were greatly cheered to know that they had such a powerful ally as Lenin in their struggle against those whom some speakers
in the October plenum had stigmatized as the "great-powerites"
(*velikoderzhavniki*). As one of the Georgians put it not long afterward, "We are in line with Lenin, they are for War Communism." [33]
The unidentified "they" referred above all to Stalin and Ordzhonikidze.

So buoyed up were the Georgians by the new turn of events
that upon returning home they reopened the federation question,
proposing at a plenum of the Tiflis Party Committee that Georgia
enter the USSR as a separate republic. Ordzhonikidze was beside
himself, and at a meeting held the next day, October 20, he cried
out: "The leadership of the Central Committee of the Georgian
Communist party is chauvinist rot which has to be thrown out
immediately." That night seven of those present, including Makharadze, called Moscow on the direct wire and dictated to Abel

32. *Ibid.*, p. 344.
33. *Ibid.*, pp. 348, 369.

Yenukidze, who came on at the other end, a bitter complaint against Ordzhonikidze to be transmitted to Lenin via Bukharin and Kamenev (they evidently did not trust Stalin to transmit it). On the following day, the Georgian Central Committee voted by a majority of nine to three to petition for Georgia's direct entry into the USSR. But Lenin, after turning over the complaint to the Secretariat, i.e., to Stalin, sent the Georgians a telegram reaffirming the decision of the October plenum and reproving them for their invective against Ordzhonikidze. And Stalin on October 22 wired Ordzhonikidze as follows: "We intend to put an end to the wrangle in Georgia and thoroughly punish the Georgian Central Committee. Let me know whom we should transfer out of Georgia beyond those other four. In my opinion we have to take a decisive line and expel any and all remnants of nationalism from the Central Committee. Did Lenin's telegram come? He is furious and extremely unhappy with the Georgian nationals." [34] At this point the Georgian Central Committee collectively resigned. The dissident majority sent Lenin a telegram apologizing for the sharpness of their language in the nocturnal message but disclaiming responsibility for the conflict. Meanwhile Ordzhonikidze proceeded, with Stalin's powerful assistance, to carry out a purge of the Georgian party, removing the oppositionists from their governmental posts.

Higher party circles in Moscow realized by now that an abnormal situation had arisen in Georgia. Both Kamenev and Bukharin proposed to the Politburo that the Central Committee should appoint a commission of inquiry. Stalin was in no position to object, but countered with the shrewd suggestion that the logical person to head the commission would be Dzerzhinsky, who was then on a holiday for his health in Sukhumi, on Georgia's Black Sea coast. Yenukidze, who was Lenin's choice for this role, prudently declined. The Secretariat proceeded to nominate Dzerzhinsky as chairman of the commission and V. S. Mitskiavichus-Kapukas and L. N. Sosnovsky as members. Remembering Dzerzhinsky's erstwhile opposition to the slogan of national self-determination, Lenin was not pleased with the composition of the commission and abstained

34. *Ibid.*, pp. 351, 352–354.

when the Politburo members were polled by phone for their votes on the nominations. Stalin, Kamenev, Kalinin, and Zinoviev voted in favor, and Trotsky said, "I don't object." Mdivani, who returned to Moscow at that time from a trip abroad, objected to the composition of the commission, Sosnovsky in particular. Stalin obliged by replacing Sosnovsky with a Ukrainian, Dimitry Manuilsky, who was in fact one of his own followers.[35]

Lacking faith in the commission's impartiality, Lenin asked Rykov, his deputy in the Council of People's Commissars, to go to Tiflis and carry out an investigation of his own. At the end of November 1922, on the eve of the Dzerzhinsky inquiry, a fateful incident occurred in Ordzhonikidze's Tiflis apartment. Rykov was chatting with one A. Kobakhidze, a supporter of Mdivani. When Ordzhonikidze broke into the conversation, Kobakhidze referred accusingly to his possession of a white horse and added an insulting remark, whereupon the enraged Ordzhonikidze slapped him in the face.[36] In memoirs written after Stalin's death, Anastas Mikoyan explained that Ordzhonikidze had received the white horse as a gift from the mountaineers upon his return to the Caucasus. After accepting the gift, which Caucasian tradition obliged him to do, he had turned the horse over to the official stables and only used it when he rode in parades in Tiflis. Kobakhidze had unjustly accused him of being corrupt.[37]

When Lenin learned of this incident from Dzerzhinsky, he reacted as though he himself had received the slap in the face. He was also indignant at the news, which had reached him from Georgian sources, that Stalin and Ordzhonikidze had stigmatized the majority of the Georgian Central Committee in open meetings as "deviationists" and that they had spoken of burning out nationalist sentiment with a red-hot iron.[38] For Lenin all this was too much.

---

35. *Ibid.,* pp. 369–370. Stalin's closeness to Manuilsky may not have been well known to others at the time.

36. *Ibid.,* p. 370.

37. A. I. Mikoyan, *Dorogoi bor'by. Kniga pervaia* (Moscow, 1971), p. 433.

38. Fotieva, *Iz vospominanii,* p. 54. The latter phrase, as noted above, was used by Stalin in his speech of July 6, 1921, in Tiflis. That speech was not published in the Moscow press.

He could not bear the thought that high-placed representatives of his regime were so conducting themselves toward a minority nation of Soviet Russia. He found Ordzhonikidze's behavior intolerable; and Stalin, for whose rude ways he had made allowances time and time again, finally began to appear to him in a sinister light. Now, at long last, he ranged himself mentally on the side of the Georgian opposition. When Dzerzhinsky came to him on December 12 to report the findings of his commission, which had held four days of hearings in Tiflis earlier in the month, Lenin was not to be put off by his exoneration of Stalin and Ordzhonikidze. He directed Dzerzhinsky to return to Georgia for more information about the incident between Ordzhonikidze and Kobakhidze. Soon after, on December 16, he succumbed to a new stroke. On December 30–31, when he was sufficiently recovered to be able to work for a brief time each day, he dictated a set of notes "On the Question of Nationalities, or About 'Autonomization.' " This memorandum—Lenin's final statement on the national question—contained a severe indictment of Stalin.

Starting with an assertion of his own guilt for not having intervened energetically enough in the question of autonomization, Lenin made reference to his discussion with Dzerzhinsky and the incident of physical violence by Ordzhonikidze. If matters had gone that far, he declared, one could imagine "what a swamp we have gotten into." Evidently, the whole notion of autonomization had been radically unsound and untimely. Unity of the apparatus was needed, so the supporters of autonomization said. But whence the demand for unity if not from the very same "Russian apparatus" that had been taken over from tsarism and barely anointed with Soviet oil? There was a great danger that the tiny percentage of truly Soviet or sovietized workers would "drown in that sea of chauvinist Great Russian riffraff, like a fly in milk." Under existing conditions, the declared freedom of exit from the union was no real protection for the minorities against invasion by that true-Russian man and Great Russian chauvinist—the typical Russian bureaucrat, a brute and scoundrel.

Steps had not been taken to protect the minorities from such individuals. "I think that here a fatal role was played by Stalin's hastiness and love of issuing orders, and also by his malice against the notorious 'social-nationalism,' " Lenin went on. "In general, malice usually plays the very worst role in politics." Dzerzhinsky too had distinguished himself on the Caucasian assignment by his true-Russianism, and here Lenin observed parenthetically that Russified minority representatives were always overdoing it on the side of true-Russianism. Ordzhonikidze's "Russian laying on of hands" was not to be excused, as Dzerzhinsky had attempted to do, by referring to his irascibility. As the man in authority in the Caucasus, he had no right to lose his self-control. Ordzhonikidze must be given an exemplary punishment, and Stalin and Dzerzhinsky must be held politically responsible for the Great Russian nationalist campaign. Viewing the problem in broad terms, Lenin insisted that the nationalism of a great oppressor nation was more to be feared than that of a small oppressed one. In dealings with the latter, it was better to err on the side of softness and conciliation. The harm that could result from disunity of Russian and national apparatuses was incomparably less than that which Soviet Russia could do to itself and to the Comintern in the eyes of the emergent Eastern peoples by showing any rudeness or injustice to its own minorities. A Georgian who overlooked the need for hyper-caution and prudence in dealings with a minority nation and who scornfully tossed around charges of "social nationalism"—such a Georgian, in addition to being himself not just a "social national" but a rude Great Russian Derzhimorda, was violating the interests of proletarian class solidarity in a most serious way.[39]

In further preparation for a statement on the national question that he hoped to make to the coming Twelfth Party Congress, Lenin toward the end of January asked his secretary, Fotieva, to obtain for him the materials of the Dzerzhinsky commission's investigation in Georgia. She had difficulty in doing so. Dzerzhinsky, now back from his second mission, referred her to Stalin. He in turn refused to hand over the materials without the Politburo's per-

39. *Lenin*, XLV, 356–362. "Derzhimorda," a Russian colloquialism deriving from a police character in Gogol's play *The Inspector General*, connotes a crude police type.

mission, and suggested that she was violating the rule now in force that Lenin should not be given information on day-to-day matters.[40] On February 1, in a session during which Stalin made plain his reluctance to grant Lenin's request, the Politburo decided to let him have the materials. After obtaining them, Lenin appointed three secretaries—Fotieva, Maria Gliasser, and Nikolai Gorbunov—as a private commission of inquiry into the Georgian affair. Its report, which came to him on March 3, spurred him to further action. On March 5, he dictated a letter to Trotsky asking him to undertake the defense of the Georgian affair in the forthcoming pre-congress Central Committee plenum. "That affair is now under 'persecution' at the hands of Stalin and Dzerzhinsky and I cannot rely on their impartiality," he said. "Indeed, quite the contrary! If you would agree to undertake its defense, I could be at rest." Next day he sent the following message to the leaders of the Georgian opposition, Mdivani and Makharadze, with copies to Trotsky and Kamenev: "I am following your affair with all my heart. I am indignant at the rudeness of Ordzhonikidze and the little indulgences of Stalin and Dzerzhinsky. I am preparing notes and a speech for you." [41] On that same day, his health took another sharp turn for the worse, and on March 10 he suffered the paralyzing stroke that finished his active life.

Along with the letter of March 5, Trotsky received a copy of Lenin's notes of December 30–31 on the national question. Through Fotieva he asked permission to make these materials known to Kamenev, who was about to leave on a trip to Georgia. After conferring with Lenin, Fotieva returned with a negative answer: "Vladimir Ilyich says: 'Kamenev will immediately show everything to Stalin, and Stalin will make a rotten compromise and then deceive us!' " When Trotsky inquired whether this meant that in Lenin's view it was no longer possible to compromise with Stalin "even on the right line," Fotieva replied: "Yes, he does not trust Stalin, and wants to

40. Fotieva, *Iz vospominanii*, p. 63. On these developments see also Lewin, *Lenin's Last Struggle*, pp. 94–95, and Pipes, *Formation of the Soviet Union*, pp. 284–286. On Lenin's medical regime see below.

41. *Lenin*, LIV, 329, 330.

come out against him openly, before the entire party. He is preparing a bomb." [42] In the sequel, however, it was Trotsky who made a "rotten compromise." He informed Kamenev that he was against removing Stalin, expelling Ordzhonikidze, and displacing Dzerzhinsky from the Commissariat of Transport. He demanded only a change of policy in the national question, no more persecution of Stalin's Georgian opponents, no more administrative oppression in the party, a firmer policy in industrialization, and "honest cooperation" in the leading organs.[43]

Stalin was only too glad to offer full satisfaction on all points, and to accept Trotsky's specific proposal that the theses on the national question (which Stalin had prepared for the coming congress) be revised to include a sharp denunciation of Great Russian chauvinism and the notion of "Russia One and Indivisible." He even proposed in the Politburo that Trotsky, as the "most popular member" of the Central Committee, give the main political report to the congress in Lenin's place.[44] Trotsky, for his part, agreed to let the Politburo decide whether and how Lenin's notes should be made known to the congress. The Politburo decided that instead of being published as a congress document, they should be read to the various delegations in closed session (not until 1956 were they published). This set the scene for the rather tame proceedings of the Twelfth Party Congress, which met in April. Given Trotsky's silence, Stalin had no difficulty weathering the debate on the national question. Although, in keeping with the agreement, he stressed the special danger of Great Russian chauvinism, he also struck out hard against his Georgian opponents. He deplored the existence of "Georgian chauvinism," and used his conflict with the "comrade-deviationists" in Georgia to illustrate the proposition that an anti-Russian "defensive nationalism" in the minority regions tended to

42. Trotsky, *My Life,* p. 484. She added that the word "bomb" was not hers but Lenin's. A little later in the day, aware that his condition was worsening, Lenin changed his mind and authorized Trotsky to acquaint Kamenev with the materials (p. 482).

43. *Ibid.,* p. 486.

44. Trotsky, *Stalin,* p. 366. Trotsky refused, as did Stalin, and Zinoviev took it upon himself to give the political report.

turn into an "offensive nationalism." He accused the Georgian opposition of resisting the federation scheme because of a wish to exploit Georgia's "privileged situation" in the Transcaucasus for nationalistic purposes. And in telling the story of his suggestion to Lenin to allow for more time to carry the scheme through the Georgian soviets, he made it appear that he, rather than Lenin, had been the voice of circumspection on that matter. In one of his congress speeches he even made the scornful statement—with reference to the Mdivani group—that "certain comrades working on a little piece of Soviet territory called Georgia apparently have something wrong in their upper story." [45]

Lenin's notes (described in several speeches as his "letter" on the national question) were communicated to the congress via the delegation caucuses, but non-publication of the document deprived it of much of its political impact. In vain did Mdivani refer to it as expressing "the Ilyich school in the national question." [46] In vain did the Ukrainian Bolshevik leader Nikolai Skrypnik castigate the "party swamp" present at the congress—those who would vote for the resolution on the national question but were Great Russian chauvinists at heart. Nor did Bukharin make much headway when he spoke up in the Georgians' defense. "I understand when our dear friend, Comrade Koba Stalin, is not so sharp in opposing Russian chauvinism, and that he, as a Georgian, opposes Georgian chauvinism," Bukharin observed. Then, as a non-Georgian, he asked leave to concentrate his own fire upon chauvinism of the Russian variety. The essence of Leninism in the national question lay in the fight against this basic form of chauvinism, which generated the other, local forms as reactions. So as to compensate for their past as a great-power nation, Bukharin went on, the Great Russians must

45. *Stalin*, V, 232, 253, 256, 262, 279. In editing these speeches for his collected works, Stalin changed "little piece" (*kusochek*) to "piece" (*kusok*) in the last passage quoted here. The original formulation is shown in *Dvenadtsatyi s"ezd rossiiskoi kommunisticheskoi partii /bol'shevikov/. Stenograficheskii otchet* (Moscow, 1923), p. 204.

46. *Dvenadtsatyi s"ezd*, p. 454. Not only was the letter not read out at the Twelfth Congress, but, according to Fotieva (*Iz vospominanii*, p. 56), it was only under pressure from Lenin's personal secretariat that Stalin arranged for it to be read to the heads of the congress delegations on the eve of the congress.

now accept a role of *in*equality vis-à-vis the smaller nations of the country. Just as it had been economically inexpedient to cut up telegraph poles into barricades and divide up the landed estates among the peasants, so, in the national question, considerations of economic expediency and administrative efficiency must take second place. Why, after all, had Lenin sounded the alarm with such savage energy in the Georgian question and said not a word in his notes about the errors of the local deviationists? As a great strategist he had seen the need to strike the *main* foe. Hence there was no point in speaking now of local chauvinism; that represented the second phase of the struggle.

It was a courageously outspoken intervention on Bukharin's part, but a far cry from the "bomb" that Lenin had intended to explode against Stalin. Bukharin himself hinted at this when he told the congress: "If Comrade Lenin were here, he would give the Russian chauvinists such a hard time that they would remember it for ten years." [47]

More than three years were to pass before Trotsky, now fighting for his own political life against overwhelming odds, finally struck out at Stalin on this issue. Lenin's notes were discussed behind closed doors at the Central Committee plenum of July 1926 and printed in the confidential proceedings of that meeting; and the materials began to be passed around in individual copies. Later that year, during their great confrontation in the enlarged meeting of the Comintern Executive Committee, Trotsky publicly accused Stalin of having committed a major error in the national question. Stalin replied:

That is untrue, comrades. That is gossip. I never had any disagreements with the party or with Lenin in the national question. Trotsky must be referring to one insignificant incident that took place when Comrade Lenin, before the Twelfth Congress of our party, reproached me for following too strict an organizational policy toward the Georgian semi-

---

47. *Dvenadtsatyi s"ezd*, pp. 562–564, 573. To illustrate the atmosphere of Great Russian domination that prevailed at the congress, Bukharin at one point cited an informal exchange with a delegate from an outlying region. "What's new with you?" Bukharin had inquired, and the man had answered: "Nothing much. We're throttling the nationals" (*ibid.*, p. 169).

A street in Gori as it must have appeared in Stalin's early years.

Stalin's birthplace in Gori before restoration.

Stalin in 1894, while a student at
the seminary in Tiflis.

A view of Tiflis.

Stalin's mother, Ekaterina.

Stalin in 1900.

Stalin (center) and other exiles in 1903.

An identification card from the secret police files in Petersburg, 1913.

Lenin in exile, 1897.

Lenin in disguise, 1917.

Stalin in 1917.

Kirov (left) and Ordzhonikidze.

Lenin speaking in Moscow, 1918.

Lenin's wife, Krupskaya.

A group of Bolshevik party members in 1919. Lenin is in the center,
with Stalin on the left and Kalinin on the right.

Lenin, Krupskaya, and others reviewing newly organized army regulars, 1919.

Kamenev, 1919.

Trotsky in Red Square, 1921.

Stalin in 1920.

Lenin and Stalin,
1922.

Krupskaya and Lenin
not long before
Lenin's death.

Lenin's casket being carried to the House of the Trade Unions by (left to right) Stalin, Kamenev, Tomsky, an unidentified man, Molotov, Zinoviev (partially hidden), Kalinin, and Bukharin.

Mikoyan, Molotov, Stalin, and others carrying Lenin's casket.

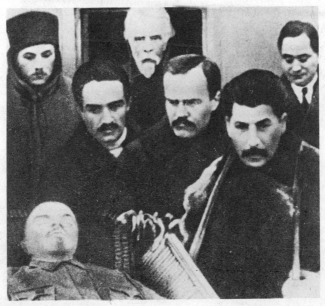

Lenin lying in state at the House of the Trade Unions.

Lenin's temporary wooden tomb, completed in 1924.
It was later replaced by a permanent structure of marble.

Trotsky leaving Moscow, 1924.

An early expression of the Lenin cult: a poster which reads,
"Great leader of the proletariat, V. I. Lenin."

Bukharin in 1926.

Zinoviev and Radek.

Above, Tomsky and Zinoviev. *Below,* Rykov, Stalin, and Voroshilov.

Members of the Politburo on the occasion of Stalin's fiftieth birthday:
(left to right) Ordzhonikidze, Voroshilov, Kuibyshev,
Stalin, Kalinin, Kaganovich, and Kirov.

The December 21, 1929, issue of *Pravda,* with tributes to Stalin
on his fiftieth birthday.

Stalin at fifty.

nationalists, semi-Communists of the type of Mdivani, who was recently commercial representative in France, saying that I was "persecuting" them. Subsequent facts showed, however, that the so-called "deviationists," the people of the Mdivani type, deserved still more severe treatment than I as one of the secretaries of the Central Committee of our party gave them. . . . Lenin did not and could not know these facts because he lay ill in bed and had no possibility of following events. But what relation could this insignificant incident have to Stalin's position in principle? [48]

But Trotsky was in a position to document his charge with most of the materials that have been cited in these pages, and did so in a party document known as his "Letter to Istpart," concerning which more will be said in Chapter Nine, "The Politics of Revolutionary Biography."

A Purge That Failed

On December 12, 1922, Lenin heard Dzerzhinsky's report on the investigation in Georgia, and the next day he had a two-hour meeting with Stalin which turned out to be their last.[49] The stroke that followed on December 16 inaugurated a period of greatly curtailed activity lasting until Lenin's paralyzing stroke of early March. He could no longer take any direct part in political events. He did insist, however, in the face of his doctors' preference for a regime of total rest, that he be permitted to dictate notes daily for what he called his "diary." On December 24, after a conference of Stalin, Bukharin, and Kamenev with the doctors, it was decided that he could dictate for five or ten minutes each day (later the period was extended), but that these notes should not bear the character of correspondence, that he should have no visitors, and that those

48. *Stalin*, IX, 65–66.
49. *Lenin*, XLV, 470–471. This information comes from the diary of Lenin's secretaries, reprinted in Vol. XLV (pp. 457–486) from *Voprosy istorii KPSS*, No. 2 (1963), where it was first published. The diary covers the time from November 21, 1922, to March 6, 1923. Fotieva reports (*Iz vospominanii*, p. 63) that Lenin told her on January 24, 1923, that what he had learned from Dzerzhinsky on December 12, particularly about the Ordzhonikidze episode, had distressed him deeply on the eve of his second attack.

around him should not keep him informed on current political developments.[50]

The conference with the doctors was preceded and perhaps provoked by an ugly incident. On December 21, with special permission from the German consulting physician, Professor Vörster, Lenin dictated to Krupskaya a short letter for Trotsky. It expressed satisfaction over the favorable outcome of their fight to preserve the foreign-trade monopoly and sought Trotsky's assistance in preparations to "continue the offensive" by placing the question of consolidation of the monopoly before the forthcoming party congress.[51] On learning of this letter, Stalin, who must have been very uneasy by now over indications of Lenin's hostility toward him, flew into a rage. Taking advantage of the fact that on December 18 the plenum of the Central Committee had entrusted him (presumably in his capacity as its general secretary) with personal responsibility for overseeing Lenin's medical regime, he phoned Krupskaya, upbraided her savagely, and threatened to have her brought before the party's Central Control Commission (the body charged with enforcement of party discipline) for violating the doctors' orders. On the following day, December 23, she wrote to Kamenev:

Lev Borisovich:

Because of a very short letter that I had written in words dictated to me by Vladimir Ilyich with the permission of the doctors, Stalin yesterday permitted himself a most rude outburst against me. This is not my first day in the party. In thirty years I have not heard a single rude word from any comrade, and the interests of the party are no less dear to me than to Stalin. I need at present the maximum of self-control. I

50. *Vladimir Ilyich Lenin. Biografiia*, 2nd ed., chief ed. P. N. Pospelov (Moscow, 1963), p. 622. Toward the end Lenin began to suspect that political considerations—presumably, in particular, Stalin's desire to isolate him from political activity—were influencing decisions concerning his medical regime. According to the entry by Fotieva in the "Diary" for February 12, 1923, "Apparently Vladimir Ilyich has acquired the impression that the doctors are not giving instructions to the Central Committee but the Central Committee to the doctors" (*Lenin*, XLV, 485).

51. *Lenin*, LIV, 327–328. Krupskaya made a notation at the top of the letter informing Trotsky that it had been dictated with Dr. Vörster's permission and another at the bottom saying that Lenin requested that he phone his reply. On this see *Lenin*, LIV, 672.

know better than any doctor what can and cannot be said to Ilyich, because I know—at any rate better than Stalin—what disturbs him and what doesn't. I am turning to you and to Grigori [Zinoviev] as much closer comrades of V. I. and I ask you to protect me from rude interference in my personal life, unworthy abuse, and threats. I have no doubt as to the unanimous decision of the Control Commission, with whose action Stalin permits himself to threaten me, but I have no time or energy to spend on this stupid squabble. I too am a living person and my nerves are strained to the utmost.[52]

We do not know precisely when Lenin learned of this incident, but he did. And on March 5, 1923, along with the letter to Trotsky asking him to undertake the defense of the Georgian affair in the Central Committee, he dictated a short note to Stalin, marked "Strictly secret" and "Personal" but with copies to Kamenev and Zinoviev. It read:

Respected Comrade Stalin:
    You had the rudeness [*grubost'*] to call my wife to the telephone and berate her. Although she expressed her willingness to forget what was said, this fact nevertheless became known, through her, to Zinoviev and Kamenev. I do not intend to forget so easily what was done against me, and there is no need to point out that what is done against my wife I consider to be against me also. Therefore I ask you to consider whether you agree to take back what you said and apologize, or whether you prefer to break relations between us.

                                        With respect.   Lenin.[53]

Lenin directed Volodicheva, the stenographer, to postpone the dispatch of this letter, evidently wanting Krupskaya to see it in advance. After seeing it, she went to Kamenev in great alarm. "Vladimir has just dictated to his stenographer a letter to Stalin saying that he breaks off all personal relations with him," she said, adding: "He would never have decided to break off personal relations if he had not thought it necessary to crush Stalin politically." [54] According to

52. *Ibid.*, pp. 674–675, where the reference to Kamenev and Zinoviev as much closer comrades of Lenin is omitted. The full text of this letter was first divulged by Khrushchev in his 1956 secret report. Robert H. McNeal, in *Bride of the Revolution: Krupskaya and Lenin* (Ann Arbor, 1972) discusses the incident at some length.
    53. *Lenin*, LIV, 329–330.
    54. Trotsky, *My Life*, p. 485.

Volodicheva's entry for March 6 in the diary of the secretaries, Krupskaya asked her not to send the letter. She insisted, however, on carrying out Lenin's instructions, and on March 7 she personally delivered the letter to Stalin, who then and there dictated, in reply, the demanded apology.[55]

Unbeknown to Krupskaya, Lenin's decision to crush Stalin politically had been taken at least two months earlier. In the last week of December 1922, he dictated the notes that came to be known as his "testament." He began on December 23 with a section which advocated increasing the size of the Central Committee to fifty or one hundred members, and which was sent to Stalin for the committee's information. Treating the remainder of the document as secret (even from Krupskaya), he continued dictating on the following two days. In this secret portion he explained that the proposed increase in the membership of the Central Committee was needed in order to prevent a split, a good half of the danger of which lay in the relations between Stalin and Trotsky. Then he went on as follows:

Comrade Stalin, having become *gensek* [general secretary], has concentrated boundless power in his hands, and I am not sure that he will always manage to use this power with sufficient caution. On the other hand, Comrade Trotsky, as was shown by his struggle against the C.C. [Central Committee] on the question of the Commissariat of Railways, is distinguished not only by his exceptional capabilities—personally he is perhaps the most able man in the present C.C.—but also by his too far-reaching self-confidence and excessive absorption in the purely administrative side of things.

These two qualities of the two outstanding leaders of the present C.C. could inadvertently lead to a split, and if our party does not take steps to prevent it, the split might come about unexpectedly.

I will not further characterize the other members of the C.C. in terms of their personal qualities. I will only recall that the October episode of Zinoviev and Kamenev was not of course accidental, but it can just as little be held against them personally as the non-Bolshevism of Trotsky.

Among the young members of the C.C. I want to say a few words about Bukharin and Piatakov. In my view, they are the most outstand-

55. *Lenin,* XLV, 486, and LIV, 675.

ing forces (of the youngest forces), and the following should be kept
in mind concerning them: Bukharin is not only the most valuable and
biggest theoretician of the party but is· rightly considered the favorite
of the whole party. But his theoretical views can only with great doubt
be considered fully Marxist, for there is something scholastic in him (he
never studied, and I do not think he has ever fully understood, dialectics).

And then Piatakov is a man of indubitably outstanding will and
outstanding capacities, but too carried away by administering and the
administrative side of things to be depended upon in a serious political
question.

Of course, both of these comments are made by me only for the
present, in case these two outstanding and devoted workers should not
find the occasion to fill out their knowledge and correct their one-sided-
ness.[56]

To this section Lenin added a postscript on January 4, 1923, recommending Stalin's removal from the post of general secretary. If he
had harbored any uncertainty when he began the notes that he
wanted to unseat Stalin from his position of power, none could have
remained by now.

The postscript read as follows·

Stalin is too rude [*Stalin slishkom grub*], and this fault, fully tolerable in
our midst and in the relations among us Communists, becomes intolerable in the office of general secretary. Therefore I propose to the comrades that they devise a way of shifting Stalin from this position and
appointing to it another man who in all other respects falls on the other
side of the scale from Comrade Stalin, namely, more tolerant, more
loyal, more polite and more considerate of comrades, less capricious,
etc. This circumstance may seem an insignificant trifle. But I think that
from the point of view of preventing a split, and from the point of view
of what I have written above about the relation between Stalin and
Trotsky, this is no trifle, or it is a trifle that may take on decisive significance.

Studying the evidence bearing upon the question of what
brought Lenin to his firm decision on this point, one finds a clue
in the word *grubost'*. Usually translated as "rudeness," this word
connotes in Russian usage not only offensiveness in speech but
rude behavior in general; and it figures very importantly in Lenin's

56. *Ibid.,* XLV, 343–348.

final utterances concerning Stalin. In the letter of March 5 demanding an apology from Stalin, he began by referring to the latter's
grubost' toward Krupskaya. It is quite possible that he learned about
the incident in late December or the beginning of January, soon
after it happened, and that Stalin's rude behavior toward his wife
was partly responsible for his decision to add the postscript.[57] But
it need not be supposed that this was the only reason. At the close
of his notes on the national question, dictated on December 30
and 31, Lenin declared that it was essential to avoid any *grubost'*
in Great Russian dealings with the minority nations. The incident
involving Ordzhonikidze's slapping of Kobakhidze was on his mind
at the time as a shocking example. So, according to Fotieva's
memoir, were reports then reaching him from Georgian sources that
Stalin and Ordzhonikidze had spoken of burning out nationalist
sentiment with a red-hot iron. To Lenin these were instances of a
grubost' that was finding expression not simply in personal relations between individuals but in the political relations between certain ruling individuals and whole social groups—the non-Russian
nationalities. Moreover, he indicated in the notes, responsibility for
rudeness on a collective scale in Georgia rested more with Stalin
than with Ordzhonikidze.

Four days later, with all this fresh in his mind, he dictated the
postscript; it is not surprising that he began it by saying: "Stalin
is too rude . . ."

The document in which the postscript appeared was in one

57. It has been suggested in both Russia and the West that since Lenin
did not write to Stalin about the incident until March 6, Krupskaya probably
did not tell him about it before the beginning of March. See, for example, the
editor's note in *Lenin*, LIV, 675, and Robert V. Daniels, *The Conscience of the
Revolution: Communist Opposition in Soviet Russia* (Cambridge, Mass., 1960),
p. 181. This reasoning seems, however, to imply that Lenin wrote the note in a
burst of anger, which is not necessarily the case. I shall suggest below an interpretation of his motives which would be consistent with the supposition that he
learned of the incident soon after it happened—a supposition made all the more
plausible by the fact that Krupskaya must have been deeply upset at the time of
the incident and hence less capable of concealing it than she would be in early
March. For these reasons I am inclined to agree with Louis Fischer (*The Life
of Lenin* [New York, 1964], p. 647) that Lenin probably learned about the incident by January 4.

sense what it later came to be called—"Lenin's testament." Lenin must have reckoned with the possibility that it would be his posthumous testament to the party leadership. Yet this designation is also deceptive in a way. *For Lenin was dictating it as a communication to a congress that he still hoped to attend in person or at the very least to guide with messages from his sickbed.* While he realized that he might die at any time or become completely incapacitated, he hoped to remain alive and reasonably active a little longer. Although he handled the document with the care and secrecy normally associated with a last will and testament, he hoped that he himself would be the one to open the sealed envelope, divulge its contents, and make political use of it. His hopes were pinned to March 30, the date on which the Twelfth Party Congress was originally scheduled to open. His doctors had indicated at one point that with a full week's total rest beforehand, he might be able to speak at the congress. Accordingly, when he began to dictate to Volodicheva on December 23, he said: "I want to dictate to you a letter to the congress. Please write." [58]

The "Letter to the Congress" (as Volodicheva entitled it) was, then, intended by Lenin to form a part of the "bomb" that he was going to explode at the Twelfth Congress in order to blast Stalin out of the office of general secretary of the party. We can see from his activities around that time and afterward that he was pursuing a methodical plan of action toward this end. All the materials he was preparing for the congress were designed, among other things, to prepare the ground for Stalin's demotion by setting forth political criticisms from which this step would flow as a natural organizational conclusion. Much of the critical indictment was to be built around Stalin's political responsibility for the Georgian affair and the encouragement of Great Russian nationalism. For this Lenin

58. *Lenin,* XLV, 474. On Lenin's hope and intention to speak before the Twelfth Congress, see *Voprosy istorii KPSS,* No. 2 (1963), p. 68. That the letter or its contents was meant for the Twelfth Congress is shown by internal evidence in its text. On this see *Vladimir Ilyich Lenin. Biografiia,* p. 643. The letter, according to Roy A. Medvedev, was typed in five copies: one for Lenin himself, three for Krupskaya, and one for Lenin's secretarial staff (*Let History Judge: The Origins and Consequences of Stalinism* [New York, 1971], p. 25).

had a preliminary text in the notes of December 30–31, and new material in his secretaries' report on the Dzerzhinsky commission's inquiry in Georgia. But he planned to base the case on other political issues as well. As noted above, he wanted to use the congress as a platform for continuing the offensive on the question of the foreign-trade monopoly, in which Stalin had stubbornly opposed him. Still another line of attack implicitly aimed at Stalin was concerned with bureaucracy in Soviet institutions.

In his last two articles, dictated respectively in January and the early part of February, Lenin mounted the campaign against bureaucracy with special reference to Rabkrin, over which Stalin had presided prior to becoming party general secretary in April 1922. The first of them, entitled "How We Should Reorganize Rabkrin (A Proposal to the Twelfth Party Congress)," began by saying that the Soviet state machine, with the exception of the Foreign Affairs Commissariat, was for the most part a relic of the Russian past. Just as the regime had sought salvation at the most dangerous moments of the Civil War by mobilizing the best workers for the Red Army, so now it should turn to the masses for help. In order to transform Rabkrin into an effective agency for reform of the state administration, it should be reduced to a force of three or four hundred picked administrative and secretarial employees, and amalgamated with the party's Central Control Commission after enlargement of the latter by seventy-five to one hundred new worker and peasant members. The administrative and secretarial employees should be endowed with the rights of Central Committee members, including the right and even duty of attending Politburo meetings in a certain number and familiarizing themselves with the papers of the Politburo. This, said Lenin, should reduce the influence of "purely personal and fortuitous circumstances" in the Central Committee and thereby lessen the danger of a split. Moreover, the Central Control Commission members "should form a cohesive group which, 'irrespective of persons involved,' should see to it that no one's authority, neither that of the *gensek* nor that of any other members of the Central Committee, could prevent them from making an interpellation, from checking on documents, and in general from keeping themselves fully informed and securing most strict propriety in the conduct of affairs." That the phrase "neither that of the *gensek* nor that of any other members of the Central Committee" was a barb aimed directly at Stalin, and understood by people as such, is perhaps best shown by its deletion from the sentence as republished in editions of Lenin's article issued during the Stalin period.[59]

In the second of the two articles, entitled "Better Less, But Better," Lenin moved from the barbed phrase to the transparent denunciation. A large part of the essay was a crushing commentary on Stalin in the guise of a further installment of Lenin's thoughts on how to reorganize Rabkrin. The condition of the state apparatus —it began—was so sad, not to say repulsive, that some way must be devised to deal with its defects. One step was to make of Rabkrin an instrument for improving the apparatus and an exemplary institution, which it had not yet become: "Let us speak bluntly. The commissariat of Rabkrin does not now enjoy a shade of authority. Everyone knows that a worse-organized institution than our Rabkrin does not exist and that under present conditions nothing can be expected from this commissariat." Lest anyone suppose that Stalin was not here under attack since he was no longer formally in charge of this institution, Lenin went on to ask whether "any of the present heads of Rabkrin—*or any persons having a connection with it*—can tell me what, in practice, is the need for such a commissariat as Rabkrin" (italics added). And before concluding, he struck a further blow at Stalin in his present capacity as chief custodian of the party apparatus: "Let it be said parenthetically that we have bureaucracy not only in Soviet institutions but in party institutions as well." [60]

59. The article originally appeared in *Pravda* on January 25, 1923. The barbed phrase was deleted when it was republished in the second edition of Lenin's works (*Sochineniia*, XXVII, 405) in 1930. That volume was prepared for the press by Stalin's aide Ivan Tovstukha, who in the same year became deputy director of the Lenin Institute. The phrase was also omitted in the fourth edition of Lenin's works (*Sochineniia*, XXXIII, 444), most of which was published in Stalin's last years, but it was restored in the fifth edition (*Lenin*, XLV, 387), this volume having been published in 1964.

60. *Lenin*, XLV, 390, 393, 394, 397.

Lenin began dictating this article on February 2 and finished on February 7. Two days later, he told Fotieva that he was going to put the question of Rabkrin before the party congress. On February 10, he instructed her to forward "Better Less, But Better" to A. D. Tsiurupa, Stalin's successor as commissar of Rabkrin, with a request that he read it within two days. A delay ensued at this point, and Lenin did not give the article a final reading until March 2.[61] During the interim, there appears to have been an attempt to prevent the article's publication. As Trotsky told the story in the "Letter to Istpart," Bukharin (who was editor of *Pravda*) hesitated to approve the article's appearance. At a special meeting of the Politburo, which was then called on Trotsky's request after Krupskaya phoned to ask his assistance in the matter, Stalin, Molotov, Kuibyshev, Rykov, Kalinin, and Bukharin opposed publication of the article, and Kuibyshev went so far as to propose that they placate Lenin by printing the article in a special copy of *Pravda* made up for him only. But Trotsky, supported by Kamenev, finally won the day with the argument that an article by Lenin simply could not be concealed from the party.[62] "Better Less, But Better" appeared in *Pravda* on March 4.

Next day Lenin dictated the brief letters to Trotsky and Stalin. The obvious aim of the first, which asked Trotsky to defend the Georgian case in the Central Committee, was to make sure that Stalin would come under attack in the pre-congress plenum of the party high council. But how the curt message to Stalin fitted into Lenin's methodical plan of action is not so immediately apparent. Contrary to a widespread impression, it did not announce a rupture of relations with Stalin. Rather, it *threatened* a rupture if Stalin failed to retract and apologize for his rude words of December 22 to Krupskaya. The letter's purpose, then, was to elicit from Stalin the confession of guilt for rudeness that Stalin in fact produced.[63]

61. *Ibid.*, pp. 478, 484–485; Fotieva, *Iz vospominanii*, p. 75.
62. Trotsky, *The Stalin School of Falsification*, p. 72.
63. Lenin's sister, Maria Ulyanova, informed the July 1926 Central Com-

Why Lenin wanted such a statement, and in writing, is not hard to explain. As we have seen, he was preparing a many-sided brief against Stalin with a view to displacing him from the office of general secretary. A key charge was Stalin's intolerable rudeness. To make the case unassailable in the face of likely efforts in some quarters to defend Stalin, Lenin—a lawyer by training—wanted to document the charge. His secretaries' report on the Georgian findings must have provided him with considerable material for this purpose, but he intended to supplement it—no doubt in closed session—with an account of Stalin's rude outburst against Krupskaya. Here the documentation would be Stalin's own written admission of guilt.

It is hard to believe that Lenin would not have won the case had his health permitted him to argue it before the court of the party congress. But when the congress opened in mid-April, he was incapacitated. And the papers containing his recommendation on Stalin's removal from office remained unopened until some time after he died in January 1924.

Although Lenin's incapacitation and death were Stalin's political salvation, there is no indication that Stalin did anything to expedite that outcome. This particularly needs to be said in view of a suspicion later expressed by Trotsky. He recalled that at a meeting of Politburo members toward the end of February 1923 Stalin reported—in the presence of Kamenev, Zinoviev, and Trotsky himself—that Lenin had suddenly called him in and asked for poison. To Trotsky's comment that Dr. Guétier (his own family physician as well as one of Lenin's) had not given up hope for Lenin's recovery, Stalin replied: "I told him all that. . . . But he wouldn't listen to reason. The Old Man is suffering. He says he wants to have the poison at hand . . . he'll use it only when he is convinced that his condition is hopeless." No vote was taken, according to Trotsky's recollection, but those present at the meeting parted with an

---

mittee plenum, in which the question of Lenin's final letter to Stalin was raised by Zinoviev, that Stalin had replied to the letter with an apology. On this see *Lenin*, LIV, 675.

implicit understanding that they could not even consider granting Lenin's request. Trotsky added that he could be mistaken on certain details of the episode, but not on the fact that it occurred.[64]

He must have been mistaken about the date because it appears from Fotieva's journal that the only official persons who saw Lenin after December 23, 1922, were the three secretaries and some medical personnel. Beyond this the question has been raised why Trotsky kept silent for so long about an episode that placed his great enemy in a sinister light.[65] Whatever the answer, it was not in Trotsky's character simply to fabricate an historical happening. It is not, moreover, implausible that Lenin, fearing that death would be preceded by a long period of paralysis, made a request for poison and did so through Stalin, who was, after all, the designated party overseer of the sick man's medical regime. Whether, as Trotsky suggests, Lenin saw in Stalin the one man in the entourage who might have been willing to grant the request for poison is wholly speculative. If he did make the request of Stalin, he must have done so on or before December 13, when the two men had their last meeting. But there is nothing to support Trotsky's further speculation that Stalin may have taken it upon himself to fulfill Lenin's request. To have taken such an action on his own, *after* the discussion with other Politburo members who all were opposed to it, would have been a politically risky thing to do (since the action could have become known to others), and this at a time when he had far less reason to fear Lenin's intentions toward himself then he was to have by early March. Apart from other inhibitions that he may have felt, Stalin was not the kind to take such risks.

64. Trotsky, *Stalin*, pp. 376–377.
65. Fischer, *Life of Lenin*, pp. 677–678. Fischer points out that Trotsky kept the matter a secret until late 1939, when he wrote a magazine article called "Did Stalin Poison Lenin?" Fischer concludes: "The detailed record of Lenin's illness before the end of February, 1923, and through March, 1923, to the end in January, 1924, offers no support for the sensational suspicion that Stalin poisoned Lenin." While in full agreement with this conclusion, I do not find it inexplicable that Trotsky made no mention of the episode and of his suspicions for so long; he might have done so for the sake of persons close to him who were still in Russia, as long as their fates remained unknown to him. Also, it seems significant that he was planning to include an account of the episode in his biography of Stalin.

Stalin and the Lenin Cult

As we have seen, Lenin's own objections were all that held public adulation of him in check during his last years. Not surprisingly, then, his final illness and death coincided with the rise of the Lenin cult. The tendency was already clearly visible in the way in which he and his teachings were spoken of at the Twelfth Congress. Kamenev set the tone when he opened the congress, saying: "We know only one antidote against any crisis, against any wrong decision: the teaching of Vladimir Ilyich."

But it was on the morrow of Lenin's death that all the earlier restraints were broken and the cult emerged full-blown as one of the institutions of Soviet Communism. The impetus was a series of official decrees issued at that time. The day of his death, which fell on January 21, was to be observed as an annual day of mourning. Petrograd was renamed Leningrad. Monuments to Lenin were to be erected in Moscow and other principal cities. A newly created "Lenin Institute" was to publish a mass edition of his writings in many languages. And, purportedly in order to give all who were unable to come to Moscow by the day of the funeral an opportunity to say farewell to Lenin, his body was to be preserved and made publicly accessible in a tomb by the Kremlin wall in Red Square. A notable comment on the latter decision came from Zinoviev in an article that appeared in *Pravda* on January 30, 1924: "How good that they decided to bury Ilyich in a tomb! How good that we thought of this in time! To bury Ilyich's body in the ground —that would be too unendurable." In time, he went on, a Lenin museum would arise nearby, and Red Square as a whole would become "a little Lenin town" to which, in future decades and centuries, hundreds of millions of grateful people would come on pilgrimage from all over Russia and the world.

So the mummified body was placed on display in a small wooden mausoleum, which become the central shrine of the Lenin cult. Hosts of the faithful or the merely curious streamed past the glass catafalque in a never-ending daily procession, and the long lines of patiently waiting people became one of the familiar sights of Red Square in all seasons. By 1929, when the wooden structure was replaced with the granite tomb that stands there now, the cult of Lenin had become an omnipresent pattern in Soviet public life. The Lenin Institute was at work on the collection and study of his writings, which were quoted as Holy Scripture to validate ideas on myriad themes. His life and thought were subjects of a great and ever-growing literature Soviet citizens encountered beginning with their school primers. Portraits, statues, and busts of him were everywhere. Even in peasant huts, according to a foreigner who traveled extensively in Russia in the later twenties, one would generally see a cheap print of Lenin's picture, often side by side with a religious icon.[66] The Lenin Museum had come into being, and the "Lenin corner" was a standard feature of all kinds of Soviet institutions, ranging from school and village reading-rooms to places of detention. Using Lenin's portrait or bust as a centerpiece and quotations from his writings as texts, the Lenin corner would show a link between the institution concerned and the leader's teachings.

How is Soviet Communism's Lenin cult to be explained? Without giving the question much systematic attention, Western scholarship has suggested a number of answers. According to one, the Bolshevik leadership was chiefly actuated by a practical political concern. Its object in sponsoring the cult of the deceased leader was to consolidate the still young revolutionary system of authority among a predominantly non-Communist peasant people accustomed to paternalistic rule under a tsar. A related but more complex interpretation speaks of the absorption of elements of old Russian culture, notably its religiosity, into a new order whose main leadership was imbued with Marxist rationalism. In the Lenin cult, with its sacred symbols and elaborate ceremonialism, this view sees something of the Byzantine tradition and the Greek Orthodox style being assimilated into Soviet Communism; and in Stalin, a Marxist of the East and the product of a Greek Orthodox theological seminary in Tiflis, it sees the principal agent of this process.[67]

66. Samuel Harper, *Civic Training in Soviet Russia* (Chicago, 1929), p. 38.
67. Isaac Deutscher, *Stalin: A Political Biography,* 2nd ed. (New York,

Stalin's remarkable "oath" speech, delivered before the Congress of Soviets on January 26, 1924, is cited in support of such an interpretation. Although Stalin's was only one of numerous speeches by prominent Bolsheviks on that occasion, it did strike a distinctive note of ritual exaltation of the dead leader. Stalin began, as we have noted earlier,[68] with a vivid representation of the party as Lenin's charismatic following. Then, in the name of the party, he made a series of vows to fulfill Lenin's "commandments": to hold high the purity of the great title of party member, to guard the party's unity as the apple of its eye, to protect and strengthen the dictatorship of the proletariat, to strengthen the alliance of the workers and peasants, to strengthen and expand the Union of Republics, and to be faithful to the principles of the Communist International. It has been remarked that in phraseology this speech was Biblical; and in form, with each commandment followed by a repetitive response, it was liturgical, carrying overtones of an Orthodox prayer book.[69]

Emphasis upon Stalin's role in the founding of the Lenin cult is justified. Apart from the contribution that he made with the "oath" speech, he appears to have had a leading part in the decision to give Communism a holy sepulcher by placing Lenin's embalmed body on public display. This was a step that provoked consternation in many Bolsheviks. It must have been foremost among the developments that led the widowed Krupskaya to raise an anguished voice of protest against the burgeoning Lenin cult. In a note published in *Pravda* on January 30, 1924, ostensibly written to thank those who had sent messages of condolence, she appealed to the people not to let their mourning for Lenin take the form of "external reverence for his person." She asked them not to raise memorials to him, name palaces after him, and hold solemn ceremonies in com-

---

1966), pp. 269–271. See also E. H. Carr, *The Interregnum 1923–1924* (New York, 1954), pp. 346–348. For an interpretation of the Lenin cult as serving the pragmatic interest of the Soviet regime in its self-consolidation, see Harper, *Civic Training,* p. 40.

68. See above, p. 130.

69. Carr, *The Interregnum,* p. 347. For the text of the speech, see *Stalin,* VI, 46–51.

memoration of him, and she concluded by saying: "If you want to honor the name of Vladimir Ilyich, build creches, kindergartens, houses, schools, libraries, medical centers, hospitals, homes for the disabled, etc., and, above all, let us put his precepts into practice." [70]

By then the decision to preserve Lenin's body in a mausoleum had been made public and was irreversible. There is evidence, however, that much earlier, when the decision could have been headed off, strong protests from individuals more powerful than Krupskaya had been similarly unavailing and that the chief force behind the embalming plan was Stalin. This evidence comes from Valentinov, who gives Bukharin himself as the source. According to his account, the embalming idea was first presented by Stalin and Kalinin in a meeting of six high Soviet leaders in late 1923, just after Lenin's health had taken a new turn for the worse. After stressing the need to carefully plan the funeral arrangements in advance so as to be prepared for the occasion, Stalin reportedly attributed to "comrades in the provinces" the opinion that Lenin, a Russian by nationality, ought to be given a funeral in accordance with Russian customs. Cremation, a commonly accepted practice for deceased party leaders, would not be in accordance with those customs, they were arguing, since Russians traditionally had seen in the burning of human remains a symbolic act of punishment. Having associated himself with this view, Stalin suggested that modern science had ways of preserving a body for a long while by embalming, sufficiently long for people to become accustomed to the thought that Lenin was no longer among them. After grasping the direction of Stalin's talk, several of those present raised strong objections. Trotsky pointed out that the embalming of Lenin's body would revive under Communist auspices the old Russian Orthodox Church practice of preserving the remains of saints as holy relics, and declared that the unnamed comrades in the provinces had absolutely nothing in common with the science of Marxism. Speaking in full agreement and with no less indignation, Bukharin argued that to make a mummy out of Lenin's remains would be both an insult to his memory and

70. McNeal, in *Bride of the Revolution,* discusses Krupskaya's role in the party after Lenin's death.

an utter negation of his dialectical materialist outlook. He referred in this connection to a proposal in party circles that Marx's remains be moved from London and reburied by the Kremlin wall so as to impart greater sacredness to the spot, and observed that "a strange aroma" was coming up out of certain crannies in the party. Kamenev spoke in the same vein, commenting that the giving of Lenin's name to Petrograd and the publishing of his works in millions of copies would be appropriate ways of venerating his memory, but that the embalming proposal smacked of that very religiosity which Lenin had castigated in his *Materialism and Empiriocriticism.*[71]

Despite this evidence of Stalin's special responsibility for the decision to preserve the body of Lenin, the tendency to depict him as the virtual demiurge of the Lenin cult is mistaken. Speaking more broadly, neither of the above views of the origin of the cult appears fully acceptable, although each contains a part of the total explanation. The Bolshevik leaders doubtless did wish to use the Lenin symbol as a propaganda device to solidify popular support of their regime, and this consideration may well have made it easier for many of them to overcome their Marxist distaste for such an act as the mummification of Lenin. There is likewise some basis in fact for the theory that the rise of the Lenin cult reflected a recrudescence of old Orthodox Russia under the auspices, at least in part, of Stalin. But these explanations are critically inadequate on at least two counts, one having to do with Stalin and the other with the Bolshevik movement.

Granted that Stalin was influential in the creation of the Lenin cult, references to his being a man of the East and to his Orthodox religious background do not go very far toward explaining why. Clearly, he was not a person of conventional religious views. Although he employed traditional religious idiom from time to time, as when he called party membership the movement's "holy of holies," he was as firm in his Marxist atheism as other Old Bolsheviks. The only god he recognized and paid homage to was the "god of history"

---

71. N. Valentinov (Vol'sky), *Novaia ekonomicheskaia politika i krizis partii posle smerti Lenina. Gody raboty v VSNKH vo vremia NEP. Vospominaniia* (Stanford, 1971), pp. 90–92.

that he invoked on revolutionary Russia's behalf in his address to
the Baku Soviet in 1920. But as this very invocation suggests, there
was a peculiarly religious cast to Stalin's Marxist outlook. He saw
history as a drama of conflict between good and evil, and the roles
that classes and countries and personalities played in it were matters
of transcendent significance. Moreover, his Marxism was a body
of dogma about things of fundamental importance. From these
standpoints, the introduction of ceremony and ritual into Russia's
evolving Communist culture, through the cult of Lenin, could only
seem natural to him—as, indeed, it did to numerous other Bolsheviks of that time.

Stalin's doctrinaire Marxism was almost from the start a
Marxism-according-to-Lenin—a "Marxism-Leninism," to employ a
phrase that would itself become dogma in Russia during the thirties.
This motive for putting Lenin and his teachings on a pedestal was
fortified by a practical political interest in accentuating the credentials of an old Leninist like Stalin as against those of a one-time
non-Leninist like Trotsky. A further, central consideration, however, has to do with the meaning of Lenin in Stalin's life. When he
formed a hero-identification with Lenin in his youth, taking Lenin
as his model figure in the revolutionary movement, the man whose
fighting partner he aspired to be, Stalin created a private personality
cult which became the axis on which his inner world revolved. It
was a dual cult in which the leader Lenin and the co-leader Stalin
were indissolubly linked in Russian Communism's historical destiny, and bathed in glory. For Stalin now to take the initiative in
developing a *public* cult of the deceased Lenin was, therefore, to
express his deep-seated way of thinking and perhaps also, if only
subconsciously, to lay the groundwork for one other leader cult
yet to come.

This last line of interpretation assumes that Stalin's basic attitude toward Lenin did not turn hostile under the tensions traced
in the foregoing pages. Virtually the only evidence of hostility that
the record shows is the slurring reference to the "national liberalism
of Comrade Lenin," and this was in hot-tempered reaction to Lenin's
reproof for having acted hastily on the constitutional issue. Stalin

no doubt really disapproved of "national liberalism" and regarded the ailing Lenin of 1922 and early 1923 as no longer the giant figure of old; he may even have blamed worsening health for what must have appeared to him a political lapse on Lenin's side. The conflict may have been brought on in part because he began somewhat too soon to act the role of co-leader, or successor-designate, which his inner life-scenario had all along envisaged for him. But his posture in the conflict was not one of aggressive hostility against Lenin. Rather, it was Lenin whose fighting spirit finally became aroused against Stalin.

For Stalin it could only have been a profoundly troubling experience to find himself at odds finally with the single most meaningful individual of his adult life, a man towards whom—judging by the few signs we have—he probably entertained some feelings of love. It must also have become an unnerving experience, for even a very ill Lenin, once his fighting spirit was aroused, was a formidable fighter. Stalin could hardly have been in any doubt of this when he received Lenin's coldly hostile final note demanding an apology for his rude outburst on the telephone against Krupskaya. When Lenin succumbed to the paralyzing stroke a few days later, Stalin very probably reacted with a huge sense of relief.

But a relationship upon which the structure of a person's self-identity rests will ordinarily resist destruction, and would be all the more resistant to destruction in this instance because the object of the private inner cult was a *hyphenate* Lenin-Stalin rather than Lenin alone. Stalin's own self-esteem was thus bound up with his veneration of Lenin. For this reason, Lenin's final incapacitation and death may have been Stalin's psychological as well as political salvation. A Lenin who no longer needed to be fought and feared was a Lenin who could be venerated in the old way and towards whose precepts one could swear undying fealty, as Stalin did in the "oath" speech. He was a Lenin toward whom one could freely feel once again those emotions of adulation and hero-worship that Stalin, who was not normally given to such intimate confessions in public, recollected in his talk of January 28 to the cadets of the Kremlin military school.

Stalin was by no means alone among Bolsheviks, however, in

having such feelings toward Lenin and in expressing them during that time of public mourning when the Lenin cult emerged. It seems, therefore, that explanations of this development which fail to take account of Bolshevism itself as a contributing factor suffer from a major deficiency. Evidence reviewed in the second chapter of this book shows that the Bolshevik movement harbored deep-seated tendencies to create a cult of Lenin. They became visible in the waves of hero-worship that arose in the party on various occasions during his last years. What must be recognized, as Lenin himself seems to have done in a horrified way, is that these were signs of things to come; they were the future Lenin cult in embryo.

When Lenin died, all inhibitions that his living presence had imposed upon the expression of Bolshevik feeling about him were removed, and striking evidence of the tendencies just mentioned was forthcoming. Reports describe a mass sobbing scene when Kalinin, on January 22, announced the news of his death to the hundreds assembled in session at the Congress of Soviets. Not only were Bolsheviks grief-stricken; there was a sense of having been orphaned by the event. Imagery expressive of this feeling appeared, for example, in the headline of an article in *Pravda* on January 24: "The Orphaned Ones." The same issue—the first one published after Lenin died—carried an article that Trotsky had hastily written in the Caucasus and dispatched by wire. "The party is orphaned," it said. "The working class is orphaned. Just this is the feeling aroused by the news of the death of our teacher and leader." In the leading article, written by Bukharin and entitled "Comrade," similar imagery appeared: "Comrade Lenin has left us forever. Let us transfer all our love for him to his own child, his heir—our party." Still more remarkable was the symbolism contained in the unsigned Central Committee proclamation to all party members and working people. The man under whose leadership the party had raised the red banner of October over the whole country was dead, the proclamation began. The founder of the Comintern, the leader of world Communism, the love and pride of the international proletariat, the banner of the oppressed East, and the head of the dictatorship of Russia, had died. Going on in this vein, the proclamation suddenly struck a quasi-mystical note: "But his physical death is not the death of his cause. Lenin lives. In the soul of every member of our party there is a particle [*chastichka*] of Lenin. Our whole Communist family is a collective embodiment of Lenin." In Trotsky's farewell article the same point was made more simply: "In each of us lives a small part of Lenin, which is the best part of each of us."

In the light of such evidence, which could be multiplied, it is impossible to share the view that the Lenin cult was somehow foreign to the spirit of Russian Communism, and that it has to be explained by the intrusion of the Russian past as represented by an Eastern Bolshevik of ecclesiastical training like Stalin. At the formative moment this cult was a collective manifestation of the party's feeling for its leader. Some of the most "Westernized" of the Bolsheviks gave the feeling its most vivid and effective expression. Bukharin's editorial, for example, may have lacked the ritual cadence of Stalin's "oath" speech, the text of which did not even appear in *Pravda* until January 30; but its emotional power was far greater, and it must have made a more significant contribution to the emerging cult of Lenin.

"It is as though there was a breakdown of the central station of proletarian mind, will, feeling, which sent its invisible currents by millions of wires to all points of the globe," wrote Bukharin. "Comrade Lenin was first of all a *vozhd'*, a *vozhd'* such as history presents to humanity once in hundreds of years, those whose names later become associated with epochs. He was the greatest organizer of the masses. Like a giant he strode at the head of the stream of humanity, directing its movement." Bukharin tried to explain Lenin's greatness as a mass leader by his possession of an extraordinary sensitivity to the masses' needs. But he also emphasized the authoritarian quality of Lenin's leadership: "He was a dictator in the best sense of the word. Drawing into himself like a sponge all the juices of life, processing in his astonishing mental laboratory the experience of hundreds and thousands of people, he at the same time led them after him with a courageous hand, as one who possesses power, as one who possesses authority, as a mighty *vozhd'*." Finally, Bukharin spoke of the attitude of Lenin's associates towards him: "It would hardly be possible in all of history to find another leader so loved by his comrades-in-arms. All of them felt a special feeling for Lenin. Their feeling for him was precisely one of love."

Citing Lenin's animadversions on the glorification of personality, post-Stalin Soviet pronouncements have condemned the cult of Stalin which flourished in the nineteen-thirties and forties as an un-Communist phenomenon. Personality cults in general, they have argued, violate the essential nature of Communism as a movement and system.[72] Our study casts doubt on that contention. It shows at least that there was nothing anomalous in the appearance of the original Communist personality cult; it was a natural and spontaneous outgrowth of Russian Communism as a movement which had, in Lenin, a charismatic central figure. His own intense dislike of adulation in no way alters this conclusion. It merely proves that the first and most enduring of Communism's leader cults owed nothing to a desire of the leader himself for personal glory.

The Aftermath

The portion of the "Letter to the Congress" kept secret at the time of writing remained unopened during the first few months after Lenin died. It was probably fortunate for Stalin's emotional equilibrium in those tense months that he continued in ignorance of the fact that Lenin had intended to unseat him from the post of general secretary. The blow was hard enough to sustain when it came.

The Thirteenth Party Congress, the first to be held after Lenin's death, met in late May 1924. Shortly beforehand, on May 18, Krupskaya turned over to the Central Committee the hitherto secret parts of the "Letter," comprising the dictated notes of December 24–25, 1922, and the postscript of January 4, 1923. In an

72. See, for example, Khrushchev's secret report to the Twentieth Congress; also the Central Committee decree of June 30, 1956, "O kul'te lichnosti i ego posledstviakh " (*Pravda*, July 1, 1956). Marx is quoted in these materials as saying: "From my antipathy to any cult of personality, I never made public during the existence of the International the numerous messages from various countries which recognized my services and which annoyed me. I did not even reply to them, except sometimes to rebuke their authors."

accompanying statement she explained that "Vladimir Ilyich expressed the firm desire that after his death these dictated notes of his should be brought to the attention of the next party congress." The material appears to have gone first to Stalin, as general secretary. According to a hearsay account reported by Trotsky, it was opened by Stalin in the presence of a personal aide, Lev Mekhlis, and a party official then working in the Central Committee offices, Sergei Syrtsov; upon reading it, Stalin burst out with invective against Lenin.[73] Then, on May 21, the testament came before the Central Committee when it met for its pre-congress plenum. An administrative assistant of Stalin who was present as secretary and who later emigrated has described the scene as Kamenev read the document aloud: "Painful embarrassment paralyzed the whole gathering. Stalin, who sat on one of the benches of the presidium's rostrum, felt small and miserable. Despite his self-control and forced calm, one could clearly read in his face the fact that his fate was being decided." [74]

As re-elected by the Twelfth Congress in the previous year, the Central Committee was a body of forty members and seventeen non-voting candidate members. Although such reliable Stalin men as Molotov, Voroshilov, Kirov, Mikoyan, and Ordzhonikidze were among the forty, the Central Committee was by no means a group which Stalin controlled. Nothing prevented it from following the specific recommendation made in Lenin's postscript of January 4. That it did not do so is a measure not of Stalin's power as general secretary but of the astuteness of his recent politicking inside the ruling group. During Lenin's incapacitation Stalin had accepted a junior partnership in an informal Politburo bloc or triumvirate with the ambitious Zinoviev and his close associate Kamenev, who still looked down on the general secretary as a person of limited political abilities and were moved above all by fear of—and in Zinoviev's

73. Trotsky, *Stalin*, p. 375. For Krupskaya's statement accompanying the material sent to the Central Committee, see *Lenin*, XLV, 594.
74. B. Bajanow, *Stalin. Der rote Diktator* (Berlin, n.d.), p. 32. This account derives credence from the fact that Trotsky, who was present, later quoted it (*Stalin*, p. 376). Trotsky himself, according to Bajanov's account, kept silent but showed his reaction by gestures and grimaces.

case rivalry with—Trotsky. Fear of Trotsky's coming to power was shared by a larger circle of men in the ruling group, and his candidacy for a role of decisive influence would be a logical result of Lenin's testament if Stalin were to be demoted. Thus, the group proved responsive to the strong pleas that both Zinoviev and Kamenev made for Stalin's retention. Zinoviev said: "Comrades, the last will, every word of Ilyich, is undoubtedly to be regarded by us as law. . . . On one point, however, we are fortunate to be able to say that Ilyich's fears have not been confirmed. I refer to the point concerning our general secretary. You have all been witnesses to our work together in the past months. Along with me, you have seen to your satisfaction that Ilyich's fears have not been realized." [75] The vote, on a motion by Zinoviev and Kamenev to close debate, was taken, according to Bajanov, by a show of hands. Stalin was saved.

It remained to decide how the sensational document should be handled, and, in particular, whether and how it should be conveyed to the party congress. A proposal by Kamenev not to convey it was protested by Krupskaya, who was present, and this led to the decision, reportedly by a vote of thirty against ten, that the testament should be communicated to the congress confidentially by being read aloud in the delegation caucuses of the major party organizations, rather than made a part of the public proceedings.[76] So it came about that the Stalin question was discussed behind the scenes of the Thirteenth Congress.

R. Terekhov, an Old Bolshevik who survived the Stalin period, later recalled from his experience as a congress participant that the testament occasioned a "stormy discussion" in the meeting of the Ukrainian delegation, with Zinoviev and Kamenev in attendance, and that it was "hotly discussed" in other delegation meetings too.[77]

75. Bajanow, *Stalin*, pp. 32–33. On fear of Trotsky as a major motive in the ruling group for leaving Stalin in office, see Jules Humbert-Droz, *De Lenine a Staline: Dix ans au service de L'internationale Communiste 1921–1931* (Neuchâtel, 1971), p. 199.

76. Max Eastman, *Since Lenin Died* (New York, 1925), p. 28. See also Deutscher, *Stalin*, p. 272, where the vote is given, presumably by error, as forty against ten. For the Central Committee decision on the manner of conveying the testament to the congress, see *Lenin*, XLV, 594.

77. *Pravda*, May 26, 1964.

At the time the testament was read to them, the delegations were evidently presented with a draft congress decision approving Stalin's continued tenure of his party office on the understanding that he would take account of Lenin's criticism of him. Stalin, for his part, offered some sort of assurances that he would rectify the faults to which the testament referred. "In deciding this question," Khrushchev stated in 1963, "the party proceeded from the real correlation of forces inside the Central Committee, and taking into account Stalin's positive aspects as a leader, believed his assurances that he would be able to overcome the deficiencies pointed out by Vladimir Ilyich." [78] When Stalin offered his resignation as general secretary in the post-congress plenum of the newly elected Central Committee, its rejection was thus a foregone conclusion.

On the ground that Lenin's "Letter" was addressed to the party congress and not meant for the press, it was decided not to publish the document. But once known to nearly twelve hundred congress delegates from all parts of the country, news of such sensational character was bound to spread through wide party circles by word of mouth. It also traveled abroad with Max Eastman, a young American supporter of Trotsky. Eastman summarized the testament and recounted the events of Lenin's last months and after in a book published in 1925, *Since Lenin Died*. Trotsky, who was Eastman's source, submitted to heavy pressure in the Politburo and published in the party journal *Bolshevik* an article that disavowed Eastman's book and branded all talk about a Lenin testament as a malicious fabrication. Before long, however, the opposition leaders, Trotsky included, were pressing the attack on Stalin with, among other things, references to Lenin's testament and demands for its publication. And opposition secret printing presses were turning out copies of the testament, which—Zinoviev protested—were being confiscated by the secret police as evidence of illegal publishing activity. "Why," he exclaimed, "has Lenin's testament become an illegal document?" [79]

78. *Ibid.*, March 10, 1963.
79. *Ibid.*, November 2, 1927.

Chapter Eight

POWER AND THE LENIN
SUCCESSION

The Stalin Machine

LIKE THE MANNER of starting biographies of Stalin, the manner of treating his rise to supremacy in the twenties is governed by certain conventions. One point regularly emphasized is that he succeeded in building the Orgburo-Secretariat complex into a formidable base of party power. Another is that he undid his principal opponents by a series of adroitly executed factional maneuvers in the intra-party politics of the post-Lenin period. Without minimizing the force of these considerations, both of which are true and important, I shall argue that they do not suffice to explain the events of that period in Bolshevism's history.

In Lenin's mind the party secretaryship was a technician's office. Reporting to the Ninth Party Congress in 1920 on how the Central Committee bodies instituted a year earlier were working, he pointedly described the secretary (Krestinsky held the office then) as strictly an executor of the will of the Central Committee, and declared that "only collegial decisions of the Central Committee, taken in the Orgburo or in the Politburo or by the Central Committee plenum, such questions exclusively were implemented by the secretary of the party Central Committee. The Central Committee cannot otherwise do its work properly." [1] But this overlooked the secretaryship's potentialities as a focal point of power, especially if

---

1. *Deviatyi s"ezd RKP/b/. Mart–Aprel' 1920 goda. Protokoly* (Moscow, 1960), p. 13.

occupied by a politically ambitious man like Stalin. The Secretariat's capacity to influence the policy-makers' agenda placed it in a highly strategic relationship to the party's higher deliberative organs, and its appointive powers made it an ideal instrument of machine politics. Lenin later showed his realization of these facts when he referred in the testament to the "boundless power" that Stalin had concentrated in his hands by becoming general secretary.

Others, too, although unaware of the testament, began to grow apprehensive over the extent of Stalin's secretarial power. Zinoviev and Kamenev were among them as they watched the junior member of the Politburo triumvirate become the dominant member during 1923–24. While seeking to use Stalin as a counterweight to Trotsky, Zinoviev became so worried by the counterweight's growing political power that in the autumn of 1923 he made a move to curb it. He called a number of vacationing party leaders to an informal meeting in a cave near the North Caucasian resort town of Kislovodsk; there he outlined a plan to "politicize" the Secretariat. He wanted to subordinate the Secretariat to the Politburo's direct control by appointing two other Politburo members—Trotsky and either Kamenev, Bukharin, or himself—as secretaries with authority co-equal to Stalin's. Nothing came of this venture, however, beyond an invitation from Stalin (who knew about the meeting) to Zinoviev, Trotsky, and Bukharin to attend sessions of the Orgburo. Without a footing in the Secretariat, participation in the Orgburo's deliberations meant very little.[2]

Further moves, similarly abortive, followed in 1925. In January of that year Kamenev suggested Stalin for the post—just vacated by Trotsky—of chairman of the Revolutionary War Council of the Republic, which would have involved his departure from the secretaryship; he was not interested. Later in the year, a number of prominent party leaders reportedly met in the apartment of an Old Bolshevik, G. I. Petrovsky, on the eve of the Fourteenth Congress

2. Alexandrov (A. S. Michelson), *Kto upravliaet Rossiei? Bol'shevitskii partiino-pravitel'stvennyi apparat i "stalinizm"* (Berlin, 1933), pp. 97–101. In telling about this "cave conspiracy" (as it became known) at the Fourteenth Congress, Zinoviev said that he and his associates wavered between the "politicizing" plan and the alternative of reducing the Secretariat to a service role.

and discussed the idea of replacing Stalin by Dzerzhinsky in the post of general secretary. Ordzhonikidze is said to have opposed this on the ground that the party would interpret it as a concession to Trotsky, and the idea was dropped.[3] The Stalin political machine and its boss were not so easy to dislodge from their entrenched position in the party-state.

A notable feature of Stalin's machine was the power structure that he constructed at its apex. Each Central Committee secretary employed the services of a number of assistants. As general secretary Stalin built up in the course of the twenties a corps of personal political aides who were chosen for their talent and acumen as well as for their loyalty. They kept him informed on every sphere of Soviet affairs, including foreign relations, and assisted him in preparing his policy positions. They also were his representatives vis-à-vis the bureaucracy.[4] No such personal chancery was created by Lenin, who dealt with the top party and government functionaries as directly as possible, employing a minimum of intermediaries. Stalin's personal aides, among whom Tovstukha and Mekhlis figured importantly in the early twenties, were given the title of "assistant central committee secretary." Tovstukha was also made assistant director and later director of the Central Committee's Secret Department, and served from 1924 to 1926 as assistant director of the Lenin Institute, in which capacity he took part in preparing the second edition of Lenin's works.

Stalin's machine politics of self-advancement were founded on the strategy of using the Secretariat to build a party clientele in the provinces and then transmuting this local power into central power. Through Uchraspred and the roving Central Committee instructors,

3. Roy A. Medvedev, *Let History Judge: The Origins and Consequences of Stalinism* (New York, 1971), p. 50. According to Medvedev, the upsetting effect of this incident upon Dzerzhinsky hastened his death, which came in 1926. On Kamenev's nomination of Stalin for Trotsky's post, see Alexandrov, *Kto upravliaet Rossiei?*, p. 137.

4. The main sources of this information are two one-time Soviet officials who recorded the facts as known to them in books written after they emigrated: S. Dmitrievsky, *Sovetskie portrety* (Stockholm, 1932), pp. 108–109; and Abdurakhman Avtorkhanov, *Stalin and the Soviet Communist Party: A Study in the Technology of Power* (New York, 1959), ch. XIV.

individuals of ability who gave promise of serving the needs of the
Stalin organization were identified. The next step was to advance
them in their political careers, particularly in the network of provincial party organizations. The province, town, and district party
committees were subject to election by local party conferences, and
the party secretaries at all three levels—these being full-time party
workers, or *apparatchiki,* in informal parlance—were subject to
election by the committees. The elective procedures continued to be
observed. Through the process of nomination, however, the electoral
results came to be governed more and more by Central Committee
recommendations having the force of directives. A former Central
Committee secretary, Preobrazhensky, complained at the Twelfth
Congress that approximately 30 per cent of the secretaries of the
party committees of provinces had been "recommended" by the
Central Committee.[5] Later in 1923, he was one of forty-six Bolsheviks of the Left who signed a secret memorandum to the Politburo
which spoke of "the ever-increasing, and now scarcely concealed,
division of the party between a secretarial hierarchy and 'quiet folk,'
between professional party officials recruited from above and the
general mass of the party which does not participate in the common
life." [6]

The general secretary's growing provincial power was not slow
to be felt in central party politics. Provincial secretaries and others
promoted to their positions by virtue of Central Committee recommendations were coming to Moscow as delegates to the annual
party congresses, and as such played a part both in congress decisions and in the voting for a new Central Committee—this body
being subject to re-election by each party congress. In these circumstances Stalin, for purposes of his own, found it expedient to espouse
Lenin's suggestion for democratizing party life in the upper spheres
through enlargement of the Central Committee and enhancement

5. *Dvenadtsatyi s"ezd rossiiskoi kommunisticheskoi partii /bol'shevikov/.
Stenograficheskii otchet* (Moscow, 1923), p. 146.
6. E. H. Carr, *The Interregnum 1923–1924* (New York, 1954), p. 368.
The memorandum, known as the "platform of the forty-six," is preserved in the
Trotsky Archives at Harvard. A full translation of the memorandum appears as an
appendix to *The Interregnum.*

of its role vis-à-vis the Politburo. There was this important difference, though: whereas Lenin had envisaged the new Central Committee members as workers, for the most part, Stalin wanted to enlarge the Central Committee with well-disposed *apparatchiki* so as to increase his own influence within it. Despite initial strong resistance from Zinoviev, who by the same token wanted to keep it from growing, the Central Committee expanded from a size of twenty-seven members and nineteen candidates in 1922 to sixty-three members and forty-three candidates in 1925, and many of the newcomers were Stalin supporters.[7] The Stalin organization's steadily rising strength in the Central Committee not only represented the beginnings of a counterbalance to Stalin's lack of a secure majority in the Politburo, but in time it affected the membership of the latter, which was subject to re-election after each party congress by the newly reconstituted Central Committee meeting in its first plenum. By the end of 1925, for example, Molotov, Voroshilov, and Kalinin joined Stalin, Trotsky, Zinoviev, Bukharin, Rykov, and Tomsky as full members of the Politburo.

The Politics of Faction

We have noted that the Tenth Party Congress passed a resolution on unity, drafted by Lenin, which banned factions in the party. Reflecting the competition of "platforms" on the trade union issue, which had divided the party in the pre-congress period, it defined factionalism as "the emergence of groups with special platforms and a certain striving to close ranks and create their own group discipline." [8] Clause seven of the resolution, not published along

7. Alexandrov, *Kto upravliaet Rossiei?*, pp. 74–83. For more detailed accounts in English of the Secretariat's role in Stalin's rise, see Robert V. Daniels, *The Conscience of the Revolution: Communist Opposition in Soviet Russia* (Cambridge, Mass., 1960), chs. 7–11; Merle Fainsod, *How Russia Is Ruled*, 2nd ed. (Cambridge, Mass., 1963), chs. 5–6; and Leonard Schapiro, *The Communist Party of the Soviet Union* (New York, 1959), chs. 13–15. A useful appendix in Daniels gives the changing composition of the Central Committee and its organs in the twenties.

8. *Desiatyi s"ezd RKP/b/. Mart 1921 goda. Stenograficheskii otchet* (Moscow, 1923), p. 571.

with the rest of the document at the time, empowered the Central Committee to enforce the ban, even against Central Committee members, by measures ranging in severity to expulsion from the party. A two-thirds vote of the combined total membership of the Central Committee and Central Party Control Commission was, however, required for demotion or expulsion of a Central Committee member.

Like the Tenth Congress' decision to abandon War Communism for the NEP, the ban on factionalism was adopted under pressure of the hard times through which the regime was passing. The Kronstadt rising was only the most dramatic expression of an unrest widespread in the country, and the ending of the Civil War did not signify to Bolshevik minds that international perils were behind them. Despite the clear victory of the "platform of the ten," any further open spectacle of division in the party seemed very inadvisable to Lenin in view of the critical internal situation and the possibility that international forces hostile to the Revolution might take advantage of it. The NEP, as he later put it, was a retreat; and on the theory that an army's need for discipline is never so great as in time of retreat, his resolution on party unity commanded the Bolsheviks to close ranks.

In the study of politics—and this may apply with special force to politics in Russia—it is essential to distinguish between formalities and realities. Formally prohibited in 1921, factionalism in fact persisted in the party, as habits formed in the past combined with the dynamics of political life in the present. How the one and the other operated may be illustrated by events that occurred during the Tenth Congress itself. On March 9, 1921, shortly after the congress opened, fifteen or so signatories and supporters of the "platform of the ten" were called to an informal meeting with Lenin in the Kremlin after the evening session. Lenin began by saying that though it was now clear that the "platform of the ten" would be adopted by the congress, there was a danger that the Central Committee would be re-elected more or less in its present composition, with many of Trotsky's supporters included, and would become engulfed again in inner conflict. To prevent this, it was essential to ensure a two-thirds majority in the new Central Committee for firm adherents of the "platform of the ten." The other third of the seats would go to prominent representatives of Trotsky's platform, to the Workers' Opposition, and to the Democratic Centralists, for these groups included many figures who were useful in the work and popular in the country, and who would be bound by party discipline to assist the Central Committee to pursue its policy line.

According to the memoirs of Mikoyan, who attended the meeting, this plan was approved and individual candidacies were discussed. Then the question arose of how to organize the congress majority to vote for the favored candidates and against those not wanted. Lenin proposed to do it by quietly caucusing with the whole group of congress delegates chosen by local party conferences as supporters of the "platform of the ten." They should be issued notices of the meeting which would serve both as invitations and entry passes. It would not be proper, Lenin went on, to use a state printing press for this purpose, so he had brought with him an old comrade, experienced in underground work, who had type and a hand printing press and who would print up the required number of notices that night. When Stalin broke in to express fear that the Trotskyists and other oppositionists might take advantage of the calling of such a meeting in order to accuse the Lenin group of factionalism, Lenin smiled good-naturedly and said to him:

What's this I hear from a zealous old factionalist?! Even he doubts the necessity of calling a meeting of adherents of the 'platform of the ten'! You must know that Trotsky has long been at work gathering the supporters of his platform and has probably called his faction together at this very moment while we sit here talking. Shliapnikov and Sapronov are doing the same. Why close our eyes to the clear fact, unpleasant as it is, that factions exist in the party? It is just the calling of this conference of adherents of the 'platform of the ten' that will bring about conditions excluding all factionalism in our party in the future.[9]

Lenin's proposed procedure was followed, and he then engaged in

9. A. I. Mikoyan, *Mysli i vospominaniia o Lenine* (Moscow, 1970), pp. 136–139.

intensive talks with various smaller groups of delegates, including representatives of the oppositions, to ensure willing acceptance of the future composition of the Central Committee desired by his group.

Ostensibly, Lenin was fighting factionalism with factionalism. But reading what a Russian might call the "sub-text" of this episode, it seems plain that factional ways were too deeply ingrained in the Bolshevik culture to be eradicated by any resolution on party unity. Although the factions were rarely close-knit and did not make public, as in 1921, their policy platforms, the ban did not eliminate them. Its real effect was, rather, to make factional politics in the party more covert, as a rule, and likewise more dangerous. Acting in the name of "the party," a victorious faction could accuse a defeated one of factionalism and then invoke against it the sanctions specified in clause seven of the resolution, which was finally made public in 1924. With sufficient support in the Central Committee and the Central Party Control Commission, the victors could demote the losers or even expel them from the party. Such, in fact, was the way in which the Stalin faction dealt with many defeated adversaries in the later twenties.

At the time of Lenin's death there were in the party four different factional groupings with representation on the Politburo. Stalin was the chief of one of them. Trotsky was the leading personality of a leftist faction which included such prominent revolutionary figures as Radek, Piatakov, Serebriakov, Krestinsky, Ioffe, Sosnovsky, Christian Rakovsky, and others who signed the "platform of the forty-six." Zinoviev and Kamenev were dual leaders of a faction whose main organizational base was the Leningrad party organization, over which Zinoviev presided. Finally, there was a faction whose leaders were a trio of Politburo moderates: the popular Bukharin, an eminent party intellectual and the chief editor of *Pravda;* Rykov, who succeeded Lenin as chairman of the Council of People's Commissars; and Mikhail Tomsky, head of the central Soviet trade union organization. The Bukharin group had a following among younger party intellectuals as well as in the government bureaucracy and the trade unions. It was strongly entrenched in the powerful Moscow city party organization, with which Bukharin himself had a long association, and it exerted dominant influence in the editorship of a number of party publications. Having led the Left Communist movement in 1918, Bukharin was now a convinced advocate of the NEP and the foremost exponent of its moderate, peasant-oriented economic policies. Indeed, it was he and his associates who originated, particularly in its economic aspects, the doctrine of socialism in one country that Stalin espoused in the intra-party controversies of the mid-twenties.[10]

The maneuvers by which Stalin steered his faction to a conclusive victory over the other three are testimony to his extraordinary skill as a political strategist; they have been cited as a textbook example of the art of coalition strategy.[11] We have seen that during Lenin's final illness, Stalin joined with Zinoviev and Kamenev as an informal leadership *troika* to give direction in the Politburo, meanwhile engaging in a covert political contest with his fellow triumvirs. At the same time, he cultivated close relations with the Bukharin group and aligned himself with their orientation in economic policy, which enjoyed wide acceptance in the party. Together with these allies he moved against his potentially most formidable rival for the Lenin succession, Trotsky. In doing so he took advantage of the fact that Trotsky and Zinoviev had a long record of mutual hostility and that Trotsky was deeply feared by the Bukharinists because of disagreements over policy, particularly having to do with the Trotsky group's advocacy of rapid industrialization at peasant expense and its reliance on further revolution abroad as a pre-condition of final success in building socialism at home. The concerted public attack on "Trotskyism" in 1924 and early 1925 marked the

10. For the political and intellectual biography of Bukharin, see Stephen F. Cohen, *Bukharin and the Bolshevik Revolution* (New York, 1973). On the priority of Bukharin and his group in devising the doctrine of socialism in one country, see also N. Valentinov, *Doktrina pravogo kommunizma* (Munich, 1960).

11. John McDonald, *Strategy in Poker, Business, and War* (New York, 1963), pp. 117–118. Speaking of the principal contestants, the author comments: "Nothing was needed more by these men than a little game theory, and only one had it."

beginning of the end for Trotsky and his political cause. It must be added that Stalin's success in this battle was substantially facilitated by Trotsky's political ineptitude during the crucial period from 1923 to 1925, as manifested, for example, in his spurning of overtures made to him by Zinoviev in the aftermath of the Twelfth Congress: the necessity of a coalition strategy for beating Stalin seems to have escaped Trotsky.

In the fall of 1925 the triumvirate broke apart as fear of Stalin and his mounting political strength came to prevail in the minds of Zinoviev and Kamenev. In September these two joined with Krupskaya and Sokolnikov in espousing an oppositionist "platform of the four," and the Fourteenth Party Congress, which met in December of that year, brought the conflict into the open. Trotsky remained aloof from this anti-Stalin effort. In a speech that proved the sensation of the congress, Kamenev not only protested Stalin's use of the Secretariat as a political instrument but directly challenged his credentials for being supreme leader of the party. "We are against creating the theory of a *'vozhd'*,' we are against making a *'vozhd'*,' " he declared, and ended his speech by saying with heavy emphasis: *"I have reached the conviction that Comrade Stalin cannot play the part of unifier* of the Bolshevik staff." [12] This direct and open opposition to Stalin's ambitions was a courageous stand, but it achieved nothing. Zinoviev and Kamenev suffered a severe defeat in the congress at the hands of the combined Stalin and Bukharin forces. The oppositionists' power sank and Stalin's rose in the reconstituted Central Committee and Politburo, and Zinoviev's Leningrad stronghold fell to the Stalin faction's attack in the aftermath. Kamenev suffered the humiliation of being demoted to candidate status in the Politburo.

In 1926, Trotsky, Zinoviev, and Kamenev belatedly joined in what was called the "united opposition." A rearguard action by two crippled factions, it was doomed to the debacle that overtook it in late 1927 when Trotsky, Zinoviev, and Kamenev, along with large numbers of their followers, were expelled from the party.

12. *XIV s"ezd vsesoiuznoi kommunisticheskoi partii /b/. 18–31 dekabria 1925 g. Stenograficheskii otchet* (Moscow, 1926), pp. 290–291.

Hardly had this phase of the struggle ended when Stalin, secure now on one flank, turned against his political allies on the other. With the anti-Stalin forces on the Left in disgrace and disarray, those on the Right succumbed after a series of bitter political battles in 1928 and early 1929. By late 1929 the Bukharinists had gone down to crushing political defeat, with the loss of their party offices and organizational bases of support, and the Stalin faction reigned supreme in the Soviet party-state.

No explanation of this outcome can fail to recognize that Stalin's use of the Secretariat as an organizational weapon and his astute maneuvers in the factional contest were essential components of his success. But an account that focused on only these factors would be critically incomplete. To picture Stalin's victory in the party struggle as an automatic result of the mechanics of the power struggle is to overlook some deeper complexities of the political process in Soviet Russia during the first post-Lenin years. To see him operating as a machine politician only, an arch-*apparatchik* supremely skilled in the arts of manipulation, is—in spite of the fact that he *was* that—to misconceive in certain ways both the protagonist and the nature of the drama in which he played a leading role.

For one thing, such a view would overlook the measure of fluidity that obtained in the historical situation of that time. In the NEP era Soviet society was not yet the tightly controlled organism that it would become during the Stalinist thirties as a result of the revolution from above that Stalin initiated in late 1929, when the power to do so was finally in his hands. The political system, in which all political parties but one were suppressed, could accurately be described as a dictatorship of the Bolshevik party. Lenin and some of his associates acknowledged this on occasion, although they maintained that the dictatorship was also democratic in a new way by virtue of being government "for" the masses and because of the involvement of millions of ordinary people in public affairs through membership in the Komsomol, the soviets, the trade unions, cooperatives, and other voluntary associations. But institutionally authoritarian as it was, the Soviet party-state of the NEP years was a far cry from the dread bureaucratic leviathan conjured up by our image of a "totalitarian system." [13]

The party-state structure still showed considerable looseness in organization and mode of functioning. The party factions themselves were loose groupings, not well-disciplined political phalanxes. Although a system of patron-client relations had taken shape among those with political position or the hope of it, clients were not always loyal to patrons—not even if the patron happened to be Stalin or one of his associates. Private enterprise flourished in much of the economy. Intellectual life was far from completely regimented.[14] The secret police, albeit an object of fear for many, was not operating as the terror machine that it was later to become and was not yet one man's political instrument. Neither the population at large nor the tens of thousands composing the politically influential class could be described (in the language of the theory of totalitarianism) as an "atomized mass."

In these conditions it was not possible for Stalin or anyone else to rise to supreme leadership of the regime simply through capable manipulating of the levers of organizational power, combined with clever tactical strategy. A would-be party chief had to develop a politically persuasive program and be convincing in his way of presenting it in higher party circles. Even power moves in some instances called for effective argumentation on other than power grounds. Thus, when Stalin at the Twelfth Congress espoused an enlargement of the Central Committee against strong covert resistance from Zinoviev, he did so by appealing in open session to the need for reinforcing a somewhat worn-out senior party leadership with a "new shift" of fresh, able, younger figures with heads on their shoulders—an argument that certainly evoked a strong posi-

13. On the idea of totalitarianism, see Hannah Arendt, *The Origins of Totalitarianism,* new ed. (New York, 1966), and Carl J. Friedrich and Zbigniew Brzezinski, *Totalitarian Dictatorship and Autocracy* (Cambridge, Mass., 1956). For a recent reconsideration of the concept, see Carl J. Friedrich, Michael R. Curtis, and Benjamin R. Barber, *Totalitarianism in Perspective: Three Views* (New York, 1969).

14. On NEP society in its pluralistic aspect, see Cohen, *Bukharin and the Bolshevik Revolution,* ch. IX.

tive response from large numbers of younger delegates who could see themselves as meeting these criteria.[15] Since, moreover, the Bolsheviks were by old habit an intensely argumentative party, given to debating their political issues in ideological terms, an aspiring leader had to be convincing theoretically as well as pragmatically. No matter how competent he might be as a technician of power, he had to prove himself as a political and ideological leader in the Lenin tradition. He had to engage in a contest not simply for power but also for the succession.

The Vacant Role

We must distinguish leadership succession from the closely related process of the rise of an individual to power; succession means legitimacy as well as power. It involves the passage to the new leader of something of the authority possessed by his predecessor, the general recognition of him as rightful head of the political community. Depending upon the character of the political order, victory in power competition, although normally necessary, is not always sufficient for this purpose. In a long-established polity with an institutionalized position of supreme leader, accession to this office, by whatever are the prescribed or permitted means, ordinarily resolves the succession problem too, or at any rate goes very far toward resolving it. But the situation is very different—and the succession problem far more difficult—in a new state in which supreme authority is centered in the personality of the leader-founder, and in which no formal office of supreme leader has been created.

The post-Lenin Bolshevik situation shows how intractable the problem of succession can be after the death of the founder of a revolutionary new order. Max Weber theorized, with the history of religions primarily in mind, that the charisma inhering in the original leader as a personal quality subsequently undergoes "routinization," meaning its institutionalization in an office and its transmission from

15. *Stalin*, V, 219. Stalin won his point. The congress raised the number of full members of the Central Committee from twenty-seven to forty.

bearer to bearer, irrespective of personal qualities, according to established rules of succession.[16] No such development occurred, however, in the case before us. It is true, as we have seen, that when Lenin died the party Central Committee proclaimed the party as a whole to be a collective embodiment and continuation of him, thus giving party membership itself a symbolically charismatic definition. But Lenin's personal charisma was neither institutionalized in an office of supreme party leadership (as we have already noted, he had held none), nor was it easily transferable to a successor. No one among the leaders of the party succeeded to Lenin's extraordinary authority. And insofar as the latter underwent "routinization," it did so in the form of the Lenin personality cult, which complicated rather than facilitated the process of leader succession. Thus Lenin, even in death, was pictured as remaining at the head of the Bolshevik movement. The problem of how he could posthumously function as supreme leader was solved (or at any rate circumvented) by the notion that, although no longer present in the flesh, he was still guiding and inspiring the movement through his teachings, through Leninism; and the presence of his embalmed body in the tomb in Red Square reinforced this notion. "Hitherto we have been able to act directly and literally 'according to Lenin,'" Zinoviev observed, for example, in the political report to the Thirteenth Party Congress. "But of late, and particularly at this congress, we are having to act according to Leninism. We have received no direct and precise instructions, no specific directives, and we must resolve the problems before us on the basis of the party's whole school of experience with Vladimir Ilyich, on the basis of our collective understanding of Leninism." [17]

A discrepancy between power and authority thus existed in early post-Lenin Bolshevism. Powerful though he had become in the party, Stalin was not yet widely perceived and accepted as Lenin's successor in the role of supreme leader of the party. Lenin's

16. Max Weber, *The Theory of Social and Economic Organization* (New York, 1947), pp. 364–371.

17. *Trinadtsatyi s"ezd RKP/b/. Mai 1924 goda. Stenograficheskii otchet* (Moscow, 1963), p. 37.

own authority lived on in the Bolshevik movement, among other ways in the idea that the movement was under the guidance of "Leninism." The oligarchical regime at the apex of party rule was officially described as one of "collective leadership," and the very idea that Lenin should have an individual successor was mentally resisted by many.

However, the problem of the Lenin succession could neither be set aside nor solved in these terms. No matter how difficult it might be to decide, the question of who would succeed Lenin had to be faced and settled. Even apart from the fact that there were ambitious men in the party and that one of them—Stalin—was already acquiring formidable personal power, the role of supreme leader that Lenin had created was in need of being filled. By virtue of both past traditions and present problems, the party needed a new political chief to unify it and give it stable direction in the coming period. The notion that Lenin himself could do this through his teachings was quite unreal. For no teaching can provide guidance for action in new historical conditions without being creatively applied. The party could not, therefore, act "according to Leninism" without living interpreters of Leninism. And in order to act in a unified way, especially at a time of great division over the main lines of internal and external policy, it needed an individual leader with authority that, even if not comparable to Lenin's, would nevertheless be very great and generally accepted. Collective leadership belonged to the Bolshevik tradition in the sense that policy questions had generally been debated in the higher Bolshevik organs and decided by majority vote. But these organs had not functioned as leaderless collectivities, and to suppose that they could do so now on a stable basis was to ignore the force of custom and precedent in political life. Indeed, it was to fly in the face of that very "school of experience" which the party had gone through under Lenin.

He had given Bolshevism strong personal leadership without being a dictator who ruled by arbitrary command. The movement had arisen as his political following in Russian Marxism and developed for twenty years under his guidance and inspiration. Although not institutionalized in an office, his role of supreme leader had entered into the unwritten constitution of Bolshevism, its habitual *modus operandi*. Lenin had been the movement's organizer, its chief strategist and tactician, the author of its distinctive version of Marxist ideology, and the authoritative interpreter of party doctrine. He had been the commander-in-chief of the party in the political struggles that led up to the revolutionary conquest of power, and in those that ensued after power was won. He had been the dominant policy-making personality of the ruling party and of the new Third International that came into being under its auspices. His unique authority enabled him to unify an extremely disputatious ruling group whose inner conflicts continually threatened to tear it apart into warring factions. As head of the Soviet government, moreover, Lenin was Bolshevism's chief executive and director of its foreign relations. Lastly, as a speaker and writer he was the foremost representative and personal symbol of the regime in its relations with its own people and the outside world. Thus, a many-sided role of supreme leader had taken shape in the crucible of the party's history under Lenin. Vacated by death, it awaited a new incumbent.

Forseeing that this would be so, Lenin himself had wrestled with the succession problem during his final months of semi-active life in 1922–23. In conversations with Bukharin, he called it "leaderology." [18] The problem preoccupied him primarily from the standpoint of preserving the stability of Bolshevik rule, for which purpose the solidarity of the leaders seemed an essential condition. Lenin's anxiety over the potential consequences of disunity in the leadership had found expression in the resolution on party unity. A year later, in 1922, he expressed it again, with greater frankness, in an unpublished letter to Molotov, who was then secretary of the Central Committee. Here he referred to the authority of the "very thin stratum that could be called the party's old guard" as the determining fact in party decision-making, and went on to warn that any inner conflict in the old guard could so weaken its authority that

18. Boris I. Nicolaevsky, *Power and the Soviet Elite,* ed. Janet D. Zagoria (New York, 1965), p. 12. Nicolaevsky was told this by Bukharin in conversations which the two men held in Paris in 1936. On the circumstances of those talks, see below, p. 424.

it would lose the power of decision.[19] When he wrote the testament
in December 1922, his anxious concern on this score was visible in
every line of the document. It showed up in his proposal that the
Central Committee's membership be enlarged to fifty or one hundred
as a means of containing its inner conflicts and thus of preventing
a "schism" that could jeopardize the continued stability of the party
and the Soviet system. It was reflected in his comment on the antagonistic relations between Stalin and Trotsky as the prime source
of the danger of a split in the Central Committee, and in his consideration of the qualifications of various possible candidates for
succession to the supreme leadership.

Lenin, it seems clear, realized that what had held the factious
party leadership together so far was his own enormous personal
authority, and therefore that his imminent passing from the scene
would remove the effective linchpin of the party's unity. Yet, as the
testament shows, the solution of the leadership question eluded him.
None of the six men whose qualifications he considered—Stalin,
Trotsky, Zinoviev, Kamenev, Bukharin, and Piatakov—was designated as his chosen candidate for the succession. No one among his
prominent revolutionary associates appeared clearly capable of unifying the Bolshevik party in the coming post-Lenin period.

Two years after his death, by which time Stalin was far along
in his march to power, the succession problem was still unresolved.
Stalin delivered the political report of the Central Committee before
the Fourteenth Congress, appearing in a role that had traditionally
been Lenin's and that Zinoviev had taken at the two preceding party
congresses. But he was not an acknowledged new supreme leader of
the party with authority in any way comparable to Lenin's. In this
regard, the proceedings of the Fourteenth Congress registered, at
most, his emergence into a dominating position in party affairs. Certainly, the fact that he was general secretary did not establish him in
Bolshevik minds as a new *vozhd'*. Originally and by design an administrative and technical function, the secretaryship had evolved
into a real political stronghold. But this was a surreptitious process
and one that the Stalin faction felt constrained to de-emphasize or

19. *Lenin*, XLV, 20.

deny in the face of charges, such as those being made by the opposition, that the Secretariat was playing an improper political role. Voroshilov, for example, countered the opposition's demand to make the Secretariat a technical organ, subordinate to the Politburo, with the claim that it already was just that, and "engages in no politics." [20]

No claim to supreme political authority could be made, either by Stalin or for him, on the basis of his tenure of the office of general secretary. Since Lenin, moreover, had not acquired or retained his supreme-leader role on the basis of office-holding but rather by force of his commanding political personality, Bolsheviks were generally disinclined to see party office itself, of whatever description, as the source of supreme leadership. Such authority was not something to be acquired at a stroke but to be built up gradually by the demonstration of outstanding prowess as a political leader. As Sokolnikov put it in his speech to the Fourteenth Congress, "Lenin was neither chairman of the Politburo nor general secretary. Nevertheless, Comrade Lenin had the decisive political voice in the party. And if we disputed with him, we thought thrice before doing so. What I have to say is this: if Comrade Stalin wants to win the confidence that Comrade Lenin had, let him win this confidence." [21]

Sokolnikov was speaking as a representative of an oppositionist group that did not receive the support of the Congress. Yet this particular statement was not one with which very many Bolsheviks (outside of Stalin's entourage) could easily have disagreed. For apart from the truth of what it said about Lenin's authority and how it had been acquired, there was as yet no general consciousness of the party's having acquired, in Stalin, a successor to Lenin in the role of *vozhd'*. Indeed a delegate to the Fourteenth Congress or a reader of its published proceedings, which came out in 1926 in an edition of 100,000 copies, might have acquired the impression that no one would succeed to Lenin's leader-role. Molotov asserted in the Central Committee's organizational report to the congress that "the significance of collective leadership is growing." Voroshilov drew applause from the floor when he stated in his speech that "we

20. *XIV s"ezd*, pp. 274, 275.
21. *Ibid.*, p. 335.

all, the whole congress and the entire party, stand for collective leadership." True, in this most openly pro-Stalin speech of the congress Voroshilov voiced the view that Stalin was the "principal member" of the Politburo, and said that "he takes the most active part in deciding questions and his proposals are carried more often than anyone else's." But he simultaneously stipulated that Stalin "never lays claim to primacy." And to show that collective leadership was operative at the top, he also observed that since Lenin's death it was Kamenev—not Stalin—who had regularly been presiding at the Politburo's meetings. Finally, Stalin himself spoke out quite categorically on this question. "To lead the party otherwise than collectively is impossible," he declared in his reply to the discussion on the political report. "Now that Ilyich is not with us, it is silly to dream of such a thing [applause], it is silly to talk about it. Collective work, collective leadership, unity in the party, unity in the organs of the Central Committee, with the minority submitting to the majority—that is what we need now." [22]

Some congress speeches, moreover, specifically rejected the idea that Lenin should have a successor. "We had Lenin, whom we all trusted and who pursued a correct line and gave general direction to the proletariat and our Communist party," said A. V. Medvedev, an Old Bolshevik of working-class origin, in his sharply anti-Zinovievist speech to the congress. "Following his death we say: it is not a question of individuals but of collective thought and work, of collective leadership." And another speaker, V. I. Polonsky, quoted the following remark of an unnamed rank-and-file party member from the Moscow province as representative of majority opinion in the party: ". . . Comrade Lenin left behind a trunkful of belongings of all kinds, and individual representatives, various members of the Central Committee, are beginning to try on his mantle. But this mantle does not fit anybody; it is not the right size for the co-reporter of the Central Committee [Zinoviev]. This inheritance should be the inheritance of our whole party and of the whole Central Committee, and no one should reach out as an individual for this inheritance, this

22. *Ibid.*, pp. 86, 396, 397.

mantle of Comrade Lenin's; nobody is the right size for it." [23] According to the published transcript of the congress proceedings, applause and shouts of "Right!" rang out from the floor at this point.

Why the anonymous Bolshevik's statement touched a responsive chord in the congress audience is not adequately explained by the unpopularity of the immediate target, Zinoviev, who had given indication of aspiring to the role of supreme leader. The fact is that the party was still under the spell of the political personality of Lenin, who in death had become an awesome presence before the minds of his Bolshevik followers. Having hero-worshiped him while he lived, they had now memorialized him in a great public personality cult, and in the process they had magnified him into a superhuman being. He loomed in retrospect as a veritable giant of world history, a figure of legendary dimensions. The stature of the surviving party leaders diminished correspondingly, and the very idea of one of them succeeding him as supreme leader seemed somehow incongruous and inadmissible. So it appeared that no one in the party could possibly be "the right size" for Lenin's mantle. The leaders, too, either shared this feeling or at least were aware of its existence among the rank-and-file membership. Thus Trotsky, writing later of his failure to speak out against Stalin during the critically important time of Lenin's final illness, explains that such a move would have been interpreted as a bid for Lenin's position in the party and state, and "the very thought of this made me shudder." [24]

Stalin, for his part, was certainly not shuddering at the thought. He was proudly conscious of being an authentic Old Bolshevik risen to high position in the party, and had long nourished the hope of succeeding to Lenin's role as *vozhd'*. He was too intelligent, however, to go against the current of party feeling just described. For the time being he was content to endorse in public the prevailing

23. *Ibid.*, pp. 173, 179.

24. L. Trotsky, *My Life* (New York, 1930), p. 482. Elsewhere he wrote: "What restrained me was the fear that any sharp conflict in the ruling group at that time, when Lenin was struggling with death, might be understood by the party as a casting of lots for Lenin's mantle" (*On the Suppressed Testament of Lenin* [New York, 1946], p. 38).

sentiment that Lenin need have no individual successor as supreme
leader and that the leadership at the top should be collective. But
this was not his actual view of the situation. Shortly after his re-
sounding statement, quoted above, on the inevitability of collective
leadership, he was saying something very different in private.

At the beginning of 1926, in the aftermath of the Fourteenth
Congress, Kirov became secretary of the Leningrad party organization. Zinoviev's old citadel was now in the Stalin faction's hands.
At a dinner held to celebrate the event, the conversation turned to
the question of how to govern the party without Lenin. As the story
has been told by Pyotr Chagin, a Leningrad leader and friend of
Kirov's who was present at the dinner, there was general agreement
that the leadership should be collective. The dissenter was Stalin.
Having listened in silence to the discussion, he got up and walked
around the table saying: "Don't forget we are living in Russia, the
land of the tsars. The Russian people like to have one man standing
at the head of the state. Of course, this man should carry out the
will of the collective." No one present, according to Chagin's reminiscence, thought at the time that Stalin had himself in mind as
this great chief of Russia.[25] If so, it only shows how little they understood him.

Opening Gambits

The political rise of Stalin in the middle of the twenties was
not, then, a simple outcome of his success in the power struggle.
We cannot account for it solely by reference to those power-build-
ing techniques at which he was so adept: the artful intrigue, the
shrewd manipulation of men, the dispensing of favors, the creation
of a personal political machine in the party. The most that he could
achieve by such means was to become the party's boss (its *khozyain,*
to use the name by which he was in fact coming to be known in
higher circles during those years). But they alone could not gain
him recognition and acceptance as the party's new *vozhd'* in succession to Lenin. Indeed, if pursued too openly or crudely, they

25. Medvedev, *Let History Judge,* p. 325.

could prove a disservice to him in this enterprise by giving him the reputation of a power-seeker. They could make him appear what Kamenev called him in a private argument with Trotsky in 1926: "just a small-town politician." [26]

To win the Lenin succession, as distinguished from the contest for power, Stalin had to legitimize himself in the supreme-leader role by acquiring special political authority in Bolshevik eyes. Moreover, anyone aspiring to become *vozhd'* would have to prove himself in Lenin's role as chief ideological spokesman of the party and Marxist thinker. This was a formidable challenge for Stalin. His *Marxism and the National Question,* although an important statement of party views on the nationality problem, was his sole significant contribution of the pre-revolutionary period to Bolshevik Marxism and, being in a specialized field, had not earned him a party reputation as a theoretician. Nor had he established theoretical credentials with his early post-revolutionary speeches and articles, which were mostly concerned with problems of Soviet policy toward the non-Russian nationalities. In the theoretical field, moreover, he had to contend with the fact that others—most notably Bukharin —had acquired large reputations among the Bolsheviks.

Stalin set about improving his standing in theory. As early as July 1921, while taking a rest cure at Nalchik, in the Caucasus, he wrote the synopsis of a planned pamphlet on "The Political Strategy and Tactics of the Russian Communists." The pamphlet was never written, but the ideas set down in the synopsis were elaborated in three published writings. The first of these was an article of August 1921 giving a sketch of the history of the party from the turn of the century to the present.[27] The second was a long essay, "Concerning the Question of the Strategy and Tactics of the Russian Communists," published in March 1923 for the twenty-fifth anniversary of the party's founding. The third and most important, *The Foundations of Leninism,* was a series of lectures that Stalin gave in 1924 at a Central Committee college for party officials known

26. L. Trotsky, *Stalin: An Appraisal of the Man and His Influence* (New York, 1967), p. 393.

27. *Stalin,* V, 62–87.

as the Sverdlov University. It was this little book that secured him wide recognition as a major ideological spokesman of the party.

One of the qualities of Stalin's mind revealed with peculiar clarity in these theoretical writings was an intense preoccupation with the theme of "strategy and tactics." In the article of March 1923, he argued that the proletarian movement is not only an objective reality as reflected in the theory and program of Marxism but also something "subjective," a conscious movement of people to reach a revolutionary goal. In the latter aspect, he went on, it is "entirely subject to the directing influence of strategy and tactics." Strategy decides the broad direction of effort during an entire period of a conflict, while tactics are concerned with ways of winning particular engagements or battles. The essence of strategy is the determination of the strategic plan, which is "a plan of the organization of the decisive blow in the direction in which the blow is most likely to achieve the maximum results." Thus, in the Civil War the question arose at the end of 1919 whether to launch the main Bolshevik blow against General Denikin's forces along the line Tsaritsyn--Novorossiisk or—as was done—along the line Voronezh–Rostov. It is the same in revolutionary political war. In 1905, for example, the basic strategic issue was whether to deliver the Revolution's main blow along the line of a coalition between proletariat and peasantry as proposed by Lenin, or along the Menshevik-favored line of a coalition between proletariat and liberal bourgeoisie, with the peasantry left out of the reckoning. Lenin's strategic plan correctly took account of the driving forces of the Russian Revolution and was confirmed by the whole ensuing development of events. After February 1917, an historic turning-point in the conflict, the radical Bolshevik strategy that Lenin formulated in terms of "All power to the soviets" came into collision with the Menshevik and Socialist-Revolutionary strategy of "All power to the Constituent Assembly." After the October Revolution, which was a new historic turning-point, the counter-revolutionary strategy of the Mensheviks and Socialist-Revolutionaries was opposed by the Bolshevik strategy of strengthening the proletarian dictatorship in Russia and extending the sphere of operation of the proletarian revolution to all countries.[28]

There was a certain originality in Stalin's choice of theme and in the emphasis he placed upon it. The classical Marxist image of revolution as class war provided an appropriate background. Yet no one in the previous history of Marxism had attached such high theoretical importance to the problem of strategy and tactics or attempted in so systematic a manner to elaborate a Marxist doctrine of political strategy. Certainly Lenin, although he was an appreciative reader of Clausewitz's famous manual on war, had not done so. On the other hand, his writings invited the kind of effort that Stalin was making, for they were studded with references to strategy and tactics and they frequently used militaristic imagery in discussing the politics of revolution. One of his most influential revolutionary treatises was entitled *Two Tactics of Social Democracy in the Democratic Revolution*, and considerations of a strategical or tactical nature figured in nearly all that he wrote.

There was consequently some basis for Stalin's prefatory description of his article of March 1923 as "a condensed and schematic exposition of the fundamental views of Comrade Lenin."[29] Nevertheless, his disclaimer of originality was somewhat misleading. The choice of topic, the impulse to systematize Lenin's thinking on strategy and tactics, and the desire to create a Marxist manual of political strategy were significant signs of Stalin's own tendency of mind. His article of March 1923, like many a first attempt to create something new, came out rather wooden. But the views expressed —whatever their source—were Stalin's own. He had formed them under the influence not simply of Lenin's writings but of other reading too, Machiavelli included, and of his personal experience. In illustrating strategic and tactical principles with military examples, he drew heavily upon his own fresh memories as a participant in the Bolshevik campaigns of the Civil War. And the ease with which he moved back and forth between the political and military realms in

28. *Ibid.*, pp. 160–180.
29. *Ibid.*, p. 160.

expounding strategy and tactics made it clear that for him, perhaps
even more than for Lenin, politics was combat.

The Foundations of Leninism, a far more ambitious piece of
work expounding Leninism as a comprehensive whole, was Stalin's
principal contribution to the spate of materials on Lenin and Leninism that appeared in the party press in the aftermath of Lenin's
death. The lectures were published in *Pravda* in April and May
1924 and then came out, together with Stalin's reminiscences of
Lenin, in a booklet entitled *On Lenin and Leninism.* Others, most
notably Bukharin and Zinoviev, had preceded him in attempts to
distill the essence of Leninism as a new phase in the development
of Marxist theory. But Stalin's work had the greatest success.

In "Lenin as a Marxist," a long report presented to the Communist Academy on February 14, 1924, and later distributed widely
in printed form, Bukharin observed that "Lenin as a theorist still
awaits his systematizer. . . ." Then, sketching the work that needed
to be done, he distinguished three epochs in the history of Marxism.
The revolutionary Marxism of Marx and Engels had been succeeded
by the degenerate reformist "Marxism of the epigones" in the period
of the Second International, but it had been revived in greatly en-
riched and up-to-date form by contemporary Leninist Marxism. This
Bukharin proceeded to summarize under such headings as the relation of theory and practice, imperialism and the national question,
the theory of the state and proletarian dictatorship, and the working class and peasantry.[30] Zinoviev discussed many of the same
themes in his major address of February 7, 1924, to the Leningrad
Soviet, "V. I. Lenin—Genius, Teacher, Leader, and Man." He held
that the five main creative contributions of Lenin to revolutionary
Marxism were his linking of the workers' revolution with the peasant
war, his linking of the proletarian class war against the bourgeoisie
with the national-liberation struggle of oppressed nationalities, his
theory of the state, his interpretation of imperialism as the final
stage of decomposing capitalism, and the theory and practice of
proletarian dictatorship. But Lenin's paramount discovery and the

30. N. I. Bukharin, *Put' k sotsializmu v Rossii,* ed. Sidney Heitman (New
York, 1967), pp. 215–224.

"most fundamental thing in Leninism," according to Zinoviev, was
the conception of the revolutionary role of the peasant. The Leninist
idea of combining the class war of the workers with the peasant war
against the landowners was not merely of Russian but of international significance.[31]

In preparing his lectures on Leninism, which he delivered at
the Sverdlov University in early April, Stalin accepted the challenge implicit in Bukharin's remark that Lenin as a theorist still
awaited his systematizer. He did not confine himself to a preliminary general sketch, as Bukharin and Zinoviev had done, but boldly
undertook a full-scale exposition of Leninism as a theoretical system and filled it out with a multitude of illustrative quotations from
Lenin's writings. Although he certainly made good use of the earlier
efforts by others, including the two just mentioned, he showed real
mastery of his Lenin materials and spoke in a voice that was unmistakably his own. Indeed, he made a subtle point of correcting
interpreters of Lenin whose theoretical authority in the party still
stood higher than his. Thus, he began by rejecting as only partial
truths the notions that Leninism was a purely Russian application
of Marxism and that it was a revival of the revolutionary Marxism
of the 1840's. The last of these points, as noted above, had been
made by Bukharin. Further on, Stalin implicitly took issue with
Zinoviev by declaring that those who considered the peasant question the fundamental thing in Leninism were "absolutely wrong";
the fundamental thing was the question of creating and consolidating the proletarian dictatorship, and the question of the peasant as
the proletariat's ally in the struggle for power was a derivative one.
As for Leninism, it was properly described as "Marxism of the era
of imperialism and the proletarian revolution"; and what it comprised, basically, was the theory and tactics of proletarian revolution in general and the theory and tactics of proletarian dictatorship
in particular.[32]

The general definition of Leninism was followed by sections
on Leninism's historical roots, Leninism as revolutionary method,

31. G. Zinoviev, *Sochineniia*, XV (Leningrad, 1924), pp. 150–152.
32. *Stalin*, VI, 70–71, 123.

the role of theory, proletarian dictatorship, the peasant question, the national question, strategy and tactics, and the doctrine of the party. Not surprisingly, the most polished section was the one on Leninist strategy and tactics as "the science of leadership in the revolutionary struggle of the proletariat," for here Stalin was developing and refining the essay written the year before. Taken as a whole, the work was rough-hewn in places, oblivious of certain subtleties of Lenin's thought, catechistic in style, and authoritarian in tone. It left something to be desired with respect to the order of topics covered, and the transitions from section to section were mostly mechanical. But for all its lack of elegance, it was a work of considerable power. Its author spoke from the pages in the manner of a heavy-handed professor of Leninism with complete command of the texts in his field and strong opinions that he knew how to defend. For better or worse, Lenin as a theorist had found a systematizer.

In an interesting concluding section of the work Stalin viewed Leninism as a special leadership style. Borrowing (without acknowledgment) an idea that Bukharin had expressed earlier, he characterized this style as a combination of "Russian revolutionary sweep" and "American efficiency." To have Russian revolutionary sweep meant to be an innovative leader with vision and wide theoretical horizons, hence one not prone to the "disease of narrow empiricism and unprincipled practicalism." But to avoid succumbing to the opposite disease of revolutionary "Manilovism," meaning the tendency to relapse into useless phrase-mongering and the concocting of beautiful schemes divorced from reality, one must combine Russian sweep with American efficiency, "that indomitable force which neither knows nor recognizes obstacles; which with its businesslike perseverance brushes aside all obstacles; which continues at a task once started until it is finished, even if it is a minor task; and without which serious constructive work is inconceivable." [33] Although Stalin duly supported these propositions with appropriate quotations from Lenin, he was rather clearly pursuing a purpose beyond that of interpreting Lenin's views. In defining the

33. *Ibid.*, pp. 186–187. The word "Manilovism" derives from the character of Manilov in Gogol's *Dead Souls*.

qualities of both positive and negative types of Bolshevik leaders, he was implicitly offering the younger party generation an ideal leader-type to emulate and at the same time casting himself as an example of it. His professorial exercise was likewise a political act in the quest for the succession. The book itself was Stalin's most effective attempt so far to prove himself a Bolshevik leader of large theoretical horizons as well as pragmatic efficiency. And by characterizing the "Leninist style" in such a way that he, Stalin, could be seen as an exponent of it, he was fighting off in advance the invidious comparison of himself with Lenin which Trotsky later formulated in a manner that many Old Bolsheviks would have accepted: "Lenin the genius and innovator, and Stalin the solid and consummate incarnation of bureaucratic mediocrity." [34]

Stalin's Leninism versus Trotsky's

The Foundations of Leninism was an avowed effort to systematize Lenin's thought and set forth the essentials of it as a theoretical credo. This was something that Trotsky feared and had openly warned against shortly before Stalin gave his lectures. In his pamphlet of January 1924, *The New Course,* Trotsky decried "a certain ideological petrification" that he saw taking place as the party came under the domination of its apparatus and the latter grew increasingly bureaucratized. He argued that a dogmatization of Lenin was contrary to the essentially non-doctrinaire, innovative, and critical-minded spirit of Leninism as a "system of revolutionary action." Citing Lenin's self-assured policy of "brusque turns"—of which October 1917, Brest-Litovsk, the creation of a regular peasant army, and the introduction of the NEP were examples—he declared that "Leninism consists in being courageously free from conservative retrospection, from being bound by precedent, purely formal references, and quotation." And further: "Lenin cannot be chopped up into quotations suited for every possible case, because for Lenin the formula never stands higher than the reality; it is always the tool that makes it possible to grasp the reality and to dominate it. . . .

34. L. Trotsky, *On the Kirov Assassination* (New York, 1935), p. 24.

The Leninist truth is always concrete!" To transform Leninism into a system of orthodoxy, "a canon which demands nothing more than interpreters appointed for good and aye," would deal a mortal blow to the spiritual life of the party and the training of its younger generation.[35]

Something can doubtless be said on both sides of this issue. Trotsky was certainly correct in calling attention to Lenin's political creativity and refusal to be bound by past precedent and party tradition. Lenin had extraordinary sensitivity to the changing needs of revolutionary practice, together with an ability to adapt Marxism to these needs and rethink it as a theory *of* practice. To codify his thought and derive a mass of party dogma from it would indeed be to make of "Leninism" something different from the mind of its creator; and Lenin, had he lived to read *The Foundations of Leninism,* might well have been moved to paraphrase Marx and say: "Thank God I am not a Leninist!" On the other hand, this very difference between the great man and the "ism" that his followers create is a normal phenomenon in history, and Trotsky was hardly being realistic in supposing—if he did so suppose—that it would not develop in the case of Lenin.

The very profusion of political ideas and intricacy of ideological argumentation in Lenin's voluminous writings invited the kind of effort that Stalin made. Moreover, there was something in the spirit of Lenin's thought that Trotsky overlooked or refused to acknowledge. For all his resistance to routine and his innovative approach to revolutionary politics. Lenin had a mind that was most doctrinaire in its way. Plekhanov and Kautsky for a while and Marx and Engels all along were his authority-figures, and dogmatic adherence to the fundamentals of Marxism (in his interpretation) became a test of political as well as intellectual soundness. In *Materialism and Empiriocriticism* he treated the whole history of philosophy as a struggle between idealist and materialist "parties" between which everyone had to choose, no third position being possible; and he anathematized the then current efforts of Russian Marxists to create an epistemology along Machian lines as veiled heresies, "deviations

35. L. Trotsky, *The New Course* (Ann Arbor, 1965), pp. 51–55.

from materialism." [36] In *The State and Revolution* and *The Proletarian Revolution and the Renegade Kautsky*, he laid down doctrinaire conditions for being a Marxist. One had not only to accept the Marxist doctrine of the class struggle, but also to believe in the dictatorship of the proletariat as the necessary and desirable outcome of the class struggle in its present historical stage. To prove in advance the Marxist legitimacy of seizing political power by violence and ruling dictatorially in the proletariat's name, Lenin in the former of these two works ransacked the whole corpus of known writings of Marx and Engels for sanctioning statements by the two great authority-figures of the revolutionary movement. *The State and Revolution* was, from this point of view, a monumental work of quotation-mongering, a model of that polemical textualism which became stylized in the discourse of Lenin's disciples and was developed to a fine art by the one-time theology student Stalin.

The truth is that both versions of Leninism—Trotsky's and Stalin's—highlighted aspects of Lenin's many-sided thought and style which the two rivals found it in their present political interests to accentuate and with which, in addition, they felt special affinity. Trotsky, who had been an independent leading figure in Russian Marxism and had made common cause with Lenin only in the midst of the 1917 Revolution, and even then as a partner in the full sense rather than as a disciple, naturally portrayed Leninism not as a body of authoritative party doctrine, but as a "method" of historical analysis and "system of revolutionary action." For this was a Leninism of which Trotsky could see himself, and be seen by others, as a foremost exponent. Stalin, the erstwhile disciple who had thoroughly mastered the Lenin texts and possessed good powers of systematizing but little theoretical originality, found it just as natural to present Leninism as a collection of dogma binding upon all Bolsheviks. As a former Bolshevik "practical worker" who had come into postrevolutionary prominence as a political organizer, he understandably emphasized businesslike practicality or "American efficiency" as an

36. Valentinov, who was one of the Marxists attacked in the book, gives a revealing account of an earlier conversation in which Lenin said to him: "Nothing in Marxism is subject to revision. There is only one reply to revision: in the face!" (*Vstrechi s Leninym* [New York, 1953], p. 255).

inalienable attribute of the Leninist style of leadership. In a sense, then, the two divergent Leninisms were projections of the revolutionary careers and political personalities of their progenitors. Both took their departure from certain authentic aspects of the Leninist legacy and exaggerated them; neither encompassed the many-sided reality of the historical Lenin.

But the question of which of the two versions of Leninism was closer to Lenin is not what chiefly concerns us here. From the standpoint of the contest for the succession, we must ask which was politically more effective in the immediate post-Lenin period, which better met the needs of the Bolshevik movement at that time and exerted the greater appeal to party minds. The answer, clearly, is that Stalin's version did, and why it did can best be explained by reference to the changing composition of the ruling party.

When the party emerged from underground in early 1917 after the deposition of the tsar, it had about twenty-four thousand members. Since then many had died, and the old guard was no more than a small and continually dwindling element of the nearly half-million-strong Bolshevik party of early 1924. Not only the great majority of the 200,000 worker-members and practically all the 125,000 peasant-members, but the bulk of the white-collar remainder as well, were party members with no pre-1917 revolutionary past, Bolsheviks who had never been revolutionaries. The relative numerical weight of the Old Bolshevik component shrank still further as a result of the "Lenin levy," the mass recruitment of factory workers which the party proclaimed at the time of Lenin's death as a dramatic demonstration of proletarian solidarity with the Soviet regime. By November 1, 1925, the number of members and candidates for membership totaled slightly over one million. The party had now become a mass organization with a membership of predominantly post-revolutionary vintage. Its pre-1917 contingent numbered only eighty-five hundred.[37]

It is true that the old guard, which still dominated the central leadership organs, exercised a political power entirely disproportion-

37. This figure was offered by Zinoviev at the Fourteenth Congress (*XIV s"ezd*, p. 460).

ate to its small numbers. A new generation of leaders was, however, on the rise. The new generation was already coming into authority at the provincial level, and was far from a negligible influence within the party. A great many of its representatives were persons of lowly social background and little formal education. One individual destined to rise far in the party, Nikita S. Khrushchev, may be taken as an example. Born into a peasant family in the village of Kalinovka in south Russia, he had received only two or three years of education in the village school when, as a boy of fifteen, he went to work in the coal mines of the Donbas. He joined the party in 1918, at the age of twenty-four, and took part in the Civil War as a Red soldier. Afterwards, he acquired further schooling and began his career as a party functionary, becoming a district party secretary in the Donbas in 1925. This was a story similar to those of thousands of other young people of humble origin whose political careers grew out of the Revolution.[38]

Stalin's early writings on Leninism were explicitly addressed to this party new guard. He introduced his article of March 1923 on Leninist strategy and tactics with the comment that it would be "of some use for our new generation of party workers," and he dedicated The Foundations of Leninism "to the Lenin levy." He was undoubtedly correct in his view that these writings would fulfill an important need of a great many in the new party generation. Not being intellectuals and not having acquired a schooling in Marxist literature through participation in the anti-tsarist revolutionary movement, the younger Bolsheviks found it no easy matter to take their bearings in Leninist Marxism by reading the mass of Lenin's own writings, the majority of which dealt with issues beyond their direct experience from a period before they had politically come of age.

The rather rarefied interpretation of Leninism offered in Trotsky's The New Course was of very little help to them, for it left open the vital question of what Leninism was as a system of sub-

38. At the end of 1927 more than 60 per cent of the secretaries of party cells were persons who had joined the party after 1921 (Schapiro, Communist Party, p. 311).

stantive belief. Stalin understood this well and took advantage of it in the anti-Trotsky campaign. In one of his speeches he referred to Trotsky's statement in *The New Course* that "Leninism as a system of revolutionary action presupposes a mentally seasoned and experienced revolutionary intuition which is the equivalent in the social realm to muscular sensation in physical labor," and commented with heavy sarcasm: "Leninism as 'muscular sensation in physical labor.' Is this not in truth something new, original, and deep? Have you understood something? All this is very picturesque, musical, and, if you like, even magnificent. Only one 'trifle' is missing: a simple and human definition of Leninism." [39] The laughter recorded in the printed text at the point where Stalin asked "Have you understood something?" is indication that his thrust struck home.

Whatever Trotsky might say about the danger of chopping Lenin up into quotations, the younger party generation as well as its mentors in the growing network of party political indoctrination needed a textbook. They required, in fact, what Stalin provided— a compendium of Leninist teachings expounded dogmatically and with abundant reference to key passages in Lenin's writings. As Zinoviev acknowledged in his concluding speech to the Fourteenth Congress, *The Foundations of Leninism* enjoyed "very great popularity." [40]

A Question of Authorship

Roy Medvedev's research into the history of *The Foundations of Leninism* has brought out Stalin's unacknowledged debt to a book by a young party intellectual, F. A. Ksenofontov: *Lenin's Doctrine of Revolution and the Proletarian Dictatorship*. This book came out in 1925, about a year after the publication of Stalin's lectures. Ksenofontov declared in the preface, however, that he wrote the book in October–November 1923, at which time he was attached to the Sverdlov University, and that in April–June 1924 it was in

39. *Stalin*, VIII, 276.
40. *XIV s"ezd*, p. 430.

Stalin's hands for final review, having prior to that been under review by M. N. Liadov, the rector of the Sverdlov University. The "comparatively late publication" of the book, according to the preface, was due to this circumstance as well as to "the author's excessive remoteness from Moscow (Tashkent)." After stating this, the author expressed "deepest comradely appreciation to Comrade I. Stalin for reviewing the manuscript and for corrections and suggestions." The preface was dated January 1925, but the date of final completion of the manuscript was given on the last page as March 13, 1924.[41]

Medvedev states that Ksenofontov had been helping Stalin in theoretical matters (whether formally, in an assistant's capacity, is not made clear), and that he was transferred to work in Tashkent soon after Stalin read his manuscript. Rumors circulated at this time that Ksenofontov was protesting Stalin's appropriation of many of his own formulas, and these rumors were substantiated when Ksenofontov's book appeared. Medvedev refers in this connection to above-mentioned particulars from Ksenofontov's preface and final page, which implicitly asserted his book's priority over Stalin's lectures of early April 1924. A simple collation of the two books, Medvedev says further, "shows their great similarity in organization, in exposition of central ideas, in basic definitions." Finally, Medvedev states that in a private letter of July 1924 to Ksenofontov, Stalin gave him some credit for helping in the preparation of *The Foundations of Leninism*. But when Ksenofontov in 1926 requested permission to cite that letter, Stalin refused. The story had a grim sequel: "Ksenofontov was arrested in 1937 and killed during interrogation."[42]

Medvedev's interpretation of the exchange of letters finds confirmation in the historical record. True, neither Stalin's letter of July 1924 nor Ksenofontov's later request to cite it has been published. But the latter's contents can be reconstructed from the text of the reply to it, which Stalin wrote on December 30, 1926, and

41. F. A. Ksenofontov, *Uchenie Lenina o revoliutsii i diktature proletariata* (Moscow and Leningrad, 1925), pp. 5, 120. The book was published by the State Publishing House.

42. Medvedev, *Let History Judge*, pp. 509–510.

much later decided to include in his collected works. This document is also well worth studying for the light it sheds upon the character and conduct of Stalin.

It appears from the reply that Ksenofontov wrote to Stalin toward the end of 1926 because of another conflict in which he had become involved. A published pamphlet of his on strategy had been attacked in an article by the Komsomol leader Lazar Shatskin, and Ksenofontov wanted to bolster his reply to Shatskin by quoting a passage from Stalin's letter to him of July 1924. It also appears that Ksenofontov, realizing far more clearly now than he had in early 1924 how powerful and difficult a man he was dealing with, avowed himself a disciple of Stalin and showed him great deference.

Stalin said to Ksenofontov in his reply:

I am opposed to your referring, in a polemic with Shatskin at the end of 1926, to my personal letter written in July 1924. All the more so since the question under discussion, the *definition of Leninism,* was formulated by me in March 1924, before the publication of the booklet *On Lenin and Leninism.* Not to mention the fact that such a reference to a passage from my letter, while doing absolutely nothing for you in the polemic with Shatskin, would confuse things and shift attention to a different plane, and could force me to come out in the press with a statement not favorable to you (which I would not like to do).

Evidently, the passage that Ksenofontov wanted permission to cite was one in which Stalin had given him some credit for helping to clarify the proper definition of Leninism. Now Stalin was claiming priority for himself in that, though without giving documentary evidence in support of his claim.

Notable in the rest of the letter is the lordly manner in which Stalin decided the dispute between the two other men. He declared that Shatskin was on the whole right, but corrected his interpretations of two fine points concerning the thought of Marx and Lenin and decried "the crudely self-assured tone of Shatskin's article: he himself preaches modesty but in fact shows the maximum of self-assurance." As for Ksenofontov, if the latter had submitted the pamphlet on strategy to Stalin in advance, he would have counseled him against publishing "such a half-baked and slipshod work con-

taining a number of most gross errors and incorrect formulations."
Taking Ksenofontov's deference to his theoretical authority as his
due, Stalin advised him finally not to continue the controversy but
instead to devote himself to a "diligent and thoughtful" study of
Leninism itself. "Furthermore," he concluded, " I advise you to give
up once and for all the habit of concocting hasty booklets on Leninism. It won't do." [43] The ugly implication of the latter remark needed
little deciphering.

Rescuing the Ksenofontov episode from possible oblivion is
one of Medvedev's many services to scholarship. We must, however,
consider on its merits his suggestion that Stalin virtually cribbed
The Foundations of Leninism from Ksenofontov's book. For such
a conclusion seems to flow, in the context of Medvedev's discussion,
from his statement on the great similarity of the two books in organization, exposition of central ideas, and basic definitions. In ampli-
fication of this statement Medvedev cites three parallels, touching
upon the general definition of Leninism, the relation between colonial movements and proletarian revolution in advanced countries,
and the treatment of the dictatorship of the proletariat. [44]

There is little doubt that Stalin, as he himself seems to have
acknowledged in the letter of July 1924, followed Ksenofontov in
his general characterization of Leninism. Ksenofontov rejected as
one-sided the views that Leninism was "Marxism in practice," or
"a revival of the revolutionary Marxism of 1848," or "a Marxism
of Russian reality." He also firmly ruled out the Zinovievist view
that the fundamental essence of Leninism lay in the "discovery of
the peasant." The "peasant question" in Lenin was to be seen as
part of the larger general question of the proletarian revolution and
the dictatorship of the proletariat. Leninism was to be defined as
"the science of the revolutionary politics of the working class in
conditions of imperialism, i.e., the theory and tactics of proletarian
revolution." [45] Stalin, who may well have seen Ksenofontov's manuscript before it came into his hands in April 1924 for final review,

43. *Stalin*, IX, 152–154.
44. Medvedev, *Let History Judge*, p. 510.
45. Ksenofontov, *Uchenie Lenina*, pp. 16, 39.

made these points in his lectures.[46] They helped give *The Foundations of Leninism* a certain momentum and intellectual distinction. If this dogmatic and rather crude little book avoided being banal, a good share of the credit belonged to Ksenofontov.

Stalin also took his cue from Ksenofontov in relating national-liberation movements in the East to proletarian revolution in the West. Observing that Lenin discovered the infantry of the world proletarian revolution in the "peasant East," Ksenofontov wrote: "For Lenin the 'national question' is a part of the general question of the proletarian dictatorship, of the proletarian revolution." Arguing in the same vein that the path of revolution in the West ran through a revolutionary alliance with the liberation movements of the colonies and dependent countries, Stalin asserted: "The national question is a part of the general question of the proletarian revolution, a part of the question of the proletarian dictatorship." [47] Although Lenin had formulated his position on this point with such studied clarity that his interpreters hardly needed much assistance to grasp it, the fact remains that Stalin pursued Ksenofontov's line of argument and went so far as to bodily appropriate the key conclusion of the other man's work. On the third parallel mentioned by Medvedev, the debt is less striking, largely because Ksenofontov's section on the proletarian dictatorship was not much more than a systematization of well-known Lenin statements. Stalin's treatment of the same subject was similar in themes, but more forceful and incisive.

Manifestly, Stalin's unacknowledged debt to Ksenofontov was substantial. But a full textual comparison does not bear out the view that his book was, as it were, lifted from the other. There is, in fact, no such great similarity in organization as Medvedev alleges. Both begin with the historical background of Leninism, but differ in their treatment of this theme. Stalin then goes on to "method," on which there is no section in Ksenofontov. The proletarian dictatorship is one of Stalin's earlier topics, whereas in Ksenofontov it comes toward the end. Ksenofontov has a polemic on reformism and a

---

46. See above, p. 317.
47. Ksenofontov, *Uchenie Lenina*, pp. 82–83; *Stalin*, VI, 141.

section on the Labour government in Britain to which there are no counterparts in Stalin, who for his part has sections on strategy and tactics·and on style in work to which there are no counterparts in Ksenofontov. The section on style, as indicated earlier, elaborated upon an idea of Bukharin's. Some of the other contributions to the public discussion on Leninism influenced Stalin too. His treatise and Ksenofontov's are not two versions of one book.

On the basis of Medvedev's information that Ksenofontov was assisting Stalin in theoretical matters, one might speculate that Stalin had requested him to assemble the materials on Leninism and various opinions about it, and that Ksenofontov, being both bright and very well versed in the subject, produced a manuscript which he then sought permission to publish. In any event, Stalin, while making good use of Ksenofontov's manuscript and failing to acknowledge this fact, produced a recognizably different work that bore his own clear imprint. Were this not so, it seems doubtful that Ksenofontov's manuscript, even in the pluralist climate of 1925, would have found a publisher in Soviet Russia.

Chapter Nine

THE POLITICS OF
REVOLUTIONARY BIOGRAPHY

LENIN'S UNIQUE AUTHORITY was not posthumously transmitted to a successor in accordance with Max Weber's conception of the "routinization" and "depersonalization" of charisma. It was never depersonalized, although it became a part of the common heritage of Bolshevism, and it was routinized only in the sense that a great public Lenin cult arose in perpetuation of Lenin's charisma, which thus remained his even in death.

But if no one among the potential successors could acquire Lenin's charisma, there was still the possibility of associating themselves with it and thus partaking of it. For this purpose it was important to have been one of Lenin's comrades-in-arms from the start of the movement, to have fought the revolutionary battles by his side, to have supported his positions in the disputes that continually racked the movement, and to have enjoyed his confidence and esteem. Accordingly, the politics of the Lenin succession revolved to a significant extent around questions of revolutionary biography. Efforts were made to show that one had been "with Lenin" and one's opponents "against Lenin" at key points in party history, or to minimize and explain away the instances in which one had been "against Lenin." By such means an individual could strive to take advantage of Lenin's prestige without taking possession of it, and to counter the strivings of rivals to do the same.

Speaking more broadly, the history of the party and the Revolution became a kind of sacred history, within which a protagonist's personal history—that is, his own party past—took on much political importance for himself and his followers. When he joined the party, what early revolutionary exploits he had to his credit, what positions he espoused or supported in the inner party debates at various times, what part he took in the actual revolutionary events, and what his relations were with the party's founder—such matters of political biography tended to enter the stuff of politics. To accentuate and embellish one's place in party history was a way of justifying pretensions to leadership in the present; to disparage the place of another, one of the methods of puncturing his pretensions. Every leading figure acquired a vested interest in his own revolutionary biography, and the writing of party history, or the collective biography of the movement, became to a special extent what the Bolshevik historian Mikhail Pokrovsky once called all history-writing—"politics projected upon the past."

The intra-party politics of revolutionary biography began in part as anti-Trotsky politics: the effort of Trotsky's chief rivals to impugn his potential claim to the Lenin succession by emphasizing his one-time non-Bolshevism and calling attention to his pre-1917 political conflicts with Lenin. Trotsky's fighting response in a long essay entitled *Lessons of October* provoked a great public polemic on questions of political biography. Afterwards, what had begun as an anti-Trotsky campaign took on an independent momentum of its own. Stalin, in particular, vigorously pursued his own version of biographical politics as one way of furthering his bid for the Lenin succession.

The Preliminaries

Although hindsight makes Stalin's victory and Trotsky's defeat in the party struggle seem a foregone conclusion, the protagonists themselves did not see things in this light as the struggle developed in 1923. Trotsky, for his part, could not yet bring himself to take Stalin seriously as a candidate for supreme leadership. Meanwhile, the triumvirs were painfully aware of the prestige that Trotsky still possessed. Any persisting doubt as to his popularity in the party would have been erased by the extraordinary outpouring of tributes to him at the Twelfth Congress in 1923. Zinoviev gave the main political report in place of the absent Lenin, but Trotsky was the man of the hour. Party cells, trade union organizations, and workers' and students' groups from all over the country paid homage to Lenin and Trotsky in messages read out at the congress.[1] The ovation that greeted Trotsky, before and again after his own report, which dealt with economic problems, surpassed by far the applause for Zinoviev and Stalin. This was one of the high points of his career in the Bolshevik movement.

The surge of pro-Trotsky feeling was an understandable response to the difficult situation in which the Bolsheviks now found themselves. For if Lenin was the party's charismatic chief, Trotsky more than any other individual in the circle of leaders partook of that charisma, or shone in its reflected light. He had a revolutionary record and proven qualities of greatness that made him the outstanding figure among Lenin's lieutenants. Lunacharsky was registering more than a personal opinion when, in *Revolutionary Silhouettes* (1923), he acclaimed Trotsky as "the second great leader of the Russian Revolution." The October Revolution was so much the joint triumph of the two men that the resulting new regime became widely known in Russia and abroad as the "Lenin-Trotsky government." Trotsky's standing in the international Communist movement was second only to Lenin's, notwithstanding the fact that Zinoviev was chairman of the Comintern Executive Committee. Small wonder, then, that in 1923, when Lenin lay ill and the problem of succession inescapably loomed on the horizon, very many in the party and the country looked to Trotsky for leadership.

Shortly before the opening of the congress, a major article by Radek helped turn Bolshevik thoughts in Trotsky's direction. Written for the special issue of *Pravda* on March 14, 1923, the twenty-fifth anniversary of the party's founding, it bore the arresting title "Lev Trotsky—Organizer of Victory," and attracted much attention. The Bolsheviks, Radek wrote, were still just learning how to run an

---

1. Isaac Deutscher, *The Prophet Unarmed: Trotsky, 1921–1929* (London, 1959), p. 94.

economy, and the state machine was creaking. The one new institution that had turned out quite well was, surprisingly, the Red Army, and this was due to the work of its creator and driving force, Trotsky, whose publicistic pen had been refashioned by the Revolution into a sword.

Radek traced Trotsky's profound grasp of war and of army problems to his pre–World War experience as a correspondent covering the Balkan war, and argued that the Red victory in the Civil War showed Trotsky's remarkable ability to apply in practice the well-known truth that the moral factor is the decisive one in war. Contrary to the advice of some military professionals, Trotsky had begun by forming volunteer units as the nucleus of the new army. He showed his organizing genius and boldness of thought again in the decision—strongly resisted by many at the time—to enlist the services of former tsarist officers in building the new military establishment. Confident that their technical knowledge could be put to use without permitting them to dictate policy, Trotsky, a man of iron will, not only subordinated the tsarist officers to his authority but managed to win the confidence of the best ones and convert them from foes of Soviet Russia to its convinced supporters. Radek cited as an example the late Admiral Altfater, one of the high old-regime officers who had been included in the Soviet delegation at Brest-Litovsk as an expert and had come suspecting a deal between the Bolsheviks and the German government. After listening for days to Trotsky as he fought for the Russian Revolution against German imperialism at the conference-table, the admiral had come to him one night and said: "I came here because I had to. I didn't believe in you. But now I am going to help you and do my duty as never before, in the deep belief that I serve the fatherland." Then, as the panegyric reached its climax, Radek spoke of "the steel figure of Trotsky," described him as a *vozhd'* of the party, and concluded: "If our party goes down in history as the first proletarian party to succeed in building a great army, this brilliant page in the history of the Russian Revolution will always be linked with the name of Lev Davidovich Trotsky, as a man whose labor and deeds will be an object not only of love but of scientific study by new working-class generations preparing to win the whole world."

Appearing as it did only a few days after the official statement of the Soviet government on the ominous new turn in Lenin's health, and at a time when rumors were beginning to circulate in Moscow that Lenin had designated Trotsky as his successor, this journalistic nomination of Trotsky for the soon-to-be-vacant role of *vozhd'* caused a sensation. No article in that special issue of *Pravda* attracted such close attention as Radek's, recalls Valentinov in his memoirs, adding: "After the more or less mandatory comment on the news of Lenin's illness, the acquaintances I met during those days would ask: 'Have you read Radek's article? What does it mean?' " From contacts that he and his friends in the Supreme Council of National Economy had with party members there and in other Soviet institutions, Valentinov learned that Radek's article had caused intense irritation in circles associated with Stalin and Voroshilov. Stalin, in particular, was reported to have called the article "idiotic babbling" and to have said of Radek that "he does not command his tongue, but rather his tongue commands him." [2]

These developments, followed by the manifestations of Trotsky's popularity when the congress met in April, spurred a series of moves by anti-Trotsky forces in the party leadership to undermine Trotsky's prestige and mobilize party sentiment against him. The triumvirs, acting behind the scenes through their agents, initiated in the midst of the congress a whispering campaign to persuade provincial delegates that Trotsky was a potential "Bonaparte" who was in danger of riding to power on his own great popularity and

2. N. Valentinov, *Novaia ekonomicheskaia politika i krizis partii posle smerti Lenina,* p. 54. Valentinov also reports here that at the opening of the Twelfth Congress the following month, Voroshilov called out as Trotsky entered the hall in the company of Radek: "Here comes the lion [in Russian *Lev* means "lion"] and behind him his tail." Radek, when the jest reached his ear, scribbled a quatrain which quickly made the rounds of the congress and Moscow. In translation it runs:

> Voroshilov's stupid,
> His mind's a jumbled mass.
> I'd rather be the lion's tail
> Than Stalin's ass.

becoming the "gravedigger" of the Bolshevik Revolution.[3] Then, in May and June, anti-Trotsky underground literature began circulating in Moscow. The authorship was anonymous, but a rumored source was Stalin's assistant, Tovstukha. A specimen shown to Valentinov by one of his co-workers on the *Torgovo-promyshlennaia gazeta* was a hectographed leaflet entitled *Small Biography of a Great Man*. Trotsky, it said, liked to consider himself an Old Bolshevik and great man, but when did he join the Bolsheviks? Only in 1917, on the eve of the October Revolution, and when the Revolution's victory was no longer in doubt. He really should call himself an Old Menshevik, because for fourteen years prior to that he had been a Menshevik and had fought constant battles against the Bolsheviks, battles that he continued to fight after finally entering the Bolshevik party in August 1917. The latter theme was taken up in another leaflet that came to Valentinov's attention. Entitled *What Ilyich Wrote and Thought about Trotsky*, it was a collection of everything negative and vituperative that Lenin had said of Trotsky from the time polemics began between the two men in 1904.[4]

It is true that Trotsky formally joined the Bolshevik organization only in 1917, although at the time it was far from clear that the Bolsheviks were going to succeed in taking power. On the other points, the anonymous pamphlets were exercises in falsification of Trotsky's revolutionary biography. Save for a short period following the 1903 congress, he had not been a Menshevik so much as a man standing between the two warring factions and striving to reunite them on a platform of revolution. For various reasons that largely had to do with his personality, Trotsky was all along something of an independent quality in the Russian Marxist movement. Even in 1917, his role was not that of a party follower of Lenin but of his first collaborator in carrying through the Bolshevik conquest of power, and he continued afterwards to take up independent positions on key political issues that arose in the party. Given this his-

---

3. Deutscher, *The Prophet Unarmed*, pp. 94–95. See also Deutscher, *Stalin: A Political Biography*, 2nd ed. (New York, 1966), p. 273, and Max Eastman, *Since Lenin Died* (New York, 1925), p. 19.
4. Valentinov, *Novaia ekonomicheskaia politika*, pp. 57–58.

torical background of his relations with Bolshevism, it is not surprising that the pre-1917 record was replete with critical statements by Lenin on Trotsky, and vice versa.

Yet, the two men had formed a revolutionary partnership in 1917 and toward the end of Lenin's active life had resumed close political and personal ties. In April 1922, just a week after Stalin formally assumed the office of general secretary, Lenin proposed in the Politburo that Trotsky be appointed vice chairman of the Council of People's Commissars. Had not Trotsky for obscure reasons refused this appointment, he would have become Lenin's deputy and potential successor in the Soviet premiership. He refused the vice chairmanship in September 1922 after Lenin, convalescing from his first stroke, sent a request from his country retreat that the Politburo consider the appointment a matter of urgency. Then, in early December, Lenin raised the proposal once more in private conversation with Trotsky, inviting him to use the vice premiership as a weapon against bureaucracy in the state administration. When Trotsky replied that he was concerned with bureaucracy not only in the state institutions but in the party as well—a plain allusion to Stalin—Lenin offered him "a bloc against bureaucracy in general and against the Organizational Bureau in particular." [5] But in mid-1923 all this evidence of Lenin's high regard for and reliance upon Trotsky remained unknown outside a tiny circle at the top. So did the testament, in which Lenin, without designating Trotsky as his chosen successor, implicitly placed him at the head of the list of candidates, and in which Trotsky's pre-1917 "non-Bolshevism" was mentioned only in the context of a warning to the party not to hold it against him.

Trotsky was undoubtedly well informed concerning the quiet campaign against him going on at this time, and he alluded to it in *The New Course*. "I came to Lenin fighting," he said with obvious reference to his pre-1917 polemics with Lenin, "but I came fully

5. L. Trotsky, *My Life* (New York, 1930), pp. 478–479. On Lenin's various efforts to make Trotsky vice premier, see Deutscher, *The Prophet Unarmed*, pp. 35 ff., 65 ff., and 84. It seems clear that he originally advanced the proposal in April 1922 as a means of creating a counterweight to the growing power of Stalin.

and all the way." If the question were to be posed in the field of biographical investigation, he went on, it would have to be asked whether all those who were faithful to the master in the small matters were faithful to him also in the great, and whether those who showed docility in his presence thereby proved their capacity to carry on his work in his absence: "Does the whole of Leninism lie in docility?" Trotsky put teeth into his argument by observing that Lenin himself was constantly accused in the party of violating tradition and going against "Old Bolshevism." Thus, it was under the aegis of "Old Bolshevism" that everything routinist in the party rose up against Lenin's "April Theses." [6] This allusion to the resistance by Kamenev and Stalin to the strategy of revolutionary maximalism that Lenin advocated in April 1917 was Trotsky's *riposte* to the charge of not being an authentic Old Bolshevik. Meanwhile, however, the charge itself was being brought into the open. Commenting on Trotsky's assertion that history contains more than one example of the degeneration of a revolutionary old guard, Stalin reproved him for implicitly including himself in the Bolshevik old guard: "It must be admitted that this readiness for self-sacrifice is a noble trait. But I must protect Trotsky from Trotsky, because, for obvious reasons, he cannot, and should not, bear responsibility for the possible degeneration of the principal cadres of the Bolshevik old guard." [7]

In the weeks and months following Lenin's death, there appeared the beginnings of a biographical literature on Lenin by his comrades in the revolutionary struggle. Trotsky's contribution—a pamphlet published in June 1924—was a personal memoir which he offered as "material for a life of Lenin." In a first section concerning Lenin in the *Iskra* period (1900–1903), the memoir beautifully evoked scenes of young Trotsky's first meeting with Lenin early one October morning of 1902 in London and a sightseeing walk on which Lenin pointed out "their" Westminster to him while discussing Russian revolutionary affairs; a visit together to Paris, where Lenin lectured on the agrarian question to an exiled

6. L. Trotsky, *The New Course* (Ann Arbor, 1965), pp. 53, 57.
7. *Stalin*, V, 384–385.

Russian professors' school and went with his friends to see *Louise* at the Opéra Comique; Lenin and others at Geneva during the Second Congress in 1903. It told the story of how Trotsky became a member of the editorial board of *Iskra* on Lenin's initiative and to the annoyance of Plekhanov. Then the memoir turned to Russia in early 1917, omitting reference to the years of conflict with Lenin and taking up the story at the point where the two came together again as revolutionary comrades-in-arms. It told how Trotsky, immediately upon his arrival in Petrograd at the beginning of May, informed Lenin that he was in full agreement with the "April Theses" and was prepared to join the Bolshevik party at once "individually" or, at the cost of some delay, to try and bring along with him the better part of the Inter-Borough group that acknowledged his leadership. Then it drew a picture of Lenin in the revolutionary maelstrom of 1917 as Trotsky, working and fighting at his side, had observed him.

Lenin was shown giving inflammatory speeches to the workers from the balcony of Kseshinskaia's palace; conquering a "conservative opposition" among the Bolsheviks in order to bring the party around from talk about armed uprising to the deed itself; facing and fighting down dissension in the party leadership at every turn in the development of events. He was described as a man consumed by anxiety lest the Kerensky government spoil everything by launching a preventive armed blow, and insisting therefore that the Bolshevik coup be carried out immediately instead of waiting, as Trotsky desired, until the convening on October 25 of the Second Congress of Soviets, in which the Bolsheviks would have majority support and which could therefore give legitimacy to the seizure of power. Then the memoir portrayed Lenin arriving at the Smolny on the twenty-fifth as the uprising was in progress, questioning Trotsky about the details of the operation, and making his peace with the latter's "refusal to seize the power by a conspiracy." It told how Lenin, arising from bed on an office floor in the Smolny the next morning to find the Revolution in power, remarked to Trotsky in German, "It makes your head swim," and circled his hand around his head. It recalled how delighted Lenin was with the revolutionary sound of "Council of People's Commissars"—Trotsky's suggestion of a name for the new Soviet government. Then it evoked memories of Lenin in connection with the talks at Brest-Litovsk, the decision to dissolve the Constituent Assembly, the beginnings of the Civil War, and the organizing of the new regime. In one of these vignettes of 1918, Trotsky remembered Lenin saying to him unexpectedly: "If the White Guards kill you and me, will Sverdlov and Bukharin be able to manage?" [8]

Trotsky placed Lenin in the limelight, calling him the "machine-driver" of the Revolution and portraying him throughout the memoir as its hero. Yet *On Lenin*, without necessarily having been planned so, was also something of a revolutionary autobiography, and as such an *apologia pro vita sua*. Since Trotsky had witnessed the October Revolution in the role of a chief actor alongside Lenin, what came out of his memories was a story of two who made a revolution. Its underlying theme was the Lenin-Trotsky revolutionary relationship, which appeared as a partnership of equals and all the more salient in view of the battles that Lenin was waging in the background against dissenters in the Bolshevik ranks. It showed how Lenin had relied upon Trotsky's advice, how he had depended on him to organize the seizure of power, how close the two men were during the crucial months, how highly Lenin came to regard Trotsky, and what complete trust he learned to place in him. Whether or not all this was communicated by conscious design of the writer, it was immediately clear to many readers. As a friendly reviewer noted in concluding his review of the memoir, "Apart from its direct task, Trotsky's work helps us to picture clearly the majestic figure of Trotsky himself. There arises before us not only the image of the honored *vozhd'* but likewise another which became inextricably interwoven with it during the revolutionary years, that of his heroic confederate." [9]

Seeing the same message, Trotsky's political opponents must

8. L. Trotsky, *Lenin* (Garden City, 1959), *passim*. The translation at some points follows the more exact form in Trotsky's *My Life*, where certain episodes are repeated.

9. G. Dayan, in *Krasnaia nov'*, No. 4 (21) (1924), p. 343.

have taken the memoir as a deliberate move on his part to enhance his role in the history of the Revolution. At any rate, on September 5, 1924, the journal *Bolshevik* came out with a critical review by a Leningrad supporter of Zinoviev named Vardin, provoking a reply from Trotsky which was subsequently printed along with an editorial rebuttal.[10] Then Trotsky took a fateful step. Under the title *Lessons of October*, he wrote a pamphlet-length introduction to an already-prepared volume of his works containing his articles and speeches of 1917. The volume appeared on the eve of the seventh anniversary of the Revolution, and set off an explosion of anti-Trotsky polemics which went down in party history as the "literary discussion."

Trotsky Opens Fire

So far in the developing controversy about his revolutionary biography, Trotsky's posture had been predominantly defensive. In *On Lenin*, for example, he had referred briefly to a series of dissensions within the party which began with the conflict over Lenin's "April Theses," continued at various times in the ensuing months, and reached a climax just before the October coup. But he did not go into detail, and he did not mention the names of those in the party who had opposed Lenin. Now, in *Lessons of October*, he threw off his earlier restraints and went over to the offensive. He exposed dark spots in the revolutionary biographies of certain members of the Bolshevik old guard, Kamenev and Zinoviev in particular. He did this, moreover, in the frame of an argument that likened their political position in the revolutionary period to the very Menshevism that they had lately been imputing to him.

The announced aim of the essay was to illuminate Russia's October for the benefit of foreign Communist parties whose Octobers still lay in the future, and whose need for edification was shown by the lost opportunities for Communist revolution in Germany and Bulgaria in 1923. Trotsky's analysis centered on an inner

10. For details, see E. H. Carr, *Socialism in One Country 1924–1926*, II, 10. Chapter 11 of this work gives a valuable account of the ensuing controversy. For Deutscher's treatment of it, see *The Prophet Unarmed*, pp. 152–162.

conflict of two tendencies within the Bolshevik party during the period from February 1917 to approximately February 1918. The true Bolshevik tendency, led by Lenin and consistently aiming at the revolutionary seizure of power, had collided with a right-wing tendency on the part of some Bolsheviks who at every critical turning-point adopted "a fatalistic, temporizing, Social Democratic, Menshevik attitude to revolution, as if the latter were an endless film." By Social Democracy, Trotsky explained, he meant the acceptance of a reformist oppositional activity within the framework of bourgeois society and its legal order. And he suggested that the Russian experience had universal significance, that a division between genuinely revolutionist and Social Democratic tendencies would reappear in every Communist party in the immediate revolutionary period when the question of power—the central issue of revolution —is posed pointblank.[11]

Supplying details for the Bolshevik case, Trotsky pointed out that prior to Lenin's return to Russia, some Bolshevik leaders there had interpreted the February Revolution as exclusively "bourgeois" or "democratic" rather than as a likely prelude to proletarian revolution, and consequently had adopted the essentially reformist tactic of exerting "pressure" on the Provisional Government to complete the democratic revolution and make peace. He proved his point by quoting pertinent excerpts from two *Pravda* editorials of mid-March, one on "No Secret Diplomacy" and the other entitled "On the War," forbearing to add that the former was written by Kamenev and the latter by Stalin. At that very time, Trotsky went on, Lenin was thundering against conciliationism from his exile in Zurich, and writing: "To turn to this government with a proposal of concluding peace is equivalent to preaching morality to the keeper of a brothel." All this had foreshadowed the conflicts that broke out between the Right Bolsheviks and Lenin after the latter arrived in Petrograd on April 4 and proclaimed in the "April Theses" a policy of revolutionary militance and no support for the Provisional Government. At the April party conference, for example, Kamenev had branded

11. L. Trotsky, *Lessons of October,* in *The Essential Trotsky* (New York, 1963), pp. 125, 157.

Lenin's position as "adventurist" and had contended that the bourgeois democratic revolution in Russia was not yet completed. "The pattern is obviously Menshevik," commented Trotsky apropos Kamenev's speech, no longer forbearing to mention names. Then he traced Lenin's recurrent conflict with the right wing through the episodes of the July days, the Democratic Conference in September, and the Pre-Parliament in early October, arguing that the right wing had favored the establishment of bourgeois parliamentarianism, on the historic Menshevik premise that a lengthy interval must intervene between the democratic and proletarian revolutions.

The intra-party conflict came to a climax, Trotsky went on, shortly before and then again after October 25. Fearing that the propitious moment for successful revolution might be allowed to pass away unutilized, Lenin all through September and October had kept pressuring the Central Committee to proceed with the armed insurrection. But some had resisted his appeals. In a letter of October 11, "On the Current Situation," which was sent to the most important party organizations, Zinoviev and Kamenev had adamantly opposed immediate armed insurrection on the ground that it would stake the fate of the party and Revolution on a single throw of the dice, and this at a time when "the prospects of our party in the elections to the Constituent Assembly are excellent." On October 18, Kamenev had published a letter in the newspaper *Novaia zhizn'* (New Life) saying that he, Zinoviev, and other "practical comrades" were opposed to the launching of an armed insurrection before the convening of the Congress of Soviets.[12] Then, on November 4, a number of party leaders had resigned from the Central Committee and the newly formed Council of People's Commissars with an ultimatum demanding the reconstitution of the Bolshevik government as a coalition of socialist parties. Revealing

12. Trotsky did not here recall the sequel to Kamenev's action, the result of which was to betray Lenin's plans for the insurrection. Lenin wrote a letter to the Central Committee describing what Kamenev and Zinoviev had done as "strike-breaking" and demanding their expulsion from the party. The Central Committee decided against expulsion but accepted Kamenev's resignation from the committee itself.

by implication the identity of some of them, Trotsky commented: "Thus, those who had opposed the armed insurrection and the seizure of power as an adventure were demanding after the victorious conclusion of the insurrection that the power be restored to those parties against whom the proletariat had to struggle in order to conquer power." [13]

Drawing the lessons of October for the Communists of other countries, Trotsky emphasized in the concluding section that there can be no proletarian revolution without a Communist party to guide and lead it. But the real main theme of the pamphlet was not the vital need for a Communist party; it was the vital need for a Communist party to have leadership of the kind that Lenin, and by implication Trotsky, gave the Bolsheviks of Russia. Trotsky was arguing that even when societies come into a revolutionary situation, as Russian society did in early 1917 and German society in 1923, there will be no successful proletarian (i.e., Communist) revolution unless revolutionary leaders of Leninist caliber come forward to direct the movement. Not only are such leaders needed to make sure that the party takes full advantage of its historic opportunity to gain power. Their function is also to overcome the resistance to resolute revolutionary action that inevitably comes from those elements of the party who have a vacillating and temporizing "Menshevik attitude to revolution." As Trotsky put it, after stating that certain of the Old Bolsheviks had taken an essentially Social Democratic position on all the fundamental questions that arose from February 1917 to February 1918, "It needed Lenin, and Lenin's exceptional influence in the party, unprecedented even at that time, to safeguard the party and the Revolution against the supreme confusion following from such a condition." As regards his own role, Trotsky had this to say in a short concluding comment: "From the very first day of my arrival in Petrograd my work was carried on in complete coordination with the Central Committee of the Bolsheviks. Lenin's course towards the conquest of power

13. *Lessons of October*, p. 153 and *passim*. Those who resigned on November 14 were Kamenev, Zinoviev, Rykov, Nogin, and Miliutin.

by the proletariat I naturally supported in whole and in part. So far as the peasantry was concerned, there was not even a shade of disagreement between Lenin and myself." [14]

The "Literary Discussion"

It is not clear that Trotsky anticipated the full extent of the storm that *Lessons of October* brought down upon his head. As a measure of caution, however, he stated toward the end of the work that the study of past party disagreements ought not to be regarded as an attack on "those comrades who pursued a false policy." Still, it was impermissible to blot out the greatest chapter in the party's history just because some party members failed to keep in step with the proletarian revolution. Further: "The tradition of a revolutionary party is built not on evasions but on critical clarity." [15] But in spite of his remarks, Trotsky had little reason to expect that his pamphlet would be received simply as a contribution to critical clarity on party history. In the context of the time, it could hardly have been taken as anything other than a declaration of open political war against "those comrades." They, at any rate, interpreted it in that manner and acted accordingly. A torrent of attacks followed, beginning with an unsigned editorial in *Pravda*, "How Not to Write the History of October." Its author, as soon became known, was Bukharin.

In defense of Kamenev and Zinoviev it pointed out that the April conference had elected Kamenev to the Central Committee on Lenin's proposal, then-existing differences notwithstanding, and that the Central Committee had appointed Kamenev to preside over the Second Congress of Soviets at the very moment of the October insurrection. As for Zinoviev, who had disagreed with the Central Committee for only a few days, the Central Committee had commissioned him not long afterwards to report to the All-Russian Central Executive Committee of the Soviet on the dissolution of the Constituent Assembly. Thus, the party had regarded the "October

14. *Lessons of October*, pp. 172, 175.
15. *Ibid.*, p. 171.

mistake" of Kamenev and Zinoviev as no more than a transient disagreement, and it had assigned extremely responsible roles to them without for a moment condoning their errors. But Bukharin's concern in the *Pravda* editorial was not so much to defend Zinoviev and Kamenev as to assail Trotsky, whom he accused of having conducted a political argument in *Lessons of October* by means of "semi-Aesopian language" and "a special sort of code" that had to be decoded.[16]

Trotsky, he asserted, had concentrated all his attention upon the immediate prelude to the capture of power, treating the whole pre-October period of party development as of secondary importance. In fact, however, the party's position in October had been prepared and determined by its entire previous history, including the history of its struggles with Trotsky over a series of fundamental issues. The October victory would never have come about if the Bolsheviks had sided with Trotsky on those issues of the preparatory period. Hence the demand for "critical clarity" must apply not only to the immediate revolutionary period but also to what went before and what came after. Nor was Trotsky's treatment of the events of 1917 acceptable. Above all, the party was missing from it·

There is Trotsky, Lenin is visible in the distance, and there is some sort of incomprehensible Central Committee. Completely absent is the Petrograd organization, the actual collective organizer of the worker insurrection. Comrade Trotsky's entire historiography moves exclusively at the "uppermost level" of the party. There is simply no use looking for the party structure itself in this enigmatic picture called "Where Is the Party?" painted with the deft brush of Comrade Trotsky. Is this the way for Marxists to write history? It is a caricature of Marxism. To write the history of October and *overlook the party* is to take the viewpoint of individualism, the standpoint of "heroes and the crowd."

Concluding that Trotsky's booklet was party history in a crooked mirror, Bukharin undertook to decode the Aesopian political message

16. *Za leninizm. Sbornik statei* (Moscow and Leningrad, 1925), pp. 9 and 14 n. Speaking of the Aesopian language, which he discerned particularly in the preface to *Lessons of October*, Bukharin stated here that Trotsky was writing in such a way that "hints and half-hints will go by unperceived by the completely inexperienced reader."

that could be read between the lines of *Lessons of October*. Was not
Trotsky saying that since it had been necessary to go against the
Central Committee in October 1917 in order to accomplish something, the same might be true now? That those who failed to pass
their crucial revolutionary test in 1917 could not be trusted to pass
present tests? That poor leadership by these people was the source
of the defeats that the Comintern was suffering nowadays in places
like Bulgaria and Germany? [17]

Kamenev's major contribution to the discussion was a speech
that laid out in great detail the record of Trotsky's pre-1917 conflicts with Lenin, thereby bringing into the open the sort of material
that had already been circulating in the anonymous literature of the
anti-Trotsky campaign. In introducing his lengthy chronicle of
Lenin's earlier polemics against Trotsky, Kamenev advanced the
thesis that the issue was not Trotsky as a personality but "Trotskyism" as a long-term political trend the function of which was to
serve as a cover for Menshevism in the working-class movement.
From the inception of Menshevism in 1903 to its final downfall in
1914, Trotsky had performed the role of an "agent of Menshevism
in the working class." Even after joining the Bolsheviks, he had
continued to fulfill his historical function by making mistakes of the
same basic type as his pre-1917 ones. Now, in *Lessons of October*,
he was cleverly attempting to supplant Leninism with Trotskyism
by insinuating that Lenin in 1917 had acted on the theory of permanent revolution. Trotsky's open attack on Zinoviev and Kamenev
was therefore to be seen as a covert attack on Lenin *through* these
two. Having said this, however, Kamenev also admitted that he and
Zinoviev had been at fault in 1917. But in extenuation he pointed
out that Lenin, despite their differences at the April conference, had
thereupon proposed and supported his candidacy for the Central
Committee; that later in the year Lenin had asked him to edit the
unfinished manuscript of *The State and Revolution* in the event that
he himself did not live to do so; that despite the differences in October over the insurrection itself, he and Zinoviev were elected—

17. *Ibid.*, pp. 12, 14–15, 24–25.

along with Lenin, Stalin, Trotsky, Sokolnikov, and Bubnov—to the original Central Committee Political Bureau, which was created to direct the insurrection; and that despite his, Kamenev's, departure from the Central Committee on November 4, the committee had, on November 18, appointed him a member of the Soviet delegation to the peace talks with Germany at Brest-Litovsk.[18]

Unlike Kamenev, Zinoviev began his attack on Trotsky with self-criticism. He had committed an "enormous mistake" at the beginning of November 1917, although he had admitted and rectified it in the space of a few days. On the other hand, Trotsky was quite wrong in assigning him to a "right wing" of Bolshevism; there had never been any such phenomenon. Bolshevism was organizationally alien to left and right wings; what it stood for was the "monolithic party, made of one piece." The long history of differences and disagreements inside the party was not to be seen in terms of a conflict between left and right wings. But if the theory of a Bolshevik right wing had no historical foundation, there was *now* a danger of one taking shape in the party and the Comintern—with Trotsky himself as its chief figure. For what was the drift of Trotsky's post-October prescriptions for party policy? Between 1921 and 1924, he had proposed at various times the incorporation of the trade unions into the state machinery, greater freedom of the state machinery from party control, greater influence for military and other non-party specialists, and delay of the currency reform; and he had raised a semi-Menshevik campaign against the party *apparatchiki* on behalf of his own peculiar version of the party's "democratization." As for his pre-October political path, it had proceeded from Menshevism of the Axelrod type (1903–5) through Menshevism of the "permanent revolution" type (1905–7) to abandonment of revolution (1909–14) and on to a halfway position during the World War. Such was the "old Trotskyism," whose political biography Lenin himself had summed up in the following words about Trotsky: "He was in 1903 a Menshevik; departed from Menshevism in 1904, returned to the Mensheviks in 1905 flaunting ultra-revolu-

18. *Ibid.,* pp. 28, 30, 60, 62, 73, 78 n.

tionary phrases; departed again in 1906; at the end of 1906, defended an electoral agreement with the Kadets, and in the spring of 1907, at the London congress, said his difference from Rosa Luxemburg was one of nuance rather than political tendency. Trotsky plagiarizes the intellectual baggage of one faction today, the other tomorrow, and on this account declares himself above both factions." [19]

Thanks to Trotsky's later exile abroad, we have an illuminating commentary by Zinoviev himself on the argumentation employed in this and other major contributions to the literary discussion. After arriving in Turkey in 1929, Trotsky released documents relating to the origin of what he called the "legend of Trotskyism." These documents concerned, in particular, some remarks by Zinoviev during a conversation at Kamenev's home in October 1926, after the two had joined with Trotsky and his followers in an oppositionist bloc against Stalin. Trotsky, some of whose followers had earlier thought the publication of *Lessons of October* a tactical blunder, asked Zinoviev on that occasion whether the literary discussion would have taken place if *Lessons* had never been written. "Yes, indeed," Zinoviev had replied. *"Lessons of October* served only as a pretext. Failing that, a different motive would have been found, and the discussion would have assumed somewhat different forms, nothing more." He said further, in an effort to quiet the minds of members of his own Leningrad faction who had taken the "legend" seriously: "You must understand it was a struggle for power. The trick was to string together old disagreements with new issues. For this purpose 'Trotskyism' was invented." [20]

The technique, in other words, was to conjure up, out of Lenin's pre-revolutionary polemics against Trotsky, an anti-Leninist political tendency—"Trotskyism"—which could then be seen as the underlying issue of the current conflicts between Trotsky and Lenin's Old Bolshevik followers. Since the only "ism" with which

19. *Ibid.*, pp. 109, 111, 124, 132, 138, 149. The quoted attack on Trotsky by Lenin appeared in an article of 1910, "The Historical Significance of the Intra-Party Struggle in Russia."

20. L. Trotsky, *The Stalin School of Falsification* (New York, 1962), pp. 89–95.

Bolsheviks wanted to identify themselves or be associated was Leninism, it could only be harmful to Trotsky to appear as the leader of a political tendency other than Leninism. What made it feasible to exploit the old arguments between Lenin and Trotsky in this manner was, of course, the fact that Lenin's supreme authority had become a basis of Bolshevik political discourse. How deeply it had done so is shown, rather ironically, by Trotsky's own acceptance of this fact in *Lessons of October,* where he vindicated himself politically, and discredited leading opponents, by demonstrating that he had fought side by side with Lenin during the revolutionary period and they had opposed him. If *Lessons of October* was a political blunder on Trotsky's part, the mistake was not that he decided to give battle openly against his adversaries but that he did so according to their rules. To all this it must be added that real programmatic differences did then exist in the leadership and were becoming associated in many party minds with the "ism" in "Trotskyism," whatever the manner in which this term originated.

Stalin, who had not been directly mentioned in the *Lessons,* nevertheless took a prominent part in the ensuing discussion. His speech of November 19, 1924, "Trotskyism or Leninism?," carried the attack on Trotsky's revolutionary biography to unprecedented lengths and was his most important pronouncement so far on questions of party history. First Stalin denied that the Central Committee had resisted the project for an uprising in the immediate pre-October period, and that Kamenev and Zinoviev had constituted a Bolshevik right wing. Then he struck out at Trotsky, whom he accused of striving to picture himself as the central figure of the October insurrection and to blot out the leading role of the party, its Central Committee, and the Petrograd organization. Trotsky had played "an indubitably important part in the insurrection," but not a "special" part. For, as president of the Petrograd Soviet he had simply effectuated the will of the proper party bodies, which had "guided Comrade Trotsky's every step." At its meeting of October 16, the Central Committee had elected a "practical center for organizational direction of the insurrection," consisting of Sverdlov, Stalin, Dzerzhinsky, Bubnov, and Uritsky. Was it not strange that

Trotsky, the rumored "inspirer," "main figure," and "only leader" of the insurrection, was not even a member of the group specially created to lead the action? Not at all, answered Stalin, for Trotsky —"a man comparatively new to our party in the October period"— did not and could not play any special role either in the party or in the October insurrection. Like all the other responsible figures of the party, he had merely been an executor of the will of the Central Committee and its organs, and talk about his special role was nothing but a legend spread by obliging party gossips. The insurrection did, however, have its inspirer and leader. "But that was Lenin, and no one else, the same Lenin whose resolutions were adopted by the Central Committee in deciding the question of the insurrection, the same Lenin whose underground status did not keep him from being, contrary to what Comrade Trotsky says, the real inspirer of the insurrection. It is stupid and absurd to try to gloss over now, with chatter about underground status, the indubitable fact that the inspirer of the uprising was the *vozhd'* of the party, V. I. Lenin." [21]

If Trotsky's special role was a legend, Stalin might have blamed himself, among others, for creating the legend. For on the first anniversary of the October Revolution, he had published an article in *Pravda* giving an account of Trotsky's role strikingly different from the one just summarized.[22] True, even then he had attributed the inspiration of the October coup to the "Central Committee of the party headed by Comrade Lenin." But he had gone on to pay tribute to Trotsky's practical directing of the uprising. Perhaps it was partly the awareness of having made such a public statement —and the awareness of its truth—which now impelled Stalin to add that "Comrade Trotsky really did fight well in October." But so, he went on, did the Left SR's. Besides, at such moments of rising insurrection and isolation of the enemy, "even laggards become heroes." The true test of revolutionaries is how they behave at times

21. *Za leninizm*, pp. 87–90. The speech appears in *Stalin*, VI, 324–357. There is no indication that the "practical center" effectively existed. On this see Carr, *Socialism in One Country*, II, p. 16.

22. See pp. 198–199, above, for this statement.

of setback and retreat, such as the period of Brest. At that difficult moment, when special courage and iron calm were needed to ensure a timely retreat and gain a breathing spell for the Revolution, Trotsky was sufficiently lacking in courage and fortitude to follow in the footsteps of the Left SR's, who went into panic and hysteria in the face of the threat from German imperialism.[23]

Next, Stalin launched into a detailed analysis of the Russian Revolution and Trotsky's treatment of it. He set the tone by ridiculing the contention of Lentsner, the editor of Trotsky's collected works, that Trotsky's letters from America in March 1917 had fully anticipated the strong revolutionary line taken in the "Letters from Afar" that Lenin wrote from Switzerland. To compare Trotsky with Lenin in this connection, said Stalin, was like comparing a wretched hovel with Mont Blanc. It was to raise higher the heap of "old legends" about the Revolution. One other such legend, Stalin added, was the widespread story that Trotsky was the "only" or "main" organizer of the Bolshevik victories in the Civil War. In fact, the party had overruled Trotsky's views on the way to meet the forces of the two chief White generals, Denikin and Kolchak, who were thus defeated by the Reds *in spite of* Trotsky's plans. "I am far from denying that Trotsky played an important role in the Civil War," Stalin asserted. "But I must emphatically declare that the high honor of being the organizer of our victories belongs not to individuals, but to the great collective of advanced workers of our country—the Russian Communist party." [24]

In the peroration of his speech, Stalin accused Trotsky of seeking, in *Lessons of October,* to discredit Lenin as the chief leader of the uprising and the party as the force that organized and carried it through—and all this for the further purpose of substituting Trotskyism for Leninism. "Trotskyism" meant, first, the theory of permanent revolution, with its ignoring of the peasant movement and its playing with the seizure of power; second, distrust of the Bolshevik party spirit (*partiinost'*) and the idea of monolithic party organi-

23. *Za leninizm,* pp. 90, 91.
24. *Ibid.,* pp. 94–95.

zation; third, distrust of the leaders of Bolshevism and attempts to discredit and defame them. Elaborating, Stalin argued that Trotsky was trying to divide Leninism into an objectionable pre-October part, which Lenin jettisoned in 1917 by adopting the theory of permanent revolution, and an acceptable post-October part. Correspondingly, he would like to treat the party's history before 1917 as a mere pre-history and only the post-October period as the genuine history of the party. But such a division of party history and of Leninism itself into two parts was grotesque. Leninism must be seen as an integral theory. Lenin himself had said that Bolshevism as a trend of political thought and as a political party came into being in 1903, and "Bolshevism and Leninism are one." [25]

In amplifying the charge that Trotskyism sought to discredit and defame the leaders of Bolshevism, Stalin made Trotsky out to be a maligner of Lenin. For evidence he went back to the booklet *On Lenin,* where Trotsky had written the following about the immediate post-October period when the German attack began and the new regime's survival was highly uncertain: "This was the period when Lenin, at every opportunity, dinned into people's heads the idea of the inevitability of terror." Stalin quoted the sentence minus the introductory phrase ("This was the period when . . ."), thereby mangling its meaning, and accused Trotsky of creating the impression that Lenin was "the most bloodthirsty of all bloodthirsty Bolsheviks." On the contrary, he said, Lenin was a cautious man who disliked reckless people and was wont to place firm restraint on those with a liking for terror. Lenin was also an exemplary party man who liked to decide questions collectively and after careful deliberation. In Trotsky's portrait of him, however, he emerged as some sort of Chinese mandarin who decided vitally important issues in the quiet of his study and by inspiration. In *On Lenin,* for example, Lenin was shown deciding on the forcible dissolution of the Constituent Assembly in a conversation with Trotsky and the Left SR leader Mark Natanson, and creating the system of political com-

25. *Ibid.,* pp. 102–104, 105–106. Lenin's characterization of Bolshevism as having existed since 1903 is to be found in his treatise *Left-Wing Communism: An Infantile Disorder.*

missars in the army on the basis of a single short talk with Trotsky, who suggested the idea. The booklet, moreover, pictured Lenin as a Blanquist-type revolutionary who during the October days had advised the party to take power conspiratorially behind the back of the Congress of Soviets. Trotsky had thus failed to represent Lenin as he really was—the greatest Marxist of the present age, a profound theoretician, and a most experienced revolutionary to whom any trace of Blanquism was alien. He had painted a portrait "not of Lenin the giant but of some kind of Blanquist dwarf." [26]

In his effort to convict Trotsky of anti-Leninism, Stalin took the further step of quoting from a hitherto unpublished private letter that Trotsky had written in 1913 to N. Chkheidze, a prominent Georgian Menshevik. It was inspired, as Trotsky much later recalled, by the fact that the official Bolshevik newspaper published in Petersburg had appropriated for itself the title of Trotsky's own Vienna publication: *Pravda—A Worker Paper*. In late 1921, when the Bureau of Party History found this letter in the tsarist police archives, its president, M. Olminsky, had written to Trotsky inquiring whether he wished it to be published. Trotsky had replied in the negative, saying that publication would only revive old quarrels now best forgotten and adding that he did not consider that he had been altogether wrong in his disputes of that time with the Bolsheviks. Now Stalin quoted from the 1913 letter—as evidence of Trotsky's hostile attitude both then and now toward Lenin and Leninism—the statement that "the whole edifice of Leninism at the present time is built on lying and falsification and bears within itself the poisoned element of its own disintegration." Further on he quoted another excerpt in which Trotsky characterized Lenin as "a professional exploiter of every kind of backwardness in the Russian working-class movement." [27] Shortly afterwards, on December 9, 1924, the full texts of both the letter to Chkheidze and the 1921 letter to Olminsky about it were published in *Pravda*.

Stalin had chosen his tactic with care, and he struck a blow that hurt Trotsky badly. Coming out now, in the prevailing atmos-

26. *Ibid.*, pp. 107–108. For the definition of Blanquism, see note 63, p. 59.
27. *Ibid.*, pp. 103, 104.

phere of cult-like reverence for Lenin and Leninism, Trotsky's old epithets sounded atrocious. As he himself acknowledged later in his autobiography, the letter to Chkheidze, although of trivial importance intrinsically and only a relic of the pre-revolutionary squabbles among the émigré Russian radicals, had a stunning effect upon a great many when disinterred in 1924 and publicized to a party three-quarters of whose members had joined it after the Revolution and possessed little understanding of its distant political past. Chronology, the fact that the letter was twelve years old and reflected the circumstances of an entirely different period, was disregarded in the face of the naked quotations, Trotsky said, and he concluded: "The use that the epigones made of my letter to Chkheidze is one of the greatest frauds in the world's history." [28] Whatever the accuracy of that assessment, the letter was used with telling effect, as was the 1921 letter to Olminsky in which Trotsky seemed to be reaffirming his views of 1913, or at any rate not apologizing for them. Having at the end of November written a long memorandum of reply to his attackers, Trotsky decided to let it go unpublished, and on January 15, 1925, he addressed to the Central Committee a letter of capitulation. In it he asked to be relieved of the duties of president of the Revolutionary War Council. His resignation from the military office was accepted by the Central Committee when it met in plenary session a few days later, and shortly thereafter Frunze was appointed to replace him as president of the council and people's commissar for war. The "literary discussion" had ended. It was a defeat of no small importance in the losing political struggle that Trotsky was waging.

Stalin on the Defensive

Both the defensive and offensive strategies of biographical politics were clearly reflected in *On Lenin* and *Lessons of October*. Somewhat in the spirit of an historian, Trotsky offered the first of

28. Trotsky, *My Life*, p. 516.

these two writings as raw material for Lenin's future biographer; it was for this reason, as he later explained, that he confined himself in it to those periods when he had been able to observe Lenin at first hand, namely, 1902–3 and 1917–19. But these also were the periods before and during the Revolution when he himself had been "with Lenin" politically. The second of them, moreover, saw not only close collaborative relations between the two men but also a reliance by Lenin upon Trotsky that was at some points greater than Trotsky's upon Lenin. Published as it was in 1924, the story of the revolutionary partnership between the two principal architects of October could not but add luster to Trotsky's biography and accentuate his suitability as Lenin's successor at the head of the party, and the laudatory reviews of the booklet by his sympathizers could hardly have come closer to making the latter thought explicit.

In one respect, however, *On Lenin* offended some Bolshevik sensibilities. Whereas the Trotsky of 1902–3 appeared here as a valued younger protégé of Lenin and no more, the Trotsky of the revolutionary period appeared as Lenin's full political equal and co-leader of the Revolution. Lenin thus emerged as something less than a superhuman demiurge of October. Not only was he shown repeatedly seeking and accepting advice from Trotsky; he was depicted, too, as having been in the wrong on certain matters on which events proved Trotsky right, notably on the question of whether to push ahead with the seizure of power in early October, as Lenin had urged out of fear that the Provisional Government might act first, or to time the action for the opening of the Congress of Soviets, as Trotsky insisted on doing and did. So Trotsky's Lenin, albeit the greatest of revolutionaries and the *sine qua non* of the Bolshevik Revolution's success, was humanly fallible. In the atmosphere of the growing Lenin cult in mid-1924, when Lenin was rapidly becoming an "icon" (as Krupskaya ruefully put it in her speech to the Thirteenth Party Congress), such a representation of Lenin began to seem offensive. Many Bolsheviks found it increasingly hard to imagine that anyone else could have been his equal at such a heroic moment of party history as the taking of power. Con-

sequently, Trotsky was open to the charge of unduly magnifying
his own role in October at the expense of Lenin's, and some of the
participants in the discussion pressed this charge vigorously. Molotov, who offered a critical dissection of *On Lenin* as his contribution
to the discussion, pictured the booklet as an act of historical self-
aggrandizement of Trotsky and belittlement of Lenin. Instead of
showing Lenin as *the* leader and inspirer of the party and masses in
October, it made him out to have played the part of "a conspirator,
and a quite unsuccessful conspirator at that." [29]

For a variety of good reasons, Stalin's approach to the politics
of revolutionary biography was very different from Trotsky's. While
establishing links between his own pre-revolutionary career and that
of Lenin, he made no effort to place himself on the same plane. On
the contrary, beginning with the "oath" speech, which represented
the entire party as a worshipful following of Lenin, he went out of his
way to place Lenin upon a pedestal high above all others, himself
included. In his speeches and writings of the middle twenties, he
helped cultivate the style of quoting Lenin as the supreme and indisputable authority on all questions concerning Marxism, revolution, and the Soviet system. More than any other leading Bolshevik
he made Lenin a cult-figure—pre-eminent like Mont Blanc, heroic,
exemplary, infallible. And in all references to himself and his party
past, he presented himself as a good and faithful disciple of Lenin's,
no more. So insistent was he on this point that when Ksenofontov in
his 1926 letter spoke of himself as "a disciple of Lenin and Stalin"
Stalin reproved him for this usage. Call yourself a disciple of Lenin,
he advised in reply, because it would be groundless and out of place
for anyone to call himself "a disciple of a disciple of Lenin's." [30]
Thus, Stalin's theme in the politics of revolutionary biography was
discipleship to Lenin rather than partnership with him. In this
connection, however, some serious problems confronted him.

In party history as it came to be told, 1917 was the climax.
The events of "this epoch of fabulous exploits, of the greatest deeds

29. *Za leninizm*, p. 186.
30. *Stalin*, IX, 152.

in history," [31] were copiously recounted and discussed, and a large literature on the year of revolution had accumulated by the mid-twenties. From Stalin's standpoint as a participant in the politics of biography, this was not fortunate. For the literature, if only by ignoring him, exposed his lack of eminence in 1917, and in some places it made reference to his failings. All this was likewise recorded in the memory of many who had participated in the revolutionary events. Caution in the treatment of Stalin's role in the Revolution was clearly dictated.

Interestingly, Stalin was himself one of the contributors to the party historical literature that reflected poorly on his conduct in 1917. In the preface to *On the Road to October,* a collection of his articles and speeches of the revolutionary period which was published in 1925, he wrote that the first three articles reflected "the well-known vacillations of the majority of our party on the questions of the war and the power of the Soviets" in March and April of 1917. It was no wonder, he went on, that Bolsheviks just back from prison and exile were unable immediately to find their bearings in the new situation and that they stopped halfway in the search for the new orientation that the party needed. The celebrated "April Theses" of Lenin were needed in order to shift the party all at once onto a new road. At this point Stalin reminded his readers that in his speech of November 19, 1924, "Trotskyism or Leninism?," he had already acknowledged sharing the position of the erring majority.[32] There, indeed, he had said that the party majority, groping for a new orientation in March, had settled upon a halfway policy of pressure on the Provisional Government—a deeply erroneous position that had given rise to pacifist illusions, provided grist for the mills of defensism, and made more difficult the revolutionary educa-

31. N. N. Sukhanov, *The Russian Revolution 1917. A Personal Record* (London, 1955), p. 356.
32. Robert H. McNeal, *Stalin's Works: An Annotated Bibliography* (Stanford, 1971), pp. 187–188. This passage of Stalin's preface was omitted when the preface was later reprinted in his *Problems of Leninism* under the title "The October Revolution and the Tactics of the Russian Communists," and also when it was reprinted in Stalin's works, Vol. VI.

tion of the masses. In his speech he had gone on to say: "This erroneous position I then shared with other party comrades and fully
abandoned only in the middle of April when I aligned myself with
Lenin's theses." [33]

Stalin's self-critical remarks in the speech and the preface were
at the same time self-serving. For they covered up, by references to
the party majority, his own special share of responsibility for foist-
ing upon the party the "deeply erroneous position." Nevertheless,
they showed how notorious his March conduct was in Bolshevik
minds—and helped to make it more so. Nor was this the end of the
matter. Stalin's revolutionary biography was finally becoming a subject of public comment by Trotsky in his polemics with the general
secretary. Speaking before an enlarged meeting of the Comintern
Executive Committee in late 1926, he declared that "after the
February Revolution Stalin preached erroneous tactics, which Lenin
characterized as a Kautskyan deviation." Stalin quoted this statement in his concluding speech at the same meeting, and replied:
"That is untrue, comrades. That is gossip. Stalin did not 'preach'
any Kautskyan deviation. That I had certain vacillations after my
return from exile, I have not concealed, and I wrote about them
myself in my pamphlet *On the Road to October*. But who among
us has not had passing vacillations?" [34] Under the stress of political
battle, self-criticism was passing over into self-justification.

Trotsky returned to the attack in a communication to the
Bureau of Party History (Istpart) called "Concerning the Falsification of the History of the October Revolution, the History of the
Revolution, and the History of the Party." Written in 1927 in reply
to a questionnaire sent out by Istpart, this unpublished "Letter to
Istpart" circulated in hundreds of typed and handwritten copies. Its
vivid style and sensational disclosures ensured for it a wide and
eager audience in party circles. Although Trotsky's primary purpose was to defend his own revolutionary record against the campaign in the party press to besmirch it, the "Letter" dealt in detail
with Stalin's record as well. "Stalin stood for unification with Tsere-

33. *Stalin*, VI, 333.
34. *Stalin*, IX, 64.

teli," Trotsky said, and then quoted the passages from the minutes of the March conference in which Stalin proposed that the Bolsheviks should meet with the Mensheviks of Tsereteli's persuasion to discuss unification, and in which he later remarked, in reply to an objection that unification might create too much heterogeneity, that "there is no party life without disagreements. We will live down trivial disagreements within the party." Then, after inquiring why the minutes of the March conference had never been published, Trotsky directly accused the Istpart directors of concealing the document "for the simple reason that it cruelly reflects upon the political physiognomy of Stalin at the end of March and the beginning of April—that is to say, in that period when Stalin *independently* tried to work out a political line." To etch this political physiognomy more sharply, Trotsky added that Stalin, as a *Pravda* editor and author of semi-defensist articles conditionally supporting the Provisional Government, was one of those implicitly under attack by Lenin when he thunderously denounced *Pravda* in the April 4 speech for demanding that the imperialist Provisional Government renounce annexations.[35]

Trotsky's "Letter" was written in October 1927, shortly before the party marked, with much fanfare, the tenth anniversary of its coming to power. Although (as Trotsky rightly alleged) the history of the Revolution was being rewritten by this time, it is important to note that Stalin was not yet being celebrated as an architect of the October victory. Trotsky's historic role was effaced in the official anniversary materials, Zinoviev and Kamenev were condemned once again for their well-known transgressions, but Stalin was not retrospectively elevated to revolutionary glory. For illustration we may refer to a study of 1917 published for the anniversary by the party historian Emelian Yaroslavsky, who by then was placing his talents at Stalin's service. As Yaroslavsky presented it, the Bolshevik Revolution had in Lenin its one great hero and single-handed leader from start to finish. Even during the 110 days spent in hiding, '

35. L. Trotsky, "Letter to the Bureau of Party History," in *The Stalin School of Falsification,* pp. 18–19. On the circulation of the "Letter" in hundreds of copies see the foreword to Trotsky's book, p. xli.

vigilantly watched over everything that happened in the country, gave a clear and precise appraisal of the situation and exact directions as to how the party should act." As for the actual organizing of the insurrection, Yaroslavsky briefly mentioned the Soviet's Military Revolutionary Committee (without saying who headed it) and then attributed the political direction of the rising to the Central and Petrograd Committees of the party, and the "practical organizational direction" to the party-appointed Military Revolutionary Center consisting of Sverdlov, Stalin, Dzerzhinsky, Bubnov, and Uritsky: "This organ (and no one else) directed all the organizations that took part in the uprising (the revolutionary military units and Red Guard)." [36]

Commenting on this, Trotsky wrote in his "Letter to Istpart" that Stalin with the help of the Yaroslavskys was trying to construct a new history of the organizing of the October insurrection, attributing the direction of it to a committee of which he, Trotsky, was not a member. The legend about this committee was being created, he went on, for the simple reason that Stalin was a member of it. Then he recalled that he had spent the decisive night of October 25–26 together with Kamenev in the quarters of the Military Revolutionary Committee, answering questions and giving orders by telephone. "But stretch my memory as I will, I cannot answer the question in just what consisted, during those decisive days, the role of Stalin. It never once happened that I turned to him for advice or cooperation. He never showed the slightest initiative. He never advanced a single independent proposal." As for the Military Revolutionary Center, it played no independent role and was of subordinate significance. The reason why Trotsky was not a member of it was easy to explain. In a note added to the "Letter" on November 2, 1927, Trotsky pointed out that *Pravda* for that day had printed an excerpt from the Central Committee minutes of October 16, 1917, saying that the five-man Military Revolutionary Center was to be a "constituent part of the Revolutionary Soviet Committee." Clearly, he remarked, it would have been superfluous to introduce

36. E. Yaroslavsky, *Partiia bol'shevikov v 1917 godu* (Moscow and Leningrad, 1927), pp. 85–86, 90.

Trotsky a second time into the organization of which he was already chairman.[37]

But even though Yaroslavsky attributed to Stalin an important role in organizing the insurrection, it was only as one member of a collective organ. Beyond that, he tried here and there to magnify Stalin's contributions. Thus he wrote that the fate of the Revolution hung on the outcome of the April conference debate on the national question, in which Stalin gave the main report, and that Stalin was already setting the party's future course toward "socialism in one country" when he told the Sixth Congress in 1917 that Russia might be the country to blaze the trail to socialism. These, however, were rather strained efforts to make Stalin's role in 1917 look more significant than it was. And while it highlighted his services, the book also made gingerly mention of his failings. True, Kamenev now became the chief culprit for *Pravda*'s defensism in March and its advocacy of pressure on the Provisional Government to end the war. But Stalin was listed among those party leaders whom the February Revolution found in exile and who were "unable immediately to take their bearings in the events which were occurring." Also, his vacillations of that period were recorded in his own words from the preface to *On the Road to October*. Yaroslavsky quoted Stalin's statement that he had shared the party majority's deeply erroneous position toward the Provisional Government, and then tried to soften the effect by adding in a footnote: "Comrade Stalin not only acknowledged this mistake of his but never again returned to it. Whereas other comrades not only did not completely acknowledge their errors but more than once displayed vacillations showing that they had not outlived these mistakes." [38]

Although it retold the story of 1917 in a manner calculated to enhance Stalin's revolutionary merits, Yaroslavsky's book stopped

37. Trotsky, *The Stalin School of Falsification*, pp. 13–15.
38. Yaroslavsky, *Partiia bol'shevikov*, pp. 24, 32–34, 50, 71. Yaroslavsky performed a further falsifying service for Stalin by writing here (p. 24) that Lenin's opinion on the Revolution as expressed in his "Letters from Afar" became known to the party some time after October. This overlooked Stalin's responsibility, as one of *Pravda*'s editors who had known of Lenin's letters earlier, for their non-disclosure.

far short of depicting him as the second great leader of the Bolshevik Revolution. On the Revolution's tenth anniversary, at a time
when his political star was clearly rising, Stalin was not yet en-
shrined in party annals as a hero of October. Nor did his name
figure prominently in the Soviet literature about the Civil War. Not
even the defense of Tsaritsyn was initially linked with him in the
public mind. When the city was renamed "Stalingrad" in 1925,
Stalin was not yet widely regarded as a hero of the Tsaritsyn events
of 1918. Ordzhonikidze, for example, had not made reference to
him in an early anniversary article about the Tenth Army, and
S. K. Minin, who was the Bolshevik mayor of the city in 1918 and
a member of the Tenth Army's revolutionary war council, paid
scant attention to him in his heroic drama, *The Encircled City*,
written in 1925.[39] Stalin went unmentioned in the press articles of
February 28, 1927, marking the ninth anniversary of the Red
Army's founding. On the same date two years later, the anniversary
articles by Voroshilov and others still did not describe him as organizer of the Red Army. Trotsky, who had just been deported to
Turkey, was no longer credited with that historic role. But Stalin
had not yet been assigned to it in his place.

The Denouement

Toward the end of his lengthy "Letter to Istpart," Trotsky
opened a new section with the ominous remark that it would be-
hoove Stalin to be extremely cautious about the last period of
Lenin's life, "when Vladimir Ilyich arrived at certain final conclusions about Stalin." Then he launched into a series of detailed disclosures. With impressive documentation, much of it drawn from
unpublished Politburo correspondence, he related how in the last
months of his life Lenin's relations with Stalin deteriorated to the
point of a complete break. Although parts of the story were known
in the party and even engraved on the public record, it had not been
told before so vividly and fully. This was the most sensational sec-

39. L. Trotsky, *Stalin: An Appraisal of the Man and His Influence* (New
York, 1967), p. 283.

tion of the widely circulated "Letter," and the most damaging to Stalin.

First, Trotsky quoted correspondence between Lenin and himself on the conflict over the foreign-trade monopoly and Stalin's role in it. Then he documented the far more serious conflict between Lenin and Stalin over the national question. He quoted the text of Lenin's letter of September 27, 1922, and the parts of Stalin's reply in which cutting reference was made to "the national liberalism of Comrade Lenin." He cited the passage of Lenin's notes on Stalin's "hastiness" and "malice," and the later one saying that Stalin and Dzerzhinsky must be held politically responsible for the Great Russian nationalist campaign. He quoted Lenin's letter of March 5, 1923, asking Trotsky to undertake the defense of the Georgian affair in the Central Committee; Lenin's message of March 6 informing the Georgian opponents of Stalin that he was wholly on their side and outraged at the conduct of Ordzhonikidze, Stalin, and Dzerzhinsky; and Lenin's remark to Fotieva that Stalin, if he found out about the notes on the national question right away, would only make a rotten compromise and then deceive.[40]

So notorious had the testament become in party circles by this time that Trotsky did not reproduce it in full in the "Letter to Istpart." He nevertheless mentioned it, spoke of it as being filled with distrust of Stalin, of his rudeness and disloyalty, and observed that the sole organizational inference indicated in the testament was: "Remove Stalin from the post of general secretary." He pointed out that Lenin's denunciation of the Rabkrin in "Better Less, But Better" was directed wholly at Stalin. He cited (without naming her) Fotieva's remark that Lenin was preparing a bomb for Stalin at the Twelfth Congress. Finally, he declared that the last letter Lenin ever sent was "a letter to Stalin breaking off all comradely relations with him." And, referring to Zinoviev's discussion of this letter in the secret proceedings of the July 1926 Central Committee plenum, he cited and questioned a statement to that plenum by Lenin's sister Maria to the effect that the letter was evoked by personal and not political causes. " 'Rudeness' and 'disloyalty' are also personal quali-

40 Trotsky, *The Stalin School of Falsification*, pp. 65–75.

ties," wrote Trotsky. "But Lenin warned the party about them not for 'personal' but for party reasons. Lenin's letter breaking off comradely relations with Stalin had exactly the same character." [41]

The drama of Lenin's testament reached its denouement in the last confrontation between Trotsky and Stalin, which occurred during the Central Committee plenum preceding the Fifteenth Party Congress. Taking the floor on October 23, 1927, to discuss the resolution calling for his and Zinoviev's expulsion from the Central Committee, Trotsky spoke not so much in his own defense as against Stalin and the course he and his faction were following. The rudeness and disloyalty of which Lenin had written in the testament, he declared, were no longer mere personal characteristics but had become the character of the ruling faction. Stalin had inspired dread in Lenin from the very day of his election as general secretary. And the fear had proved well founded. The Central Committee Secretariat, which played a subordinate role in politics so long as Lenin remained in active charge of affairs, had begun to usurp power as soon as he fell ill. That was why Lenin had given the party his last counsel: "Remove Stalin, who may carry the party to a split and to ruin." [42]

That day Stalin rose before the high party body to fire a parting fusillade against Trotsky. Since the speech was printed in *Pravda* a few days later, its audience was the whole Soviet population. Stalin began by dismissing as of small consequence the "personal factor" —the opposition's attacks upon him personally. They were only a reflection of the fact that he was harder than some other comrades to fool, better able to see through the opposition's tricks. Let them attack him to their hearts' content. Stalin, after all, was only a little man; consider what things they had said about Lenin! Here Stalin

41. *Ibid.,* pp. 75–77. The statement that Lenin's last letter broke off comradely relations with Stalin is inaccurate, though Trotsky, not having seen the text of the letter, may not have known this. He repeated the inaccuracy in his biography (*Stalin,* p. 375). These statements probably account for the widespread misapprehension that Lenin's letter actually broke off relations with Stalin instead of threatening to do so.

42. L. Trotsky, *The Real Situation in Russia* (New York, 1928), pp. 7–8.

quoted once again the passage in Trotsky's 1913 letter to Chkheidze calling Lenin a professional exploiter of everything backward in the working-class movement, and exclaimed: "What language, comrades, take note of the language. This is Trotsky writing, writing of Lenin. Is it any wonder that this Trotsky who so unceremoniously slights the great Lenin, although he is not worth the sole of Lenin's boot, should now hurl abuse at one of Lenin's disciples—Comrade Stalin?" And having started the speech as an exercise in biographical politics, Stalin ended it in the same way. In closing, he wished Trotsky godspeed to his "dear teacher, Pavel Borisovich Axelrod." Thus had Trotsky dedicated his pamphlet of 1904, *Our Political Tasks,* which attacked the organizational principles that Lenin had expounded in his *One Step Forward, Two Steps Back.* In that work Trotsky had never called Lenin anything but "Maximilien Lenin," thus hinting that Lenin was a new Robespierre with a hankering for personal dictatorship. It was, said Stalin, a purely Menshevik pamphlet expressing Trotsky's typically Menshevik disdain for the Leninist conception of the party and party discipline. Let him, then, go to his "dear teacher," the émigré Menshevik leader Axelrod; and he had better hurry lest the senile old man die before his arrival.

That was Stalin's peroration. Meanwhile, he had come to grips with Lenin's testament in an opening section of the speech headed "Some Petty Questions." First he denied the opposition's claim that the Central Committee was concealing the controversial document. The testament had been addressed to the Thirteenth Congress, had been divulged at that congress, and by the latter's unanimous decision had been withheld from publication because, among other reasons, Lenin himself had neither desired nor demanded its publication. Was it not rather Trotsky who had tried to conceal the testament's existence when he denounced Eastman's book in *Bolshevik?* It was absolutely true—Stalin went on—that Comrade Lenin had proposed in the testament that the congress think of a way of removing Stalin, in view of his "rudeness," from the post of general secretary. Then he quoted the full text of Lenin's postscript of January 4, and went on:

Yes, I am rude, comrades, toward those who rudely and treacherously wreck and split the party. I have never concealed this and do not do so now. It may be that a certain softness should be shown toward splitters. But it doesn't come off with me. At the very first plenary meeting of the Central Committee after the Thirteenth Congress, I requested the Central Committee plenum to release me from the duties of general secretary. The congress itself discussed this question. Each delegation discussed this question, and all the delegations, including Trotsky, Kamenev, and Zinoviev, *obliged* Stalin to remain at his post. What, then, could I do? Flee the post? That is not in my character. I have never run away from any posts and have no right to run away, for that would be desertion. As I have already said before, I am an unfree man, and when the party imposes an obligation, I must obey. A year later I again submitted a statement to the plenum asking to be released, but was again obliged to stay at the post. What else could I do? [43]

Having quoted the part of the testament that concerned his negative personal qualities, Stalin contended that the opposition had no basis for regarding the document as a trump card. On the contrary, it was fatally damaging to the opposition leaders. For had it not accused Trotsky of "non-Bolshevism" and stated that there was nothing "accidental" in the October error of Kamenev and Zinoviev? But this meant that Trotsky was *politically* untrustworthy, in view of his non-Bolshevism, and that the errors of Kamenev and Zinoviev, being no accident, could and would be repeated. As for Stalin, the testament contained not a word, not even a hint, concerning errors on his part. "It refers only to the rudeness of Stalin. But rudeness is not and cannot be a defect of the *political* line or position of Stalin."

The ugly wrangle over the testament must have dimmed the satisfaction that Stalin derived from his political triumph at this time over the united opposition. Bulletins containing the text of the testament were, according to Medvedev, distributed to the 1,669 delegates who gathered in Moscow in December for the Fifteenth Party Congress; judging by the fact that they were printed up in an edition of 13,500, they were intended for a larger party audience. The unpublished papers of E. P. Frolov, who was one of the delegates,

43. *Pravda,* November 2, 1927.

reveal that the congress on December 9, 1927, passed a decision, on a motion by Rykov, that the testament and other previously unpublished Lenin letters on intra-party matters should be published as part of the congress record.[44] This was not done, however, nor were the surplus copies of the bulletins distributed to party organizations after the congress. Nearly all the delegates who failed to destroy their personal copies of the bulletins in good time were among the victims of Stalin's purges of the thirties, at which time party members were condemned to death or long terms of confinement for possessing "a counter-revolutionary document, the so-called testament of Lenin." [45]

None of the principals emerged well from the biographical controversy. All now figured in the party mind, in various ways, as men with blemished biographies. Whether this was seriously harmful to Stalin as a politician involved in the struggle for party supremacy is debatable. But it clearly did not serve his need and wish for recognition by the political community as Lenin's rightful successor, and it was painful to him as a person. For he was, as we have noted, a man whose revolutionary biography was all important to him.

44. Roy A. Medvedev, *Let History Judge: The Origins and Consequences of Stalinism* (New York, 1971), pp. 28–29.

45. *Ibid.*, p. 29.

Chapter Ten

SOCIALISM IN ONE
COUNTRY

Lenin's Guidelines

NOT LEAST among the sources of intra-party conflict after Lenin died were real differences over the direction of the regime's policy. The NEP was accepted as the framework within which socialism would be built in Soviet Russia, but fundamental disagreements emerged over the question of how the development should take place.

A major modification of the classical Marxist scheme of history was implicit in the very notion of "building socialism." Marx and Engels had expected the proletarian revolution to occur in societies already industrialized and urbanized under capitalism and hence ready for very rapid reconstruction along radically new lines. They therefore envisaged society on the morrow of the great workers' revolt as already in the "first phase" of communism, which in the later development of the Marxist movement became known as "socialism." In this transitional first phase, which Marx appears to have viewed as a matter of months or years rather than decades, people would be remunerated according to their work and society would be governed by a revolutionary dictatorship of the proletariat. In the ensuing "higher phase" of communist society, which became known among Marxists as "communism" or "full communism," the modern productive powers that had been developed but fettered by capitalism would be completely liberated, material plenty would be achieved, people would be remunerated according to need, and government in the old repressive sense would cease to exist.[1]

Such was classical Marxism's prospectus for the post-revolutionary future. Leninist Marxism's innovation was to interpose—for a backward country like Russia—a whole historical epoch between the proletarian revolution and the advent of socialism. To Lenin, Russia on the morrow of the taking of power was Soviet but not yet socialist. It had undergone a political revolution that placed the state in the hands of the working class led by a party of Marxist socialists, but the country's way of life had not yet become socialist, or had done so only in part. Nationalization of the land, resources, and main means of production did not make Russia socialist, notwithstanding the use of the phrase "War Communism" as a label for the initial period of Bolshevik rule. For "socialism" meant more than collective ownership of the means of production. It signified an economically and culturally advanced society with machine technology and an educated populace imbued with socialist consciousness, participating actively in the management of public affairs and engaging voluntarily in cooperative forms of work. To make NEP Russia socialist, it would therefore be necessary to carry out a thoroughgoing renovation of the society, overcoming its age-old legacy of backwardness, poverty, illiteracy, religiosity, bureaucracy, sloth, and corruption. The socialist revolution was thus projected beyond the capture of power as a long-range developmental process, and the Bolshevik party claimed legitimacy for its power monopoly on the ground that it alone knew how to supervise the many-sided work of constructing a socialist society. The development of Marxist thought along these lines was one of Lenin's contributions to communism as an ideology and culture.

He and his colleagues were understandably preoccupied with economic aspects of the developmental process, industrialization in particular. Even before taking power, Lenin had posed the question

1. Karl Marx, "Critique of the Gotha Program," in *The Marx-Engels Reader,* ed. Robert C. Tucker (New York, 1972), pp. 386–388, 395.

of "either perishing or else overtaking the advanced countries and outstripping them *economically* as well." [2] In the aftermath he became so enthusiastic about electricity as a key to Russia's economic advance that he advanced the formula: "Communism equals the Soviet regime plus the electrification of the whole country." Unlike pre-revolutionary Russia and the still poor, backward, and agrarian NEP Russia, the future socialist Russia would be an urbanized land of relative plenty, with a modern machine industry resting especially upon electric-power development under the ten-year GOELRO (State Commission for the Electrification of Russia) plan that was worked out under Lenin's inspiration. The task, as Lenin put it in "Better Less, But Better," his last article, was "to change horses, to change from the peasant, *muzhik* horse of poverty, from the horse of economy fit for a ruined peasant country, to the horse which the proletariat is seeking and cannot but seek—the horse of large-scale machine industry, of electrification, of Volkhovstroi, etc." [3]

The internal developmental process was always connected in Lenin's mind with external events, in particular with the prospects of assistance resulting from worker revolutions in other countries. "The complete victory of socialist revolution is unthinkable in one country," he said on November 8, 1918. "It requires the most active *cooperation* of at least several advanced countries, *among which we cannot classify Russia.*" [4] At the Tenth Congress, he stated that in a country such as Russia, with a minority of industrial workers and a huge majority of small farmers, a socialist revolution could have final success only on two conditions: support for it in good time by socialist revolution in one or several advanced countries, and agreement between the proletariat and the majority of the peasant population. Such was the generally accepted Bolshevik view. And it continued to be accepted despite developments abroad —culminating in the Communist failure in Germany in the autumn of 1923—which dimmed the Bolshevik belief in the imminence of socialist revolutions in Europe. So Stalin was merely restating the orthodox Leninist position when he wrote in *The Foundations of Leninism:* "To overthrow the bourgeoisie the efforts of one country are sufficient; this is proved by the history of our revolution. For the final victory of socialism, for the organization of socialist production, the efforts of one country, particularly of a peasant country like Russia, are insufficient; for that, the efforts of the proletarians of several advanced countries are required." [5]

The linkage of the successful completion of Russia's socialist transformation with external revolutionary developments was a constant of Lenin's thinking. But the "building of socialism" doctrine underwent certain changes in his final period. The Lenin of 1921–23 placed stronger emphasis upon gradualness in constructing a socialist Russia. In an article of November 1921 (in which he made his famous forecast that gold would be used for building public lavatories in major world cities after the victory of the revolution on a world scale), Lenin contrasted the War Communism period's "revolutionary approach" to economic development with the slow, cautious "reformist approach" that was correctly being adopted under the NEP, and defined the development of internal trade as the key link in the chain of events for the Bolsheviks to grasp now. [6] In this final period, moreover, Lenin found a cardinal formula for socialist construction in what he called the "cooperating of Russia," the enlistment of the population in cooperatives. He wrote that early socialists like Robert Owen were not wrong in their fantasies of socialism as a society of cooperatives; their error lay in the failure to see that class struggle and a political revolution were the essential prerequisites of realizing the cooperative dream. Now the party must shift the center of gravity from revolution and political struggle to peaceful organizing and cultural work—in a word, to "cultural-

5. Robert H. McNeal, *Stalin's Works: An Annotated Bibliography* (Stanford, 1961), pp. 110–111. This passage was in the original version of *The Foundations of Leninism* as published in *Pravda* but has been deleted from the version reprinted in Stalin's works.

6. "On the Significance of Gold Now and After the Complete Victory of Socialism," in *Lenin,* XLIV, 222–223, 225.

izing" (*kul'turnichestvo*). Through the spread of enlightenment, combined with economic inducements, it must persuade the peasants and other strata to work in cooperatives. A whole historical epoch, comprising a decade or two at a minimum, would be needed, however, to effect such a "cultural revolution" in Russia and build socialism through the NEP.[7]

The Industrialization Debate

Such were Lenin's guidelines for party policy after his death. While taking account of them, his heirs inevitably had to define the situation for themselves in the light of changing conditions and pressures as well as their own differing policy preferences. Confronted with urgent practical problems centering in the need to industrialize without delay, the collective party leadership shifted the center of gravity more to economics than to "culturalizing." The party debate on how best to build socialism in Russia turned largely into a debate about industrialization, and opinion in leadership circles divided along Right-Left lines. Bukharin and Preobrazhensky, who had collaborated on a major theoretical manifesto of the War Communism period, *The ABC of Communism,* now became the principal spokesmen of the opposing positions. Both claimed fidelity to Leninism in their policy prescriptions. Each had a basis for doing so, yet each deviated from the Leninist legacy in one or another way.

Bukharin took his departure from the Lenin of the final period who had stressed reformism, the crucial role of trade, the cooperating of Russia, and the cultural revolution. He advocated what he liked to call—ascribing the idea to Lenin—"agrarian-cooperative socialism," which was to be constructed very gradually through the NEP. Industrialization was to be achieved through the stimulation of trade by low or lowered prices for manufactured goods, on the theory that an expansion of effective demand would call forth increased peasant production for the market and, deriving from this,

7. "On Cooperation," in *Lenin,* XLV, 370–372, 376.

a growing surplus which the government could tax for purposes of industrial investment.[8]

Bukharin emphasized that the path to socialism would necessarily be "very long" in Russia's backward conditions, and that what would emerge in the absence of technical-economic aid from other countries could at best be a relatively "backward socialism." Nevertheless, the task of building socialism could be accomplished in Russia provided the party pursued a correct policy toward the peasantry. This would be a policy oriented primarily toward the middle peasant as, in Lenin's words, "the central figure of our agriculture." On the one hand, it would, by extending the NEP in the countryside, allow and encourage the industrious, relatively well-to-do middle peasant and even the kulak to prosper—to "get rich," as Bukharin on one occasion expressed it in a phrase that he later had to retract. It would use market relations as a means of ultimately overcoming market relations. On the other hand, the workers' state would compete with the rural bourgeoisie by all peaceful means of persuasion for the future of the mass of the peasantry. Through material incentives it would induce the middle peasant to join diverse kinds of cooperative organizations—sales, purchase, and credit cooperatives in particular. The system of peasant cooperatives would, little by little, "grow into" the system of state economic agencies. The hundred-million-strong peasantry and its twenty-two million farmsteads would be drawn into socialist construction along the highroad of rural cooperatives. To achieve all this would not be easy for a country just emerging from terrible poverty, dirt, darkness, barbarism, and inertia, but it could be done.[9]

As early as February 1924, Bukharin injected into a discussion

8. Bukharin's economic views are discussed in Alexander Erlich, *The Soviet Industrialization Debate 1924–1928* (Cambridge, Mass., 1967), ch. I and *passim*, as well as in Stephen F. Cohen, *Bukharin and the Bolshevik Revolution* (New York, 1973).

9. This argument is summarized from Bukharin's tract of 1925, "The Path to Socialism and the Worker-Peasant Alliance." See Bukharin, *Put' k sotsializmu v Rossii*, ed. Sidney Heitman (New York, 1967), pp. 271, 279, 288, 290, 315–316. The phrase "get rich," directed to the peasantry, was used by Bukharin in a speech of June 1925. On this episode, see Erlich, *The Soviet Industrialization Debate,* p. 16.

of the building of socialism a parenthetical observation that he was talking about "one country in isolation." [10] Contrary to the orthodox Bolshevik assumption, he was detaching the program of socialist construction at home from prospects for further revolutionary developments abroad. True, he did not accentuate the "one country" theme at this time. But he and close associates in the moderate group, like Rykov and Leonid Krasin, were well aware of its significance. They had become convinced that a Soviet Russia engaged in the slow fostering of an agrarian-cooperative socialism—an effort that could succeed only with external peace and perhaps some economic assistance from non-Communist countries—must abandon reliance upon international Communist revolution as a serious element and concern of its national policy. The refusal of Trotsky and his associates on the party Left to do this was a major source of their political hostility toward Trotsky and willingness to make common cause with Stalin against him. As they saw it, the abandonment of the world revolutionary perspective flowed logically from the grand strategic switch of 1921 from War Communism to the NEP, a switch that had been necessitated by the absence of the further revolutions on which Lenin had heavily banked in 1917. Lenin himself, they felt, was moving in their direction toward the end of his life. As one of them, Abel Yenukidze, put it in private to a sympathetic American journalist, once the world revolution failed to materialize "it was up to us to uncook the *kasha*." [11]

Apart from being disinclined to abandon hope in the further progress of international Communist revolution, the Left opposition was uninspired by the later Lenin's counsel of gradualism and his vision of a Russia of cooperatives at the end of a very long cultural revolution. Its program, as Preobrazhensky formulated it in late 1924, found the key to both the industrializing of Russia and the building of socialism in "accumulation." The state must accumulate resources for the accelerated growth of the socialist (state-owned) economic sector, which was also predominantly the industrialized

10. "Lenin as a Marxist," in Bukharin, *Put' k sotsializmu*, p. 238.
11. William Reswick, *I Dreamt Revolution* (Chicago, 1952), pp. 119, 165, 254. Yenukidze was secretary of the Central Executive Committee of Soviets.

sector, at the expense of the predominantly agrarian private sector. Preobrazhensky reasoned that the Soviet state's position in this regard was analogous in a certain sense to that of the entrepreneurs at the dawn of the modern age who had set in motion the mechanism of capitalist economy by such accumulative processes as colonial plunder and the dispossession of peasants through land enclosure—processes that Marx treated in *Capital* under the heading of "primitive capitalist accumulation." Soviet industrialization would proceed through "primitive socialist accumulation," by which Preobrazhensky meant, mainly, the use of fiscal measures (taxation, prices, etc.) to tap resources from the private sector for investment in the growth of state-owned industry. The economic relations of the two sectors would thus be based on "non-equivalent exchange." Preobrazhensky formulated it as the "fundamental law" of primitive socialist accumulation that:

The more backward economically, petty-bourgeois, peasant a particular country is which has gone over to the socialist organization of production, and the smaller the inheritance received by the socialist accumulation fund of the proletariat of this country when the social revolution takes place, by so much the more, in proportion, will socialist accumulation be obliged to rely on alienating part of the surplus product of pre-socialist forms of economy and the smaller will be the relative weight of accumulation on its own production basis, that is, the less will it be nourished by the surplus product of workers in socialist industry.[12]

On December 12, 1924, Bukharin published in *Pravda* a blistering polemical reply to Preobrazhensky entitled "A New Revelation on the Soviet Economy, or How to Wreck the Worker-Peasant Bloc." It denounced Preobrazhensky's "law" as an inadmissible approach to the building of socialism in Russia. The very idea of projecting "primitive socialist accumulation" on the analogy

12. E. Preobrazhensky, *The New Economics* (Oxford, 1965), p. 124. The essay, entitled "The Fundamental Law of Socialist Accumulation," was originally published as an article in *Vestnik kommunisticheskoi akademii* (Herald of the Communist Academy), and was republished in 1926 as a chapter in Preobrazhensky's book. For analysis of Preobrazhensky's economic views, see Erlich, *The Soviet Industrialization Debate*, ch. II, and Nicolas Spulber, *Soviet Strategy for Economic Growth* (Bloomington, Ind., 1964), ch. 2.

of the cruelly exploitative processes treated by Marx under the heading of primitive capitalist accumulation was "monstrous." To the plunder of the peasants in Marx's scheme corresponded their "exploitation" in Preobrazhensky's, and what Marx described as the catastrophically swift "devouring" of the old economic forms in the period of primitive accumulation was to be repeated. Here was a model of socialist industrialization in which the working class sits astride the small producers, like a plantation-owner in relation to a colonial object of exploitation. It would cast socialist industry in the role of a "metropolitan country," and the peasant economy as a set of "petty-bourgeois colonies." Such a policy reflected the Trotskyist view of the peasantry as an inevitable enemy and would, if put into practice, threaten to rupture or gravely undermine the axis of the Soviet system—the worker-peasant bloc. It fundamentally contradicted Lenin's agrarian-cooperative socialism, according to which the peasant must remain an *ally* of the working class, "albeit a grumbling one," throughout the whole period of transition to socialism. And it ignored the Leninist conception of the cooperatives as the prime means of leading the peasantry to socialism.

Responding to the onslaught, Preobrazhensky declared that the works of Lenin were not a Talmud, and Leninists should not be Talmudists. He also pointed out, however, that his conception of the mixed economy of the NEP as an arena of competitive struggle between socialist and capitalist sectors had a Leninist foundation. So it had. In a major speech of October 1921, for example, Lenin had characterized the Soviet situation under the NEP as a new, non-military form of war in which "the enemy among us is anarchic capitalism and anarchic product exchange." NEP Russia had a proletarian dictatorship and an internal bourgeoisie, and the great issue still to be decided was: "Who will beat whom [*Kto kogo*]? Which side will prevail?" [13] This reading of the situation was serving as Preobrazhensky's text. He dismissed Bukharin's proposal for maximum concessions to the peasant as a "vulgar conception of Lenin-

---

13. "The New Economic Policy and the Tasks of the Political Propagandists," in *Lenin*, XLIV, 163.

ism." More, it was "a Slavophile, nationally limited interpretation of Leninism" along the lines of the old peasant-oriented Russian populism, reflecting the pressure of the country's twenty-two million peasant households. Bukharin's price-reduction prescription could lead to economic trouble. The task was to take production rather than consumption as the starting-point. Lenin had taught that in politics, where situations are ever changing, one should always strive to seize the decisive link in the chain. At present, a time of industrial underproduction and rising retail prices, the decisive link was the struggle for a faster rate of industrialization, implying more rapid accumulation in industry.[14]

Besting Trotsky

Stalin made no particular contribution to the industrialization debate in its earlier phases. He echoed the Bukharinist position, albeit with certain oblique indications—to be mentioned further on—that he was not a Bukharinist at heart. But he did play a commanding part in the larger party controversy of the time by taking up "socialism in one country" as a political and ideological platform. This he did at the end of 1924, when he spoke out for the first time on building socialism in an isolated Soviet Russia.

Stalin's systematization of Lenin in *The Foundations of Leninism* had been both a contribution to the needs of the movement and a significant success for him on the road to the succession. Yet the success was incomplete. For he had still to come forward with a doctrine that was in some sense distinctively his own. To achieve the salience required by a new supreme leader, he had to espouse a position that would meet with widespread approval in the party and at the same time be associated in Bolshevik minds with him personally. What made it possible for him to do so, notwithstanding Bukharin's authorship of the concept of socialism in one country, was the fact that Bukharin did not at first stress the "one country" aspect. This was the very thing that Stalin championed. While Bu-

14. Preobrazhensky, *The New Economics*, pp. 230–231, 235, 253, 303–304.

kharin concentrated upon "socialism," especially in economic terms, Stalin seized upon the "one country" theme and went forth with it to do battle with Trotsky over the grand ideological issues of party policy. In the process he did great service to his own cause in the struggle for party supremacy.

Opportune as this course was, there is no reason to think that Stalin chose it in the spirit of a political technician who opts for an issue just because it is available and potent. It was a case, rather, of the confluence of expediency and political belief. Whatever reservations he harbored concerning Bukharin's agrarian-cooperative socialism and willingness to build it (as Bukharin said on one occasion) at a tortoise pace, Stalin was so constituted as a political personality that he could not help responding enthusiastically to the "one country" idea. It appealed to the strong streak of "Russian Red patriotism" that we have seen in him. It was in full accord with the position he had taken when he declared in August 1917: "The possibility is not excluded that Russia will be the country that blazes the trail to socialism. . . . It is necessary to give up the outworn notion that Europe alone can show us the way. There is a dogmatic Marxism and a creative Marxism. I take my stand on the latter." What the "one country" idea meant to Stalin, as became quite clear from his many speeches of the middle twenties, was that Russia, which had shown the world the way to proletarian revolution, would now be able, with or *without* help from outside, at the cost of great exertions, to accomplish the second historic feat of constructing a full socialist society.

Since it was by now axiomatic in the party that an idea had to be Leninist in order to be right, Stalin made no claim to originality when he espoused the view that it was possible to construct a full socialist society in an isolated Soviet Russia. On the contrary, he insistently called it "Lenin's theory of the victory of socialism in one country," and expressly denied any originality of his own in the matter.[15] Much of his polemical ammunition at the time con-

15. For Stalin's denial of originality, see his speech of December 7, 1926, "Once More on the Social Democratic Deviation in Our Party" (*Stalin,* IX, 29 ff.). His first public espousal of "socialism in one country" came in his article "The

sisted of quotations from Lenin which supported, or seemed to support, the position that he himself was now defending. Thus, in his article of 1915 on "The United States of Europe Slogan" Lenin had formulated the law of unequal economic and political development under capitalism and derived from it the conclusion that "the victory of socialism is possible first in several countries or even in one capitalist country, taken singly." At the conclusion of his final public speech, delivered in November 1922 before the Moscow Soviet, he had predicted that "out of NEP Russia will come socialist Russia." And in "On Cooperation," he had written that state control of the large-scale means of production and the class alliance between the proletariat and the many millions of small and poor peasants gave Russia "all that is necessary for the purpose of building a complete socialist society." Citing these passages again and again in his speeches and writings of 1925–26, Stalin maintained that "it was Lenin, and no one else, who discovered the truth that the victory of socialism in one country is possible." [16]

When Stalin at the end of 1924 began preaching the view that it was possible to complete the building of socialism in Russia by the efforts of its people alone, he had to disavow his own earlier formulation, which was deleted from subsequent editions of *The Foundations of Leninism*.[17] But in correcting himself, he did not acknowledge that he was changing the Bolshevik ideology. Instead, he repudiated his earlier formulation (that complete victory of socialism called for the efforts of the proletarians of several countries) on the ground that it was not an adequate statement of Lenin's real position, and he casuistically re-interpreted the latter in such a way that what Lenin had said about "complete victory" was reconciled with the doctrine of socialism in one country. What "complete victory" really meant in Leninist thinking, it now transpired, was not the complete building of socialism in the USSR; it was the *safety* of Soviet social-

October Revolution and the Tactics of the Russian Communists," which was written in December 1924 and first appeared as the preface to his collection *On the Road to October*.

16. *Stalin*, VIII, 304.

17. For the disavowal, see *Stalin*, VIII, 61–62.

ism from external danger, from military intervention by the hostile capitalist encirclement. The Soviet people could create a socialist society entirely by their own efforts, with no more help from the foreign proletariat than it was already receiving in the form of moral support and the readiness of foreign workers to come to its aid in case of need. But no amount of constructive effort by the Soviet people could provide a "complete guarantee against the restoration of the old order." For that, the proletariat must be victorious "at least in several other countries." [18] Only in the further progress of world revolution lay final security—and in that sense final victory—for the Soviet Revolution. On this point Stalin laid heavy emphasis. His version of the theory of socialism in one country in no way abandoned the postulate that the Communist revolution would, in time, spread beyond Soviet borders, and would eventually become worldwide. The innovation lay in asserting the autonomy of the Russian national revolutionary process, in making the construction of a socialist society at home independent of the international revolution.

Armed with the new distinction between "complete building" and "complete victory," Stalin opened a frontal ideological attack upon Trotsky. The strategy of attack was to draw a fundamental contrast between "Leninism," now identified with belief in the possibility of socialism's victory in one country, and "Trotskyism." Stalin depicted "Trotskyism" as a semi-Menshevik, anti-Leninist tendency associated particularly with the theory of "permanent revolution" that Trotsky presented in his book *Results and Prospects,* written in 1904–6. Trotsky had seen in the Revolution of 1905 an opportunity for a workers' government to come to power and initiate a socialist transformation of Russia. Should the European proletariat be inspired to successful revolution by the Russian example, he had reasoned, the temporary rule of the Russian workers might be converted into a lasting socialist dictatorship. Left to its own resources, however, the Russian working class would "inevitably be crushed by the counter-revolution the moment the peasantry turns

18. *Ibid.,* pp. 262–263.

its back on it." [19] This revolutionary strategy was not basically different from the one that Lenin then expounded under the title of "uninterrupted revolution," save that Lenin envisaged the revolutionary Russian government as a "democratic dictatorship of the proletariat and peasantry." Lenin, however, allotted at least a subordinate revolutionary role to the peasant, and saw the government as addressing itself to the tasks of the bourgeois democratic revolution rather than proceeding at once to socialist revolutionary measures. But given the great importance that the Russian Marxists attached to the niceties of ideological formulation, these differences were inevitably controversial. In an article of 1915, for example, Lenin ironically spoke of "permanent revolution" as Trotsky's "original theory," and described it as taking from the Bolsheviks their appeal to the workers to conquer power and from the Mensheviks their denial of the role of the peasantry.[20]

Raking over the coals of this old controversy, Stalin now made it out to be the forerunner of a burning issue of the present—whither the Revolution in Russia? In doing so he took advantage of the fact that in 1922 Trotsky had summarized the theory of permanent revolution in the preface to his book *The Year 1905*, concluding the summary with the words: "The contradictions in the position of a workers' government in a backward country with an overwhelmingly peasant population could be solved only on an international scale, in the arena of the world proletarian revolution." These words were written in the context of an intellectual autobiography, but Stalin treated them as a contribution to contemporary political debate. He cited them as proof of Trotsky's continuing underestimation of the potentialities of the peasant, his alleged opposition to Lenin's notion of an *alliance* between workers and laboring peasants as the basis of the proletarian dictatorship. And what if the world revolution was fated to come with some delay? Trotsky offered no ray of hope; he left the Russian Revolution no prospect but "to

19. L. Trotsky, *Permanent Revolution and Results and Prospects* (London, 1962), p. 247.
20. *Lenin*, XXVII, 80.

vegetate in its own contradictions and rot away while waiting for the world revolution." No wonder, then, that Trotsky had lately been talking about a possible "degeneration" of the party and prophesying doom. The theory of permanent revolution was a doctrine of " 'permanent' hopelessness." "Lack of faith in the strength and capacities of our revolution, lack of faith in the strength and capacity of the Russian proletariat—that is what lies at the root of the theory of 'permanent revolution.' " [21]

Stalin's assault was formidable, but not because of anything Trotsky had said to justify it. Trotsky had not been preaching "permanent revolution" as a policy line that the Soviet regime should adopt at the present time. His recent references to it had been historical; he had maintained, in retrospective self-defense, that the Russian Revolution of 1917 confirmed the correctness of the general conception of revolutionary strategy set forth in his book *Results and Prospects* twelve years before. He was not, moreover, denying the possibility of progressing toward socialism in Russia in the absence of revolutions elsewhere in the near future. On the contrary, at about this time he began a pamphlet, *To Socialism or to Capitalism?*, by saying that "the splendid historical music of growing socialism" could be heard in the dry statistical columns of Gosplan's control figures for the Soviet economy in 1925–26. His answer to the title question was one of qualified hope. NEP Russia, he argued, was an arena of cooperation and conflict between socialist and capitalist tendencies, the latter represented chiefly in peasant agriculture. Given judicious use of fiscal and other devices comprised in the "system of socialist protectionism," the workers' state could keep the capitalist tendencies in check and foster the eventual victory of socialism through the growth of industry, the improvement of technology, and the expansion of foreign trade. The problem would be simpler to solve if one assumed an outbreak of proletarian revolution in Europe in the coming few years. For the joining of the economies of Soviet Russia and Soviet Europe would resolve the issue of comparative growth curves of socialist and capitalist production decisively in favor of socialism and against

21. *Stalin*, VI, 367–368, 377–378.

capitalism, which would still prevail in America. But even on the pessimistic alternative assumption that capitalism was fated to hold on in the surrounding world for several more decades, the socialist prospect would be dim only in the highly unlikely event of a new era of swift capitalist economic development comparable to 1871–1914.[22] Such was Trotsky's analysis in 1925. Politically speaking, it was neither a counsel of internal passivity in the coming period nor a call to foment revolutions abroad as the way of solving Soviet problems at home.

Much of this he pointed out in his own defense when he finally took the floor to reply to a new ideological broadside that Stalin delivered at the Fifteenth Party Conference in October 1926. He declared that the theory of permanent revolution had no relation to the present dispute and that he considered this question long ago consigned to the archives. He denied the charge of disbelief in the building of socialism, and cited his pamphlet of 1925 as proof that he considered it possible for the form of the proletarian state to be filled in with the economic content of socialism. He called for accelerated industrialization, particularly through higher taxation of the kulak, as a means of achieving this goal. But he stood his ground on the issue of whether Russia could build a complete socialist society entirely on her own, observing that not only he but also Lenin and even Stalin (in the first edition of *The Foundations of Leninism*) were on record as opposing that assumption. Russia, he went on, was still a very poor country. Only in 1930, according to present expectations, would its average per capita consumption of industrial goods reach the 1913 level, which was one of poverty, backwardness, and barbarism. Meanwhile, the countryside was swelling the surplus labor force by two millions annually, and industry was expected to absorb only 100,000 of the half-million or so coming each year to the towns. But socialism meant the end of contradictions between town and countryside, general prosperity, plenty, high culture. The accomplishments so far, although something

22. L. Trotsky, *K sotsializmu ili k kapitalizmu?* (*Analiz sovetskogo khoziaistva i tendentsii ego razvitiia*) (Moscow and Leningrad, 1925), pp. 1, 53–54, 59–61. Gosplan was the State Planning Commission.

to be proud of, represented only the first serious steps on the long bridge connecting capitalism with socialism. And this process could not realistically be conceived of as taking place in isolation from international affairs and the world economy. Imports alone showed that socialist construction in one country was internationally conditioned. To ask whether the country could build socialism in thirty or fifty years by its own resources and efforts, irrespective of world developments, was an incorrect way of posing the problem, for the world revolutionary proletariat had as much or more chance of winning power in ten, twenty, or thirty years than Russia had of building socialism.[23]

Zinoviev and Kamenev were by this time aligned with Trotsky in an opposition bloc. As early as the Fourteenth Congress, the previous year, Zinoviev had opposed the theory of "socialism in one country" on the ground that it breathed a spirit of "national narrow-mindedness." [24] Now he made his position more explicit. It was false to accuse the opposition of wanting to do away with the NEP and go back to War Communism. Only through the NEP could the party lead the country to socialism. But it was wrong to suppose, as Bukharin did in putting forward his notion about the "growing of the kulak into socialism," that the country could proceed to socialism through the NEP *smoothly,* i.e., practically without class struggle. Furthermore, the process should not be envisaged as a strictly internal affair: "The theory of international proletarian revolution, founded by Marx and Engels and developed by Lenin, remains our banner. The final victory of socialism in one country is impossible. The theory of final victory in one country is wrong. *We are building and will build socialism in the USSR with the aid of the world proletariat in alliance with the main mass of our peasantry.* We will win final victory because revolution in other countries is inevitable." [25]

23. XV konferentsiia vsesoiuznoi kommunisticheskoi partii /b/. 26 oktiabria–3 noiabria 1926 g. Stenograficheskii otchet (Moscow and Leningrad, 1927), pp. 514–517, 524–526, 530–531.

24. XIV s"ezd vsesoiuznoi kommunisticheskoi partii /b/. 18–31 dekabria 1925 g. Stenograficheskii otchet (Moscow, 1926), p. 430.

25. XV konferentsiia, pp. 564, 566.

The offensive to which the opposition leaders were replying was probably the greatest polemical performance of Stalin's political career. After reviewing the emergence of the opposition bloc and describing it—to the amusement of much of his audience—as "a combination of castrated forces," he defined the basic issue as follows: "Is the victory of socialism possible in our country, bearing in mind that it is so far the only country of the dictatorship of the proletariat, that the proletarian revolution has not yet been victorious in other countries, and that the tempo of the world revolution has slowed down?" Starting his argument with an unusual excursus into the history of Marxist thought, Stalin stated that Engels had erred when he wrote in the first draft of the *Communist Manifesto* in 1847 that the communist revolution could not take place in one country alone. Although he gave the credit for discovering Engels' error to Lenin, whose greatness lay in the fact that "he was never a slave to the letter of Marxism," it is notable (as Kamenev pointed out) that Lenin himself had never taken issue with Engels on this point. Then, marshaling his quotations once again, Stalin contended that Lenin and Leninism gave an affirmative answer to the question about the possibility of socialism's victory in one country. On the other hand, Trotskyism—a Social Democratic deviation in the party—"denies the possibility of the victory of socialism in our country through the internal forces of our Revolution."

Stalin hammered mercilessly upon the opposition's "disbelief" in the internal forces of the Revolution, and accused it on this ground of weakening the proletariat's will to build socialism and thereby of "fostering a spirit of capitulation." Citing Trotsky's words on "the splendid historical music of growing socialism," he dismissed them as a "musical evasion" of the real question: "We can, Trotsky says, move towards socialism. But can we *arrive* at socialism—that is the question. To move towards socialism knowing that you cannot arrive there—is that not folly?" Again and again Stalin returned to the psychological theme that there must be a clear conception of the goal and confidence in the possibility of attaining it: "We cannot build without prospects, without the certainty that having begun to build a socialist economy we can complete it. . . . Further, if the prospects of our constructive work are not clear, if there is no certainty that the building of socialism can be completed, the working masses cannot *consciously* participate in this constructive work, and cannot *consciously* lead the peasantry. If there is no certainty that the building of socialism can be completed, there can be no will to build socialism. Who wants to build knowing that he cannot complete what he is building?" Giving the psychological argument a paradoxical anti-Trotsky twist, Stalin declared that any weakening of the Russian proletariat's will to build socialism was bad for world revolution, since it would strengthen capitalist tendencies in the Soviet economy and hence extinguish the foreign workers' hope for the victory of socialism in Russia—which in turn would delay the outbreak of revolutions in other countries. For had not Lenin written after 1917: "At the present time we are exercising our main influence on the international revolution by our economic policy. All eyes are turned on the Soviet Russian republic. . . . If we solve this problem, we shall have won on an international scale *surely and finally*. That is why questions of economic construction assume absolutely exceptional significance for us. On this front we must win victory by slow, gradual—it cannot be fast—but steady progress upward and forward." [26]

Stalin's style of argument was ungraceful, his language at times was crude, and some of his points were highly forced. He could not match the sophisticated economic reasoning of Trotsky, and on any objective judgment he lost the battle of Lenin quotations. Yet he appears to have scored a political triumph at the Fifteenth Conference, and the key to it lay in his message of sturdy confidence in "the internal forces of our Revolution." He was speaking before an assembly in which half of the 194 voting delegates and well over a third of the 640 delegates with advisory vote were people with no pre-1917 party past. A great many of these men of the new party generation (only 30 out of the 834 delegates were women), as well

26. *Ibid.*, pp. 428, 433–456.

as a good proportion of the former "undergrounders," were receptive to Stalin's theme. For what he said about the need of the "proletariat" for a clear conception of the goal and faith in the possibility of its attainment was especially true of the leadership—as he must have known. Stalin's theme undoubtedly appealed to their sense of the need for "prospects," their will to revolutionary accomplishment on the vast arena of Russian economy and society regardless of what happened abroad.

Stalin was giving this outlook ideological legitimacy by invoking the main authority symbols—Lenin and Leninism—on its behalf. At the same time, he was careful to legitimize the practice of ideological innovation—for example, by explicitly revising Engels' 1847 formula on the simultaneity of Communist revolution in all major countries—and in this way he assumed Lenin's old role of giving Bolshevism ideological direction. Indeed, he subtly invited comparison of himself with Lenin by noting, in self-justification, that Lenin, in *The State and Revolution,* had revised Marx's opinion that the workers of America and Britain could attain their revolutionary goal by peaceful means. And in replying to the discussion on his conference report, he effectively argued for a creative approach in ideology. Rebutting Zinoviev's critical comments on his attempted revision of Engels, he enumerated the measures that Engels had envisaged a revolutionary government taking on the morrow of coming to power, contended that nine-tenths of them had now been carried out in Soviet Russia, and then evoked laughter with the barbed remark: "It may very well be that we were guilty of a certain 'national narrow-mindedness' in putting through these measures." If Engels were now living, Stalin went on, he would not cling to his old formula but would say: "To hell with all the old formulas, long live the victorious Revolution in the USSR!" Whatever Engels would have said, this was clearly Stalin's message. In effect, he was declaring the national independence of Russian Communism, its ability to carry through the post-revolutionary social transformation to a finish regardless of delay in the further progress of world Communist revolution.

The receptivity of the conference audience to this message

made the opposition's position politically hopeless from the outset, no matter how capably it might be argued. However unsubstantiated many of Stalin's accusations against the opposition leaders were, he could make an effective case against them because, in the final analysis, they were unwilling to give up the postulate that the future of the Soviet Revolution was, as Trotsky put it, "internationally conditioned." The inherent plausibility of the postulate and the fact that it was demonstrably Leninist could not save its defenders from defeat at a time when the party was getting ready to move on, when large and growing forces in it were prepared or even eager to adopt the new, post-Leninist orientation that Stalin, Bukharin, Rykov, and others were championing under the name of "Leninism." Stalin realized this and pressed his advantage relentlessly. The decisive issue, as he summed it up again in his reply to the discussion, was that "the party regards our Revolution as a socialist revolution, as a revolution that represents a certain independent power, capable of doing battle against the capitalist world, whereas the opposition regards our Revolution as a free bonus on the future, still unvictorious revolution in the West, as an appendage to the future revolution in the West, as something without any independent power." Further: "Whereas Lenin appraises the proletarian dictatorship as a force with the greatest initiative, which after organizing a socialist economy must then give direct support to the world proletariat and do battle with the capitalist world, the opposition on the contrary looks on the proletarian dictatorship in our country as a passive force, living in fear of immediate loss of power 'in the face of conservative Europe.' " [27] The symbolism here recalls that with which Stalin opened the attack on the opposition in the main report. He had called the opposition leaders "a combination of castrated forces," explaining that to be castrated means to be "deprived of power." Now he was saying that the political eunuchs had a view of the Revolution which deprived *it* of its own internal, independent power and condemned it to a passive role in international relations. This was a frank appeal to the pride of po-

27. *Ibid.*, p. 751.

litical virility in the rising Soviet ruling class, its will to believe in
the potency and world mission of the Russian Revolution.

Stalin was unquestionably making conscious use of this appeal as a vehicle of his drive for the succession. But as one of those
for whom the world of Russian revolution had always been the great
revolutionary arena, he was also giving expression to an outlook
that he himself shared. He was personally predisposed to become
the mouthpiece of a Russian great-power Communism that would
concentrate attention and effort upon internal developmental tasks
without renouncing international Communist revolution as a later
prospect. For such was the political substance of the doctrine of
socialism in one country in his formulations.

The Bolshevik political milieu had by now grown decidedly
receptive to just such an outlook and policy. As a younger representative of the party elite of that time recalled in a memoir he
wrote much later, as an émigré:

Our general mood was one of healthy optimism. We were sure of ourselves and of the future. We believed that, provided no war came to interrupt the reconstruction of Russian industry, our Socialist country
would be able, within a few years, to offer the world an example of a
society based on principles of liberty and equality. How could it be
otherwise? The old capitalist Europe was moving from crisis to crisis,
while we were soon to present to the eyes of humanity the spectacle of
a steady rise of production and of worker and peasant masses living in
happy abundance under a planned economy. This conviction was shared
by almost all of us.[28]

Stalin, moreover, found politically cogent ways of presenting the
case. He cannily preached his Russia-oriented "creative Marxism" between the lines of a dogmatic Leninism. He pushed and
prodded his prominent opponents into taking positions that he knew
would be ill received by a great many in the party. And he effectively rationalized the Russia-first orientation in terms of the idea
that Soviet Russia could best contribute to eventual world revolu-

28. Alexander Barmine, *One Who Survived: The Life Story of a Russian under the Soviets* (New York, 1945), p. 161.

tion by developing itself into a socialist society, since its successes in socialist construction would foster the revolutionizing of foreign workers.

A Russian Thermidor?

Toward the close of his autobiography, written in 1929, Trotsky addressed himself to a question that he said many had put to him: "How could you lose power?" He sketched in reply the Thermidor theory that had been taking shape in his mind since about 1923. What had been happening in the USSR in the twenties was, he suggested, comparable to the conservative takeover in revolutionary France following the overthrow of Robespierre on the ninth of Thermidor. The difference was that France's Thermidor had broken out in a single blow whereas Russia's was a slow process of political backsliding. As October receded into the past and the international revolutionary prospects grew dim, the bureaucratic ruling stratum of Bolshevism yielded more and more to a "new psychology" compounded of moral relaxation, complacency, desire for easy living, and outright philistinism. The baiting of the theory of permanent revolution grew from just such psychological sources, said Trotsky, and an austere revolutionary personality like himself came to appear increasingly alien in these circumstances.

As for Stalin, he was significant simply as a symptomatic figure, an instrument of the Thermidorian process: "For the thing that matters is not Stalin, but the forces that he expresses without even realizing it." In this connection, Trotsky related a conversation he had in 1925 with his former deputy in the war commissariat, Sklyansky. "What is Stalin?" Sklyansky had asked, and after a minute's reflection Trotsky had replied: "Stalin is the outstanding mediocrity in the party." Now he added: "In that conversation, I realized for the first time with absolute clarity the problem of the Thermidor." The essence of the Thermidor, he explained, was the upward thrust of self-satisfied mediocrity in all spheres of Soviet life. Hence Stalin, precisely as mediocrity, was the Thermidor's ideal leader. His political success was due to the very limitations that had always made him seem a man destined to play second and third fiddle: restricted political horizon, stubborn empiricism, lack of creative imagination, ignorance of foreign life and languages, and primitive theoretical equipment, as shown in *The Foundations of Leninism,* which was just a work of compilation and full of sophomoric errors at that.[29]

Elsewhere Trotsky recounts a further conversation of that time in which he told his friend Ivan Smirnov that Stalin was destined to become dictator of the Soviet Union. When Smirnov remonstrated, "But he is a mediocrity, a colorless nonentity," Trotsky demurred:

"Mediocrity, yes; nonentity, no," I answered him. "The dialectics of history have already hooked him and will raise him up. He is needed by all of them—by the tired radicals, by the bureaucrats, by the *nepmen,* the kulaks, the upstarts, the sneaks, by all the worms that are crawling out of the upturned soil of the manured revolution. He knows how to meet them on their own ground, he speaks their language and he knows how to lead them. He has the deserved reputation of an old revolutionist, which makes him invaluable to them as a blinder on the eyes of the country. . . . Of course, great developments in Europe, in Asia, and in our country may intervene and upset all the speculations. But if everything continues to go automatically as it is going now, Stalin will just as automatically become dictator." [30]

But even as dictator, Trotsky implied, Stalin would remain the instrument and representative of the Thermidorian bureaucracy that had elevated him to this position; it, rather than he, would be in power.

Trotsky's theory of the Soviet Thermidor, although not without elements of truth, was seriously flawed. As later events showed, it erred in its image of the Bolshevik ruling stratum as a soddenly conservative if not counter-revolutionary force. It is true, as noted earlier here, that the Old Bolsheviks were diminishing in numbers and influence in the twenties, that a new party generation was beginning to come to the fore, and that the spirit of Bolshevism was undergoing significant change. But the ruling bureaucracy, in which

29. L. Trotsky, *My Life* (New York, 1930), pp. 481, 502–506, 512–513.
30. Trotsky, *Stalin,* pp. 393–394. This conversation took place, according to Trotsky, in 1924.

many Old Bolsheviks were still represented in leading positions, was not accurately described as "Thermidorian." Its unresponsiveness to Trotsky's position was not rooted in counter-revolutionary inclinations. Nor was its receptivity to "socialism in one country" a sign of indifference to socialism as a universal goal. Undoubtedly, the Bolshevik movement had by this time entered upon the process of de-radicalization that takes place in most radical movements eventually.[31] But the process still had a long way to go before Bolshevism's revolutionary spirit would become only a memory, as it is today. Not without justification did Stalin, for example, still find it expedient in 1926 to speak to his party audience of the impetus that the USSR could give to world revolution by its success in building a socialist society.

If Trotsky's picture of the bureaucracy as a Thermidorian group was inaccurate, he was likewise mistaken in his view of Stalin as its mere instrument and personification, who owed his political success to his very mediocrity. There was nothing "automatic" about the process of Stalin's elevation during the twenties. It took an uncommonly gifted man to navigate the treacherous waters of Bolshevik politics with the skill that he showed in those years. Trotsky badly misread him as a dull, plodding empiricist without political imagination or range of mind. Although he did not display notable originality in the field of theory, his systematizing of Lenin was an achievement. More important, to have taken up the notion of socialism in one country as Stalin did and made it his platform was the act of a man with political insight and imagination, and he showed very impressive powers of mind and speech in the polemical campaigns that he conducted against such doughty controversialists as Trotsky, Zinoviev, and Kamenev. Granted that the theory of socialism in one country originated with Bukharin, it was Stalin who became its great popularizer and who managed to identify himself with it, and it with himself, in the very process of arguing its Leninist paternity. Furthermore, he elaborated this theory in a manner that was distinctively his own and not Bukharinist. It was

31. On the concept of de-radicalization, see Robert C. Tucker, *The Marxian Revolutionary Idea* (New York, 1969), ch. 6.

not by being mediocre that he won the fight for party primacy, but by being a master politician and by furnishing the Bolsheviks with leadership of a kind to which a great many responded.

It is hard to resist the thought that elements of unconscious rationalization were involved in Trotsky's theory of Thermidor and its associated conception of Stalin. At the time of its formulation, Trotsky was losing out to Stalin in the leadership contest. To succumb to a man whom he saw as a third-rater must have been intensely galling to this proud revolutionary, but less so if what he was succumbing to was a whole new social stratum of which Stalin was merely the representative figure and symptom. In Trotsky's view, nothing less than a tide of social history was responsible for his own defeat. What he failed to see was that Stalin had bested him in the political struggle.

Yet Stalin's success and Trotsky's failure have also a sociological explanation, to which the theory of Thermidor is at least a clue. Lenin, as we have seen, provided the Bolsheviks with charismatic— that is, messianic—leadership at various key points in party history, 1917 in particular. Paradoxically, however, a leader of messianic tendency was not what the movement required as a *successor* to Lenin. The Bolshevik political community felt no need of a savior-leader in the mid-twenties because it was not, basically, in a state of distress. Having achieved power in the largest country in the world, it was a ruling group with a stake in the stability and success of the new Soviet order. The dominant mood was one of cautious optimism about the domestic prospect, combined with fear of any international complications which might endanger the Soviet regime or interrupt internal development.

This was a situation that greatly favored Stalin's victory and Trotsky's defeat in the leadership contest. For Stalin, by virtue of both his seemingly plain and earthy personality and his sanguine platform of socialist construction in one country, offered the Bolsheviks non-charismatic leadership, although he continually invoked the sacred authority of Lenin in its support. Trotsky, on the other hand, wittingly or unwittingly stood before the party as a potential savior-leader. This was what seemed to follow from his belief that the Revolution was in danger owing to the impossibility of completing the construction of socialism in Russia without help from revolution abroad. A revolution in danger was implicitly a revolution needing salvation—hence also one needing leadership of truly Leninist revolutionary caliber. Such, for example, was the message that could easily be read between the lines of *The New Course*. Trotsky was therefore in the hapless position of appealing to a sense of political distress that was felt by no more than a small minority in the party, and of seeming to offer a brand of leadership that the dominant majority did not consider necessary or desirable in the existing circumstances.

Stalin, for his part, shrewdly pressed him deeper into this disadvantageous position by accusing him over and over again of alarmism over the fate of the Revolution. Here Stalin showed that sensitive appreciation of an opponent's sore spots which was one of his own greatest strengths in politics. Years earlier he had discerned a subtle messianic tendency in Trotsky. In a private letter of March 1921 to Lenin, in which he unfavorably compared Trotsky's plan of Russian economic revival with the GOELRO plan sponsored by Lenin, he scornfully referred to Trotsky as a "medieval artisan who imagines himself an Ibsen hero destined to 'save' Russia with an ancient saga." [32] And now, at a time when not many politically influential people in Russia saw the country or the system as being in need of salvation, Stalin kept reminding them that Trotsky did.

32. *Stalin*, V, 51.

Chapter Eleven

THE EMERGENCE OF
STALINISM

Stalin and Bukharinism

CONSIDERING THE super-industrialization policies that Stalin adopted at the end of the twenties, we may suspect that even earlier he had serious reservations concerning Bukharin's program of gradualism in socialist construction. But in the mid-twenties he also had compelling political reasons for keeping any such reservations to himself. He imperatively needed the political support of the Bukharin group in the fight against the Trotskyist and united oppositions. Further, Bukharin's program gave economic substance to the doctrine of socialism in one country. Finally, it would have been hard to press against Trotsky the standard charge of "underestimation of the peasant" without, as a correlative, supporting Bukharin's optimistic thesis that the mass of peasants, kulaks included, were amenable to "growing into socialism." So, albeit with occasional subtle lapses, Stalin in this period repeated Bukharinist views on the economics of socialism in one country.

In his report to the Fourteenth Congress, for example, he called for a policy of winning over the middle peasant (the officially recognized intermediate category between "kulak" and "poor peasant") and decried the tendency of some to go into a panic in the face of the "kulak danger." As between the deviation that treated the kulak danger as nonexistent and the opposite one that magnified this danger unduly, the party should concentrate its fire upon the latter. For an overestimation of the kulak danger pointed in practice to class struggle in the countryside, a revival of the "de-kulakization" practiced under War Communism. Commenting critically on this part of Stalin's report, Kamenev said that he had previously thought Stalin unsympathetic to Bukharin's position, "but now I see, comrades, that Comrade Stalin has been completely taken in by the incorrect political line of which Comrade Bukharin is the author and real representative." [1]

As the fight against the united opposition approached its climax in the ensuing months, Stalin made statements calculated to reinforce such an impression. In his treatise of January 1926, *Concerning Questions of Leninism,* he sketched a Bukharinist picture of the private peasant economy gradually being drawn into the channel of socialist development by the mass organization of the peasants into cooperatives for marketing, supply, credit, and ultimately production; and he held that the mass of peasants would take this path voluntarily because of the material incentives for doing so. Further, he took the opposition to task for its disbelief in "this new path of development of the peasantry," its panic in the face of the kulak, and its forgetfulness of the fact that "the middle peasant is the central figure in our agriculture." Criticizing the oppositionist view of the NEP as a restoration of capitalism and mainly a "retreat," he argued that the NEP had only *begun* as a retreat and that it should be seen as a complex, two-way process of development of capitalism on the one hand and socialism on the other, "a process in which the socialist elements are overcoming the capitalist elements." In support of this contention, Stalin pointed out that the cooperatives already had over ten million members. In other words, the retreat was over, and the advance towards socialism was already taking place in the circumstances of the NEP: "In actual fact, we have been on the offensive for several years now, and are attacking successfully, developing our industry, developing Soviet trade, and ousting private capital." [2]

1. *XIV s"ezd vsesoiuznoi kommunisticheskoi partii /b/. 18–31 dekabria 1925 g. Stenograficheskii otchet* (Moscow, 1926), pp. 47, 48, 254.
2. *Stalin,* VIII, 79–89.

Although Stalin began speaking at this time about the importance of the development of heavy industry in Soviet industrialization, he nevertheless emphatically associated himself with the Bukharinist attack upon Preobrazhensky. "There are people in the party who look upon the laboring mass of the peasantry as a foreign body, as an object of exploitation for industry, as something in the nature of a colony for our industry," he said in a speech of April 1926 in Leningrad. "These are dangerous people, comrades." The raising of peasant living standards, Stalin went on, was one of the prerequisites of the development of industry. Consequently, it was impossible to agree with those who urged that greater pressure be exerted on the peasantry through excessive increases of taxation and higher prices of manufactured goods. For that would undermine the worker-peasant alliance and thereby shake the foundations of the proletarian dictatorship.[3]

In his speech at the Fifteenth Conference, Stalin sharpened the attack by directly quoting Preobrazhensky on the law of primitive socialist accumulation, and saying: "I consider that, in likening peasant economy to a 'colony' and trying to make the relations between the proletariat and the peasantry take the form of relations of *exploitation*, Preobrazhensky, without himself realizing it, is undermining or trying to undermine all possibility of socialist industrialization." Preobrazhensky, Stalin argued further, was in effect recommending the "capitalist method of industrialization," under which the interests of industrialization are set against those of the laboring masses, the internal contradictions in the given country are aggravated, the great bulk of the workers and peasants are impoverished, and profits are used not for raising the people's living standards but for export of capital and extension of the base of capitalist exploitation at home and abroad. By contrast, the "socialist method of industrialization" is one that harmonizes the interests of industrialization and those of the laboring masses, brings not impoverishment but higher living standards to the vast masses, assuages and overcomes the internal contradictions of the country,

3. *Ibid.*, p. 142.

and steadily enlarges the home market and its absorptive capacity, thereby creating a solid domestic base for the development of industrialization. This socialist way of industrialization through "steady improvement" of the living standards of the masses, including the main mass of the peasantry, was the Soviet way.[4]

Such was Stalin's message to the ruling party. Its appeal was enhanced by a significant difference between his way of formulating it and Bukharin's. Whereas Bukharin warned that it would take a very long time to build socialism in Russia, that the movement would necessarily proceed at a tortoise pace, Stalin subtly encouraged a more optimistic view of the timetable. In his report to the Executive Committee of the Comintern in December 1926, he severely attacked Trotsky for suggesting that it might take some fifty or even a hundred years for an isolated socialist state like Russia to develop productive forces more powerful than those of capitalism. It had taken about two centuries for the feudal system of economy to show its superiority over the slave system, Stalin said, and about a hundred years or less for the bourgeois system to prove its superiority over feudal economy. Because technological progress had now greatly accelerated the pace of development and change, however, the socialist system of economy could advance with "giant strides" and out-perform capitalism in a much shorter period. Being a unified and concentrated economy, and one conducted on planned lines, the socialist system should show its superiority over the contradiction-ridden capitalist system in a comparatively short time. "In view of all this, is it not clear that to hold out here a perspective of fifty or a hundred years means to suffer from the superstitious faith of the scared petty bourgeois in the almighty power of the capitalist system of economy?"[5] This sanguine outlook on the prospects for socialist construction must have contributed much to Stalin's political success. Not only was he appealing to the urge prevalent in the party to concentrate attention and effort on the tasks of Soviet development, he was hinting that a fully socialist economy could be created in a comparatively short time.

4. *Ibid.*, pp. 286–289.
5. *Ibid.*, IX, 136–138.

Stalin's association with the moderates stood him in good stead during a critical phase of his drive for the succession. He took advantage of their political strength, of Bukharin's personal popularity in party circles, and of the appeal of his agrarian-cooperative socialism. But Stalin was not simply echoing Bukharin's position in his contributions to the debate over socialism in one country. The case he built was subtly his own. His distinction between "complete victory" and "complete guarantee," for example, tied the theory of socialism in one country to the postulate of a continuing international Communist revolution, and that was an un-Bukharinist thing to do. Stalin's fundamental theme, moreover, was the "internal forces" of the Revolution, the feasibility of creating a fully socialist Soviet Russia without assistance from further revolutions abroad. What Bukharin offered was something rather different: a vision of a particular *way* of creating socialism in Russia. Apart from the fact that this was not the way Stalin chose at the end of the twenties, there is reason to wonder whether he really accepted Bukharinism even when he appeared to do so during 1924–26. One piece of negative evidence is his above-noted optimism about the timetable of socialist construction. If one took seriously Bukharin's idea about the way of constructing a socialist society, then it was hardly possible to visualize it happening save at the tortoise pace of which he spoke. Not only was Stalin's hint of a rapid pace a decidedly un-Bukharinist note in his argumentation; it suggests that even then he was envisaging a different way of construction, *a revolutionary rather than evolutionary approach to the problem.*

We have some testimony from Stalin bearing upon this point. On November 7, 1925, the eighth anniversary of the Revolution, he published in *Pravda* an article entitled "October, Lenin, and Prospects of Our Development." It was constructed around the theme of a fundamental similarity between the period of preparation for the October rising and the present. Both represented "a turning-point in the development of our Revolution." Before October, the task had been to make the transition from bourgeois to proletarian power; now, it was to make the transition from the NEP economy to a socialist one. Before October, the external situation had been defined by the war between two European coalitions, and the internal by various signs of the revolutionizing of the masses in Russia. Now, correspondingly, the world was split into capitalist and socialist camps, and economic and social conditions inside Russia had improved sufficiently to make possible a forward push on the front of economic construction. In 1917, the party had vanquished bourgeois rule because of the Leninist hardness (*tverdost'*) with which it carried out the tasks of the proletariat in the face of incredible difficulties and vacillations in certain party quarters. Now, with the outcome still undecided, the party had every opportunity to vanquish the capitalist elements of the economy, provided that it managed to show the old Leninist hardness in the face of a mass of difficulties and possible vacillation in certain party quarters. Such Leninist hardness, Stalin declared, was in fact one of the most necessary conditions of victory in the building of socialism.

Evidently, he had conceptualized the Soviet present as an analogue of 1917. The building of socialism figured in his mind as a revolutionary undertaking comparable in historic meaning to the Bolsheviks' taking of power in October. He was ready to take a hard line, just as Lenin had been in 1917, in carrying through the internal revolutionary transformation. He was ready, too, to overcome the vacillations or resistance that would arise in certain party quarters, just as before, in the face of the necessity for Lenin-like bold and decisive action. Such were the implications of his anniversary article. If they were not widely perceived at the time (and there is no indication that they were), this may be because few if any other party minds were attuned to Stalin's sense of the historical present as an analogue of 1917, with a new October impending. The very idea of such a parallel must have seemed rather farfetched during that time of high NEP: why should the near historical future resemble the huge revolutionary upheaval brought on in Russia by the World War? So the party public does not seem to have attached much importance to his article or to have read it as the portent of things to come that it was.

A revolutionary approach to socialist construction, harking back to War Communism, with its forcible grain requisitions and civil war in the countryside, was what Bukharin most feared. His animus against the party Left, in whose policy prescriptions a revolutionary approach seemed implicit (though they themselves denied it), drew force from this fear. The fundamental impulse of his agrarian-cooperative socialism was the reformism, gradualism, and preservation of civil peace that Lenin had counseled in his last articles. The population, almost three-quarters of which still consisted of peasants, must be brought to socialism by the methods of persuasion inherent in the NEP, Bukharin insisted, rather than by War Communism's methods of coercion. This necessitated the evolutionary approach. The party's task, he said, was not to orient itself toward "some sort of a new third revolution" but to press forward by peaceful organizing work, carrying on the class struggle primarily in economic forms, not cutting itself off from the main mass of the peasantry. Although the internal class struggle might yet undergo periods of aggravation, on the whole "the class struggle in our country will diminish little by little until it dies out in communist society without any third revolution." [6]

The "no third revolution" theme was as antithetical to Stalin's socialist *Weltanschauung* as it had become central to Bukharin's. Stalin's whole mode of being in the world militated against the renunciation of the idea of a new revolutionary period. The perspective of an ever-diminishing internal class struggle as the right way to socialism was totally alien to his makeup. Fighting, struggle and conquest were what he lived for as a Marxist and a Leninist. Socialism had always meant to him a gospel of class war and it still did, whatever Lenin might have said toward the end about civil peace and reformism. Stalin's Lenin was the one who defined the task of building socialism in the doctrine of *kto kogo?*—who would beat whom in the internal class contest between the proletarian dictatorship and the Soviet bourgeoisie? Stalin frankly formulated the problem in those terms in his address of December 1926 to the

6. Bukharin, *Put' k sotsializmu v Rosii,* ed. Sidney Heitman (New York, 1967), pp. 322, 323. The references to a "third revolution" occur in a speech that he gave in Leningrad in 1926. From the fact that he elsewhere spoke of the Revolution of 1905 as Russia's first, we may surmise that he meant to include both the February and October phases of 1917 under the heading of the second.

Comintern Executive: "But what does building socialism mean if we translate this formula into concrete class language? Building socialism in the USSR means overcoming our Soviet bourgeoisie by our own forces in the course of a struggle." [7] At a deeper level, the "no third revolution" theme collided with Stalin's inner vision of himself and his destiny. How could he prove himself as a new revolutionary hero in succession to Lenin without facing and surmounting the challenge of a new heroic period comparable to 1917? Without a third revolution to carry off, there could be no second Lenin.

For these reasons and still others, Bukharin's insistent call to eradicate from party practice the surviving remnants of War Communism, its "methods of orders and command" in particular, found no favor with Stalin. His deep-seated predilection for issuing peremptory orders and commands has been amply noted in these pages. It was a characteristic, however, which he shared with many others in the party, especially those who, like himself, had occupied or risen to leading positions during the Civil War. The later Lenin was so concerned over this phenomenon that he gave it a special derogatory name, "Communist arrogance" (komchvanstvo), meaning that "a man belonging to the Communist party and not yet turned out of it imagines that he can solve all tasks by handing down Communist edicts." [8] But this element would not prove easy to dislodge from party office.

War Communism had given way to the NEP as a matter of general policy, but its imprint upon the thought and behavior of a great many party members had not been effaced. For Stalin, as for many others of his generation and those younger, the Civil War had been a formative influence. It showed in their style, their approach to people and problems, even their mode of dress. Their very Bolshevism had undergone a certain militarization. Four or five years of the NEP, though a time of great changes, had not remade these people and their political ethos. Many of them still felt a certain hankering for the Sturm und Drang of the earlier years of combat,

7. Stalin, IX, 21.
8. Lenin, XLIV, 173.

still fresh in their memories. Stalin himself drew attention to this fact, or to an implication of it, during one of the moments of his public identification with the Bukharinist position. He stated in his report to the Fourteenth Congress:

If you were to ask Communists which the party is better prepared for— to strip the kulak or, instead, to enter an alliance with the middle peasant—I think that ninety-nine out of a hundred would say that the party is best prepared for the slogan, "Beat the kulak." Just say the word and they will instantly strip the kulak. Not so easily assimilated is the idea of refraining from de-kulakization and pursuing a more complex policy of isolating the kulak through an alliance with the middle peasant.[9]

Even if Stalin was exaggerating the "beat the kulak" sentiment for purposes of argument, there is little doubt that it existed on a sizable scale in the party. What he understandably forebore to say was that he himself tended to share it.

The upshot of the discussion is that "socialism in one country" had more than one meaning as a political and ideological current in post-Lenin Bolshevism. Although the duality would not emerge with full clarity until late in the twenties, the doctrine signified in Stalin's mind something different from what it signified in Bukharin's. The Stalinist version pointedly upheld the postulate of international Communist revolution even as it placed its emphasis upon the one country's ability to achieve "complete victory" in building socialism by its own efforts. It took a much more optimistic view of the timetable. It breathed an expansive and even truculent spirit of "Russian Red patriotism" that was lacking in the Bukharinist version. Without repudiating the NEP, it drew inspiration from the War Communism heritage that Bukharin resolutely rejected. It found authoritative guidance in different Lenin texts. And contrary to Bukharin's evolutionary approach and perspective of an ever-diminishing internal class struggle, the Stalinist version

9. Stalin, VII, p. 334. See in this connection Alec Nove, An Economic History of the USSR (London, 1969), pp. 74–82. Nove writes: "Some felt that the days of 1918–20 were not only heroic and glorious days of struggle, leading to victory against heavy odds, but were also stages toward socialism or even the gateway to full communism" (p. 78).

tended toward a revolutionary mode of socialist construction, a perspective of class struggle, and "Leninist hardness."

The cleavage of orientations within the school of "socialism in one country" remained obscure during the mid-twenties. One reason may have been that Stalin was not as far along as Bukharin in working out the specifics of his position. But the exigencies of co-alition war against the Left opposition were the chief force that kept underlying differences from coming into the open sooner than they did. So long as this contest continued, Stalin and Bukharin were compelled to maintain a common front and keep their latent disagreements submerged. Moreover, the need to accentuate issues with the Left made it opportune for Bukharin to elaborate his evolutionary conception of socialist construction with emphatic clarity, whereas Stalin, whose emergent position had certain affini-ties with the thinking of the Left, was forced to keep these aspects of his thinking muted and even to parrot Bukharin's debating points in ways that made him appear at times an outright Bukharinist. The falseness of that impression became clear as soon as the crushing of the Left opposition removed the constraints imposed upon Stalin by the struggle against it.

The Fifteenth Party Congress

The expulsion of Trotsky, Zinoviev, and Kamenev from the Politburo in the latter part of 1926 foreshadowed the fall of the united opposition, which made a hopeless last stand in the Central Committee plenum of October 1927 and went down to defeat. Its platform, subsequently published abroad, was suppressed inside Russia. Its efforts to arouse worker support by clandestinely dis-tributing such materials as the text of Lenin's testament and by or-ganizing street demonstrations in Moscow and Leningrad on November 7, 1927, the tenth anniversary of the Revolution, were foiled by the authorities. One week after the latter episode, the Central Committee and the Central Control Commission issued a joint decree expelling Trotsky and Zinoviev from the party and submitting the question of the opposition to the impending Fifteenth

Party Congress. Meanwhile, a purge of opposition sympathizers went on quietly at lower levels of the party, and police measures were taken.

The congress opened in early December. Stalin, who delivered the main political report, declared in it that the opposition's theses had received the votes of only 4,000 out of 728,000 voting members in the pre-congress discussions held by party organizations around the country. Referring to the opposition's proposal to disband its factional organization and submit to the party majority's decisions, subject only to the right to continue defending its views within the limits of the party rules, he rejected it on the ground that there was no place in the party for privileged "nobles" as against "peasants devoid of these privileges," and "we do not want nobles in the party." [10] His no-compromise attitude prevailed. A resolution reported out by a special commission under the chairmanship of Ordzhonikidze pronounced adherence to the Trotskyist opposition incompatible with party membership and ordered the expulsion of seventy-five prominent oppositionists, including Kamenev and Piatakov. It was adopted by acclamation over the courageous but ineffectual protest of one of the seventy five, Smilga, who was allowed to read a dignified statement of principle on behalf of himself and three others who were being expelled—Radek, Rakovsky, and Nikolai Muralov. In the wake of this action by the congress, some thirty of the opposition leaders, headed by Trotsky, were exiled to remote parts of the country in early 1928, Trotsky's place of exile being Alma-Ata, near the Chinese border. Many others submitted public statements of political capitulation and sought readmission to the party. As a political force the Left opposition was crushed.

In the congress report Stalin listed seven basic political differences between "the party" and the opposition. The first, and the one to which he devoted by far the greatest space, was the opposition's alleged denial of the possibility of victoriously constructing socialism in the USSR. Whatever leftist phrases and revolutionary

10. *Piatnadtsatyi s"ezd VKP/b/. Dekabr' 1927 goda. Stenograficheskii otchet* (Moscow, 1961–62), I, 81, 89–90.

gesticulations the opposition might produce, Stalin said, such denial was tantamount to "capitulation" to capitalist elements in the country and to the international bourgeoisie. Significantly, Stalin returned to 1917 in elaborating upon the charge of capitulation. Zinoviev and Kamenev, he asserted in a long historical excursus, had declined to go into the October action, and Trotsky, who did go into it, had done so only "with a reservation." For in June 1917 he had re-issued his old pamphlet, *The Peace Program,* which argued that a revolutionary Russia could never hold out against a conservative Europe unless revolutions also broke out elsewhere. Lenin, on the contrary, had gone into the October insurrection "without reservations," contending that proletarian power in Russia itself would serve as a base for assisting the workers of other countries to get rid of their bourgeoisie.[11] Once again Stalin was revealing the association in his mind between the revolutionary situation of 1917 and the one that he felt was impending in the Russia of the present.

Breakneck industrialization, with priority for heavy industry, and forcible mass collectivization of the peasantry would be the twin hallmarks of the revolution from above that Stalin inaugurated in 1929. Here at the Fifteenth Congress, which sealed the Stalin-Bukharin coalition's victory over the Trotsky-Zinoviev coalition, he subtly signalized a new phase of the party struggle by adumbrating both themes. He stated, first, that the already-existing "elements of a goods famine" would unavoidably continue through "a number of coming years" owing to the needs of industrialization, in which industries producing means of production must develop more rapidly than light industry. In the next breath he misrepresented Trotskyist "super-industrialization" as a prescription for overcoming the goods famine by full-scale expansion of *light industry* at the expense of heavy-industry development—thereby clearing the way for his own later sponsorship of super-industrialization of a different kind. Then he went on to say that not enough was being done to restrict and isolate the kulak class by economic means, such as with-

11. *Ibid.,* pp. 82–84.

holding agricultural credit. Putting an end to the kulak by administrative measures, by the services of the GPU (the new name for the Cheka), was not the answer, Stalin added, although "this of course does not exclude the use of certain necessary administrative measures against the kulak." This cautious step toward espousal of an anti-Bukharinist policy of de-kulakization put teeth into Stalin's statement, made earlier in the congress report, that the way out for agriculture lay in "the changeover of the small and dispersed peasant holdings into large and amalgamated farms on the basis of social cultivation of the soil." During the final moments of the congress, as its resolution on farm policy was being voted, an amendment was hurriedly inserted saying: "At the present time, the task of transformation and amalgamation of small individual farms into large-scale collective farms must be set as the party's fundamental task in the countryside." [12] Thus was Stalin's call for collective farming incorporated into official policy, causing the Fifteenth Congress to be described in later party histories as the "congress of collectivization."

The Defeat of the Right Opposition

Now that changed political circumstances made it possible for Stalin to begin moving toward a showdown with the Bukharinists, new economic circumstances offered a basis for doing so. At the end of 1927 and in the early months of 1928 the Soviet regime was confronted with a critical shortage of grain procurements. Among the reasons for peasant withholding of grain from the market was an intensified goods famine brought on in part by fiscal policies espoused earlier under the influence of Bukharinist low-price philosophy.[13] In an effort to galvanize the lagging grain procurements campaign, the party leaders fanned out to the main grain-growing

12. *Ibid.*, I, 63, 66–67; II, 1419.
13. Roy A. Medvedev, *Let History Judge: The Origins and Consequences of Stalinism* (New York, 1971), pp. 75–77. For a full account of the procurements crisis of 1928 and its political repercussions, see Moshe Lewin, *Russian Peasants and Soviet Power: A Study of Collectivization* (Evanston, Ill., 1968), ch. 9.

regions. Stalin chose Siberia as his destination on what must have seemed—as his train pulled out of Moscow on January 15, 1928—a rerun of his grain-expediting mission of a decade ago to Tsaritsyn. He spent the next three weeks in the Siberian centers of Novosibirsk, Barnaul, Rubtsovsk, and Omsk conferring with local party and government officials and dictating the line they were to follow. Here at last he found an opportunity to practice the "Leninist hardness" that he had foreseen would be necessary in the revolutionary process of building Soviet socialism.

A digest of his remarks to the Siberian officials was first published in his collected works twenty-four years after. It reveals that whereas the local officials were responding to the situation in the NEP spirit, he responded in the spirit of War Communism. Informed that the kulaks were withholding their grain surplus in expectation of threefold higher prices, he directed the officials to demand surrender of the stocks at existing prices and, in the event of refusal, to confiscate them, distributing 25 per cent to poorer peasants at fixed low prices or on credit—a throwback to the "committees of the poor." Further, he ordered the officials to bring the recalcitrant to justice under Article 107 of the Criminal Code, prescribing stiff punishments for activities defined as "speculation." When they objected that this would be an "emergency measure" for which the judges and prosecutors were not prepared, Stalin said: "Let's allow that it will be an emergency measure. So what?" Emergency measures would give splendid results, he went on, and any court workers unprepared to apply them should be purged. As for the danger that the kulaks would react by sabotaging next year's grain deliveries, sabotage was an ever-present danger, and the solution lay in still further measures. Specifically, the organizing of collective and state farms (*kolkhozy* and *sovkhozy*). Soviet industry must be made independent of kulak caprice by setting up enough collective and state farms in the next three or four years to provide the state with at least a third of its grain requirement. As the mandate for such action Stalin invoked the provision on collectivization that had been inserted at the last minute into the Fifteenth Congress' resolution on farm policy, and concluded: "Our obligation is to carry out those instructions." [14]

Stalin's championship of the "Uralo-Siberian method of grain procurement," as he himself later called it, has rightly been described as a great turning-point in Russian history, since "it upset once and for all the delicate psychological balance upon which the relations between party and peasants rested. . . ." [15] Stalin's Siberian statements show that he was without illusions on this score. The prescribed harsh emergency measures, reminiscent of War Communism's forcible grain requisitions, would predictably stimulate greater peasant recalcitrance the next time around, which in turn would stimulate and justify more radical measures culminating in the mass collectivization campaign on which Stalin's sights were set; and so it went in reality in 1928–29. In taking this policy course, he was concerned not only to solve the grain procurements crisis in accordance with his revolutionary approach in socialist construction, but also to win the final round in the leadership contest. The strategy was to push and prod the party establishment into adopting a Stalinist hard line toward the peasantry and thereby to maneuver the Bukharin group into a disadvantageous oppositionist stance. Given success along the former line, he could also count on success along the latter because he knew, as he put it during the April 1929 Central Committee plenum, that "Bukharin flees from emergency measures as the devil from incense." [16]

The strategy succeeded, but not without a protracted struggle in the party, one of the bitterest battles of Stalin's career. In the course of it he had to backtrack more than once in the face of party hesitation about entering upon a trial of strength with the better-off strata of the peasantry, including the economically vital middle

14. *Stalin*, XI, 2–9.

15. Nove, *An Economic History*, p. 153. Nove adds that this is also the first time that a major policy departure was undertaken by Stalin personally without even the pretence of a Central Committee or Politburo decision. For Stalin's use of the term "Uralo-Siberian method of grain procurement" and his defense of the method, see his Central Committee plenum speech of April 1929 (*Stalin*, XII, 88, 90).

16. *Stalin*, XII, 61.

peasant as well as the kulak. Led by Bukharin, Rykov, and Tomsky, the moderates waged a determined fight behind the scenes, and as far as possible in the party press, to keep the pendulum of policy from moving to a Stalinist extreme. Having gone along with the "Uralo-Siberian methods" of procurement in early 1928, they sought to head off repeated resort to those methods and opposed de-kulakization. They advocated raising grain prices sufficiently to induce the peasants to part with their surpluses voluntarily. They fought for a balanced investment policy that would combat the goods famine by maintaining a modicum of development in light industry rather than concentrating nearly all available resources on heavy-industry expansion. Finally, they opposed early mass collectivization as a nostrum for the regime's economic woes. In rebuttal of Stalin's contention that the production collective, or *kolkhoz*, was chiefly what Lenin's "cooperating of Russia" called for, they continued to argue that purchase, credit, and marketing cooperatives were the highroad of socialist construction in the countryside. Not until a higher level of mechanization had been achieved in the country would collectivization be desirable. As Bukharin put it in unpublished memoranda of May and June 1928 to the Central Committee, "If all of salvation lies in *kolkhozy*, whence the money for mechanization? And is it really right to suppose that the *kolkhozy* must grow up in our country on poverty and dispersion?" [17]

Although Stalin was by this time clearly embarked upon an anti-Bukharinist course, and the Bukharinists were strenuously resisting it in intra-party councils, he stopped short of an open collision with them. Even in late November 1928, when he declared in a published speech before a Central Committee plenum that there existed a "Right deviation" in the party, he did not identify Bukharin, Rykov, and Tomsky as its leaders. His need to go slowly in bringing the conflict into the open was testimony to, among other

17. F. M. Vaganov, *Pravyi uklon v VKP(b) i ego razgrom (1928–1930 gg.)* (Moscow, 1970), pp. 63, 91–92, 105, 112, 115. For detailed accounts of the fight waged by Bukharin and his group in 1928–29, see Stephen F. Cohen, *Bukharin and the Bolshevik Revolution* (New York, 1973), and Robert V. Daniels, *The Conscience of the Revolution: Communist Opposition in Soviet Russia* (Cambridge, Mass., 1960), ch. 13.

things, the political strength of those whom he was now challenging. One of the sources of this strength was the continuing influence of Bukharinist thinking in some party quarters; another was organizational.

The Bukharinist group was less a cohesive faction like Stalin's and more a coalition of like-minded party elements. Still, it represented a serious force organizationally. It had profited in this respect from Stalin's very need to collaborate with it in the earlier fight against the Trotskyist and united oppositions. All three of its leading figures were numbered among the nine full members of the Politburo as reconstituted after the Fifteenth Congress. The Bukharinists were strong in the influential Moscow party organization, in part through the support of its secretary, N. A. Uglanov, who was a candidate member of the Politburo and held seats on the Secretariat and Orgburo. They had considerable influence in the Soviet governmental bureaucracy, over which Rykov presided as premier, and in Tomsky's trade union hierarchy. Another of their strong points was the USSR's first newspaper, *Pravda*. Bukharin was its editor-in-chief, and in 1928 its editorial board was still filled with his followers— Alexander Slepkov, Valentin Astrov, D. Maretsky, A Zaitsev, and Efim Tseitlin. Although it did not operate as a partisan Bukharinist organ, Bukharin's views could still count on outlet in its pages. He himself, as their leading expositor, was able to publish in *Pravda* such major statements of the Bukharinist position as "Leninism and the Problem of Cultural Revolution" and "Notes of an Economist" in 1928, and, on the fifth anniversary of Lenin's death in January 1929, his powerful address on "Lenin's Political Testament."

If the Bukharinists proved no match for the Stalinists in the party infighting of 1928–29, this was due in no small measure to the superior strength of the political machine that Stalin and his associates had built up in the party-state. But it would be an error to view the Bukharinists' defeat as a victory of naked organizational power on the part of the Stalin faction. As in the earlier phase of the leadership contest, the outcome also reflected the persuasiveness of Stalin's case and his crude effectiveness in the arena of intra-party controversy. The forum before which the debates took place was, at some points, the so-called enlarged plenum in which the Central Committee, currently numbering 121 members and candidates, joined forces with the 195-member Central Party Control Commission. Although well populated by now with persons whose career success was due in one or another degree to the Stalin organization, the Bolshevik ruling stratum was not a mere Stalinist claque like the Central Committee as constituted during later times of terror. Stalin was a figure of formidable power but not yet a tyrannical master. He had to do battle with his adversaries before a Central Committee whose members' votes in many instances could go either way depending upon the relative cogency of the contending programs and arguments.

Freed now from his earlier constraints, Stalin elaborated the Stalinist version of building socialism into a coherent ideological doctrine. Certain thoughts expressed before only by hint or indirection were made explicit and presented with the forcefulness of which he had shown himself capable in his controversies with Trotsky, Zinoviev, and Kamenev. In effect, he amalgamated his earlier Russocentric, great-power gospel of socialism in one country with the programmatic content of high-speed industrialization and collectivization; yet he was flexible on certain points or adopted a moderate tone so as to allay fears concerning the possible implications of this program.

A landmark in the arguing of the case was Stalin's principal address during the Central Committee plenum of July 4–12, 1928. Speaking on July 9, he found the key to industrialization, as Preobrazhensky had done, in "accumulation." The prime source of accumulation was the "scissors" between town and countryside: charging the peasant high prices for manufactured goods while paying him low ones for farm products. Avoiding Preobrazhensky's impolitic term "exploitation," Stalin called this "something on the order of 'tribute,' something on the order of a supertax." As for the nexus (*smychka*) between working class and peasantry—the need to preserve which was a fundamental article of faith in the party—there existed, said Stalin, not only a "nexus through textiles" but also a "nexus through metal" or mechanization, and the latter had the advantage that it would ensure the "remaking of the peasant in the spirit of collectivism." But was a course based on collectivization and all-out heavy-industry expansion compatible with the NEP, which the party still believed itself to be following? Stalin casuistically disposed of this question by re-interpreting the NEP inself in militant revolutionary terms as "a victorious and systematic offensive against capitalist elements of our economy." The capitalist elements, kulaks included, would naturally resist the offensive in all ways open to them. Hence class struggle, of which the recent emergency measures were an expression, must be seen as a normal phenomenon under the NEP. Having thus blurred the very distinction between War Communism and the NEP, Stalin propounded the novel, directly anti-Bukharinist thesis, henceforth central to Stalinism, that the class struggle inevitably grows sharper with the country's advance toward socialism.[18]

In 1925 Stalin had said that there was latent "beat the kulak" sentiment in the party. Valentinov confirms, from his personal experience in the Moscow bureaucracy and political circles of those years, that such a feeling was widespread among party members. He also attests that Preobrazhensky's industrialization scheme evoked a certain positive response in a party that had never gotten over suspecting that the NEP was a danger to it because of the opportunity given the internal bourgeoisie to wax wealthy and strong. He goes so far as to say that "the party, particularly in its *lower cells,* was instinctively, subconsciously antagonistic toward the NEP."[19] Even if this acute participant-observer of the early Soviet scene overstates the point somewhat, there can be no doubt that the attitudes he reports had considerable currency in the ambivalent party mind of the twenties.

Stalin's program was bound to appeal to Bolsheviks who har-

18. *Stalin,* XI, 158–159, 162, 166, 172. Stalin's speech was first published in 1952 in this volume.

19. N. Valentinov, "Ot NEPA k stalinskoi kollektivizatsii," *Novy zhurnal,* No. 72 (1963), pp. 238, 239, 241, 243.

bored such attitudes, and his argumentation shows how conscious of this he was. "We cannot live like gypsies without grain reserves," he said in the speech of July 9, 1928. "Isn't it clear that a great state covering a sixth of the earth's surface can't get along without grain reserves for internal and external needs?" Speaking before a Leningrad party audience in public a few days later, he touched upon themes that he had discussed behind closed doors at the plenum. In a veiled riposte to Rykov, who had defended there the needs of light industry, Stalin said scornfully that anyone who thought the nexus could be preserved only through textiles, forgetting about metal and machines, was perpetuating the class division between proletariat and peasantry, and hence was "not a proletarian revolutionary but a 'peasant philosopher.' " [20] In the November plenum speech he directly appealed to the latent "beat the kulak" feeling in the party leadership by saying, "It is not a matter of caressing the peasant and seeing in this the way to establish correct relations with him, for you won't go far on caresses. . . ." [21]

As in the earlier debate over "socialism in one country," Stalin studded his speeches with Lenin quotations and represented the views he was advocating as Leninism. There was never any suggestion that his special amalgam of Russocentrism and a revolutionary approach in building socialism could be called "Stalinism." The Lenin to whom he ascribed authorship of the doctrine differed, however, from the one whose authority Bukharin invoked. Stalin's was the Lenin who had said when introducing the NEP, "Now we retreat, move backward as it were, but we do it in order to draw back, run, and make a greater leap forward." It was the Lenin of *kto kogo?* As Stalin put it in his speech to the Central Committee plenum of April 1929, when he branded Bukharin, Rykov, and Tomsky as the leaders of the "Right deviation" in the party, "The situation is that we live according to Lenin's formula of '*kto kogo*': either we shall pin them, the capitalists, to the ground and give

---

20. *Stalin*, XI, 214. The above-cited statements in the speech of July 9 appear in the same volume, p. 170.
21. *Ibid.*, p. 256.

them, as Lenin expressed it, final decisive battle, or they will pin our shoulders to the ground." [22] This metaphorical depiction of the Soviet situation as a great wrestling match of opposing classes was at once a manifesto of Stalin's Leninism and a clear revelation of his lifelong need to "beat" in the twofold sense of "strike" and "be victorious."

It may be argued from a scholarly point of view that this time, just as before, Stalin lost the battle of Lenin quotations. Moreover, Lenin, had he been resurrected long enough to take part in one of those plenums of 1928–29, would undoubtedly have said that the moderates' position represented, as Bukharin argued, his "political testament," and that Stalin, giving vent now to a *grubost'* against the peasant, was impelling the party onto a terribly dangerous course of policy. But given the party as it was five years after Lenin's death, and the situation in the country, Stalinist Leninism had a powerful attraction for many. In addition, it had a certain claim of its own to the legacy of Lenin, whose political testament was in some sense the whole of his thought and not simply the views set forth in his last articles.

Among the Bolsheviks who saw Leninism more in Stalin's light was no less a figure than Piatakov, one of the seventy-five expelled Left oppositionists. His petition for re-admission to party membership was granted, and he was appointed in 1928 to the post of Soviet trade representative in France. Valentinov, who knew him from his own work on the *Torgovo-promyshlennaia gazeta,* received permission at that time to go abroad for medical treatment, and the two men chanced to meet in Paris. Long after Piatakov's execution following a Stalinist treason trial in 1937, Valentinov published abroad an account of their private conversation of 1928. Piatakov had confided that he himself and many others, "including Politburo members," considered Lenin's last articles "unfortunate." They were written, he said, under the influence of Lenin's depress-

22. *Ibid.,* XII, 37. Lenin's statement at the time of the NEP's introduction was quoted by Stalin in his article of November 7, 1929, "The Great Turning-Point Year."

ing final sickness. No one who knew him well could take the NEP to represent his real philosophy. His authentic outlook was the view that had found expression in *one* of the last articles, "Our Revolution." It argued—with a reference to Napoleon's saying "On s'engage et puis . . . on voit"—that the Bolsheviks had rightly taken power without waiting for Russia to reach a level of culture adequate for socialism. The whole of Lenin, affirmed Piatakov, lay in this scorning of "objective prerequisites," this bold willingness to disregard them, this appeal to the creative will as the all-important factor.[23]

It was baseless to dismiss Lenin's last articles as a product of sickness, all the more so as Piatakov saw in one of them "the whole of Lenin." But he was on strong ground in stressing the spirit of revolutionary militance and voluntarism in Lenin. Ten years after the Revolution, this spirit was not dead in the party. The idea of a return to the offensive still exerted an appeal. Trotsky and his followers did not succeed in giving effective ideological expression and political leadership to this current in Bolshevism; Stalin did.

By mid-1928, the contest behind the scenes had become a no-quarter fight, and the atmosphere was so tense that Stalin and Bukharin were no longer on speaking terms. Fearful that Stalin was about to make overtures to Zinoviev and Kamenev in order to enlist their help on his side, Bukharin took the risky step of approaching them first. Using Sokolnikov as a go-between, he invited Kamenev, who was then living in the provincial town of Kaluga, to come to Moscow for a meeting. On July 11, two days after Stalin's big plenum speech, Bukharin appeared at Kamenev's Moscow apartment. They had a long talk which was continued the following morning and which Bukharin asked Kamenev, who took notes, to keep confidential. Bukharin urged Kamenev, and indirectly Zinoviev, not to yield to Stalin's probable blandishments and to support the moderates against him rather than vice versa. And in a voice that (as Kamenev noted in his record of the conversation) quivered

---

23. N. Valentinov, "Sut' bol'shevizma v izobrazhenii Iu. Piatakova," *Novy zhurnal*, No. 52 (1958), pp. 146–149. Valentinov subsequently broke off his Soviet connection and remained abroad for the remainder of his life.

with excitement, he gave a vivid inside account of the fierce conflict raging in higher party spheres.[24]

Stalin, he said, was pursuing a line of internal policy ruinous for the Revolution. His only solution to repeated difficulties with grain procurements was repeated emergency measures. That meant War Communism and the end of everything. His policy was leading to civil war, to an uprising that Stalin would have to drown in blood. His idea of "tribute" from the peasantry was Preobrazhensky's theory all over again. His notion that resistance must grow in proportion to the growth of socialism was "idiotic illiteracy," a formula for catastrophe of the whole Soviet cause. He himself was a Genghis Khan, an unprincipled intriguer who subordinated everything to the maintenance of his power, one whose only formula was vengeance, by means of the knife in the back. "Let us recall," added Bukharin at this point, "his theory of 'sweet revenge.'"

The picture that Bukharin gave of the political struggle itself was at once optimistic and pessimistic. When Kamenev asked, "What are your forces?" he spoke of a hard core consisting of himself, Rykov, Tomsky, and Uglanov; of support among the Leningrad Communists; of the Orgburo being on his group's side. So were two prominent secret police officials, Henrikh Yagoda and M. A. Trilisser, both influenced by the spectacle of 150 small-scale outbreaks of violence around the country. Voroshilov and Kalinin had deserted the group at the last minute, apparently because of some sort of hold that Stalin had over them. Ordzhonikidze had come to Bukharin and denounced Stalin in private, but then, at the decisive moment, betrayed the anti-Stalin cause. Everything depended now upon gradually explaining Stalin's ruinous role and persuading the "middle" (i.e., undecided) Central Committeemen of the necessity of removing him. "But so far he is removing you," Kamenev interjected at this point, and that indeed was the upshot of Bukharin's story. Stalin's strategy was working. He was ma-

24. A copy of Kamenev's record of the conversation is in the Trotsky Archives at Harvard University (Document T1897), and will henceforth be cited from that source as "Bukharin-Kamenev Conversation." A published text based on Kamenev's record appeared in *Sotsialisticheskii vestnik*, No. 9 (199) (May 4, 1929), pp. 9–11.

neuvering the Bukharinists into a dilemma: "To come out openly or not to come out? If we do, they will cut us down under the no-splitting clause. If we don't they will cut us down with a series of little chess moves, and heap the blame on us if there is no grain in October." It is no wonder that during the interview Bukharin displayed what Kamenev described as an extremely distraught and tortured face, and at times gave the impression of a man who knew he was doomed.

Bukharin's approach to the former opposition leaders was a service to history, but not to his own cause. A coldly unmoved Kamenev penned this marginal comment on his record of the long first day's meeting: "All this was fawning. I find no other word for it; politically, of course." Soon copies of the sensational document were circulating in oppositionist circles through the *samizdat* of that time, and accounts of it appeared some months later in the Trotskyist *Biulleten' oppozitsii* (Bulletin of the Opposition), published in Paris, and elsewhere. All this was grist for the mills of Stalin's strategy, providing him with material with which to convict his opponents of conspiring behind the party's back for oppositional ends.

The backstage fight came to a climax in a prolonged joint session of the Politburo and the presidium of the Central Control Commission at the close of January and the beginning of February 1929. Under fire for factional conspiring, Bukharin, Rykov, and Tomsky attacked Stalin in statements presented to the session. He counter-attacked in a speech which began: "Sad as it is, one must register the fact of the formation in our party of a special Bukharin group consisting of Bukharin, Tomsky, and Rykov." It was, he went on to allege, a Right deviationist group with a platform that called for slowing down industrialization, winding up collectivization, and giving free scope to private trade. Its members had a naïve faith in the savior role of the kulak. Their misfortune was that they did not understand the mechanics of the class struggle and failed to see the kulak as the mortal enemy of the Soviet system that he was. Lenin had been a thousand times right when he wrote to Shliapnikov way back in 1916 that Bukharin was "devilishly unstable in politics." And now, in addition to all else, it was established that Bukharin, by authorization of the group, had carried on behind-the-scenes negotiations with Kamenev to form a factional bloc of Bukharinists and Trotskyists against the party and its Central Committee.[25]

The January–February session was decisive. In a resolution that accepted Stalin's position *in toto,* the combined Politburo and Control Commission presidium censured the Bukharinists for their stand and actions. This paved the way for the April 1929 joint plenum of the Central Committee and Central Control Commission. They approved the earlier resolution; decreed that Bukharin and Tomsky should be relieved of their posts on *Pravda,* the Comintern, and the Central Trade Union Council; and warned that the slightest further attempt on their part at opposition would cost them their seats on the Politburo.

Stalin marked this triumphal occasion with a great polemical broadside against Bukharin and his friends. It was an indictment of the opposition on all counts, and implicitly a platform of the Stalinist revolutionary version of building socialism in Russia. At one point Stalin drew upon memories of the Turukhansk exile and found imagery of compelling force to express his message:

Have you ever seen fishermen before the storm on a great river like the Yenisei? I have more than once. It happens that one group of fishermen mobilizes all its forces in the face of the oncoming storm, inspires its people, and boldly heads the boat into the storm, saying, "Hold fast, boys, tighter on the rudder, cut through the waves, we'll win!"

But there is another kind of fishermen who lose heart when they see the storm coming, start to whine, and demoralize their own ranks: "Oh, woe, the storm is breaking, lie down, boys, on the bottom of the boat, close your eyes, maybe we'll somehow be borne onto the shore." [*General laughter.*]

Need it be demonstrated that the Bukharin group's outlook and behavior are as similar as two drops of water to the outlook and be-

25. *Stalin,* XI, 318–322. A digest of Stalin's statements to the January–February 1929 session was first published here.

havior of the second group of fishermen, those who retreat in panic in the face of difficulties? [26]

The rest was anticlimax. The moderates were politically crushed. A measured capitulatory document submitted by Bukharin, Rykov, and Tomsky was rejected by the Central Committee plenum of November 1929 as a factional maneuver, and Bukharin was expelled from the Politburo. Then the three men submitted an unconditional recantation, which *Pravda* printed on November 26. Meanwhile, a purge of Bukharin supporters went on at lower levels.

Earlier in the year, Trotsky had been shipped into exile in Turkey. Organized opposition was now at an end. The struggle for leadership was over, and Stalin was the victor. As if to mark this fact and formalize the outcome, his fiftieth birthday, on December 21, 1929, was officially celebrated with great fanfare. The party, over which the Stalin faction reigned supreme, saluted him on that occasion as Lenin's successor—the new *vozhd'*.

26. *Ibid.*, XII, 17–18.

Chapter Twelve

THE DECISIVE TRIFLE

As Others Saw Him

APART FROM their attitude toward Lenin, Bolsheviks were not generally inclined to attach much importance to the personal factor in politics. To their Marxist-trained minds, what mainly mattered about a comrade was not his personality but his political beliefs, his ideological commitment, the rightness or wrongness of his positions in party councils. Lenin was taking account of this ingrained assumption when he wrote in the postscript to the testament that the question of Stalin's personal qualities "may seem an insignificant trifle." And he was taking issue with it when he went on to contend that in this instance the personality trifle might prove of *decisive* historical significance.

In later years some other party leaders came around to his view under the pressure of their own further experiences with Stalin, but they, too, found it hard to overcome the Bolshevik tendency to deprecate the role of personality. Stalin made it even harder by maintaining that oppositionist attacks impugning him on personal grounds were a red herring. We have seen, for example, that in his confrontation with Trotsky in October 1927 he dismissed the personal factor as something of no real consequence—one of those "petty questions" that had to be cleared away before coming to the serious substance of the dispute. Again, in addressing the Central Committee in April 1929 on his conflict with the Bukharin group, which had accused him of lusting after despotic power, he began by saying: "Comrades, I shall not touch on the personal factor, although it played a rather conspicuous part in the speeches of some comrades of Bukharin's group. I shall not touch upon it because it is a trifle, and it is not worthwhile dwelling on trifles." The personal accusations, he said, were only a cheap trick designed to "cover up the underlying political basis of our disagreements." [1] And in the lengthy speech that followed, Stalin presented the conflict strictly in terms of fundamental differences over party policy. Although these differences existed, Stalin owed part of his success to the Central Committee's willingness to view the personal factor as the "trifle" that he said it was.

Lenin, albeit tardily, realized that Stalin's personality very much mattered. But neither he nor others who later arrived at the same realization succeeded in supporting this insight with anything like an adequate analysis of Stalin's character. Lenin, as we have seen, became alarmed about Stalin's rudeness; his administrative peremptoriness; his Great Russian nationalism; his tendency to give animosity free rein in official conduct; and his lack of tolerance, loyalty, and considerateness toward others. It was a weighty catalogue of politically significant character defects, but not a reasoned analysis. The others, too, even as their horror of Stalin deepened, stood somehow mentally paralyzed before the enigma of the man's personality. Krestinsky, for example, described him privately as "a bad man with yellow eyes." [2]

Trotsky, in whose writings we find very many valuable observations on Stalin as an individual, took the position that he was important not in his own right but only as a personification of the Thermidorean bureaucracy. As he summed up his view in *The Revolution Betrayed,* "Stalin is the personification of the bureaucracy. That is the substance of his political personality." [3] Even Stalin's personal traits, such as the notorious rudeness, seemed significant to Trotsky primarily as manifestations of a social phenomenon: the characteristics of the new bureaucratic ruling stratum as a group.[4] So the problem of Stalin as a personality was partially set

1. *Stalin,* XII, 1–2.
2. L. Trotsky, *My Life* (New York, 1930), p. 449.
3. L. Trotsky, *The Revolution Betrayed* (New York, 1945), p. 277.
4. In his speech in the Central Committee session of October 23, 1927, on

aside by the one man who combined a wealth of pertinent knowledge and recent observation with full freedom to communicate his thoughts in writing during the years that remained to him after he was deported from Russia in 1929. And the full-scale biography of Stalin in which he was trying finally to come to grips with the personal factor remained in raw and unfinished condition when the assassin sent by Stalin struck him down in 1940.

Bukharin was more inclined to consider the personal factor in its own terms. He enjoyed excellent opportunities to observe Stalin at close range over a long period of years, and it appears that even after his fall in 1929 he continued, on occasion, to be a summer guest of the Stalins at Zubalovo.[5] We have seen the importance that he attached to Stalin's theory of "sweet revenge." Along with others in high Soviet circles, he came to believe that a motivating mainspring of Stalin's personality was the need for a vindictive triumph over those whom he regarded as his enemies. But what aroused his vindictive feelings, and whom did he regard as his enemies? It was in offering a clue to the answer to this crucial question that Bukharin made his best contribution to a deeper understanding of Stalin. Briefly, he saw that Stalin was psychologically driven to feel enviously vengeful toward all who surpassed him in qualities or capacities in which he considered *himself* to be pre-eminent. "Stalin's first quality is laziness," Bukharin told Trotsky on one occasion. "And his second is an implacable jealousy of anyone who knows more or does things better than he." [6]

---

the motion for his expulsion, Trotsky said: "The rudeness and disloyalty of which Lenin wrote are no longer mere personal characteristics. They have become the character of the ruling faction . . ." (*The Real Situation in Russia* [New York, 1928], p. 7).

5. Svetlana Alliluyeva, *Twenty Letters to a Friend* (New York, 1967), p. 31.

6. Trotsky, *My Life*, p. 450. Trotsky evidently agreed with at least the latter part of the statement, for he himself spoke here (p. 477) of Stalin's "enormous envy and ambition." Elsewhere he wrote that the mainspring of Stalin's personality, besides love of power, was "ambition, envy—active, never-slumbering envy of all who are more gifted, more powerful, rank higher than he." And further, that "he tirelessly schemed, with people and circumstances, in order to push aside, derogate, blacken, belittle anyone who in one way or another eclipsed him or interfered with his ambition" (Trotsky, *Stalin: An Appraisal of the Man and His Influence* [New York, 1967], pp. 237, 336).

Fate gave Bukharin an opportunity to express this view of Stalin to persons living abroad, who preserved it for posterity. In early 1936 he was sent to Paris as the head of a three-man Soviet delegation to negotiate for the purchase of Marx archives belonging to the German Social Democratic party. These archives had been sent from Berlin to Paris and Copenhagen in 1933 by Boris Nicolaevsky, editor of the émigré Menshevik *Sotsialisticheskii vestnik* (Socialist Herald). Nicolaevsky and a colleague, the prominent Menshevik Fyodor Dan, were intermediaries in the negotiations and saw Bukharin frequently over a period of about two months.[7] One day he appeared unexpectedly and unaccompanied at the Dans' apartment and stayed for several hours, during which he spoke at length of Stalin. Perhaps he wanted to take advantage of a unique opportunity to say something for the historical record on a subject concerning which the world remained very largely in the dark. Dan, who had known Stalin a little in earlier years, found Bukharin's characterization of him not only disturbing but surprising. In a memoir published years later, after both Bukharin and Dan were dead, Mrs. Dan revealed it.

In one of the early negotiating sessions with Dan and Nicolaevsky, Bukharin had said jocularly that the Bolsheviks were so interested in everything pertaining to Marx that they would even be willing to buy his remains for transfer to Moscow. If that were to happen—he now remarked in private to the Dans—a monument to Marx would be erected on the spot. But it would not be a very tall one, and beside it would be built a taller monument to Stalin. He would be shown reading *Capital,* with pencil in hand in the event he should find it necessary to make some marginal corrections in Marx's book. Elaborating, Bukharin went on:

You say you don't know him well, but we do! He is unhappy at not being able to convince everyone, himself included, that he is greater than everyone; and this unhappiness of his may be his most human trait, perhaps the only human trait in him. But what is not human, but rather something devilish, is that because of this unhappiness he cannot help

7. For Boris Nicolaevsky's account of Bukharin's stay in Paris, see his *Power and the Soviet Elite* (New York, 1965), pp. 3–7.

taking revenge on people, on all people but especially those who are in any way higher or better than he. If someone speaks better than he does, that man is doomed! Stalin will not let him live, because that man is a perpetual reminder that he, Stalin, is not the first and the best. If someone writes better, matters are bad for him because *he,* Stalin, has to be the premier Russian writer. Marx, of course, no longer has anything to fear from him, save possibly to appear small to the Russian worker in comparison with the great Stalin. No, no, Fyodor, he is a small-minded, malicious man—no, not a man, but a devil! [8]

Future history was to provide abundant corroboration of Bukharin's words. For all its emotionalism, his characterization pointed to a fact of cardinal importance for an understanding of Stalin: his sense of himself as a very great man and his imperative need to have his greatness acknowledged by others.

How Stalin became in early life the kind of person who has to be "the first and best" has been shown in a previous chapter. Now we must take up the inner story again, as it was unfolding during his middle years.

As He Saw Himself

To comprehend the mental world of Stalin, we must be aware that those who peopled it fell into two classes: friends, whom one could trust, and enemies, whom one must fight against and strive to overcome. There was hardly any possibility of escaping this dichotomy. If a given individual was neither friend nor foe, he was still *potentially* the one or the other, and for Stalin this was always a fact of cardinal significance about him.

Character and culture coalesced and reinforced each other in this way of perceiving other people. A gifted and unusually sensitive child suffered bad early experiences, including his father's brutality toward himself and his mother, and emerged as a hardened, vigilant youngster with a self-idealizing tendency, on the one hand, and a vengeful streak and indomitable will to fight and to win, on the other. The Georgian social setting and its Russifying overseers

8. Lydia Dan, "Bukharin o Staline," *Novy zhurnal,* No. 75 (1964), pp. 181–182.

offered him a ready-made hostile division of people into friends and enemies, together with such cultural traditions as the blood feud and such dramatizations of the situation as the Koba story. As a youth in the seminary he immersed himself in the Marxian revolutionary sub-culture; what particularly appealed to him in that, as we have seen, was the ideological symbolism that split the social universe into two great warring classes of oppressed and oppressors: friends and enemies on the scale of all mankind and all recorded history. Within the sub-culture he gravitated unerringly to the militant version of the ideology that Lenin presented. As has been noted earlier, Lenin's was an angry Marxism, replete with invective and imagery that projected the class enemy as irremediably evil and hostile. Stalin found in his writings a wealth of material that he wrought into his own image of the enemy. Moreover, Lenin's notion of the revolutionary party as a comradely band of fighters for the people, united in mutual trust, defined for him an idealized conception of what it would—or should—mean to have friends.

Implicit in this discussion is a further fact of great importance in understanding Stalin. The distinction between "personal" relationships and "political" ones, something we may take for granted, was foreign to his mind. Of course, the personalizing of political relationships, and the politicalizing of personal ones, is a familiar phenomenon in revolutionary movements and perhaps in political life generally. What may have been somewhat peculiar to Stalin was the extreme form that this merger took in his case. His political life was as intensely personal in its meaning to him as his personal life was absorbed in the political realm. One of the contributing factors was his early background in a traditional society, the Georgian, where the distinction between private and public relationships was undeveloped as a cultural pattern. Another was the pronounced asocial tendency that we have observed in him, the small number of personal ties outside the political milieu. But not least among the explanations was the highly political character of his personal self-concept as Stalin. As we shall now try to make clear, because of the terms in which he defined *himself*, he could never extrude the play of personal passion from his relations with political associates, particularly other party members.

But how did Stalin define himself in his middle years? We are fortunate in having a statement that represents in a way his own answer to this question. In June 1926, while on a visit to Tiflis, Stalin gave a sketch of his revolutionary biography as he liked to view it. Replying to acclaim from workers of the local railway shops, he chided them for flattery. It was quite an unnecessary exaggeration, he said, to picture him as a hero of the October Revolution, a leader of the party and the Communist International, a legendary warrior-knight, etc. That was how people usually spoke at the graveside of departed revolutionaries—and he had no intention of dying yet. The true story of his revolutionary career, he explained, was one of apprenticeship, of learning from worker-teachers first in Tiflis, then in Baku, and finally in Leningrad. In 1898, when he was put in charge of a study-circle of workers from the Tiflis railway yards, older comrades like Djibladze, Chodrishvili, and Chkheidze, who perhaps had less book learning than he but possessed more experience, had given him practical instruction in propaganda activity. That was his first "baptism" in the revolutionary struggle. Here, among his first teachers, the Tiflis railroaders, he had become an "apprentice of revolution." Then, in the years 1907 to 1909, spent in Baku, where he had learned to lead large masses of workers in the oil-fields, he had received his second baptism in the revolutionary struggle and become a "journeyman of revolution." And in Leningrad in 1917, operating among the Russian workers and in direct proximity to the great teacher of the proletarians of all countries, Lenin, in the maelstrom of class war, he had learned what it means to be one of the leaders of the party. That had been his third revolutionary baptism. In Russia, under Lenin's leadership, he had become a "master-workman of revolution," said Stalin, and concluded: "Such, comrades, without exaggeration and in all conscience, is the true picture of what I was and what I became." [9]

This revealing essay in revolutionary autobiography laid the

9. *Stalin*, VIII, 173–175.

groundwork for a full biography of Stalin by his assistant, Tovstukha. Prepared for a special volume of the *Granat entsiklopediia*
containing the autobiographies or authorized biographies of some
250 leading Soviet figures, the Tovstukha biography was also published in 1927 as a separate pamphlet in an edition of fifty thousand
copies. Reading this account of Stalin's pre-1917 years, and comparing it with the careers of other prominent Bolsheviks recounted
in the same biographical volume, one is struck by several distinctive
features of Tovstukha's treatment. True, it followed a general styli-
zation that was visible in this Bolshevik "lives of the revolutionaries." In substance it was a laconic listing of revolutionary actions
participated in, conferences attended, punishments suffered, etc.
What distinguished it from the others was not simply that it modified
historical reality in a number of subtle ways flattering to its subject.
More than that, it showed a solemnity of tone, a reaching for super-
latives, and even an occasional grandiloquence that deviated from
the volume's general tendency to understatement. Thus Stalin did
not simply move to Baku. Rather, "From 1907 commences the Baku
period in the revolutionary activity of Stalin." His arrival in Petersburg in 1911 marked the beginning of "the Petersburg period in the
revolutionary activity of Stalin." Here, with some revision, is the
three-stage progress to "master-workman of revolution" which Stalin
had set forth to the Tiflis railroaders. We sense that a revolutionary
biography is being recast in retrospect according to certain canons
of drama.[10]

From this and other evidence we may infer that the psychological forces which impelled the younger Djugashvili to form a
heroic revolutionary identity for himself as "Koba Stalin" remained
active in the older Djugashvili, and prevented him from accepting
himself on any other terms. As a man in his forties he continued to
believe in the vision of himself as a leader and fighter of genius. His
life appeared to him in retrospect as a realization of his youthful
dream of playing Koba to Lenin's Shamil. Such was the message

10. I. P. Tovstukha, *Iosif Vissarionovich Stalin. Kratkaia biografiia* (Moscow, 1927).

of the dramatic sketch of his political biography that he gave in
1926. He presented it as a saga of one man's rise to revolutionary
greatness alongside Lenin, and his concluding expression of gratitude to the Russian workers and Lenin conveyed a sense of himself
as the latter's chosen continuator and heir: "Permit me to extend
my sincere comradely gratitude to my Russian teachers and to bow
my head before the memory of my great teacher—Lenin."

Stalin's accomplishments, it must be granted, were sufficient to
encourage him in his *hubris*. By all worldly tests, his career up to
the mid-twenties was a dazzling success story. He had come out of
nowhere, a son of poor and illiterate parents living in a provincial
corner of one of the non-Russian borderlands of the Empire. Yet,
by the time of his arrest on the eve of the World War he had risen to
a leading position in the Bolshevik party and was in direct collaborative association with Lenin, who entrusted him with the treatment of one of the movement's most important theoretical problems.
He had returned from exile in March 1917 to join the leadership of
the party that then carried off one of the stunning revolutionary
feats of history. He had gone on to play an active part in the Civil
War and in organizing the institutions of the Soviet state. Finally,
he was now emerging as the party's new supreme leader in succession to Lenin. Surely he had gone very far toward realizing his
"bright hope" of rising "higher than the great mountains." What
more was needed to prove that he was a political man of genius?

On the other hand, Stalin had failed in many ways to fulfill
the demands of his heroic revolutionary persona. He had not become a leader of renown second only to Lenin's. For all his formidable talents and commitment to the party's cause, he lacked the
extraordinary qualities needed to make him a star of the first magnitude on the Russian revolutionary horizon. Not only Lenin but
many of the other major Bolshevik figures eclipsed him in one way
or another. Not even in his native Caucasian milieu had he been
a notable success as a revolutionary. His poor performance during
the March days of 1917 was so notorious in the party that he had
felt constrained to apologize publicly for it, and the remainder of

his record in the Revolution was spotty. If he became a "master-workman of revolution" in 1917, this fact failed to impress itself upon the party mind.

Far from starring in the Civil War, he had created difficulties at Tsaritsyn, carried on a feud with Trotsky, and disgraced himself by his insubordination in the futile effort to capture Lvov. Not he but Trotsky had risen to the heights of glory as Lenin's right-hand man in the Revolution and the Civil War. A former non-Bolshevik had thus enacted the role that the young Stalin had foreseen for himself, and as if in mockery of his vision of linking his own name with Lenin's in history, the party had become known as that of "Lenin-Trotsky." To make matters worse, the dying Lenin had turned against him and advised the party to remove him from his position of power. No event could have been more cruelly incongruent with the younger Stalin's life-scenario.

There was, similarly, a discrepancy between Stalin's acquired sense of Russian self-identity and the fact of his being Georgian. All his "true-Russianness" could not erase from people's minds, his own included, the fact of his Georgian nationality. It was obvious in his appearance, in his generally known family name, and in his speech. Despite the fluency of his Russian, the traces of a Georgian accent were as ineradicable from his speech as those of his childhood smallpox were from his face. He could never really pass for a Russian. He was in the position of continually reminding others, if not also himself, that Stalin was Djugashvili.

Dealing with Discrepancies

But chastening experience did not cause him to question his idealized image of himself. Nor did his political victories of the post-Lenin period incline him toward realistic retrospection concerning himself and his career. Rather, they fortified him in his grandiosity. Instead of scaling down his self-estimate in the face of clear evidence of disparity between the man he had aspired to be and the man he actually was, he took the opposite path of rejecting the evidence. Extremely powerful feelings drove him to do this. From all that we know concretely of him on the one hand and his general personality type on the other,[11] it appears that any failure to measure up to his lofty standards and self-expectations was unbearably painful to him. Violation of the norms of achievement implicit in his revolutionary self-concept would arouse, or threaten to arouse, shame, self-accusation, and self-hatred. To guard against such tormenting experiences, he employed a number of internal security operations familiar to students of modern depth psychology, notably repression, rationalization, and projection.

In repression, he would ignore, deny, or forget the potentially disturbing fact, thrust it out of conscious awareness. In rationalization, he would subject the fact to an interpretation that made it consistent with his self-image. An example of Stalin's use of rationalization is provided by his concluding speech to the Fourteenth Congress in 1925. In a passage criticizing Zinoviev's "The Philosophy of an Epoch," he mentioned that Molotov had sent him a copy of this article while he was away on a trip and that he had reacted rudely and sharply. "Yes, comrades," he went on, "I am forthright and rude, that is true and I don't deny it." But then: "I sent back a rude criticism, *because it is intolerable that Zinoviev should for a whole year systematically ignore or distort the most characteristic features of Leninism in regard to the peasant question. . . .*" [12] The final phrase transmuted the offensive rudeness into a manifestation of zeal for preserving the purity of Leninist doctrine.

Stalin returned to the question of his rudeness in his speech of October 23, 1927, quoting the postscript to Lenin's testament and acknowledging the justice of the charge that Lenin had brought against him. But he did this in a special way, saying: "Yes, I am rude, comrades, *toward those who rudely and treacherously smash and split the party*. I have not concealed this and do not do so now. It may be that a certain softness should be shown toward splitters. But it doesn't come off with me." [13] This was to emasculate Lenin's

11. His form of personality development corresponds closely to that delineated by Karen Horney in her work *Neurosis and Human Growth* (New York, 1950). See in particular chs. 1, 4, and 8, esp. pp. 197–212.

12. *Stalin*, VII, 375. Italics added.

13. *Ibid.*, X, 175. Italics added.

accusation in the act of pleading guilty to it. What had worried Lenin was Stalin's tendency to antagonize party comrades and potential political allies (like the Georgians) by his *grubost'*. In Stalin's speech, and doubtless in his mind as well, that grave personal defect was now transformed into a forgivable fault: hardness toward *enemies* of the party. An excess of such hardness could even be seen as a virtue in a Bolshevik. In all probability, it was by means of just this rationalization that Stalin learned to live with the memory of the postscript to Lenin's testament. Even so, however, he preferred to forget—that is, he repressed—the episode. Thus, the text of the postscript was omitted from the speech of October 23, 1927, as later reprinted in Stalin's collected works, of which Stalin himself was the chief editor.[14] And, as noted earlier, the decision of the Fifteenth Congress to publish the testament was never carried out.

Stalin's attempt to repress awareness of his Georgian nationality was shown even in his manner of speech. "He could read Georgian but used to say that he had largely forgotten the language," reports his daughter.[15] He spoke Russian in a low, monotonous voice, which he sometimes softened further at points where the Georgian accent would be most audible. An Old Bolshevik who heard him speak at the Sixth Congress in 1917 later wrote: "He had on a gray modest jacket and boots, and was speaking in a low, unhurried, completely calm voice. I noted that Nogin, sitting in the same row as I, could not suppress a slight smile when the speaker uttered a certain word *in a somehow especially soft tone with his special accent.*" [16] Further, Stalin expunged from his family life most of what might recall his Georgian origins. His daughter describes him as a man who in certain of his living habits remained Georgian all his life. He liked, for example, to conduct business while sitting at the dinner table with his associates and sipping

14. Robert H. McNeal, *Stalin's Works: An Annotated Bibliography* (Stanford, 1971), p. 129. The speech, with the text of Lenin's postscript included, appeared in *Pravda* on November 2, 1927.

15. Svetlana Alliluyeva, *Only One Year* (New York, 1969), p. 379.

16. I. G. Korolev, in *Voprosy istorii*, No. 2 (1956), pp. 12–13. Italics added. See also Alliluyeva, *Twenty Letters*, p. 31, where reference is made to Stalin's habit of speaking in a low monotone.

Georgian wines. But she makes clear that he was a person who thought of himself—and wanted to be thought of—as Russian. He did not, for example, bring up the two children of his second marriage, Vasily and Svetlana, to think of themselves as partly Georgian or to take pride in the Georgian side of their ancestry. Observing that "in general, Georgian ways were not cultivated in our home—father was completely Russified," Svetlana recalls a day in 1931 or so when Vasily said to her: "You know, our father *used to be* a Georgian once." In another passage, Svetlana writes that because of her mother and grandparents, Georgia remained a living presence in their home. But this had nothing to do with her father: "He was the one, I think, who cared about it least. It was Russia that he loved. He loved Siberia, with its stark beauty and its rough, silent people." And elsewhere: "I know no other Georgian who had so completely sloughed off his qualities as a Georgian and loved everything Russian the way he did." [17]

Stalin's attitude toward Yakov, the son of his early marriage, shows how painful it was for him to be confronted with the fact that he himself was Georgian. After being brought up by his mother's sister in Georgia and attending school there, Yakov came to Moscow during the twenties at the insistence of his uncle, Alexander Svanidze, and joined his father's household. Since he not only was Georgian in appearance and upbringing but at first found it hard to learn to speak Russian, he was a living reminder of his father's Georgianness. Doubtless on this account Stalin disapproved of his coming and of everything about him. So great was his contempt that when Yakov shot himself in 1928 or 1929, in despair over his father's hostility, Stalin ridiculed him for bungling the suicide attempt, exclaiming: "Ha! He couldn't even shoot straight!" After that Yakov went to Leningrad to live with the elder Alliluyevs.[18] Later he became a Red Army officer and was one of the thousands

17. Alliluyeva, *Twenty Letters*, pp. 31, 32, 67, 119–120.
18. *Ibid.*, pp. 101, 158–159. Svetlana explains her father's contempt for Yakov on the basis of temperamental difference, suggesting that "Yakov's gentleness and composure were irritating to my father, who was quick-tempered and impetuous, even in his later years." The feelings that caused Stalin to reject his son were no doubt numerous as well as complex.

captured by the invading Germans in the early period of the Soviet-German war. Stalin rejected a German offer to trade him for some German prisoners in Russian hands. He died in the Sachsenhausen concentration camp, reportedly by making a suicidal escape gesture after the fact was broadcast over the camp's radio that his father had said in reply to a foreign correspondent's question that there were no Russian prisoners-of-war in Hitler's camps, only Russian traitors who would be done away with after the war, and: "I have no son called Yakov." [19]

Violent rages for which there seems small cause commonly express feelings about oneself that are turned outward against others. There is reason to believe that the anger with which Stalin reacted to Yakov's appearance in Moscow was really anger against himself. It is very likely, in other words, that the arrival upon the scene of an unmistakably Georgian son activated Stalin's intense but normally repressed feelings of shame and self-contempt about being a Georgian himself, feelings that he could not bear to experience in relation to himself and therefore experienced as contempt for Yakov. This turning outward—or projection—of self-recriminatory feelings aroused by lapses from his self-ideal or violations of his standards of accomplishment was a cardinal characteristic of Stalin's. He could not tolerate in himself any deviation from his idealized self-image. But, on the other hand, neither could he help registering them unconsciously, and he habitually experienced the resulting rage against himself and self-accusations as rage and accusations against others. Here, it may be added, is part of the explanation for the moodiness, irascibility, and outbursts of ill temper which were frequent with Stalin.

Failure to perceive one's own flaws and shortcomings is a common human trait. What made Stalin's case an extreme one was his intolerance of anything short of perfection in himself. He totally identified himself with the ideal Stalin of his imagination, and became oblivious of everything in himself that detracted from this picture. Not only gross defects but any departures from the self-ideal,

19. Alliluyeva, *Only One Year,* p. 370.

any failings in the revolutionary biography, were censored. Since the internal censorship became habitual and automatic, Stalin developed an extraordinary blindness to his own blemishes. This made it possible for him to read moral lectures to others without any apparent realization of their applicability to himself.

For example, speaking in 1929 to a group of American Communist leaders gathered in Moscow, he declared that the Comintern was not a stock market but the "holy of holies of the working class," and went on:

Either we are Leninists, and our relations one with another, as well as the relations of the section with the Comintern, and vice versa, must be built on mutual confidence, must be as clean and pure as crystal—in which case there should be no room in our ranks for rotten diplomatic intrigue; *or* we are not Leninists—in which case rotten diplomacy and unprincipled factional struggle will have full scope in our relations. One or the other. We must choose, Comrades.

An American present on that occasion recalled later that Stalin put the tip of his thumb and index finger together when he spoke the words "clean and pure as crystal," and said them with a straight face. Knowing how far Stalin himself was from being the "angel of purity" that he affected to be, the American viewed the statement as "rank hypocrisy." [20] This not unreasonable interpretation overlooked the inner complexity of Stalin, his capacity for self-deception. Because of his imperative need to be perfect (in accordance with his own special definition of perfection) and the associated habit of not taking cognizance of his faults and deficiencies, Stalin could believe in himself as a paragon of political virtue while behaving like any other factional politician. What appeared to others as rank hypocrisy could thus be unconscious duplicity. Cynical about much in life, Stalin was a true believer where he himself was concerned, and as such he was prey to illusions. Lenin may have had an inkling of this when he remarked to Krupskaya toward the

20. Benjamin Gitlow, *I Confess: The Truth about American Communism* (New York, 1929), p. 15. For the text of Stalin's statement, see *Stalin's Speeches on the American Communist Party* (New York, n.d.), p. 15.

end of his life that Stalin was "devoid of the most elementary honesty, the most simple human honesty." [21]

All this underlines the significance of the self-dramatizing tendency that we have observed in Stalin at a number of points in his career. Others, too, including some who observed him close up, were struck by a certain theatricality in his nature. Former American Ambassador in Moscow George F. Kennan has described him as "a consummate actor." [22] Milovan Djilas, to whom we owe a vivid character sketch of Stalin drawn from life, found him to be a role-player for whom the roles were real, a person with whom "pretence was so spontaneous that it seemed he himself became convinced of the truth and sincerity of what he was saying." As Djilas saw him, Stalin had a "passionate and many-sided nature—though all sides were equal and so convincing that it seemed he never dissembled but was always truly experiencing each of his roles. . . ." The Yugoslav visitor also noted, while attending one of the after-dinner movie showings which were a regular feature of life in Stalin's Kremlin, that "throughout the showing Stalin made comments—reactions to what was going on, in the manner of uneducated men who mistake artistic reality for actuality." [23] It should be mentioned in this context that Stalin showed a strong liking for dramatic productions on stage and screen, including historical dramas like *Lenin in October,* in which he himself figured as a character. Yuri Yelagin, one of our sources on this point, recalls from his own experience an occasion when Stalin appeared at Moscow's Vakhtangova Theater for a special Lenin anniversary showing of the last act of the heroic revolutionary drama *Man with a Rifle.* In it Lenin stands on the Smolny steps greeting the Red Guards as they march off to bat-

---

21. Trotsky, *Stalin,* p. 375. Trotsky learned of the remark directly from Krupskaya after Lenin's death.

22. George F. Kennan, *Russia and the West under Lenin and Stalin* (Boston, 1960), p. 248. According to Erving Goffman, a "performer" may or may not believe in his own act. "At one extreme, one finds that the performer can be fully taken in by his own act; he can be sincerely convinced that the impression of reality which he stages is the reality" (*The Presentation of Self in Everyday Life* [Garden City, 1959], p. 17). As an actor Stalin falls into the latter category.

23. Milovan Djilas, *Conversations with Stalin* (New York, 1962), pp. 69–70, 97, 103.

tle, and Stalin appears at his side. Yelagin, who was playing the drum in the orchestra that evening, observed Stalin seated in his special box, applauding Ruben Simonov in the role of Stalin and evidently deriving great pleasure from the performance.[24]

Stalin gave sensitive observers like Djilas the impression of being a role-player because, at bottom, that is what he was: a person whose life was dedicated to the enactment of a role of historical glory. It started with his early hero-identification with Lenin, which gave rise to the conception of himself as the Lenin II of Bolshevism. An element of unconscious acting is inevitably involved in the psychological process of identification, for the identifying person is patterning himself on someone else. Role-playing was therefore integral to Stalin's political personality from the outset. In later years he did not outgrow it. Rather, the original role of being Bolshevism's second Lenin evolved into a whole cluster of hero-roles that he believed himself to have played or to be playing in the still unfolding drama of party history, Russian history, and world history. The word to be emphasized here is *belief*. Of course, Stalin was also capable of conscious play-acting when political situations called for it, although even at such moments, as Djilas perceived, he actually experienced the role he was playing. But underlying the surface displays of expedient histrionic behavior was the serious drama of a personality whose chosen role of greatness was a lifelong identity-commitment. To understand Stalin we must see him as a person for whom *"genial'ny* Stalin" [25]—a phrase that the Soviet media regularly applied to him after the mid-thirties—represented his fundamental belief about himself.

The Need for Affirmation

When an individual is driven to repress many facts concerning himself in order to maintain a façade of perfection in his own

24. Yu. Yelagin, *Ukroshchenie iskusstv* (New York, 1952), p. 381. (English translation: Jury Jelagin, *The Taming of the Arts* [New York, 1951], pp. 287–288).

25. Since English lacks the adjectival form of "genius" ("genial" having another meaning), the closest translation would be "Stalin the genius." To avoid that clumsy phrase, I will employ the Russian word *genial'ny*.

mind, he becomes inwardly insecure. So it was with Stalin. Despite his characteristic show of complete self-confidence, he was not a genuinely self-confident person. His repressed thoughts lived on at the subconscious level, and so did the self-doubts, self-recrimina-tions, and self-accusations that they provoked. His resulting inse-curity was manifested, among other ways, in the extreme touchiness that we have repeatedly had occasion to note in him, his "un-Georgian" inability to take a joke.

One illustration is an episode out of *Pravda*'s history near the end of the twenties. The prominent cartoonist Boris Efimov submitted a friendly caricature of Stalin for publication in the paper's picture magazine, *Prozhektor* (The Searchlight). It showed him in a characteristic pose, with one arm thrust inside his jacket and the other held behind his back, smoking his pipe, and wearing ex-aggeratedly big boots polished to a gleam. As Efimov told the story in reminiscences published after Stalin's death, the editors sat there looking the sketch over and scratching their heads. They remem-bered how heartily Lenin, Gorky, and others had laughed when they saw comparable cartoons of themselves in *Pravda*. Still, some-thing about the saturnine figure of Stalin gave them pause. So, in-stead of deciding the matter on their own, they sent the drawing to Stalin's office with a request for permission to publish it. Next day it came back with Tovstukha's reply: "Not to be printed." [26]

Nor did subsequent success ease Stalin's painful sensitivity about being seen humorously. In his year of supreme triumph, 1945, when Roosevelt confided to him over a dinner table at Yalta that he and Churchill between them called him "Uncle Joe," Stalin showed genuine pique. Churchill's personal interpreter, Mr. Hugh Lunghi, who observed that scene, grew convinced from six years of close watching of Stalin at such meetings that he had a "basic inferiority complex." One of the signs of it was his way of jockeying for a position on a step higher than anyone else when photographs were being taken. A further expression of the uneasiness that he evidently felt because of his short stature was his habit of wearing

26. *M. I. Ulyanova. Sekretar' "Pravdy,"* ed. Z. D. Bliskovsky *et al.* (Mos-cow, 1965), pp. 199–200.

shoes with built-up heels which were only just revealed by his wide and sharply creased trousers.[27]

Bukharin put his finger upon the source of Stalin's insecurity when he observed in his conversation with Fyodor Dan that Stalin was unhappy at not being able to convince everyone, "himself included," that he was greater than everyone. In other words, Stalin was nagged by an undercurrent of suspicion that he might not really be the unblemished hero-figure that he took himself to be. This in turn made him highly dependent upon the attitudes of others, no less so after he attained the pinnacle of power than before. To assuage his underlying uncertainty and doubts, his suppressed awareness of not always fulfilling the dictates of his pride, he thirsted for others' admiration and devotion, their recognition of him as a great man, their affirmation of his view of himself as the *genial'ny* Stalin. Some close associates grew uncomfortably aware of the compulsive strength of this need in Stalin. Thus, Yenukidze complained of him in a private conversation of the mid-twenties: "I am doing everything he has asked me to do, but it is not enough for him. He wants me to admit that he is a genius." [28] Having been brought up by a mother who lavished praise and admiration upon him, Stalin now needed more of the same to bolster his unconsciously shaky ego.

In the post-revolutionary years his immediate social milieu was both satisfying and unsatisfying from this viewpoint. On the positive side, he had a wife who at first rendered him not only wifely devotion but glowing admiration as one of the great figures of the Revolution. At the time of her marriage to Stalin, Nadya Alliluyeva was seventeen and he was forty. In the eyes of this ardent daughter of the Revolution, he represented the ideal of the revolutionary New Man.[29] In time, his brusque and inconsiderate manner sorely tried her feeling for him, and at the beginning of the thirties a political estrangement occurred as well. Once in 1926, after a quarrel pro-

27. Hugh Lunghi, "Stalin Face to Face," *The Observer Weekend Review,* February 24, 1963, p. 25.

28. Trotsky, *Stalin,* p. 389. The remark was made to Trotsky's good friend Serebriakov.

29. Alliluyeva, *Twenty Letters,* p. 105.

voked by some act of rudeness on his part, she took the children and went off to Leningrad to live with her parents. A conciliatory phone call from him led her to relent and return, however, and life resumed its normal pattern.[30]

As mentioned earlier, the Stalins at Zubalovo received a constant flow of guests from among their relatives and friends. The guests, along with the children and the children's friends, stayed in the rooms downstairs, while Nadya and Stalin occupied the upper story. The elder Alliluyevs; Nadya's brothers, Fyodor and Pavel, and their wives; and her sister, Anna, and Anna's husband, Stanislav Redens, were frequent visitors, as were the relatives of Stalin's first wife: her sisters, Alexandra and Mariko; her brother, Alexander Svanidze, and his wife, Maria. Among the friends whom Svetlana recalls as house guests were the Ordzhonikidzes, who would stay for long stretches; the Bukharins, who would often come for the summer; and Sergei Kirov, who in addition to being a close personal friend of Stalin's had friendly ties with the Alliluyevs dating from pre-revolutionary days. Guests on family social occasions or companions of the Stalins on the summer trips to the Black Sea resort of Sochi that became their custom during the twenties included Yenukidze (who was Nadya's godfather as well as Stalin's old party comrade), the Molotovs, the Voroshilovs, the Mikoyans, and Budenny.[31]

The people of the Stalins' circle, most of them Old Bolsheviks, were pursuing a wide variety of public careers. Stalin's factional associates each had a sphere of leadership in the Soviet system: Ordzhonikidze as head of the Transcaucasian party organization and later of the Party Control Commission; Kirov as chief of the Leningrad party organization; Yenukidze as secretary of the Central Executive Committee of the Soviets; Molotov as Stalin's deputy in the Central Committee Secretariat; Voroshilov as war commissar; Mikoyan as trade commissar. The relatives, too, were involved in public affairs. Nadya's father was active in electric power plant

30. *Ibid.*, p. 103. Svetlana Alliluyeva learned these facts from her Aunt Anna, after Stalin died.

31. *Ibid.*, pp. 24–36, 138.

construction. Alexander Svanidze served in Soviet financial posts abroad, and his sister Mariko worked as `Yenukidze's secretary. Pavel Alliluyev, a soldier by profession, served on the General Staff and in the Military Academy. Redens, a one-time colleague of Dzerzhinsky's in the Cheka, was a secret police official. These people contributed a wealth of knowledge and experience to the conversations at Zubalovo and were inclined to speak their minds freely. "In this house," writes Svetlana, "my father was neither a god nor a 'cult,' but just the father of a family." [32]

That judgment calls for a certain qualification. At Zubalovo in the later twenties Stalin was living in an atmosphere of friendly recognition of him, if not deference to him, as a man not only of great power but of merited authority, an atmosphere of esteem for his positive strengths and talents as a leader as well as for his services to the party's cause on the revolutionary road to power. In addition to esteem, there existed in the circle—first of all among such men as Ordzhonikidze and Yenukidze who had known Stalin long and well—an awareness of his need for affirmation and his extreme sensitivity to anything he perceived as a slight. Although constitutionally incapable of paying fulsome tribute to his genius (as the earlier-quoted remark by Yenukidze attests), such men must have taken care not to offend his pride and not to appear overly critical of him. Subordinates like Molotov and Voroshilov must have done likewise, probably with less effort.

Still, it is true that Stalin was not a cult figure in the Zubalovo circle before the end of the decade, and this helps to explain why a man like Lavrenti Beria was becoming significant in his life. A Georgian twenty years Stalin's junior, Beria had joined the Cheka during the turbulent post-1917 period in the Transcaucasus. He was suspected by some leading Bolsheviks involved in the protracted Transcaucasian revolution of having played a double game as the fortunes of competing Bolshevik and anti-Bolshevik forces rose and fell. He also became known in those circles as a despicable, wholly unscrupulous character. By around 1930 he had become head of

32. *Ibid.*, pp. 24, 35–36, 39.

the Transcaucasian secret police administration. Just when he and Stalin first met is not known, but it was probably before the end of the twenties.[33] He was hated by the Svanidzes, the Redenses, and others of the Zubalovo circle who knew about his past. Much later Stalin told his daughter that Nadya had "made scenes" and had insisted, as early as 1929, that "that man must not be allowed to set foot in our house." He recalled: "I asked her what was wrong with him. Give me facts. I'm not convinced. I see no facts! But she just cried out, 'What facts do you need? I just see he's a scoundrel! I won't have him here.' I told her to go to hell. He's my friend. He's a good Chekist." [34]

What attracted Stalin to Beria was not just the fact that he saw in him a useful tool as a "good Chekist." Sensing Stalin's craving for admiration, Beria won a place in his good graces through flattery, an art in which he excelled. "He flattered my father with a shamelessness that was nothing if not Oriental," states Svetlana. "He praised him and made up to him in a way that caused old friends, accustomed to looking on my father as an equal, to wince with embarrassment." [35] Whether these recollections refer to the time of which we are writing or to a later period, we may be sure that Beria employed these deferential devices from the start in his relations with Stalin. His future services as one of the architects of the personality cult must have been prefigured in the worshipful attitude that he assumed toward Stalin even then.

The fact that he tolerated Beria's extravagant praise bespoke

33. Roy A. Medvedev suggests that it was in the summer of 1931, when, as he also reports, Stalin went south for a rest cure and Beria took personal charge of his bodyguard. But Medvedev's position is internally inconsistent on this point, for he also reports that later in 1931, when a deputation of Transcaucasian party officials called on Ordzhonikidze in Moscow to protest Stalin's intention to promote Beria to second secretary of the Transcaucasian Party Committee, Ordzhonikidze said: "For a long time I've been telling Stalin that Beria is a crook, but Stalin won't listen to me, and no one can make him change his mind" (*Let History Judge: The Origins and Consequences of Stalinism* [New York, 1971], p. 243).

34. Alliluyeva, *Twenty Letters,* pp. 19–20. The author writes that this conversation with her father took place when she was grown up.

35. *Ibid.,* p. 137.

Stalin's receptivity to it. For a long time, however, this hankering for adulation was something that he felt constrained to conceal, particularly from the party at large. Personal vanity was frowned upon in Bolshevik circles, and Lenin's freedom from it was well known. One of Trotsky's disadvantages in the succession contest had been the suspicion in many party minds that he was a vain and ambitious man. In *Revolutionary Silhouettes* Lunacharsky dismissed the suspicion as groundless, but contrasted Lenin's and Trotsky's attitudes toward themselves. Lenin, he wrote, was a man who never contemplated himself, never looked at himself in the mirror of history, and never even considered what posterity would say of him, but simply did his work, actuated by an enormous confidence in his own rightness combined with a certain inability to see things from his opponent's point of view. Trotsky, on the other hand, was one who without doubt frequently contemplated himself, valued his role in history, and would make any personal sacrifice, even life itself, to remain wreathed in mankind's memory as a true revolutionary leader.[36] Given such a climate of opinion in the party, it was contrary to Stalin's interest to be seen as another who liked to view himself in the mirror of history. So he carefully avoided conveying such an impression. He cultivated a public image of himself as a simple, modest, unassuming man, devoid of vanity like Lenin; a man whose whole being was selflessly absorbed in the party's political affairs, the concerns of Communism as a movement.

In his talk to the Kremlin cadets in January 1924, for example, he invoked the memory of Tammerfors, where Lenin had set him an instructive example of the simplicity and modesty characteristic of a true proletarian *vozhd'*. Earlier, in his speech at the meeting for Lenin's fiftieth birthday, he had singled out "the modesty of Comrade Lenin" as his special theme and illustrated it with two examples of the courageous way in which "this giant" admitted his mistakes. The emphasis on modesty as a Bolshevik virtue recurred in his statements of subsequent years, as when he saluted a deceased

36. A. V. Lunacharsky, *Revoliutsionnye siluety* (Moscow, 1923), pp. 26, 27.

Civil War leader of his acquaintance as "the bravest among our modest commanders and the most modest among the brave." [37] In keeping with this, he portrayed himself as Lenin's disciple and insistently ascribed his views to Lenin even when, as in the case of the doctrine of socialism in one country, they were essentially post-Leninist. When a participant in the party discussions of early 1927 described the slogan of a "worker-peasant government" as "Comrade Stalin's formula," Stalin replied that he was only repeating Lenin, and then pedantically proved his point by giving the page references to thirty passages in Lenin's works where the formula appeared.[38] The purpose of showing that the formula was Leninist merged with that of presenting himself as Lenin's self-effacing disciple. His simple style of dress accentuated the impression. As a result of all this, Stalin's enormous egocentricity remained hidden from general view. Probably very few persons outside the narrow circle of close associates realized what a swollen and sensitive self-esteem lurked behind the pipe-smoking *gensek*'s gruff, unassuming exterior.

The Vindictive Response

The other side of his swollen self-esteem was Stalin's painful sensitivity to whatever he interpreted as a slight or aspersion. If the surest way of pleasing him was to affirm his idealized version of himself, the surest way of incurring his displeasure or wrath was to negate it. For the same reason that adulation was balm to his insecurity, anything resembling disparagement aggravated it. If the disparagement was justified, Stalin would have to plead guilty before his inner tribunal and accept its condemnatory judgment. That being intolerable, he had to assume that the disparagement was unmerited, in which case the person who failed to give him due recognition and deference must be intentionally maligning him, and Stalin characteristically responded by striking out in anger against the maligner.

37. *Stalin*, VIII, 99. The statement was made in 1926.
38. *Ibid.*, IX, 180.

There were many occasions during Stalin's time of post-Lenin struggle and triumph when fellow party members behaved toward him in ways that impugned his exalted self-concept. One section of the party, the Left opposition, not only failed to recognize him as a great leader but fought his policy views, rejected his theoretical argumentation as un-Leninist and invalid, and let it be known that they considered him a mediocrity. Kamenev rose before the Fourteenth Congress in 1925 to contest his credentials for becoming the new *vozhd'*. As the intra-party battle reached its climax in October of the following year, Trotsky depicted Stalin as a man whose leadership threatened ruination of the Revolution. Before very long, accusations of comparable gravity were coming from leaders of the embattled Right opposition. There were instances, too, in which old revolutionaries treated Stalin condescendingly not because they were active in the oppositions but simply because they were unable to take him seriously in the role of Bolshevik supreme leader or Marxist theoretician. Finally, there were a great many in the party who, whatever they said openly, entertained a view of Stalin greatly at variance with his own. He had not, as we have seen, become one of the legendary figures of Bolshevism. Not even on the tenth anniversary of October did he figure in Soviet publicity as its co-leader. Although Trotsky's name was now rapidly being expunged from the record, everyone still knew that he was "the second great leader of the Russian Revolution," as Lunacharsky had written in *Revolutionary Silhouettes* [39]—in which, as noted earlier, there was no "silhouette" of Stalin. This was but one of numerous instances in which Stalin was confronted by *non*-affirmation of his self-concept inside the party.

Unable to question his fundamental beliefs about himself in the light of all this, Stalin questioned the motives and the political character of the people who were—as he saw it—underestimating his revolutionary services, disparaging his abilities, maligning his policies, and generally vilifying *him*. He reacted with resentment, anger, and the resolve to gain a vindictive triumph over those who did not affirm his view of himself. It was not always politic for him

39. *Revoliutsionnye siluety*, p. 27.

to voice such feelings openly, but they came to the surface in various ways. Trotsky points out, for example, that Stalin found a subtle means of expressing his resentment against Lunacharsky for omitting him from *Revolutionary Silhouettes*. He did it by alluding, in a speech of 1925, to Lunacharsky's less than courageous conduct while in police custody in Petrograd in July 1917.[40] On some occasions, he reacted with an explosion of wrath. When Trotsky dramatically pointed to Stalin during a stormy Politburo session of 1926 attended by many Central Committee members and exclaimed: "The first secretary poses his candidature to the post of gravedigger of the Revolution!" [41] Stalin "turned pale, rose, first contained himself with difficulty, and then rushed out of the hall, slamming the door." Soon afterwards Piatakov, one of the Central Committee members who had been present at the meeting, arrived pale and shaken at Trotsky's apartment:

He poured out a glass of water, gulped it down, and said: "You know I have smelt gunpowder, but I have never seen anything like this! This was worse than anything! And why, why did Lev Davidovich say this? Stalin will never forgive him until the third and fourth generation!" Piatakov was so upset that he was unable to relate clearly what had happened. When Lev Davidovich at last entered the dining room, Piatakov rushed at him asking: "But why, why have you said this?" With a wave of his hand Lev Davidovich brushed the question aside. He was exhausted but calm. He had shouted at Stalin: "Gravedigger of the revolution." . . . We understood that the breach was irreparable.[42]

In this instance everyone realized instinctively that no matter how ill-disposed Stalin might have been toward Trotsky hitherto, his will to vengeance would now be utterly implacable. The challenge that Trotsky had flung down was so flagrant that Stalin could never desist from the quest for revenge. What remained far less clear

40. Trotsky, *Stalin,* pp. 389, 394.
41. Isaac Deutscher, *The Prophet Unarmed: Trotsky, 1921–1929* (London, 1959), p. 296. For Trotsky's account of the episode, see *Trotsky's Diary in Exile, 1935* (New York, 1963), p. 69.
42. Deutscher, *The Prophet Unarmed,* pp. 296–297. The eyewitness account of the scene in Trotsky's apartment is quoted by Deutscher from Victor Serge, *Vie et mort de Trotsky* (Paris, 1951), pp. 180–181, some parts of which were written by Trotsky's wife, Sedova.

at the time was that he would respond in the same basic manner to incomparably less serious provocations than Trotsky's terrible epithet. Any statement or omission that appeared derogatory to himself—and this meant anything that detracted from the image of the *genial'ny* Stalin—could call forth his vengeful anger. It was not necessary to directly impugn one or another of his claims to greatness. Simply by taking issue with him on a theoretical problem or point of party history, and particularly by persisting in one's position after he had once argued its erroneousness, one could implicitly disparage his picture of himself as a pre-eminent Marxist thinker and evoke the vindictive response.

Stalin's correspondence with one S. Pokrovsky in 1927 is an illustration. In a first exchange, Pokrovsky contested and Stalin upheld the view that in 1917 the party had dropped its previous strategic slogan of "alliance *with the whole* peasantry" in favor of a new one calling for "alliance *with the poor* peasantry." An important issue of current peasant policy was implicit in this historical debate, but that would not explain the emotional outburst that Pokrovsky provoked from Stalin by writing him a second letter in which, while retreating on the slogan question, he asserted that he had been guilty only of a "verbal" inaccuracy and then taxed Stalin with "having given no reply" on the matter of neutralizing the middle peasants. Stalin began his second and final letter, which remained unpublished for twenty-one years, by saying that he had thought he was dealing with someone in search of the truth, but that now, after Pokrovsky's second letter, he could see that he was corresponding with a conceited, insolent man who placed the interests of his ego higher than those of truth. A terrible tongue-lashing followed, replete with epithets like "you and many other political philistines" and language such as the following: "Carried away by the 'artistry' of your own pen and conveniently forgetting your first letter, you assert that I have failed to understand the question of the *growing over* of the bourgeois revolution into the socialist revolution. That is indeed a case of laying one's own fault at another's door!" Stalin ended: "Conclusion: one must possess the effrontery of an ignoramus and the self-complacency of a narrow-minded equilibrist to turn things upside down as unceremoniously as you do, esteemed Pokrovsky. I think the time has come to stop corresponding with you. *I. Stalin.*" [43]

A similar episode, which also remained private for many years, occurred in 1930 when a party member responded to one of Stalin's public speeches by writing him a note in which he apparently said something about contradictions between the proletariat and the kulaks. In Stalin's reply, which as later published in his collected works identified the correspondent only as "Comrade Ch-e," Stalin said that the note reflected a confusion. The speech had been concerned only with resolvable contradictions between the proletariat and the mass of working peasants. "Plain? I think so," remarked Stalin, ending his reply: "With Communist greetings." Whereupon Comrade Ch-e made the mistake of continuing the discussion in a second letter. Stalin, now infuriated, took him to task in his own second reply for playing a "game of words" instead of honestly admitting his mistake. The diplomatic blurring over of the difference between the two sorts of contradictions was highly characteristic of Trotskyist-Zinovievist thinking, he said. "I did not think you were infected with this disease, but now I have to reckon with this too," ran the ominous conclusion. "Since I do not know what kind of a game you will play next and I am devilishly overburdened with current work, in view of which I have no time left for games, permit me to say good-bye to you, Comrade Ch-e." This time there were no Communist greetings. [44]

There were many other such episodes in which party members unwittingly wounded Stalin's pride. They were acting in the tradition of sanctioned intra-party discussion, remembering how Lenin had respected the right of Bolsheviks to disagree with him on questions of party policy. Stalin's very insistence upon his faithful discipleship to the master, his assurances that the Leninist style of leadership was his model, afforded them encouragement in this. For these reasons, the widespread acceptance of Stalin as the party's new supreme leader did not bring automatic acquiescence in all his

43. *Stalin*, IX, 315–321.
44. *Ibid.*, X, 20–22.

views. Many went on voicing opinions at variance with his, only to discover later that they had been acting as "enemies." For this was his characteristic conclusion concerning those who aroused the vindictive response.

Stalin's daughter has given a graphic description of him in the act of drawing such conclusions. If he was told that someone "has been saying bad things about you" or "opposes you," and that there were facts to prove this, a "psychological metamorphosis" would come over him. No matter how long and well he had known the person concerned, he would now put him down as an enemy. According to Svetlana, "At this point—and this was where his cruel, implacable nature showed itself—the past ceased to exist for him. Years of friendship and fighting side by side in a common cause might as well never have been. . . . 'So you've betrayed me,' some inner demon would whisper. 'I don't even know you anymore.' " [45]

In an individual who had thus incurred his vindictive hostility Stalin was compelled to see not simply a personal enemy but also an enemy of the Soviet cause. The Bolshevik political culture provided a strong foundation for this in its conception of the class struggle as a continuing phenomenon in Soviet society and as a fact of international life in a world divided into two hostile camps. This doctrine, in both of its aspects, found no more fervent exponent among the party leaders than Stalin, who summed it up in a 1928 speech by saying: "We have internal enemies. We have external enemies. This, comrades, must not be forgotten for a single moment." [46] In expounding the two-camp theory, moreover, his reasoning was more schematic and his rhetoric more violent than Lenin's. "The world has split decisively and irrevocably into two camps," he wrote in 1919. "The struggle between them is the entire axis of contemporary life, the whole substance of the internal and external policies of the leaders of the old world and the new." [47] In another article of that time he showed his tendency to highlight anything stealthy, devious, or conspiratorial in the class enemy's behavior.

45. Alliluyeva, *Twenty Letters*, p. 78.
46. *Stalin*, XI, 63.
47. *Ibid.*, IV, 232.

The imperialist camp, he said, was "not dozing." Its agents were "on the prowl through all the countries from Finland to the Caucasus, from Siberia to Turkestan, supplying the counter-revolutionaries, hatching criminal conspiracies, organizing a crusade against Soviet Russia, and forging chains for the peoples of the West." [48] Elsewhere he wrote that the Entente, having failed in its open intervention against Soviet Russia, was now going over to a new policy of "disguised" or "masked" intervention involving the use of Rumania, Poland, Galicia, Finland, and Germany for counter-revolutionary operations.[49] Although these statements were not devoid of some factual basis, it is worth noting here that the conspiracy theme, which would be one of the hallmarks of Stalinist thinking, was making its appearance in Stalin's writings of the revolutionary era.

He did not necessarily harbor any great personal animosity against people who by definition fell in the category of class enemies —heads of foreign states, for example. But the converse did not hold true. When his personal animosity was aroused against persons in his own milieu, he had to see them as class enemies rather than simply as party critics or opponents of Stalin. This ominous inference was necessitated, first, by the fact that it provided justification for voicing and acting upon his rage against these people, his urge to take revenge upon them. For if they were class enemies, they fully deserved to be mercilessly exposed and harshly punished. But equally important, the categorizing of his critics as class enemies was for Stalin a necessary way of rationalizing their derogatory attitudes toward him. He thereby warded off any need to confront himself in a self-questioning way and accept the painful possibility that these attitudes had some foundation.

It was out of the question for him to regard such an individual —we may call him X—as an honorable anti-Stalin Bolshevik. For this would be an implicit admission that a party person in good standing could conceivably find some political failing or imperfection in Stalin, which in turn would threaten to arouse Stalin's latent

48. *Ibid.*, pp. 181–182.
49. *Ibid.*, pp. 246–248.

self-doubts and suppressed self-condemnatory feelings. So, he identified X as an anti-*party* person, an enemy of the Bolshevik *cause*.
Now he could take full account of X's critical or unfriendly view
without a twinge of self-questioning, *or even construe it as an in-
direct confirmation of his idealized image of himself*. For if X was
an enemy of the Bolshevik cause, then he would naturally and
necessarily be opposed to a Stalin who was the best of Leninists
and the principal defender of that cause. He would be critical of
Stalin's ideas and policies precisely *because* they were in the interests of Communism. He would belittle Stalin's revolutionary past
and disparage him as a political personality precisely *because* he
perceived his historic merits and his genius as a Marxist-Leninist
leader. Far from expressing X's real opinion of Stalin, the belittlement and disparagement would be his way of trying to tear Stalin
down in the eyes of the party, to keep the younger generation from
realizing what a great revolutionary Stalin had been, to discredit
Stalin as the foremost figure of the movement after Lenin, and thereby to hurt the movement.

By this logic, the very attributes of personal and political greatness which made Stalin an outstanding party leader would make him
also, inevitably, the chief target of hatred and opposition on the part
of all deviationists, ill-wishers of the party, and the like: they were
against him precisely *because* he was the man of genius that he conceived himself to be. Here, then, was a line of reasoning that made
it possible for him to interpret anti-Stalin attitudes as evidence in
favor of his heroic self-image. As a result, the picture of his detractors as enemies of the party and people became an integral part
of his identity structure. Instead of having a restraining effect upon
his self-estimate, the unflattering view that many in the party took
of him only made him all the more adamantly insistent upon its
validity, and all the more avid for others' affirmation that they saw
him as he saw himself. And having rationalized opposition to himself as a twisted kind of tribute to his genius, he could welcome attacks on the part of those he had put down as "enemies"; they
were flattery in disguise. Let the Trotskyists attack me to their
hearts' content, he said in his speech of October 23, 1927, in the

Central Committee. They rightly choose me as their main target, for I am the one who best sees through them and their machinations. And consider the abuse that Trotsky once poured on Lenin! Is it any wonder that one who disparaged Lenin as he did in his letter of 1913 to Chkheidze should now be vilifying Stalin?

Stalin's way of rationalizing derogatory attitudes was not lost upon perceptive persons around him. *Pravda*'s leading article for his fiftieth birthday on December 21, 1929, which must have been written under the direction of his former assistant Mekhlis, who was now the editor, said: "Stalin stands at the head of the Leninist Central Committee. Therefore he is invariably the object of savage abuse on the part of the world bourgeoisie and the Social Democrats. All the oppositions inside the party always aim their arrows at Comrade Stalin as the most unbending, the most authoritative Bolshevik, the most implacable defender of Leninism against any and all perversions." To cite a further example, G. Krumin observed in his birthday article on Stalin's merits as a theoretician that "countless enemies of the party" were *right,* from their own point of view, in denying these merits. Not for nothing, he went on, did the world bourgeoisie and the Social Democratic press assail Stalin with such malice and bestial hatred, and heap filthy slander upon him. And by the same token, attacks on Stalin were the telltale sign of each new opposition arising in the party under the influence of hostile elements and classes. "For the enemies of the party know that a blow against Stalin is a blow against the party, a blow against the most faithful disciple and confederate of Lenin. . . ." [50]

But if the maligners of Stalin were enemies of the party, they would not admit to being such. If it was hostility toward the Bolshevik cause that made them hate Stalin and strive to besmirch him, the hostility was concealed. Derogatory attitudes toward Stalin were strongest, after all, in Old Bolshevik circles. Although Trotsky and some of his colleagues had not joined the Bolshevik organization until 1917, many members of the Left as well as the Right opposition, and still others who were not friendly to Stalin, had

50. *Pravda,* December 21, 1929.

illustrious Bolshevik records going as far back as Stalin's or farther. Ostensibly they had been and remained loyal party men and good Leninists, and they purported to be acting as such when they attacked, opposed, criticized, and belittled Stalin. As enemies of the party, therefore, they must be *covert* enemies operating behind the masks of friends. Their Bolshevism must be a masquerade. That such was the trend of Stalin's thinking would become abundantly clear in the thirties, but this was beginning to be apparent still earlier, as was his general readiness, noted above, to perceive class enemies as conspiratorial in their conduct. The word "mask," for example, came readily to his lips or pen. Thus, in his furious final letter to S. Pokrovsky he commented, apropos Pokrovsky's point that his earlier letter had not dealt with the question of neutralizing the middle peasant: "One or the other: either you are too naïve or you are deliberately putting on a mask of naïveté for some purpose that is by no means scientific." [51] In his Central Committee speech of April 1929, he accused Bukharin of trying to "mask" his treacherous position toward the party with talk about collective leadership. Moreover, he said, Bukharin had talked in the same way when, as leader of the Left opposition against the Brest agreement in 1918, he "conspired" with the Left SR "enemies of our party," who for their part had intended to arrest Lenin and carry out an anti-Soviet coup.[52]

Before his final victory in the post-Lenin power struggle, Stalin was beginning to manifest his tendency to view Bolsheviks hostile toward him as enemies who had spent much of their lives wearing a mask of loyalty and conspiring against the very party to which they claimed to be totally dedicated. This being the direction of his thinking, it is no wonder that a "psychological metamorphosis" would come over him when he concluded that one whom he had considered a friend was really an enemy. In general, no enemy is so evil and dangerous, so important to expose and so deserving of harsh treatment, as one who has worn the mask of a friend. Stalin therefore grew mercilessly hostile toward any individual whom he

51. *Stalin*, IX, 317.
52. *Ibid.*, XII, 100–101.

had come to see in this light, regardless of how long and close their association had been. As his daughter has further testified, years of friendship and common struggle meant nothing to him in these circumstances. Once his condemnatory judgment had been pronounced, he could not retract it: "Once he had cast out of his heart someone he had known a long time, once he had mentally relegated that someone to the ranks of his enemies, it was impossible to talk to him about that person anymore. He was constitutionally incapable of the reversal that would turn a fancied enemy back into a friend. Any effort to persuade him only made him furious." [53] Stalin's inability to reverse the judgment of condemnation is understandable. For if someone had been an enemy in disguise all along, then his manifestations of loyalty and good will must have been feigned; and the greater the false show of friendship had been, the more evil and depraved an enemy he must be. Naturally, it was hopeless under these conditions to appeal to Stalin with reminders of the past record of friendly association. For him, that very record now stood as evidence of the unmasked individual's perfidy.

In Stalin's mind, then, the hero-image of himself was in symbiosis with a villain-image of the enemy. Counterposed to the picture of himself as a great revolutionary and Marxist, the truest of Lenin's disciples and his rightful successor at the head of the movement, was a picture of the enemy inside the party as would-be betrayer of it and the Revolution. The enemy was everything that the *genial'ny* Stalin was not: an opponent of Lenin, a disguised counter-revolutionary, a military bungler, a pseudo-Marxist in theory, and a saboteur of the construction of a socialist society in Russia. Because he was all these things, the enemy was also, necessarily, a vicious hater and maligner of Stalin. In addition, he was morally loathsome in his duplicity and his willingness to resort to the most devious, underhanded, conspiratorial means in pursuit of his anti-party ends. Such was Stalin's generic view of those party comrades whom he mentally classified as enemies. He was willing to admit that individual cases differed from one another, but ultimately the differences seemed inessential. The crucial question was whether a

53. Alliluyeva, *Twenty Letters*, p. 59.

given person belonged to the category of "friend" or that of "enemy." Those Bolsheviks who by word or deed convinced Stalin that his image of the enemy applied to them did so at their peril and, in a great many instances, to their subsequent sorrow.

The Projected Stalin

Stalin has gone down in history with a merited reputation for being, among other things, a fighter without scruples, a Machiavellian power-seeker, a master at double-dealing, and a cynical realist in politics. He showed this side of himself in small ways as well as large. Duplicity was second nature to him. He used coarse language at times and was given to obscenity in private conversations with associates. The esteem in which he held the physical realities of power was later to be immortalized in his question: "How many divisions has the Pope?" Many biographers have stressed these qualities of Stalin. Trotsky, who came by his knowledge of them through harsh experience, was planning to entitle an unfinished chapter of his biography *"Kinto in Power." Kinto,* in Georgian, was a slang term referring to the tough, sly street youth of old Tiflis. Trotsky recalled Makharadze saying of Stalin at some point in the twenties: "He's a—*kinto*!" [54]

While keeping the *kinto* side of Stalin clearly in view, we should take care not to assume that it was part of Stalin's self-image: the evidence presented in these pages testifies that it was not. His self-consciousness was focused upon the attributes and exploits of genius that made up the lofty paragon-self. Insofar as he could not help being aware of such elements of his nature as rudeness, underhandedness, duplicity, meanness, and cruelty, he attempted to reconcile them with the idealized image of himself by rationalization. As shown above, by rationalization he transmuted the rudeness for which Lenin had faulted him into, in one instance, a zeal for preserving the purity of Leninist doctrine and, in another, a hardness toward enemies of the party. In both cases the offensive trait underwent a metamorphosis and emerged as something Stalin could prop-

54. Trotsky, *Stalin,* p. 414.

erly take pride in; indeed, as an attribute of his heroic revolutionary persona.

In yet another episode of rationalizing, Stalin justified an unbecoming course of conduct by reference to the final goals of the Revolution. A certain Shinkevich wrote to him in protest against a party decision to reopen the vodka trade as a governmental monopoly. In old Russia vodka had served as the common man's consolation for a grim life, and many revolutionaries—including Lenin, whom Shinkevich now quoted—had denounced the state vodka trade as an evil. In his reply to Shinkevich, dated March 20, 1927, but first published twenty-five years later, Stalin admitted that this had been Lenin's position but explained that in 1922 Lenin had agreed with members of the the Central Committee that it was necessary to re-introduce the vodka monopoly. Had the Genoa conference of that year (at which economic problems were discussed by Soviet Russia and the major European powers) resulted in a large foreign loan or long-range credits, such a decision would not have become necessary. As it was, however, vodka remained the only possible source of funds for industrial development. Stalin went on: "Which was better: enslavement to foreign capital or the introduction of vodka? This was how the question stood before us. It is clear that we came down on the side of the vodka because we believed and continue to believe that *if we have to dirty our hands a little bit* for the sake of the final victory of the proletariat and the peasantry, *we will go to this extreme for the sake of the interests of our cause.*" [55] In this instance the action being rationalized was one taken by the party Central Committee, though evidently with Stalin's strong concurrence. Undoubtedly, however, "the interests of our cause" was a formula by which he also rationalized many actions of his own that involved the dirtying of hands.

But there was much in Stalin's character, conduct, and past career that did not easily lend itself to rationalization by reference to the Revolution's goals or the need to resort to foul means in combating foul enemies. Here, as already indicated, repression played a great role in his mental life, helping him to hold on to his pride

55. *Stalin,* IX, 191–192. Italics added.

system and preserve his rigidly self-righteous posture in spite of everything. He kept the *genial'ny* Stalin in clear focus by censoring out or blurring discordant aspects of himself. Repression operated as a defense mechanism, however, in tandem with projection. Facts thrust out of awareness because of their inconsistency with the self-concept tended to re-appear in his perceptions of others; and then he could and would give vent to the self-recriminatory feelings that these discordancies aroused in him as *recriminatory feelings toward these others*. So projection performed the cathartic service of permitting him not only to admit painful or embarrassing facts into consciousness but also to give uninhibited expression to the emotions associated with them.

Let us consider his characteristic way of coming to terms with his mistakes and the blame for them. Sooner or later the mistakes would be attributed to and blamed on others. Of course, politicians under all forms of government have an interest in shifting responsibility for their own mistakes onto others, preferably their opponents. But in Stalin this went along with an intense psychological aversion to admitting errors and being blamed, an aversion arising from the incompatibility of blameworthy mistakes with the paragon-self. If he was truly the *genial'ny* Stalin, he could hardly have taken a whole series of wrong stands in the revolutionary politics of 1917. He could not have considered even hypothetically the possibility of Lenin's volunteering to appear before a court of the Provisional Government. He could not have been recalled from the southwestern front in 1920 for costly insubordination. But it was not sufficient for him to shut these and other transgressions out of awareness; he had to go further and impute them to others, upon whom he could then heap the blame that he found it intolerable to take upon himself. The others may in fact have committed mistakes of the type ascribed to them, or they may not have. Kamenev, for example, had taken some stands similar to Stalin's in 1917, whereas there was no basis for accusing Bukharin, as would one day be done, of advocating Lenin's surrender for trial by the Provisional Government. Or for casting Trotsky in Stalin's historical role as a political commissar who had to be recalled from the front during the Civil

War because of military failures, although this was beginning to be done in Soviet writings by 1929.

If Stalin was under inner pressure to impute his own mistakes and failings to others and then to visit upon them the self-accusations and self-punitive feelings that these mistakes and failings caused in him, the most suitable targets—although not the only possible ones—were people already identified in his mind as enemies of the Revolution. They, after all, were in many instances the people for whom he already harbored vindictive hostility as a result of some sin of commission or omission against his pride. Since they were already objects of his hatred, the projection of his self-hatred upon them only intensified an established enmity and reinforced his conviction that those people deserved whatever punishment he might inflict upon them. Moreover, who but his enemies were the logical repository of all that he felt enmity toward in himself?

So it was that the villain-image of the enemy came to represent, as was suggested above, everything that Stalin rejected and condemned in himself. All that belonged to the rejected evil Stalin— the errors, flaws, and elements of villainy that had no place in his hero-image of himself—tended to be incorporated into his picture of the enemy, especially the picture of the internal enemy as villain of party history. Whatever he inwardly censored from the record of his past deeds and misdeeds was likely to re-appear in characterizations of his enemies. Further, Stalin had a remarkable propensity for seeing and condemning in enemies the qualities that he condemned *without seeing* in himself. We can infer from his idealized version of himself as an extremely modest man that one of the qualities he unconsciously rejected and condemned in himself was his monstrously inflated self-esteem, his arrogance. Accordingly, it comes as no surprise to find him ascribing "swollen pretentiousness" in the field of theory to Bukharin, who was actually the soul of modesty as well as the recognized chief theorist of Bolshevism, or to find him berating the hapless Pokrovsky for placing the "interests of his ego higher than those of truth." Or, finally, to be accusing this same Pokrovsky of doing precisely what he, Stalin, was doing in these and very many other instances—"laying one's own fault at another's door."

One further facet of the projected Stalin especially merits mention at this point. Stalin, we have seen, was acting out in life a role of historical greatness. Fully identified in his own mind with the revolutionary persona, he experienced himself as the Lenin II of Bolshevism. In a great many ways, however, the persona made demands that the real Stalin simply could not fulfill; the role was too much for him. He was in the position of attempting throughout life to be something that he was not, yet of never being able to face this fact. Consequently, there was unconscious pretense in him, which may explain the histrionic impression that he made on sensitive observers like Kennan and Djilas. Symbolizing as it did his ultimate incapacity to carry out his life-project, this pretense was supremely unacceptable to him, hence most stringently in need of repression and projection. This made Stalin prone to perceive pretense all around him. One of the telltale signs was his above-mentioned tendency to see those hostile to him as people wearing masks. To wear a mask means, of course, to put on an alien identity, to pretend to be something that one is not. Stalin's mental world was full of enemies wearing masks. External enemies were wont to wear masks, which they themselves sometimes took off. "Following the Nanking events," said Stalin in 1927, "imperialism is throwing aside unctuous speeches, non-intervention, the League of Nations, and any other mask. Now imperialism stands before the world in all its nakedness as an open predator and oppressor." [56] The masks of internal enemies, on the other hand, always had to be ripped off in order for them to be revealed in all their nakedness. Stalin's passion for vindictive exposure of internal enemies who, he thought, had lived lives of pretense behind masks of Bolshevism would become horrifyingly evident in the coming decade of the thirties.

Owing to the habit of projecting his unacceptable traits and self-accusations upon others, Stalin's accusations were very often self-revelatory. The villain-image of the enemy became a sort of

56. *Ibid.*, IX, 198–199.

dumping-ground for the rejected evil Stalin. The personal and political shortcomings, biographical blemishes, lapses, failures, mistakes, scandals—all the facts and memories that Stalin had to
repress because there was no place for them in the *genial'ny* Stalin
—could be emptied into his image of the enemy and by this means
mentally projected onto real persons in the environment whom he
identified as enemies. Then he could admit the incriminating facts
and memories into consciousness as facts and memories that related
not to him but to them. In the same way, feelings too painful to be
consciously felt with reference to himself could be felt with reference
to enemies "out there." Stalin could feel his own guilt as theirs, his
own self-condemnation as condemnation of them, his own self-
accusations as accusations against them. In addition, he could act
upon the feelings thus admitted into consciousness. He could expose the guilty ones and inflict punishment upon the accused.

Finally, the mechanism of projection made it possible for
Stalin to experience certain particularly inadmissible feelings as
enemy feelings toward himself. This is how he appears to have dealt
with his unconscious hatred and contempt of himself for not measur-
ing up to his standards of perfection. One piece of evidence is the
fact that the villain-image envisaged the enemy as a terrible hater
of Stalin. There were, of course, Bolsheviks who disliked him intensely, and some who loathed him. But the savage, slow-burning,
anti-Stalin fury that he imputed to "enemies of the party" bore a
strange resemblance to his own special way of hating. By projecting
his self-hatred not only as hatred of them but also, in part, as *their
hatred of him,* he could consider himself all the more justified in
repaying them in kind. He could take the offensive against them in
the belief that he was acting in self-defense. He could more freely
turn others into the objects of his self-destructive rage.

"We are surrounded by enemies—that is clear to all," said
Stalin to a party congress in 1923. "The wolves of imperialism who
surround us are not dozing. Not a moment passes without our enemies trying to seize some little chink through which they could
crawl and do harm to us." [57] But it was not only the world beyond

the Soviet borders that Stalin saw in this way. Inside Russia, too, and even within its Communist party, he felt himself to be in a besieged fortress. He was driven by unconscious needs and drives to people the party world around him with Stalin-hating enemies who pretended to be loyal Bolsheviks while watchfully waiting for an opportunity to strike a blow against the Communist cause and against him as its leader. Were such enemies lacking in sufficient numbers, he would have to invent them. And invent them he did.

Chapter Thirteen

THE NEW HERO

A Cult Is Born

THE PUBLIC CELEBRATION of Stalin's fiftieth birthday marked the effective beginning of his personality cult, a phenomenon destined to grow to gigantic proportions in the thirties and forties. Earlier intimations of the cult had been few and minor. The celebration of Stalin's forty-sixth birthday in 1925 was a local Georgian event reflected in the Tiflis press only. Still earlier, the paper of his Commissariat for Nationality Affairs had published a message from minority-nationality representatives saluting him as the architect of Soviet nationality policy. The message prophesied the advent of "a worldwide, united, fraternal Communist family which we will teach to value the great merits that belong to you—*vozhd*' of the oppressed nations." [1] There was also the obsequious welcoming statement on his arrival in Baku in late 1920. But all these were small straws in the wind by comparison with the 1929 event.

Its cause was a combination of political motives and psychological needs. The crushing defeat of the oppositions gave the Stalin faction an unprecedented freedom of maneuver in Soviet politics, making the move to start a Stalin cult possible. The cult of Lenin, an established institution of Soviet public life in 1929, constituted a precedent. The desire of Stalin and others of his faction to consolidate their enhanced power position was a political motive,

---

1. *Zhizn' natsional'nostei*, December 24, 1920. Bertram D. Wolfe, who unearthed this item, sees it as evidence that "the craving for flattery, and the will to exact it where he had the power, was inherent in Stalin's nature . . ." (*Khrushchev and Stalin's Ghost* [New York, 1957], p. 155 n.).

particularly at this time of incipient national upheaval in the collectivization and industrialization campaigns.[2] We should also reckon with the private political motives of some of the figures around Stalin, their wish to advance their own political careers by advocating and assisting in a move that they knew would please him.

From the psychological point of view, it need not be assumed that Stalin instigated or cooperated in the celebration out of a conscious craving for public acclaim. In approving the plan (without his approval, the celebration would not have occurred), he was very likely consciously influenced by his notion of the proper relationship between leader and followers. One of the characteristics of a heroic leader is that he is recognized as such and enjoys the complete trust and devotion of his followers. Such a picture of the leader-follower relation had been in Stalin's mind ever since he read in Kazbegi of the Caucasian mountaineers' adoration for their "man of iron" on a white charger, the warrior chicftain Shamil. His Bolshevik experience had reinforced it. In the person of Lenin the Bolsheviks had possessed a hero-*vozhd'*. In addition to his personal memory of this, Stalin had a constant reminder of it in the posthumous cult of Lenin. Accordingly, a merely powerful role of leadership could not satisfy him. He could not feel himself to be truly the "man of steel" while remaining the unsung boss of the party machine. He could not be Lenin II without a measure of the adulation and acclaim that had gone, and was still going, to Lenin I.

The paradox of his situation, however, was that he had achieved wide acceptance as the party's new supreme leader not only without being personally charismatic but in part *because* he was not. As we have noted, leadership of messianic caliber was not what the preponderance of party leaders and functionaries desired in those times. They were looking not for a great revolutionary and new charismatic personality in the role of *vozhd'* but for a practical and sober-minded manager who would steer a steady course toward socialism and pursue a prudent foreign policy. Stalin had recom-

2. For an interpretation of the rise of the Stalin cult that stresses this theme, see Moshe Lewin, *Russian Peasants and Soviet Power: A Study of Collectivization* (Evanston, Ill., 1968), pp. 452–453.

mended himself as just such a man. Even after his advance to the supreme leadership, therefore, no one saw him as a savior-hero. The popularity that he enjoyed in party circles by the later twenties had nothing in common with the feelings Lenin had inspired. He was accepted as the leader not by virtue of extraordinary personal qualities but because a great many agreed with the policies he advocated and were confident of his ability to supervise their implementation. Nor did the existence of the Lenin cult imply to Bolshevik minds that there ought to be a cult of his successor. Lenin remained the revered leader even after Stalin had become the generally accepted new chief. *Khozyain* ("boss"), the name by which Stalin was familiarly known in governmental circles, was a fair reflection of the attitude widely held toward him in the Soviet hierarchy. As late as the middle of 1929 there was not only no Stalin cult in Soviet Russia but no indication of substantial sentiment in the ruling party that such a thing was desirable.

The very success in political life which reinforced Stalin in his lofty self-estimate thus made his position vis-à-vis the party psychologically vulnerable. The rise to supreme leadership made him all the more desirous of admiration that he was not yet being accorded, hence all the more keenly aware of its absence. As his power in the party grew, moreover, the psychological need for recognition was undoubtedly intensified by his sense of the practical political importance of personal prestige, especially at the present juncture, and by his awareness that a merely factual supreme leader, a boss in the post of general secretary, was not what *vozhd'* meant in the Bolshevik leadership tradition. He had expressed this awareness in a still unpublished letter of 1925 to a German Communist leader: "Leaders [*vozhdi*] of the party can be real leaders only if they are not merely feared but also respected in the party, if their authority is recognized." [3]

Since there was no formal office of *vozhd'*, however, the only way in which Stalin could finally establish and consolidate himself in the successor role was to gain general party recognition in it.

---

3. *Stalin*, VII, 45. The letter, dated February 28, 1925, was addressed to a "Comrade Me—rt," not otherwise identified.

To *be* the supreme leader, he had to be publicly acknowledged and acclaimed as such. A further major move was called for in the politics of biography—a celebration of Stalin as party chief.

A convenient pretext for such a celebration—his fiftieth birthday—presented itself at the very time when events in the party made it politically opportune. Here we may recall that while Lenin suppressed the incipient manifestations of a Lenin cult, he did submit —albeit with extreme reluctance and distaste—to the desire in party circles to hold a meeting in honor of his fiftieth birthday. Hence party history contained a precedent for the honoring of Stalin that now occurred. Given the precedent, and the Stalin faction's political ascendancy at this time, it was probably not difficult for persons in Stalin's entourage to arrange the event. Just at this time Stalin men were moving into important positions in the apparatus that they had not previously held. Stalin's assistant Mekhlis, for example, was appointed managing secretary of *Pravda* following the resignation of Bukharin as editor-in-chief in April 1929 and not long afterward became editor himself.

The birthday was not celebrated in a party meeting as Lenin's had been, possibly because Stalin remembered how Lenin had absented himself from the ceremony in 1920 and had then expressed disapproval of it during his brief appearance. This affair was no mere gathering of friends but a bureaucratic extravaganza. Workers from all over the Soviet Union were reported to be adopting resolutions expressing birthday greetings to "dear Leader," and *Pravda* over a five-day period listed hundreds of organizations that had sent him messages of this character. On December 21, the Soviet newspapers printed special birthday issues filled with eulogies. The leitmotif of all the messages was that Stalin had succeeded Lenin as— in the words of *Pravda*'s editorial—"the leader and *vozhd'* of the party." A message from the party Central Committee and Central Control Commission saluted him as "the best Leninist and senior member of the Central Committee and its Politburo." Birthday articles by his party associates paid tribute to him as Lenin's supremely gifted disciple and successor. An official biography was issued, with the following concluding paragraph: "In these years since Lenin's death, Stalin, the most outstanding continuator of Lenin's cause and his most orthodox disciple, the inspirer of all the most important party measures in the struggle to build socialism, has become the generally acknowledged *vozhd'* of the party and the Comintern." A collection of these materials in book form came out in a first edition of 300,000 copies.[4] Altogether, it was an impressive inauguration of what the Soviet Union would one day look back upon as Stalin's "cult of personality" (*kul't lichnosti*).

The most significant difference between the two fiftieth-birthday celebrations was not, however, the grand scale of the publicity in the later one or its non-spontaneous character as compared with the gathering for Lenin; it was the difference in the attitudes of the two men toward the event. For Lenin the personal adulation was an obvious ordeal; for Stalin, it appears to have been an hour of triumph. The gratification that it gave him showed through in his message of thanks to all who sent greetings:

> Your congratulations and greetings I place to the credit of the great party of the working class which bore me and reared me in its own image and likeness. It is precisely because I place them to the credit of our glorious Leninist party that I make bold to tender you my Bolshevik thanks.
>
> You need have no doubt, comrades, that I am prepared in the future, too, to devote to the cause of the working class, to the cause of the proletarian revolution and world Communism, all my strength, all my ability, and, if need be, all my blood, drop by drop.[5]

For all its careful phrasing, this was an extraordinarily self-revelatory statement. Notable, first, is Stalin's transparent attempt to preserve his modest pose amid the eulogies by pretending that they were really meant for the party rather than for him, which was manifestly not the case. Secondly, the remarkable imagery of birth and rearing by implication placed the party and Stalin in a mother-son relationship and thereby suggested that he saw in the party— or wanted to see—another source of the trust, loving devotion, and

---

4. *Stalin. Sbornik statei k piatidesiatiletiiu so dnia rozhdeniia* (Moscow and Leningrad, 1929). A second mass edition came out in 1930. Unless otherwise indicated, the birthday materials cited in this chapter are cited from this source.

5. *Pravda*, December 22, 1929.

complete admiration that he had originally received from his own mother. In place of the doting mother of his childhood, he needed a doting party.

Finally, and as if in confirmation of this hidden confession, Stalin drew a striking picture of himself in the heroic mode—as one who would be prepared to die a martyr's death for the Communist cause by shedding his blood, if necessary, drop by drop. It was a remarkable display of the self-dramatizing that we have repeatedly had occasion to note in him. A witticism heard at the time in party circles not friendly to him testified to the statement's melodramatic quality: "Why all this modesty about shedding it drop by drop, can't he give all his blood at once?" [6]

The Best Leninist

The fiftieth-birthday celebration was at once a crowning act in the post-Lenin politics of biography and a means of satisfying Stalin's psychological need for recognition as a great man of the Communist movement. In the former aspect, its principal purpose was to create a public image of him as Lenin's successor, or "generally acknowledged *vozhd'*." The event basically accomplished this purpose simply by being what it was—a pageant of party and public acceptance of Stalin in the role of supreme leader. The aim was further promoted by portraying his revolutionary biography and political personality in terms befitting the supreme-leader role. Here, however, the other aspect of the celebration also emerges. The public acclaim of Stalin as an outstanding revolutionary leader—the "rock-hard Bolshevik" that many of the anniversary articles called him—served his need for affirmation in this capacity. Stalin's friends and associates were aware of this need in him, and of the forms of recognition that especially gratified him. Hence *their* eulogies told something of *his* self-image. The revolutionary virtues they ascribed to him were those he believed himself to possess. The exploits they praised were his past deeds as he liked to remember them. Con-

6. Abdurakhman Avtorkhanov, *Stalin and the Soviet Communist Party: A Study in the Technology of Power* (New York, 1959), p. 157.

sequently, and paradoxically, this most secretive of modern political men, who was always so reticent in all that concerned himself personally, opened himself up to an extraordinary extent. The words of others revealed something of his inner world of heroic make-believe.

Among the hero-roles that he imagined himself to be playing in the history of the Russian and world revolution, that of "best Leninist"—a phrase appearing frequently in the anniversary materials—stands out in first place. This is not at all surprising in view of the hero-identification with Lenin that Stalin had formed in his youth. In his early revolutionary persona as a member of the Bolshevik movement, he and Lenin were indissolubly linked as leader and lieutenant. As a self-concept in Djugashvili's mind, "Stalin" carried from the start the connotation of "best Leninist." Now, on his fiftieth birthday, he was hailed as just this.

Stalin was affirmed in various ways as the figure he had set out to become in the revolutionary movement: Lenin's truest disciple, comrade-in-arms, trusty helper and alter ego. His life was described precisely as the life he had wished for himself: "From the very first days of your work as a professional revolutionary building the first cells of the Bolshevik organization under the leadership of Lenin, you showed yourself to be the faithful best disciple of Lenin. Among the immediate disciples and comrades-in-arms of Lenin you proved the most staunch and consistent-to-the-end Leninist. Not once in your entire career have you deviated from Lenin either in your theoretical positions of principle or in all your practical work." So stated the message from the Central Committee and Central Control Commission. The same theme ran through most of the anniversary articles, those by Yenukidze and Ordzhonikidze in particular. "Stalin was always with Lenin, never departed from him, never betrayed him," wrote Yenukidze. As if to blot out all memory of the "tempest in a teacup" phrase of 1908, Ordzhonikidze falsely testified that when Lenin broke with Bogdanov, "the Baku Bolsheviks, headed by Comrade Stalin, without the slightest hesitation took Lenin's side." Never once did Stalin part company with Lenin, he continued, adding: "Lenin knew with whom he was dealing. Highly valued and trusted him." And contrasting Lenin's devoted disciple with the "Messrs. Trotskys" who were waging a hard fight against Lenin at the time, Ordzhonikidze observed that one had to be boundlessly faithful in order to remain true to the great teacher during those years of ideological confusion and organizational chaos. "Such an unshakably faithful one was Comrade Stalin."

In the same vein, Emelian Yaroslavsky evoked a memory of Trotsky forming the August bloc with the Menshevik liquidators while "Stalin together with Lenin was dealing one blow after another against this bloc." He and others likewise stressed Lenin's high regard for Stalin and heavy reliance upon him for advice. Digging deeply into Lenin's pre-revolutionary correspondence, they came up with a statement of 1911 praising an article in which Koba had defended the necessity of an illegal party: "Comrade K's article merits the closest attention of all who value our party." To illustrate Lenin's habit of taking counsel with the best Leninist at critical moments, Maximilian Saveliev, the editor of *Izvestia*, quoted his message to Trotsky over the direct wire on February 15, 1918, in reply to the latter's request from Brest for instructions: "Reply to Trotsky. I would like to confer first with Stalin before answering your question." And three days later: "To Trotsky. Stalin has just arrived, we'll discuss it and give you our joint reply right away. Lenin. . . ."

The anniversary writings cast Stalin in the role of best Leninist not only during Lenin's lifetime but also after his death. His struggles against the party oppositions were depicted as continuations under new conditions of Lenin's own battles against intra-party opposition to the Leninist course. In the post-Lenin period, Stalin was playing the part of best Leninist by his successful effort to defend and realize Lenin's designs for the Communist future. A prominent Soviet journalist, Mikhail Koltsov, offered an interesting elaboration of this theme in an article entitled "The Riddle of Stalin." The Stalin who was such a riddle to the world bourgeoisie—"Stalin the enigma," "the Communist sphinx," "Stalin the incomprehensible personality"—was not at all enigmatic to the Soviet worker, he wrote, no more so than were such favorite ideas of his as "socialism in one country," "five-year plan," and "self-criticism." Any secretary of a workshop party cell could solve the riddle of Stalin simply by paraphrasing Stalin's own description of Lenin as "the greatest Marxist and *vozhd'* of the working class in the epoch of imperialism and proletarian revolution." He could tell you that "Stalin is the strongest Leninist of the difficult post-Lenin era, with its new contradictions and class battles." [7]

Had Koltsov guessed at Stalin's hero-identification with Lenin and its psychological implications? His use of a Stalin statement about Lenin as a key to the "riddle" of Stalin himself suggests so. But it was left to the poet-publicist Demyan Bedny to hypothesize openly that Stalin's characterizations of Lenin possessed a self-referential meaning. He began by mentioning the extreme sensitivity of Stalin to any attempt to pry into his inner life. Lenin, being both beyond pride and beyond modesty, had merely been amused by things said about him personally or had taken no notice of them. Stalin, on the contrary, was irritated when anyone undertook to "write intimately" about him. The personal approach aroused his suspicions. This guardedness had its source, Bedny suggested, in Stalin's "heroic past" of constant struggle and his experience of others' desertions, betrayals, hypocrisies, fawning, and vain efforts to deceive.

Then the poet observed that he had been greatly struck in 1924 by Stalin's recollection that Lenin originally appeared to him a "mountain eagle" fearlessly leading the party along the trackless paths of the Russian revolutionary movement. Only much later, however, had he grasped the full meaning of Stalin's use of this "essentially artistic" formulation. An image had lain in his mind since childhood as a symbol of the one thing still higher than the majestic Caucasian mountain peaks—the eagle flying above them. In later applying it to the greatest of great men, Stalin had expressed his boundless admiration in an artist's way. Like any other artistic image, moreover, this one told more about the artist himself than about his object. "We therefore have the right," wrote Bedny, "to look on the Stalin portrait of Lenin as a subconsciously executed

7. *Pravda,* December 21, 1929.

self-characterization." The portrait expressed Stalin's ideal of the revolutionary. The qualities of Lenin singled out in his pamphlet *On Lenin* represented a catechism of the revolutionary virtues that he himself prized: modesty and simplicity, great strength of conviction, clarity of argumentation, compelling force of logic, absence of oratorical gestures and phrases, hatred for whining at times of defeat and for whining intellectuals, sober weighing of the enemy's forces, respect for the party majority's opinion, principle in politics, faith in the masses. Here, in Stalin's Lenin-ideal, was his measure of all people. He would never say to another person "Know thyself," but "Tell me your understanding of Lenin, and I'll tell you who you are." Others might shy away from this direct question, some to the Right and some to the Left, but not Stalin. He could no more shy away from Lenin than from himself: "Try to characterize Stalin and you will find yourself using the lexicon of Stalin's brochure on Lenin. *Lenin is the supreme measure.* And there are varying degrees of approximation to this measure. *The degree of approximation determines the party and revolutionary price of each one of us. It determines the price of Stalin too. The party knows that price. And won't come down from it.''* At the height of the struggle with the Left opposition, Bedny said in conclusion, some Trotskyists sent him a parcel marked "Caucasian mountains," and inside he had found a picture of Stalin. Without wishing to, they had told the truth about Stalin. He was made of mountain granite. His revolutionary name was in astonishing accord with his real essence: steel. Not a toy spring with a dancing political clown up above, but a fighting blade made of steel.[8]

Because it made a real probe of Stalin's personality, Bedny's contribution to the birthday celebration was daring. What he saw and made bold to say was that Stalin's hero-identification with Lenin rendered all that he had ever said about him self-revelatory—an implicit confession of his own self-ideal as a revolutionary. At the climax, however, the poet fell into the classic role of the court pane-

8. "On Lenin" was the title of Stalin's talk of January 28, 1924, to the Kremlin cadets. Later a pamphlet was published under this title containing both the talk and Stalin's other articles and speeches about Lenin.

gyrist. He drew an equation between the self-ideal and what Stalin really was, treated his beliefs about himself as true. By ascribing to Stalin all the qualities that he admired in Lenin, Bedny portrayed the "best Leninist" as virtually a reincarnation of Lenin himself. How Stalin reacted to this adulatory portrait is not known. But had his response not been positive, Bedny's article would not have been republished in the collection of birthday materials that circulated through the country in hundreds of thousands of copies.

The Great Revolutionary

Conceiving himself as the best Leninist, Stalin needed an appropriately eminent role in the revolutionary movement and overthrow of tsarism. The short biography by Tovstukha was no more than a start toward the reworking of the past that this involved. The fiftieth-birthday celebration opened a new phase. Although the official biography released for the occasion was only a reproduction of Tovstukha's work with a few paragraphs added at the end, many of the anniversary articles offered embellishments and sought to magnify Stalin's place in party history. They affirmed him as the heroic revolutionary figure that he considered himself to have been —and to be.

Demyan Bedny made a remarkable contribution in this vein with a second birthday article. In an unusual departure from Soviet journalistic practice, he drew his material from the émigré Russian press. Vereshchak's memoir of Stalin in the Baku prison had appeared in the Paris Russian émigré paper *Dni* (Days) on January 22 and 24, 1928. Parts of it that reflected favorably on Stalin were now reprinted in *Pravda,* along with commentary by Bedny in blank verse. The passage on Stalin's formidable Marxist knowledge and his reputation in the Transcaucasus as a "second Lenin" was one of those quoted. Another recounted an incident that occurred on Easter day in 1909, when the political prisoners were made to run the gauntlet of a company of soldiers from the Saliansky regiment. "Koba," wrote Vereshchak, "walked between the rows with a book in his hand, not bending his head under the blows of the rifle butts." Bedny's commentary ran as follows:

> Consider this, will you!
> How the enemy's criticism has disgraced itself!
> Stalin is no hero of an SR novel.
> But truth penetrates all barriers.
> Wouldn't "Stalin Walking the Gauntlet"
> Be a subject for a heroic picture?![9]

Pravda underlined Bedny's point by adding an editorial note saying that his poetic *feuilleton* had given artistic expression to "one of the moments out of Comrade Stalin's heroic past." The editor or editors must have realized, as Bedny himself obviously did, that Stalin desired to remember himself, and to be remembered, as an early hero-figure of the revolutionary movement.

Others who knew him well showed a similar awareness. Ordzhonikidze wrote that Stalin became the recognized leader of the Georgian Bolsheviks by the beginning of 1905, and then of all the Bolsheviks in the Transcaucasus. Yenukidze presented the same theme against a background of personal reminiscences. He had first met Stalin in 1900 when Lado Ketskhoveli, then getting his underground press started in Baku, sent him to Tiflis for materials and suggested that he seek Stalin's assistance. A very short conversation had sufficed, for then as now brevity, clarity, and precision were Stalin's distinctive qualities. Although still quite young, he enjoyed great authority among the Tiflis workers because of his natural simplicity of speech and manner, his absolute unconcern for his own comfort and convenience, his total lack of vanity, and his formidable knowledge. "Our Soso," they would call him. Yet never in any way did he seek the personal popularity that he so obviously enjoyed. Party-building activity absorbed him completely. More than any other Old Bolshevik, he had the qualifications for work as a professional revolutionary.

9. *Pravda*, December 20, 1929. Bedny's article was dated February 7, 1928, but I have not been able to ascertain whether or not it appeared in print before the birthday celebration in 1929.

In his talk before the Moscow Old Bolsheviks' club in 1923 on the underground printing presses in the Transcaucasus, Yenukidze had not portrayed Stalin as the foremost Bolshevik on the Caucasian scene in the early years of the century. Now, mindful of his old comrade's craving for recognition as a revolutionary of genius, he did. "In a word," he wrote, "Stalin was the intellectual and practical leader of our organizations in the Transcaucasus." He was so, it transpired, from the first beginnings of the division between Bolsheviks and Mensheviks in that region. From 1904 to 1908 he bore on his shoulders "literally the whole burden" of the fight against the Mensheviks in the Caucasus. The Bolshevik newspapers in Tiflis relied chiefly upon him. He spoke at all the important conferences. He played a great part in the peasant movement of 1905–6 in western Georgia—so great that even now, twenty-four years after, many of the peasants there could still remember his speeches. Later, he made Bolshevism dominant among the oil workers of Baku. In the period of reaction he did not emigrate, yet he remained in constant contact with Lenin, and whenever exiled he would escape at the first opportunity. He went on to become, in 1917, "one of the very foremost organizers and leaders of October and its victories."

This statement of Yenukidze's was one of several that retrospectively elevated Stalin to a new role of revolutionary greatness in 1917. Said the Central Committee and Central Control Commission in their birthday message: "In the victorious days of great October, you, in contrast to certain other disciples of Lenin, proved his first, closest, and most faithful assistant as a most prominent organizer of the October victory." When Lenin issued his "April Theses," asserted *Pravda*'s birthday editorial, "he found in Comrade Stalin a most close adherent and direct assistant." Then it pictured Stalin fighting alongside Lenin against the "wavering opportunists" in the party, charting the party's revolutionary prospects at the Sixth Congress in place of the absent Lenin, and upholding the Leninist line against all obstacles in the subsequent period of the taking of power. The editorial concluded: "Everyone knows what *an outstanding part Comrade Stalin played in the immediate preparation and carry-*

ing through of the October coup." When the tenth anniversary of
October was celebrated two years earlier, it will be remembered,
Trotsky's signal services were ignored. Now these services showed
signs of re-appearing in party annals—with a new actor in the hero-
role that Trotsky historically played. The glory of having been the
second great leader of the Bolshevik Revolution was beginning to be
appropriated for Stalin.

Further, he was now being cast as leader of the *international*
Communist revolution and its organizational spearhead, the Comintern. This, too, involved his retrospective aggrandizement at
others' expense. In the early years of the Comintern, Lenin, Trotsky, and Zinoviev were the dominant Russian Communist personalities in its affairs. Zinoviev was chairman of the organization from
its founding in 1919 to his resignation in 1926. Although Bukharin
did not succeed him in this office, which was abolished, he was *de
facto* the leading figure in the following two years, and drafted the
program that the Comintern adopted at its Sixth Congress in 1928.[10]
Stalin, who by this time was a power in Comintern affairs, influenced the final form of the document in a manner that Bukharin
described to Kamenev during their conversation of July 11–12,
1928, by saying: "Stalin spoiled the program for me in many
places." Before the mid-twenties, however, the Comintern was not
a major arena of Stalin's activity. Not until the Comintern's Fifth
Congress, in 1924, did he become a member of its Executive Committee.

Now a birthday editorial in the Executive Committee's theoretical journal, *Kommunisticheskii internatsional'* (The Communist
International), saluted him as leader of the Comintern and world
proletariat. Messages from many of the Communist parties of the
world did the same. Two of Stalin's lieutenants in the Comintern,
Otto Kuusinen and Dimitry Manuilsky, contributed glowing accounts of his services to the organization, past as well as present.
Kuusinen wrote that Stalin's direct participation in leadership of

10. Kermit E. McKenzie, *Comintern and World Revolution 1928–1943.
The Shaping of Doctrine* (New York, 1964), pp. 29–30, 40–42. On Bukharin's
authorship of the program, see Theodore Draper, "The Strange Case of the
Comintern," *Survey*, No. 3 (84) (Summer 1972), p. 134.

the Comintern proved necessary after Lenin died. And as if to underline that Stalin was the Comintern's new Lenin, he added that for some years the Comintern Executive Committee's line "in all the main questions" had been formulated on the basis of Stalin's advice. Manuilsky, in one of the most adulatory of the articles for Stalin's fiftieth birthday, described him as "a concentrated bundle of the most enormous revolutionary experience of the Soviet Communist party, transferred to the world Communist movement." He suggested that the capitalist press was making a great mistake by picturing Stalin as simply a "national figure," thus overlooking the international significance of the man who had defined Leninism as the Marxism of the epoch of imperialism and proletarian revolution. True, said Manuilsky, Stalin's leading role in the world Communist movement was not generally known. Much of the story was still concealed in the Comintern archives, and the time had not yet come to reveal how his leadership had saved a number of Communist parties from making grave political errors. But no document of major importance had issued from the Comintern without his most active participation in its drafting, and he had edited the program with great theoretical care. Manuilsky dwelt upon the implications for the world movement of Stalin's views on the national question, his fights against the Left and Right oppositions, and his theory of socialism in one country; he concluded by conjuring up a vision of Stalin as hero of the international revolution. Referring to the episode of his walking the gauntlet in 1909, as recounted by Demyan Bedny, he wrote:

And now, twenty years after, Stalin walks at the head of the proletarian movement through the gauntlet of the world bourgeoisie's hatred, carrying the banner of Leninism and working-class liberation. In over thirty years of selfless service to the working-class cause, of strict devotion to a revolutionary duty, Stalin has never bent his head, his hand has never trembled. . . . From Lenin he learned to perfection the indispensable art of brusque turns in directing the party and Comintern, and he masters as no one else does these qualities of the revolutionary strategist and tactician. . . . They are a guarantee of firm leadership of the Comintern in the coming decisive battles of the international working class.

The anniversary articles laid some of the foundations upon which Stalin's revolutionary biography would be more radically reconstructed in later years. Mikoyan, by now a candidate member of the Politburo, issued a call for more work along these lines. Important aspects of Stalin's revolutionary biography remained unknown to broad circles in spite of their great significance for the party, he wrote in a birthday article entitled "Steel Soldier of the Bolshevik Guard." This unsatisfactory situation was to be explained both by the remissness of Stalin's former comrades in the struggle and by his own "excessive modesty," which hampered the wide-scale publicizing of his life career. But Mikoyan expressed the hope that the fiftieth-birthday jubilee would give impetus to an effort to overcome these obstacles. It was necessary to meet the "just demands of the masses" by elaborating Stalin's biography and making it accessible to all.

The Civil War Fighter

It is one of the ironies of Soviet history that Voroshilov, whom Trotsky described to Lenin in 1918 as fit to command a regiment but not an army of fifty thousand, succeeded to Trotsky's old post of war commissar after the death of the immediate successor, Frunze, in 1925. The article that Voroshilov contributed in honor of Stalin's fiftieth birthday was something of a sensation when it first appeared. Entitled "Stalin and the Red Army," it was a major exercise in the rewriting of military history, and became the basis of the Stalinist historiography of the Civil War as it evolved during the thirties. Since it was both republished in the collection of birthday materials and issued as a separate pamphlet in 100,000 copies, the article must have pleased Stalin greatly.

And no wonder, for it was an essay in the historical might-have-been, written by one who knew Stalin intimately, had often reminisced with him about the Civil War, and well understood what would appeal to him. Based on real incidents and events, the article idealized the part Stalin had played in them. Everything positive was highlighted, everything negative blotted out. Furthermore, the events in which Stalin had participated became the decisive ones of the war. He emerged in the center of the historical picture, by Lenin's side, as the great front-line organizer of victory, the outstanding Civil War hero on the Red side.

In Voroshilov's account, Stalin was a superb success wherever he went during the war. By his interventions as political commissar he regularly forged victory out of threatened defeat. When confronted at Tsaritsyn with the failure of the military specialists to cope with their tasks and the inability of the local staff headquarters to quell counter-revolutionary activities, he assumed supreme military authority and quickly saved the situation. His indomitable will to victory inspired those around him with confidence; Tsaritsyn was held, and the enemy was hurled far back toward the Don. When he went east after the fall of Perm, he did not simply investigate the causes of the catastrophe but took timely and effective steps to eliminate them, thereby making it possible for the eastern front to go over to the offensive. Again, when Petrograd was endangered in the spring of 1919 by a combination of Yudenich's offensive from without and counter-revolutionary plots inside the city, the Central Committee sent Stalin to take charge, and within three weeks the situation was transformed. In telling this part of the story, Voroshilov omitted all reference to Yudenich's major offensive in the fall of the year, when Trotsky organized the city's defense. In effect, Trotsky's role as the savior of Red Petrograd was transferred to Stalin.

Much later, the Soviet playwright Vsevelod Vishnevsky made this theme the basis of his heroic drama *Unforgettable 1919,* which was written in 1949 to honor Stalin on his seventieth birthday. In the opening scene, Lenin seeks Stalin's counsel on dangerous developments in the Petrograd area and dispatches him to the north with plenipotentiary powers of command and a mandate to defend the city. In Petrograd and its environs Stalin copes brilliantly with a situation made desperate by White conspiracy and Trotskyite-Zinovievist defeatism. At the end his armored train rolls up to Krasnaia Gorka, the key coastal fort taken by the Baltic fleet in accordance with his boldly unorthodox plan. Receiving the acclaim of the sailors, Stalin sends off to Lenin his triumphant telegram on the taking of the fort in contravention of all the laws of naval science. *Unforgettable 1919* was translated into most of the languages of the Soviet peoples, shown in the majority of the country's drama theaters, made into a film, published in book form, and awarded a Stalin prize (first class) in 1950. Khrushchev has borne witness to Stalin's great fondness for it: "Stalin loved to see the film *Unforgettable 1919*, in which he was shown on the steps of an armored train and where he was practically vanquishing the foe with his own saber." [11]

In the birthday article of 1929, Voroshilov also portrayed Stalin as the strategic mastermind of the victory over Denikin. Taking his cue from one of Stalin's own earlier speeches, he wrote that Stalin accepted the Central Committee's assignment to the southern front in the fall of 1919 only on condition that Trotsky not interfere in its affairs or even cross its lines of demarcation. Then he offered Stalin's letter to Lenin from the southern front (without dating it) as evidence that Stalin devised the counteroffensive strategy successfully employed against Denikin. The facts, as noted earlier, are that Trotsky had propounded the strategic plan that Stalin defended in his letter to Lenin, and that this plan was already beginning to be implemented when Stalin arrived on the southern front in early October. He was not, therefore, the strategic innovator on the southern front that Voroshilov made him out to be. Nor is there any known foundation for the claim that Stalin made Trotsky's non-interference in the affairs of the southern front a condition of his own going there. Trotsky "withdrew" from that theater in the fall of 1919 in order to rush to the aid of beleaguered Petrograd.

While on the southern front, Voroshilov continued, Stalin developed into a fine art his method of action by means of shock groups: choose the main line of attack, concentrate the best units there, and crush the enemy. In the face of resistance from the center,

11. "Special Report to the Soviet Twentieth Party Congress," *The New York Times*, June 5, 1956. For the text of the play, see V. Vishnevsky, *P'esy. 1929–1950 gg.* (Moscow, 1954), pp. 440–558.

moreover, he took the initiative in the creation of a mounted army by combining cavalry divisions into a large formation. Consequently, Budenny's famous First Mounted Army was Stalin's "brainchild." Here again Voroshilov was trying to present Stalin as an innovative military mind of the first order, and again the claim ran afoul of chronology. Budenny himself, an ex–sergeant major in the cavalry, conceived the idea of the mounted army. And before Stalin went to the southern front in October 1919, Trotsky had posed the question of creating large-scale bodies of cavalry in his article "Proletarians, to Horse!" [12]

The topic of Stalin's role in the Russo-Polish war was unavoidable for Voroshilov because of its importance, yet disadvantageous because of the widely known facts concerning the way in which Stalin had conducted himself. He solved the dilemma by confining his treatment to a few short sentences that sought to put Stalin in the right. Stalin, wrote Voroshilov, furnished skillful leadership that contributed in large measure to the defeat of the Polish armies in the Ukraine, the liberation of Kiev, the penetration into Galicia, and the organizing of the famous raid that brought the First Mounted Army to the gates of Lvov. And only the failure of the Red forces near Warsaw prevented the mounted army, then only ten kilometers from Lvov, from carrying through its planned attack upon the city. This was stated baldly, without any supporting evidence. The truth, as informed Bolsheviks knew, was just the reverse: Stalin's obstinate insistence upon the capture of Lvov had dashed all Soviet hope for a successful outcome of the march on Warsaw.

In his summation, Voroshilov wrote that Stalin was perhaps the one man whom the Central Committee was shifting from one fighting front to another in 1918–20, sending him always to the most dangerous spots where the threat to the Revolution was greatest. He was not to be seen where things were going smoothly. But wherever the Red armies were suffering reverses, wherever the counter-revolutionary forces were endangering the Soviet regime's ex-

---

12. Isaac Deutscher, *Stalin: A Political Biography,* 2nd ed. (New York, 1966), p. 199; Erich Wollenberg, *The Red Army* (London, 1938), p. 97.

istence and at any moment panic could turn into helplessness and disaster—there Stalin would appear. Forsaking sleep, he would organize, take leadership into his firm hands, break all obstacles, act ruthlessly, and rectify the situation.

In the Civil War legend that Voroshilov fashioned for his friend, Stalin strikingly resembled the historical Trotsky. He was the talented organizer; the great Red troubleshooter roving from one critical sector to another; Lenin's staunch right hand on the far-flung fronts; the savior of Petrograd; the stickler for discipline. Just as Stalin was now beginning to displace Trotsky as the co-leader of the October Revolution, so he was being assigned the heroic part that Trotsky actually played as the chief organizer of victory in the Bolshevik regime's military struggle for survival. And Trotsky, as we have noted, was now being cast in Stalin's role as one who had to be recalled from the front on occasion because of failings as a political commissar. The repressed *bad* Civil War Stalin was being retrospectively projected onto Trotsky.

The Eminent Marxist Theorizer

As late as the mid-twenties, few people in Russia were aware of Stalin's desire for theoretical eminence and renown. Bukharin was widely regarded as the party's best theoretical brain after Lenin. Although Stalin's work as a codifier of Leninism was a notable po-litical success, his reputation as a *praktik* without strong credentials in general Marxist theory was not easily overcome among the Old Bolsheviks. In 1927, according to one report, he was blackballed for membership in a select body of leading Marxist intellectuals called the Communist Academy because of his "lack of specialized research in the realm of Marxism." [13] Another incident involved David Riazanov, the distinguished Marx scholar and director of the Marx-Engels Institute. Riazanov went up to Stalin after hearing him argue the doctrine of socialism in one country at a party meet-

13. Avtorkhanov, *Stalin and the Soviet Communist Party*, p. 135. The author was at that time a member of the Institute of Red Professors in Moscow. According to more recent, unofficial, information which has reached the West via *samizdat*, the report of Stalin's blackballing is not true. On this see *Politicheskii dnevnik 1964–70* (Amsterdam, 1972), p. 512.

ing of the mid-twenties, and said: "Stop it, Koba, don't make a fool of yourself. Everybody knows that theory is not exactly your field." [14]

Besides being an outspoken man, Riazanov probably did not know Stalin well enough to understand how galling this remark would be to him. He did not realize that theory was one of the fields in which Stalin coveted greatness. Personal as well as political motives spurred Stalin to assume the role of ideological spokesman of Bolshevism in the policy debates of the post-Lenin period. How, indeed, could he prove himself as "best Leninist" unless he was the most accurate, the most incisive, the most erudite, and generally the most truly Leninist of all the party interpreters of Lenin and Leninism? Little by little, people in close contact with Stalin became conscious of his desire for recognition as a party theoretician second only to Lenin. "He is consumed by the craving to become a recognized theoretician," Bukharin said of Stalin in his conversation of July 11–12, 1928, with Kamenev. "He feels that this is the only thing he lacks."

By then Bukharin must have been uncomfortably aware that Stalin envied him his reputation as the party's first theoretician. If he had any doubts about this, Stalin dispelled them in the course of his great polemic in the April 1929 plenum. For here he undertook to demolish Bukharin's theoretical reputation, calling him a theoretician who was "not fully Marxist" and still needed to "complete his education." Stalin cited in evidence the passage on Bukharin in Lenin's testament. After describing Bukharin as the biggest theoretician and "the favorite of the whole party," Lenin had added that his theoretical views "can only with great doubt be considered fully Marxist, for there is something scholastic in him (he never studied and I do not think he has ever fully understood dialectics)." Stalin now italicized this addendum, and branded Bukharin as "a theoretician without dialectics"—dialectics in turn being "the soul of Marxism." Then he raked over the coals of an old controversy in an effort to convict Bukharin of immodestly seeking to "teach our

14. Deutscher, *Stalin*, p. 290.

teacher, Lenin." In an article of 1916, Lenin had reproved Bukharin for suggesting that Marxists as well as anarchists wanted to "blow up" the state. Recalling the incident in an article of 1925 on the theory of the state, Bukharin mentioned that Lenin had come around to his view. Upon his arrival in Petrograd from America in August 1917, at which time Lenin was in hiding, Krupskaya's first words to him had been: "V. I. asked me to tell you that he no longer has any disagreements with you on the question of the state." Stalin now pounced upon Bukharin's reminiscence as an example of the "hypertrophied pretentiousness of an undereducated theoretician." Instead of being Leninists, he added sarcastically, Lenin's disciples and Lenin himself were apparently Bukharinists. "It's a little funny, comrades. But what is one to do when he comes up against the swollen pretentiousness of Bukharin?" [15]

The birthday celebration brought Stalin official recognition as the party's leading theoretician. One of *Pravda*'s editorials on December 21, 1929, hailed him as "the most outstanding theoretician of Leninism not only for the All-Union Communist party but for the whole Comintern as well." Several of the other birthday messages and articles elaborated upon this theme. The Institute of Red Professors commended Stalin's works on Leninism as models of Marxist-Leninist revolutionary dialectics and examples of creative, as distinguished from dogmatic and scholastic, Marxism. The Communist Academy and the Institute of Lenin congratulated him in messages addressed to him, respectively, as "the party theoretician" and "the militant materialist and dialectician." He was praised as Lenin's collaborator in laying the theoretical foundations of party policy on the national question and as the author of the constitutional structure of the Soviet multi-national state.

V. V. Adoratsky, a well-known Marx scholar and party philosopher, devoted his birthday article to the thesis that Stalin was not only the political leader that everyone acknowledged him to be but also "the most eminent theoretician of Leninism." Another

15. *Stalin*, XII, 69–78. On the Lenin-Bukharin controversy concerning the state, see Stephen F. Cohen, *Bukharin and the Bolshevik Revolution* (New York, 1973).

contributor, G. Krumin, defined the issue more sharply by attacking those who considered Stalin a practical man only and denied his significance as a theoretician. He explained Stalin's success in becoming leader of the party by the fact that he was *both* a theoretician and a practician of revolution. Among his most conspicuous qualities as a Marxist theorizer were precision and depth of thought, skillful mastery of the dialectic, and the capacity to go to the heart of a question with astonishing clarity and simplicity. It was unimaginable for anyone to work on problems of Leninism nowadays without making use of *The Foundations of Leninism*. Stalin, however, was not only a faithful disciple and interpreter of the great teachers but a "profound continuator" of their work. He was advancing Marxist thought with "truly revolutionary dialectical formulations" that gave theoretical expression to new facts and the experience of the world revolutionary movement.

Stalin took these tributes as his due. During the week following the birthday celebration, he made a public appearance in the role of the party's first theoretical mind. Addressing a conference of agrarian Marxists called by the Communist Academy, he declared that Soviet successes in theoretical work in the economic field were not keeping pace with practical successes. There was, in fact, a certain divorce between the practical successes and the development of theoretical thought, as shown by the continued currency among Communists of various bourgeois and petty-bourgeois theories like the theory of "equilibrium" of different economic sectors, the theory of "drift" in socialist construction, and the theory of the small-peasant economy's "stability." This lag had to be eliminated, for "theory, if it is really theory, gives the practical workers strength of orientation, clarity of perspective, confidence in the work, and faith in the victory of our cause." [16]

The Builder of Socialism

To go down in history as the builder of a socialist society in the USSR was one of Stalin's most cherished ambitions. Such, in-

16. *Stalin*, XII, 141–143, 147, 149.

deed, was the hidden message of his article for the eighth anniversary of the Revolution in 1925. There, it will be recalled, he saw the historical present as an analogue of 1917, which carried the corollary that a breakthrough comparable in significance to the Bolsheviks' seizure of power in October was in the offing.

That this was his settled viewpoint and not a passing fancy is indicated by his reversion to it in theses that he submitted to the Fifteenth Party Conference in October 1926. Here he spoke of the present period as one of intensified struggle between capitalism and socialism both internationally and at home, and accused the Left opposition of voicing the pessimism and defeatism felt by one section of the party. In this sense, he went on,

the present period of radical change is to some extent reminiscent of the period of radical change of October 1917. Just as then, in October 1917, the complicated situation and difficulties of transition from bourgeois to proletarian revolution engendered in one section of the party vacillation, defeatism, and disbelief in the possibility of the proletariat's taking and retaining power (Kamenev, Zinoviev), so now, in the present period of radical change, the difficulties of the transition to the new phase of socialist construction are giving rise to vacillations in certain circles of our party, disbelief in the possibility of the victory of the socialist elements of our country over the capitalist elements, disbelief in the possibility of the victorious building of socialism in the USSR.[17]

Although he made no direct reference to himself here, Stalin was implicitly including himself in the picture. A 1917-like situation with its Zinoviev- and Kamenev-like vacillating disbelievers in determined revolutionary action ineluctably called for the Leninist hardness and inspired leadership that only a new Lenin-like party *vozhd'*—that is, a Stalin—could provide.

Stalin could not be glorified as the "builder" on his fiftieth birthday because at that time socialism, by general agreement, remained to be built. But some of the birthday articles showed an awareness that this was one of his hero-roles. Kuibyshev, who now headed the Supreme Council of National Economy and had recently been elevated to the Politburo, called Stalin the "flaming champion

17. *Ibid.,* VIII, 215.

of the idea of industrialization" and the man destined to lead the
party and the working class in resolving the problem of building
socialism in the USSR. To demonstrate Stalin's long practical involvement with this problem, Kuibyshev cited the letter, then still
unpublished, that Stalin had written to Lenin in March 1921 praising the GOELRO ten-year electrification plan in comparison with
Trotsky's economic-revival proposals and suggesting a series of
practical steps to implement the plan. This was the letter in which
Stalin (in an impulse of unconscious self-projection?) had accused
Trotsky of being "a medieval handicraftsman imagining himself
an Ibsen hero destined to 'save' Russia with an ancient saga."

Kuibyshev also reviewed Stalin's pronouncements on industrialization, starting with the statement at the Fourteenth Congress
that the party's general line was to transform the USSR from an
agrarian into an industrial country. He emphasized Stalin's argument of 1926 that industrialization refers not to industrial development as such but specifically to expanded production of capital
goods. To create socialism and uphold the USSR's independence in
spite of capitalist encirclement, Stalin had further argued in 1928,
it was necessary to possess an adequate industrial base for defense
and to industrialize at an accelerated pace. Such, concluded Kuibyshev, was the visage of Stalin as ideologue of an industrializing
country. "Comrade Stalin upholds the idea of industrialization of
the country with an iron hand, with Bolshevik indomitability and
tenacity, and with the greatest energy, mercilessly exposing those
who try to divert the party from this path."

Saveliev's article was more penetrating in that it characterized Stalin's own interpretation of the role of builder. A former
professional revolutionary who had taken a doctorate at Leipzig in
1910 and was editor of the party journal *Prosveshchenie* in 1913
when Stalin's study of the national question appeared in it, Saveliev,
who was younger than Stalin by five years, had linked himself with
the general secretary's faction and had served during the late
twenties in such sensitive posts as head of the Lenin Institute and
editor of *Proletarskaia revoliutsiia*. His birthday encomium drew a
vivid image of Stalin as industrializer, stressing his orientation toward

a "decisive offensive" against capitalist elements in town and countryside. But its special significance lay in the way it related Stalin as builder of socialism to Stalin as the latter-day Lenin. Saveliev said that it was absolutely impossible to understand Stalin's role as "best Leninist" and "successor to Lenin's cause under contemporary conditions" without bringing to light his present-day role in the building of a socialist economy. Elaborating, he particularly underlined Stalin's view that socialism must embrace the countryside as well as the towns, and his statement at the Fifteenth Congress that the way out of Russia's agrarian backwardness was to transform the small peasant farms into large collective ones. This pointed to Stalin as the inspirer of the revolution of collectivization that was developing in the Soviet countryside when the article appeared at the end of 1929.

In the Bolshevik mind, as we know, the Lenin symbol signified above all the revolutionary hero. Lenin's supreme service to the party and to history had been the October Revolution itself, his decisive contribution to its success. Saveliev's reasoning was based upon this symbolism. In order to understand Stalin as the contemporary personification of Lenin, he was saying, one must realize that he is now embarking upon an enterprise of truly revolutionary scope and character. Precisely as collectivizer of agriculture and industrializer he is seeking to prove himself as another Lenin. Stalin sees the coming revolutionary transformation of Russia as his October.

The scholarly Old Bolshevik had read Stalin's writings well, and through them his mind.

Chapter Fourteen

THE AMBIGUOUS OUTCOME

Men live in dreams and in realities.[1]

THE CONCEPTION OF political man as power-seeker is one of the age-old archetypes of political thought, and Stalin has often been seen as a classic case in point, almost a textbook example of the power-centered personality. To some of his biographers, just as to some of his political associates, he was a man for whom power—personal, absolute power, for its own sake—was the supreme and all-absorbing goal.

Our study of his life up to the winning of recognition as leader of the Russian Communist movement has brought out many facts that lend superficial plausibility to such a view of him. Stalin's urge to dominate others became evident in him from early boyhood, when, as Iremashvili later testified, he was a good friend so long as one submitted to his imperious will. His craving for power showed up in his relations with fellow young socialists in the Tiflis seminary and in dealings with party comrades during his subsequent career as a Marxist revolutionary. In addition to prizing power itself, he took a keen interest in the art of acquiring it and developed the requisite skills to something close to perfection. So unswerving was his dedication to the aim of building power for himself in the Soviet party-state that some Bolsheviks put it down as the only aim he had.

They were mistaken in taking such a view. In spite of his concentration upon acquiring and accentuating power, the goal Stalin

1. Milovan Djilas, *Conversations with Stalin* (New York, 1962).

sought was something greater, something to which this power was ultimately no more than a necessary means. His goal was the Lenin succession. The aim of his life was to be—and be recognized as—Russian Communism's second Lenin, a supremely gifted *vozhd'* leading the movement in new revolutionary exploits comparable in historic significance to the Bolshevik Revolution of 1917. He believed in the caption of a widely distributed Soviet picture of the thirties which showed his profile against a background of Lenin's and read: "Stalin is Lenin today." If his motivation remained a mystery to other Bolsheviks, it may have been in part because so few of them could see in such an equation anything other than propaganda for the masses. Not taking it seriously themselves, they failed to understand that Stalin did.

But before he could prove his revolutionary greatness by leading the movement in new world-historic actions, he had to become its acknowledged leader. This, rather than power per se, was his aim throughout the twenties. His very zeal in positioning himself for the succession contest while Lenin was still alive was one of the forces that brought him into conflict with the man he aspired to succeed. To gain the supreme prize he was prepared to fight with Lenin himself if necessary. If Lenin failed to see Stalin as his rightful successor, this could only be—in Stalin's mind—because he was ill and no longer the Lenin of old.

What was the outcome of Stalin's quest for the Lenin succession? To this concluding question there seems to be no unequivocal answer. In one respect he fulfilled his ambition; in another he did not. The ambiguity of the outcome would plague him for the remainder of his long life, with far-reaching and at times tragic consequences for Communism, Russia, and the world.

On the one hand, he was victorious in the post-Lenin struggle for party primacy. He won not only power but a strong measure of acceptance in the role of Bolshevism's chief. He ousted his party opponents on the Left and the Right, all the prominent people who opposed his candidacy for leadership. Above all, he defeated his most important single rival for political supremacy: Trotsky. Moreover, it was not merely by manipulating the levers of power that he accomplished this. He did it, as we have seen, partly by establishing political rapport with the party constituency, by espousing positions that made sense to the upcoming new generation of Bolshevik men of power and to many of their party elders. At the close of the twenties, as a result, he stood at the head of a party and movement that, by and large, acknowledged him as its leader. He was not yet a dictator ruling by terror.

In terms of what are often regarded as the realities of political life, this was a time of triumph for Stalin. His quest for the succession might seem to have reached its victorious end. But such a view would both oversimplify and misrepresent the situation. For while Stalin was accepted by the party as its new leader, he was not perceived as a second Lenin; and in this sense the succession remained unconsummated even after he had attained the pinnacle of party leadership. He now enjoyed not only great power as general secretary but also far-reaching authority as the political chief of Bolshevism. But this leader-follower relation bore little resemblance to that which had existed between Lenin and the Bolshevik movement. Stalin did not possess a personal authority at all comparable to Lenin's. Notwithstanding the extravagance of the fiftieth-birthday tributes, he was no charismatic figure in Bolshevik eyes. He was not thought of in the party, even by those who most willingly accepted his leadership, as "Lenin today." Apart from the most ardent of his political protégés, not even the men of the Stalin faction saw him in this light.

In one way he was farther from such recognition than he had been earlier. For while he won the debates over party policy in national development and industrialization, the prolonged battle over revolutionary biographies was, on balance, damaging to his cause. He had done much to hurt the political reputations of his rivals, but they had badly tarnished his. Even as they went down to defeat in the power contest, they dealt him telling blows in the biographical fight. They were able to do this because they knew and could document some deeply incriminating facts about Stalin, particularly about his final relations with Lenin. Indeed, they ultimately reduced him to blurting out to a nationwide audience the passage in Lenin's testament that was most damaging to him—the passage in which the party's dying leader rejected Stalin. And although he argued that Lenin's failure to point to any political failings on his part, as distinguished from personal ones, made the testament less damaging to him than it was to Trotsky, Zinoviev, and Kamenev, even he must have had some sense of the lameness of this contention.

If Stalin had been only the hard-headed political realist and pragmatist that many then and later took him to be, the incompleteness of his victory in the succession struggle would have given him little pause. His truly impressive success in gaining the leadership would have seemed sufficient reward. The fact that few if any in the party perceived him as the second Lenin of Bolshevism would not have been oppressive. Like other Bolsheviks he might have taken it for granted that no one could *really* be a second Lenin. But Stalin, as we have seen, was not like other Bolsheviks in this regard. Simply winning power and achieving the supreme leadership could not appease his ambition. Ever since the early years, when he enlisted from afar in the revolutionary band of his "mountain eagle," he had cherished the goal of becoming not simply a man of power but a great and heroic leader like Lenin. That vision of himself made it seem natural later on that he rather than any other prominent Bolshevik should be Lenin's successor. And now that he had finally won the role of *vozhd'*, he felt an imperative need for recognition as the hero-leader that he believed himself to be. He wanted to be the successor in *every* sense.

If this was not generally understood in the party, Stalin bore major responsibility. Between a political leader and his following there exists as a rule a compact, explicit or implicit, involving his undertaking to provide leadership of a certain kind in a certain direction. Stalin's is a case in which one party to the compact—the would-be leader—misled the other. In the mid-twenties, as we noted, the Bolshevik movement was not in need of another messianic leader as successor to Lenin. Not being in distress, it was not in search of salvation. It did not want a new revolutionary hero to guide it through great new vicissitudes to the farther shores of history—as Trotsky seemed ready to do. What it wanted was a competent and forceful chairman who believed in the independent development of the Revolution and would foster the prosperity and power of Soviet Russia under socialism. Stalin, whose very lack of brilliance was an advantage under those conditions, presented himself in his speeches and manner as just such a leader: plain, solid, businesslike, matter-of-fact, a good manager. He shrewdly perceived the party's outlook and adapted himself to it.

But this self-projection was deceptive in some ways, reflecting the constraints under which Stalin was operating in the struggle for party supremacy. The genius and heroic mission that he lacked in the eyes of his fellow Bolsheviks were evident to his own. Once his political rivals were vanquished and his claim to the leader-role was uncontested, he could not help wanting to show himself as a Lenin-like *vozhd'*, and to be acknowledged as such. He could not help striving to demonstrate that the birthday tributes were no more than his due, that the idealized version of himself symbolized to his own mind by the name "Stalin" was the truth. He was driven to consummate the Lenin succession.

Although not yet an autocrat at the end of 1929, Stalin by then was in a position to shape policy pretty much according to his desires. This was shown, for example, by the way in which he influenced the agricultural collectivization plan, making it a more radical blueprint for rapid change than other party leaders generally favored. Coming events would show, too, that Stalin could quell protest and resistance in the party in the event of his policy's miscarriage, becoming in the process a dictator in the full and classic sense of the term. What placed him in this position was in part the formidable organizational power that he had accumulated in the post of general secretary and in part the unstructured nature of the leader-role itself, its lack of institutional definition.

Lenin had bequeathed to the party the example of a supreme leader who led primarily by consultation and persuasion on the basis of matchless energy, talent, imagination, personal charm, and tactical genius. A lesser figure in this role, particularly in the event of serious policy setbacks—such as were soon to occur—would come under strong inner pressure to compensate for the lack of comparable leadership powers by mobilizing his potential coercive power, his power to dominate and tyrannize the party. This would be especially true if, like Stalin, he was a man of dictatorial tendency who saw his party critics as class enemies and was unprepared at bottom to recognize how inferior he was to his predecessor in ability as a leader.

Here, then, was an historic instance—neither the first nor the last—in which a leader's personality acquired critical importance. A basic element of the ominous situation taking shape in the Soviet Communist party at the end of 1929 was the discrepancy between Stalin's way of perceiving himself and the way a great many in the party perceived him. He was under stringent inner pressure to keep the idealized Stalin-figure steadily and clearly in focus and to shut out everything in himself or his past that marred it. His fellow Communists, even those who were strongly pro-Stalin and convinced supporters of his policies, operated under no such compulsion. While aware of his impressive strengths as a leader, they felt no need to deny his limitations, or to repress or rationalize away their memories—if they had them—of such facts as Stalin's conditional support of the Provisional Government in March 1917, his harmful conduct in the Polish war, and the postscript to Lenin's testament. Nor did these politically informed people realize, in their psychological naïveté, how important it was to him that they should share his view of himself in all major particulars; hence they likewise failed to appreciate what deadly dangers were latent in this situation.

In fact, it contained the makings of a catastrophe for the country and its ruling party. In the terror of the thirties, untold thousands of loyal party members and other Soviet citizens would have to be condemned as covert enemies of the people so that Djugashvili could prove to himself and Russia that he was really Stalin.

BIBLIOGRAPHY

THIS BIBLIOGRAPHY lists books cited or referred to in the footnotes, transcripts and some other documents, and selected articles of major significance to which reference is made in the present volume.

1. Books

Alexandrov (A. S. Michelson). *Kto upravliaet Rossiei? Bol'shevitskii partiino-pravitel'stvennyi apparati i "stalinizm."* Berlin, 1933.

Alliluyev, Sergei. *Proidennyi put'.* Moscow, 1946.

Alliluyeva, A. S. *Vospominaniia.* Moscow, 1946.

Alliluyeva, Svetlana. *Twenty Letters to a Friend.* New York, 1967.

———. *Only One Year.* New York, 1969.

Arendt, Hannah. *The Origins of Totalitarianism.* New ed. New York, 1966.

Arkomed, S. T. *Rabochee dvizhenie i sotsial-demokratiia na Kavkaze (s 80-kh godov po 1903 g.).* 2nd ed. Moscow, 1923.

Avtorkhanov, Abdurakhman. *Stalin and the Soviet Communist Party: A Study in the Technology of Power.* New York, 1959.

Bajanow, B. *Stalin, der rote Diktator.* Berlin, n.d.

Barmine, Alexander. *One Who Survived: The Life Story of a Russian under the Soviets.* New York, 1945.

Baron (Bibineishvili). *Za chetvert' veka (Revoliutsionnaia bor'ba v Gruzii).* Moscow and Leningrad, 1931.

Billington, James H. *Mikhailovsky and Russian Populism.* London, 1958.

Bonch-Bruevich, V. D. *Na boevykh postakh fevral'skoi i oktiabr'skoi revoliutsii.* Moscow, 1931.

———. *Izbrannie sochineniia.* Vol. III. *Vospominaniia o V. I. Lenine 1917–1924 gg.* Moscow, 1963.

Bukharin, N. I. *Put' k sotsializmu v Rossii,* ed. Sidney Heitman. New York, 1967.

Carr, Edward Hallett. *The Bolshevik Revolution 1917–1923.* 2 vols. Vol. I. New York, 1951.

———. *The Interregnum 1923–1924.* New York, 1954.

———. *Socialism in One Country 1924–1926.* 2 vols. Vol. II. New York, 1960.

Chamberlin, W. H. *The Russian Revolution.* 2 vols. New York, 1965.

Cherniavsky, Michael. *Tsar and People: Studies in Russian Ruler Myths.* New Haven, 1961.

Chernyshevsky, N. G. *Polnoe sobranie sochinenii.* Volume I. Moscow, 1939.

Cohen, Stephen F. *Bukharin and the Bolshevik Revolution.* New York, 1973.

Dan, Theodore. *The Origins of Bolshevism.* New York, 1964.

Daniels, Robert V. *The Conscience of the Revolution: Communist Opposition in Soviet Russia.* Cambridge, Mass., 1960.

Deutscher, Isaac. *The Prophet Armed: Trotsky, 1879–1921.* London, 1954.

———. *The Prophet Unarmed: Trotsky, 1921–1929.* London, 1959.

———. *The Prophet Outcast: Trotsky, 1929–1940.* London, 1963.

———. *Stalin: A Political Biography.* 2nd ed. New York, 1966.

Djilas, Mllovan. *Conversations with Stalin.* New York, 1962.

Dmitrievsky, S. *Sovetskie portrety.* Stockholm, 1932.

Dubinsky-Mukhadze, I. *Ordzhonikidze.* Moscow, 1963. 2nd ed., Moscow, 1967.

Duranty, Walter. *Duranty Reports Russia.* New York, 1934.

Eastman, Max. *Since Lenin Died.* London, 1925.

———. *Love and Revolution: My Journey Through an Epoch.* New York, 1964.

Erikson, Erik H. *Childhood and Society.* New York, 1963.

———. *Insight and Responsibility.* New York, 1964.

———. *Identity: Youth and Crisis.* New York, 1968.

Erlich, Alexander. *The Soviet Industrialization Debate 1924–1928.* Cambridge, Mass., 1967.

Essays Presented to Sir Lewis Namier, ed. Richard Pares and A. J. P. Taylor. London, 1956.

Fainsod, Merle. *How Russia Is Ruled.* 2nd ed. Cambridge, Mass., 1963.

Fischer, Louis. *The Life of Lenin.* New York, 1964.

Florinsky, Michael T. *Russia: A History and an Interpretation.* 2 vols. New York, 1955.

Fotieva, L. A. *Iz vospominanii o V. I. Lenine. Dekabr' 1922 g.–mart 1923 g.* Moscow, 1964.

Freud, Sigmund. *Collected Papers.* 5 vols. Vol. IV. London, 1952.

————. *Group Psychology and the Analysis of the Ego.* New York, 1960.

Friedrich, Carl J., and Zbigniew Brzezinski, *Totalitarian Dictatorship and Autocracy.* Cambridge, Mass., 1956.

Friedrich, Carl J., Michael R. Curtis, and Benjamin R. Barber. *Totalitarianism in Perspective: Three Views.* New York, 1969.

From Max Weber: Essays in Sociology, ed. H. G. Gerth and C. Wright Mills. New York, 1958.

Fromm, Erich. *Sigmund Freud's Mission: An Analysis of His Personality and Influence.* New York, 1959.

Fülöp-Miller, René. *The Mind and Face of Bolshevism. An Examination of Cultural Life in Soviet Russia.* New York, 1928.

Gertsen, A. I. (Herzen). *Izbrannye filosofskie proizvedeniia.* Moscow, 1946.

Gitlow, Benjamin. *I Confess: The Truth about American Communism.* New York, 1929.

Goffman, Erving. *The Presentation of Self in Everyday Life.* Garden City, 1959.

Gorodetsky, E. N. *Rozhdenie sovetskogo gosudarstva (1917–1918 gg.).* Moscow, 1964.

Gorodetsky, E., and Ia. Sharapov. *Sverdlov. Zhizn' i deiatel'nost'.* Moscow, 1961.

Hare, Richard. *Pioneers of Russian Social Thought.* London, 1951.

Harper, Samuel. *Civic Training in Soviet Russia.* Chicago, 1929.

Hook, Sidney. *The Hero in History.* Boston, 1955.

Horney, Karen. *Neurosis and Human Growth.* New York, 1950.

Hugo, Victor. *Ninety-Three.* Boston, 1888.

Humbert-Droz, Jules. *De Lénine à Staline: Dix ans au service de L'Internationale Communiste 1921–1931.* Neuchâtel, 1971.

Iosif Vissarionovich Stalin: Kratkaia biografiia. Moscow, 1947.

Iremaschwili, Joseph. *Stalin und die Tragödie Georgiens.* Berlin, 1932.

Iroshnikov, M. P. *Sozdanie sovetskogo tsentral'nogo gosudarstvennogo apparata: sovet narodnykh kommissarov i narodnye kommissariaty. Oktiabr' 1917 g.–ianvar' 1918 g.* 2nd ed. Leningrad, 1967.

Istoriia kommunisticheskoi partii Sovetskogo Soiuza, chief ed. P. N. Pospelov. Vol. III. Moscow, 1967.

Istoricheskie mesta Tbilisi: putevoditel' po mestam sviazannym s zhizn'iu i deiatel'nost'iu I. V. Stalina. 2nd revised and enlarged ed. Tbilisi, 1944.

Kazbegi, Alexander. *Izbrannye proizvedeniia*. Tbilisi, 1957.

Kazemzadeh, Firuz. *The Struggle for Transcaucasia (1917–1921)*. New York, 1951.

Keep, J. L. H. *The Rise of Social Democracy in Russia*. London, 1963.

Kennan, George F. *Russia and the West under Lenin and Stalin*. Boston, 1960.

Kharmandarian, S. V. *Lenin i stanovlenie zakavkazskoi federatsii. 1921–1923*. Erevan, 1969.

Konstantinov, A. P., *et al. Leninskie traditsii partiino-gosudarstvennogo kontrolia*. Leningrad, 1963.

Krupskaya, Nadezhda. *Memories of Lenin*. Vol. II. New York, n.d.

Ksenofontov, F. A. *Uchenie Lenina o revoliutsii i diktature proletariata*. Moscow and Leningrad, 1925.

Lang, David M. *A Modern History of Soviet Georgia*. New York, 1962.

Lavrov, P. L. *Filosofiia i sotsiologiia. Izbrannye proizvedeniia*. Moscow, 1965.

Lenin, V. I. *Sochineniia*. 2nd ed. Vol. XXV. Moscow, 1928.

———. *Polnoe sobranie sochinenii*. 5th ed. 55 vols. Moscow, 1958–1965. (Cited in the text as *Lenin*.)

———. *Selected Works*. 3 vols. Moscow, 1970–71.

Lerner, Warren. *Karl Radek: The Last Internationalist*. Stanford, 1970.

Levine, Isaac Don. *Stalin's Great Secret*. New York, 1956.

Levitsky, V. O. *Za chetvert' veka*. Moscow and Leningrad, 1926.

Lewin, Moshe. *Lenin's Last Struggle*. New York, 1968.

———. *Russian Peasants and Soviet Power: A Study of Collectivization*. Evanston, 1968.

Liberman, Simon. *Building Lenin's Russia*. Chicago, 1945.

Lunacharsky, A. V. *Revoliutsionnye siluety*. Moscow, 1923. (English translation: *Revolutionary Silhouettes*. New York, 1968.)

Makharadze, Filipp. *Ocherki revoliutsionnogo dvizheniia v Zakavkaz'i*. Tbilisi, 1927.

Malia, Martin. *Alexander Herzen and the Birth of Russian Socialism 1812–1855*. Cambridge, Mass., 1961.

Marx and Engels. *Basic Writings on Politics and Philosophy,* ed. Lewis S. Feuer. Garden City, 1959.

The Marx-Engels Reader, ed. Robert C. Tucker. New York, 1972.

Materialy vsesoiuznogo soveshchaniia zaveduiushchikh kafedrami obshchestvennykh nauk. Moscow, 1958.

McDonald, John. *Strategy in Poker, Business, and War*. New York, 1963.

McKenzie, Kermit E. *Comintern and World Revolution 1928–1943: The Shaping of Doctrine*. New York 1964.

McNeal, Robert H., ed. *Stalin's Works: An Annotated Bibliography.* Hoover Institution Bibliographical Series, XXVI. Stanford, 1967.

———. *Bride of the Revolution: Krupskaya and Lenin.* Ann Arbor, 1972.

Medvedev, Roy A. *Let History Judge: The Origins and Consequences of Stalinism,* ed. David Joravsky and Georges Haupt. New York, 1971.

Michels, Robert. *Political Parties.* New York, 1959.

Mikoyan, A. I. *Mysli i vospominaniia o Lenine.* Moscow, 1970.

———. *Dorogoi bor'by.* Kniga pervaia. Moscow, 1971.

Miliukov, Paul. *Russia and Its Crisis.* New York, 1962.

M.I. Ulyanova. Sekretar' "Pravdy," ed. Z. D. Bliskovsky *et al.* Moscow, 1965.

Mosse, W. E. *Alexander II and the Modernization of Russia.* New York, 1962.

Nicolaevsky, Boris. *Power and the Soviet Elite,* ed. Janet D. Zagoria. New York, 1965.

Nove, Alec. *An Economic History of the USSR.* London, 1960.

Ocherki istorii kommunisticheskikh organizatsii Zakavkaz'ia. Chast' pervaia. 1883–1921 gg. Tbilisi, 1967. (Cited in the text as *Ocherki istorii.*)

Ocherki po istoriografii sovetskogo obshchestva, chief ed. P. A. Zhilin. Moscow, 1965.

Pipes, Richard. *The Formation of the Soviet Union: Communism and Nationalism, 1917–1923.* Rev. ed. New York, 1968.

Plekhanov, G. V. *Selected Philosophical Works.* Vol. I. Moscow, n.d.

———. *Sochineniia.* Vol. XIII. Moscow and Leningrad, 1926.

———. *Sotsializm i politicheskaia bor'ba. Nashi raznoglasiia.* Moscow, 1939.

———. *The Role of Individuals in History.* New York, 1940.

Pokrovsky, M. N. *Russkaia istoriia s drevneishikh vremen.* 3rd ed. 4 vols. Moscow, 1920.

Politicheskii slovar', ed. G. Alexandrov *et al.* Moscow, 1940.

Potresov, A. N. *Posmertny sbornik proizvedenii.* Paris, 1937.

Preobrazhensky, E. *The New Economics.* New York, 1965.

Rabinowitch, Alexander. *Prelude to Revolution: The Petrograd Bolsheviks and the July 1917 Uprising.* Bloomington, 1968.

Rasskazy starykh rabochikh zakavkaz'ia o velikom Staline. Moscow, 1937.

Reed, John. *Ten Days That Shook the World.* New York, 1960.

Reswick, William. *I Dreamt Revolution.* Chicago, 1952.

Sbornik statei k piatidesiatiletiiu so dnia rozhdeniia I. V. Stalina. Moscow and Leningrad, 1929.

Schapiro, Leonard. *The Origin of the Communist Autocracy.* Cambridge, Mass., 1955.

————. *The Communist Party of the Soviet Union.* New York, 1959.

Seifullina, L. *Sobranie sochinenii.* Vol. II. Moscow and Leningrad, 1928.

Shliapnikov, A. G. *Semnadtsaty god. Kniga vtoraia.* Moscow and Petrograd, 1923.

Smith, Edward Ellis. *The Young Stalin. The Early Years of an Elusive Revolutionary.* New York, 1967.

Souvarine, Boris. *Stalin: A Critical Survey of Bolshevism.* New York, 1972.

Spulber, Nicolas. *Soviet Strategy for Economic Growth.* Bloomington, 1964.

Stalin, I. V. *Sochineniia.* 13 vols. Moscow, 1946–1952. (English translation: *Works.* 13 vols. Moscow, 1952–1955.) (Cited in the text as *Stalin.*)

————. *Stalin's Speeches on the American Communist Party.* New York, n.d.

Stasova, E. D. *Vospominaniia.* Moscow, 1969.

Stopani, A. *Iz proshlogo: Stat'i i vospominaniia iz istorii bakinskoi organizatsii i rabochego dvizheniia v Baku.* Baku, 1923.

Sukhanov, N. N. *The Russian Revolution 1917. A Personal Record.* Edited, abridged, and translated by Joel Carmichael from *Zapiski o revolutsii.* London, 1955.

Suny, Ronald Grigor. *The Baku Commune 1917–1918: Class and Nationality in the Russian Revolution.* Princeton, 1972.

Sverdlov, Ia. M. *Izbrannye proizvedeniia.* Vol. I. Moscow, 1957.

Takim byl Lenin. Vospominaniia sovremennikov, ed. G. Zhuk. Moscow, 1965.

Tovstukha, I. P. *Iosif Vissarionovich Stalin. Kratkaia biografiia.* Moscow and Leningrad, 1927.

Trifonov, Iu. *Otblesk kostra.* Moscow, 1966.

Trotsky, L. *K sotsializmu ili k kapitalizmu? (Analiz sovetskogo khoziaistva i tendentsii ego razvitiia).* Moscow and Leningrad, 1925.

————. *The Real Situation in Russia.* New York, 1928.

————. *My Life.* New York, 1930.

————. *On the Kirov Assassination.* New York, 1935.

————. *The Revolution Betrayed.* New York, 1945.

————. *On the Suppressed Testament of Lenin.* New York, 1946.

————. *The History of the Russian Revolution.* Ann Arbor, 1957.

————. *Lenin.* Garden City, 1957.

————. *Permanent Revolution and Results and Prospects.* London, 1962.

————. *The Stalin School of Falsification.* New York, 1962.

————. *The Essential Trotsky.* New York, 1963.

————. *Trotsky's Diary in Exile, 1935.* New York, 1963.

————. *The New Course.* Ann Arbor, 1965.

————. *Stalin: An Appraisal of the Man and His Influence.* New ed. New York, 1967.

The Trotsky Papers, ed. Jan M. Meijer. The Hague, 1971.

Tucker, Robert C. *The Marxian Revolutionary Idea.* New York, 1969.

Tukhachevsky, M. N. *Izbrannye proizvedeniia.* Vol. I, *1919–1927.* Moscow, 1964.

Uratadze, Grigori. *Vospominaniia gruzinskogo sotsial-demokrata.* Stanford, 1968.

Vaganov, F. M. *Pravyi uklon v VKP(b) i ego razgrom (1928–1930 gg.).* Moscow, 1970.

Valentinov, Nikolai (N. V. Volski). *Vstrechy s Leninym.* New York, 1953. (English translation: *Encounters with Lenin.* London, 1968.)

————. *Doktrina pravogo kommunizma: 1924–1926 gody v istorii sovetskogo gosudarstva.* Munich, 1960.

————. *The Early Years of Lenin,* trans. and ed. Rolf H. W. Theen. Ann Arbor, 1969.

————. *Novaia ekonomicheskaia politika i krizis partii posle smerti Lenina. Gody raboty v VSNKH vo vremia NEP. Vospominaniia.* Stanford, 1971.

Venturi, Franco. *Roots of Revolution: A History of the Populist and Socialist Movements in Nineteenth-Century Russia.* New York, 1960.

Vishnevsky, V. *P'esy 1929–1950 gg.* Moscow, 1954.

Vladimir Ilyich Lenin. Biografiia, chief ed. P. N. Pospelov. 2nd ed. Moscow, 1963.

Volin, B. M. *Dvenadtsats biografy.* Moscow, 1924.

Voroshilov, K. *Stalin and the Armed Forces of the USSR.* Moscow, 1951.

————. *Rasskazy o zhizni. Vospominaniia.* Kniga pervaia. Moscow, 1968

Wallace, Sir Donald Mackenzie. *Russia.* London, 1912.

Weber, Max. *The Theory of Social and Economic Organization.* New York, 1947.

Wolfe, Bertram D. *Three Who Made a Revolution.* New York, 1948.

————. *Khrushchev and Stalin's Ghost*. New York, 1957.

Wollenberg, Erich. *The Red Army*. London, 1938.

Yaroslavsky, E. *Partiia bol'shevikov v 1917 godu*. Moscow and Leningrad, 1927.

Yelagin, Iu. *Ukroshchenie iskusstv*. New York, 1952. (English translation: Jury Jelagin. *The Taming of the Arts*. New York, 1951.)

Yenukidze, A. *Nashi podpol'nye tipografii na Kavkaze*. Moscow, 1925.

Za leninizm. Sbornik statei. Moscow and Leningrad, 1925.

Zhivoi Lenin. Vospominaniia pisaltelei o V. I. Lenine, ed. N. I. Krutikova. Moscow, 1965.

Zhordania, N. *Moia zhizn'*. Stanford, 1968.

Zhvaniia, G. K. *V. I. Lenin, Ts. K. partii i bol'sheviki Zakavkaz'ia*. Tbilisi, 1969.

Zinoviev, G. *Sochineniia*. Vol. XV. Leningrad, 1924.

————. *Lenin. Speech to the Petrograd Soviet Celebrating Lenin's Recovery from Wounds Received in the Attempt Made on His Life on August 30, 1918*. London, 1966.

2. Transcripts and Other Documents

Bukharin-Kamenev Conversation. Trotsky Archives (T1897), Harvard University.

Desiatyi s"ezd RKP/b/. Mart 1921 goda. Stenograficheskii otchet. Moscow, 1963.

Deviatyi s"ezd RKP/b/. Mart–aprel' 1920 goda. Protokoly. Moscow, 1960.

Dvenadtsatyi s"ezd rossiiskoi kommunisticheskoi partii /bol'shevikov/. Stenograficheskii otchet. Moscow, 1923.

Khrushchev, Nikita. "Special Report to the Soviet Twentieth Party Congress," *The New York Times*, June 5, 1956, pp. 13–16.

Odinnadtsatyi s"ezd RKP/b/. Mart–aprel' 1922 goda. Stenograficheskii otchet. Moscow, 1961.

Piatnadtsatyi s"ezd VKP/b/. Dekabr' 1927 goda. Stenograficheskii otchet. 2 vols. Moscow, 1961–1962.

Piatyi (londonskii) s"ezd RSDRP. Aprel'–mai 1907 goda. Protokoly. Moscow, 1963.

Protokoly tsentral'nogo komiteta RSDRP/b/. Avgust 1917–fevral' 1918. Moscow, 1958.

Sed'maia ('aprel'skaia') vserossiiskaia i petrogradskaia obshchegorodskaia konferentsii RSDRP/b/. Aprel' 1917 g., ed. M. D. Orakhelashvili. Moscow, 1934.

Shestoi s"ezd RSDRP /bol'shevikov/. Avgust 1917 goda. Protokoly. Moscow, 1958.

Trinadtsatyi s"ezd RKP/b/. Mai 1924 goda. Stenograficheskii otchet. Moscow, 1963.

Vos'moi s"ezd RKP/b/. Mart 1918 goda. Protokoly. Moscow, 1959.

XIV s"ezd vsesoiuznoi kommunisticheskoi partii /b/. 18–31 dekabria 1925 g. Stenograficheskii otchet. Moscow, 1926.

XV konferentsiia vsesoiuznoi kommunisticheskoi partii /b/. 26 oktiabria–3 noiabria 1926 g. Stenograficheskii otchet. Moscow and Leningrad, 1927.

3. Selected Articles

Aronson, Gregory. "Stalinskii protsess protiv Martova," *Sotsialisticheskii vestnik*, Nos. 7–8 (1939), pp. 84–85.

———. "Was Stalin a Tsarist Agent?," *The New Leader*, August 20, 1956, pp. 23–24.

Arsenidze, R. "Iz vospominanii o Staline," *Novy zhurnal*, No. 72 (June 1963), pp. 218–236.

Baikalov, A. "Moi vstrechi s Osipom Djugashvili," *Vozrozhdenie* (Paris), March–April 1950, pp. 116–119.

Burdzhalov, E. N. "O taktike bol'shevikov v marte–aprele 1917 goda," *Voprosy istorii*, No. 4 (1956), pp. 38–56.

———. "Eshche o taktike bol'shevikov v marte–aprele 1917 goda," *Voprosy istorii*, No. 8 (1956), 109–114.

Dan, Lydia. "Bukharin o Staline," *Novy zhurnal*, No. 75 (March 1964), pp. 176–184.

Denisov, A. "Narodnyi kommissariat po delam national'nostei." In *Bol'shaia sovetskaia entsiklopediia*, Vol. 41, pp. 213–214. Moscow, 1931.

Donskoi, V., and S. Ikonnikov. "Razvitie leninskikh idei o partiino-gosudarstvennom kontrole," *Kommunist*, No. 18 (December 1962), pp. 30–39.

Draper, Theodore, "The Strange Case of the Comintern," *Survey*, No. 3 (84) (Summer 1972), pp. 91–137.

"Iosif Vissarionovich Stalin: Kratkaia biografiia." In *Malaia sovetskaia entsiklopediia*, Vol. 10, pp. 319–391. Moscow, 1940. (Cited in the text as *Malaia* biography.)

Kaminsky, V., and I. Vereshchagin. "Detstvo i iunost' vozhdia: dokumenty, zapisi, rasskazy," *Molodaia gvardiia*, No. 12 (1939), pp. 22–100.

Kennan, George F. Review of Edward Ellis Smith, *The Young Stalin*, in *The American Historical Review*, October 1968, pp. 230–232.

Kuzmin, N., S. Naida, Iu. Petrov, and S. Shishkin. "O nekotorykh voprosakh istorii grazhdanskoi voiny," *Kommunist*, No. 12 (1956), pp. 54–71.

Levinson, Daniel J. "Role, Personality, and Social Structure in the Organizational Setting," *Journal of Abnormal and Social Psychology*, 58 (1959), 170–180.

Lunghi, Hugh. "Stalin Face to Face," *The Observer Weekend Review*, February 24, 1963, pp. 1, 25.

McNeal, Robert H. "Trotsky's Interpretation of Stalin," *Canadian Slavonic Papers*, No. 5 (1961).

Pentkovskaia, V. V. "Rol' V. I. Lenina v obrazovanii SSSR," *Voprosy istorii*, No. 3 (1956), pp. 13–24.

Pestkovsky, S. "Vospominiia o rabote v narkomnatse (1917–1919 gg.)," *Proletarskaia revoliutsiia*, No. 6 (June 1930), pp. 124–131.

"Protokoly i rezoliutsii Biuro Tsk RSDRP/b/ (mart 1917 g.)," *Voprosy istorii KPSS*, No. 3 (1962), pp. 134–157.

"Protokoly vserossiiskogo (martovskogo) soveshchaniia partinnykh rabotnikov (27 marta–2 aprelia 1917 goda)," *Voprosy istorii KPSS*, Nos. 5 and 6 (1962), pp. 106–125 (No. 5), 130–135 (No. 6).

Radek Karl. "Lev Trotsky—organizator pobedy," *Pravda*, March 14, 1923.

Reichenbach, Bernard. "Moscow, 1921. Meetings in the Kremlin," *Survey*, No. 53 (October 1964), pp. 16–22.

Sanford, Nevitt. "The Dynamics of Identification," *Psychological Review*, No. 2 (1955), pp. 106–118.

Semenov, Iu. I. "Iz istorii teoreticheskoi razrabotki V. I. Leninym natsional'nogo voprosa," *Narody Azii i Afriki*, No. 4 (1966), pp. 106–129.

Suny, Ronald Grigor. "A Journeyman for the Revolution: Stalin and the Labour Movement in Baku, June 1907–May 1908," *Soviet Studies*, January 1972, pp. 373–394.

Tucker, Robert C. "The Theory of Charismatic Leadership," *Daedalus*, Summer 1968, pp. 731–756.

Tytell, Martin K. "Exposing a Documentary Hoax." Paper presented at the New York meeting of the American Association for the Advancement of Science, December 29, 1956.

Vakar, N. "Stalin po vospominaniiam N. N. Zhordania," *Poslednye novosti* (Paris), December 16, 1936.

Valentinov, N. (N. V. Volski). "Sut' bol'shevizma v izobrazhenii Iu. Piatakova," *Novy zhurnal*, No. 52 (1958), pp. 140–161.

————. "Ot Nepa k stalinskoi kollektivizatsii," *Novy zhurnal,* No. 72 (1963).

Vereshchak, Simeon. "Stalin v tiur'me (Vospominaniia politicheskogo zakliuchennogo)," *Dni,* January 22 and 24, 1928.

Zhvaniia, G. K. "V. I. Lenin i partiinaia organizatsiia Gruzii v period bor'by za sovetskuiu vlast'," *Zaria vostoka,* April 21, 1961.

INDEX

EUROPEAN HISTORY TITLES IN
NORTON PAPERBOUND EDITIONS

Menéndez, Pidal, Ramón. *The Spaniards in Their History.* N353

Newhouse, John. *Collision in Brussels: The Common Market Crisis of 30 June 1965.*

Nichols, J. Alden. *Germany After Bismarck: The Caprivi Era, 1890-1894.* N463

Pirenne, Henri. *Early Democracies in the Low Countries.* N565

Roth, Cecil. *The Spanish Inquisition.* N255

Rowse, A. L. *Appeasement.* N139

Russell, Bertrand. *Freedom versus Organization: 1814-1914.* N136

Salvemini, Gaetano. *The French Revolution, 1788-1792.* N179

Sontag, Raymond J. *Germany and England: Background of Conflict, 1848-1894.* N180

Stansky, Peter and William Abrahams. *Journey to the Frontier: Two Roads to the Spanish Civil War.* N509

Talmon, J. L. *The Origins of Totalitarian Democracy.* N510

Taylor, A. J. P. *Germany's First Bid for Colonies, 1884-1885.* N530

Thompson, J. M. *Louis Napoleon and the Second Empire.* N403

Tucker, Robert C. *The Marxian Revolutionary Idea.* N539

Waite, Robert G. L. *Vanguard of Nazism: The Free Corps Movement in Postwar Germany, 1918-1923.* N181

Wedgwood, C. V. *William the Silent.* N185

Wheeler-Bennett, John W. *Brest-Litovsk: The Forgotten Peace, March 1918.* N576

Wheeler-Bennett, John W. and Anthony Nicholls. *The Semblance of Peace: The Political Settlement After the Second World War.* N709

Whyte, A. J. *The Evolution of Modern Italy.* N298

Wolfers, Arnold. *Britain and France between Two Wars.* N343

Wolf, John B. *Louis XIV.*

Wolff, Robert Lee. *The Balkans in Our Time.* N305

Zeldin, Theodore. *The Political System of Napoleon III.* N580

THE NORTON HISTORY OF
MODERN EUROPE

Rice, Eugene F., Jr. *The Foundations of Early Modern Europe, 1460-1559*

Dunn, Richard S. *The Age of Religious Wars, 1559-1689*

Krieger, Leonard. *Kings and Philosophers, 1689-1789*

Breunig, Charles. *The Age of Revolution and Reaction, 1789-1850*

Rich, Norman. *The Age of Nationalism and Reform, 1850-1890*

Gilbert, Felix. *The End of the European Era, 1890 to the Present*